Plan of the book

Contents

Part
one

Teaching and learning French

1 To the teacher: using *French Grammar Explained* in the language class

1.1	**The language class**
1.2	**Layout of *French Grammar Explained***
1.3	**Grammar**
1.4	**Exercises**

As teachers of French as a foreign language, we are probably all agreed on one thing: the language has to be learnt, as well as acquired. Here is one reason why:

'certains adolescents et adultes qui acquièrent une langue seconde en milieu naturel (travailleurs immigrés, par exemple, en 'immersion' et en 'interactions' constantes avec les natifs) ne parviennent jamais à 'parler comme on parle', en raison du fait qu'ils s'en tiennent à une interlangue, plus ou moins 'fossilisée' mais relativement efficace dans leurs échanges avec les natifs.' (H Besse, R Porquier, *Grammaire et didactique des langues*, 1991, p157)

1.1 The language class

In the language class, not all activities can always be communicative; but non-communicative activities (such as presentation, explanation and discussion of grammar points), and pre-communicative activities (such as individual/pair/group practice exercises), should be explicitly formulated in terms of the communicative functions that students will be helped to carry out by using new structures: what students can expect to do with the grammar they have learnt. Listening and reading should, except in the case of preparation of written notes prior to a spoken contribution, precede speaking and writing. A set of activities should, whenever possible, proceed from individual preparation, through pair and group work (or round-the-class contributions), to whole-class activities, and involve communicative activities at one or more stages.

During communicative activities, the tutor should note down students' errors: if the same error is made by more than one student, the grammar point(s) involved can be dealt with in a follow-up session, working from the appropriate grammar section(s) in this book, and using the corresponding exercises. Students should be encouraged to bring problem sentences and cases (whether in English or in French) to the language class, and to share their thoughts on these with the rest of the class, in particular by asking 'What happens if ... (a particular modification is made to the sentence)?', and by discussing possible generalisations and solutions to a problem among themselves (in pairs) before the point is discussed and practised by the class as a whole. Students should also be encouraged to formulate their own rules and explanations: they do this anyway, unconsciously, but their 'interlanguage' **(see 2.2)** may contain serious misapprehensions, and remain uncorrected, if it is not made explicit, pooled and tested in the language class.

This way of proceeding will not address all students' needs all the time, but it represents a learning method which all students can benefit from, as it encourages them, whenever communication (whether productive or receptive) has broken down, to carry out self-diagnosis, turning to the grammar 'first aid' provided by the book, not only when the teacher does, but whenever they feel that repairs are needed to their understanding and use of French.

1.2 Layout of *French Grammar Explained*

The plan of this book is designed to help students to diagnose their errors so that they have some idea of where to begin putting them right; for this purpose, a comprehensive three-part **Index (Section 59)** is provided, listing separately:

- English grammatical terms **(59.1)**;
- English words **(59.2)**;
- French words **(59.3)**.

Points of grammar are presented with the following objectives in mind:

- to make students aware of basic grammatical concepts, such as direct/indirect object **(see 18)**, or aspect **(see 54)**;
- to set out, sometimes in the form of **Tables**, the basic forms and structures (of the passé composé or the passive, for example) in which these concepts are expressed in French;
- to compare and contrast these forms and structures in French with equivalent forms and structures in English (such as compound forms of nouns and verbs **(see 16)**, verb constructions + noun or + infinitive **(see 38)**);
- to highlight points which English-speaking learners need to be aware of, such as demonstratives and relatives (*celui* and *lequel*: **see 21.5** and **42.3**), word order, such as negative passé composé (*je ne l'ai pas vu*: **see 34.3**), passive constructions (including *donner* and *permettre* **see 35.3**);
- to make students aware of which points are worth paying most attention to, and why;

3

- to show the communicative functions which these forms and structures can be used to perform.

Progression

The sequence of points explained, illustrated and practised in this book builds up from:

- forms (**5–16**): sounds, words and groups of words, to
- syntax (**17–49**): combinations of words and groups in phrases and sentences, and concludes with the construction of
- texts (**50–55**).

Forms are the WHAT of language, the basic building bricks: forms must either be absorbed by the learner through years spent in a French-speaking environment, or studied and learnt by heart.

Syntax is the HOW of language, building with the bricks: syntax has to be observed, explained and practised.

This approach allows students to focus on one feature of the language at a time, but the cumulative progression from syllables to texts is not meant to be a straitjacket for teachers or students: it is not expected that students or teachers will want to work through all the sections in the order in which they appear.

Appeal is made throughout to students' knowledge of both English and French. Reference to English rules can make students aware of how certain notions and functions are expressed in English, as a point of comparison and contrast with how these notions and functions are expressed in French. English examples are also used to demonstrate the difference between formal and informal usage.

Cross-references in each section enable students to trace important grammatical structures from their most basic forms up to the more complex structures and uses dealt with in later sections of the book: students can pinpoint the nature and the level of problems they are having in understanding or using French, instead of obscuring the problem under the blanket heading of 'grammar'.

The **Tables** in the book are accompanied by **Exercises (see 1.4)** designed to reinforce students' grasp of the different meanings and uses of the items in the table.

1.3 Grammar

Grammatical rules are a matter of statistics, not legislation. Wherever possible, students are led to make generalisations which will serve them well in the majority of cases. Emphasis is given to forms and structures in common use. Special attention is given to words and phrases which are often confused by students.

Grammar points seldom occur in isolation: to understand and produce authentic and acceptable sentences in French, one often needs to apply two or more rules at the same time: but which rules, and in which order? In this book, points are presented and explained one at a time, and step-by-step.

The grammar explanations include model sentences as a basis for grammar explanation. Grammatical knowledge is presented as a springboard to expression: the ways in which knowledge can be put to use. Students are directed towards:

- noticing when native speakers use certain constructions;
- being aware of what effect these have on them as listener/reader, and;
- including these constructions at appropriate points in their own productions as speaker or writer, whenever they wish to achieve similar effects.

Terms that might mislead students unfamiliar with grammatical terminology (such as 'the passive') are explained, either early in the relevant section, or in the **Glossary** of grammatical terms (**see 58**). An inductive approach (from examples to generalisations) is followed wherever possible, but deductive methods are applied when necessary.

> **Variation**
> Certain examples are labelled N1, N2, N3, N4: these four labels correspond to four broad types of situation: **very formal (N4)**, **relatively formal (N3)**, **relatively informal (N2)**, **very informal (N1)**, and indicate that the form of language in the example thus labelled might not be appropriate in a different situation, for example *pourquoi* with or without inversion of verb and subject. Most examples, however, are unlabelled. This means that they can be used in all situations, formal and informal: they are part of both standard French (N3) and everyday French (N2). (**See 55**).

1.4 Exercises

Most exercises are French–French. As appropriate, exercises are:

- **individual:** capable of being worked through in private study time, and the results checked by referring to the **Key** at the end of the book;
- **pair/group:** suitable to encourage discussion and mutual enlightenment when worked through in pairs or groups;
- **oral:** suitable for practice in a small group, a class, or during a lecture to the whole year group;
- **written:** as a follow-up to individual, pair or group work, or as a test.

Many exercises are suitable for use twice: when the new point has been studied for the first time, and later, for revision. At either of these stages, it may be helpful to ask students to work out the English equivalents of the sentences in the exercises.

Many exercises are structured in two or more stages: *Travail individuel > Travail à deux > Mise en commun*. The teacher is placed in the role of adviser rather than instigator (a top-down role can lead to inhibition and lack of participation on the part of students). Students are encouraged to share ideas in pairs (and to tackle many of the exercises outside the language class hours) and then to submit these ideas to the rest of the group (students can also be invited to prepare for tests in pairs).

Wherever possible, exercises invite students to consider the meaning of the sentences to be produced, and to explore possibilities of reformulating the sentence to produce different meanings: the aim is to enable students to build up a grammar for choice:

> *mieux vaut que l'élève pense 'Qu'est-ce que je peux dire, compte tenu des contraintes syntagmatiques propres à la langue étrangère', plutôt que de penser 'Qu'est-ce que le professeur veut que je dise?'* (H Besse, R Porquier, op. cit., 1991, p130).

2 To the student: studying French

2.1   **Memory**
2.2   **Interlanguage**
2.3   **Priorities**
2.4   **Mistakes and motivation**

There are no short cuts to learning a foreign language: for example, you have to build up vocabulary (words and phrases) systematically, week after week. Spending periods abroad, among French-speaking people, will help your listening comprehension; whether at home or abroad, you will make progress not by learning the language mechanically or absorbing it passively, but by actively comparing what you hear and read with your previous ideas about how French sounds and works, and by being prepared to change these ideas.

Four aspects of language learning are discussed in this section: the importance of training and using your memory; taking account of your interlanguage; deciding on priorities for study; overcoming your dislike of making mistakes by being clear about your motivation to learn French.

2.1 Memory

Language learning, in common with many useful human activities, involves exercising your memory:

- by deliberate memorisation: learning selected words and phrases;
- through short-term recall: reproducing words or phrases immediately after hearing them, in class or in the laboratory;
- through long-term memory: absorbing and retaining new material. Unlike imitation or rote-learning, this involves integrating new bits of language, patterns or rules with what you know already, rearranging some of your knowledge and ideas about French **(see 2.2, Interlanguage)**;
- through spontaneous recall: retrieving vital words from your memory.

We all use our memory in different ways: what works for one individual is useless or unacceptable to another. But for all of us, successful language learning is about integrating new material into what we know already: not merely noticing something new, and parking it in a notebook, never to be used again.

Always link the sound and spelling of French words in your mind. Move your attention to and fro between sound and spelling: this will help you iron out discrepancies between what you say and spell and what you think you have said or written. Beyond individual words, pay attention to the 'melody' of a sentence in French: the intonation and the stress patterns which should be included in your sound map of French.

Successful language learning is like learning to play a musical instrument well: it takes constant practice. With each practice session, you learn to modify your reflexes, not only in order to play one particular piece, but to improve tone, rhythm, and the way you produce notes and runs, whatever you are playing.

2.2 Interlanguage

Ever since you were a small child, you have had in your head your own personal map of how grammar works in English: a set of ideas and assumptions, partly made up of conscious rules, which you are aware of applying, but mainly consisting of unconscious assumptions, which you act on without thinking about them.

Ever since you began to learn French, you have had in your head your own personal map of how grammar works in French, consisting of assumptions transferred from your grammar of English, together with ideas about French (and any other language you've been learning). Some of these ideas and assumptions may be close to those of a native speaker of French, but many are significantly different, and thus a source of repeated errors. All of these combine and interact to form your personal map of French. This is called your **interlanguage**, and it affects both the way you attempt to make sense of French when listening or reading, and the way you attempt to produce French: you have probably noticed that many of the mistakes you make when speaking or writing French are caused by applying English patterns to French.

However accurate or inaccurate your map of French, or interlanguage, it exists, so you have to work on it, piece by piece, in order to make progress. When studying grammar, do not pretend to yourself that all you have to do is add new ideas about 'French grammar' to the ones you have already. To help you revise and improve your map of French, this book shows you:

- some of the grammatical rules governing constructions in English;
- whether these rules can be applied directly to French.

By comparing English and French in this way, you will become more aware of certain general principles of grammar, and of how these principles apply in the particular cases of English and French, including whether you need to apply a different rule. Knowing about the mechanics of French grammar will not, in itself, enable you to understand or pronounce French more easily and proficiently. What it can do for you is increase your confidence in using the language, just as understanding some of the handling characteristics of the car you are driving can help you to become a more confident (and safer) driver.

2.3 Priorities

As a learner of French, you can acquire only gradually a set of reflexes similar to those of someone for whom French is their first or only language. Many learners of a foreign language remain at a relatively low level of proficiency or authenticity, perhaps all their lives: some migrant workers, for example, who learn to understand and make themselves understood sufficiently well for their purposes, make no further progress, even though this may exclude them from promotion, a change of occupation or career, or from being accepted among particular groups of people in the host country. No one can decide for you what level of proficiency or authenticity you wish to reach in French, but work out for yourself what you are aiming at, and how much time and effort you are prepared to put into achieving it.

Whether you are studying French in order to pass an exam (or achieve a particular grade), to improve your career prospects, to make travel more of a pleasure, out of personal or cultural interest, or any combination of these, you should aim, one step at a time, to make your map of French more like what it is for a native speaker of French. To do this you will need to prioritise, working systematically on each point (whether of pronunciation, endings, constructions, etc.) one by one, observing your own mistakes, and applying more rules, more complex rules, and thus more accurate rules.

This book is designed to help you to understand and classify vocabulary, and to know and practise grammatical structures and patterns which are frequently used by French speakers and writers. It is intended as a practical, working grammar manual, not a comprehensive reference grammar.

Vocabulary

Make a point of learning vocabulary regularly and systematically, in order to build up a stock of words and phrases, but not blindly: follow your own interests. Don't stare at lists of words taken out of context: select, from a text or transcript you've found interesting, 10–20 words and phrases, and learn these.

Learn idioms, phrases and constructions as well as individual words. Learn the forms of verbs: their stem (*boire*, for example, has two stems, *boi-* and *buv-* (**see 9.3**), and the different endings for persons and tenses (such as *on boit, vous buvez; j'ai bu, ils ont bu*: **see 9** and **10**), nouns with their gender (**see 11.1**), groups of words with the same stem but different suffixes, such as *le voyage, le voyageur, voyager* (**see 14**).

Structures

Knowledge about language is best applied to phrases and sentences with which you are already familiar; years ago, in your beginner's French lessons, you needed no grammatical knowledge in order to understand and use correctly an expression such as *Qu'est-ce que c'est?* Now, awareness of how this phrase has a similar structure to the question forms *Est-ce que* + subject + verb and *Qu'est-ce que* + subject + verb can help you to form correctly a wider range of sentences, following these models.

As far as possible, learn new grammar using familiar vocabulary, so that you can concentrate on one thing at a time. When writing French, or preparing spoken talks or presentations, try to include phrases and structures you have learnt recently, so that you are constantly extending your powers of expression, and not just relying on things you knew already.

Using a language for communication is not the same as putting together pieces of Lego (there is no point in communicating in French if you have nothing to say), but you do need to understand how the pieces fit together: learn to diagnose the strong and weak points of your competence in French, and concentrate, one point at a time, on the things that keep getting in your way. In French, as in any language, you have a good deal of freedom, especially when speaking, to choose the phrases and structures which best suit your mood and meaning **(see 50–54)**. But remember that freedom to say what you want to say comes from understanding and accepting constraints, choosing words and using structures in such a way that people can understand you.

2.4 Mistakes and motivation

Mistakes

Nobody likes to make mistakes, and many of us react badly when we have our mistakes pointed out to us. But in fact your mistakes of French are your best guide to how to make progress:

- do you keep making the same kind of mistake?
- can you formulate to yourself what rule you are applying when you say or write something which turns out to be a mistake?

As your proficiency in French improves, you will continue to make some of your old mistakes, and even begin to make new ones; at other times, you will be inconsistent, applying a rule correctly one moment, and apparently forgetting it in the next breath. It's a process we all went through as small children acquiring our own language; perhaps you have noticed it taking place with younger members of your family: for you, it is part of the process of learning French.

Motivation

Most of you started to learn French after the age of 5–8; you first learned about yourself and the world around you in terms of a language that was not French. When it comes to speaking or writing French, you will often find that you know how to express what you mean in English, but your French-speaking listeners will only understand you if you speak their language. Because you know more than you can say in French, you have to simplify your message in order to achieve any kind of communication at all. Successful second or foreign language learning therefore requires you to be motivated enough to practise the language, sitting down on your own to learn vocabulary and phrases, to do written practice exercises, and trying to understand how the language works, so that you gradually narrow the gap between what you can say in English, and what you can say in French.

In foreign language classes, so-called 'communicative activities' take place between learners who could nearly all communicate better in English than in French, and in the presence of teachers for whom English is their first or second language. In order to become sufficiently involved in these practice activities for you to derive benefit from them, you need to be sufficiently motivated to overcome the artificiality of the classroom situation.

You also need patience and stamina – there is no short cut – and your only satisfaction will be that of successfully climbing a mountain, not by cable-car or other mechanically assisted means (quite quickly, with little expenditure of energy, but with little time to enjoy the views on the way up), but by using only your own body (slowly, with greater expenditure of energy, but with time to enjoy the views on the way). The views are the same, but the viewer is different. *C'est le bonheur que je vous souhaite!*

Pairwork activity

What kind of language learner are you?

Do any of these descriptions fit you? Look through them with a partner, and see if you can both agree as to which ones apply (in some ways or to some extent) to either or both of you. Then see if you both agree with the comments and advice that follow each description.

1 'I daren't open my mouth to speak French in class/in a group/with a French person, for fear of making a lot of mistakes.'

If you are making good progress with writing French, you have nothing to fear but fear itself! Take the plunge, and get started on saying something before you've worked out how you will finish: that's what you do in English, and that's what French speakers do all the time – and they make slips of the tongue, repeat themselves, change their mind in mid-stream, leave sentences unfinished and so on. Speak the way the French speak French, not the way you write French.

2 'When I write French, I can't think of anything to say.'

If you quite like speaking French, and manage to keep going even though it may not all be very accurate, you probably do have a lot of usable ideas, but these always seem to run away from you when you sit down to plan a piece of writing. Try taking a blank sheet of paper and noting down (in English and/or in French) all the ideas, examples etc. that come into your head, even if you feel that some of them will not be usable. Then look through this jumbled mass of ideas and examples: some of them are similar, related, linked etc. – label these A, then B for another group, and so on (you will only need 2–4 main groups!). Next, try to work out which group of points you think should come first, which group you'd like to come last, and so on. Then try to see, within each group, whether points can be put in a particular order. (You will find that some of your original jottings won't fit in anywhere: be prepared to abandon these.) Above all, don't start worrying about your French (vocabulary, grammar, style etc.) until you've gone through the process outlined above which, as you can see, is aimed at making you concentrate first on ideas, then on organisation, and finally on your French (last but not least!).

3 'When I write French, I keep making the same mistakes over and over again.'

If you know you're making the same mistakes, you've taken the first step in self-diagnosis, which is to see where you are going wrong. The next, all-important step can only be taken if you want to take it: what are you prepared to do about it? Whatever it is that you keep getting wrong, it is a part of your interlanguage, and therefore a part of you: it cannot be eliminated just by deciding to eliminate it (like making a New Year resolution), or by reading over and over again a page of explanations and examples in this book, or even by working through the exercises. In many cases, you need to understand how the grammar point is expressed in English, in order to check whether you are simply translating the English structure word-for-word into French. You also need to check whether you have understood the mechanics of the corresponding French structure (if need be by translating it literally into English: this will also show you in what way the French structure is different from its English equivalent). You are then ready to practise identifying and reproducing the correct French structure in a number of contexts, perhaps using the exercises in this book (on your own, with a fellow-student, and in class with your teacher). Finally, you should make a point of using this new, corrected structure as soon and as often as possible, in your spoken and written work.

4 'I can read French quite easily, but when I hear it, it never makes sense.'

Studying French is like learning two languages at once: French as it is spoken, and French as it is written. In fact, there is only one French language, which can take on either spoken or written form (with different regional varieties, and various conventions as to what constitutes correct usage). Develop the habit of making conscious links between these two forms, for example by listening to short recorded extracts while looking at a written transcription, and comparing the two. This is best done selectively, focussing on particular words, types of word or structure, rather than trying to take in everything at once. Conversely, you could try listening to a reading of a text that you are already familiar with as written French: again, looking out for the way in which particular syllables, words or phrases are pronounced.

5 'I don't see the point of all these exercises.'

Exercises are no substitute for the real thing: understanding and making yourself understood in French. The first thing an exercise tests is your motivation: are you willing to identify for yourself what your weak points are, to compare what you think is correct French with what is in the examples and explanations and then, when it comes to the exercises themselves, can you motivate yourself to think, speak and/or write French in a situation which you know is artificial?

6 'I'm bored with French because (most of) the others are so slow.'

Why let this hold you back? Your teacher is expecting each student in your group to make progress from whatever point they have reached, and in whatever way best suits them. This applies to you as well: choose the most challenging assignments for written and spoken work and practice; read and listen to more French and try to make use of French writers' and speakers' words and phrases to express your ideas. When working in pairs, try to explain points to your partner: you will learn by teaching!

Part two

How language conveys meaning

3 Language and meaning

- **3.1 Communication**
- **3.2 The four major parts of speech**
- **3.3 Grammar and meaning in French and English**

3.1 Communication

Non-verbal communication

In our everyday lives, we communicate a lot of meaning without using language at all. For example:

- facial expression: our eyes and mouth show our thoughts, feelings, opinions, reactions and intentions;
- body language: our posture, our gestures and movements, whether sitting or standing, send unmistakable signals to other people;
- voice: 'it's not what you say, but how you say it'. As well as the words we use, volume, pitch, delivery, hesitations and so on, all send out messages about us.

Most of the time, we do not exercise conscious control over our expression, gestures and voice, and even when we try to our efforts will not always be interpreted in the way we intend. But we know how important all these non-verbal means are in enabling us to communicate with others: speaking on the telephone (where we cannot fall back on expression or gesture to help convey our message) may be easy in a conversation with a friend, but this is less easy when speaking to a stranger or in a foreign language, when we have to think about what we are saying, and how it will be received.

Conversely, we respond to, and sometimes depend on, non-verbal signals from other people: many of us are tongue-tied when faced by a telephone answering machine instead of the person we were expecting to speak to; we generally find presenting our ideas in the form of a monologue (such as a formal presentation to a group) more stressful than participating in a one-to-one conversation or in an informal discussion group.

Elementary verbal communication

Language begins as noises and individual sounds: babies soon learn to experiment with the production of sounds, and to imitate the sounds they hear around them. Throughout our lives we feel the need (not just when talking to babies) to communicate by elementary verbal means: onomatopoeia ('Bang!'), exclamations ('Wow!'), interjections ('Hey!', 'Quick!') and expletives ('Drat!'), often with accompanying gestures or expression. In such cases our tone of voice is a vital part of the message being conveyed.

Bridging the information gap

Non-verbal and elementary verbal communication together represent a large part of human communication, particularly in close-knit groups, or to deter or exclude total strangers. This is possible because both parties already know what is going on, and how the other will react: making a simple gesture or saying a word is enough, and often does no more than confirm what both parties know. There is little or no information gap between speaker and listener.

In many situations, however, a simple sound or word is not enough to convey either what the speaker needs or wishes to communicate, or what the listener needs or wishes to hear. The wider the information gap, the more complex language needs to become, in order to bridge it. If this gap is too wide, or if one or both of the parties does not dispose of sufficient and appropriate linguistic means of conveying and understanding meaning, communication does not take place, is incomplete, or is in some way unsatisfactory.

The first steps in using language

The first steps in using language usually consist of a noun + something else, which need not be a verb:

Noun + Verb	baby cry	ball gone
Verb + Noun	kick ball	
Noun + Noun	baby toy	
Noun + Adverb	ball here	here ball

These examples from English show that, even at this stage, word order plays a part in the communication of meaning: the first word announces the topic, the second word makes a comment on this topic (see 52.2).

When there are three or more words or elements in the sentence, word order becomes particularly important in languages such as English or French, where nouns sound the same whether they are the subject (baby kick ball) or the object (baby kick ball) of the verb:

Noun + Verb + Noun   baby want toy   man clean car

Now the verb, not a noun, is the pivot of the sentence, and the logical order topic + comment has been replaced by the conventional grammatical order subject + verb + object (see 32.1). This shows that, as soon as our message becomes more complex, we need to use language, not simply in strings of unrelated and undifferentiated words, but to express different types of idea, and to show how different words or groups of words are linked or related.

3.2 The four major parts of speech

The four major parts of speech, or grammatical classes, are:

- nouns and verbs: these are the two basic building blocks of the sentence;
- adjectives and adverbs: these enable the meaning of nouns and verbs to be extended.

(For minor parts of speech, **see 17.1.**)

The following table shows how the four major parts of speech relate to one another, with examples of phrases and sentences made up from combinations of two different parts of speech:

	Static	**Dynamic**
Basic	Noun ────────────────	Verb
	│	│
Additional	Adjective ────────────	Adverb

Nouns and adjectives are static: they describe objects (real or imaginary).
Verbs and adverbs are dynamic: they describe processes, actions.

Examples:

Adjective + noun
argent liquide ready cash

Noun + verb
Marie chante Marie sings

Verb + adverb
marchons lentement let's walk slowly

Adverb + adjective
trop facile too easy

Nouns

Nouns represent substance; they can be thought of as 'names' (in French, *un nom* is used to mean both 'a noun' and 'a name'): not only proper names such as Paul or Mary, but the name or label for people (*une femme*), creatures (*une girafe*), inanimate objects (*une pierre*) and more general or abstract ideas or concepts such as *les mathématiques, le plaisir*.

Verbs

Verbs represent process; they are often called 'doing words'; this can be a useful starting-point for understanding what a verb is or does, so long as one extends this definition to include not only actions, but processes and states:

*Paul **aime** Marie*	Paul loves Marie
*Paul **ressemble** à Pierre*	Paul looks like Pierre
*Marie **est** contente*	Marie is pleased
*Pierre **reste** inquiet*	Pierre is still concerned
*Paul **reçoit** un coup mortel*	Paul suffers a mortal blow

Adjectives

Adjectives represent quality; they can be said to 'describe a noun', so long as 'describe' is understood to include almost any kind of detail about the noun. For example, *un discours présidentiel* could, depending on the context, mean 'a speech of presidential class' or simply 'a speech by the president'.

Adverbs

Adverbs represent time, manner, place; as the name suggests, they often 'qualify the verb': they say in what manner, or circumstances, an action is done:

*elle a parlé **vite***	she spoke quickly
*il a **rapidement** résumé la discussion*	he rapidly summarised the discussion

An adverb (single word, or a group of words) can also qualify an adjective or another adverb (**see 31.4 Intensifiers**):

*elle était **très** contente*	she was very pleased
*il est parti **bien** vite*	he left pretty quickly

It can also occupy a free-standing position in the sentence, describing the circumstances in which something takes place (**see 43.1**):

***aujourd'hui**, on va bien rigoler*	today we'll have a good laugh
***en fin de compte**, c'était la meilleure solution*	at the end of the day, it was the best way out

or acting as a modaliser (**see 50.2**), indicating to the listener or reader the speaker's or the writer's attitude to what follows:

***curieusement**, elle n'a rien dit*	strangely enough, she didn't say anything

3.3 Grammar and meaning in French and English

Grammar and meaning are distinct: one can exist without the other. In English, for example, Chomsky's famous sentence 'colorless green ideas sleep furiously' is perfectly grammatical, but it is meaningless in terms of our usual notions of reality. Nevertheless, it could become meaningful in a particular context, if it were understood that 'ideas' and 'sleep' had been given unconventional meanings: for example in Rumer Godden's *Black Narcissus*, one reads that 'The nuns' heads nodded above the ponies, they rode in a shade of green dark sleep'.

In French, *il le lui donne* ('it/he gives it/him to him/her/it') is a perfectly formed sentence, but on its own it is meaningless: it tells us about an action, but who or what are *il*, *le* and *lui*? The sentence becomes meaningful only from its context, from something outside itself: information available to the speaker or writer and the listener or reader.

> Grammar comes from the structures of a language; meaning comes from the users of the language.

A grammatical description of the French language can help you to understand ways in which it can help you to communicate meaning, but it does not decide for you what meanings you wish to communicate.

French and English grammar

French and English have many basic grammatical features (or principles) in common:

- the small number of verb endings in spoken French, and in both spoken and written English;   **(see 9–10)**
- normal word order is SV or SVO (subject, verb, object).   **(see 32.1)**

In other cases, a basic feature is the same in both languages, but its application is different:

- in both English and French, object pronouns are placed next to the verb, but in English they come after, and in French before, the verb;   **(see 18.2)**
- in both English and French, an adjective is placed next to the noun it qualifies, but in English it is placed before the noun, and in French it is most often placed after the noun.   **(see 26)**

More fundamental differences include the following:

- there is a far larger number of verb endings in written French, compared to English;   **(see 9–10)**
- adjectives agree in French, but not in English, with the noun they qualify.   **(see 12)**

You need to have a clear idea of all these differences between French and English grammar, so that you can make the necessary changes to your map of French as you learn more about the language **(see 2.2 Interlanguage)**.

French
Grammar
Explained

4 Words and meaning

4.1   Using a dictionary
4.2   Synonyms

4.1 Using a dictionary

What kind of dictionary?

You probably own a bilingual (French–English/English–French) dictionary, and have found it useful for checking the meanings of French words or phrases, and for finding French equivalents of English words or phrases. The smaller your dictionary, the more likely you are to find yourself confronted with two or more possible words or phrases, with no guidance as to which one corresponds to the meaning you want. For this you will need to use a larger dictionary. Larger dictionaries tend to:

- give examples of words in use;
- list other words and phrases with which they are often used;
- show which area(s) of knowledge or activity they are associated with.

You have probably also looked at, in a library, a monolingual (French–French) dictionary, and wondered whether you would be able to make good use of it. In fact, because words are explained and illustrated in French, instead of simply giving one or more English equivalents, a monolingual dictionary can, if used appropriately, be more helpful to you than a bilingual dictionary.

Exercice 4/1   **Comment se servir d'un dictionnaire monolingue**
Travail individuel ou Travail à deux

Notez par écrit cinq mots français (pas trop techniques, ni trop spécialisés!) que vous avez déjà utilisés vous-même, à l'oral ou à l'écrit.

Dans un dictionnaire monolingue, lisez la définition (avec les phrases illustratives) d'un des mots que vous avez notés.

a   Cette définition correspond-elle au sens que vous donnez vous-même à ce mot?

b   Y a-t-il **d'autres** définitions du même mot? Les connaissiez-vous déjà?

c   Essayez, pour les mots dont la ou les définitions vous ont **surpris**, de retrouver l'origine de votre erreur!

WHEN TO USE A DICTIONARY

Reading and listening

If you are reading a text in French, or listening to a recorded text, do not stop and open the dictionary each time you come across a word you don't understand. On a first reading or listening, try to get an idea of the text as a whole: the writer or speaker, the intended audience, the main topic or issue, the main points covered, the kinds of ideas and attitudes being expressed. It may be that one or two words keep appearing: if you are not sure what they mean, look these words up first. Then read or listen to the text again, one section at a time, to gain a clearer idea of the contents of this section; this time, it may be one particular word that is blocking your understanding of the section as a whole: try to work out what kind of word it is (noun or verb; singular or plural; tense, etc.), what it might mean, and then check your idea in the dictionary.

If you use a dictionary without thinking first, you are likely to be unable to decide which of several possible meanings given in the dictionary is the right one in this text. If you use a dictionary too often, you will spoil the pleasure of the text you are reading or listening to. Use a French–English dictionary for topic-based, specific, concrete words, and a French–French dictionary for more general or abstract words and phrases: in short, be selective in your use of the dictionary. Follow up your work on a text by noting down and learning in their context 5–10 new words and phrases which you think will be worth knowing and using in the future.

Writing and speaking

If you are preparing a piece of written work, or making notes for a spoken presentation, use the dictionary several times: not automatically every time you can't think of a word, but whenever you need to know, or check, a word or phrase that is vital for what you want to say. If you are preparing a spoken presentation, try to avoid technical words and terms: your aim is to interest and inform your audience, who will not have the opportunity to look up these words as you speak!

Parts of speech

All dictionary entries show to which part of speech a word, or a particular use of a word, belongs: e.g. **n.** for *nom* (noun), **v.** or **vb** for *verbe* (verb). One reason for being clear about grammatical classes and categories **(see 3.2** and **17.1)** is so that, when you look up 'drop', you already know whether this is a noun (*une goutte*) or a verb (*laisser tomber*), or whether 'stick' is a noun (*un bâton*) or a verb (*coller*).

4.2 Synonyms

Synonyms are often thought of as two or more words or phrases with the same meaning, but in practice it is rare for two words to have exactly the same meaning, or to be used in exactly the same context or situation. Each language in the world is a storehouse, in simplified or distorted form, of the history and culture of all those who ever spoke it, so that many words in language A do not have exactly the same meaning as the apparently equivalent words in language B. That is one reason why it would represent a devastating form of cultural impoverishment if everyone in the world spoke (only) the same language.

If you look up a word in a monolingual dictionary, the definition is usually given in a combination of four ways:

- a list of synonyms of the word in question;
- an indication of the context(s) in which the word is used, e.g. the nouns with which an adjective is commonly used, or the verbs with which a noun is commonly used;
- an indication of the situation(s) in which the word is used, e.g. literary, vulgar;
- a set of examples showing the word in particular phrases or sentences.

If you look up a word in a bilingual dictionary, you will find a similar set of entries which make up the definition of the word – except that this is sometimes wrongly called 'looking up the translation' of a word. In fact, all the dictionary can provide you with is a series of synonyms (with contexts, situations and examples) which are not necessarily exact translations.

Exercice 4/   **Verbes: sens et synonymes**

a   Travail individuel

En consultant un dictionnaire français–français (ou français–anglais), étudiez et notez les similarités et les différences de **sens** et d'**emploi** des verbes suivants (pour le **sens**, comparez les **définitions** (ou les équivalents en anglais); pour l'**emploi**: est-ce que le verbe s'emploie avec une personne ou une chose (comme sujet, et comme objet)? avec quels mots ou quels types de mots?):

s'en aller	laisser	partir	quitter	sortir
rentrer	retourner	revenir		
achever	arriver à	atteindre		
éprouver	ressentir	sentir	se sentir	

b Travail en classe (oral) ou individuel (écrit)

Complétez chacune des phrases suivantes en choisissant, parmi les verbes proposés, celui qui vous semble convenir le mieux au contexte. N'oubliez pas de mettre le verbe à la **personne** et au **temps** corrects!

s'en aller   laisser   partir   quitter   sortir

1   Ils ne _ pas beaucoup le soir; ils préfèrent rester à la maison.
2   Il fait trop chaud dans la salle, et il y a trop de bruit: je _.
3   Il ne faut jamais _ les petits enfants seuls à la maison.
4   Tu vois, on va manquer le train! On _ trop tard.
5   Aujourd'hui les gens ont peur de _ leur emploi avant d'en avoir trouvé un autre.

rentrer   retourner   revenir

6   Elle habite en Écosse, mais elle est née au Canada, et elle a toujours eu envie de _ là-bas.
7   Son chien était parti il y a dix jours, mais hier il _.
8   Quand il a commencé à pleuvoir, nous _ à la maison.

c Travail à deux > Mise en commun

Composez, pour chacun des verbes suivants, une phrase où ce verbe est employé dans un contexte qui convient au(x) **sens**, et à la **personne** et au **temps** appropriés:

achever   arriver à   sentir   se sentir

Exercice 4/   **Noms: sens et synonymes**

a Travail individuel

En consultant un dictionnaire français–français (ou français–anglais), étudiez et notez les similarités et les différences de **sens** et d'**emploi** des noms suivants (pour le **sens**, comparez les **définitions** (ou les équivalents en anglais); pour l'**emploi**: avec une personne ou une chose (comme sujet, et comme objet)? avec quels mots ou types de mots?):

l'endroit	le lieu	la place	
l'époque	la fois	la période	le temps
l'étage	l'étape	le stade	le stage
la famille	les parents	les relations	

b Travail en classe (oral) ou individuel (écrit)

Complétez chacune des phrases suivantes en choisissant, parmi les noms proposés, celui qui vous semble convenir le mieux au contexte.

le lieu   l'endroit   la place

1   Ils ont compris qu'ils étaient perdus dans la forêt, quand ils sont revenus au même _.

2   Nom. Adresse. Date et _ de naissance.

3   C'est un homme très ordonné: il veut que chaque objet soit à sa _.

l'époque   la fois   la période   le temps

4   C'était une machine très avancée pour son _.

5   Avez-vous vu le film de Chaplin, 'Les _ modernes'?

6   C'est la première _ qu'un véhicule a traversé le mur du son.

7   Après la chute du gouvernement, on va traverser une _ difficile.

c   Travail à deux > Mise en commun

Composez, pour chacun des noms suivants, une phrase où ce nom est employé dans un contexte qui convient au(x) sens:

l'étape   le stage   la famille   les relations

Exercice 4/   **Adjectifs: sens et synonymes**

a   Travail individuel

En consultant un dictionnaire français-français (ou français-anglais), étudiez et notez les similarités et les différences de **sens** et d'**emploi** des adjectifs suivants (pour le **sens**, comparez les **définitions** (ou les équivalents en anglais); pour l'**emploi**: avec une personne ou une chose (comme sujet, et comme objet)? avec quels mots ou types de mots?):

agréable   aimable   amical

fatal   grave   mortel   sérieux

b   Travail en classe (oral) ou individuel (écrit)

Complétez chacune des phrases suivantes en choisissant, parmi les adjectifs proposés, celui qui vous semble convenir le mieux au contexte. N'oubliez pas de faire l'accord de l'adjectif:

agréable   aimable   amical

1   Merci de nous avoir invités: c'était une soirée bien _.

2   Quand il m'a vu, il m'a adressé un sourire _.

3   Connaissez-vous les Dupont? Ce sont des gens très _.

fatal   grave   mortel   sérieux

4   A l'hôpital, on nous a dit que les blessures étaient _ mais pas _.

5   Ce problème mérite une étude _.

6   Une fois libéré, il a commis le même crime: c'était _.

Part three

Language, sounds and spelling

Why try to improve your pronunciation of French?

Very few learners of a foreign language achieve anything like perfect pronunciation. 'Perfect pronunciation' is an unhelpful concept: even when speaking our own language, we all have an accent, which tells our listener something about our social and geographical origins. All the same, there are four very good reasons for you to try to improve your pronunciation of French and these are:

1   How you pronounce French affects how well you are understood by French speakers. There is no point in your being able to compose, write down or memorise well-formed sentences in French, if when you try to say them people cannot make out what you mean. Making yourself understood depends on a number of other factors, of course: having a wide vocabulary, knowing verb endings, knowing how to use tenses being able to use certain grammatical constructions and expressions correctly, and so on. However, certain points of pronunciation can be crucial in making yourself understood.

2   How you speak affects how people think of you. Speaking in such a way that you can be understood is a form of politeness towards your listener: the less they have to concentrate on deciphering poorly-articulated or mispronounced words, the more they will be open to what you have to say. This is more important than striving for a perfect accent: all sorts of regional and social accents are acceptable to most unprejudiced people, and in any case, a French-speaking listener who knows your first language is not French will not expect your accent to be perfect.

3   Your idea of how French is pronounced affects your ability to understand French when it is spoken to you, so it is worth your while to know all the basic sounds of French, even if

you cannot yet manage to pronounce them all as well as you would like. Being able to understand, like being able to make yourself understood, is a form of politeness, and one which pays dividends.

4   The better you are at linking sound and spelling in French, the better you will be at picking up new words and phrases: you will be learning one language with two forms of expression, instead of having to treat spoken French and written French as two separate languages!

Reading French, or studying phonetic symbols, will not, of itself, improve your pronunciation of French. Identify specific points where you need to improve. Listen closely to French speakers (in person, on tape/video/TV); sometimes, listen out for one particular sound at a time, and try to imitate what you hear. Compare, when listening to spoken French, how a word is pronounced with how you thought or assumed it was pronounced, and be prepared to change your mind! Make a note of these differences, and practise them: on your own, with a fellow-student, or with a native speaker, and by using the exercises in this book.

In the next four sections (5–8), you will have some opportunity to see how French pronunciation differs from English, and how spoken French and spelling are related:

5   **Speech and writing**
6   **Consonants**
7   **Syllables and stress**
8   **Sound and spelling**

5

Speech and writing

5.1	**The sounds of French**
5.2	**Vowels: open vowels**
5.3	**Nasal vowels**
5.4	**Semivowels**

The origin of human language and of particular languages is in speech, not writing. This is true:

● for individual human beings in the early stages of their life (language);
● for human societies in the early stages of their development (languages).

Most of the 3000 languages in the world today exist only as spoken languages, but a certain number of languages, including English and French, have developed a written code which is now essential, in many countries, for full participation as a citizen in society. It is pointless to argue whether proficiency in the spoken code is more or less important than proficiency in the written code: anyone who cannot understand and produce both the spoken and the written code of a language is at a serious disadvantage in everyday life.

Although we use the terms 'English speakers', or 'the English-speaking' countries to refer to people who habitually communicate in English (and the terms *francophones* and *francophonie* for (members of) the 'French-speaking' community), literacy is usually understood to mean 'being able to read and write'.

We tend to associate each of the two codes (spoken or written) with particular activities or characteristics (**see 55**):

● *spoken* language is associated with spontaneity, family, friends, leisure, entertainment, but it is also used in formal speeches, lectures, etc.;
● *written* language is associated with studying, work, formality, official communication, serious culture, but it is also used in informal letters, email, etc.

In the rest of this section, we look at the sounds of French, and differences between French and English, and then at French vowel sounds.

5.1 The sounds of French

The trouble with French

Of the most widely-used European languages, French is one in which the system (the set of conventional signs) used for spelling is furthest away from the system (the set of sounds) used in speech: any child growing up in a French-speaking community, and any young or not-so-young person learning French as a second language, has to accept, for example, that the sounds [wa zo] and the letters *oiseau* correspond to the same mental image of a 'bird', just as [lə kɛ̃ zu] and *le quinze août* refer to the same thing: 'the 15th of August'.

The origins of the mismatch between the sound and spelling systems of French go back several centuries, to periods when changes took place in the way certain sounds were pronounced; these changes were inadequately reflected in changes in spelling. In addition, changes were made to the spelling system in order to make French look more like its distant ancestor, Latin.

One result of these changes is that, in French, certain groups of two (or three) vowels correspond to a single vowel sound:

au, eau	are pronounced the same as *o* in *photo:*	*autre, beau*
ai, ei	are pronounced either the same as *è* or *ê* in *la règle, la fête:*	
		je boirai, la maison, la peine
	or the same as *é* in *répéter:*	*la mairie, peiner*
ais, ait, aient	are pronounced the same as *è* in *très, près:*	*je boirais, il buvait*
eu	is pronounced as a single vowel:	*un peu*
œ	is pronounced as a single vowel:	*ma sœur*
ou	is pronounced as a single vowel:	*la bouche, un jour*

For the last two centuries, the standard systems of French sounds and spellings have remained relatively unchanged; through universal education, the press and the audio-visual media, these sounds and spellings now reach every French citizen.

Vowels and consonants

Written French and English use the same alphabet of 26 letters. In addition French spelling relies on a system of accents **(see 8.3)**. (In English, these are used mainly in words of French origin, such as café, attaché.) Of these 26 letters, 5 (or 6) are vowels: *a e i o u* (and *y*), and the rest are consonants. These 26 letters, together with accents, represent the spelling system of French; however, this spelling system corresponds only approximately (particularly in the case of vowels) to the sound system of standard French, where one can distinguish 36 different sounds (compared to 44 different sounds in standard English).

■ The sound systems of English and French

	English	(Similar in English and French)	French
Open vowels	12	(6)	11–12
Nasal vowels	0	(0)	3–4
Diphthongs	8	(0)	0
Semivowels	2	(2)	3
Consonants	22	(17)	18
Total	**44**	**(25)**	**36**

The English-speaking learner of French has to learn how to produce 11 wholly new sounds (36 minus 25). For the French-speaking learner of English, the corresponding figure is 19 (44 minus 25). To these we must add the six vowel sounds described above as 'similar', and certain consonant sounds, such as [p], [t], [k] and particularly [r], where there are noticeable differences between English and French.

In order to be sure which sounds are being described in the pages that follow, you should familiarise yourself with the phonetic symbols (taken from the International Phonetic Alphabet, or IPA) for the sounds of French: **see 5.2**: Table of French vowel sounds and **6**: Table of French consonant sounds.

5.2 Vowels

■ Table of French vowel sounds

Open vowels				**Nasal vowels**			
[i]	*ville*	*île*	*mardi*	[ɛ̃]	*ancien*	*main*	*plein*
[e]	*idée*	*les*	*régler*	[ɑ̃]	*écran*	*quand*	*central*
[ɛ]	*faible*	*fête*	*problème*	[ɔ̃]	*bon*	*oncle*	*ronde*
[a]	*chat*	*pas*	*espace*	[œ̃]	*un*	*aucun*	*parfum*
[o]	*beau*	*aux*	*rose*				
[ɔ]	*bonne*	*note*	*alcool*	**Semivowels**			
[u]	*tout*	*fou*	*coûter*	[j]	*oeil*	*yeux*	*pièce*
[y]	*russe*	*eu*	*virus*	[w]	*ouest*	*trois*	*noyer*
[ø]	*eux*	*feu*	*Europe*	[ɥ]	*lui*	*huit*	*actuel*
[œ]	*heure*	*club*	*jeune*				
[ə]	*je*	*de*	*que*				

As the above table shows, the French vowel system is simpler than in English, but there are some vowel sounds in French which are quite unlike any of those in English, especially the vowel spelt *u* (*sur, dû, bu, but*) and nasal vowels (**see 5.3**; for semivowels, **see 5.4**).

There are two other differences between vowel sounds in French and in English which you need to know about, and practise carefully, if you want your spoken French to sound like that of a French native speaker.

These two differences are that:

> **a** There are no diphthongs in spoken French, and
> **b** Vowels in French are pronounced with their full sound value.

a No diphthongs

A **diphthong** is a sound that is produced as (or as part of) a single syllable, but is actually made up of two different vowels run together: when pronouncing it, one starts with one vowel sound, and ends with a different vowel sound.

Try saying aloud several times the English word 'say' (with a London/SE England accent!), each time making the sound last longer; eventually, you will find that you are making three different sounds: the consonant [s], the vowel [e] and finally a long drawn-out vowel rather like an [i] in French. In short, a diphthong is a vowel that changes direction in mid-stream. This does not happen in spoken French.

Exercice 5/1   Travail à deux

Avec un(e) partenaire, lisez tour à tour à haute voix une des phrases (ou groupes de mots) ci-dessous. Ecoutez bien votre partenaire: la valeur de la voyelle dans la syllabe soulignée est-elle maintenue? Répétez vous-même la phrase, et invitez votre partenaire à vous imiter.

1   [ɛ]   Je <u>sais</u> ce qu'elle a <u>fait</u>
           Ils a<u>vaient</u> <u>fait</u> des pro<u>grès</u>
2   [e]   Liber<u>té</u>, <u>Egalité</u>, Fraterni<u>té</u>
           Elle s'est cou<u>chée</u> sans rien man<u>ger</u>
3   [i]   Je vais lui <u>dire</u> de ralen<u>tir</u>
4   [o]   Quels sont les princi<u>paux</u> jour<u>naux</u> régio<u>naux</u> en France?

---

b Full value

IN ENGLISH many vowels in unstressed position tend to lose their value, and to be pronounced as [ə]: something like 'Uh!' or 'Er . . .'. When one says the English word 'organisation' for example, the second and last syllables are unstressed, with the result that the vowels in '-ga-' and in '-tion' are reduced to this very neutral sound [ə].

Try saying these English words aloud:

    organisation   government   official   environment

How many times, in each word, did you 'reduce' a vowel to [ə]? Which ones?

Sometimes, in English, an unstressed vowel is not pronounced at all: the consonants that come just before and just after it are joined up, so that for example 'police', 'policeman' are pronounced as if they began with 'pl-', not 'pol-'.

IN FRENCH, all vowels are pronounced with their full value, even in an unstressed position **(see 7.2)**. In the French word *organisation*, for example, there are five syllables, and the vowel in each syllable is pronounced with its full value:

    [ɔr ga ni za sjɔ̃]

Try saying these French words aloud:

    organisation   *gouvernement*   *officiel*   *environnement*

Are you sure you haven't pronounced any syllable in an 'English' way, reducing the vowel to [ə]? (The sound [ə] does exist in French: **see 7.4**).

Exercice 5/2   Travail à deux

Avec votre partenaire, lisez tour à tour à haute voix le mot **anglais** (colonne de gauche), puis le mot **français** (colonne de droite). Écoutez bien votre partenaire: les différences entre les prononciations 'anglaise' et 'française' du mot ont-elles été bien marquées?

Anglais	Français
cigarette	une cigarette
comfortable	confortable
dialogue	le dialogue
industry	l'industrie
problem	un problème
religion	la religion
responsible	responsable
structure	la structure

Open (or oral) vowels and nasal vowels

There are two types of vowel in French: open vowels and nasal vowels.

As the name suggests, an **open** (or **oral**) **vowel** is pronounced by air from the throat passing through the open mouth; for a **nasal vowel (see 5.3)**, air passes through the nasal passages as well as through the open mouth.

Open vowels

When practising French vowels with the aim of maintaining the correct value, the most important ones are as follows: [i], [y], [u]; [e], [ɛ]; [ɔ], [o]. By far the most important one to practise is the vowel [y], which does not exist in English: practise it until you can produce it reasonably well.

The exercise that follows gives practice in producing the open vowel sounds of French when pronouncing a number of familiar words.

Exercice 5/3   Travail à deux > avec le professeur

Lisez tour à tour à haute voix les mots dans la liste ci-dessous, en faisant surtout attention au son de la voyelle indiquée à gauche, et en écoutant attentivement la prononciation de votre partenaire.

1   [i], [y], [u]

[i]	le système	imiter	joli
[y]	russe	public	l'individu
[u]	fou	tout	la soupe
[u] + [y]	j'ai voulu	surtout	pas du tout

2   [e], [ɛ]

| [e] | l'été | ayant | préféré |
| [ɛ] | faible | un problème | français |

3   [ɔ], [o]

| [ɔ] | la police | folle | l'alcool |
| [o] | rose | de l'eau | le bureau |

Vowel + [r]

If you speak English with a Scottish accent, you will have no problem with the next item; if your spoken English is closer to the SE England variety, then this section is for you! Say these English words aloud:

beat	beer		clean	clear
peg	pair		shed	share
school	sure		food	tour

If you do not pronounce the 'r' in any of the second words in each pair, you will also have altered the value of the vowel from what it was in the first word. For you, when speaking English, the sole effect of the 'r' is to change the value of the preceding vowel, making it into a diphthong: the 'r' itself is not pronounced. This is precisely what you must avoid when speaking French!

IN FRENCH, the value of most vowels followed by [r] is the same as usual, whether the [r] is at the end of the syllable, or at the start of the following syllable (**see 7.1**), except that:

- in the case of [e] followed by [r] in the same syllable, the sound changes to [ɛr];
- in the case of [ø] followed by [r] in the same syllable, the sound changes to [œr];
- in the case of [o] followed by [r] in the same syllable, the sound changes to [ɔr].

The next exercise gives practice in producing the open vowel sounds of French when pronouncing a number of familiar words where they are followed by [r]. When saying these words, try to pronounce the vowel exactly as it was pronounced when not followed by [r].

Exercice 5/4   Travail à deux > avec le professeur

Lisez tour à tour à haute voix les mots dans la liste ci-dessous, en faisant surtout attention au son de la voyelle indiquée à gauche, et en écoutant attentivement la prononciation de votre partenaire.

1   **[i] + [r]**
    [i] + [r]   un virage   tirer   admirer
    [ir]   dire   la firme   choisir

2   **[y] + [r]**
    [y] + [r]   durer   durable   puritain
    [yr]   urgent   la voiture   futur

3   **[u] + [r]**
    [u] + [r]   la Touraine   un touriste   le courage
    [ur]   l'amour   le cours   la course

4   **[a] + [r]**
    [a] + [r]   varier   les parents
    [ar]   large   les marchandises

5   **[ɔ] + [r]**
    [ɔ] + [r]   la Lorraine   un orage
    [ɔr]   mort   la force   la Normandie

Now practise the vowel sounds which change when followed by [r].

Exercice 5/5   Travail à deux > avec le professeur

Lisez tour à tour à haute voix les mots dans la liste ci-dessous, en faisant le changement indiqué pour la valeur de la voyelle indiquée à gauche, et en écoutant attentivement la prononciation de votre partenaire.

1   **[e]+ [r]; [ɛr]**

| [e] + [r] | le numéro | différent | exagéré |
| [ɛr] | le service | une personne | le cancer |

2   **[ø] + [r]; [œr]**

| [ø] + [r] | l'Europe | européen | |
| [œr] | la peur | la couleur | |

5.3 Nasal vowels

All the vowel sounds described above are open vowels (also called oral vowels): they are pronounced through the mouth, which stays open while the vowel is being pronounced.

IN ENGLISH, all vowels are open (oral), except for those in certain words of French origin, such as *ambiance, détente, lingerie, impasse.*

IN FRENCH, there are a number of **nasal vowels**. As their name suggests, nasal vowels in French are pronounced by allowing air to pass through both the nose and the mouth, which remains open while the nasal vowel is being pronounced.

These nasal vowels are written as a vowel + nasal consonant (*n* or *m*), but this consonant is not pronounced in standard northern French. When practising French nasal vowels, try not to pronounce an *n* or an *m*, which you will find yourself doing if you close your mouth before moving on to the next sound!

[ã]   Spellings which correspond to this nasal vowel:

an   am   en*   em

*(at the beginning or in the middle of a word, but not at the end of a word)

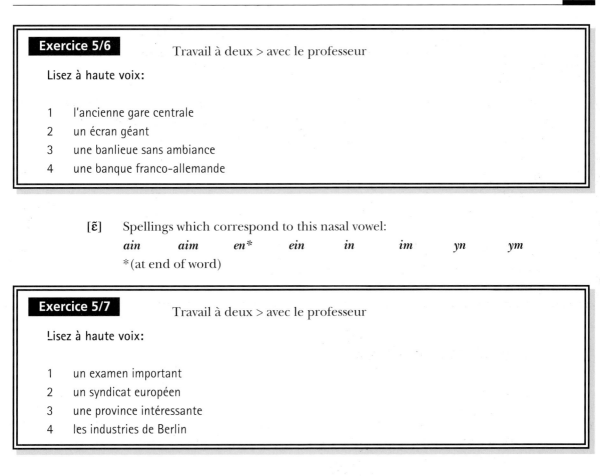

Exercice 5/6   Travail à deux > avec le professeur

Lisez à haute voix:

1   l'ancienne gare centrale
2   un écran géant
3   une banlieue sans ambiance
4   une banque franco-allemande

[ɛ̃]   Spellings which correspond to this nasal vowel:
        ain   aim   en   ein   in   im   yn   ym*
        *(at end of word)

Exercice 5/7   Travail à deux > avec le professeur

Lisez à haute voix:

1   un examen important
2   un syndicat européen
3   une province intéressante
4   les industries de Berlin

[œ̃]   Spellings which correspond to this nasal vowel:
        un   um

Exercice 5/8   Travail à deux > avec le professeur

Lisez à haute voix:

1   un nouveau parfum
2   aucun n'est brun
3   quelques-uns sont communs

In some parts of France (including Paris), this sound is not used: *un* and *um* are pronounced in the same way as *ain, in* and *aim, im.*

[ɔ̃]   Spellings which correspond to this nasal vowel:
        on   om

Exercice 5/9   Travail à deux > avec le professeur

Lisez à haute voix:

1   le son du violon
2   son nom? Simon
3   on fait des comparaisons

When to pronounce a nasal vowel, and when to pronounce an open vowel + [n] or [m]

A nasal vowel occurs in French when:

- it is followed by a new consonant, which starts the next syllable:

  la campagne [la kã paɲ]   *l'industrie* [lɛ̃ dy stri]   *la montagne* [la mɔ̃ taɲ]

- or when it is at the end of a group of words.

  je l'ai vue à l'écran   *on est allé à Berlin*   *elle a joué du violon*

An open vowel occurs when:

- the next sound after *n* or *m* is a vowel, and *n* or *m* is pronounced at the start of the next syllable:

  mes camarades [me ka ma rad]   *c'est inutile* [se ti ny til]   *monotone* [mɔ nɔ tɔn]

As well as practising the words in the exercise below, make yourself familiar with the ways in which French words and phrases are divided into syllables **(see 7.1)**.

Exercice 5/10   Travail à deux/avec le professeur

Avec un(e) partenaire, lisez à haute voix les mots suivants, en prononçant une **voyelle nasale** ou une **voyelle orale** + [n] ou [m], selon le cas:

	Voyelle nasale	Voyelle orale + n ou m
1	la campagne	une camarade
2	l'industrie	inutile
3	intéressant	inévitable
4	l'intention	l'inégalité
5	Berlin	un Berlinois
6	un magasin	un magazine
7	il prend	ils prennent
8	elle vient	elles viennent

If the vowel + *n* or *m* at the end of a word is followed by *e* (for example, when an adjective ending in *n* agrees with a feminine noun), then the nasal vowel becomes an open vowel + *n*:

Masculine form: nasal vowel	Feminine form: open vowel + *n/m*
aucun	*aucune*
certain	*certaine*
plein	*pleine*

Double *n* is required in the feminine form of words ending in *-an*, *-ien* and *-on* (**see 12.3** and **6.3**):

indien	*indienne*		*bon*	*bonne*

Exercice 5/11   Travail à deux/avec le professeur

Avec un(e) partenaire, lisez à haute voix les mots suivants, en prononçant une **voyelle nasale** ou une **voyelle ouverte + [n]**, selon le cas:

	Masculin	Féminin
1	humain	humaine
2	voisin	voisine
3	ancien	ancienne
4	italien	italienne
5	paysan	paysanne
6	européen	européenne
7	Jean	Jeanne
8	quelques-uns	quelques-unes

A vowel + double consonant (*nn* or *mm*) is always pronounced as an open vowel, with *n* or *m* pronounced at the start of the next syllable:

innocent [i no sã]   *récemment* [re sa mã]   *immense* [i mãs]

Exercice 5/12   Travail à deux/avec le professeur

Lisez à haute voix les mots suivants, en ayant soin de prononcer une voyelle orale + [n] ou [m], chaque fois qu'il y a nn ou mm:

1   l'innocence
2   une innovation
3   les immigrés
4   immense

5.4 Semivowels (also called semiconsonants, or glides)

IN ENGLISH, there are two semivowels, [j] and [w], which function as consonants:

[j]   yellow, young, Yarmouth   [w]   water, watch, Wimbledon

IN FRENCH, these two semivowels function as consonants in words taken from English:

[j]   *un yacht, un yaourt, le yoga*   [w]   *le water-polo, le whisky, la williams*

There are three semivowels in French:

[j]	as in	*travail*	[tra vaj]	*société*	[sɔ sje te]
[ɥ]	as in	*huit*	[ɥit]	*actuel*	[ak tɥɛl]
[w]	as in	*croire*	[krwar]	*jouer*	[ʒwe]

They can be seen as **semivowels** because each of them is the contracted form of a particular vowel in French:

Semivowel	Vowel
[j]	[i]
[ɥ]	[y]
[w]	[u]

They can also be seen as **semiconsonants**, because, like consonants, they are pronounced with a vowel, and do not form part of a separate syllable (a syllable is formed from a vowel, with or without one or more consonants (**see 7.1**)):

[j]   the word *société* has three syllables, not four
[ɥ]   the word *actuel* has two syllables, not three
[w]   the word *jouer* has one syllable, not two

They can also be described as **glides**, because they help certain sequences of sounds to be pronounced without a break. This *enchaînement* is characteristic of the way words and groups of words are spoken in French (**see 7.3**):
- between a consonant and a vowel:

[mje] *premier*   [ʒɥi] *juillet*   [fwa] *quelquefois*
- between two vowels:

[aje] *un cahier*   [aje] *travailler*   [ije] *fusiller*

In this function as a glide, [j] is particularly useful: for example, it is difficult to pronounce the sequence *li* + vowel or *ri* + vowel unless the *i* is used twice: [ij]:

[li je] *j'avais oublié*   I'd forgotten   [ri jɛ] *elle riait*   she was laughing

The following Exercise provides practice in saying certain French words which include a semivowel.

Exercice 5/13   Travail à deux/avec le professeur

Lisez à haute voix les mots suivants, en ayant soin de prononcer une semi-voyelle quand il le faut:

1   [j]
    la violence   une pièce   s'inquiéter   la société
    le travail   ayant   un conseil   une bouteille

2   [ɥ]
    huit   juillet   actuel   l'ennui

3   [w]
    croire   quelquefois   moins   le besoin

6 Consonants

6.1	**Single consonants**
6.2	**Final consonants**
6.3	**Double consonants**

There are more similarities than differences between English and French in regard to the pronunciation and spelling of consonants.

■ Table of French consonant sounds

[p]	*peur*	*premier*	*frapper*
[b]	*beau*	*blanc*	*tabac*
[t]	*table*	*très*	*quatre*
[d]	*dont*	*droit*	*bande*
[k]	*quatre*	*Québec*	*cinq*
[g]	*gare*	*grand*	*vague*
[f]	*fort*	*froid*	*phrase*
[v]	*valeur*	*vrai*	*devoir*
[s]	*centre*	*salon*	*passer*
[z]	*zéro*	*douze*	*loisir*
[ʃ]	*chercher*	*tâche*	*fasciste*
[ʒ]	*jamais*	*nager*	*rouge*
[m]	*matin*	*âme*	*caméra*
[n]	*note*	*nuit*	*année*
[ɲ]	*ignorer*	*signe*	*magnifique*
[ŋ]	*camping*	*parking*	*shopping*
[l]	*livre*	*filer*	*ville*
[r]	*raison*	*arriver*	*octobre*

In this section, certain key differences between English and French are highlighted.

6.1 Single consonants

c

Before a consonant, and before *a*, *o* and *u*, *c* is pronounced [k]:

capable	*encore*	*encourager*	*curieux*
capable	again	to encourage	curious

Before *e* and *i*, *c* is pronounced [s]:

la céramique	*s'efforcer*	*la société*	*un exercice*
pottery	to try	society	an exercise

In *-cer* verbs, *c* is spelt *ç* with endings beginning with *o* or *a*:

nous commençons	*il commençait*
we're beginning	he was beginning

And in *recevoir*, *décevoir*, *concevoir* etc., with endings beginning with *o* or *u*:

je reçois	*reçu*	*déçu*
I receive	received	disappointed

ch

The usual pronunciation of *ch* before a vowel is [ʃ]:

un chat	*acheter*	*la recherche*	*l'architecture*
a cat	to buy	research	architecture

But in certain words, *ch* before a vowel is pronounced [k]:

archaïque	*l'archéologie*	*Michel-Ange*
archaic	archeology	Michelangelo

Before a consonant (usually *r*), *ch* is pronounced [k]:

chronologique	*chrétien*
chronological	Christian

c or cc?

Before or after a consonant, or in final position, *c* is written as a single letter, pronounced [k]:

une activité	*l'action*	*exact*	*le lac*	*le sac*
activity	action	exact	lake	bag

But in *l'aspect* and *le respect*, final *-ct* is silent: [las pɛ], [lə rɛs pɛ]

Between two vowels, *c* or *cc* are pronounced [k] before *a*, *o* and *u*:

le chocolat	*l'agriculture*	*le baccalauréat*	*un accord*
chocolate	farming	18+ exam	an agreement

Before *e* and *i*, *cc* is pronounced [ks]:

le succès	*un accident*	*occidental*
success	accident	Western

g

Before a consonant, and before *a*, *o* and *u*, *g* is pronounced [g]:

la margarine	*l'argot*	*une virgule*	*entre guillemets*
margarine	slang	a comma	in quotation marks

In the groups *ge*, *gi*, *g* is pronounced [ʒ]:

imaginaire	*exagérer*
imaginary	to exaggerate

In *-ger* verbs ending in *-ger*, *e* is added between *g* and endings beginning with *o* or *a*:

nous nous changeons   we're getting changed

elle mangeait   she was eating

g or gg?

In the group *-aggl-*, the spelling corresponds to a single sound: [g]:

l'agglomération	*s'agglutiner*
the built-up area	to congregate

The group *-agr-*, on the other hand, is spelt with a single *g* [g]:

agressif	*agresser*	*(s')agrandir*
aggressive	to attack, assault	to enlarge (grow larger)

Exception:	*(s')aggraver*	to make worse (get worse)

In the verb *suggérer* and the noun *la suggestion* the spelling *gg* corresponds to two sounds in French: [gʒ], a hard *g* followed by a soft *g*:

il suggère	*je suggérais*	*elle a suggéré*
he suggests	I was suggesting	she suggested

gn

gn is pronounced [ɲ], a sound which has no exact equivalent in English: it is neither [n] as in 'on', nor [ŋ] as in 'song'.

Try saying aloud the following words, where the sound is in final position; do not pronounce the final *-e*:

le champagne	*l'Allemagne*	*la vigne*
[lə ʃɑ̃ paɲ]	[lal maɲ]	[la viɲ]
champagne	Germany	the vine

In internal position, followed by a vowel, the sound [ɲ] is harder to produce. Try saying these words, where it is followed by [i] or [ɔ]:

signifier	*magnifique*	*ignorer*
[si ɲi fje]	[ma ɲi fik]	[i ɲɔ re]
to mean	magnificent	not to know about

Almost certainly, you will have found yourself producing the sound [nj] ([n] followed by the semivowel [j]), as in Spanish *mañana*, 'tomorrow'. This is how many French speakers pronounce *gn*, so you are in good company!

EXCEPTIONS: in *un gnou* and *stagnant*, *g* and *n* are pronounced separately: [gnu], [stag nã]

l or *ll*?

In initial or internal position, a single *l* is pronounced [l]:

le livre	*un palais*	*Malte*	*symbolique*

In final position, *-l* is usually silent after *i*:

un outil   a tool

but it is pronounced [l] after *a* and *e*:

un canal	*le total*	*Chanel*	*le tunnel*

Verbs in *-eler*

The spelling of verbs in *-eler* varies between single *l* and double *ll*, depending on whether *l* is followed by a sounded vowel, or by a 'mute e' **(see 7.4)**.

In every case (single *l* or double *ll*), *l* is pronounced [l]:

l + vowel	*appeler*	*appelé*	*appelons*	*appelait*
ll + silent *e*	*elle appelle*	*ils appellent*	*j'appellerai*	*il appellerait*

With the endings *-eler*, *-elé*, *-elons*, *-elez*; *-elais*, *-elait*, *-elaient*, the sound [l] is the start of a new syllable; with the endings *-elle*, *-elles*, *-ellent*, the sound [l] is at the end of a syllable.

-ail, *-eil*, *-euil* (and *-aille*, *-eille*, *-euille*; also *-ille*)

After *ai* and *ei*, *l* is not pronounced [l], but [j] **(see 5.4)**; the group *ail* (or *aille*) is pronounced [aj], and *eil* (or *eille*) is pronounced [ej]:

ail	[aj]	*le travail*		*les rails*	
aille	[aj]	*je travaille*	*travailler*	*Versailles*	
eil	[ej]	*un conseil*	advice	*un appareil*	a camera
eille	[ej]	*un conseiller*	an adviser	*une bouteille*	
euil	[œj]	*le seuil*	the threshold		also: *un œil*
euille	[œj]	*la feuille*	the leaf		

In the group *ille*, *ll* is also pronounced [j]:

la fille	*la vanille*	*la Bastille*

EXCEPTIONS: *ll* is pronounced [l] in:

mille [mil]	*le village* [vi laʒ]	*la ville* [vil]

The group *illi* is pronounced [ilj]:

un million [mi ljɔ̃]   *un milliard* [mi ljar]

ps is pronounced as two consonants, [p] and [s]:

la psychologie   *le psychiatre*
psychology   the psychiatrist

The group *bs* is also pronounced [ps]:

observer   *absolu*   *absurde*   *abstrait*

qu is, in most cases, pronounced as a single consonant, [k]:

l'équilibre   *le Québec*   *un questionnaire*   *quasi-*
balance   Quebec   a questionnaire   almost

But, in a small number of words, *qu* is pronounced as consonant + semivowel, [kw]:

une équation   *quadruple*   *l'Équateur*
an equation   four-fold   Ecuador

r

Pronunciation of the letter *r* varies widely across Western Europe, from the very forward articulation in Southern German to articulation at the back of the mouth, as in Northern French. The relatively neutral articulation of *r* in standard Southern English stands out as 'foreign' if used by English speakers when speaking in French.

rh, pronounced the same as *r*, is used in a number of words in French:

	le Rhin	the Rhine	*le Rhône*	the Rhone
	le rhum	rum	*un rhume*	a cold
But:	*un rime*	a rhyme	*le rythme*	rhythm

Similarly, *th* is pronounced as [t]:

le théâtre   theatre   *le thé*   tea

s: pronounced [s] or [z]?

The letter *s* is pronounced as [s] or as [z], depending on its position in a word or group of words. The rules for the choice of [s] or [z] are not the same in French as they are in English.

Initial s

At the beginning of a word, *s* is pronounced [s] in French, whether it is followed by a vowel or a consonant:

silencieux   silent   *s'inquiéter*   to be worried
un scandale   a scandal   *la stabilité*   stability

Internal s

In the middle of a word, *s* is pronounced [s] after or before a consonant (even if the consonant is *n* or *m*, forming part of a nasal vowel, as in the last example below):

Israélien	Israeli	*Istanbul*	
un décapsuleur	a bottle-opener	*une récompense*	a reward

Between two vowels, *s* is pronounced [z]:

épuisé	exhausted	*une occasion*	an opportunity

EXCEPTION: *vraisemblable*, 'likely', and a small number of other words.

The sound [s], between two vowels, is spelt *ss*:

choisissez!	choose!	*saisissant*	startling

Final *s*

At the end of a word, *s* is usually silent **(see 6.2)**.

Exercice 6/1   **La lettre *s*: prononcée [s] ou [z]?**   Travail à deux ou avec le professeur

Indiquez à votre partenaire un des mots suivants, et demandez-lui de le dire à voix haute. Êtes-vous d'accord avec sa prononciation? En tout cas, dites le mot à votre tour. Ensuite, c'est à votre partenaire d'indiquer un mot, et ainsi de suite.

peser	une comparaison
islam	la conséquence
une névrose	renverser
économiser	la législation

Exercice 6/2   ***s* ou *ss*?**   Travail individuel

Complétez les phrases suivantes en ajoutant s ou ss dans les blancs:

1   C'est une entrepri( )e réu( )ie.
2   Il s'intére( )e à ses po( )e( )ions.
3   Choi( )i( )ez le succè( )!
4   Ils sai( )i( )ent l'occa( )ion.
5   Quelqu'un dans l'a( )i( )tance a perdu connai( )ance.

---

sc

In *sca*, *sco*, *scu*, and *scl*, *scr*, *sc* is pronounced [sk]:

scolaire	(to do with) school	*la sculpture*	
s'inscrire	to sign up	*une transcription*	

In *sce, sci, sc* is pronounced [s]:

scénique	scenic	*la science*	science
sceptique	sceptical	(pronounced the same as *septique*, 'septic')	
un ascenseur	a lift	*fascinant*	fascinating

EXCEPTION: [ʃ] in *fasciste*

In *sch, sc* is pronounced [ʃ]:

un schéma   a diagram

EXCEPTION: [sk] in *schizophrénique*

x

x is always pronounced as two consonants, [k] + [s], or [g] + [z]

The usual pronunciation is [ks]:
- before a consonant: *exceptionnel*   *s'excuser*
- between two vowels: *un taxi*   *un réflexe*   *fixer*   *l'oxygène*   *le luxe*

But in a word beginning with *ex* + vowel, *x* is pronounced [gz]:

exagérer   *un exercice*   *un examen*   *exhaustif*

Final x
At the end of a word, *x* is usually silent **(see 6.2)**.

6.2 Final consonants

Final consonants are often silent in French. In the case of words ending in *-d, -t, -s, -x, -z, -p* and *-er*, you should assume that the consonant is silent, unless:

- you are sure that you have heard it sounded in a particular word (a list of some words where these final consonants are sounded is given later), or
- the next word begins with a vowel, in which case the consonant is sounded in liaison **(see below** and **7.5)**.

Final *-s* is silent:
- in plural subject and object pronouns:
      nous, vous, ils, elles; les
- in plural articles:
      les, des
- in plural possessive and demonstrative adjectives:
      mes, tes, ses, nos, vos, leurs; ces
- in plural adjective forms:
      importants, importantes; moyens, moyennes

- in plural nouns:

   les Allemands, les Allemandes; les Écossais, les Écossaises

- in verb forms ending in *-s*:

   je vais, tu prends, nous sommes, vous êtes

In verb forms ending in *-ez*, the *-z* is silent, but the *e* is pronounced [e]:

   partez!   *vous travaillez bien*

Final *-t* is silent:

- in verb forms ending in *-t*:

Person 3	*il est, il vient, il savait*
Person 6:	*ils sont, ils viennent, ils savaient*
Present participle:	*étant, venant, sachant*
Past participle:	*mort, ouvert; j'ai écrit, tu as dit*

- in adjectives and nouns ending in *-ant* and *-ent*:

   important   un étudiant   différent   le présent

- in adjectives and nouns ending in *-at* and *-et*:

   l'État   the State   *muet*   silent   *secret*   secret   *l'intérêt*   interest

- in the word ***tout***:

   j'ai tout vu   I've seen everything   *c'est tout?*   is that all?

Final *-d* is silent:

- in all words except those taken from English;
- in ***Nord*** (but *-d* is sounded in ***Sud***)

Final *-x* is silent:

- in words ending in ***-aux, -eaux, -eux, -oux***, including place names: *Bordeaux*
- in the numerals ***six*** and ***dix*** when followed by a noun beginning with a consonant:

   six fois   [si fwa]   six times   *dix francs*   [di frã]   ten francs

Liaison

When a silent final consonant is followed by a vowel in certain groups of words such as article + noun, subject pronoun + verb, liaison takes place: the final consonant is sounded. In these cases, *-d* and *-t* are always sounded as [t] and *-s*, *-x* and *-z* are always sounded as [z] **(see 7.5)**.

Sounded final consonant

The final consonant is sounded in the following words:

-d	*Sud*	*David*	*le week-end*		*août* (but *le quinze août*: [lə kɛ̃ zu])
-t	*sept*	*huit*	*net*	*le fait*	
-s	*mars*	*le fils*	*le sens*	*le campus*	*le virus*
-st	*Est*	*Ouest*			
-x	(pronounced [s])	*six*	*dix*	(pronounced [ks])	*Astérix*

-*ax* in place names: *Aix*   *Dax*   *Oyonnax*

-*z*   *le gaz*   *le jazz*

-*p*   *stop*   *un slip*

-*c*   *le parc*   *le trafic*   (but *le tabac*: [ta ba])

Final consonant + *e*

Final *e* is not pronounced in standard Northern French **(see 7.4)**, but the presence of *e* at the end of a word has the effect of converting a silent final consonant into a sounded consonant. This means that there is a clear distinction, in spoken French, between the masculine and feminine forms of many adjectives and nouns (and participles used as adjectives).

Masculine		Last syllable	Feminine		Last syllable
Silent -*d*	*allemand*	[mã]	Sounded [d]	*allemande*	[mãd]
Silent -*t*	*un étudiant*	[djã]	Sounded [t]	*une étudiante*	[djãt]
Silent -*s* after consonant					
	divers	[vɛr]	Sounded [s]	*diverses*	[vɛrs]
Silent -*s* after vowel					
	des Français	[sɛ]		*des Françaises*	[sɛz]

The same distinction is made between the singular and plural of certain -*re* verbs, where the plural ending -*ent*, itself silent, activates the preceding silent consonant:

Singular		Last syllable	Plural		Last syllable
Silent -*d(s)*	*je les vends*	[vã]	Sounded [d]	*elles vendent*	[vãd]
	on m'attend	[tã]		*ils nous attendent*	[tãd]

Exercice 6/3   **Consonne finale: muette ou prononcée?**   Travail à deux ou avec le professeur

Avec votre partenaire, indiquez tour à tour un des groupes de mots choisis au hasard dans la liste ci-dessous. Votre partenaire doit prononcer aussitôt le groupe de mots indiqué; écoutez-le/la attentivement: la consonne finale est-elle restée muette, ou a-t-elle été prononcée, là où il le fallait? Prononcez vous-même le groupe de mots en question, puis c'est au tour de votre partenaire de choisir un autre groupe de mots, et ainsi de suite.

1	les Anglais	les Anglaises
2	un marché couvert	une piscine couverte
3	c'est évident	la réponse est évidente
4	tout le monde	toute la terre
5	un grand secret	une chambre secrète
6	un personnage important	une personne importante
7	les Écossais	les Écossaises
8	en haut	la ville haute

French
Grammar
Explained

6.3 Double consonants

Pronunciation

Unless they are pronounced as two different sounds (**see 6.1**, *cc*, *gg*, for example), most double consonants in French are pronounced as if they were a single consonant:

bb   *ff*   *mm*   *nn*   *pp*   *rr*   *tt*

EXCEPTION: *rr* in certain verb forms. A small number of verbs such as *courir* and *mourir* are formed with *r* in the present and imperfect tenses, and with *rr* in the future and conditional. In these cases, a double *rr* is sounded in the future and conditional forms:

Present	*nous courons*	we run	**Future**	*nous courrons*	we shall run
Imperfect	*il mourait*	he was dying	**Conditional**	*il mourrait*	he would die

Spelling

How can one decide whether a word is spelt with a single or a double consonant? A few generalisations can be made:

With words made up of more than one element, such as prefix + verb or noun (**see 13**), the spelling can reflect the spelling of the individual elements:

m	*amener*	to fetch	(*à* + *mener*)
mm	*emmener*	to take away	(*en* + *mener*)
m	*imiter*	to imitate	(no prefix)
mm	*immobile*	motionless	(*in* + *mobile*)

When a verb ending (**see 9.3**) or a suffix (**see 14**) is added to words ending in *-ion*, the *n* is usually doubled to *nn*:

n	*la raison*	reason
nn	*raisonner*	to reason (with)
n	*la tradition*	tradition
nn	*traditionnel*	traditional

Note the double *nn* in *la personne* and words formed from it:

un personnage   a character (in book, play, etc.)
la personnalité   personality, character

But *n* is not doubled before the suffix *-al*:

la nation   the nation   *le nationalisme, la nationalité*

The feminine form of the adjective suffix *-al* is *-ale*, but the feminine form of the adjective suffix *-el* is *-elle* (**see 12.4**):

-el, *-elle*   *universel, universelle*   *industriel, industrielle*   *individuel, individuelle*
In every case (*-al*, *-ale*, *-el*, *-elle*), the *l* is pronounced [l].

The suffix *-el* changes to *-al-* when a further suffix is added:

industrialiser   *l'industrialisation*   *individualisé*   *l'individualisme*

The spelling of words such as the following has to be learnt individually; sometimes the English spelling of the word is a guide, but in other cases it can lead you astray:

m	*une imitation*	an imitation	*mm*	*l'immigration*	immigration
n	*la résonance*	resonance	*nn*	*résonner*	to resonate, resound
p	*attraper*	to catch	*pp*	*frapper*	to hit, strike
r	*des carottes*	carrots	*rr*	*la carrosserie*	bodywork (of car etc.)
t	*un atelier*	a workshop	*tt*	*un attelage*	a team (of horses)

7 Syllables and stress; *Enchaînement*, elision, liaison

7.1 Syllables

Understanding how to divide a word (or sequence of words) into syllables is the key to your ability to pronounce words in a reasonably French way, and to spell words correctly.

A **syllable** consists of one vowel (V), together with any number of consonants (C) from none to five. For example, the following words all consist of a single syllable:

hé!	[e]	hey!	(V)
très	[trɛ]	very	(CCV)
l'heure	[lœr]	the time	(CVC)
strict	[strikt]	strict	(CCCVCC)

A semivowel (**see 5.4**) does not form a separate syllable: it is counted as a consonant. The following words consist of one syllable, therefore:

trois	[trwa]	three	(CCCV)
(un) pied	[pje]	(a) foot	(CCV)

Open and closed syllables
A syllable that ends in a vowel (an oral vowel or a nasal vowel) is an open syllable: when you pronounce it, your mouth opens to produce the vowel, and remains open. For example, the following words consist of one open syllable:

l'eau	[lo]	water	(CV)
vingt	[vɛ̃]	twenty	(CV)
hein?	[ɛ̃]	eh?	(V)

A syllable that ends in a consonant is a closed syllable: when you pronounce it, your mouth opens to produce the vowel, then closes to produce the consonant(s) at the end of the syllable. For example, the following words consist of one closed syllable:

(un) but	[byt]	(a) goal	(CVC)
août	[ut]	August	(VC)
(un) texte	[tekst]	(a) text	(CVCCC)

In spoken French, 80% of syllables are open (V, CV, CCV etc.), and only 20% are closed (VC, CVC, CVCC etc.). This contrasts sharply with German, for example, where only 30% of syllables are open, and 70% are closed.

The basic unit of sounds in French is consonant + vowel (CV), as are the first words we all uttered as babies: 'baba', 'dada', 'mama' etc. 55% of all syllables in adult French speech consist of this basic unit, CV.

Words of more than one syllable

IN SPOKEN ENGLISH, two-syllable words tend to be divided as follows:

| | | | | |
| par-ents | col-our | var-ied | park-ing | prob-lem |

IN SPOKEN FRENCH, where stress patterns are determined by groups of words, not within individual words **(see 7.2)**, syllables in a long word are divided more evenly: wherever possible, a word is spoken as a succession of open syllables (V, CV, CCV etc.):

| *(les) pa-rents* | | | *(la) cou-leur* | |
| CV | CV | | CV | CVC |

When two or more sounded consonants occur in succession, they are divided between two syllables:

| *(le) par-king* | | CVC | CVC |

EXCEPTION: if *l* or *r* occur after another consonant, they stick with that consonant:

| *(le) pro-blème* | | CCV | CCVC |

The following exercise provides practice in dividing long words into syllables, and then pronouncing them appropriately.

Exercice 7/1   **Syllabes et prononciation**   Travail à deux > Mise en commun

a   Avec un(e) partenaire, décidez comment les mots suivants se divisent en syllabes.
b   Ensuite, lisez-les à haute voix.

Syllabes ouvertes:		Syllabes ouvertes et fermées:	
1	premier	5	la structure
2	la sévérité	6	étranger
3	l'opéra	7	surtout
4	s'occuper	8	responsable

Groups of words

In spontaneous spoken French, there are no separate words, only sequences of syllables, with pauses for breath, or for emphasis, between groups of words. Wherever possible, a group of words is spoken as a succession of open syllables, even if these consist of a consonant from the end of a word, plus a vowel at the beginning of the next word:

une heure et quart	[y nœ re kar]	a quarter past one
il y aura huit entrées	[i ljɔ ra ɥi tã tre]	there will be eight entrances

This feature, known as *enchaînement* (see 7.3), affects the way any group of words is spoken in French.

It leads to **elision (see 7.3)** of the final *-e* of certain words, when the next word begins with a vowel or mute *h*:

*une salle **de** bain*	but	*une salle **d'**attente*
*il **se** lève*	but	*il **s'**habille*

It also causes **liaison (see 7.5)**: a silent final consonant such as *-s* or *-t* is pronounced when the next word in a group begins with a vowel or mute *h*:

les garçons	[le gar sɔ̃]	but	*les enfants*	[le zã fã]
ils sont	[i sɔ̃]	but	*ils ont*	[i zɔ̃]

7.2 Stress and intonation

In order to make yourself understood when speaking a foreign language, several factors are important (in addition to vocabulary and grammar):

● **Pronunciation**: saying vowels and consonants in ways that your listener can recognise **(see 5–6)**;

● **Articulation**: producing the sounds of the language clearly;

● **Delivery**: not too slow, or the meaning of groups of words will be lost; not too fast, or your listener will be lost;

● **Register**: using words and structures appropriate to the situation: formal (N3) or informal (N2) **(see 55)**;

● **Intonation**: attempting to imitate the melody of speech of native speakers – a rising, falling or steady tone of voice within each group of words (see below);

● **Stress**: when to make syllables longer or louder, at the end of a group or for emphasis.

The importance of stress patterns in French

The main reason for trying to use the right stress patterns is to make it easier for French speakers to understand what you are saying, just as it is easier for you to understand someone speaking English, if they get the stress patterns right:

'Failure to use the right stress patterns in English often leads to unintelligibility for the native English speaker' (S Romaine, *Bilingualism*, 1989, p53).

Word stress and group stress

Several European languages, including English, German and Russian, have word stress: any word of more than one syllable is pronounced with the same stress pattern, wherever it appears in a group of words:

parliament amazing operation to operate

Some English words are always stressed on the first syllable if they are used as a noun, and on the second syllable if they are used as a verb:

conduct (noun) to conduct (verb)

French, on the other hand, has group stress: any word of more than one syllable can be pronounced with stress on the first or the last syllable, depending on its position in a group of words:

Group-final stress (the basic stress pattern in French):

qu'est-ce qu'on fait maintenant? what shall we do now?

Group-initial stress (used in French for emphasis):

maintenant, vous allez voir! now you'll see!

Final stress is the normal stress pattern in French: in a group of words spoken without a pause, there is stress on the final syllable of the last word in the group:

Monsieur Dupont n'est pas là aujourd'hui Mr Dupont isn't in today

This stress on the final syllable (*-pont*, *là* and *-d'hui*) is achieved by making the vowel longer, momentarily slowing down the rate of delivery.

Initial stress is the means used in French to emphasise a word or phrase: the first syllable of a group of words is spoken more loudly than usual.

Here are some examples of initial stress in French:

Tonic pronouns **(see 19 and 51):**

lui, il n'a rien dit he didn't say anything
eux, au moins, ils ont compris at least they understood
moi je trouve qu'elle a raison I think she's right

(*moi je*, instead of *je*, is widely used in conversational French (N2); it is not particularly emphatic)

Numbers (when ordering drinks, etc.):

trois cafés, s'il vous plaît! three coffees, please!

Exclamations **(see 32.5):**

qu'est-ce qu'il fait chaud! my, it's hot! (N2)

Questions; asking WH- questions   **(see 33):**

> *quand est-ce qu'on part?*   when are we leaving?

Adverbs used as modalisers or fillers   **(see 50.2):**

> *heureusement, j'étais déjà parti*   luckily, I'd already left

Initial stress is also used, if emphasis is needed during the course of a sentence or statement, on the first syllable of a group:

> *il a pris ma place!*   he's taken <u>my</u> (parking) place!
> *je vais m'en occuper personnellement*   I'll deal with the matter my<u>self</u>
> *c'est une erreur monumentale!*   that's a <u>big</u> mistake!

Within a group there is no pause (unless there is hesitation), and there is no stress on internal syllables:

(in words)

> *une réservation*   (no stress on -*ser*- or -*va*-)   a booking
> *malheureusement*   (no stress on -*lheu*- or -*reuse*)   unfortunately

(in groups)

> *il y a eu un accident*   (no stress on *a* or *eu*)   there's been an accident
> *je lui ai dit de partir*   (no stress on *lui*, *ai* or *de*)   I told him/her to leave

EXCEPTION: if the first syllable begins with a vowel, emphasis, if required, is placed on the second syllable:

> *c'est épouvantable!*   (with stress on -*pou*-)   that's dreadful!

Intonation

The rise and fall of the tone of voice in everyday conversation is similar in French and in English:

- a rising tone at the end of a group indicates that one has not finished speaking;
- a falling tone indicates that one has finished.

In questions **(see 33)**, however, intonation patterns are different.

Yes/No questions

In Yes/No questions where the usual word order (subject–verb–object: **see 32.1**) is not changed, there is a rising intonation in French, in order to make clear to the listener that it is a question, and not a statement:

> *tu l'as vu?*   have you seen him?
> *on y va?*   shall we make a start?

WH- questions

In WH- questions ('who?', 'where?', 'why?', etc.), on the other hand, there is a falling intonation in French:

> *qui a dit ça?*   who said that?
> *où est-ce que tu l'as vu?*   where did you see him?

English-speaking learners, when speaking French, tend not to begin a sentence on a high enough tone, making it difficult to sustain a falling intonation when one is required. It pays, when speaking French, to start a sentence sounding bright and cheerful!

The best way to study intonation is to listen repeatedly to recordings of short spontaneous conversations, and to attempt to imitate the melody of one of the speakers. The words 'melody' and 'tone of voice' are particularly appropriate when discussing intonation: what you are practising is the music of the (spoken) language.

7.3 *Enchaînement*; elision

Enchaînement

Words and groups of words are spoken in French without a break. In this uninterrupted flow of sounds within and between words, syllables are formed consisting as far as possible of CV or CVC (**see 7.1**). A consonant which is spelt at the end of a word can, in speech, become the start of the next syllable; this phenomenon is known as *enchaînement*.

Here are some examples of how *enchaînement* affects the way words and groups of words are pronounced:

Words

If there are two consecutive vowels in a word, each is pronounced with its full value (**see 5.2**), but they are run together without a break:

créer	[kre e]	to create
le pays	[lə pe i]	the country
l'aéroport	[la e ro pɔr]	the airport
le chaos	[lə ka o]	chaos

Groups

If there are two or more consecutive vowels in a group of words, each is pronounced with its full value, and they are run together without a break:

j'ai oublié	[ʒɛ u bli je]	I've forgotten
il y a eu un accident	[i li a y]	there's been an accident

When you are listening to French, *enchaînement* is what makes it difficult for you to distinguish individual words. When you are speaking French, if you can avoid making a pause between each separate word, you will sound more authentically French.

Exercice 7/2   *Enchaînement*: **groupes de mots**   Travail à deux > Mise en commun

Avec un(e) partenaire, lisez tour à tour chacune des phrases suivantes, en **enchaînant** les mots quand il le faut.

1   J'ai été très surpris.
2   Il va arriver ce soir.
3   J'ai vu un taxi arrêté au feu.
4   Elle a eu un sourire forcé.
5   Je n'ai eu peur à aucun moment.

Elision

Elision occurs in French when a vowel is not pronounced at the end of a word, before a following word beginning with a vowel. In certain words, elision is indicated in written French by replacing the elided vowel by an apostrophe: for example, the *-e* of *ce* is elided in *c'est* and *c'était*, and the *-e* of *que* is elided in *qu'il, qu'elle, qu'est-ce que*, etc.

Elision occurs in the following specific cases:

		Followed by a consonant: no elision	Followed by a vowel: elision
Subject pronouns	*je*	*je sais*	*j'arrive*
	ce	*ce sera, ce fut*	*c'est, c'était*
Object pronouns	*me*	*ça me surprend*	*ça m'étonne*
	te	*tu te trompes*	*tu t'égares*
	se	*il/elle se lève*	*il/elle s'habille*
	le	*tu le vois*	*tu l'as vu*
	la	*tu la vois*	*tu l'as vue*
Definite articles	*le*	*le garçon*	*l'homme*
	la	*la comédienne*	*l'actrice*
Prepositions	*de*	*la salle de bains*	*la salle d'attente*
	jusque	*jusque-là*	*jusqu'ici, jusqu'à minuit*
Relative pronoun	*que*	*la femme que j'aime*	*l'homme qu'elle aime*
Interrogative pronoun	*que*	*que fait-il?*	*qu'est-ce qu'il fait?*
Adverb	*que*	*il n'y a que lui*	*il n'y a qu'elle*
Conjunction	*que*	*il sait que j'ai raison*	*je sais qu'il a raison*

Elision also occurs in the following cases:

● *quelque* in the pronoun ***quelqu'un*** ('someone') but not otherwise;
● *presque* in the noun ***une presqu'île*** ('a peninsula') but not otherwise;

● the conjunctions *lorsque* ('when'), *puisque* ('since'), *quoique* ('although'), except when followed by a proper name;

● the conjunction *si* ('if') when followed by *il* or *ils*: *s'il vous plaît, s'ils arrivent*, but not when followed by *on, elle* or *elles*: *si on gagne, si elle veut*.

Note: in very casual speech (N1), *-u* can elide in *tu* (*t'as vu?* 'did you see?'), and *-i* can elide in the relative pronoun *qui* (*c'est lui qu'a gagné* 'he's the one that won'). This fact is to be noted, but not imitated!

7.4 The letter e

Almost all cases of elision (**see 7.3**) involve the letter *e*. The letter *e* (spelt without an accent, and pronounced rather like the sound a French speaker makes when hesitating: *euh*...) is the only vowel which, in standard Northern French, can be either sounded or silent, depending on whether a word or phrase is easier to say with, or without it.

Final *e*

Look again at the list of words (see above, Elision) where final *-e* is elided before a vowel, and say them aloud: you will probably find that the phrases in the left-hand column (no elision) are easier for you to say with *-e*, and the phrases in the right-hand column (with elision) are easier for you to say without *-e*.

In standard Northern French, final *-e* is not pronounced in words of more than one syllable. This means that it does not form a separate syllable in speech: a word ending in consonant + *e* ends with a closed syllable (**see 6.2**):

(la) police	[pɔ lis]	*(un) athlète*	[a tlɛt]

Practise saying the following words without pronouncing the final *-e*:

Final consonant + *-e*

la violence	*une minute*	*pittoresque*	*un véhicule*

Final consonant + *-le* or *-re*

responsable	*impossible*	*le théâtre*	*le Louvre*

In many Southern varieties of French, and in poetry and song, final *-e* is pronounced, and thus forms, with the preceding consonant, a separate syllable:

Toulouse	[tu lu zə]	*Barcelone*	[bar sə lɔ nə]
je ne regrette rien	[ʒə nə rə grɛ tə rjɛ̃]		

Effect of final *e*

Although final *-e* is not pronounced, its presence affects the pronunciation of the preceding syllable:

● a mute final consonant is pronounced (**see 6.2**):

français	[frɑ̃ sɛ]	*française*	[frɑ̃ sɛz]

- a nasal vowel in final position is pronounced as an oral vowel + nasal consonant (**see 5.3**):

bon	[bɔ̃]	*bonne*	[bɔn]
ancien	[ɑ̃ sjɛ̃]	*ancienne*	[ɑ̃ sjɛn]

If the object pronoun *le* appears at the end of a group of words, the *-e* is pronounced:

prends-le!   take it!

Internal *e*

Look at the following words:

maintenant	now	*l'Allemagne*	Germany
la charcuterie	the delicatessen	*la pâtisserie*	the cake shop

Each of these words has an unstressed internal syllable consisting of consonant + *e*. If you were reading these words aloud, for example in a list of words, you might wish to pronounce this internal syllable: *main-te-nant, l'Al-le-magne*, and so on. But in the normal flow of speech, *e* is not pronounced in internal position; practise saying these four words without pronouncing the *e*.

maintenant	[mɛ̃t nɑ̃]	*l'Allemagne*	[lal maɲ]
charcuterie	[ʃar ky tri]	*pâtisserie*	[pa ti sri]

As you can hear, the consonant in the internal syllable has been redistributed, either to the end of the preceding syllable (*maintenant, l'Allemagne*) or to the beginning of the next syllable (*charcuterie, pâtisserie*).

You should try, as far as possible, not to pronounce *e* in internal position:

- you will find long words easier to pronounce, since there will be fewer syllables;
- you will be imitating the spontaneous pronunciation of Northern French speakers.

Verb forms

Internal *e* is not pronounced in a number of verb forms:

Infinitive and past participle

qu'est-ce que tu vas acheter?	[aʃ te]	What are you going to buy?
je l'ai jeté	[ʒə lɛʒ te]	I threw it away

Future and conditional

il achètera, il achèterait	[i la ʃɛ tra]	[i la ʃɛ trɛ]
elle jettera, elle jetterait	[ɛl ʒɛ tra]	[ɛl ʒɛ trɛ]
j'étudierai, j'étudierais	[ʒe ty di rɛ]	
tu oublieras, tu oublierais	[ty u bli ra]	[ty u bli rɛ]

'Three consonants rule'

If making internal *e* silent would lead to a cluster of three consonant sounds (which is not easy to pronounce), internal *e* is pronounced:

le parlement	Parliament	*le gouvernement*	government
autre chose	something else	*un entretien*	an interview, a conversation

---

Exercice 7/3   **Suppression de e interne**   Travail à deux > Mise en commun

a   Avec un(e) partenaire, lisez simultanément, à haute voix, une des phrases suivantes; avez-vous, tous les deux, supprimé les deux e internes qui se trouvent dans la phrase?

b   Essayez de décider, dans le cas de chaque mot, quelle est la prononciation (avec ou sans e interne) que vous préférez:

1   C'est un développement dangereux.
2   C'était également un événement important.
3   Qu'est-ce qu'elle va acheter à la charcuterie?
4   Il parlera rapidement, comme d'habitude.
5   Elle touchera une somme importante.

Initial *e*

In the first syllable of a word, *e* can be pronounced:

demain   *regarder*   *des mesures*   *Besançon*

But in a group of words spoken without a break (**see 7.3**), the first syllable of a word can become an internal syllable within the group. In these cases, *e* need not be pronounced:

à demain!   [ad mɛ̃]   instead of [a də mɛ̃]
see you tomorrow!

je vais regarder   [ʒvɛr gar de]   instead of [ʒə vɛ rə gar de]
I'll have a look

In these examples, either pronunciation is acceptable.

Sometimes it is essential to pronounce initial *e*, in order to distinguish between two words:

dehors! [də ɔr]   out!   *dors!* [dɔr]   (go to) sleep!

Strings of *e*

One-syllable words ending in *e* are so common in French that many sentences include a string of two or more successive syllables consisting of consonant + *e*:

dans ce chemin   on this/that track
je ne le regarderai pas   I won't look at it

Try to say these sequences aloud: you will find that it is impossible to say them if you make every *e* silent, and yet if you pronounce each one, the result is very strange! Ideally, you should pronounce *e* in the initial syllable (and in the third syllable). For example:

dans ce chemin   [dɑ̃ sə ʃmɛ̃]
je ne le regarderai pas   [ʒən lər gar drɛ pa]

7.5 Liaison; the letter *h*

Liaison occurs when a final consonant that is normally silent is sounded in front of a following vowel.

For example, in *les garçons* or *des garçons*, the final *-s* of *les* and *des* is silent: the next sound after the vowel is the consonant [g]. But in *les enfants* or *des enfants*, where the following noun begins with a vowel, the final *-s* of *les* and *des* is sounded, as [z]. This [z] is pronounced at the start of the next syllable, not at the end of the previous one: [le] [zã] [fã]. This is called *enchaînement* (**see 7.3**).

The most common final consonants which are silent in most words, but sounded in liaison are:

-d and *-t*, both sounded in liaison as [t];
-s, *x* and *z*, all sounded in liaison as [z];
-n, sounded in liaison as [n].

Examples:
grand(e)(s) has five possible pronunciations:

M singular + consonant, M plural + consonant
   -d or *-ds*   silent   *un grand plaisir, de grands progrès*

M singular + vowel or mute *h*
   -d   sounded as [t]   *un grand homme*

M plural + vowel or mute *h*
   -ds   sounded as [z]   *de grands hommes*

F singular + consonant or vowel or mute *h*, F plural + consonant
   -de or *-des*   sounded as [d]   *une grande joie, de grandes qualités*

F plural + vowel or mute *h*
   -des   sounded as [dz]   *de grandes illusions*

quand Although *quand* is spelt with a *-d*, the *-d* is never pronounced as a [d].
Before a consonant, *-d* is silent: *quand nos amis sont là*
In liaison, *-d* is sounded as [t]:   *quand ils sont là*

six, dix The numerals *six* and *dix* have three pronunciations:
Before a consonant, *-x* is silent: *six mille, dix millions*
In liaison, *-x* is sounded as [z]:   *six élèves, dix étudiants*
On its own, *-x* is sounded as [s]:   *Tu en as combien? – Six*
                                        Ils ont combien de points? – Dix

When does liaison take place?

Liaison is not universal: a French speaker does not automatically pronounce a mute final consonant every time it happens to be followed by a vowel. There are three categories of liaison:

a Invariable (or obligatory) liaison

In these cases, the great majority of French speakers automatically make the liaison, and you should try to do so.

b Variable (or optional) liaison

In these cases, liaison takes place in formal situations (N3/N4), but not in informal situations (N2/N1): these cases are not vital for your spoken French.

c Blocked (or forbidden) liaison

In these cases, the great majority of French speakers automatically pronounce the sequence without making the liaison, and you should try to follow this.

Examples:
a Invariable liaison

Say the following groups of words aloud, making the liaison:
- between articles, numerals, adjectives, possessive/demonstrative/indefinite adjectives and a noun beginning with a vowel:

les années	*des années*	*deux ans*	*six ans, dix ans*
un grand immeuble	*un petit enfant*	*les mêmes heures*	
ses amis	*leurs amis*	*ces enfants*	*certains enfants*

- between the prepositions *dans, en, sans, sous, chez* and (an article +) a noun beginning with a vowel:

dans une heure	*en une heure*	*sans hésitation*	*chez eux*

- between the adverbs *plus, moins, très, bien, tout* and an adjective beginning with a vowel:

c'est plus important	*c'est moins important*	*tout à l'heure*
il est très intelligent	*c'est bien évident*	

- between a subject or object pronoun and a verb beginning with a vowel, or between a verb and one of these pronouns beginning with a vowel:

nous avons	*ils aiment*	*je les ai vus*	*on nous aime*
nous y voilà	*ils en ont*		
quand finit-on?	*allons-y!*	*allez-vous-en!*	

b Variable liaison

In formal situations (N3), liaison is made:
- after the verbs ***être*** and ***avoir***, used as an auxiliary, and after an auxiliary verb:

je suis arrivé(e)	*elle est arrivée*
elle avait eu un accident	*il peut y avoir une raison*

- after a negative:

    elle n'est pas arrivée   *elle n'est pas encore arrivée*

c   Blocked liaison

Practise not making a liaison in the following cases:

- between a singular noun and an adjective, adverb, preposition, conjunction or verb:

    le temps utile   *pas de temps à perdre*   *cet étudiant a gagné le prix*

- after *et*:   *un homme et une femme*   *femmes et enfants*

- before an aspirate *h* (see below).

The letter *h*

IN ENGLISH, pronunciation of the sound corresponding to the letter 'h' causes problems for speakers of languages (such as French) where the sound does not exist.

IN FRENCH the spelling of several words begins with *h*, and several others are spelt with an internal *h*, but *h* is not pronounced in French.

'Mute' *h*

Certain everyday words are spelt with an initial *h*, but they and the preceding word are pronounced as if the *h* were not there at all:

Elision takes place: *l'hôtel*   *l'heure*   *comme **d'**habitude* *s'habiller*

Liaison takes place: *un hôtel*   *trois heures*   *des huîtres*   *vous vous habillez*

'Aspirate' *h*

Other words beginning with *h* are marked in dictionaries with an asterisk, or other distinguishing mark. This *h* is sometimes called an 'aspirate *h*'; although it is not pronounced, it affects the pronunciation of the word and the one before it:

Elision is blocked: *le héros*   [lə e ro]   *la haie*   [la ɛ]

Liaison is blocked: *les héros*   [le ero]   *les haies*   [le ɛ]

The effect of 'aspirate' *h* is to create a sequence of two vowels, which are pronounced without a break **(see 7.3)**.

This *h* is also found in internal position, where it has the same effect as initial 'aspirate' *h*: it creates a sequence of two vowels (or vowel + semivowel):

    le Sahara   [sa a ra]   the Sahara

    un cahier   [ka je]   an exercise-book

    souhaiter   [swɛ te]   to wish

8 Sound and spelling

- **8.1 Forms of words: sound, spelling and meaning**
- **8.2 Some differences between French and English**
- **8.3 Accents and capital letters**

8.1 Forms of words: sound, spelling and meaning

Words that sound the same but have different meanings

A number of words in French look and sound exactly alike, but have completely different meanings or grammatical functions. These include:

ce   il   le   l'   la   les   leur   que

Ce

- used before a noun, *ce* is one of the set of demonstrative adjectives *ce, cet, cette, ces* etc. (**see 21**) and means 'this' or 'that':

ce film est ennuyeux   this/that film is boring

- used before the verb *être* (*c'est, c'était, ce fut* etc.), *ce* is a neuter subject pronoun (**see 52**), and means 'it' or 'that':

c'est une bonne idée, ça!   that's a good idea!

- used with *qui/que*, *ce* forms a neuter relative pronoun *ce qui, ce que*, (**see 42**) to mean 'what':

je n'ai pas compris ce qu'elle me disait   I didn't understand what she was saying

Il

- used before a verb, *il* is one of the set of personal subject pronouns *il, elle, ils, elles* (**see 9** and **52**) and means 'he':

tu n'as pas vu Paul? Il était là tout à l'heure

haven't you seen Paul? He was here/there just now

- used before a verb, *il* is part of an impersonal verb or construction (**see 37** and **52**), and means 'it':

il fait beau　　　　　　　　　it's fine
il faut y aller　　　　　　　　you must go
il est difficile de le croire　　it's hard to believe it

Le, l', la, and les

● used before a noun, *le, l', la,* and *les* are definite articles (**see 22**), and mean 'the' (or no article at all in English):
l'homme est un produit récent de l'évolution
Man is a recent product of evolution

● used before a verb, *le, l', la,* and *les* are direct object pronouns (**see 18**), and mean 'him', 'her', 'it', and 'them':
elle lui a dit qu'elle l'aimait toujours
she told him she still loved him

Leur

● used before a noun, *leur* is one of the set of possessive adjectives *notre, nos, votre, vos, leur, leurs* etc. (**see 20**), and means 'their':
les Européens sont très attachés à leur pays, et à leur région
Europeans are very attached to their home country and region

● used before a verb, *leur* is one of the series of indirect object pronouns *lui, leur* etc. (**see 18**), and means 'to them':
les délégués sont arrivés: allons leur demander leur avis
the delegates are here: let's go and ask them what they think

Que

● used as the direct object of a verb in a question (**see 33**), *que* is one of the series of interrogative pronouns *qui* ('who'?), *que* ('what?') etc.:
qu'est-ce que tu vas faire, alors? or *que vas-tu faire, alors?*
so what are you going to do?

● used as the direct object of the verb in a relative clause (**see 42**), *que* is one of the series of relative pronouns *qui* ('who', 'that' (subject)), *que* ('whom', 'that' (direct object)), etc.:
tu vois cette femme-là? c'est celle que j'ai vue hier
do you see that woman? she's the one I saw yesterday

● used to introduce a completive construction (**see 49**), *que* corresponds to 'that' in English (although 'that' is often omitted in English):
je pense qu'il est temps de rentrer　　　　I think it's time to go home
on m'a dit que c'est un bon joueur　　　　I was told he's a good player

8.2 Some differences between French and English

Many words are common to English and French, either because a word has passed from one language to the other, or because both languages have adapted the same word from another language, such as Latin or Greek.

Many words which are common to English and French, and have quite similar meanings, are formed differently in terms of both pronunciation and spelling. The main difference can often be a matter of one vowel:

		French		**English**
a	[a]	*les marchandises*	e	merchandise, goods
a	[a]	*responsable*	i	responsible
ai	[ɛ]	*une comparaison*	i	a comparison
au	[o]	*la communauté*	i	community
ou	[u]	*un pourcentage*	e	a percentage
ou	[u]	*approuver*	o	to approve

The examples that follow provide an opportunity for you to focus on certain words where your pronunciation and/or spelling is at risk of falling between two stools: their form in English and their form in French. Say each of the French words aloud as you read through the following list.

Individual words
The final syllable of certain nouns is different in French from what it is in English:

un changement	a change
un civil	a civilian
une habitude	a habit
un individu	an individual
le résultat	the result
la valeur	the value

Nouns ending in -*ment*
Several nouns end in -*ment* in both languages, but with significant differences in what comes before:

un développement	a development
l'environnement	the environment
le gouvernement	government

(For adverbs ending in -*ment*, **see 30.1**.)

Adjectives
The ending of certain adjectives is different in French from what it is in English:

chimique	chemical
continu	continuous

égalitaire	egalitarian
financier	financial
hypocrite	hypocritical
interne	internal
philosophique	philosophical
significatif	significant

Pairs of words

Certain pairs of words in French have endings which are quite similar, but the endings in English are no help:

l'humeur/l'humour

de mauvaise humeur	in a bad mood
l'humour anglais	English humour

le ministre/le ministère

le ministre a parlé	the minister spoke
le dossier est au ministère	the file is at the ministry

le or **la photographe/la photographie**

un(e) photographe	a photographer
une photo(graphie)	a photo(graph)

romain/roman

une ville romaine	a Roman city
l'architecture romane	romanesque architecture

Nouns: singular and plural

'Singular' and 'plural' are grammatical terms; in reality, we think of things as units, pairs or groups, or as uncountable, as well as 'one' or 'more than one'. Most nouns are **countable**: they refer to either one of a kind (*une girafe*) or more than one of a kind (*des girafes*). But several nouns are massive, or **uncountable** (marked U in some English dictionaries): they are not used in the plural.

The grammatical notions of singular and plural are very similar in English and French, but there are differences in the way certain objects and ideas are allocated to either 'singular' or 'plural':

Abstract nouns

	donner un conseil	to give (a piece of) advice, some advice
but	*donner des conseils*	to give advice
	le progrès	progress (the idea of 'progress')
but	*faire des progrès*	to make progress
	un séjour (de vacances)	a holiday
	de bonnes vacances	a good holiday
	les vacances	the holidays

Clothes

un collant	(a pair of) tights; ski pants; cycling shorts
une culotte, un slip	(under)pants
un pantalon	(a pair of) trousers
un short	(a pair of) shorts

69

8.3 Accents and capital letters

Accents

Many European languages, including French, German, Spanish and Italian, make use of one or more accents:

- ● to indicate how a particular letter should be pronounced;
- ● to indicate that there is stress on a particular syllable (not applicable to French);
- ● to distinguish between two words that are spelt the same.

IN FRENCH, there are five types of accent:

L'accent aigu (acute accent) is only used over *e* and is usually pronounced [e]:

préférer	*préféré*	*préférée*
créer	*créé*	*créée*

L'accent grave (grave accent) is used
- over *e*; it is usually pronounced [ɛ]:

très	*près*	*père*	*mère*

- over *a* and *u*, without affecting the sound, to distinguish:

à	(to, at)	from	*a*	(has)
là	(there)	from	*la*	(the, her, it)
où	(where)	from	*ou*	(or)

L'accent circonflexe (circumflex accent) is used
- over *e*; it is usually pronounced [ɛ]; *è* and *ê* are therefore pronounced the same:

bête	*fête*	*fenêtre*

- over *a*, *o*, with the effect of lengthening the vowel sound:

pâtisserie	*chômage*	*côté*

- over *i*, *u*, without affecting the sound (**see 8.4**):

boîte	*dû*	*sûr*

La cédille (cedilla) is a sign like a small *c*, back-to-front, and is used in French to indicate that *ça, ço, çu* are to be pronounced [sa], [so], [sy], and not [ka], [ko], [ky]:

façade	*leçon*	*reçu*

There is never a cedilla on *c* before *e* or *i*: *ce, ci* are always pronounced [sə], [si]:

céléri	*ancêtre*	*ici*

In the same way, in *ga, go, gu*, the *g* is 'hard' [g], but in *ge, gi*, it is 'soft' [ʒ]; instead of an accent, an *e* is added to make *gea, geo, geu* 'soft', or a *u* to make *gue, gui* 'hard'.

Le tréma is used
- over *e* or *i*, to indicate that two vowels are to be pronounced separately:

héroïne	*naïf, naïve*	*Noël*	*Israël*

- over *i* between two other vowels, to indicate that the *ï* is to be pronounced as a semivowel, [j] (**see 5.4**):

    aïeul   *glaïeul*

- after *g*, over *ü*, to indicate that the *ü* forms part of a new syllable (these are the new spellings introduced in 1990):

aigu, aigüe	[ε gy]	*ambigu, ambigüe*	[ã bi gy]
compare:		*longue*	[lɔ̃g]

When does *e* have an accent, and when not?

You will find it helpful to link the sounds and spellings of *e* as follows:

Pronunciation	Spelling		
[ə]	*e*		
[e]	*é*	*er*	
[ε]	*ê*	*è*	*ès*
	ai	*ais*	*ait* *aient*

In order for your spelling to be correct, you also need to pay attention to:

- how the syllable containing *e* is pronounced;
- whether the syllable containing *e* is open or closed (**see 7.1**);
- the consonant(s) at the beginning of the next syllable.

Here are some guidelines which you can apply:

'Mute *e*' [ə] at the end of an open syllable is always spelt *e*:

    la religion   *lever*   *un partenaire*

At the end of an open syllable, [e] and [ε] are written with an accent, *é* for [e] and *è* or *ê* for [ε], if the next syllable begins

- with a vowel:	*é*	*réa*liser	*réa*nimer
- with a single consonant:	*é*	*répo*ndre	*diffé*rent
	è	*chère*	*un problème*
	ê	*une fête*	
- with consonant + *l* or *r*:	*é*	*régler*	*névrose*
	è	*règle*	*allègre*
- at the end of a word:	*é*	*arrivé*	*protégé*
	è	*très*	*le succès*

In all the above examples, the spelling (*é*, *è*/*ê*) corresponds to the sound. However, if the sounds [e] or [ε] at the end of an open syllable are followed by a double consonant there is no accent on the *e*, but it is pronounced [e] or [ε]:

[e]	*un effort*	*effrayant*	*le dessert*	*essayer*
[ε]	*l'intelligence*	*l'Angleterre*	*la guerre*	*on jette*

At the end of a word, *-er* is pronounced [e] in most cases:

    arriver   *protéger*

But at the end of some words (including words taken from English), -er is pronounced [ɛr], making a closed syllable (one ending with a consonant):

cher [ʃɛr]	dear, expensive	*le fer* [fɛr]	iron
un corner		*Westminster*	

In one-syllable words, -es is pronounced [e]:

ces	*des*	*les*	*mes ses tes*

Finally, in a syllable spelt with a final consonant, the sounds [e] and [ɛ] are written without an accent:

[e]	*la clef*	*le nez*	*le pied*
[ɛ]	*cher*	*le fer*	*une personne*
	*dés**espéré*	*le **pres**tige*	*la **tech**nologie*

Note: the single letter *x* corresponds to two sounds: [g] + [z], or [k] + [s] (see 6.1), and so the first syllable of the words below ends with a consonant:

[gz]	*l'ex**amen*	*l'ex**emple*	*ex**ister*
[ks]	*ex**pliquer*	*l'ex**térieur*	*ex**traordinaire*

Exercice 8/1   **La lettre e: avec ou sans accent?**   Travail individuel ou à deux

Dans cet extrait du roman de Camus, La Peste, trouvez les **douze** mots où il faut un accent sur la lettre e. Quel accent? Comment le mot, avec accent, se prononce-t-il?

Le matin du 16 avril, le docteur Bernard Rieux sortit de son cabinet et buta sur un rat mort, au milieu du palier. Sur le moment, il ecarta la bete sans y prendre garde et descendit l'escalier. Mais, arrive dans la rue, la pensee lui vint que ce rat n'etait pas à sa place et il retourna sur ses pas pour avertir le concierge. Devant la reaction du vieux M. Michel, il sentit mieux ce que sa decouverte avait d'insolite. La presence de ce rat mort lui avait paru seulement bizarre tandis que, pour le concierge, elle constituait un scandale. La position de ce dernier etait d'ailleurs categorique: il n'y avait pas de rats dans la maison. Le docteur eut beau l'assurer qu'il y en avait un sur le palier du premier etage, et probablement mort, la conviction de M. Michel restait entiere. Il n'y avait pas de rats dans la maison, il fallait donc qu'on eût apporte celui-ci du dehors. Bref, il s'agissait d'une farce.

© Éditions Gallimard

Capital letters

Capital letters in French are used as in English, with the following exceptions or differences:

A capital letter is used with names of continents, countries, regions, places (see 29.4):

l'Asie	*l'Australie*	*la Normandie*	*Caen*	*Bayeux*

including both names of compound names of countries:

la Grande-Bretagne	*le Royaume-Uni*	*les États-Unis*

A capital letter is used with the names of inhabitants, if these are nouns (**see 14.6**):

les Français   *les Anglais*   *les Normands*   *les Parisiens*

A small letter is used with the names of inhabitants, if these are adjectives (**see 14.6**):

elle est française   but   *c'est une Française*

and with all other adjectives formed from place names:

la vie parisienne   *les vaches normandes*

A language is always spelt with a small letter:

| *l'anglais* | *le français* | *l'allemand* | *l'hébreu* |
| English | French | German | Hebrew |

A small letter should to be used for days and months, but you will also see them spelt with a capital:

jeudi   *vendredi*   *mars*   *avril*

A capital letter is used when referring to a noun which has already been named:

le Général   *le Directeur le Plan*

or to specific historical events and entities which do not need further qualification:

la Révolution   *la République*   *la Libération*

But a small letter is used when the name appears with the noun:

le gouvernement Jospin   *le lycée Lakanal*
le lac Léman   *la mer Noire*
la mer Méditerranée (or: *la Méditerranée*)

Exercice 8/2   **Avec ou sans majuscule?**   Travail individuel ou à deux

Dans les phrases ci-dessous, les mots entre parenthèses doivent-ils s'écrire avec ou sans majuscule?

1   Tous les (bretons/Bretons) ne parlent pas (breton/Breton).
2   La (mer/Mer) du (nord/Nord) est très polluée.
3   Le nouveau directeur est un (anglais/Anglais), mais sa femme est (française/Française).
4   Le (président/Président) de la (république/République) est élu pour sept ans.
5   L'(italien/Italien) est une langue facile pour les (français/Français).

Part four

How words are made up

We have seen how meaning can be conveyed by simple strings of words **(see 3.1)** such as 'me want milk now', in which the order of these words plays a part in the communication of meaning **(see 32)**, but word order on its own is seldom sufficient. The communication of meaning usually calls for additional indications as to how the various words in a statement are related: who is doing what, to or with whom, how, where, when and why.

The function of grammar is to enable speakers and writers to communicate such details as these, using the vocabulary of their particular language, but following grammatical categories which are common to all languages. Grammar is universal because the things it enables humans to express are universal. For each particular language, a set of conventions evolves, governing the ways in which the relations between the different parts of a statement are related. These conventions constitute the grammar of a particular language.

Parts Four and **Five** of this book present some of the ways in which grammar operates in the French language.

In Part Four, we look at ways in which the form of words contributes to the expression of meaning through the explicit expression of grammatical links between different parts of a statement. Part Four contains grammatical rules which say 'if you want to express this idea in this way, you must use a particular form of certain words'.

In Part Five, we will look at ways in which the choice of words contributes to the expression of meaning through the explicit expression of grammatical links between different parts of a statement. Part Five contains grammatical rules which say 'if you want to express this idea in this way, you must choose certain words, and not others'.

What you have to learn as 'rules' are in fact a set of shared expectations among speakers of French as to what particular word endings, or choices of word, mean in terms of grammar. French speakers' expectations about their language allow for a degree of variation in pronunciation, vocabulary and grammar, depending on a speaker's age, geographical origins and socioeconomic status, and the degree of formality or informality of the situation in which communication takes place (**see 55**). Not only that, but conventions can change over a period of time. Grammar rules are therefore descriptive in that they describe how people use a language; but a learner of a language has to treat these rules as prescriptive, in order to have relatively straightforward guidelines for making sense of the language, and for using it with confidence.

In general, the 'rules' described in this book represent the kind of French that a native speaker might expect to hear or read from an educated foreigner.

In Part Four, the forms of words are presented under the following headings:

 9 **Verbs 1: agreement**
10 **Verbs 2: markers of tense**
11 **Gender of nouns**
12 **Adjective agreement and adjective endings**
13 **Prefixes**
14 **Suffixes: verb, noun and adjective suffixes**
15 **When one word is not enough**
16 **When words are too many or too long**

9 Verbs 1: agreement

9.1 **Subject pronouns**
9.2 **Agreement of verb with subject**
9.3 **Present tense of regular and irregular verbs**

9.1 Subject pronouns

It is usual to distinguish six 'Persons of the verb'. These persons, and the subject pronouns associated with them, are listed below:

Singular			Plural		
Person	Subject pronoun		Person	Subject pronoun	
1	*je* (*j'* before a vowel)	I	4	*nous*	we
2	*tu* (informal singular)	you	5	*vous* (plural, and formal singular)	you
3	*il* (for persons and things)	he, it	6	*ils* (Masculine and mixed)	they
	elle	she, it		*elles* (Feminine)	they
	on	one			
	(or any person, depending on meaning and context)				

The subject pronouns *je*, *tu*, *nous* and *vous* do not 'replace a noun': they refer directly to the person concerned. In certain circumstances, these pronouns are replaced by indirect forms of address:

- the subject pronoun *on* (see below);
- polite forms of address including the use of Person 3, or a passive construction (**see 35**), avoiding the use of *je* or *vous*:
  Madame désire-t-elle du thé?   Would Madam like some tea?   (N4)

The subject pronouns *il*, *elle*, *ils* and *elles*, on the other hand, do 'replace a noun': they are used to refer to a noun (person or thing) which has already been mentioned:

*j'ai vu **Marie** hier. **Elle** va beaucoup mieux*   I saw Marie yesterday. She's a lot better
*tu as vu **leur bateau**? **Il** est superbe!*   have you seen their boat? It's fantastic!

On

The subject pronoun *on* has been called 'the most dishonest pronoun in the French language', and indeed it is impossible to pin it down to a set of definite meanings: depending on the context, its meaning can be impersonal, or it can refer to any one of the six persons (*je, tu, il/elle, nous, vous, ils/elles*).

Impersonal use of *on*

This use corresponds to the original form and function of the pronoun *on*, which is a 'double' of the noun *homme* (in the same way as *man* and *der Mann*, in German), and can be used in the same way as the English impersonal pronoun 'one':

on ne sait jamais	one never knows/you never know
ici on parle français	French spoken here

The form *l'on* is largely restricted to literary (N4) usage, and to this impersonal meaning of *on*.

But *ils* is used, instead of *on*, with a similar meaning to 'they' in English, referring to distant and impersonal authorities, or to any other group one wishes to distance oneself from:

qu'est-ce qu'ils vont nous sortir encore à la rentrée?
what've they got in store for us next, after the holidays?
à Paris, ils conduisent comme des fous
in Paris, they drive like madmen

In everyday speech (N2), *tu* can be used, in place of impersonal *on*, just as 'one' is replaced in English by 'you':

*sur les petites routes, **tu** vois pas beaucoup de voitures* (N2)
on the smaller roads, you don't see many cars

In everyday speech (N2), *on* usually refers to a group consisting of or including the speaker and the listener (see below).

Use of *on* instead of, or with, *nous*

This is the most common use of *on* in everyday conversation (N2), but if you are in a formal situation (N3) such as an interview, or with older people, it may be more acceptable to your listeners if you use *nous*, not *on*.

The use of *on* instead of *nous* assumes a certain solidarity or unity of purpose between speaker and listener: one is speaking as one of a group of like-minded people:

*bon, qu'est-ce qu'**on** va faire maintenant?* (N2)
right, what shall we do now?
***on** a été obligés d'attendre trois heures à l'aéroport* (N2)
we had to wait three hours at the airport

Note: when this use of *on* with plural meaning is written down, adjectives and past participles can agree.

In casual conversation (N2/N1), *on* can be used to replace not *nous* but *je*:

avec ma soeur, **on** *est allées au bord de la mer*	(N2)
on *est allées au bord de la mer avec ma soeur*	(N2)
me and my sister went to the seaside	(N1)

On is so widely used in French that one can find it twice in the same sentence, but in a different disguise each time:

> *Aujourd'hui, quand* **on** *ment sur notre âge,* **on** *nous croit* (from *Elle* magazine)
> Nowadays, when we lie about our age, people believe us

The subject pronouns *je, tu, on* and, to a lesser extent, *nous* and *vous,* can be used together with a tonic pronoun *moi, toi* etc. (**see 19.3**).

The subject pronouns *il, elle, ils* and *elles* can be used alongside the noun to which they refer, particularly in informal situations (N2), but also in certain constructions used in formal situations (N3):

mes parents ils n'ont rien dit	(N2)
my parents didn't say anything	
pourquoi les autorités n'ont-elles rien fait?	(N3)
why did the authorities do nothing?	
(For further examples, see **33.3c** and **51.1b**.)	

IN ENGLISH, subject pronouns can be stressed to give emphasis: '<u>he</u> did it', '<u>I</u> saw you', etc. IN FRENCH, this is possible, but unusual:

> *La rentrée, c'est quand je veux!* (from a poster advertising a supermarket chain)
> I do my end-of-summer shopping when <u>I</u> choose!

Function of subject pronouns in French

The main function of subject pronouns in French is to indicate the person of the verb: other languages derived from Latin, such as Spanish or Italian, tend to use subject pronouns only to provide additional emphasis: in these two languages, the person of the verb is almost always indicated by the verb ending.

Many verb endings, which originally served to indicate the person of the verb, have become reduced or eliminated in spoken French, while remaining present in written French. The 'subject pronoun' is not really a pronoun at all: it is more like a 'verb ending' which is placed before the verb.

9.2 Agreement of verb with subject

Agreement is:

● when the (spoken and/or written) form of a verb changes according to the subject of the verb;

● when the (spoken and/or written) form of an adjective changes according to the gender and number of the noun which it qualifies **(see 12)**.

Verb agreement

IN ENGLISH, most verbs keep the same form in Persons 1 2 4 5 6 in the present tense; only in Person 3 is there a marker of agreement:

Persons 1 2 4 5 6	I/you/we/they	run
Person 3	he/she/it/one	run**s**

IN FRENCH, in the present tense, the situation is more complex than in English: there are many more markers of agreement, but several of them appear only in the written forms of the verb, not in the spoken forms. This means that, by and large, 'making a verb agree with its subject' is a simpler matter in spoken than in written French.

9.3 Present tense of regular and irregular verbs: spoken and written forms

a   1 2 3 6: no ending in spoken French

In spoken French, the largest class of verbs (with infinitive in *-er*, also *ouvrir, couvrir* etc. and *cueillir, accueillir* etc.) has just three forms in the present indicative tense:

Person	Spoken endings	Written forms			
1 2 3 6	no ending	*parle*	*parles*	*parle*	*parlent*
4	[ɔ̃]	*parlons*			
5	[e]	*parlez*			

This list is simplified when *on* or *nous on* (Person 3) is used instead of *nous* (Person 4) **(see 9.1)**. Also *voir* to see, *croire* to believe, *rire* to laugh, where the written endings for Persons 1 2 3 and 6 are *-s -s -t* and *-ent*, and [j], spelt *y* or *i*, is added to the stem for Persons 4 and 5.

b   1 2 3 versus 4 5 6

Other groups of verbs show a contrast in the present tense between singular (Persons 1 2 3) and plural (Persons 4 5 6), where there is an additional consonant, [s], [d], [t], [z], [v], [m], [ɲ], [n]:

+ **[s]**: regular *-ir* verbs such as *finir*, also *connaître, paraître, naître*;

+ **[d]**: regular *-re* verbs such as *rendre, vendre, répondre*;

+ **[t]**: irregular *-ir* verbs such as *partir, sortir, (se) sentir*, also *(se) battre, mettre*;

+ **[z]**: irregular *-re* verbs such as *lire, conduire, produire*;

+ **[v]**: irregular *-re* and *-ir* verbs such as *vivre, écrire, suivre, (se) servir*, also, with a change to the vowel value in the stem, *savoir*;

+ **[m]**: irregular *-ir* verbs such as *dormir*;

+ **[ɲ]**: irregular *-dre* verbs such as *craindre, rejoindre, peindre, (se) plaindre*;

+ [n] (with a change to the vowel value in the stem): *prendre*; also *venir, devenir, revenir, tenir.*

c 1 2 3 6 versus 4 5

The present indicative tense of several irregular verbs (*devoir, recevoir, boire, pouvoir, vouloir*) shows a double contrast between Persons 1 2 3 and 6 and Persons 4 and 5, and a consonant is added ([v] or [l]); the vowel value in the stem changes.

d   dire, faire, être, avoir, aller

Finally, five of the most commonly-used verbs (*dire, faire, être, avoir, aller*) show the widest variety of forms of all.

All the above forms and groupings of verbs are for the present indicative only; for the present subjunctive **see 48.1** and **56.2**. You should study the present indicative forms of regular and irregular verbs (**see 56.2**), before attempting to learn or revise other tense forms.

The exercise that follows is intended to give you practice in forming the present indicative of commonly-used verbs. For the forms of other tenses, **see 10** and **56.2**.

Exercice 9/1   **Formes du présent**   Travail à deux

A tour de rôle, dites à haute voix un des verbes ci-dessous; si vous choisissez la forme au singulier (Personne 3), votre partenaire doit aussitôt dire, sans regarder la liste, la forme au pluriel (Personne 6), et vice-versa.

Singulier	Pluriel	Singulier	Pluriel
attend	attendent	se bat	se battent
conçoit	conçoivent	conduit	conduisent
connaît	connaissent	détruit	détruisent
écrit	écrivent	interdit	interdisent
met	mettent	part	partent
produit	produisent	reçoit	reçoivent
répond	répondent	sort	sortent
vit	vivent		

---

10 Markers of tense

10.1 Simple forms: the future tense; the conditional; the imperfect tense and the past historic
10.2 The past participle
10.3 Compound forms: the passé composé; the pluperfect; the past conditional and the future perfect

10.1 Simple forms: the future tense; the conditional; the imperfect tense and the past historic

The future tense in English and French

IN ENGLISH, the future tense is a compound tense, formed from the auxiliary 'will', together with the infinitive form of the verb: 'you will go', they will see'. In everyday speech (N2), 'will' is shortened: 'you'll go', 'they'll see'.

Although the future tense in English is indicated by the word 'will', the word 'will' does not always indicate the future tense: it can also be the equivalent of 'want to':

    I <u>will</u> finish this work   *je veux finir ce travail*
                  or   *j'ai l'intention de finir ce travail*

IN FRENCH, the future tense is a simple tense, formed by using the verb stem with certain endings:

    *tu **iras***   you will go   *ils **verront***   they will see

> The future tense in French always includes the sound and letter *r* (from the infinitive form of the verb), between the stem and the ending. This *r* is also present, between the verb stem and a different set of endings, in the conditional in French.

Future tense: endings (spoken and written forms)

In spoken French, there are three different endings in the Future tense, but six in written French:

Person	Spoken forms	Written forms	
1 5	stem + [r] + [ɛ] or [e]	*parlerai*	*parlerez*
2 3	stem + [r] + [a]	*parleras*	*parlera*
4 6	stem + [r] + [ɔ̃]	*parlerons*	*parleront*

Future tense: stem

We have seen that the stem of certain irregular verbs varies in the present indicative e.g. *doit, devez* or *reçoit, recevez* **(see 9.3)**. This is also true, though for a smaller number of verbs, in the future tense.

a   No change to stem

For all regular *-er, -ir* and *-re* verbs, and for the great majority of irregular *-ir* verbs, the stem does not change: all you have to do is apply the formula stem + *r* + ending:

-er verbs

Infinitive	Stem	Future (Person 3)	Pronunciation
étudier	*étudi(e)-*	*étudiera*	[e ty di ra]
parler	*parle-*	*parlera*	[par lə ra]

Note: in the future tense of *-er* verbs, the *e* in the stem is not pronounced, unless this would create a cluster **(see 7.4)** of three consonants.

For *-er* verbs where the stem changes (*préférer, (se) lever, (s')appeler,* etc.) **see 56.2**.

-ir verbs

regular *se réunir*		*réuni-*	*se réunira*
irregular *sortir*		*sorti-*	*sortira*

irregular -ire verbs

dire		*di-*	*dira*
boire		*boi-*	*boira*

-re verbs

regular *-dre* verbs *répondre*	*répond-*	*répondra*
irregular *-dre* verbs *rejoindre*	*rejoind-*	*rejoindra*
irregular *-tre* verbs *mettre*	*mett-*	*mettra*
irregular *-vre* verbs *vivre*	*viv-*	*vivra*

b   Change to stem

	New stem		
Loss of *i* *mourir*	*mour-*	*mourra*	
Loss of *-oi* *recevoir*	*recev-*	*recevra*	
v becomes *r* *pouvoir*	*pour-*	*pourra*	
Loss of *oi*; *av* becomes *au* *savoir*	*sau-*	*saura*	[sɔ ra]
avoir	*au-*	*aura*	[ɔ ra]
Loss of *oi*; *l* becomes *d* *vouloir*	*voud-*	*voudra*	

Change of vowel in stem *venir*	*viend-*	*viendra*
voir	*ver-*	*verra* [vɛ ra]
envoyer	*enver-*	*enverra*
faire	*f(e)-*	*fera* [fra]
être	*s(e)-*	*sera* [sra]
aller	*i-*	*ira*

The conditional in English and French

IN ENGLISH, the conditional, like the future tense, is a compound tense, formed from the auxiliary 'would' plus the verb: 'you would go', 'they would see'. In everyday speech (N2), 'would' is shortened: 'you'd go', 'they'd see'.

Although the conditional in English is indicated by the word 'would', the word 'would' does not always indicate the conditional; like the future, it can also be the equivalent of 'wanted to', especially in the negative:

he <u>wouldn't</u> do it	*il ne voulait pas le faire*
or	*il refusait de le faire*

IN FRENCH, the conditional, like the future tense, is a simple tense: no auxiliary is used, and the conditional meaning is shown by using the verb stem with certain endings:

*tu **irais***	you would go	*ils **verraient***	they would see

As with the future tense, the conditional in French always includes the sound and letter *r* between the stem and the ending.

The conditional: endings (spoken and written forms)

In spoken French, there are three different endings in the conditional, and five in written French. These endings are identical to the endings of the imperfect tense (see below):

Person	Spoken forms	Written forms			
1 2 3 6	stem + [r] + [ɛ]	*parlerais*	*parlerais*	*parlerait*	*parleraient*
4	stem + [r] + [jõ]	*parlerions*			
5	stem + [r] + [je]	*parleriez*			

The conditional: stem

For all verbs, the conditional is formed on the same stem as the future tense.

The conditional: use

The conditional is formed like a tense of the verb, but it is often used as a mood of the verb: in other words, it can have a modal function (**see 39.2**) instead of a temporal function (**see 47**).

This modal function of the conditional occurs in certain situations where the use of a present tense, passé composé or past historic is not appropriate.

For politeness: instead of the present tense, which would be felt as too abrupt:

je voudrais un kilo de poires, s'il vous plaît

I'd like a kilo of pears, please

auriez-vous la monnaie de dix francs, s'il vous plaît?

would you (happen to) have change for ten francs, please?

In news reports when a fact is not yet established as certain: instead of a past tense, which would be saying that the fact is certain:

selon les premières estimations, il y aurait une vingtaine de blessés

according to first reports, about twenty people (are thought to) have been injured

ce financier aurait conclu plusieurs affaires douteuses

this/that/the financier is thought to have done several shady deals

See also **Exercice 10/3**, below.

The imperfect tense in English and French

IN ENGLISH, the imperfect tense (called the past continuous) is a compound tense, formed from the auxiliary 'was', 'were', together with the present participle of the verb: 'it **was** raining', 'they **were** having a good time'.

IN FRENCH, the imperfect tense is a simple tense, formed by using the verb stem with certain endings:

il pleuvait	it was raining
ils s'amusaient	they were having a good time

The imperfect tense: endings (spoken and written forms)

In spoken French, there are three different endings in the imperfect tense, and five in written French. These endings are identical to the endings of the conditional (see above):

Person	Spoken forms	Written forms			
1 2 3 6	stem + [ɛ]	*parlais*	*parlais*	*parlait*	*parlaient*
4	stem + [jɔ̃]	*parlions*			
5	stem + [je]	*parliez*			

> The characteristic sound of the imperfect tense is the [ɛ] which forms the ending of Persons 1 2 3 and 6.

The imperfect tense: stem

For all verbs (except *être*), the stem for the imperfect tense is formed from Persons 4 and 5 (*nous* and *vous*) of the present tense, minus the ending (*-ons*, *-ez*); in other words, you cannot form the imperfect tense with confidence unless you know the present tense of the verb in question.

Examples:

Infinitive	Stem	Imperfect (Person 3)
étudier	*étudi-*	*étudiait*
finir	*finiss-*	*finissait*
apprendre	*appren-*	*apprenait*
devenir	*deven-*	*devenait*
lire	*lis-*	*lisait*
boire	*buv-*	*buvait*
faire	*fais-*	*faisait*

EXCEPTION:

être	*ét-*	*était*

The imperfect tense: use

The imperfect tense is associated with continuing, uncompleted actions, with situations for which a definite starting or finishing point is not stated.

IN ENGLISH, the imperfect tense is not necessarily used in cases where the imperfect is required in French; sometimes a simple past tense or the auxiliary 'did' + negative or the auxiliary 'used to' + infinitive is used:

*je **ne savais pas** que la route **était** barrée*
I didn't know that the road was blocked
*quand j'**étais** petit, on **allait** à l'école à pied*
when I was a child, we used to walk to school

For when to use the imperfect tense, and when to use the passé composé (or the past historic): **see 54.1**.

The past historic tense: use

IN ENGLISH, the simple past tense ('I saw', 'she went', etc.) is used in three different contexts:

- to refer to habitual actions ('used to'), where the imperfect tense is used in French;
- in everyday conversation (N2), to describe an event or series of events in the past (in French, the passé composé (see **10.3**) is used in such cases);
- in formal situations (N3), to describe a sequence of events in history or fiction.

IN FRENCH, the past historic (also called the passé simple) is used only in this last context: to narrate a story or history. This includes children's stories, whether these are in a book or spoken aloud: every French-speaking child is familiar with the past historic, from a very early age.

The past historic: formation

The past historic is formed by the addition of the following endings to the stem of the verb:

Person	Verb type		
	-er	*-ir*, *-re* (regular)	*-oir*, *-re* (certain verbs only)
1	*-ai*	*-is*	*-us*
2	*-as*	*-is*	*-us*
3	*-a*	*-it*	*-ut*
4	*-âmes*	*-îmes*	*-ûmes*
5	*-âtes*	*-îtes*	*-ûtes*
6	*-èrent*	*-irent*	*-urent*

In practice, you are unlikely to come across the past historic in Persons 2, 4 or 5, and Person 1 is found only in stories told in the first person.

10.2 The past participle

The past participle **(see 44)** is one of the most versatile parts of a verb:

- it is used to form several tenses: passé composé, pluperfect, past conditional, future perfect (see below), and also the past subjunctive **(see 48)**;
- it is used to form the passive **(see 35)**;
- it is used on its own in a number of constructions **(see 44.3)**.

This means that you need to be able to formulate the past participle of commonly-used verbs as quickly as you can. Always learn the infinitive and the past participle side-by-side.

In order to form the passé composé, or other compound tenses **(see 10.3)** of a verb, you need to know how to form the past participle of that verb:

	Infinitive		Past participle	
French	*acheter*	*vendre*	*acheté*	*vendu*
English	to buy	to sell	bought	sold

IN ENGLISH, the past participle ends in either '-d' or '-t' in most cases.

IN FRENCH, the past participle has one of a number of endings:

Infinitive	Spoken ending	Written ending	Written form	
étudier, être	[e]	*-é*	*étudié*	*été*
définir, choisir	[i]	*-i*	*défini*	*choisi*
comprendre, mettre		*-is*	*compris*	*mis*
écrire, interdire		*-it*	*écrit*	*interdit*
conduire, produire	[ɥi]	*-uit*	*conduit*	*produit*
vouloir, avoir	[y]	*-u*	*voulu*	*eu*
faire	[ɛ]	*-ait*	*fait*	

Infinitive	Spoken ending	Written ending	Written form	
craindre	[ɛ̃]	*-aint*	*craint*	
peindre		*-eint*	*peint*	
rejoindre	[wɛ̃]	*-oint*	*rejoint*	
ouvrir, souffrir	[ɛr]	*-ert*	*ouvert*	*souffert*

(For these and other verb forms **see 56.2**.)

10.3 Compound forms: the passé composé; the pluperfect; the past conditional and the future perfect

Formation of the passé composé (spoken and written forms)

IN ENGLISH, the passé composé (called the present perfect tense) is formed from the auxiliary 'has', 'have', together with the past participle of the verb: 'she **has** gone', 'they **have** spoken'. In everyday speech (N2), 'has' and 'have' are shortened: 'she's gone', 'they've spoken'.

IN FRENCH, the passé composé is formed in the same way as in English: from the present tense of an auxiliary, together with the past participle of the verb. The auxiliary used in French is either *avoir* or, in the case of a handful of verbs, including all pronominal verbs, *être*.

*ils **ont** parlé*	they have spoken, they've spoken, they spoke
*elle **est** partie*	she has gone, she's gone, she left
*ils **se sont** réveillés*	they have woken up, they've woken up, they woke up

(For the past subjunctive (forms and uses), **see 48.1**.)

The passé composé: use

The passé composé is associated with completed actions (one or a series), with events for which a definite starting or finishing point is stated.

IN ENGLISH, the passé composé tense is not necessarily used in cases where the passé composé is required in French; sometimes a simple past tense (or the auxiliary 'did' + negative) is used in English:

*je **suis allé** regarder, mais **je n'ai** rien **vu***
I **went** to have a look, but I **didn't see** anything
*ce matin, je me **suis réveillé** de bonne heure*
this morning I **woke up** early

(For when to use the passé composé, and when to use the imperfect tense, **see 54.1**.)

a   Passé composé + *avoir*

The following exercise gives you practice in producing the correct form of the past participle. Doing such exercises can only help you check whether you have learnt these forms successfully: it cannot teach you these forms if you don't know them already!

Exercice 10/1   Présent et passé composé   Travail à deux

A tour de rôle, dites à haute voix un des verbes suivants; si vous choisissez la forme au **présent**, votre partenaire doit aussitôt dire, sans regarder la liste, la forme au **passé composé**, et vice-versa.

Présent	Passé composé
tu commets	tu as commis
il conçoit	il a conçu
on connaît	on a connu
nous craignons	nous avons craint
vous décrivez	vous avez décrit
ils détruisent	ils ont détruit
je dois	j'ai dû
ils font	ils ont fait
nous interdisons	nous avons interdit
je lis	j'ai lu
elle met	elle a mis
j'ouvre	j'ai ouvert
ils peignent	ils ont peint
vous pouvez	vous avez pu
ils reçoivent	ils ont reçu
je sais	j'ai su
il vit	il a vécu
elle voit	elle a vu

---

b   Passé composé + *être*

Note: the passé composé of some verbs is formed with *être*, not with *avoir*, in which case the past participle always agrees with the subject (**see 44.4**).

Here is a list of the verbs with which you should use *être* for the passé composé and other compound tenses, such as the pluperfect:

Infinitive		Passé composé	Pluperfect
arriver	to arrive	*je suis arrivé(e)*	*j'étais arrivé(e)*
descendre	to go down	*on est descendu(s)*	*on était descendu(s)*
redescendre	to go back down		
entrer	to enter	*on est entré(s)*	*on était entré(s)*
rentrer	to go back into		
monter	to go up	*tu es monté(e)*	*tu étais monté(e)*
remonter	to go back up		
mourir	to die	*il est mort*	*il était mort*
naître	to be born	*elle est née*	*elle était née*
partir	to leave	*vous êtes parti(e)(s)*	*vous étiez parti(e)(s)*
sortir	to go out	*elle est sortie*	*elle était sortie*
tomber	to fall	*il est tombé*	*il était tombé*
retomber	to fall back		
retourner	to go back	*je suis retourné(e)*	*j'étais retourné(e)*
venir	to come	*je suis venu(e)*	*j'étais venu(e)*
devenir	to become		
revenir	to come back		

The construction of these verbs with *être* means that in compound tenses, two meanings are often possible, depending on whether one is referring to an action in the past or to a result or state in the present (**see 54.1**). See also Exercice 10/2, below.

c Passé composé of pronominal verbs: (**see 36**)
Agreement of the past participle
In certain circumstances, the past participle, when used in a compound tense (passé composé, pluperfect, etc.) agrees with a particular noun or pronoun, that is to say that *-e*, *-s* or *-es* are added, indicating feminine singular, masculine plural or feminine plural agreement (**see 44.4**).

The pluperfect tense

IN ENGLISH, the pluperfect (called the past perfect) tense is formed from the auxiliary 'had', together with the past participle of the verb: 'she **had** left', 'they **had** finished'. In everyday speech (N2), 'had' is shortened: 'she'd left', 'they'd finished'.

IN FRENCH, the pluperfect is formed the same way as in English, using the imperfect tense of the auxiliary (*avoir* or *être*), together with the past participle of the verb:

*ils **avaient parlé***	they had spoken, they'd spoken
*elle **était partie***	she had left, she'd left
*ils **s'étaient réveillés***	they had woken up, they'd woken up

USE

The pluperfect tense is associated with actions or events situated at an earlier period in time than an action or series of events in the past (**see 53.1**):

*elle m'**a dit** qu'elle **avait perdu** sa montre*

she told me she'd lost her watch

*nous **sommes redescendus** parce qu'il avait commencé à neiger*

we came down because it had started to snow

Exercice 10/2   **Passé composé (et plus-que-parfait) + *être***   Travail individuel ou à deux

a   Lisez à haute voix chacune des phrases suivantes;
b   Récrivez-la au **passé composé**;
c   Vérifiez vos réponses et faites les **corrections** nécessaires;
d   Lisez à haute voix la phrase au passé composé;
e   Récrivez les phrases au **plus-que-parfait**;
f   Vérifiez vos réponses et faites les **corrections** nécessaires;
g   Lisez à haute voix la phrase au plus-que-parfait.

1   Elle reste à la maison.
2   Ils deviennent très riches.
3   Nous sortons faire une promenade.
4   Il naît prématurément.
5   Ils meurent à un âge avancé.
6   Vous partez faire du ski.

The past conditional

MEANING AND FORMATION

IN ENGLISH: 'would have' + past participle: 'she **would have** left', 'they **would have** finished'. In everyday speech (N2), 'would' is shortened: 'she'd have left', 'they'd have finished'.

IN FRENCH: conditional of *avoir* or *être* + past participle:

*ils **auraient fini***	they would have finished
*elle **serait partie***	she would have left
*ils **se seraient réveillés***	they would have woken up

USE

The past conditional is associated with actions or events that did not take place in reality, but which are being described as something that would have happened under certain conditions (**see 47**).

Exercice 10/3   **Conditionnel et conditionnel passé**   Travail à deux

A tour de rôle, dites à haute voix **un** des verbes suivants: si vous choisissez le **conditionnel**, votre partenaire doit aussitôt dire, sans regarder la liste, la forme au **conditionnel passé**, et vice-versa.

Conditionnel	Conditionnel passé
il commettrait	il aurait commis
je couvrirais	j'aurais couvert
on deviendrait	on serait devenu(s)
elle mourrait	elle serait morte
tu recevrais	tu aurais reçu
vous reconnaîtriez	vous auriez reconnu
nous rejoindrions	nous aurions rejoint
ils rentreraient	ils seraient rentrés
cela vaudrait	cela aurait valu
elle vivait	elle aurait vécu

The future perfect

MEANING AND FORMATION

IN ENGLISH: 'will have' + past participle: 'she **will have** left', 'they **will have** finished'.

IN FRENCH: future of *avoir* or *être* + past participle:

*ils **auront fini***	they will have finished
*elle **sera partie***	she will have left
*ils **se seront réveillés***	they will have woken up

USE

The future perfect is associated with future actions or events which are being described as likely to take place before some other event or point in time in the future:

> on **pourra** passer chez Marie, mais je suis sûr qu'elle **sera** déjà **partie**
> we can call for Marie but I'm sure she will have left already

In English, the future perfect is not always used: instead, one could say: '. . . but I'm sure she's left already'.

11 Gender of nouns

11.1 Gender, form and meaning
11.2 Status and occupation

11.1 Gender, form and meaning

IN FRENCH, every noun has a grammatical gender: it is either masculine or feminine.

Except for nouns denoting people's status or occupation (see below), the grammatical gender of nouns in French does not affect their meaning. For example, there is nothing particularly 'masculine' about *un placard* ('a cupboard') or *un fauteuil* ('an armchair'), or particularly 'feminine' about *une armoire* ('a wardrobe') or *une chaise* ('a chair').

IN ENGLISH, people sometimes refer to ships (or even cars) as 'she', but in most other cases the neuter subject or object pronoun 'it' is used to refer to things and ideas.

IN FRENCH, *il* and *ce* (in *c'est* etc.) can function as neuter subject pronouns, and *cela/ça* as neuter tonic pronouns **(see 52)**, but there is no 'neuter gender' as such. The existence of grammatical gender ('masculine' and 'feminine') affects almost every sentence in French, in one or more of the following ways:

Articles (see 22): singular articles are either *le* or *la* (or *l'* before a noun beginning with a vowel), either *un* or *une*, either *du* or *de la*.

Adjectives (see 12): an adjective agrees (masculine/feminine, singular/plural) with the noun it refers to.

Pronouns (see 9, 18, 19): the masculine or the feminine form of a subject, object or tonic pronoun is used, depending on the gender of the noun it refers to.

Past participles (see 10, 35, 36, 44): in certain cases, the past participle agrees with a particular noun.

For these reasons, it is best always to learn the gender of a noun, as well as its pronunciation and spelling. You may remember the gender either in terms of *le/la* (but what about *l'*?), or of *un/une* (but make sure you pronounce these two little words differently: **see 5.3**).

You will also find it useful to note certain groups of nouns, and certain noun endings **(see 14.3 and 14.4)** which tend to be masculine, or feminine.

Here are some pairs or groups of nouns which are identical (a), or similar (b), in pronunciation and/or spelling, but which are of different gender:

	Masculine		Feminine	
a	**Nouns that are identical in form**			
	un crème	a coffee with milk	*une crème*	a cream (dessert)
	un livre	a book	*une livre*	a pound
	un mode	a way, a style	*une mode*	a fashion
	un poste	a job	*une poste*	a post office
b	**Nouns that are similar in form**			
	un choix	a choice	*une croix*	a cross
	un côté	a side, a direction	*une côte*	an incline, a hillside
	un crime	a crime	*une crise*	a crisis
	un étage	a floor, a storey	*une étape*	a phase, a stage
	un foie	a liver	*une foi*	a faith
			une fois	a time, an occasion
	un manque	a lack	*une marque*	a (trade) mark, a sign
	un sourire	a smile	*une souris*	a mouse

Exercice 11/1   **Masculin ou féminin?**   Travail individuel

Connaissez-vous les noms suivants?

a   Écrivez chacun avec un ou une

b   Donnez sa signification en anglais

1	banlieue	7	façon	13	régime
2	chiffre	8	fierté	14	risque
3	cimetière	9	fin	15	saison
4	comité	10	honte	16	siècle
5	commerce	11	luxe	17	trimestre
6	enquête	12	modèle		

11.2 Status and occupation

In the case of nouns used in French to denote a person's status or occupation, grammatical tradition and social change come into conflict. In some cases, it is difficult to see how this conflict could be resolved without creating new anomalies.

Certainly there are anomalies in the language as it stands. For example, whether male or female, we all come into the world as *un bébé*, but eventually we become *une personne âgée*. No one seems to object to this change of gender: perhaps because, on the way, we become either *un enfant, un adolescent* then *un adulte*, or *une enfant, une adolescente* and *une adulte*.

When it comes to the names of occupations, however, certain conflicts emerge: some have been resolved, but others remain.

Until the middle of the 20th century, certain occupations were regarded (whether or not this corresponded to the law or reality) as being for men. So that *la présidente*, or *la générale*, for example, referred, not to a woman in that position (since there were none), but to 'the chairman's/the president's wife', and 'the general's wife'.

This is no longer the case: the names of many positions and occupations have both a masculine and a feminine form which is widely used:

un conseiller	*une conseillère*	a councillor
un député	*une députée*	an MP
un écrivain	*une écrivaine*	a writer
un président	*une présidente*	a president, a chair
un principal	*une principale*	a principal

The feminine forms of the above names follow the precedent set by the names of several roles or occupations which have established feminine forms:

un avocat	*une avocate*	a barrister
un directeur	*une directrice*	a headteacher
un héros	*une héroïne*	a hero, a heroine
un instituteur	*une institutrice*	a primary-school teacher
un ouvrier	*une ouvrière*	a worker

Most nouns ending in a silent *-e* present no problem:

un dentiste	*une dentiste*	a dentist
un linguiste	*une linguiste*	a linguist
un ministre	*une ministre*	a minister

Two words illustrate the nature and extent of the problem, and how French speakers have tried to solve it: *professeur* and *docteur*.

Professeur

The widespread use of the abbreviated form *prof* means that, in informal situations (N2), *une prof* is used automatically for a female teacher. But attempts to introduce a feminine form, *une professeure*, for use in formal situations (N3) have so far been unsuccessful.

Docteur

The feminine form *doctoresse*, which was formerly used to refer, in informal situations (N2), to a female medical doctor, has gone out of favour, and there is no feminine form available for the more official term *médecin*: *la médecine* refers to the practice of medicine.

A transitional solution, when a feminine form of the noun is not yet available or established, is to use *une femme* + the masculine form as an adjective:

une femme député	a woman MP
une femme écrivain	a woman writer
une femme médecin	a woman doctor
une femme professeur	a woman teacher

This solution is felt by many French speakers to be unsatisfactory, and is being abandoned.

By and large, French speakers are not concerned to iron out each and every anomaly in this area. Indeed, they are quite happy to use certain nouns which have a grammatical gender contrary to their meaning:

- *un top-model*, 'a fashion model', usually refers to a woman;
- *une star*, 'a film/show-business star', refers to a man or a woman;
- *une basse*, 'a bass (singer)' is usually a man.

Mode of address

In formal situations (N3), it is polite to address men or women as *Monsieur* or *Madame*, together with the name of their status or occupation:

Monsieur l'agent	officer
Madame le directeur or *Madame la directrice*	(Madam)

The above remarks point out some general conventions and trends which you need to be aware of, but you will also have noticed that many individual words have their own distinctive 'case history'. **Exercice 11/2** may help to make you more aware of the extent and complexity of the issues involved:

Exercice 11/2   **Le vocabulaire des professions**   Travail à deux > Mise en commun

Imaginez qu'on vous a demandé de participer aux travaux d'une commission sur le vocabulaire français, afin de proposer des solutions aux problèmes suscités par l'adaptation du vocabulaire traditionnel des professions aux réalités sociales d'aujourd'hui, où la quasi-totalité des fonctions professionnelles sont ouvertes aux femmes.

a   Avec un(e) partenaire, discutez le cas spécifique des quatre noms suivants: député, écrivain, docteur/médecin, professeur. Dans chaque cas, essayez de décider comment il convient de désigner ces occupations, quand elles sont exercées par une femme. Vous pourrez discuter, entre autres considérations, les possibilités suivantes:

- faut-il toujours employer l'article au féminin (la, une)?
- la formulation femme écrivain (etc.) est-elle acceptable?
- faut-il créer des formes spécifiques du nom au féminin (professeure, etc.)?
- dans les formules de politesse, faut-il adopter systématiquement Madame la directrice (etc.) de préférence à Madame le directeur (etc.)?
- ou au contraire, ne faut-il rien imposer du tout, laissant les personnes concernées libres d'adopter le titre qu'elles préfèrent?

b   Avec le reste du groupe, présentez les principes que vous avez essayé de suivre, et vos propositions.

12 Adjective agreement and adjective endings

12.1 **Adjective agreement**
12.2 **When adjectives do not agree**
12.3 **Adjective forms and endings**
12.4 **Endings of certain groups of adjectives**

12.1 Adjective agreement

IN ENGLISH, an adjective stays the same whatever kind of noun it refers to, and whether the noun is singular or plural.

IN FRENCH, an adjective agrees in gender (masculine or feminine) and in number (singular or plural) with the noun or pronoun it refers to. This agreement is marked in writing by the addition of *-e*, *-s* or *-es*:

  un ciel bleu   *une robe bleue*   *des yeux bleus*   *des fleurs bleues*

In speech, this agreement is not always audible: the word *bleu(e)(s)* is pronounced exactly the same in each of the above examples.

The adjective agrees with its noun wherever the adjective comes in the sentence:

- before or after the noun (epithet adjective):
  *une **grande** occasion*   a great occasion
  *des espaces **verts***   green spaces

- after *être* and verbs such as *devenir*, *rester*; also after *paraître*, *sembler*, *avoir l'air* (attributive adjective) (**see 38.2** and **37.5**):
  *elle est restée **silencieuse***   she stayed silent
  *elle a l'air **fatiguée***   she looks tired

- separated from the noun, for example by a comma (apposed adjective): (**see 43.1**)
  ***désespérée**, elle a appelé SOS Amitié*   in despair, she phoned the Samaritans
  *les hommes, **inquiets**, ont pris la fuite*   worried, the men ran away

If one or more adjectives qualify two or more nouns, the adjectives agree in the plural:
  *une tension et une violence **extraordinaires***   amazing tension and violence

If the same adjective refers to both masculine and feminine nouns, it takes the masculine form, and if possible the masculine noun is placed next to the adjective:

j'ai vu des femmes et des enfants terrifiés	I saw terrified women and children
j'ai vu des femmes et des hommes terrifiés	I saw terrified men and women

12.2 When adjectives do not agree

An adjective agrees with a noun only if: the adjective directly qualifies that noun, and not a whole phrase or sentence in which the noun happens to appear:

	*une/la/cette/sa voiture est **blanche***	one/the/this/his (etc.) car is white
but	***conduire** une voiture est **intéressant***	driving a car is interesting
	les vacances** sont trop **longues	holidays are too long
but	*les vacances, **c'est essentiel***	holidays are essential **(see also 52.2)**

Certain nouns can form part of a group which, although containing a feminine noun, is itself neuter, in which case there is no agreement:

	une chose sensationnelle	a sensational thing
but	*quelque chose **de** sensationnel*	something sensational
and	*rien **de** sensationnel*	nothing sensational
	une personne active	an active individual
but	*c'est quelqu'un **d'**actif*	he's/she's someone active
and	*je n'ai vu personne **d'**actif*	I saw no one who was active

---

Exercice 12/1   *Une chose, quelque chose etc.*   Travail individuel

a   Dans les phrases suivantes, remplacez le **nom** entre parenthèses par un pronom **indéfini** (quelqu'un ou quelque chose). N'oubliez pas d'ajouter de entre le pronom et l'adjectif, et de **supprimer** l'accord de l'adjectif.

Exemple: J'ai vu (une chose) exceptionnelle.
Réponse: J'ai vu **quelque chose d'**exceptionnel.

1   Elle a trouvé (une personne) active pour le poste.
2   Il cherche (une chose) différente dans sa vie.
3   C'est (une femme) exceptionnelle.
4   Son livre contient (une idée) passionnante.
5   Ce changement offre (une possibilité) nouvelle.
6   Il a rencontré (une jeune femme) intéressante.

b   Vérifiez vos réponses, puis récrivez les six phrases **au négatif**, en remplaçant le pronom indéfini par un mot négatif (personne ou rien).

Exemple: J'ai vu (quelque chose) d'exceptionnel.
Réponse: Je **n'**ai **rien** vu **d'**exceptionnel.

Invariable adjectives

Certain adjectives in French are invariable: they never agree with a noun they qualify:

Adjectives formed from other parts of speech:

(noun)	*marron*	*une ceinture **marron***	a brown belt
(exclamation)	*chic*	*une femme **chic***	a fashionable woman
(adverb)	*bien*	*elle est **bien**, ta chemise*	your shirt is great

Adjectives formed from foreign words:

cool	*des parents **cool***	easy-going parents

If such words become adopted as a permanent feature of the language, they may eventually agree: for example, with a plural noun, *chics* is sometimes used.

An adjective used as a noun (***une chemise bleu marine***) does not agree (**see 17.3d**). An adjective used as an adverb (*coûter **cher***, etc.) does not agree (**see 17.3e**).

12.3 Adjective forms and endings

In spoken French, two-thirds of feminine forms of adjectives are identical to the masculine forms:

Adjectives which always end in *-e*:

immense	*impossible*	*jaune*	*rouge*

Many adjectives for which the masculine form ends in a sounded consonant such as *-r* or *-t*:

clair, claire	*cher, chère*	*net, nette*

Certain adjectives for which the masculine form ends in *-i* or *-u*:

joli, jolie	*poli, polie*	*pointu, pointue*

In written French, on the other hand, over half of feminine forms of adjectives are different from the masculine forms.

The following tables show the main adjective forms and endings, with examples. When studying these, read the examples (on the right) aloud to yourself (or to a partner), so that you can check what is said about the spoken forms and endings. The following codes are used: M = masculine, F = feminine, C = consonant and V = vowel.

■ **Table 1 Adjective forms and endings (1) singular**

	Spoken ending		Written ending		Examples	
			M	**F**	**M**	**F**
1	M & F forms: identical		-e	-e	rouge	rouge
					tranquille	tranquille
2	M & F forms: identical		-(i)al	-(i)ale	social	sociale
			-(i)el	-(i)elle	naturel	naturelle
			-eil	-eille	pareil	pareille
			-ic	-ique	public	publique
			-ect	-ecte	direct	directe
			-et	-ette	net	nette
			-er	-ère	cher	chère
			-eur	-eure	meilleur	meilleure
3	M & F forms: identical		-i	-ie	joli	jolie
			-u	-ue	aigu	aigüe
4	F form: change	[r]	-(i)er	-(i)ère	premier	première
	vowel, add consonant	[l]	-ou	-olle	fou	folle
		[l]	-eau	-elle	nouveau	nouvelle
		[j]	-ieux	-ieille	vieux	vieille
5	F form: add	[d]	-and	-ande	grand	grande
	consonant	[t]	it	-ite	petit	petite
		[t]	-et	-ette	muet	muette
		[s]	-as	-asse	bas	basse
		[s]	-oux	-ouce	doux	douce
		[z]	-eux	-euse	dangereux	dangereuse
		[ʃ]	-anc	-anche	blanc	blanche
6	F form: denasalise		-ain	-aine	urbain	urbaine
	nasal vowel, add		-in	-ine	citadin	citadine
	consonant		-an	-anne	paysan	paysanne
			-ien	-ienne	parisien	parisienne
7	F form: change		-ec	-èche	sec	sèche
	consonant		-ef	-ève	bref	brève
			-if	-ive	actif	active
			-eur	-euse	prometteur	prometteuse
	F form: change		-eur	-rice	conservateur	conservatrice
	vowel and consonant		-eur	-eresse	vengeur	vengeresse

■ **Table 2   Adjective forms and endings (2) plural**

	Spoken ending	Written ending MS	MP	Examples MS	MP	FP
1	S & P forms: identical	-e	-es	rouge	rouges	rouges
2	S & P forms: identical	-(i)el	-(i)els	naturel	naturels	naturelles
		-eil	-eils	pareil	pareils	pareilles
		-er	-ers	cher	chers	chères
		-et	-ets	net	nets	nettes
	S & FP forms: [al], MP forms: [o]	**-(i)al**	**-(i)aux**	**général**	**généraux**	**générales**
				social	**sociaux**	**sociales**
3	S & P forms: identical	-i	-is	joli	jolis	jolies
		-u	-us	aigu	aigus	aigües
4	S & P forms: identical	-(i)er	-(i)ers	premier	premiers	premières
		-ou	-ous	fou	fous	folles
		-eau	-eaux	nouveau	nouveaux	nouvelles
5	S & P forms: identical	-and	-ands	grand	grands	grandes
		-it	-its	petit	petits	petites
		-as	-as	bas	bas	basses
		-eux	-eux	dangereux	dangereux	dangereuses
6	S & P forms: identical	-ain	-ains	urbain	urbains	urbaines
		-in	-ins	citadin	citadins	citadines
		-an	-ans	paysan	paysans	paysannes
		-ien	-iens	ancien	anciens	anciennes
7	S & P forms: identical	-ec	-ecs	sec	secs	sèches
		-if	-ifs	actif	actifs	actives
		-eur	-eurs	prometteur	prometteurs	prometteuses

12.4 Endings of certain groups of adjectives

Adjectives ending in -al and -ial; -el, -iel and -eil

These two adjective suffixes (see group 2 in the tables above) are widely used in French (**see 14.5**); both correspond to equivalent English words with the suffix '-al'.

They show marked differences when it comes to feminine or plural endings:

-el

The feminine ending is spelt with *-ll-*:

| *industriel(s)* | *industrielle(s)* | *traditionnel(s)* | *traditionnelle(s)* |

-al

These adjectives (and some nouns, including some ending in *-ail*) alternate between a singular ending with a consonant (or semivowel) and a plural ending with a vowel:

Singular	**Masculine plural**
-al, pronounced [al]:	*-aux*, pronounced [o]:
social, national, le total, le cheval	*sociaux, nationaux, les totaux, les chevaux*
-ail, pronounced [aj]:	*-aux*, pronounced [o]:
le travail work	*les travaux* (road-)works

EXCEPTIONS:

| *banal* | commonplace | **banals** |
| *naval* | naval | **navals** |

Adjectives ending in *-eau, -ou* etc.

These adjectives (see group 4 in the tables above) alternate between a masculine ending with a vowel and a feminine ending with a consonant (or semivowel):

Masculine		**Feminine**	
-eau, pronounced [o]:	*beau*	*-elle*, pronounced [ɛl]:	*belle*
-ieux, pronounced [jø]:	*vieux*	*-ieille*, pronounced [jej]:	*vieille*
-ou, pronounced [u]:	*fou*	*-olle*, pronounced [ɔl]:	*folle*

Beau, nouveau, vieux, which are usually placed before a noun (**see 26.1**), have the ending *-el/-eil* before a masculine noun beginning with a vowel:

c'est un bel endroit	it's a lovely spot
'Le Nouvel Observateur'	(Paris weekly news magazine)
'Le vieil homme et la mer'	'The old man and the sea' (Hemingway)

Exercice 12/2   **Adjectifs: masculin et féminin**   Travail individuel

Écrivez au féminin singulier:

1	amical	6	naturel
2	familial	7	normal
3	individuel	8	principal
4	industriel	9	traditionnel
5	local	10	universel

Exercice 12/3 **Adjectifs: singulier et pluriel** Travail individuel

Écrivez au masculin pluriel:

1	commercial	6	principal
2	égal	7	professionnel
3	local	8	social
4	mondial	9	spécial
5	naturel	10	traditionnel

Adjectives ending in a mute consonant

This category (group 5 in the tables above) includes a large number of adjectives which:

● in the masculine form, end with a vowel in speech and a consonant in writing;
● in the feminine form, end in an additional consonant in speech, and an additional vowel in writing:

français	[frã sɛ]	*française*	[frã sɛz]
différent	[di fe rã]	*différente*	[di fe rãt]

The rule for writing such adjectives ('add -e in the feminine') is easy to remember; for help with saying them, **see 6.2**.

13 Prefixes

13.1 How prefixes are used

A **prefix** is a letter or group of letters which, added at the beginning of a word (verb, noun, adjective or adverb), forms a new word with a different meaning from the original word:

	Word	Meaning	Prefix	New word	New meaning
Verbs					
	faire	to do	***dé-***	*défaire*	to undo
	sortir	to go out	***re(s)-***	*ressortir*	to go out again
	voir	to see	***pré-***	*prévoir*	to foresee
Nouns					
	un poison	poison	***contre-***	*un contrepoison*	an antidote
Adjectives					
	doué	gifted	***sur-***	*surdoué*	hyperintelligent

In the above examples, a prefix is used to form a new word in the same grammatical class as the original word.

In other cases, the addition of a prefix creates a word in a different grammatical class:

Noun > adjective

un gang	a gang	***anti-***	*(la brigade) antigang* (the) organised crime (division)

Noun > verb

le courage	bravery	***en-***	*encourager*	to encourage
la terre	the earth	***en-***	*enterrer*	to bury

Adjective > verb

la mer	the sea	***a-***	*amerrir*	to splashdown

A prefix is a unit of meaning rather than a word in its own right (*pré-*, *anti-*, in the above examples), but certain prepositions (*contre-*, *en-*, in the above examples) are also used as prefixes.

Certain words can combine with several different prefixes, including verbs such as:

mettre	*démettre*	*remettre*	*soumettre*		
	to dismiss	to put back	to submit		
tenir	*contenir*	*détenir*	*maintenir*	*retenir*	*soutenir*
	to contain	to detain	to maintain	to hold back	to sustain
venir	*convenir*	*devenir*	*prévenir*	*revenir*	
	to agree	to become	to warn	to come back	

In other cases, the verb without a prefix does not exist:

(-clure)	*conclure*	*exclure*	*inclure*
	to conclude	to exclude	to include
(-duire)	*déduire*	*produire*	*réduire*
	to deduce	to produce	to reduce

The adaptability of prefixes means that new combinations of prefix + verb/noun/adjective are constantly being created: this is one area of the French language where you can make up new words yourself, and still be understood!

In speech, there is no break between a prefix and the rest of the noun (**see 7.1**), and in writing, the majority of prefixed words are spelt as a single word, without a hyphen.

EXCEPTIONS to this general rule include:

● the prepositions *après*, *avant*, *sans* and *sous* and the noun *arrière*, when used as prefixes, and the prefixes *mi-*and *non-*:

(le service) après-vente	after-sales (service)
un avant-goût	a foretaste
les sans-emploi	the unemployed
sous-estimer	to underestimate
à mi-mollet	calf-length
non-violent	nonviolent

● the prepositions *contre* and *entre*, when followed by a vowel or another prefix:

une contre-expertise	a second opinion
s'entre-dévorer	to tear one another to pieces

13.2 Meaning of prefixes

Broadly speaking, prefixes are used in order to specify:
a Position (in time, space or thought), **b Quality** and **c Status**.

a Position

anti	*un anticorps*	an antibody
anti-	*un antivol*	a (car or bicycle) lock
	(une campagne) anti-tabac	(an) anti-smoking (campaign)
après	*après-demain*	the day after tomorrow
after		
arrière	*un arrière-goût*	an aftertaste
behind	*l'arrière-pays*	the hinterland
avant	*avant-hier*	the day before yesterday
before		
co	*un coauteur*	a coauthor
together	*une coopérative*	a co-op (producers or distributors)
con	*la concurrence*	(economic/commercial) competition
together	*des confettis*	confetti
com	*composer*	to compose, to make up
(used instead of *con* when followed by *b*, *m*, *p*)		
contre	*la contrepartie*	compensation; the opposite view
counter-	*la contre-allée*	service road, side track
entre	*une entreprise*	a firm/business/company
between	*entre-temps*	meanwhile
ex	*exclure*	to exclude, leave out
out of, ex-		
extra	*(une activité) extrascolaire*	(an) out-of-school (activity)
out of, extra-	*extraterrestre*	extraterrestrial
inter	*intervenir*	to intervene
between, inter-	*un intervalle*	a gap, an interval
mi	*à mi-chemin*	halfway
half, mid-	*à mi-temps*	part-time
para	*paramédical*	paramedical
para-		
pré	*prémédité*	premeditated
pre-	*la préretraite*	early retirement
pro	*(jouer) les prolongations*	(to play) extra time
pro-		
sous	*sous-estimer*	to underestimate
under-	*un sous-officier*	an NCO
sur	*surmonter*	to overcome
over-	*un surcroît (de travail)*	extra (work)
trans	*transmettre*	to transmit, broadcast
trans-		

b   Quality

auto	*un autocollant*	a sticker
self-	*(une économie d')*	(a) subsistence (economy)
	autoconsommation	
mal	*un malentendant*	(someone who is) hard-of-hearing
badly	*malencontreusement*	ill-advisedly
micro	*un microprocesseur*	a microprocessor
micro-		
mini	*une minijupe*	a miniskirt
mini-		
non-	*la non-assistance*	failure to assist (a person in danger)
non-	*(à personne en danger)*	
	non-syndiqué	non-union(ised)
sans-	*les sans-papiers*	illegal immigrant (workers)
without		
uni	*unilatéral*	unilateral
uni-		

Certain prefixes are used as intensifiers of nouns and adjectives: *archi-*, *extra-*, *hyper-*, *super-*: for other intensifiers, **see 31.4**.

c   Status   (see 13.3 and 13.4)

The one-syllable prefixes ***a-***, ***dé***, ***é-***, ***en-***, ***in-***, and ***re-*** in French are similar to the English prefixes 'de-', 'dis-', 'in-', 're-', 'un-' in that they are used with a large number of words, to the point of scarcely being perceived as prefixes at all.

13.3 Prefixes with more than one meaning

The prefixes ***a-***, ***é-***, ***en-***, ***in-*** have more than one meaning, and ***dé-/dés-*** has a wide range of meaning:

a-

In everyday words, ***a-*** refers to position or movement towards:

affolé	*approcher*	*atterrir*
panic-stricken	to move/get nearer	to land

Note that in many words the initial consonant is doubled after the prefix *a-*.

In learned or technical words, the prefix ***a-*** means 'non-', 'un-':

asymétrique	*athée*	*atone*
asymmetric(al)	atheist	lifeless, expressionless

In everyday words, the prefix ***non-*** is used **(see 13.2b)**.

é-

The usual meaning of **é-** is 'out of', 'away from':

éjecter	*éloigné*	*une évasion*
to eject, kick out	distant, remote	an escape

But this meaning is less obvious in:

échanger	*éclairer*	*une épreuve*	*l'épuration*
to exchange	to light up	a test	purification

en-

en- (spelt **em-** before **b**, **m** and **p**) often carries the meaning of position, movement towards, etc.:

embellir	*un embouteillage*	*enterrer*	*s'entraîner*
to decorate, adorn	a traffic jam	to bury	to train

But in certain words the meaning is of movement away:

emmener	*emporter*	*un enlèvement*
to take away	to carry away	a kidnapping

Compare:

amener	*apporter*
to bring	to fetch

in-

in- appears in a number of disguises, depending on the consonant that follows it:

imb-, imp-	nasal vowel + *b*, *p*	*impossible*
ill-, imm-, irr-	open vowel + *l*, *m*, *r*	*immédiat*
in-	open vowel + *n* + vowel	*inutile*
in-	nasal vowel + *c*, *d*, *f*, *g*, *j*, *s*, *t*, *v*	*intéressant*

(**See 5.2** and **5.3** for examples of open and nasal vowels.)

The meaning of **in-** (etc.) is often the opposite of the word without this prefix:

possible	possible	*impossible*	impossible
utile	useful	*inutile*	useless
le mobilier	furniture	*l'immobilier*	property, real estate

But in certain uses the meaning of **in-** (etc.) is that of movement towards:

un investissement	*l'irradiation*
an investment	(exposure to) radiation

dé- and dés-

dé- and **dés-** have a wide range of meaning around the central idea of removal of something, or reversal of a process (compare English 'un-', 'de-').

The form is generally **dé-** before a consonant, and **dés-** before a vowel or mute *h*:

démodé	*démonter*	*démontrer*
old-fashioned	to dismantle	to demonstrate
désespéré	*se déshabiller*	*un désherbant*
desperate	to get undressed	a weed-killer

13.4 The prefix *re-*

Re-, **ré-** is the most commonly used prefix in French (closely followed by *dé-*, *dés-*); it presents three main problems for the learner of French:

- pronunciation and spelling: sometimes **re-**, sometimes **ré-**;
- meaning: it is equivalent in meaning to the prefix 're-' in English, but it also appears in a number of words where it seems to have no distinct meaning;
- form: when added to words beginning with **a-**, the prefix **re-** is often shortened to **r-**.

Pronunciation and spelling: *re-* or *ré-?*

The spelling of *re-/ré-* is determined by the pronunciation; in some cases, this depends on the letter that comes next – the initial letter of the word to which *re-/ré-* has been added. Here are two general rules, with examples:

re-
no accent; pronounced [rɛ] before *j*, *l*, *m*, *n*:

rej-	*rejeter*	*rejoindre*	
	to reject	to catch up with	
EXCEPTION:		*(se) réjouir*	
		to delight (be delighted)	
rel-	*relevé*	*relier*	*religieux*	*la religion*
	spicy (food)	to connect	religious	religion
rem-	*un remède*	*remettre*	*une remise*	*remuer*
	a remedy	to put back	a discount	to move
EXCEPTIONS:	*la rémission*	*rémunérer*		
	remission	to remunerate, pay		
ren-	*une rencontre*	*renouveler*		
	an encounter	to repeat, renew		
EXCEPTION:	*rénover*			
	to renovate, restore			

ré

acute accent; pronounced [re] before *a*, *é*, *e*, *i*, *o*, *u*:

réa-	*une réaction*	*réagir*	*réapprendre*	(see also *ra-*, below)
	a reaction	to react	to learn again	
réé-	*rééditer*	*réélire*	*réécrire* or *récrire*	
	to republish	to reelect	to rewrite	
rée-	*réemployer* or *remployer*		*se réengager* or *se rengager*	
	to re-employ		to re-enlist	
réi-	*réinstaller*		*réintégrer*	
	to reinstall		to reinstate	
réo-	*la réouverture*	but	*rouvrir*	
	the reopening		to reopen	
réu-	*réunir*		*une réunion*	
	to join together		a meeting	

rés- + vowel

réserver	*la résidence*	*la résistance*
to reserve, book	residence	resistance

res- + consonant

responsable	*ressembler*	*ressentir*	*les ressources*
responsible	to resemble, look like	to feel, be affected by	resources

re- + other consonants

Here, your only guide is the pronunciation of the word itself. In some cases, there are two different words, one with *ré-*, one with *re-*:

réformer	to reform
reformer	to form again, set up again

In most cases each word has to be learnt separately, with its pronunciation:

ré-	*réchauffer*	to warm up	*re-*	*rechercher*	to search for
[re]	*récompenser*	to reward	[rə]	*recomposer*	to put together (again)
	réconcilier	to reconcile		*reconduire*	to see someone home
	réfuter	to disprove		*refuser*	to refuse
	régaler	to (give someone a) treat		*regarder*	to look at

ra-

We have seen how, in some cases, *ré-* + vowel reduces to *ré-*, *rou-* etc. This reduction is common before the vowel *a*:

rapprocher	*rassembler*	*ramasser*	*rappeler*
to bring closer	to gather, collect	to pick up	to call back

Also: *réanimer* or *ranimer*   to revive someone

Meaning

The basic meaning of *ré-/re-* as a prefix in French is similar to the meaning of 're-' in English: one of repetition, copying something or putting something back. However, certain words are formed with the prefix **ré-/re-** in French, whereas the prefix 're-' is not necessarily present in their English equivalents:

> *elle ouvrit la porte puis la **referma** doucement* (N3)
>
> she opened the door and then **closed it (again)** quietly

Also:	*ralentir*	*(se) rapprocher*	*rebondir*	*réchauffer*
	to slow down	to come closer	to bounce	to warm up
	reconnaître	*remercier*	*remplir*	*rencontrer*
	to recognise	to thank	to fill up	to meet

In these and many other cases, the original meaning of the prefix has become weakened.

Many words beginning with **ré-**, **re-** or **r-** are not thought of as containing a prefix at all:

regarder	rencontrer	(se) réveiller
to look at	*to meet*	*to wake up*

Some verb forms with *ré-/re-* are in more frequent use than related words which do not have the prefix:

(regarder)	*à l'égard de*	towards, with regard to
(rencontrer)	*aller à l'encontre de*	to run counter to, go against
(se réveiller)	*s'éveiller*	to be aroused, come to life

French
Grammar
Explained

Exercice 13/1   **Préfixes et sens**   Travail individuel ou à deux

a   Proposez un **préfixe** pour les mots ci–dessous (dans certains cas, le mot nouveau est dans une classe grammaticale différente).

b   Écrivez l'équivalent **en anglais** de chaque mot (1) sans préfixe, (2) avec le préfixe que vous avez proposé.

c   **Vérifiez** vos réponses à l'aide d'un dictionnaire.

Verbes		Noms		Adjectifs et Adverbes	
1	composer	1	l'abri	1	entendu
2	conseiller	2	le développement	2	équilibré
3	couvrir	3	dimanche	3	national
4	espérer	4	le droit	4	réel
5	finir	5	la forme	5	responsable
6	passer	6	le gel	6	utile
7	finir	7	la pluie	7	visible
8	présenter	8	la prise	8	constitutionnellement
9	prouver	9	la route	9	loin
10	voler	10	le ski	10	tout

d   **Contrôle**   Travail à deux

Quelque temps après avoir fait cet exercice, vérifiez avec un(e) partenaire que vous avez gardé en mémoire ces mots avec préfixe: tour à tour, choisissez au hasard un des trente mots sans préfixe; votre partenaire doit dire le mot avec un préfixe approprié.

14 Suffixes: verb, noun and adjective suffixes

14.1   **How suffixes are used**
14.2   **Verb suffixes**
14.3   **Noun suffixes**
14.4   **Noun and adjective suffixes**
14.5   **Adjective suffixes**
14.6   **Geographical nouns and adjectives**

14.1 How suffixes are used

The **ending** of a verb, noun or adjective is the part that varies in order to give grammatical information about the word:

- verb endings indicate the Person of the subject of the verb **(see 9.2)**, and the tense of the verb **(see 10)**;
- noun endings indicate number (and in some cases gender) **(see 11.1)**;
- adjective endings indicate both gender and number **(see 12.1)**.

An ending does not create a new word: *je travaille, je travaillais, je travaillerais* are different forms, with different endings, of the verb *travailler*; *blanche, blancs, blanches* are different forms, with different endings, of the adjective *blanc*.

A **suffix**, on the other hand, is a group of letters which, when added at the end of a word, creates a new word. This new word often belongs to a different grammatical class from the original word. For example, from the noun *le travail* one can create *travailler* (verb), *travailleur/travailleuse* (adjective), *un travailleur* (noun).

A suffix (*-eur*, for example) does not form a word in its own right: its function is to allocate a word to a grammatical class, and to give some indication of meaning. For example, a masculine noun ending in *-eur* is usually 'one who does'.

A suffix can itself carry an ending, to indicate Person and tense of verbs, or gender and number of nouns and adjectives.

14.2 Verb suffixes

Verb suffixes fall into two broad categories of meaning:

- those which convert an adjective or a noun into a process;
- those which weaken the meaning of a verb, or add an unfavourable meaning.

Process: adjective or noun > verb

-is(er)	*réel*	real	*réaliser*	to achieve
	(un) total	(a) total	*totaliser*	to add up
-ifi(er)	*pur*	pure	*purifier*	to purify
	un plan	a plan	*planifier*	to plan
-el(er)	*un marteau*	a hammer	*marteler*	to beat out

Weakening: verb with full meaning > verb with diminished meaning

-ass(er)	*rêver*	to dream	*rêvasser*	to daydream
-ich(er)	*pleurer*	to cry	*pleurnicher*	to whine
-in(er)	*trotter*	to run, trot	*trottiner*	to trot along
-onn(er)	*chanter*	to sing	*chantonner*	to hum (a tune)
-ot(er)	*taper*	to bang, hit hard	*tapoter*	to pat, tap

14.3 Noun suffixes

Noun suffixes can be presented in three main groups:

a suffixes that form names of objects;
b suffixes that form names of places;
c suffixes that form abstract nouns.

a   Names of objects

A number of suffixes are used to designate objects (including machines); in some cases the noun is masculine (*-eur, -(i)er, -oir*), in others it is feminine (*-euse, -(i)ère, oire*):

Masculine	Feminine	Examples	
-eur		*un moteur*	an engine
	-euse	*une tondeuse*	a mower
-er/-ier		*un oranger*	an orange tree
		un olivier	an olive tree
	-ière	*une cafetière*	a coffee pot
-oir		*un arrosoir*	a watering-can
	-oire	*une baignoire*	a bath (tub)

The suffix *-ette* is used for a wide variety of nouns, with a diminutive meaning:

une fille	*a girl, a daughter*	une fillette	*a little girl*
une maison	*a house*	une maisonnette	*a small house*

b   Names of places

Certain noun suffixes indicate a place (including places of production or sale):

Masculine	Feminine	Examples	
	-ade	*une rocade*	a bypass
	-aie	*une oliv(er)aie*	an olive grove
-ée		*un lycée*	a high school
(words taken from Latin)		*un musée*	a museum
-ère		*le ministère*	the ministry
	-erie	*la crémerie*	(dairy) food shop
	-ure	*une filature*	mill (factory)
-us		*un campus*	a campus
(words taken from Latin)		*le terminus*	the terminus

c   Abstract nouns

Many abstract nouns are formed by the addition of a suffix to a verb, an adjective or another noun. Some of these suffixes form a masculine noun, others a feminine noun:

Masculine	Feminine	Examples	
-age		*l'esclavage*	slavery
		un personnage	a character
	-ance	*la croyance*	belief
		l'élégance	elegance
-at		*le patronat*	employers
		le salariat	wage earners
	-ée	(see below: noun suffix: **-ée**)	
	-ence	*l'incohérence*	incoherence
	-erie	*la tricherie*	cheating
	-esse	*la tristesse*	sadness
	-eur	*la hauteur*	height
		la valeur	value
-ing		*le parking*	the car park
(words taken from English)		*le shopping*	shopping
-is		*un gâchis*	a waste, a mess
	-ise	*la sottise*	silliness
-isme		*l'humanisme*	humanism
	-ison	*une comparaison*	a comparison
-ment		*un changement*	a change
		le rendement	output, yield

-nce	*l'existence*	existence
-té	*la bonté*	kindness
	la pauvreté	poverty
-tion	*une compensation*	compensation
-tude	*la solitude*	loneliness

Some of these words, which were originally abstract terms, have come to be applied to people, places, etc.

Noun suffix: *-ée*

This suffix often has a meaning corresponding to '-ful' or 'full' in English:

une poignée	a handful
une pelletée	a spadeful
la maisonnée	the whole household, everyone in the house
une assemblée	a gathering, a meeting

Several words in French denoting (periods of) time have two forms, one with, one without the suffix *-ée*. By and large, the form without the suffix is used when the period of time is seen as one in a series; the form with *-ée* is used when the focus is on the quality of the period of time itself, or the activities that take place during it:

Le jour/la journée

*à la fin du **jour*** — at the end of the day
(day as opposed to night)

*à la fin d'une **journée** chargée* — at the end of a busy day
(emphasis on what kind of day it's been)

Le matin/la matinée

*le lendemain **matin**, elle était guérie* — the next morning, she was cured
(morning, as opposed to afternoon or evening)

*la **matinée** s'est très bien passée* — the morning went very well
(emphasis on the events of the morning)

Le soir/la soirée

*on passera les voir demain **soir*** — we'll drop in and see them tomorrow evening
(in the evening, and not during the daytime)

*on a passé une excellente **soirée*** — we('ve) had a splendid evening
(emphasis on what kind of evening it's been)

L'an/l'année

*ils ont vécu deux **ans** au Pérou, puis dix **ans** en Chine* — they lived in Peru for two years, then in China for ten years
(emphasis on the number of years, not on what those years were like)

*on a passé cinq merveilleuses **années** à Florence* — we spent five wonderful years in Florence
(emphasis on what the five years were like)

Exercice 14/1   **Suffixes nominaux**   Travail individuel

a   Ajoutez un suffixe aux mots ci–dessous, de façon à former un **nom abstrait**.

Exemple: haut
Réponse: la hauteur

Exemple: exister
Réponse: l'existence

1	bon	11	inévitable
2	commun	12	inquiet
3	compter	13	loger
4	évident	14	masculin
5	exagéré	15	organiser
6	faible	16	rentrer
7	féminin	17	sauver
8	gouverner	18	sentir
9	habiter	19	suggérer
10	ignorer	20	violent

b   **Contrôle**   Travail à deux

Quelque temps après avoir fait cet exercice, vérifiez, avec un(e) partenaire, que vous avez gardé en mémoire ces noms: tour à tour, choisissez au hasard un des vingt mots dans la liste ci–dessus; votre partenaire doit dire le nom qu'on peut former à partir de ce mot.

14.4 Noun and adjective suffixes

Certain suffixes are used to designate people associated with a particular activity or condition. In most cases, the noun that is produced using these suffixes can also function as an adjective (**see 17.3c**). This is also true of suffixes used to form geographical nouns and adjectives (**see 14.6**):

Masculine	Feminine	Examples	
-aire	*-aire*	*(un) célibataire, (une) célibataire*	(an) unmarried (person)
		(un) milliardaire, (une) milliardaire	a multi-millionaire
-an	*-anne*	*(un) paysan, (une) paysanne*	a farmer (rural)
-ard	*-arde*	*(un) montagnard, (une) montagnarde*	(a) highland(er)
-en, -ien	*-enne, -ienne*	*un pharmacien, une pharmacienne*	a pharmacist
		(un) végétarien, (une) végétarienne	(a) vegetarian

-er, -ier	-ère, -ière	(un) étranger, (une) étrangère	(a) foreign(er)
		(un) ouvrier, (une) ouvrière	a worker (working-class)
-eur	-euse	un skieur, une skieuse	a skier
-teur	-trice	(un) conservateur, (une) conservatrice	(a) conservative
		un lecteur, une lectrice	a reader
-iste, -yste	-iste, -yste	un analyste, une analyste	an analyst
		(un) travailliste, (une) travailliste	(a) Labour (supporter)
-ois	-oise	(un) villageois, (une) villageoise	(a) village(r)

14.5 Adjective suffixes

As well as the suffixes which can be used to form a noun or adjective designating a person associated with a particular activity or condition (see 14.4), other suffixes are used to form adjectives from verbs or nouns:

Masculine	Feminine	Examples	
-able	-able	remarquable	remarkable
-ain	-aine	humain	human
-al	-ale	familial	family
		hexagonal	to do with France	('l'Hexagone': France)
-ant	-ante	(present participle: see 44.1)	
-âtre	-âtre	blanchâtre	pallid
-é	-ée	stéréotypé	stereotyped
-el	-elle	personnel	personal
-ent	-ente	équivalent	equivalent
-esque	-esque	romanesque	fictional
-eur	-eure	inférieur	inferior
-eux	-euse	paresseux	lazy
-ible	-ible	résistible	resistible
-ième	-ième	(numerals: see 25)	
-if	-ive	éducatif	educational
-ique	-ique	chimique	chemical
-ite	-ite	cosmopolite	cosmopolitan
-oire	-oire	notoire	notorious
-ole	-ole	agricole	agricultural
-u	-ue	barbu	with a beard

-al/-ale and **-el/-elle**   (see 12.4)

The suffix **-al/-ale** is common to many adjectives in both English and French:

    local   *national*   *normal*   *social*

But many adjectives which, in English, have the suffix '-al', have the suffix *-el/-elle* in French:

personnel *professionnel* *traditionnel* *universel*

And the French equivalents of several adjectives which, in English, have the suffix '-al', have a quite different suffix:

-e	*hypocrite*	hypocritical	*interne*	internal
-que	*chimique*	chemical	*philosophique*	philosophical
-é	*controversé*	controversial		
-er	*financier*	financial		

Exercice 14/2 **Suffixes adjectivaux** Travail individuel

a Ajoutez un suffixe aux noms ci-dessous, de façon à former un **adjectif**.

Exemple: une personne
Réponse: personnel

1	le commerce	6	une femme	11	l'individu
2	la communauté	7	la finance	12	le luxe
3	le coût	8	le gouvernement	13	le monde
4	l'égalité	9	l'histoire	14	la norme
5	la famille	10	la honte	15	le système

b **Contrôle** Travail à deux
Quelque temps après avoir fait cet exercice, vérifiez, avec un(e) partenaire, que vous avez gardé en mémoire ces adjectifs: tour à tour, choisissez au hasard un des vingt noms dans la liste ci-dessus; votre partenaire doit dire l'adjectif qu'on peut former à partir de ce nom.

14.6 Geographical nouns and adjectives

These are formed from the names of the corresponding countries, regions, towns, etc., by the addition of certain suffixes. It is important, when learning place names in French, to learn also the corresponding adjective (which always takes a small letter) and noun (which always take a capital letter) forms, as these are used more widely in French than in English:

Endings		Examples		
M	F	Place name	adjective	Noun
-ain	*-aine*	*Rome*	*romain, romaine*	*un Romain, une Romaine*
-ais	*-aise*	*l'Irlande*	*irlandais, irlandaise*	*un Irlandais, une Irlandaise*
-al	*-ale*	*la Provence*	*provençal, provençale*	*un Provençal, une Provençale*
-an	*-ane*	*Texas*	*texan, texane*	*un Texan, une Texane*
-and	*-ande*	*la Normandie*	*normand, normande*	*un Normand, une Normande*
-ard	*-arde*	*la Savoie*	*savoyard, savoyarde*	*un Savoyard, une Savoyarde*
-e	*-e*	*la Russie*	*russe, russe*	*un Russe, une Russe*
		la Belgique	*belge, belge*	*un Belge, une Belge*
-eau	*-elle*	*Tours, la Touraine*	*tourangeau, tourangelle*	*un Tourangeau, une Tourangelle*
-éen	*-éenne*	*l'Europe*	*européen, européenne*	*un Européen, une Européenne*
-ien	*-ienne*	*Israël*	*israélien, israélienne*	*un Israélien, une Israélienne*
-in	*-ine*	*le Maghreb*	*maghrébin, maghrébine* (North African)	*un Maghrébin, une Maghrébine*
-ique	*-ique*	*l'Asie*	*asiatique, asiatique*	*un Asiatique, une Asiatique*
-ois	*-oise*	*Berlin*	*berlinois, berlinoise*	*un Berlinois, une Berlinoise*
		le Québec	*québécois, québécoise*	*un Québécois, une Québécoise*
-ol	*-ole*	*l'Espagne*	*espagnol, espagnole*	*un Espagnol, une Espagnole*
-on	*-onne*	*la Bretagne*	*breton, bretonne*	*un Breton, une Bretonne*

Exercice 14/3   **Pays (etc.) et habitants**   Travail individuel

a   Écrivez, au **masculin** et au **féminin**, l'**adjectif** (sans majuscule) et le **nom** (avec majuscule) qui correspondent aux noms de pays et de villes (etc.) ci-dessous.

Exemple: Paris

Réponse: parisien, parisienne; un Parisien, une Parisienne

1	l'Allemagne	11	le Japon
2	l'Alsace	12	la Lorraine
3	la Bavière	13	Lyon
4	la Californie	14	Marseille
5	le Canada	15	Naples
6	la Catalogne	16	la Norvège
7	Florence	17	les Pays-Bas
8	le pays de Galles	18	le Portugal
9	la Grande-Bretagne	19	Strasbourg
10	Hambourg	20	la Suède

b   **Contrôle**   Travail à deux

Quelque temps après avoir fait cet exercice, vérifiez, avec un(e) partenaire, que vous avez gardé en mémoire ces noms et ces adjectifs: tour à tour, choisissez au hasard un des vingt noms de pays, de villes, etc., dans la liste ci-dessus; votre partenaire doit dire, au masculin et au féminin, l'adjectif et le nom qui désignent les habitants.

French
Grammar
Explained

15 When one word is not enough

15.1 **Compound nouns**
15.2 **Compound forms of verbs**
15.3 **Set phrases**

15.1 Compound nouns

IN ENGLISH and FRENCH, many compound nouns consist of noun (+ *de*) + noun, or verb + noun (for compound nouns formed of noun 1 + *à/de* + noun 2, and noun + *à/de* + infinitive, **see 41.2**):

Noun (+ *de*) + noun:	*une leçon de conduite*	a driving lesson
	la pâte de soja	bean curd
	une porte-fenêtre	a French window
Verb + noun:	*un porte-clefs*	a key ring

IN ENGLISH and FRENCH, many compound nouns are spelt with a hyphen, indicating that although they are two distinct words, they are being used as a single unit of meaning (for compound nouns formed from preposition + noun, **see 13.1** and **13.2**):

Noun + noun:	*une auto-école*	a driving school
	le centre-ville	the city/town centre
	une station-service	a service station
Verb + noun:	*un chasse-neige*	a snowplough

Several compound nouns are commonly used in a truncated form (**see 16.2**):

l'autostop	>	*du stop*	hitch-hiking
du supercarburant	>	*du super*	premium grade (petrol)
un blue-jean(s)	>	*un jeans*	(a pair of) jeans

Compound nouns spelt as single words

IN ENGLISH and FRENCH, many compound nouns have ceased to be thought of as two separate words, even when spelt with a hyphen, and are spelt as a single word:

un stylo à bille	a ballpoint pen	*un canot de sauvetage*	a lifeboat
un hautparleur	a loudspeaker	*un téléfilm*	a film made for TV
un piquenique	a picnic	*un tirebouchon*	a corkscrew
à contrecœur	reluctantly	*un portemanteau*	a coat rack

The formation of one new word from two existing words is a continual process: one of the recommendations in the 1990 spelling reforms was that a large number of words should be spelt as a single word, instead of with a hyphen.

15.2 Compound forms of verbs

A compound form of a verb consists of two or more words which, when used together, function as a single unit.

IN ENGLISH, many compound forms of verbs consist of verb + adverb: 'get up', 'go out', 'stay in', 'roll over', and so on; some consist of verb + two adverbs: 'get up to', 'be over with', etc.

IN FRENCH, compound forms of verbs consist of verb + noun: *prendre feu* ('catch fire'), *faire partie (de)* ('form part of'), or verb + preposition + noun.

Certain verbs are used with nouns to form a large number of compounds: ***avoir***, ***faire***, ***mettre*** and ***prendre***. Other verbs used in this way include: *donner, laisser, perdre, tenir.* (For verb + infinitive constructions, such as *faire/laisser* + infinitive, **see 39.3.**)

MEANING

The majority of compound forms of verbs consist of a verb which describes an action (or, in the case of *avoir*, a state), followed by an abstract noun, often describing a feeling. The meaning of the resultant compound often concerns a process within one individual, or an intervention by an individual.

FUNCTION

A compound form of a verb combines the function of a verb (by showing that a process is taking place) and that of a noun (by showing what kind of process it is): see verbs and nouns in **3.2**. One could say that the function of the verb, in these compounds, is to convert a noun into a verb.

FORM

The noun can be linked to the verb in one of three ways:
- without an article: *avoir lieu*   to take place
- with a preposition: *se mettre **en** route*   to set out
- with an article: *faire **de la** peine (à quelqu'un)*   to distress (someone)

Here are some further examples:

Without an article (verb and noun come closest to forming a single unit)

       avoir envie (de)   to want
       avoir hâte (de)   to be in a hurry to

avoir honte (de)	to be ashamed to
avoir intérêt (à)	to be (well) advised to
avoir soin (de)	to take care of
avoir tendance (à)	to tend to
donner lieu (à)	to give rise to
faire mal (à)	to harm, hurt
faire partie (de)	to be/form part of
but: *être une grande partie (de)*	to form a large part of
faire peur (à)	to frighten
faire plaisir (à)	to do a favour for
perdre connaissance	to faint
prendre forme	to take shape
prendre plaisir (à)	to take pleasure in
se rendre compte (de)	to realise

(*Se rendre compte (de)* is used in fixed expressions such as *je ne me rendais pas compte* ('I didn't realise') and the exclamation *tu te rends compte!* ('can you believe it!') otherwise, *réaliser* is used.)

With a preposition (the preposition is usually *à* or *en*)

avoir à cœur (de)	to set one's heart on
se mettre en colère	to get angry
mettre en marche	to start up (a machine)
prendre en compte	to take account of
tenir à cœur	to mean a lot to
(*cela me tient à cœur*	that means a lot to me)

With an article (verb and noun come less close to forming a single unit)

avoir l'air (de)	to look like
avoir des chances (de)	to be likely to
avoir le droit (de)	to have the right to
avoir du mal (à)	to have difficulty in
faire l'effet (de)	to work/act like
faire de la peine (à)	to distress, upset
mettre du temps (à)	to take time
passer du temps (à)	to spend time (-ing)
prendre l'air	to take off, become airborne

Exercice 15/1

Avoir, faire, mettre, prendre: verbes composés   Travail individuel

a   Complétez les phrases ci-dessous en ajoutant un des quatre verbes *avoir, faire, mettre, prendre*.
     N'oubliez pas d'employer la forme qui convient (infinitif, participe passé, etc.).

Exemple: Sa nouvelle m'a – de la peine.
Réponse: Sa nouvelle m'a **fait** de la peine.

1   Il a couru parce qu'il – peur d'arriver en retard.
2   S'il ne veut rien faire, c'est à vous de – l'initiative.
3   Ils ont vendu leur maison six mois après l'avoir – en vente.
4   Peu à peu, son grand projet a commencé à – forme.
5   Il prétend l'avoir construit lui-même, mais on – du mal à le croire.
6   Bon! assez parlé. On va se – au travail.
7   Ne crie pas comme ça; tu m'as – peur!
8   Dix heures déjà! Il est temps de nous – en route.
9   On a découvert à sa mort qu'il avait – de côté une somme importante.
10   Ferme la fenêtre! je n'aimerais pas que tu – froid.
11   Avec un vent favorable, on – des chances d'arriver au port avant le soir.
12   Faute d'argent, son projet risque de – long feu.

b   Vérifiez vos réponses, puis donnez leur équivalent en anglais.

15.3 Set phrases

FORM

A set phrase is a group of words (verb + article + noun, or noun 1 + preposition + noun 2) which are used together often enough for most French speakers to make an automatic association between them, and to use the group of words readily in particular circumstances.

FUNCTION

A compound form of a verb **(see 15.2)** performs a communicative function: it extends the range of notions which can be expressed by single-word verbs; a set phrase, on the other hand, performs an expressive function: it describes a situation, a process, an action using words that are colourful, exaggerated, etc. However, because the speaker and listener expect this combination of words to be used in a given situation, the meaning of the individual words is considerably diluted, reducing the communicative usefulness of the set phrase.

Examples:

(verb + noun)

attraper la crève	to catch your death (of cold)	(N2)
crever de faim	to be famished, to be starving	
peser le pour et le contre	to consider both sides of the argument	
prendre une veste	to be sent packing	
avoir roulé sa bosse	to have knocked around	

(noun 1 + noun 2)

c'est la fin des haricots	it's the end of the world
le revers de la médaille	the other side of the coin

As you can see from some of these examples, the result is often a 'cliché'; use a few of these, in the right place, and French speakers will admire your command of vocabulary and idiom; over-use them, and people will begin to wonder whether you have anything worthwhile to say.

16 When words are too many or too long

16.1 Reduction

16.2 Truncation

16.3 Acronymns

In spontaneous speech in informal situations (N2), we tend to increase the number of words we say, and the time we take to say them: we add words or phrases as fillers (**see 50.1**), we repeat words or phrases, leave sentences unfinished, hesitate, and so on. By these means, we give ourselves longer to think out, and our listener longer to take in, what we have to say.

At the same time, we tend to shorten individual words and phrases, including many that are in common use, and which can be easily recognised by our listener in their shortened form.

Some of these shortened forms eventually become adopted as part of the standard language, in place of the original form which is eventually forgotten. For example:

un stylo	(from *un stylographe*)	a pen
un vélo	(from *un vélocipède*)	a bike

This process of shortening words and phrases usually involves nouns or adjectives, and takes three main forms:

Reduction of a noun phrase or compound form to a single word:

	le chemin de fer métropolitain	the metropolitan railway
is reduced to:	*le métropolitain*	the metropolitan

Truncation of a single noun or adjective, reducing it to one or two syllables:

	le métropolitain	the metropolitan
is reduced to:	*le métro*	the underground, the tube

Acronyms: the initials of a group of words are used to form a new word:

la Régie autonome des transports parisiens	the Paris Transport Authority

becomes: *la RATP*

16.1 Reduction

Some official names and titles are reduced for ease of reference, in speech and writing:

une route nationale	> *une nationale*	an A road
une route départementale	> *une départementale*	a B road
la Compagnie générale des eaux	> *la Générale des eaux*	(the) General Water (company)
la Compagnie lyonnaise des eaux	> *la Lyonnaise des eaux*	(the) Lyon Water (company)

Compound nouns that are reduced in everyday speech include:

faire de l'autostop	> *faire du stop*	to hitch-hike

Some compound adjectives can be reduced:

bleu marine	> *marine*	navy (blue)

16.2 Truncation

Truncated nouns (some of which were originally compound nouns) in everyday use include:

le baccalauréat (N3)	> *le bac*	18+ exam
	avoir son bac	to have passed one's 18+
	passer le bac	to sit the 18+
une cafétéria	> *une cafète* (N2)	a cafeteria, self-service restaurant
la faculté (N3)	> *la fac* (N2)	university, 'college'
	aller en fac	to go to university
une manifestation	> *une manif* (N2)	a demonstration, a demo
la météorologie (N4)	> *la météo*	the weather forecast

Le cinéma, originally a truncation of *le cinématographe*, is truncated to *le ciné* (N2): 'the pictures', 'the movies'. This shortened form of the word can be lengthened by the addition of a suffix (**see 14**):

le ciné	> *le cinoche* (N1)	the flicks
le directeur	> *le dirlo* (N1)	the boss

Auto, bus and *car* are all truncated nouns (*automobile, autobus, autocar*), two of which, in their turn, form part of new compound nouns (**see 15.1**):

une auto-école	a driving school
l'Airbus	(the) Airbus (European civil aircraft)
un bibliobus	a mobile library

The names of some newspapers and magazines are truncated:

'Libération'	> *'Libé'* (N2)	(a Paris daily)
'Le Nouvel Observateur'	> *'Le Nouvel Obs'* (N2)	(a Paris weekly)

Truncation originates, very often, in a desire to appear 'in the know'; the truncated form eventually either passes into general usage, or dies out.

16.3 Acronyms

IN FRENCH, even more than in English, acronyms form part of the everyday language and their use is taken for granted. In part, this may be because the names of the letters of the alphabet in French sound more like actual syllables found in words than do the names of the letters in the English alphabet (say the two alphabets aloud, and see if you agree).

Acronyms are pronounced as far as possible as a word, not as a sequence of letters; this means without pauses:

le PS	[pe ɛs]	le Parti socialiste	the Socialist Party
le RPR	[ɛr pe ɛr]	le Rassemblement pour la République	the Conservative Party

In some cases, two initials are combined as if they were letters in a word:

le DEUG	[dœg]	le Diplôme d'études universitaires générales	two-year university diploma
l'ENA	[le na]	l'École nationale d'administration	National School of Administration

The punctuation of acronyms in French is subject to variation. The simplest solution is to use capitals and no full stops: *SNCF*. One can also use capitals with full stops: *S.N.C.F.*, and a capital for the first initial only: *Sncf* or *S.n.c.f.*

As with truncation, so with acronyms: many examples make a brief appearance and are then forgotten (or replaced when the organisation changes its name), but others become an established part of the vocabulary, and are used more often than the full version. This is particularly true of the names of political, economic and international organisations, and also of aspects of the educational system in France.

Some organisations are listed below, together with their acronyms:

Politics

le PC	le Parti communiste	the Communist Party
l'UDF	l'Union des démocrates français	(centre-right party)
le FN	le Front national	the National Front

Economics

le CNPF	le Conseil national du patronat français	(employers' organisation)
la CGT	la Confédération générale du travail	(union close to the PC)
FO	Force ouvrière	(centre-left union)

International

l'ONU	*l'Organisation des nations unies*	the United Nations
l'UE	*l'Union européenne*	the European Union

In some cases, the widespread use of an acronym can lead to the loss of any sense of what the letters stand for. This can result in the creation of a hybrid expression, which includes the main word in full as a noun, followed by the acronym as an adjective:

	les habitations à loyer modéré > les HLM	low rent housing
becomes	*les habitations HLM*	HLM-type housing

From acronym to new word

Some acronyms become used as words in their own right: *un laser* and *le radar*, for example, were originally (English) acronyms of the five words used to describe these two inventions. By way of contrast, many funding programmes of the European Union are given acronyms which form a word that is known already, such as ERASMUS and SOCRATES.

Certain French acronyms have become used as words in their own right, by the addition of a suffix **(see 14)**:

-ard	*un(e) smicard(e)*	person earning the national minimum wage
-arque	*un(e) énarque*	graduate of the ENA
-iste	*un(e) cégétiste*	member of the CGT union
	un(e) RMiste	person receiving the RMI (minimum guaranteed national income)

Only a small number of acronyms become lexicalised (used as a word in their own right) and, as the last example above shows, the process can stop at a halfway stage.

Part five

How words combine in groups

In **Part Four**, we saw how the form of many words contributes to the communication of meaning by representing a particular grammatical function; in **Part Five**, we look at how the choice of certain words contributes to the communication of meaning by representing a particular grammatical function.

These grammatical functions are presented in **17**, with particular emphasis on the distinction between grammatical form (when one says that a particular word 'is' a noun, for example) and grammatical function (when one says that this same word which 'is' a noun can also function as an adjective, for example).

In 18–26, some of the functions of pronouns and determiners ('minor' parts of speech) are presented:

18	**Object pronouns** the choice of which is determined by their relation to a verb
19	**Tonic pronouns** which are independent of the verb, but are often dependent on a preposition
20–21	**Possessive** and **demonstrative adjectives** and **pronouns** the choice of which is determined by their relation to a particular noun
22–25	**Determiners** and **qualifiers/quantifiers**, including numerals the choice of which is governed not only by their meaning, but also their relation to a particular noun
26	**Adjectives** and their place relative to a noun they qualify

17 Parts of speech: grammatical definition and grammatical function

17.1 **The eight parts of speech**
17.2 **Grammatical definition and grammatical function**
17.3 **Words that can have more than one grammatical function**

17.1 The eight parts of speech

The four major parts of speech are nouns, verbs, adjectives and adverbs (**see 3.2**).

The four minor parts of speech are: determiners, pronouns, prepositions and conjunctions.

The differences between the four major and the four minor parts of speech can be summarised as follows:

Major parts of speech:	**Minor parts of speech:**
- are content words	- are function words
- express specific ideas	- specify kinds of information (such as tense of verbs, gender of nouns)
- represent the world	- show how ideas are related
- link together to construct sentences	- are tools enabling the four major parts of speech to link together

The following table shows how the four minor parts of speech relate to the four major parts of speech:

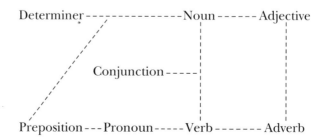

Pronouns function like nouns, which they replace or represent: *il/elle* represent a singular noun, *ils/elles* represent a plural noun which is the subject of a verb:

Pierre travaille > *il travaille*	**(see 9.1)**

le/la/les represent a noun as direct object of a verb:

je vois la colline > *je la vois*	**(see 18.3)**

lui/leur represent a noun as indirect object of a verb:

je parle aux enfants > *je leur parle*	**(see 18.3)**

celui-là etc. represent a noun which is being pointed out:

quelle chemise? > *celle-là*	**(see 21.3)**

qui/que etc. represent a noun in a relative construction:

cet homme parle peu > *c'est un homme qui parle peu*	**(see 42.1)**

Determiners specify a particular function of a noun.

Definite/indefinite/partitive article + noun	*un homme mystérieux*	**(see 22)**
Demonstrative adjective + noun	*cet homme est dangereux*	**(see 21.1)**
Possessive adjective + noun	*on connaît sa carrière*	**(see 20.1)**

Prepositions introduce phrases centred on nouns or pronouns:

Preposition + pronoun	*devant moi*	
Preposition + determiner + noun	*derrière cet arbre*	**(see 27–30)**

Conjunctions introduce clauses centred on verbs:

Conjunction + noun + verb	*quand Marie arrivera*	
Conjunction + pronoun + verb	*s'il fait beau*	**(see 45–49)**

Examples of combinations:

conj	pron	pron	**verb**	det	**noun**	**verb**	**adverb**	prepos	det	**noun**
dès	*qu'il*	*nous*	*a vus,*	*l'*	*animal*	*a passé*	*rapidement*	*derrière*	*l'*	*arbre*

det	**adj**	**noun**	**verb**	**adverb**	prepos	det	**adj**	**noun**
votre	*nouvelle*	*maison*	*ressemble*	*beaucoup*	*à*	*un*	*petit*	*palais*

*

Exercise 17/1 **Parts of speech in English** Individual or pair work

Read this extract from the beginning of T Zeldin's *A History of French Passions* (vol 1, 1973, p11), then answer the questions below it:

The bourgeois <u>is</u> a central <u>figure</u> in every <u>modern</u> history. In France more than <u>anywhere</u> else, <u>because</u> aristocracy and monarchy were defeated in <u>the</u> great Revolution, the bourgeois <u>appeared</u> <u>manifestly</u> supreme <u>for</u> a century and a half after <u>it</u>, to the extent that the two words have been combined into a single idea: *la France bourgeoise*. It is argued that it was in this period that the bourgeois attained self-confidence, ceased to aspire to enter the old hierarchy, and sought rather to replace it. He developed his own moral and economic doctrine and formed an original class with a spiritual unity. At the same time he became an object of attack, satire and animosity, far more concerted than ever before.

a   At the beginning of the above text, ten words are underlined: say what part of speech each one belongs to.

b   Check your answers in the Key to the Exercises (57), then read through the rest of the extract and write down sixteen words: two examples of each of the eight parts of speech.

Exercice 17/2 **Les parties du discours en français** Travail individuel ou à deux

Lisez ces deux sketches de R Devos, puis répondez aux questions ci-dessous:

Les parcmètres

Les <u>parcmètres</u>, c'est <u>une</u> tricherie!
Vous savez <u>que</u> ça <u>rapporte</u> une fortune aux <u>pouvoirs</u> publics?
Une fortune!
Je <u>le</u> sais <u>parce que</u> mon voisin
s'est fait installer un
<u>petit</u> parcmètre clandestin devant chez lui ...
Tous les soirs, il va <u>retirer</u> la recette ...
Il vit <u>bien</u>!
Il s'est même acheté une voiture!
Évidemment, il l'a mise devant
son parcmètre.
Depuis, il ne fait plus un rond.
Mais ça, c'est de sa faute!   (*Sens dessus dessous*, 1976, p97)

Ceinture de sécurité

Mesdames et messieurs, je ne voudrais pas
vous affoler, mais des fous, il y en a!
Dand la rue, on en côtoie ...
Récemment, je rencontre un monsieur.
Il portait sa voiture en bandoulière!
Il me dit:
"Vous ne savez pas comment
on détache cette ceinture?"
Je lui dis:
"Dites-moi! Lorsque vous l'avez bouclée,
est-ce que vous avez entendu un petit déclic?"
Il me dit:
"Oui, dans ma tête!"
Je me dis: "Ce type, il est fou à lier!"
J'ai eu envie de le ceinturer ...
mais quand j'ai vu que sa ceinture
était noire ...
je l'ai bouclée!!!   (*A plus d'un titre*, 1989, p27)

a   Au début du premier sketch, dix mots ont été soulignés: décidez à **quelle partie du discours**
     appartient chacun de ces dix mots.
b   **Vérifiez** vos réponses, puis relisez les deux sketches. Notez seize mots: **deux** exemples pour
     chacune des huit parties du discours.

17.2 Grammatical definition and grammatical function

So far, we have described the parts of speech (nouns, verbs, etc.) as if one word 'is' a
noun, another word 'is' a verb, and so on. For some purposes, this way of describing words
and parts of speech is adequate, but quite often it is not: in order to understand how
French (or any other language) works, we need to distinguish between the grammatical
definition of the word itself, and its grammatical function.

Here are two illustrations of this distinction:

Un homme-grenouille
The term *(un) homme-grenouille* ('a frogman') is made up of two words, both of which are
defined as nouns:
    homme (grammatical definition: noun); *grenouille* (grammatical definition: noun)

But the second word, the noun *grenouille*, functions as an adjective, describing *homme*, which functions as a noun:

> *homme* (grammatical function: noun); *grenouille* (grammatical function: adjective)

The result is a new compound word:

> **un homme-grenouille** (grammatical function: noun) (for compound nouns, **see 15.1**)

Le prêt-à-porter

The term *(le) prêt-à-porter* ('(the) ready-to-wear clothing (industry)') is made up of three words:

> *prêt* (grammatical definition: adjective); *à* (grammatical definition: preposition);
> *porter* (grammatical definition: verb, in the infinitive form)

The two words *à porter* function together as an adverb qualifying the adjective *prêt*.

The result is a new word, which can function either as a noun or as an adjective:

> *l'industrie* **du prêt-à-porter** *se porte bien* (grammatical function: noun)
> the ready-to-wear industry is in good shape
> *elle a acheté un nouveau tailleur* **prêt-à-porter** (grammatical function: adjective)
> she bought a new off-the-peg suit

Many words which are regularly used with a different grammatical function are regarded as having more than one grammatical definition; these are shown separately in dictionaries.

In the case of the verb **passer**, for example, the past participle (*passé*), as well as being used as an adjective (*le temps passé*: past time, time past), is used as a noun (*le passé*), to the extent that one thinks of *le passé* as a noun in its own right, by definition as well as by function.

Another example is the adverb **bien** which, as well as being used as an adjective (**see 17.3f**), is used as a noun:

> *je l'ai fait pour* **ton bien**   I did it for your own good
> *il attache trop d'importance* **aux biens** *de ce monde*
> he attaches too much importance to worldly goods

The following table gives examples of words which can have a different grammatical function from their usual grammatical definition.

■ Grammatical definition and grammatical function

	Function of underlined word:			
Definition of underlined word:	**Noun**	**Adjective**	**Adverb**	**Preposition**
Verb (infinitive,	*prendre le pouvoir*; to take power			
present participle,	*avoir du répondant* to have money	*une histoire passionnante*, an exciting story	*jouer gagnant*; to hold all the trumps	*moyennant finances*; in exchange for money
past participle)	*les frustrés* frustrated people	*un homme passionné* a passionate man	*jouer serré* to play a tight game	*vu son passé* in view of his/her past
Noun	–	*un homme grenouille* a frogman	*s'habiller rive gauche* to dress in Left Bank style	*côté travail* work-wise
Adjective	*c'est du propre!* what a mess!	–	*travailler dur* to work hard	*sauf lui* except for him
Adverb	*avoir le dessus* to have the upper hand	*il est bien, ce film* this film's good	–	*à part lui* apart from him
Preposition	*les avants* the forwards	*c'est un jour sans* there's none today	*comme avant* as before	–
Pronoun	*un rien* a mere trifle			
Conjunction	*avec des si* with ifs and buts			

Travail à deux > Mise en commun

Chacun des mots ci-dessous peut remplir plus d'une fonction grammaticale.

a   Pour chaque mot, décidez quelles sont ces fonctions.

b   Composez, pour chaque fonction de chaque mot, une phrase où le mot est employé avec cette fonction.

c   Lisez au reste du groupe les phrases que vous avez composées.

Exemple: rapide

Réponse: (a)   adjectif; nom

Réponses possibles: (b)   Elle avait juste le temps de manger un repas **rapide**.

Arrivé à la gare, il a sauté dans **le rapide** qui allait partir.

1	pouvoir	5	passé	9	avant
2	savoir	6	permis	10	chocolat
3	vouloir	7	mobile	11	pas
4	assises	8	devant		

17.3 Words that can have more than one grammatical function

Here, with examples, are the main cases where the grammatical function of a word is different from its grammatical definition:

a   Verb used as noun

Strictly speaking, a verb only functions as a verb when it is used to express tenses: *je travaille* (present tense), *je travaillais* (imperfect tense), *j'avais travaillé* (pluperfect tense), etc. (**see 9–10**).

Three forms of a verb which do not express tenses, *travailler* (infinitive), *travaillant* (present participle), *travaillé* (past participle), can, in the case of many verbs, function as a noun:

infinitive

le devoir	duty	*le pouvoir*	power
le savoir	knowledge	*le souvenir*	memory
le rire	laughter	*le boire et le manger*	eating and drinking
present participle		*un passant*	a passer-by
past participle		*le vécu*	real life

b   Verb used as adjective

The present and past participles of many verbs are used as adjectives, in which case they agree with the noun they qualify:

*une rue **passante***	a busy street
*une sauce **piquante***	a spicy sauce
*une sauce **relevée***	a highly-seasoned sauce
*un projet **réussi***	a successful plan
*une histoire **vécue***	a real-life story

c   Noun used as adjective

IN ENGLISH, when a noun functions as an adjective, it is placed before the noun it qualifies:

my car keys	a log jam	a fun thing (N2)

IN FRENCH it is placed after the noun it qualifies (**see 26**):

*l'autoroute **A75***	the A75 motorway
*il a un culot **monstre!***	he's got some cheek! (N2)

When a noun functions as an adjective, it is invariable:

une sauce chasseur	mushroom sauce
des gants bon marché	inexpensive gloves

The group *bon marché* can also function as the equivalent of an adverb:

*j'ai acheté ces gants **bon marché***	I bought these gloves cheaply

The construction noun + noun, where the second noun functions as an adjective, can be distinguished from the construction noun + *de* + noun, where the group *de* + noun, not the noun on its own, functions as an adjective (**see 41.2**).

d   Adjective used as noun

Many adjectives can also function as nouns:

le vide	emptiness	*un vide*	a vacuum
un express	espresso (strong black coffee; from *un café express*)		
un rapide	an express (train; from *un train rapide*)		
un indépendant	an independent (candidate, etc.)		

Adjectives of colour can function as nouns:

***le bleu** te va très bien*	blue really suits you
*ajoutez **trois blancs** d'oeuf*	add three egg whites
*aujourd'hui, elle broie **du noir***	she's got the blues today

An adjective of colour can be described by another adjective or a noun, in which case the adjective group is invariable:

Adjective + adjective	*des chaussures **gris clair***	pale grey shoes
Adjective + noun	*un ensemble **bleu marine***	a navy blue outfit
	*une cravate **vert bouteille***	a bottle green tie

In the last two examples, *marine* and *bouteille* are nouns functioning as an adjective describing the colours *bleu* and *vert*.

e   Adjective used as adverb

This category includes a number of adjectives which are habitually used as an adverb with a particular verb or group of verbs, forming a compound verb **(see 15.2)**. In this construction the adjective, since it qualifies the verb, not a noun, is invariable:

bas	*parler bas*	to speak quietly
cher	*les fraises coûtent cher au mois d'avril*	strawberries are expensive in April
court	*elle s'est fait couper les cheveux très court*	she's had her hair cut very short
dur	*travailler dur*	to work hard
fort	*crier fort*	to shout loudly
haut	*parler haut*	to speak aloud
net	*s'arrêter net*	to stop dead

In other cases, the bond between an adjective used as an adverb and a particular verb is less close, but the two are often to be found together:

faux	*chanter faux*	to sing off-key
	sonner faux	to sound odd, suspicious
gros	*gagner gros*	to earn lots of money
utile	*voter utile*	to vote effectively (tactically)

If the verb and adjective do not form a group, the attributive adjective agrees **(see 12.1)**:

ils sont rentrés ivres   they came home drunk

Exercice 17/4   **Adjectifs employés comme adverbes**   Travail individuel ou à deux

Complétez les phrases ci-dessous en employant, comme adverbe, un des adjectifs suivants: *bas, cher, court, dur, faux, fort, gros, haut, net.* Dans certains cas, plus d'une réponse est possible:

Exemple: Le cheval s'arrêta – et ne voulut plus avancer.
Réponse: Le cheval s'arrêta **net** (ou: **court**) et ne voulut plus avancer.

1   On a travaillé très – sur ce projet.
2   C'est une erreur qui lui a coûté –.
3   J'ignore son salaire, mais je sais qu'elle gagne –.
4   Parlons plus –: on pourrait nous entendre.
5   Le juge a coupé – aux protestations de l'avocat de la défense.
6   Le branche a cassé –; heureusement, elle n'est pas tombée sur la maison.
7   Ses paroles paraissaient sincères, mais sa voix sonnait –.
8   Ne criez pas si –, les enfants: j'essaie de me détendre.
9   Il faut le dire – et –: cette solution est inacceptable.

f   Adverb used as adjective

Bien

The adverb *bien* is used as an adjective in a number of contexts. The table below shows how the meaning of *bien* is different from the meaning of *bon*, when used in similar constructions:

Bon	*Bien*
c'est bon	*c'est bien*
that's all right, that'll do; that tastes good!	well done! (that's) good (work)
c'est pas très bon (N2)	*c'est pas très bien* (N2)
that's not very good; that doesn't taste very good	that's not very nice (behaviour)
cet homme est (très) bon	*tu es (très) bien comme ça*
this man is (very) kind	you look fine (as you are)
	je suis (très) bien comme ça
	I'm comfortable (as I am)

g   Adverb used as preposition, preposition used as adverb (see also 27)

(adverb)	*mettre un document à part*	to put a paper to one side
(preposition)	*à part lui, il n'y a personne*	there's no-one apart from him
(preposition)	*voter pour le changement*	to vote for change
(adverb)	*voter pour*	to vote in favour, to vote yes

18 Object pronouns

18.1 **Subject and object**
18.2 **Object pronouns in English and French**
18.3 **Direct object and indirect object**
18.4 **The indirect object pronouns *y* and *en***
18.5 **Two object pronouns together**

18.1 Subject and object

The **subject** of a verb (**see 9.1**) is a noun or pronoun which is the agent of the action described by the verb:

elle chante   she sings   *il souffre*   he is in pain

The **object** of a verb is a noun or pronoun which is not the agent of the action described by the verb; on the contrary, it is on the receiving end of the action:

*je regarde **les singes***   I'm looking at the monkeys
*Pierre ouvre **la porte***   Pierre opens the door

This grammatical definition of subject and object holds good whatever the meaning of the verb. For example, in:

***Paul** a reçu **un coup** sur la tête*   Paul got hit on the head

Paul is the grammatical subject, and *un coup* the grammatical object of the verb *recevoir*.

The same unfortunate event could be described in other ways; for example:

***quelqu'un** a frappé **Paul** à la tête*   someone hit Paul on the head

Now the grammatical subject (of the verb *frapper*) is *quelqu'un*, and *Paul* is the (direct) object of the verb.

The above examples illustrate the importance of the order of words in both English and French: the assumption is that the word (or group) before the verb is the grammatical subject, and the word (or group) after the verb is the grammatical object (**see 32.1**).

In the above examples, the object of the verb is a noun: what happens when the object is a pronoun?

18.2 Object pronouns in English and French

IN ENGLISH, object pronouns are relatively straightforward in formation and use:

■ Object pronouns in English

Person	1	2	3			4	5	6
Object	me	you	him	her	it	us	you	them

If a pronoun is the indirect object of the verb (**see 18.3**), one simply adds 'to', 'from' or another preposition to the above pronouns: 'to you', 'from him', etc.; the pronoun itself stays the same.

The order of words is the same with object pronouns as with nouns:

  he reads **a lot of books**   and   he reads **them** quickly

IN FRENCH, unlike English, there are two sets of object pronouns, one for use with verbs constructed with a direct object, and another for use with verbs constructed with an indirect object (**see 18.3** for how to distinguish between a direct object and an indirect object).

■ Object pronouns in French

Person	1	2	3			4	5	6	
Direct object	*me*	*te*	*se**	*le*	*la*	*nous*	*vous*	*se**	*les*
Indirect object	*me*	*te*	*se**	*lui*	*lui*	*nous*	*vous*	*se**	*leur*
			(also *y* and *en*: see below)						

*The reflexive pronoun *se* is used with pronominal verbs and constructions (**see 36**).

These object pronouns cannot be used with prepositions: for preposition + pronoun, **see 19.2**.

Some object pronouns in French have the same form, whether they are the direct or the indirect object of a verb:

  me   *te*   *se*   *nous*   *vous*

But other object pronouns have two forms, depending on whether they are the direct or the indirect object of a verb:

Direct object   *le*   *la*   *les*

Indirect object *lui*   *lui*   *leur*   (also *y* and *en*: **see 18.4**)

WORD ORDER

IN FRENCH, the order of words is not the same with object pronouns as with nouns; object pronouns come between the subject and the verb:

  *il lit **beaucoup de livres***   but   *il **les** lit vite*
  he reads lots of books   he reads them quickly

One consequence of this word order is that, in spoken French, object pronouns cannot be emphasised (**see 7.2**): this is because the usual stress, or 'tonic accent', falls on the last syllable in a group. In *il les lit*, for example, the tonic accent falls on *lit*, and in *il les lit vite* it falls on *vite*, but in neither case does any stress fall on *les*.

To emphasise an object pronoun in French, one uses a different construction, perhaps involving a demonstrative pronoun (**see 21.3**) and dislocation (**see 51.1**):

    celui-là**, il l'a lu très vite*   or   *il l'a lu très vite, **celui-là
    he read that one very quickly

Some object pronouns in French, used before a verb beginning with a vowel, reduce to a single consonant, which becomes part of the first syllable of the verb (**see 7.3**):

    me > m'   *te > t'*   *se > s'*   *le/la > l'*

18.3 Direct object and indirect object

How to distinguish between a direct object and an indirect object

The correct use of certain object pronouns in French (*le/la/ les* or *lui/leur/y/en*) depends on being able to tell a direct object from an indirect object.

Direct object

When a verb is constructed without a preposition (**see 38.1**) between it and a noun which is the object of the verb, the noun is the **direct object** of the verb. Many French verbs and their English equivalents are constructed without a preposition:

		+ noun (no preposition)	+ direct object pronoun
aider	to help	*elle aide son frère*	*elle l'aide*
		she helps her brother	she helps him
comprendre	to understand	*je comprenais les manifestants*	*je **les** comprenais*
		I understood the demonstrators	I understood them

Indirect object

When a verb is constructed with a preposition (*à, de, par, pour* etc.: **see 38.1**) between it and a noun which is the object of the verb, the noun is the **indirect object** of the verb. Many French verbs and their English equivalents are constructed with an indirect object, but this is expressed differently in each language.

IN ENGLISH, the indirect object pronoun can be used with any preposition.

IN FRENCH, only a verb constructed with the preposition *à* can be used with the indirect object pronouns *lui, leur,* and *y* (**see 18.4**), except for the indirect object pronoun *en*, which is used with verbs constructed with *de* (**see 18.4**).

Examples (the object is a person):

+ preposition + noun	+ indirect object pronoun

Écrire à to write to

il a écrit à ses parents   *il **leur** a écrit*

he wrote **to** his parents   he wrote **to them**

Répondre à to reply to

la mairie n'a pas répondu à Pierre   *la mairie ne **lui** a pas répondu*

the Town Hall didn't reply **to** Pierre   the Town Hall didn't reply **to him**

Parler à to speak to someone about something

*je parlerai **de** cette affaire **à** mon patron*   *je **lui en** parlerai*

I'll speak **to** my boss **about** this matter   I'll speak **to him about it**

But the construction of some verbs is not the same in English and in French:

Écouter to listen to	+ noun	+ object pronoun
French: + direct object	*elle écoute son frère*	*elle **l'**écoute*
English: + indirect object	she listens **to** her brother	she listens **to** him

Regarder to look at

| French: + direct object | *j'ai regardé les manifestants* | *je **les** ai regardés* |
| English: + indirect object | I looked **at** the demonstrators | I looked **at** them |

Exercice 18/1   **Pronoms: objet direct ou indirect?**   Travail individuel

a   Dans les phrases ci-dessous, remplacez les mots soulignés par un pronom.

Exemple: Elle aide <u>son frère.</u>
Réponse: Elle l'aide.

Exemple: Il répond <u>à son frère.</u>
Réponse: Il lui répond.

1   Je connais <u>le directeur.</u>
2   Vous ne savez pas <u>la réponse.</u>
3   Il ne racontera pas tout cela <u>à ses parents.</u>
4   Elle téléphonait souvent <u>à son copain.</u>
5   Vous cherchiez <u>le gardien.</u>
6   Nous ne mangerons pas <u>les restes.</u>
7   J'apporterai <u>le pain.</u>
8   Je transmettrai votre demande <u>à la personne concernée.</u>
9   Elle ne conduisait pas <u>la voiture.</u>

10   Il accueillait <u>les visiteurs</u>.

11   Ils ne détruiront pas <u>l'environnement</u>.

12   Nous repeindrons <u>les murs</u>.

13   Vous n'écrivez pas <u>aux autorités</u>.

14   Je choisirai <u>la couleur</u>.

15   Je parlerai <u>au responsable</u>.

b   Contrôle   Travail à deux

Quelque temps après avoir fait cet exercice, regardez les **réponses** (voir **Key**, p000–000) et essayez de reconstituer la phrase (avec nom).

18.4 The object pronouns *y* and *en*

The object pronoun y

Perhaps because of *il y a* ('there is', 'there are'), it is tempting to think of the neuter object pronoun *y* as meaning 'there'. This holds good in some cases:

> *Elle va à Paris. Quand est-ce qu'elle y va?*
> She's going **to** Paris. When's she going (**there**)?

But it is more useful, and a more reliable guide, to define *y* in terms of its grammatical function:

> *Y* is used as a neuter object pronoun replacing or representing *à* + **noun**.

Once you have made the mental association between '*à* + **noun** (thing or idea)' and '**y**', you can be more confident when using verbs constructed with *à*:

Examples (the object is a thing or idea):

+ *à* + **noun**	+ indirect object pronoun (*y*)
Répondre à to reply to	
la mairie n'a pas répondu à sa lettre	*la mairie n'y a pas répondu*
the Town Hall didn't answer/reply **to** his letter	the Town Hall didn't answer/reply **to it**
Croire à to believe in	
je n'ai jamais cru à cette histoire	*je n'y ai jamais cru*
I never believed (**in**) this/that/the story	I never believed **in it**
Tenir à to care about	
elle tient beaucoup à son indépendance	*elle y tient beaucoup*
she cares a lot **about** her independence	she cares a lot **about it**

Penser à to think about, to have in mind (thing, place)

*elle pensait souvent **au** pays où elle était née*   *elle **y** pensait souvent*

she often thought **about** the country where   she often thought **about it**
she was born

Verbs constructed with *à lui/à elle* (for persons), but with *y* (for things, ideas)

In the case of several verbs constructed with *à*, an indirect object pronoun (such as *lui*, *leur*) is not used when referring to a person; instead, *à* + tonic pronoun is used; but *y* is used when referring to a thing, an idea etc.:

Example:

S'intéresser à   to be interested in

person

*cette femme? il ne s'intéresse pas **à elle***   this/that/the woman? he's not interested **in her**

thing, idea

*l'histoire? je m'**y** intéresse beaucoup*   history? I'm very interested **in it**

Also:

faire attention à	to pay attention to
renoncer à	to give up
s'habituer à	to get used to

and

penser à (+ person)	to think about, to have in mind
*(je pense **à elle***	I'm thinking **about her**)

(preposition + tonic pronoun: **see 19.2**)

The object pronoun *en*

If you think of the neuter object pronoun *en* as meaning 'of it', 'of them', you can be more confident when forming sentences such as:

*Tu as acheté son livre? Oui, mais je n'**en** ai pas lu beaucoup*

Have you bought his/her book? Yes, but I haven't read much **of it**

*Tu as mangé des fraises? Oui, j'**en** ai mangé beaucoup*

Have you eaten any strawberries? Yes, I've eaten a lot (**of them**)

However, it is also useful, as with *y*, to define *en* in terms of its grammatical function:

> ***En*** is used as a neuter object pronoun replacing or representing *de* + **noun**.

This association is apparent in sentences such as the following, all involving verbs constructed with *de*:

+ *de* + **noun**	+ **indirect object pronoun** (*en*)
Dépendre de to depend on	
*votre avenir dépend **de** votre esprit d'initiative*	*votre avenir **en** dépend*
your future depends **on** your sense of initiative	your future depends **on it**
Douter de to doubt	
*je doute **de** sa capacité à réussir*	*j'**en** doute*
I doubt his/her ability to succeed	I doubt **it**
Se douter de to suspect, think as much	
*je me doutais déjà **de** sa réaction*	*je m'**en** doutais déjà*
I already had an idea he'd/she'd react in that way	I suspected it already/I already thought as much

The above explanations and examples can be summarised as follows:

■ Object pronouns (direct and indirect object) in French

Verb construction	Object pronoun (person)			(thing, idea)		
+ direct object (**no** preposition) (such as *aider*)	*le*	*la*	*les*	*le**	*la*	*les*
+ indirect object (preposition is *à*) (such as *répondre à*)	*lui*	*lui*	*leur*	*y*	*y*	*y*
+ indirect object (preposition is *de*) (such as *parler de*)	–	–	–	*en*	*en*	*en*
+ indirect object (**other** preposition) (such as *discuter avec*)	–	–	–	–	–	–

*For the use of *le* as a neuter direct object pronoun, **see 52.5**.

Exercice 18/2   **Emploi de *y* et de *en***   Travail individuel

a   Remplacez les mots soulignés dans les phrases ci-dessous par *y* ou *en*, selon la construction du verbe.

Exemple: Tu crois <u>à son histoire</u>?   **Exemple:**   Je doute <u>de sa sincérité</u>.
Réponse: Tu **y** crois?   *Réponse:*   J'**en** doute.

1   Le train s'approchait <u>de la gare</u>.
2   On s'adressera <u>à la mairie</u>.
3   Je pense souvent <u>à ce problème</u>.
4   Elle résistera <u>à toutes les pressions</u>.
5   Il ne renonce pas <u>à son projet</u>.
6   Je ne m'occuperai pas <u>de cette affaire</u>.
7   Ils dépendaient entièrement <u>de l'État</u>.
8   Je me doutais <u>de sa réponse</u>.
9   Il participait souvent <u>à leurs discussions</u>.
10   C'est la première fois que j'entends parler <u>de cette histoire</u>.

b   **Contrôle**   Travail à deux

Quelque temps après avoir fait cet exercice, essayez, avec un(e) partenaire, de retrouver, à partir des **réponses** avec les pronoms *y* et *en* (voir **Key**, 57), de recomposer les phrases avec *à* ou *de* + nom.

18.5 Two object pronouns together

Several verbs in English and French can be constructed with two or more objects:

dire quelque chose de quelqu'un	to say something about someone
dire quelque chose à quelqu'un	to tell someone something
donner quelque chose à quelqu'un	to give someone something
prendre quelque chose à quelqu'un	to take something from someone

IN ENGLISH, as the second and third examples above show, a verb can appear to have two direct objects, but the distinction between direct and indirect object reappears if the sentence is rearranged:

tell him that story	but	tell that story **to** him
give me the book	but	give the book **to** me

IN FRENCH, a verb can have only one direct object: if you find yourself writing a sentence with two objects to a verb, neither of which has a preposition or is an indirect object pronoun, something is wrong!

A verb describing a person or thing being changed from one state to another can appear to have two direct objects:

*ils l'ont fait **roi***	they made him king
*ils l'ont élu **député***	they elected him as an MP

In fact, both the pronoun and the noun refer to the same person.

Two object pronouns: word order
When there are two object pronouns, the word order is as follows:

■ Order of object pronouns

Direct object/ ind obj + à	Direct object	Indirect obj + à (usually persons)	Ind obj + à Ind obj + de (usually things, ideas, etc.)	
me *te* *se* *nous* *vous*	*le* *la* *les*	*lui* *leur*	*y*	*en*

Restrictions

a Two object pronouns from the same column are not used together

b Pronouns from column 1 and column 3 are not used together

Présenter to introduce someone to someone else

With *présenter*, which is constructed with two objects, certain combinations of object pronoun are not used; one of the pronouns takes the form of a tonic pronoun (**see 19**):

*tu vas **me le** présenter?*	but	*je vais **te** présenter **à lui***
are you going to introduce him to me?		I'll introduce you to him

Object pronouns: word order with compound tenses and the infinitive
Compound tenses (passé composé, pluperfect, etc. **see 10.3**)
The position of any object pronoun(s) is immediately before the auxiliary verb (*avoir*):

*Tu as vu l'avion? Oui, je **l'**ai vu*	Did you see the plane? Yes, I saw it
*ils **nous** ont parlé de leur voyage*	they told us about their trip
*je **les lui** ai donné(e)s tout de suite*	I gave him/her them straight away

In negative sentences (**see 34.3**), the position of the object pronoun(s) is also immediately before the auxiliary verb:

*je ne **les lui ai** pas donné(e)s*   I didn't give them to him

*personne ne **m'en avait** parlé* nobody had told me about it

(For agreement of the past participle, **see 44.4**.)

Exercice 18/3 **Temps composés: ordre des mots** Travail individuel ou à deux

Écrivez **deux** réponses aux questions suivantes:

a une commençant par *Oui,* ...

b l'autre commençant par *Non,* ...

Dans chaque réponse, remplacez les mots soulignés dans la question par un pronom (object direct ou indirect, selon la construction du verbe); employez le même temps du verbe que dans la question.

Exemple: Tu as vu <u>les éléphants</u>?

Réponse a: Oui, je les ai vus.

Réponse b: Non, je ne les ai pas vus.

1 Est-ce que Marie a aidé <u>ses parents</u>?
2 En aviez-vous parlé <u>au directeur</u>?
3 Est-ce que Paul a rendu visite <u>à son oncle</u>?
4 Est-ce qu'ils avaient prévenu <u>les autres</u>?
5 Tu as demandé la réponse <u>à tes camarades</u>?
6 Est-ce que vous avez fini <u>cet exercice</u>?

Auxiliary verbs (such as *devoir, pouvoir, aller.* **see 39.1** and **39.2**) **used with an infinitive**
Here, the position of the object pronoun(s) is different: it is immediately before the infinitive:

*tu devrais **y aller** tout de suite* you ought to/should go (there) straight away

*je vais **leur en parler** demain* I'll talk to them about it tomorrow

In negative sentences, the position of the object pronoun(s) is also immediately before the infinitive:

*je ne peux pas **en parler** maintenant* I can't talk about it now

Exercice 18/4 **Auxiliaire + infinitif: ordre des mots** Travail individuel ou à deux

Récrivez les phrases ci-dessous en ajoutant, au temps du verbe original, le verbe auxiliaire indiqué entre parenthèses; le verbe original doit être récrit à l'infinitif. Attention à l'ordre des mots!

Exemple: Je l'aide. (aller)
Réponse: Je vais l'aider.

1	Je ne l'écoute pas.	(vouloir)
2	On les surveille.	(devoir)
3	Je vous dis un secret.	(aller)
4	Ils nous écrivaient souvent.	(pouvoir)
5	Personne ne lui parle.	(devoir)
6	On les voyait tous les jours.	(pouvoir)
7	Je leur disais au revoir.	(aller)
8	Il m'a oublié.	(devoir)
9	Ils nous avaient donné un cadeau.	(vouloir)
10	Je ne leur ai pas parlé.	(pouvoir)

19 Tonic pronouns

19.1 **Form and use of tonic pronouns**
19.2 **Use of tonic pronouns after prepositions**
19.3 **Use of tonic pronouns with subject pronouns**
19.4 **Use of tonic pronouns with the imperative**

19.1 Form and use of tonic pronouns

IN ENGLISH, there are no tonic pronouns: the usual subject and object forms of pronouns are used, at least in formal situations (N3):

■ Subject and object pronouns in English

	Person							
	1	2	3			4	5	6
Used as:								
Subject	I	you	he	she	it	we	you	they
Object	me	you	him	her	it	us	you	them

IN FRENCH, there is a set of tonic pronouns (some of which are the same as the corresponding subject or object pronouns) which can be used as or with the subject or object of the verb, after prepositions, and in isolation:

■ Tonic pronouns in French

Person	1	2	3			4	5	6
			(person)	(thing, idea)		(impersonal)		
Tonic pronoun								
	moi	*toi*	*lui/elle*	*ça*	*soi*	*nous*	*vous*	*eux/elles*
Corresponding **subject pronoun**								
	je	*tu*	*il/elle*	*ça*	*on*	*nous*	*vous*	*ils/elles*
				ce (in *c'est*)				

155

Tonic pronouns are sometimes called 'emphatic pronouns', but this label is inaccurate, since they can be used (after prepositions, for example) without emphasis.

Tonic pronouns are used:
- at the end of a group of words (**see 7.2**), where they receive the usual tonic accent, but no particular emphasis:

à côté de lui	next to him	*avec eux*	with them	(**see 19.2**)

- in a detached position (**see 51.1a**) at the end of a group:

je la connais, ***moi***   **I** know her

- at the beginning of a group, where they can receive stress for emphasis:

toi *aussi, tu la connais*   **you** know her as well

Object pronouns (such as ***la*** in the last two examples above) always occur in the middle of a breath group; they do not receive either tonic or emphatic stress. In order to emphasise a pronoun (subject or object) in French, one uses a tonic pronoun, as well or instead.

Tonic pronouns can also be used, with or without emphasis, after prepositions, although *à* + tonic pronoun (person or thing) and *de* + tonic pronoun (thing) are used only for emphasis. When there is no emphasis, indirect object pronouns are used.

19.2 Use of tonic pronouns after prepositions

The most obvious use of tonic pronouns is after prepositions: you should make the association preposition + tonic pronoun automatic in your mind. You will need to practise, above all, the tonic pronouns *lui, eux* and *soi*, and also, for conversation etc., *ça*:

celui-là c'est Dupont, et celui ***à côté de lui****, c'est Durand*

that's Dupont, and the one next to him is Durand

sans eux*, l'opération de sauvetage aurait échoué*

had it not been for them, the rescue operation would have failed

quelle confusion! c'est vraiment chacun ***pour soi***

what chaos! it's a case of everyone for himself

Un kilo de pommes? Oui, madame. Et ***avec ça****?*

A kilo of apples? Right. Will that be all?

Mon idée à moi*:* '<u>my</u> idea', etc.; ***il/elle est à moi*** etc: **see 20.2**

19.3 Use of tonic pronouns with subject pronouns

A tonic pronoun can be added at the beginning of a group, with, or in certain cases instead of (see Persons 3 and 6, below), a subject pronoun:

Persons 1 and 4

(*moi, nous*)

In the case of *moi je* and *nous on*, there is little emphasis: the two words are spoken without a pause (and written without a comma), as if they formed a single subject pronoun:

moi je trouve qu'il exagère	I think he's going too far	(N2)
nous on va au cinéma	we're going to the cinema	(N2)
nous on est là pour regarder	we just came to look	(N2)

Persons 2 and 5

(*toi, vous*)

Toi, tu and *vous, vous* can be used instead of the imperative (**see 50.3**) form of the verb:

Imperative form		Use with tonic pronoun	
reste là!	stay here!	*toi, tu restes là!*	you stay where you are!
allez devant!	go in front!	*vous, vous allez devant*	(you can) go in front!

Persons 3 and 6

(*lui, elle, eux, elles*; *ça* and *ce* in *c'est*)

These forms are used with a subject pronoun to give emphasis, marked in speech by a pause, and in writing by a comma:

lui, il y va souvent	he often goes there
eux, ils n'ont rien dit	they said nothing

There is also emphasis when the tonic pronoun (including *moi, toi, nous* and *vous*) is placed at the end of a sentence:

il y va souvent, lui	he often goes there, he does
ils n'ont rien dit, eux	they said nothing
je n'en sais rien, moi!	I've no idea!

Note: because of the repetition involved, *elle, elle* and *elles, elles* are used less often.

Lui, elle, eux and *elles* can also be used for emphasis without the subject pronoun:

lui sait la réponse	he knows the answer
elles n'ont rien vu	they saw nothing

Ça

The neuter pronoun **ça** can be used in most of the above ways:

ça, c'est une bonne idée!	that's a good idea!

or *c'est une bonne idée, ça!*

ça, ça me dépasse!	that's beyond me!

or *ça me dépasse, ça*

Soi

Soi is the tonic form of the impersonal subject pronoun *on*, when *on* means 'one':

> *chaque campeur doit apporter son matériel **avec soi***
>
> all campers must bring their equipment with them

The above sentence is a general instruction, and this is reflected in the use of *soi*; *lui* is also possible in such contexts: this would make the instruction sound more specifically directed at each individual camper.

Use with -*même*

The adjective -*même* can be added to a tonic pronoun, in the same way as '-self' can be added to pronouns and possessive adjectives in English:

> *si tu ne trouves personne pour t'aider, il faudra faire le travail **toi-même***
>
> if you can't find anyone to help, you'll have to do the work yourself
>
> ***moi-même**, j'en ai fait l'expérience*
>
> I myself have been through the same experience

Use with *aussi* and *seul*

A tonic pronoun can be followed by *aussi* or *seul*:

> ***eux aussi** sont concernés*
>
> or ***eux aussi**, ils sont concernés*
>
> or *ils sont concernés, **eux aussi***   they're involved as well
>
> ***elle seule** a donné la bonne réponse*   she was the only one to give the correct answer

---

Exercice 19/1   **Pronoms toniques**   Travail individuel

Dans chacune des phrases ci-dessous, ajoutez le pronom tonique qui convient (parfois, plus d'une réponse est possible).

Exemple: Je n'en sais rien, –!
Réponse: Je n'en sais rien, **moi**!

Exemple: – seul sait la réponse.
Réponse: **Lui** seul sait la réponse.

1   – , tu viens avec moi!
2   – , ils sont tranquilles.
3   – je trouve qu'il a raison.
4   Il a toujours sa photo avec –.
5   On n'a rien vu, –.

6   Tu y vas, –?
7   – sait la réponse, mais pas –.
8   Si tu n'y vas pas, j'irai – même.
9   – aussi ont le droit de parler.
10 Aucune solidarité: c'était chacun pour –.

19.4 Use of tonic pronouns with the imperative

Object pronouns used with the imperative form of verbs **(see 50.3)** take the form of tonic pronouns in some cases, but not in others:

Persons 1 2 4 5: use tonic pronouns

(direct or indirect object: *-moi, -toi, -nous, -vous*):

*apprenez-**moi**!*	teach me!	*écoutez-**nous**!*	listen to us!

Persons 3 and 6: use object pronouns

(direct object: *-le, -la, -les*; indirect object: *-lui, -leur, -y, -en*):

*regardez-**les**!*	look at them!	*demande-**lui**!*	ask him!
*parlons-**en**!*	let's talk about it!		

Order of pronouns with two object pronouns: Person 3/6 before Person 1/2/4/5:

*donne-**le-moi**!*	give me it!/give it to me!

Negative imperative

All object pronouns are placed before the verb; tonic pronouns are not used:

*ne **les** regardez pas!*	don't look at them!
*ne **m'en** parlez pas!*	don't talk to me about it!

This includes the reflexive pronoun in pronominal verbs:

*ne **nous** énervons pas!*	let's not get worked up!

Imperative of pronominal verbs (for pronominal verbs, see 36)

The imperative is formed with *-toi, -nous* and *-vous*:

*réveille-**toi**!*	*réveillez-**vous**!*	wake up!
*reposons-**nous**!*		let's have a rest!

Certain pronominal verbs are also used as simple verbs with a direct object:

*réveille-**moi**!*	wake me up!
*réveillons-**le**!*	let's wake him up!

These two forms (simple and pronominal) are easily confused, especially when forming imperatives and questions:

Aller:

Imperative without object pronoun

allez à la ferme!	go to the farm!

Imperative with object pronoun

*allez-**y**!*	go to it!

Question with subject pronoun

où ***allez-vous?*** where are you going?

S'en aller:

Imperative of pronominal verb, with reflexive pronoun and object pronoun

allez-vous-en! go away!

Exercice 19/2   **Pronoms employés avec l'impératif**   Travail individuel

a   Récrivez au **négatif** les phrases ci-dessous:

Exemple: Donnez-moi ce livre!

Réponse: Ne me donnez pas ce livre!

1   Regardez-le!
2   Réveille-toi!
3   Surprenez-moi!
4   Demande-leur!
5   Aidons-la!
6   Écoutez-nous!

b   Récrivez au **positif** les phrases ci-dessous:

Exemple: Ne te pose pas cette question!

Réponse: Pose-toi cette question!

1   Ne l'abandonnons pas!
2   Ne t'imagine pas!
3   Ne lui parle pas!
4   Ne vous asseyez pas!
5   Ne me raconte pas cette histoire!
6   Ne les écoutez pas!

---

20 Possessive adjectives and pronouns

20.1 Possessive adjectives
20.2 Emphasising possessive adjectives
20.3 Use of possessive adjective, or definite article, with parts of the body
20.4 Possessive pronouns

20.1 Possessive adjectives

Possessive adjectives are used before a noun to indicate who or what the noun belongs to, or is associated with:

ENGLISH	my book	her face	his leg	their house
FRENCH	*mon livre*	*son visage*	*sa jambe*	*leur maison*

Possessive adjectives are constructed according to much the same general principles in both English and French, apart from two important differences:

The 'owner' and the 'owned'

IN ENGLISH, the possessive adjective indicates only the owner, and says nothing about the noun that is owned: for example, 'my' is invariable, whether one is saying 'my book', 'my school', my shirt' or 'my exams'.

IN FRENCH, the possessive adjective indicates the owner, and says something about the noun that is owned: for example, to make the correct choice between *mon, ma* and *mes,* you need to consider whether the noun that is owned is masculine or feminine, whether it is singular or plural, and even whether the noun begins with a vowel.

Person 3

IN ENGLISH, there are more forms of the possessive adjective for Person 3 ('his, her, one's, their, its') than for all the other five persons put together ('my, your, our, their'). This means that a learner of English has to become particularly sensitive to the choice of possessive adjective for Person 3, including the problem of saying 'his/her', 'his or her' (the neutral alternative 'their' is acceptable to most people).

IN FRENCH, *son, sa, ses* are used for any Person 3 owner. As a learner of French, you can forget about who or what, or what gender, a Person 3 owner is – but you have to remember whether the noun owned is masculine or feminine, singular or plural, or whether it begins with a vowel.

■ Possessive adjectives in French and English

	Noun owned: Singular			Plural
Owner:	masculine	feminine (+ vowel)	feminine (+ consonant)	masculine or feminine
Person				
1	*mon livre* my book	*mon école* my school	*ma chemise* my shirt	*mes examens* my exams
2	*ton style* your style	*ton idée* your idea	*ta maison* your house	*tes disques* your records
3	*son pouvoir* his/her/one's/ its power	*son énergie* his/her/one's/ its energy	*sa force* his/her/one's/ its strength	*ses possibilités* his/her/one's its possibilities
	Singular (masculine or feminine)			**Plural**
4		*notre invention* our invention		*nos droits* our rights
5		*votre service* your service		*vos responsabilités* your responsibilities
6		*leur surprise* their surprise		*leurs chiffres* their figures

---

Exercice 20/1   **Adjectifs possessifs**   Travail individuel

a   Récrivez au singulier les phrases ci-dessous.

Exemple: Ils perdent leur temps.
Réponse: Il perd son temps.

1   Ils ont augmenté leur offre.
2   Nous cherchons notre inspiration.
3   Elles connaissent leur public.
4   Vous vous intéressez à votre travail.
5   Ils s'ennuient à leur école.

b   Récrivez au pluriel les phrases ci-dessous.

Exemple: Elle s'occupe de ses enfants.
Réponse: Elles s'occupent de leurs enfants.

1   Il augmente ses revenus.
2   Je suis mes propres idées.
3   Elle réforme ses organisations.
4   Tu cultives tes légumes.
5   Il soigne ses malades.

When to use *mon, ton, son* and when to use *ma, ta, sa*

Mon, ton, son are used with all singular masculine nouns, and also with singular feminine nouns that begin with a vowel; *ma, ta, sa* are used only with singular feminine nouns beginning with a consonant.

This means that if you associate *mon, ton, son* with masculine nouns, and *ma, ta, sa* with feminine nouns, you will be confused when faced with possessive adjective + feminine nouns such as: *indépendance, idée, importance, école.*

Exercice 20/2   *Mon, ton, son* ou *ma, ta, sa*?   Travail à deux

Avec un(e) partenaire, lisez tour à tour à haute voix un des groupes de mots (article + nom) ci-dessous. Votre partenaire doit dire aussitôt le même nom, mais précédé de *mon/ton/son* ou de *ma/ta/sa*, selon que le nom est masculin ou féminin, et qu'il commence avec une voyelle ou une consonne.

Exemple: une idée
Réponses possibles: mon idée   ton idée   son idée

1 une photo	4 une enquête	7 une couleur	10 une image
2 un choix	5 une surprise	8 une invention	
3 un exercice	6 une histoire	9 un système	

When to use *son, sa, ses*, and when to use *leur, leurs*

You will not get this one right just by asking yourself 'is it singular or plural?', since in French the correct choice of one of these words depends on the answers to two questions:

● Is the owner singular (in which case use *son/sa/ses*)? or plural (in which case use *leur/leurs*)?

● Is the noun owned singular (in which case use *son/sa/leur*)? or plural (in which case use *ses/leurs*)?

The following exercise gives practice in asking yourself both questions – and in getting both answers right! This is the kind of exercise that you should come back to some weeks or months later, to see whether you can complete the sentences correctly and more quickly.

Exercice 20/3   *Son, sa, ses; leur, leurs*   Travail individuel

a   Complétez les phrases suivantes, en ajoutant *son*, *sa*, *ses* ou *leur*, *leurs*, selon le cas.
b   Après avoir vérifié et corrigé vos réponses, lisez chaque phrase à haute voix.

1   Les premiers jours, ma sœur n'a pas du tout aimé _ école.
2   Les spectateurs ont montré _ enthousiasme pour le nouveau joueur.
3   Quand on conduit en ville, il faut maîtriser _ impatience.
4   Sylvie est allée chercher _ parents à la gare.
5   Ces perles ne risquent pas de perdre _ valeur.
6   Les Dupont ont invité _ amis à dîner.
7   Ce projet a _ avantages et _ inconvénients.

20.2 Emphasising possessive adjectives

IN ENGLISH, if one wishes to emphasise ownership, one can put stress (in speech or in writing) on the possessive adjective:

> it's <u>my</u> book! *(implying: 'and not his/hers')*

IN SPOKEN FRENCH, the same device can be used, especially in the case of *mon/ma/mes*:

c'est <u>mon</u> livre!	*dans <u>ma</u> maison*	*avec <u>mes</u> idées*
that's <u>my</u> book!	in <u>my</u> house	with <u>my</u> ideas

IN WRITTEN FRENCH (and in speech) emphasis on ownership can also be provided by adding *à moi* etc. (for tonic pronouns, **see 19**):

*c'était **mon** idée **à moi***	that was <u>my</u> idea
*ses livres **à lui***	<u>his</u> books
*ses livres **à elle***	<u>her</u> books
*leur famille **à eux***	<u>their</u> family

20.3 Use of possessive adjective or definite article with parts of the body

IN ENGLISH, a possessive adjective is widely used with a noun referring to parts of the body, even if the ownership is clearly signalled (by the subject of the verb, for example), as in **a**, **b** and **d** below:

a **Movement of** part of the body:

he closed his eyes   she raised her hand

b **Action done to** part of the body:

I broke my wrist   she washed her hair

c **Description** of part of the body:

his hair was black   their arms were long

d **Action done with** part of the body:

he banged the table with his fist   she moved the chair with her foot

IN FRENCH, each of these four types of statement involving ownership is constructed in a different way; only in **d** is a possessive adjective used.

a   Movement of part of the body

In statements of this type, a definite article, not a possessive adjective, is used:

*il a fermé **les** yeux*   he closed his eyes

*elle a levé **la** main*   she raised her hand

However, a possessive adjective can be used to emphasise the unexpected or unusual nature of a movement:

*soudain, il a baissé **sa** tête jusqu'à la table*

suddenly, he brought his head down as far as the table

If the part of the body is the subject of the verb, a possessive adjective is used:

***ses** yeux, lentement, se fermaient*   his/her eyes were slowly closing

*brusquement, **sa** main se leva*   his/her hand shot up

b   Action done to part of the body

In these cases, a pronominal verb construction (**see 36**) is used, to indicate that the person is both agent and recipient of the action:

*je **me** suis cassé **le** poignet*   I broke my wrist

*elle **s'**est lavé **les** cheveux*   she washed her hair

A similar construction is used, but with an indirect object pronoun, to describe actions done to someone else:

*je **leur** ai serré **la** main*   I shook their hand

*je **lui** ai caressé **le** dos*   I stroked its back

165

c Description of part of the body

Here, a construction using *avoir* + definite article is used in French, similar to the use of 'have', without a definite article, in English:

il avait les cheveux noirs	he had black hair	or	his hair was black
ils avaient les bras longs	they had long arms	or	their arms were long

This construction, like the one in **a** above, is used for straightforward descriptions of physical features. If what is being described is particularly unusual, or a temporary phenomenon, then the part of the body is placed in the subject position, and a possessive adjective is used:

leurs mains étaient couvertes de farine
their hands were covered in flour
ses bras émergeaient d'une chemise volumineuse
his/her arms emerged from a voluminous shirt

d Action done with part of the body

Here, unlike **b**, the part of the body is the instrument of the action; a possessive adjective is used:

*il a tapé sur la table **avec son** poing*	he banged the table with his fist
*elle a déplacé la chaise **avec son** pied*	she moved the chair with her foot

But a construction involving *de* + definite article is also possible:

*il a tapé **du** poing sur la table*
*d'un mouvement **du** pied, elle a déplacé la chaise*

For constructions such as *les mains dans les poches, il . . .*, see **43.2**.

Exercice 20/4   **Adjectif possessif ou article défini?**   Travail à deux

Avec un(e) partenaire, complétez les phrases ci-dessous en employant un adjectif **possessif** ou un article **défini**, selon le cas. Avant de passer à la phrase suivante, mettez-vous d'accord sur les raisons de votre choix.

Exemple: Elle a fermé _ yeux.
Réponse: Elle a fermé **les** yeux.

1 Tout le monde a levé _ main.
2 Je l'ai regardée de plus près: _ visage était presque blanc.
3 Le boulanger m'a salué; _ mains étaient couvertes de farine.
4 J'aimerais faire du ski, mais j'ai peur de me casser _ jambe.
5 Malgré ce qui s'était passé entre lui et moi, je lui ai serré _ main.
6 Soudain, l'orateur a levé _ bras vers le ciel.

7 Refusant de participer, il a croisé _ bras.

8 Elle a chassé la mouche d'un geste de _ main.

9 Je ne l'avais pas reconnue, parce que _ visage était caché par _ chapeau.

10 On a dit aux prisonniers de garder _ mains sur _ tête.

20.4 Possessive pronouns

Possessive pronouns are used to indicate ownership of a noun which has already been mentioned or referred to:

> vos **fleurs** sont plus jolies que **les miennes**
> *your flowers are prettier than mine*

As with possessive adjectives (*mon/ma/mes* etc.), the correct choice of words depends on:

● whether the owner is Person 1 or 2 etc.;

● whether the noun owned is masculine or feminine, singular or plural.

■ Table of Possessive pronouns in French and English

Person	English	French			
1	mine	*le mien*	*la mienne*	*les miens*	*les miennes*
2	yours	*le tien*	*la tienne*	*les tiens*	*les tiennes*
3	his/hers/ theirs/its	*le sien*	*la sienne*	*les siens*	*les siennes*
4	ours	*le nôtre*	*la nôtre*		*les nôtres*
5	yours	*le vôtre*	*la vôtre*		*les vôtres*
6	theirs	*le leur*	*la leur*		*les leurs*

The definite article *le, la, les* can be used after *de*, becoming *du, de la, des* (**see 29.2**):

> *occupe-toi de tes affaires, et pas **des miennes**!*
> mind your own business, and not mine!

Certain forms of these pronouns are used in set expressions, with a particular meaning:

il faut y mettre du sien	you have to make an effort
à la vôtre! (= à votre santé!)	here's to you! (your good health!)
il/elle sait s'occuper des siens	he/she knows how to look after his/her own (children, family, etc.)
je me suis senti(e) aussitôt un(e) des leurs	I felt accepted straight away (as a member of the group)
il/elle a encore fait des siennes	he's/she's still up to his/her old tricks

C'est le mien **and** *il/elle est à moi*

As well as *c'est le mien* etc., one can also say *il/elle est à moi* etc.:

C'est le mien (etc.):

> *à qui est ce sac? c'est **le mien***
>
> whose is this bag? it's mine
>
> *cette place est occupée! oh, pardon! je ne savais pas que c'était **la vôtre***
>
> this seat is taken! oh, sorry! I didn't know it was yours

Il/elle est à moi (etc.):   (for tonic pronouns, **see 19**)

> *à qui est cette canne? **elle** est **à moi***
>
> whose is this stick? it's mine/it belongs to me
>
> *ce chien est **à vous**, madame? (or: il est **à vous**, ce chien, madame?)*
>
> is this dog yours?

C'est à moi (etc.) is used in a different construction, where ownership is not involved:

> *à qui le tour? (c'est) à moi (= c'est à moi de jouer)*
>
> whose turn/whose go is it? (it's) mine/it's my turn (to play)

21 Demonstrative adjectives and pronouns

21.1 **Demonstrative adjectives in English and French**
21.2 **Demonstrative adjectives with expressions of time**
21.3 **Demonstrative pronouns: *celui*, etc.**
21.4 ***Celui-là* or *cela/ça*?**
21.5 ***Celui-là, celui qui* etc. or *lequel* etc.?**

21.1 Demonstrative adjectives in English and French

IN ENGLISH, the system of demonstrative adjectives (and pronouns) is binary; there is an immediate either/or choice: 'this/these' or 'that/those':

'**this/these**' refers to someone or something close to the speaker, or to future time:
    this book of instructions is useless   (demonstrative adjective)
    tell me **this**: how did he get out?   (demonstrative pronoun)

'**that/those**' refers to someone or something further away from the speaker; or to past time:
    I don't like **that** sort of thing   (demonstrative adjective)
    why did you tell me **that**?   (demonstrative pronoun)

IN FRENCH, the system of demonstrative adjectives works in three stages: there is no immediate choice between 'this' and 'that'.

Stage one   *cet homme*
The demonstrative adjective *ce, cet, cette, ces* is like a definite article (*le, l', la, les*), but more emphatic: it is used to refer to someone or something that has just been mentioned, or which is obvious to both speaker and listener:
    *alors, tu l'as vu, **cet** homme?*   well, did you see the/this/that man?
    (the man in question is not present, but has just been mentioned)
    ***cette** idée est ridicule*   the/this/that idea is ridiculous
    (the idea in question has just been referred to by someone)

Stage two   *cet homme-là*
IN FRENCH, therefore, there is no equivalent to the immediate distinction, made in English, between 'this' and 'that'. *Ce, cet, cette, ces* on their own refer to something that is

169

already in view or in mind: the obvious choice. To single out a noun in French (as is done in English by stressing '<u>this</u>' or '<u>that</u>'), one adds *-là* after the noun, as a signal to the listener or reader to focus on something which is visible or conceivable, but not completely obvious:

> *comment est-ce qu'elle s'appelle, cette fleur-là?*
>
> what's the name of this/that flower?

(*-là* is used, whether the flower is very close to the speaker (English: 'this'), or farther away (English: 'that'))

The distinction between Stage one (demonstrative without *-là*) and Stage two (demonstrative with *là*) also applies when referring to situation in time:

Without *-là*

> *qu'est-ce qu'on fait **ce** soir?*   what shall we do this evening/tonight? (N2)
> (clearly inviting a choice for the coming evening: *-là* is not needed)
> *j'ai pas fait grand-chose **cette** année*   I've not done much this year   (N2)
> (the past tense shows clearly that one is talking about the past year)

With *-là*

> *ce soir-**là**, je me suis vraiment amusé(e)*
>
> that evening/that night, I had a really good time

(*ce soir* on its own would refer to the coming evening, or the one that is just finishing; adding *-là* shows that the speaker is talking about a particular evening which is neither of these)

> *cette année-**là**, je vivais encore chez mes parents*
>
> that year, I was still living at home

(*cette année* on its own would refer to the current year; adding *-là* shows that the speaker is referring to a particular year other than the current one)

Stage three   *cet homme-ci; cet homme là-bas*

Only when neither *ce* (etc.) on its own, nor *ce* (etc.) + *-là*, make the meaning clear, is *-ci* or *là-bas* used:

Ce (etc.) + *-ci* carries the idea: '. . . and not (the other one/ones)':
- when two objects or people are presented simultaneously:

> *préférez-vous ce pull-**ci**, ou celui-**là**?*   do you prefer this sweater, or that one?

(*celui-là*, demonstrative pronoun: **see 21.3**)
- when the implied meaning is 'this . . . and not that':

> *ces jours-**ci***   these days/recently (and not at a previous period)
> *ce mois-**ci***   this month (and not any other month)
> *cette fois-**ci***   this time/on this occasion (and not any other time)
> *à cette heure-**ci***   at this time (and not at any other time)

Là-bas is used when referring to someone or something some distance away; one might say it with an accompanying gesture:

-*là*	*je n'aime pas cet homme-là*	I don't like that man
	(the man in question is present, or not far away, or has just been mentioned)	
là-bas	*tiens! regarde cet homme là-bas!*	hey! look at that man over there!

IN FRENCH, therefore, there is a three-stage system of demonstrative adjectives:
Stage one: the basic demonstrative adjective;
Stage two: the addition of *-là*, if this is necessary to make the meaning clear;
Stage three: the use of *-ci* or *là-bas*, if neither of the above is sufficient to make the meaning clear:

Stage one	Stage two	Stage three		
ce livre	*ce livre-là*	*ce livre-ci*	or	*ce livre là-bas*
cette table	*cette table-là*	*cette table-ci*	or	*cette table là-bas*

As we have seen, the central choice is between *ce* on its own and *ce* used with *-là*.

21.2 Demonstrative adjectives with expressions of time

The table below shows how the basic system (without or with *-là*) works with *matin/ après-midi/soir/nuit/semaine/mois/année* (for *an* and *année* etc., **see 14.3**).

The main distinction is between the form *ce/cet/cette/ces* + noun, used to refer to now, to the current period, or to the immediate past or future, and the form with *-là*, used to refer to a particular occasion or span of time, in the past, or in the future.

■ **Demonstrative adjectives with expressions of time**

Stage one (simple demonstrative: current, imminent)		Stage two (addition of *-là*: more distant; past or future)	
ce matin	this morning	*ce matin-là*	that (particular) morning
cet/cette après-midi	this afternoon	*cet après-midi-là*	that (particular) afternoon
ce soir	this evening, tonight	*ce soir-là*	that (particular) evening
cette nuit	tonight, last night	*cette nuit-là*	that (particular) night
cette semaine	this week	*cette semaine-là*	that (particular) week
ce mois	this month	*ce mois-là*	that (particular) month
cette année	this year	*cette année-là*	that (particular) year

The demonstrative adjective is only one way of situating something in space or time; a definite or indefinite article, and/or certain adjectives, are also used:

171

Past	Future	Past	Future
le mois dernier	*le mois prochain*	*l'autre jour*	*un de ces jours*
last month	next month	the other day	one of these days
le mois passé	*le mois qui vient*	*un jour*	*un jour*
last month	the coming month	one day	one day

Situation in time is indicated by one or more of the following:

- the tense of the verb (**see 10** and **53**);
- adverb phrases (**see 29**) and detached complements (**see 43**);
- demonstratives.

In other words, the use of demonstratives is an additional means, but not the only one, of indicating situation in time.

Exercice 21/1 Démonstratifs: quand faut-il ajouter *-là* (ou *-ci* ou *là-bas*?)

Travail à deux

Dans chacune des phrases ci-dessous, un adjectif **démonstratif** est employé. Avec un(e) partenaire, décidez si le sens de la phrase est évident telle qu'elle est, ou s'il faut ajouter *-là*, ou peut-être *-ci* ou *là-bas*, pour rendre le sens plus clair. Mettez-vous d'accord, dans chaque cas, sur les raisons de votre choix.

Exemple: Qu'est-ce qu'on fait ce soir?
Réponse: (rien à changer)

Exemple: Ce soir j'ai eu un choc terrible!
Réponse: Ce soir-là j'ai eu un choc terrible!
(sans *-là*, la phrase est possible, mais on dirait plutôt:
je viens d'avoir un choc terrible)

1   Ce vin est vraiment délicieux: tu veux l'essayer?
2   J'aurais bien aimé participer, mais ce mois je suis vraiment trop occupé.
3   On est passé(s) chez eux, mais ce jour ils étaient sortis.
4   Comment rassurer Henri? Depuis quelque temps, cette question me tourmente.
5   Lesquelles tu préfères? Ces fleurs, ou celles-ci?
6   Qu'est-ce qu'il fait, cet homme, sur le lac?
7   Pour moi, cette maison est pleine de souvenirs.
8   Quelqu'un a proposé d'aller au cinéma, mais cette idée ne me disait rien.

21.3 Demonstrative pronouns: *celui, celle, ceux, celles*

FORM

Demonstrative pronouns are formed from *c(e)* + tonic pronoun (**see 19.1**):

Tonic pronoun	*lui*	*elle*	*eux*	*elles*
Demonstrative pronoun	*celui*	*celle*	*ceux*	*celles*

MEANING

Celui, celle, ceux, celles correspond to English 'the one' 'the ones', 'those (ones)', and can refer to persons or to things.

They are mainly used instead of repeating a specific noun, which is indicated by the form (masculine/feminine; singular/plural) of the demonstrative pronoun:

Masculine singular: *celui*

> *Elle a pris **quel train**? Mais, **celui** qu'elle prend tous les jours*
> Which train did she get? The one she gets every day

Feminine singular: *celle*

> *il préférait **sa voiture** à **celle** de son frère*
> he preferred her car to her brother's/to the one belonging to her brother

Masculine plural: *ceux*

> ***les livres** imprimés les plus précieux sont **ceux** publiés au 16ᵉ siècle*
> the most valuable printed books are those published in the 16th century

Feminine plural: *celles*

> ***Quelles fleurs** est-ce qu'on va acheter? **Celles**-ci ou **celles**-là?*
> Which flowers shall we buy? These (ones) or those (ones)?

They can also be used (generally with *qui*) to refer to an unnamed person, corresponding to English 'the man/woman/person', 'men/women/people':

> ***celui qui** a dit ça est un imbécile*
> the man who said that is a fool
> ***ceux qui** ont fini leur travail peuvent sortir*
> those who have finished their work can leave

In relative constructions referring to a thing, an idea, etc., and not a person, *ce* is used with *qui/que*, not *celui* etc.:

> *ce qui m'inquiète, c'est que . . .*   what worries me is that . . .
> *ce qu'elle pense ne m'intéresse pas*   what she thinks is of no interest to me
> (**see 42.3** and **51.3**)

USE

Demonstrative pronouns are used in a number of constructions:

+ Preposition

*celui **de***	*sa maison et **celle de** ses amis*	
	his/her house and his/her friends' (house)	
*celui **à***	*quelle femme? **celle aux** yeux verts*	
	which woman? the one with green eyes	
*celui **avec***	*quel bâtiment? **celui avec** le toit enfoncé*	
	which building? the one with the collapsed roof	
*celui **derrière***	*quels arbres? **ceux derrière** la haie*	
	which trees? the ones behind the hedge	

+ Relative pronoun

*celui **qui***	*celui **que***	*celui **dont***	*celui **où***

+ Past participle

+ Past participle   *Quelle lettre? Celle écrite avant-hier*

Which letter? The one written the day before yesterday

+ -ci, -là

When two or more objects or groups are mentioned, both **-ci** and **-là** are used:

Singular	*celui-**ci**/celle-**ci** ou celui-**là**/celle-**là**?*	this one or that one?
Plural	*ceux-**ci**/celles-**ci** ou ceux-**là**/celles-**là**?*	these (ones) or those (ones)?

When only one object or group is mentioned, **-là** is sufficient:

Singular	*celui-**là**/celle-**là***	this one	or	that one
Plural	*ceux-**là**/celles-**là***	these (ones)	or	those (ones)

Exercice 21/2   *Celui, celle, ceux ou celles?*   Travail individuel

Complétez chacune des phrases ci-dessous en employant *celui, celle, ceux ou celles*.

Exemple: La Rolls Corniche, c'est _ qu'il préfère.
Réponse: La Rolls Corniche, c'est **celle** qu'il préfère.

1   Je vais prendre des tomates: _ -là, peut-être.
2   _ qui sourient ne sont pas toujours les plus sincères.
3   Il préférait les légumes de son jardin à _ du supermarché.
4   _ qui faisait rêver mon grand-père, c'était Marlène Dietrich.
5   Il y aura une récompense pour _ qui trouvera la réponse aujourd'hui.
6   _ qui sait la réponse à ça n'est pas encore né.

Exercice 21/3   *Celui* (etc.) + préposition, pronom relatif ou *-ci/-là*?   Travail individuel

Complétez les phrases ci–dessous en employant une préposition, un pronom relatif ou
-ci/-là.

Exemple: De tous ses romans, j'aime celui _ l'action se passe en Alaska.
Réponse: De tous ses romans, j'aime celui **où** l'action se passe en Alaska.

1   Celui _ me fait rire, c'est Devos.
2   Allons, vite! Choisis tes chaussures: celles _, ou celles _ ?
3   L'eau avait inondé notre jardin et celui _ nos voisins.
4   Le meilleur musée Van Gogh, c'est celui _ Amsterdam.
5   Celles _ elle admirait surtout, c'étaient les infirmières.
6   Quelle collection! Mais pour moi, la plus belle pièce, c'est celle _.

21.4 *Celui-là* etc. or *cela, ça?*

Celui-là etc. refer to a specific noun; this is shown in English by the use of 'this one', 'that one', 'these ones', 'those ones'.

Cela (N3) and *ça* (N2), on the other hand, correspond to the English neuter pronoun 'that', and refer, not to a specific noun, but to an action, a state, an idea, a phrase or a sentence (**see 52.3**):

Celui-là etc. + a specific noun
*Tu connais **Paul Martin**? Ah, **celui-là**!*
Do you know Paul Martin? Oh, him!
***celle-là**, c'est une drôle de **femme**!*
she's a strange **woman**, **she is/that one**!
*Voulez-vous **des cerises**, Monsieur? Oui, donnez-moi un kilo de **celles-là***
Would you like some cherries? Yes, a kilo of these/those, please

Cela, ça + an idea, a phrase etc.
*il **a plu** toute la nuit, et à cause de **cela**, le match a dû être annulé*
it rained all night, and because of that/and so the match had to be cancelled
*boire **du café** le soir, moi **ça** m'empêche de dormir*   (N2)
if I drink coffee in the evening, it stops me sleeping

175

Exercice 21/4   *Celui* (etc.) *-là* ou *cela/ça*?   Travail individuel

Complétez les phrases ci-dessous en ajoutant *celui* (etc.) *-là* ou *cela/ça*, selon le sens.

Exemple: Tu connais Jean Dupont? Ah oui, je le connais, _!
   Réponse: Tu connais Jean Dupont? Ah oui, je le connais, **celui-là**!

Exemple: Tu sais que Jean Dupont a eu son permis? Non; _, c'est extraordinaire!
   Réponse: Tu sais que Jean Dupont a eu son permis? Non; **ça**, c'est extraordinaire!

1   Aller au cinéma ce soir-là, _ ne lui disait rien.
2   Ces olives sont trop petites; donnez-moi plutôt un kilo de _.
3   Il n'est pas chez lui. C'est pour _ que je te téléphone.
4   De toutes les propositions, pourquoi avoir choisi _? Elle n'est pas cohérente!
5   La neige a bloqué la route; à cause de _, le médecin a dû y aller en hélicoptère.
6   Jeanne Dupont serait parfaite dans ce rôle. Tiens! Je n'avais pas pensé à _.

21.5 *Celui-là, celui qui* etc. or *lequel* etc.?

Distinguish between the demonstrative pronouns *celui* etc. and the relative pronouns *lequel* etc.:

Lequel etc. is used in questions (**see 33.2**), generally when asking someone to make a choice. It corresponds to English 'which (one)?', 'which (one)s?'

Celui-là etc., even in a question, corresponds to English 'this/that one', 'these/those (ones)':

> [buying shoes]
> *Bon, il faut te décider. **Lesquelles** tu veux, **celles-ci** ou **celles-là**?*
> Right, make up your mind. Which ones do you want, these or those?

Lequel etc. is also used a relative pronoun (**see 42.2**), for example in *pour lequel, auxquelles* etc. ('for which', to which' etc., referring back to a specific noun).

Celui qui etc. corresponds to English 'the one(s) who/which', 'those/people who/which'.

Examples:

Lequel etc.:   *voilà les raisons pour **lesquelles** l'expédition a échoué*
                   those are the reasons why/because of which the expedition failed
                   *c'est la conclusion à **laquelle** il est venu, lui aussi*
                   that's the conclusion he reached, too

French
Grammar
Explained

Celui qui etc.:   *je suis aimable avec tous **ceux qui** sont aimables avec moi*
I'm pleasant with everyone who/all people who are pleasant with me
*de toutes les Renault, **celle que** je préfère c'est la Laguna*
of all the Renault models, the one I like best is the Laguna

The following sentence, where ***celui*** etc. and ***lequel*** etc. are used together, illustrates their different meanings and functions in a relative construction:

*cette conclusion n'est pas **celle** à **laquelle** il aurait voulu venir*
this/that conclusion is not the one which he would have preferred to reach

22 Articles

22.1 Differences between English and French
22.2 Definite and indefinite articles
22.3 Partitive articles
22.4 Which article to use in negative expressions
22.5 When a noun can be used without an article

22.1 Differences between English and French

An **article** is a grammatical word used with a noun to indicate what category of meaning the noun is being placed in, ranging from general to specific.

In English and in French, a certain number of words are used as articles, but no French article is the exact equivalent of a particular English article: the system of articles is different in each of the two languages. For example, in English, there are two categories of meaning where a noun is used on its own, without an article or any other determiner (see Tables, p180 and p181),whereas in French a noun is always used with an article (or other determiner), except in certain specific cases, quite different from English, where a noun can be used without an article (**see 22.5**).

Words used as articles

IN ENGLISH, the words used as articles are 'the', 'some, 'any' and 'a'/'an'. One can think of 'the' as the definite article, 'some', 'any' as partitive articles and 'a'/'an'/'any' as singular indefinite articles.

IN FRENCH, *le/l'/la/les* are usually described as definite articles, *du/de l'/de la* as partitive articles, *un/une* as singular indefinite articles, and *des* as a plural indefinite article.

FORM

IN ENGLISH articles, the only variations in form are between singular ('a'/'an') and plural ('some') forms of the indefinite article, and between 'a' and 'an', depending on whether the following word begins with a consonant or a vowel.

IN FRENCH, the form of articles varies between singular and plural, masculine and feminine and also depending on whether the following word begins with a consonant or a vowel (see Table, p180).

USE AND NON-USE OF ARTICLES

IN ENGLISH, there is no article before a noun being used in a general sense ('pigs don't fly'), or when referring to a substance ('this product contains butter'). In both these cases, an article is used in French, but it is a different article in each case:

> *les cochons ne volent pas*   (definite article in French)
>
> and   *ce produit contient **du** beurre*   (partitive article in French)

To form these and similar statements correctly IN FRENCH, you have first to decide which article is 'left out' in English. If the word 'some' could be used with the noun in English, then the article in French must be either partitive or indefinite. For example, how do you decide which article to use in the French equivalent of 'books are useful', or 'he reads books all day'?

If you are not sure which article to use in each case (*les* for the first one, where 'books' is understood in a general sense, referring to all and any books not just 'some' books, and *des* for the second one, where 'books' is understood to refer to certain books, 'some' books: an unspecified selection from the total number of books available), you may find it helpful to study the two tables (p180 and p181).

What is a definite article in French?

The **definite article** in English is what its name suggests: the opposite of an indefinite article. If you say 'the book', 'the clouds', your listener already knows, or you are about to say, which specific book (the one you borrowed last week) or which specific clouds (the ones that were there this morning) you are referring to. If this is not the case, an indefinite article, or no article, is used in English: 'a book', '(some) clouds'.

IN FRENCH, on the other hand, the definite article is used with two very different meanings: either to refer to a specific item, as in English:

> *les livres que j'ai achetés*   the books I bought

or, in a quite different category of meaning, to refer to the whole class of such items:

> *les livres sont chers*   books are expensive
>
> *le fromage est fabriqué avec du lait*   cheese is made with milk

To form these and similar statements correctly in French, you need to develop a different set of rules from those that you automatically apply in the case of English.

The table on page 180 shows the different articles in English and in French, and the categories of meaning (ranging from general to specific) for which they are used:

■ Table of articles in English and in French

Category of meaning	Article used in English	Article used in French			
General: 'all items in the class of …'	(no article)	*le*	*l'*	*la*	*les*
Referring to a substance: 'what something is made of'	(no article)	*du*	*de l'*	*de la*	
Partitive: 'an amount, a portion of …'	some, any	*du*	*de l'*	*de la*	
Indefinite: **singular:** 'one example (not yet specified) of …'	a, an, any	*un*	*un/une*	*une*	
plural: 'some examples (not yet specified) of …'	(no article)/some, any				*des*
Specific: 'this/these specific example(s), and no other(s), of …'	the	*le*	*l'*	*la*	*les*
Demonstrative adjective: **(see 21)**	this, that, these, those	*ce*	*cet/cette*	*cette*	*ces*
Possessive adjective: **(see 20)**	my, your, his/her etc.	*mon*	*mon*	*ma*	*mes* (etc.)

Demonstrative adjectives and possessive adjectives are included in the above table to show that *ce/cet/cette/ces* and *son/sa/ses* (etc.) also refer to specific items, and are thus a form of definite article, as well as *le/l'/la/les*. So much so that *ce/cet/cette/ces* are used in French in some cases where an English speaker would expect *le/l'/la/les* (**see 21.1**), and conversely, *le/l'/la/les* are used in French, in certain constructions, with parts of the body (**see 20.3**), where an English speaker would expect *son/sa/ses* etc.

You will have noted, from the above table, that as well as the double entry (general, and specific) for definite articles, there is also a double entry (referring to a substance, and partitive) for partitive articles. These two distinctions are made in the English system of articles (no article versus 'the', and no article versus 'some', 'any'), but not in the French system of articles.

The next table gives examples of how the system of articles is used in English and in French, highlighting the differences – and the similarities – between the two systems:

■ **Table of definite, indefinite and partitive articles in English and French**

Category of meaning:	
General, universal	
Do you like [ ] cheese?	*Aimez-vous **le** fromage?*
[ ] water is essential for life	***L'eau** est essentielle pour la vie*
I don't like [ ] flan	*Je n'aime pas **la** tarte*
I don't like [ ] onions	*Je n'aime pas **les** oignons*
Referring to a substance	
What's that? It's [ ] cheese	*Qu'est-ce que c'est? C'est **du** fromage*
What's that? It's [ ] water	*Qu'est-ce que c'est? C'est **de l'**eau*
What's that? It's [ ] flan	*Qu'est-ce que c'est? C'est **de la** tarte*
What's that? It's [ ] potted meat	*Qu'est-ce que c'est? C'est **des** rillettes*
Partitive	
Would you like some cheese?	*Voulez-vous **du** fromage?*
Would you like some water?	*Voulez-vous **de l'**eau?*
Would you like some flan?	*Voulez-vous **de la** tarte?*
Indefinite	
I bought a cheese	*J'ai acheté **un** fromage*
I bought a flan	*J'ai acheté **une** tarte*
I bought [ ]/some onions	*J'ai acheté **des** oignons*
Specific	
That's the cheese I told you about	*Voilà **le** fromage dont je vous ai parlé*
There's the rainwater I've collected	*Voilà **l'**eau de pluie que j'ai recueillie*
There's the flan she made	*Voilà **la** tarte qu'elle a préparée*
Those are the onions I bought	*Voilà **les** oignons que j'ai achetés*

How *à* and *de* combine with articles (*au, aux; du, des; de*): **see 29.1** and **29.2**.

22.2 Definite and indefinite articles

The singular indefinite articles *un* and *une* are used in French when 'a'/'an' is used in English:

> ***un** homme ne sait pas toujours ce qu'il veut*
> a man doesn't always know what he wants
> ***une** femme a téléphoné*
> a woman phoned

With a plural noun, the correct choice of *les* or *des* presents difficulties for many learners of French, especially when the noun is used in English without any article at all (look again at the English examples without article in the tables in **22.1**).

For example, the article used with *habitants* is not the same in the following two cases:

> *Est-ce qu'il y a (?) habitants qui n'ont pas été affectés par le nuage defumée?*
>
> *Non, tous (?) habitants ont été affectés par le nuage de fumée*

The reply is clearly a general statement about all the residents, whereas the question asks whether, among all the residents, some were not affected. So: *les habitants* ('all the residents') in the reply, but *des habitants* ('some residents') in the question. Perhaps you need to practise a few more . . .

Exercice 22/1   *Des* or *les*?   Travail individuel

a   Complétez les phrases ci-dessous en ajoutant *des* ou *les*, selon le sens:

Exemple: Dans cette ville, est-ce qu'il y a _ enfants sans problèmes respiratoires? Non, ici tous _ enfants ont des problèmes respiratoires.

Réponse: Dans cette ville, est-ce qu'il y a **des** enfants sans problèmes respiratoires? Non, ici tous **les** enfants ont des problèmes respiratoires.

1   Si M. le Maire était là, j'aurais _ questions à lui poser.
2   _ magazines féminins sont tous _ mêmes.
3   Il y a eu tant d'accidents que _ services d'urgence étaient débordés.
4   Les manifestants réclamaient _ négociations, mais on ne leur a offert que _   discussions.
5   La police arrêtait tous _ véhicules, sauf _ voitures étrangères.
6   Pour cet examen, _ questions sont rédigées par un seul homme.
7   Il a affirmé que c'était vrai, mais elle avait _ raisons de croire le contraire.

b   Après avoir vérifié vos réponses, écrivez l'équivalent en anglais de chaque phrase, en faisant bien attention à l'article employé (ou absent!) en anglais.

Definite article in titles, etc.

The definite article is used in French (but not in English) before a title followed by a name:

> *le général de Gaulle*   General De Gaulle
>
> *le président Clinton*   President Clinton

French
Grammar
Explained

22.3 Partitive articles

Partitive articles **(see 22.1)** are used in two categories: when one is speaking about a noun as a substance, and when one is speaking of a limited amount or portion:

*dans cette boisson colorée, il y a essentiellement **de l'eau** et **du sucre***

this coloured drink consists mainly of water and sugar

*Un apéritif? Rien que **de l'eau** minérale, s'il vous plaît*

An aperitive? Just (some) mineral water, please

But other articles can be used with such nouns, depending on how they are being presented:

General (everyone's water):

*depuis dix ans, **l'eau** a beaucoup augmenté*

(the price of) water has gone up a lot in the past ten years

Indefinite (a type or quality of water):

*au fond de ce puits on trouve **une eau** plus pure que partout ailleurs dans la région*

in this well you get purer water than anywhere else round here

---

Exercice 22/2   **Article partitif ou défini?**   Travail individuel

a   Complétez les phrases ci-dessous en ajoutant un article partitif ou défini, selon le sens:

Exemple: On les accusait d'avoir ajouté _ eau à leur charcuterie.

Réponse: On les accusait d'avoir ajouté **de l'eau** à leur charcuterie.

Exemple: Dans ce puits, _ eau est très pure.

Réponse: Dans ce puits, l'eau est très pure.

1   _ sucre est bon pour la santé, mais mauvais pour les dents.
2   Je sais que c'est vrai, parce que j'ai pris _ peine de vérifier.
3   Voulez-vous _ lait ou _ crème dans votre café?
4   _ thé et _ café sont des produits dont le prix fluctue énormément.
5   Je suis ravi de voir _ succès de votre entreprise.
6   Pour cette recette, il faut _ sucre, mais pas trop.
7   Cette histoire d'enfants abandonnés m'a fait _ peine.
8   Il parle si bas qu'on a _ mal à le comprendre.

b   Après avoir vérifié vos réponses, écrivez l'équivalent en anglais de chaque phrase, en faisant bien attention à l'article employé (ou absent!) en anglais.

22.4 Which article to use in negative expressions (*pas de, plus de* etc.)?

In negative sentences, the partitive forms *du/de l'/de la/des* all reduce to *de*:

du fromage	cheese	*pas de* fromage	no cheese
de l'eau	water	*plus d'eau*	no water left
de la crème	cream	*plus de* crème	no cream left
des fruits	fruit	*pas de* fruits	no fruit

However, this does not mean that *pas* is always followed by *de* with a noun:

Definite articles do not reduce after *pas* etc.:

c'est la même chose	it's the same thing
ce n'est plus la même chose	it's not the same thing any more
les autres jours, je travaille	(on) the other days, I work
je suis libre le dimanche, mais pas les autres jours	I'm free on Sundays, but not the other days
elle aime les oranges	she likes oranges
elle n'aime pas les oranges	she doesn't like oranges

Indefinite articles reduce to *(pas) de* if the noun is being negated:

il n'y a pas eu de feu d'artifice cette année

there was no firework display this year

je ne donnerai pas d'excuses

I won't make any excuses

but they remain as *un/une/des* if the verb is being negated:

ce n'était pas un feu d'artifice sensationnel

it wasn't a particularly good firework display

je ne veux pas des excuses

I don't want excuses

or if a distinction is being made between two nouns:

elle n'a pas mangé d'oranges cette semaine

she's eaten no oranges/she hasn't eaten any oranges this week

elle ne mange pas des oranges, elle mange des pommes

she doesn't eat oranges, she eats apples

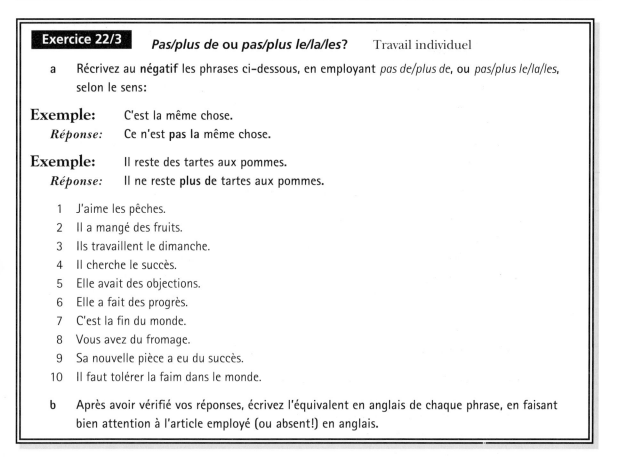

Exercice 22/3   *Pas/plus de* ou *pas/plus le/la/les*?   Travail individuel

a   Récrivez au **négatif** les phrases ci–dessous, en employant *pas de/plus de*, ou *pas/plus le/la/les*, selon le sens:

Exemple: C'est la même chose.
Réponse: Ce n'est **pas** la même chose.

Exemple: Il reste des tartes aux pommes.
Réponse: Il ne reste **plus de** tartes aux pommes.

1   J'aime les pêches.
2   Il a mangé des fruits.
3   Ils travaillent le dimanche.
4   Il cherche le succès.
5   Elle avait des objections.
6   Elle a fait des progrès.
7   C'est la fin du monde.
8   Vous avez du fromage.
9   Sa nouvelle pièce a eu du succès.
10   Il faut tolérer la faim dans le monde.

b   Après avoir vérifié vos réponses, écrivez l'équivalent en anglais de chaque phrase, en faisant bien attention à l'article employé (ou absent!) en anglais.

22.5 Noun used without article

Some of the cases are given below where a noun is used without any article in French.

In lists
There is no article before nouns in lists (of two or more) when the list is exhaustive – that is to say, when it covers all sub-sets within a particular category:

> *tous furent sauvés: **hommes**, **femmes** et **enfants*** (N3)
> all were rescued: men, women and children

> ***orages**, **avalanches**, **froid extrême**: autant de raisons de craindre la montagne* (N3)
> storms, avalanches, extreme cold: all reasons for fearing mountain heights

In announcements
This category includes:
- **messages** such as small ads:

> ***studio** à louer dans **immeuble** neuf*   one-room flat to let in new block

- **headlines** in the press:

    Tremblement de terre en Iran   Earthquake in Iran

- **signs** and **notices**:

    Entrée interdite   No admittance

    Ralentir. **Travaux**   Slow down. Roadworks ahead

- **labels**:

    Fromage fermier   Farmhouse cheese

Exercice 22/4   **Messages, titres, annonces**   Travail à deux > Mise en commun

Voici des phrases qui contiennent des informations, des conseils, des avertissements, etc. A partir de chaque phrase, composez un message, un titre (dans un journal, etc.), une annonce, etc.

Exemple: Il y a un appartement à louer.

Réponse: **Appartement** à louer.

Exemple: C'est dangereux à cause des travaux.

Réponse: **Danger. Travaux.**

1   Il est interdit de fumer.
2   Je vends une Fiat 500 pour le prix de 10 000 francs.
3   C'est le dernier jour de nos soldes d'été.
4   Gardez le silence près de cet hôpital.
5   Nous vendons du lait frais.
6   Il est interdit de rouler dans ce sens.
7   La route est barrée par une chute de pierres.
8   Les produits dans ce camion ne sont pas toxiques.
9   Il y a eu un rebondissement dans l'affaire des missiles en Irak.
10   Adressez-vous ici pour vous renseigner et pour vous inscrire.

In apposition

When a noun is used to define or describe another noun, and is placed immediately after it, it is said to be 'in apposition'. In this role, it can be used without an article, to emphasise that one is talking about status (here, of Chenonceau, or of M. Dupont):

    Chenonceau, **joyau** *des châteaux de la Loire*   (N3)

    Chenonceau, (the) showpiece of the Loire châteaux

    M. Dupont, **président-directeur général** *de Vastco*   (N3)

    M. Dupont, chairman and chief executive of Vastco

A definite article could be used (*le joyau, le P-D G*), if the statement is more personal and less solemn. Similarly:

M Durand, **un** *P-D G* **dynamique et clairvoyant**

M Durand, a dynamic and far-sighted boss

le mont Saint-Michel, **le** *site* **le plus visité de France**

the Mont St Michel, the most popular tourist spot in France

In this last example, *le* is required because of the superlative construction (**see 31.2**).

As attribute

When a noun is used after a verb introducing a particular status (high or low), there is no article:

il est **devenu président**	he became chairman
il est **devenu chômeur**	he became unemployed
on l'a **élu député**	he was elected an MP
il a été *prisonnier de guerre*	he has been a P.O.W.
qu'est-ce qu'elle fait dans la vie? **elle est** *médecin*	what's her job? she's a doctor

But if the noun appears with additional information (an adjective, for example), it takes an article:

    que fait sa femme? elle **est avocate**

    what does his wife do? she's a barrister

but   *elle est maintenant* **une** *avocate* **célèbre**

    she's now a famous barrister

Other examples:

    il est devenu **le** *plus jeune député* **de son pays**

    he became his country's youngest MP

    le matricule 345? **c'est un** *prisonnier modèle*

    inmate 345? he's a model prisoner

After prepositions   (see 30)

Many adjective or adverb phrases consist of preposition + noun, without an article:

elle est **en réunion**	she's in a meeting
(but *elle est* **dans une** *réunion* **importante**	she's in an important meeting)
une chambre **sans confort**	a room without facilities
qu'est-ce qu'il y a **comme dessert?**	what is there for pudding?
le théâtre est fermé **pour travaux**	the theatre is closed for alterations
travailler **avec sérieux**	to work seriously
arriver **par hasard**	to happen by chance
(but *par* **un** *hasard* **extraordinaire**	by an amazing coincidence)
partir **à pied**	to set out on foot

Also in the group noun 1 + *de* + noun 2: **(see 41.2)**

   *une salle **de bains***   a bathroom   *un donneur **de sang***   a blood donor

In compound verbs   **(see 15.2)**

Many compound verbs are composed of *avoir/mettre/prendre* + noun, without an article:

   avoir lieu   to take place   *prendre feu*   to catch fire

23 Qualifiers: indefinite adjectives (+ noun)

23.1 *Tout, tous; chaque*
23.2 *Tout, chacun*
23.3 *Plusieurs, quelques, certains*
23.4 *Autre*

Qualifiers are indefinite adjectives, which can be used

- with a noun
  plusieurs personnes   several individuals
- on their own, as a pronoun
  plusieurs   several people
- as a pronoun   + *de* + article + noun
  *plusieurs des personnes**   several of the people
- + *de* + demonstrative + noun
  plusieurs de ces personnes   several of these people
- + *de* + possessive + noun
  plusieurs de ses amis   several of his/of her friends

* How *de* combines with definite articles: **see 29.2**.

The following table shows qualifiers which can be used as adjectives + noun, or as pronouns (+ *de* + noun):

■ Indefinite adjectives and the corresponding pronouns

Indefinite adjective + noun	Pronoun used alone	Pronoun + *de* + *les/ces/ses* (etc.) + noun
Tout, tous; chaque (see **23.1**); *tout, chacun* (see **23.2**)		
à toute heure at any time	*tout est possible* everything/anything is possible	–
tous les coureurs all the runners	*tous sont arrivés* all of them have arrived	–
chaque enfant each child	*chacun(e) a reçu un prix* each one got a prize	*chacun(e) des enfants* each (one) of the children

Aucun, nul (see 34)

aucun(e) enfant	*aucun(e)* n'est arrivé(e)	*aucun(e)* des enfants
no/not one child	none/not one has arrived	not one of the children
nul doute (N4)	*nul* ne le sait (N4)	*aucun(e)* de mes enfants
no doubt at all	no one knows	not one of my children

Plusieurs, quelques, certains (see 23.3)

plusieurs femmes	*plusieurs* sont tombé(e)s	*plusieurs* des femmes
several women	several fell/have fallen	several of the women
quelques auditeurs	*quelques-un(e)s* sont d'accord	*quelques-uns* des auditeurs
some/a few listeners	some/a few agree	some/a few of the listeners
quelqu'un		*quelques-uns* de nos auditeurs
someone		some/a few of our listeners
certaines réponses	*certaines* sont inexactes	*certaines* des réponses
some/certain answers	some are wrong	some of the answers
une *certaine* idée		*certaines* de ces réponses
a certain idea		some of these/those answers

Autre; le même, un tel (see 23.4)

une *autre* fois	un(e) *autre*	–
another time	another person/another one	
d'*autres* occasions	d'*autres*	
other occasions	others/other people	
l'*autre* jour	l'*autre*	–
the other day	the other one	
les *autres* jours	les *autres*	
the other days	the other ones/the others	
la *même* chose	le/la *même*	–
the same thing	the same one	
les *mêmes* idées	les *mêmes*	
the same ideas	the same ones	
un *tel* bruit	un(e) *tel(le)*	*telle* ou *telle* de ses idées
such a noise	so-and-so	one or other of his/her ideas
de *telles* idées		
such ideas		

(Le)quel (see 33.2, 33.4)

quelles réponses?	*le(s)quel(le)(s)*?	*le(s)quel(s)* de ces arbres?
which answers?	which one(s)?	which of these/those trees?
n'importe *quelle* chemise		n'importe *laquelle* de ces chemises
any shirt (whatever)		any one of these/those shirts

23.1 *Tout, toute, tous, toutes* and *chaque*, adjectives

Tout le/toute la + singular noun means 'all the', without interruption; *chaque* + singular noun means 'each', 'every', without exception:

> *elle a pleuré **toute la nuit***
>
> she cried all night (long)

but *pendant une semaine, ella a pleuré **chaque nuit***

> for a week, she cried every night
>
> *arrête de parler **tout le temps**!*
>
> stop talking all the time!

but ***chaque fois** qu'elle parle, il l'interrompt*

> each time she speaks, he interrupts her

Tous les/toutes les + plural noun means 'every . . .', 'without exception'; *chaque* + singular noun means 'each and every':

> *le gardien passe **toutes les heures***
>
> the caretaker comes round every hour

and *(à) **chaque heure**, il y a un gardien qui passe*

> every hour, there's a caretaker who comes round
>
> ***tous les bruits** le rendaient malade*
>
> all noises/any noise made him ill

and ***chaque bruit** lui causait un nouveau tourment*

> each noise meant more torture for him
>
> *on apprend quelque chose de nouveau **tous les jours/chaque jour***
>
> you learn something new every day/each day

Tout/toute (without *le/la*) + noun, like *tous les/toutes les*, focuses on the fact that there is no exception to what is being described. It tends to be used in fixed expressions, such as:

> *casse-croûte **à toute heure***
>
> snacks at all hours/at any time (of day)
>
> *attention! ils peuvent arriver **à tout moment**!*
>
> watch out! they might turn up at any time!
>
> *téléphone-lui **à tout hasard***
>
> ring him/her just in case (he's/she's in)

Tout, in the above examples, corresponds to English 'any'; to emphasise the idea that choice, timing, etc. are irrelevant, *n'importe quel* (etc.) + noun is used.

Exercice 23/1   *Tout, tous, chaque*   Travail individuel > Mise en commun

a   Complétez les phrases ci-dessous en ajoutant:

  chaque + nom au singulier

ou   *tout le/toute la* + nom au singulier

ou   *tous les/toutes les* + nom au pluriel

ou   *tout/toute* + nom au singulier

Si deux (ou trois) constructions sont possibles, écrivez-les toutes. Si vous choisissez *tou(te)s les*, n'oubliez pas de faire les accords nécessaires au pluriel.

b   Pour chaque phrase que vous jugez possible, écrivez l'équivalent en anglais.

c   Ensuite, vérifiez vos réponses avec le professeur: on demandera à chacun(e) des étudiant(e)s de lire une de leurs phrases au reste du groupe.

Exemple: Il a plu _ nuit.

Réponses possibles: Il a plu **chaque** nuit   (it rained each/every night)

              Il a plu **toute la** nuit   (it rained all night (long))

              Il a plu **toutes** les nuits   (it rained every night)

1   _ fois qu'on allait la voir, elle nous servait le thé.

2   _ infraction sera punie.

3   Si tu cries _ temps, on ne pourra rien entendre.

4   _ lettre aura une réponse.

5   Je ne peux pas m'occuper de lui _ cinq minutes.

6   _ spectateur avait une bonne vue du terrain.

7   _ matin, il passait lui dire bonjour.

8   Les murs étaient si épais que _ idée d'évasion était impossible.

23.2 *Tout* (invariable), *chacun, chacune,* pronouns

Tout or *tous?*

Tout, used on its own,

- means 'everything'
- is pronounced [tu]
- is invariable
- is singular, so a following verb must be in the singular

Tous, used on its own,

- means 'everyone'
- is pronounced [tus]
- is masculine; the feminine form is *toutes*
- is plural, so a following verb must be in the plural

Examples:

Tout	*Tous*
tout *cela*	**tous** *ceux-là, toutes celles-là*
all that	all those (people/things)
merci pour **tout**!	*bonjour à* **tous**!
thanks for everything!	hello (to) everyone!
cette machine fait **tout**	**tous** *étaient arrivés*
this machine does everything	everyone had arrived

Tou(te)s and *chacun(e)* are similar in meaning: *tou(te)s* emphasises the whole group, *chacun(e)* each individual:

> *le président les a* **tous/toutes** *salué(e)s*
>
> the chairman greeted them all
>
> *le président leur a dit un mot à* **chacun**
>
> the chairman said something to each one of them
>
> *je les connais* **tous/toutes**
>
> I know them all
>
> *je les connais* **chacun(e)**
>
> I know each and every one of them

Exercice 23/2   *Tout* ou *tous*?   Travail individuel > Mise en commun

a Complétez les phrases ci-dessous, en ajoutant *tout* ou *tous*, selon le sens.
b Proposez un équivalent en anglais pour chaque phrase.
c Vérifiez vos réponses avec le professeur.

Exemple: Ils sont _ arrivés.
Réponse: Ils sont **tous** arrivés.

Exemple: Ce n'est pas le moment de parler de _ cela.
Réponse: Ce n'est pas le moment de parler de **tout** cela.

1 Il savait qu'il pouvait lui dire _.
2 Je vous souhaite une bonne nuit à _.
3 _ sont contents qu'elle soit là.
4 Voilà: ça fait 80 francs en _.
5 Avant _, je voulais savoir que tu allais bien.
6 L'émission s'appelle 'La musique pour _'.
7 J'ai vu _ ceux que je voulais voir.
8 C'est _ ce que j'ai pu faire.

For *tout* + **adjective** (e.g. *tout neuf*, 'brand new', etc.): **see 31.4.**

23.3 *Plusieurs, quelques, certains*

Plusieurs ('several') suggests that there are more than expected ('as many as'), whereas *quelques* ('a few') suggests that there are fewer than expected ('as few as').

> The same form, *plusieurs*, is used with both masculine and feminine nouns.

Plusieurs + noun

Used before a noun, *plusieurs* means 'several':

plusieurs choses
several things, quite a lot of things
pour plusieurs raisons
for several reasons, for a good number of reasons

Plusieurs des/de ses/de ces + noun

Used as a pronoun, followed by *de* + noun, *plusieurs de* means 'several of':

elle m'a dit plusieurs choses
she told me several things
plusieurs des choses qu'elle a dites sont vraies
several of the things she said are true
plusieurs spectateurs sont partis avant la fin
several spectators left before the end
plusieurs des supporteurs de Tours FC sont partis avant la fin
several of the Tours FC supporters left before the end

Quelques + noun

Used before a noun, *quelques* means 'a few':

quelques spectateurs	a few spectators, a small number of spectators
quelques exceptions	a few exceptions, a certain number of exceptions

Quelques-un(e)s

The pronoun *quelques-un(e)s*, used on its own, means 'some (people)', 'a few (people)'. It is, in effect, the plural form of the singular pronoun *quelqu'un*, 'someone':

quelqu'un a sonné à la porte
someone rang at the door
quelques-uns pensaient qu'il était coupable
some/a few (people) thought he was guilty
(see also *certains*, below)

Quelques is not used with the noun *gens*: for 'a few people' use *quelques-uns*.

Quelques-un(e)s des/de ces/de ses (etc.) + noun

Followed by *de* + noun, *quelques-un(e)s de* means 'a few of':

   quelques-uns *de nos auditeurs ont protesté*

   a few/a small number of our listeners complained

Certain(e)s + noun

   certaines personnes disent qu'ils l'ont vu

   some people say they've seen him

The noun *personne* is feminine: for 'some people' use *certains*.

Certaines is used before a noun in phrases such as:

certains jours	*certaines fois*	*certaines choses*
some days	on some occasions	certain things

Used as a pronoun, *certain(e)s* is similar in meaning to *quelques-un(e)s* (see above):

   certains *pensaient qu'il était coupable*   (N3)

   some people thought he was guilty

Exercice 23/3   *Plusieurs, quelques, certains* etc.   Travail individuel

a   Complétez les phrases ci-dessous en ajoutant *plusieurs, plusieurs de* + article, *quelques,*
     quelques-un(e)s, certain(e)s, selon le sens et la construction grammaticale. Dans certaines
     phrases, plus d'une réponse est possible.

b   Donnez l'équivalent en anglais de chaque phrase que vous avez complétée.

Exemple: La salle était presque vide: _ spectateurs au fond, et c'était tout.
Réponse: La salle était presque vide: **quelques** spectateurs au fond, et c'était tout.

Exemple: Tout le monde était d'accord, sauf _ qui ont protesté.
Réponse: Tout le monde était d'accord, sauf **quelques-uns** qui ont protesté.

1   On pourrait se voir bientôt? J'ai _ choses à te dire.
2   _ jours, il se sentait découragé.
3   Il ne me reste que _ dizaines d'enveloppes à adresser.
4   J'ai écouté _ de ses discours: c'est un bon orateur.
5   Il n'a pas eu à attendre longtemps: la réponse est arrivée _ jours plus tard.
6   Tous ses tableaux sont excellents, et _ sont des chefs d'oeuvre.
7   On voit qu'il est intelligent: _ de ses réponses sont intéressantes.
8   Ce feuilleton est suivi par _ millions de téléspectateurs.

23.4 *Autre, autres*

Autre, *autres* are used, without article, in a number of fixed expressions:

<table>
<tr><td>*autre chose*</td><td>*autres pays, autres moeurs*</td></tr>
<tr><td>something else</td><td>each country has its own customs</td></tr>
</table>

In all other cases, *autre(s)* is used with an article:

<table>
<tr><td>*un(e)* autre</td><td>*l'autre*</td><td>*d'autres*</td><td>*les* autres</td></tr>
</table>

D'autres

> ***certains*** *pensent qu'il a raison,* ***d'autres*** *pensent qu'il a tort*   (N3)
> some think he's right, some think he's wrong

Distinguish between ***d'autres*** and ***les autres***:

- ***d'autres*** is partitive (**see 22**): it refers to one group which is being distinguished from another, as in the above example;
- ***les autres*** includes the definite article (**see 22**), in its general sense:

> *on a toujours un peu peur* ***des autres*** *(de + les = des:* **see 29.2***)*
> one is always a little afraid of other people

or in its specific sense:

> ***les autres*** *sont partis, mais moi je suis resté*
> the others left, but I stayed behind

Compare:

> ***d'autres*** *sont partis*
> more people left (in addition to some who had already left)

D'autres + noun

> *il me faut* ***d'autres*** *emballages, tout de suite!*
> I need more wrappers, at once!

Encore des *emballages* and ***de nouveaux*** *emballages* are also possible

---

Exercice 23/4   ***D'autres* ou *les autres*?**   Travail individuel

Complétez les phrases ci-dessous en ajoutant *d'autres* ou *les autres* (*de + les autres = des autres*), selon le sens.

Exemple: Quelques-uns approuvent son action, mais _ la condamnent.
Réponse: Quelques-uns approuvent son action, mais **d'autres** la condamnent.

Exemple: Il est timide: il a peur _ autres.
Réponse: Il est timide: il a peur **des autres** (de + les autres).

---

1 Le problème numéro un, c'est le chômage, mais il y a _ questions aussi.
2 Ceux qui ont fini peuvent sortir, mais _ doivent rester.
3 Auriez-vous _ chaussures dans le même style?
4 On dit qu'il va abandonner son projet, mais moi, je pense qu'il a _ idées en tête.
5 Tous _ ont acheté quelque chose, mais moi je n'ai rien trouvé d'intéressant.
6 Il est toujours dangereux de dire du mal _.

L'un(e) et l'autre, les un(e)s et les autres

These correspond to English 'both of (them)', 'all (of them)'. Their meaning is similar to *tou(te)s les deux* and *tou(te)s*, respectively (**see 23.1** and **23.2**), except that using *l'un(e) et l'autre, les un(e)s et les autres* emphasises that there are two separate individuals or groups, whereas *tou(te)s les deux* and *tou(te)s* emphasise the group as a whole.

Examples:

'Both'   *je vous préviens, **l'un(e) et l'autre***   I'm warning both of you
          *vous avez raison **tou(te)s les deux***   you're both right
'All'   *je crois qu'on est **tou(te)s là**, maintenant*   I think we're all here now
          *mettez-vous d'accord, **les un(e)s et les autres!*** come to some agreement, all of you!

L'un(e) l'autre, l'un(e) à l'autre etc.: reciprocal action

IN ENGLISH, reciprocal action is described using expressions such as 'each other', 'one another'; if a preposition is required, it comes first: '**to** each other', '**for** one another'. The use of the word 'each' in English leads learners of French to try to use the word *chaque* with *autre*, but there is no way of making this work in French.

IN FRENCH, reciprocal action is described using the expressions *l'un(e) l'autre, les un(e)s les autres*; if a preposition is required, it is placed between the two parts of the expression: *l'un(e) à l'autre, les un(e)s **pour** les autres*. *L'un(e) l'autre, l'un(e) **à** l'autre* (etc.) are used when two individuals are involved; *les un(e)s les autres, les un(e)s **aux** autres* (etc.) are used when two groups are involved.

Examples when there is a preposition:

Two individuals

*les deux hommes se tenaient **l'un près de l'autre***

the two men were standing close to one another

Two groups

*toutes les chaises étaient rempilées **les unes sur les autres***

all the chairs were stacked on top of one another

Reciprocal action: use of pronominal verb

If 'each other', 'one another' are the object of a verb, a pronominal verb (**see 36**) is used in French, and *l'un(e) l'autre, les un(e)s les autres* are added only if this is necessary to make the meaning clear, or for emphasis:

Two individuals

*elles ne **se** sont pas parlé*   they didn't speak to each other

*elles ne **se** sont pas parlé **l'une à l'autre***   neither of them spoke to the other

Two groups

*nous devons **nous** aider*   we must help one another

*nous devons **nous** aider **les uns les autres***   we must all help one another

---

Exercice 23/5   *L'un/les uns . . . l'autre/les autres* etc.   Travail individuel

Complétez les phrases ci-dessous en ajoutant *l'un(e)/les un(e)s . . .* (+ préposition s'il le faut) *l'autre/les autres*, selon le sens.

Exemple: Il faut nous aider _.
Réponse: Il faut nous aider **les uns les autres.**

Exemple: Les oiseaux étaient serrés _.
Réponse: Les oiseaux étaient serrés **les uns près des autres.**

1   Les deux soeurs avaient réussi, _.
2   C'était un couple très uni: ils ne pouvaient pas vivre _.
3   Tous les enfants s'excitaient _ à tourmenter le malheureux professeur.
4   ⁻Les pays européens sont obligés de s'entendre _.
5   En les observant tous les deux, on voyait qu'ils étaient jaloux _.
6   Ils se parlaient très bruyamment _.
7   Bon, maintenant écoutez-moi bien, _.
8   Ces deux hommes se détestaient _.

---

24 Quantifying adverbs (+ *de* + noun)

24.1 *Beaucoup*
24.2 *Tant*
24.3 *La plupart*

Quantifying adverbs

Quantifying adverbs (*beaucoup, trop, combien* etc.) can be used

- with *de* + noun
  *combien **de** spectateurs?*   how many spectators?
- on their own
  combien?   how much?/how many?
- with *de* + definite article + noun
  *combien **des** spectateurs?**   how many of the spectators?
- with *de* + demonstrative + noun
  *combien **de ces** spectateurs?*   how many of these spectators?
- with *de* + possessive + noun
  *combien **de leurs** spectateurs?*   how many of their spectators?

* How *de* combines with definite articles: **see 29.2**.

Beaucoup, trop etc. can be used in three ways:

- on their own;
- + *de* + noun;
- + *de* + definite article + noun.

In most cases, these adverbs can be used with a singular or a plural noun.

The following table shows quantifying adverbs which, when used with a noun, are followed by *de*:

■ Quantifying adverbs: use with/without *de* + noun

Partitive use (+ *de* + noun)	Used alone	Use with definite article (+ *de* + *les/ses/ces* + noun)
***Beaucoup* (see 24.1)**		
beaucoup de fierté a lot of/much pride	**beaucoup** a lot	*beaucoup de sa fierté* a lot of his/her pride
beaucoup d'ennuis lots of/many problems	**beaucoup** lots (of people)	*beaucoup des ennuis* lots of the problems
Combien, (un) peu		
combien d'argent? how much money?	**combien?** how much?	*combien de cet argent?* how much of this/that money?
combien d'enfants? how many children?	**combien?** how many (people)?	*combien des enfants?* how many of the children?
un peu de satisfaction a bit of satisfaction	**un peu** a bit	*un peu de sa satisfaction* a bit of his/her satisfaction
peu de satisfaction not much satisfaction	**peu** not much	*peu de cette satisfaction* not much of this satisfaction
peu d'idées not many/few ideas	**peu** not many/few (people)	*peu de ses idées* not many/few of his/her ideas
***Tant* (see 24.2)**		
tant de bruit so much noise	**tant** so much	–
tant de clients so many customers	**tant** so many	*tant des clients* so many of the customers
Assez, trop		
assez d'argent enough money	**assez** enough	–
trop d'argent too much money	**trop** too much	*trop de cet argent* too much of this money
trop de questions too many questions	**trop** too many	*trop des questions* too many of the questions
***La plupart* (see 24.3)**		
–	**la majeure partie** most (of it)	*la majeure partie du champ* most of the field
–	**la plupart** most (people)	*la plupart de ses habitants* most of its occupants

Comparative expressions (see 31.1)

plus de bruit	***plus***	*plus du gâteau*
more noise	more	more of the cake
plus de clients	***plus***	*plus de ses clients*
more customers	more	more of his/her customers
moins de bruit	***moins***	*moins du gâteau*
less noise	less	less of the cake
moins de clients	***moins***	*moins de ses clients*
less/fewer customers	less/fewer	less/fewer of his/her customers
autant de bruit	***autant***	*autant de son gâteau*
as much noise	as much	as much of his/her cake
autant de clients	***autant***	*autant des clients*
as many customers	as many	as many of the customers

Exercice 24/1   *Beaucoup, (un) peu, assez, trop (+ de)*   Travail à deux

a   Après avoir étudié la **Table** ci-dessus, choisissez **une** des questions dans la liste
ci-dessous, et posez-la à haute voix à votre partenaire. La réponse doit commencer par *Oui, ...,*
ou par *Non, pas* ... + un des (groupes de) mots suivants:
beaucoup (un) peu assez trop tant plus moins autant.

Exemple: Tu as de l'argent?
Réponses possibles: Oui, **un peu** d'argent
                        Non, **pas beaucoup** d'argent.

b   Aussitôt après avoir donné sa réponse, votre partenaire doit donner aussi un commentaire ou
une explication.

Exemple: (un peu d'argent)
Explications possibles: ... mais pas assez.
                        ... parce que je viens d'hériter de mon grand-père.

c   Ensuite, c'est au tour de votre partenaire de vous poser une question, et ainsi de suite.

1   Est-ce que tu as du travail en ce moment?
2   Est-ce que le prof pose des questions?
3   Est-ce que tes voisins font du bruit?
4   Est-ce que tu as eu des ennuis récemment?
5   Est-ce que tu as des projets pour l'été prochain?
6   Est-ce que le gouvernement fait des erreurs?

24.1 *Beaucoup*

Used with *de* + singular or plural noun, *beaucoup* means 'much', 'a lot', or 'many', 'lots'. In informal situations (N2), but not in formal speech or writing, *plein de* is often used instead:

> *cette nouvelle m'a causé **beaucoup de** chagrin* (N3)
> this news caused me much distress
>
> *j'ai **plein de** choses à te dire* (N2)
> I've lots of things to tell you

Used on its own, *beaucoup* can mean 'many people'; this is typical of formal usage (**see also** *certains*, **23.3**):

> ***beaucoup de** gens pensent comme lui*
> lots of people think the way he does
>
> ***beaucoup** pensent comme lui* (N3)
> many people think the way he does

Intensifiers, with and without *beaucoup*

Beaucoup cannot be used after *assez, si, très* or *trop*: note carefully the French equivalent of the following English phrases:

French intensifier	English intensifier
assez de, pas mal de (N2)	quite a lot of
énormément de	a great deal of
tant de	so much, so many
trop de	too much, too many

But *beaucoup* can be used as an intensifier before *trop, plus* and *moins*:

beaucoup trop important	much/far too important
beaucoup plus important	much/far more important
beaucoup moins important	much/far less important

(see also **31.4**)

Use of *beaucoup* etc. with *il y en a, j'en ai* etc.

In this construction. the neuter object pronoun *en* (**see 18.4**) stands for *de* + noun:

j'en ai, je n'en ai pas . . .	*. . . beaucoup, un peu, assez*
I have, I haven't . . .	. . . many/a lot, a few, enough
il y en a, il n'y en a pas . . .	*. . . des milliers, des millions*
there are, there aren't . . .	. . . thousands, millions (of them) (etc.)
j'en vois, je n'en vois pas . . .	
I can see, I can't see . . .	

Bien can also be used, in formal situations (N3), instead of *beaucoup de*. The construction is quite different; *bien* functions as an intensifier (**see 31.4**), not a quantifier:

*cette nouvelle leur a fait **bien de la** peine* (N3)
*cette nouvelle leur a fait **beaucoup de** peine*
this news caused them much sorrow
*j'ai fait **bien des** erreurs au cours de ma vie* (N3)
*j'ai fait **beaucoup d'**erreurs au cours de ma vie*
I have made many mistakes in the course of my life

24.2 *Tant* and *autant*

Tant is used in expressions emphasising quantity, when no comparison is implied; ***autant*** is used when a comparison is stated or implied:

*il a **tant de** jouets qu'il ne sait pas jouer*	he has so many toys that he doesn't know how to play
*il n'a pas **autant de** jouets **que** son cousin*	he hasn't as many toys as his cousin
*elle a **tant** pleuré, ce soir-là!*	she cried such a lot that evening!
*elle n'avait jamais ri **autant***	she'd never laughed as much before
*des possibilités? mais il y en a **tant**!*	openings? there are scores of them!
*il n'était pas rassuré pour **autant***	(despite this,) he still wasn't reassured

Pas de: for articles in negative expressions, **see 22.4**.

Exercice 24/2   ***Tant* ou *autant*?**   Travail individuel

Complétez les phrases ci-dessous en ajoutant *tant* ou *autant*, selon le sens.

Exemple: J'ai _ de choses à te dire!
Réponse: J'ai **tant** de choses à te dire!

Exemple: Des ennuis? J'en ai _ qu'elle.
Réponse: Des ennuis? J'en ai **autant** qu'elle.

1   On a eu beaucoup de neige l'hiver dernier, mais pas _ cet hiver.
2   Il avait _ travaillé qu'il était épuisé.
3   Vivre sur la Côte? J'en ai _ rêvé!
4   Je le regrette _ que toi.
5   Autrefois il buvait trop, mais maintenant il ne boit plus _.
6   Ils ont _ ri qu'ils en avaient mal aux côtes.
7   J'ai vu _ de micro-ordinateurs que je m'y perds.
8   L'avalanche est passée loin d'eux, mais ils n'étaient pas hors de danger pour _.

24.3 *La plupart*

This quantifier is used only with a plural noun, and only with *de + les* (= *des*), demonstrative adjective (*ces*) or possessive adjective (*ses, leurs* etc.). There is no way of distinguishing between 'most' + noun and 'most of the' + noun in French:

*la plupart **des** innovations*	most (of the) innovations
*la plupart **de ces** innovations*	most of these/those innovations
*la plupart **de leurs** innovations*	most of their innovations

La majorité

One can also use *la majorité* in the same way as *la plupart*, and with a similar meaning.

La plus grande partie, la majeure partie

These are the equivalents in French of 'most of' + singular noun:

la plus grande partie de la vieille ville a été restaurée

most of the old town has been restored

la majeure partie de la récolte a été détruite

most of the crop was destroyed

There is one fixed phrase where *la plupart* is used with a singular noun:

la plupart du temps	most of the time

Exercice 24/3   *La plupart* ou *la plus grande partie*?   Travail individuel

Complétez les phrases ci-dessous en ajoutant *la plupart* ou *la plus grande partie*, selon qu'il s'agit d'un nom au pluriel ou au singulier.

Exemple: _ de l'hiver
Réponse: la plus grande partie de l'hiver

Exemple: _ des habitants
Réponse: la plupart des habitants

1   _ de ses réponses étaient incompréhensibles.
2   _ de l'inscription était indéchiffrable.
3   Il a perdu _ de sa collection de disques dans l'incendie.
4   J'ai lu _ de ses livres maintenant.
5   Quelques spectateurs sont partis, mais _ sont restés.
6   _ de l'année, il habite au bord de la mer.

French
Grammar
Explained

25 Numerical quantity

25.1 **Numbers**
25.2 **Approximate numbers**
25.3 **Percentages, fractions, proportions**
25.4 **Rank, order**

25.1 Numbers

English and French use the same system for counting; some differences of detail, which you need to study and practise, are set out below. These include numbers from 60–99, very large numbers, and approximate numbers.

Spoken and written forms

One of the most difficult aspects of a foreign language to master is to make clear associations between the various ways in which a number is represented in speech, writing and printing.

Here are some activities in which you might need to convert numbers between English and French, and between spoken and written forms:

- saying in French a telephone or other number which you have in front of you, in written or printed figures;
- writing down in figures a number which is being said to you in French;
- repeating aloud in French a number which you have just heard, to confirm that you have written it down correctly.

Numbers from 60–99

In France and Quebec, a counting system based on units of 20 is used for numbers from 60–99:

70	*soixante-dix*		80	*quatre-vingts*
71	*soixante et onze*		81	*quatre-vingt-un*
72	*soixante-douze*		90	*quatre-vingt-dix*
79	*soixante-dix-neuf*		91	*quatre-vingt-onze*

In Belgium and Switzerland a system based on units of 10 is used, as in English:

70   *septante*

80   *octante* or *huitante*

90   *nonante*

Telephone numbers

Telephone numbers in France are spoken or printed in groups of two figures:

02 47 86 00 79

(zéro deux, quarante-sept, quatre-vingt-six, zéro zéro, soixante-dix-neuf)

This is one reason why you need to master numbers in French from 60–99: hearing the above set of figures, you might be tempted to note down 60 19 at the end, instead of 79 – only the absence of a pause makes the difference!

A specific source of confusion is the pair *24* and *80 (vingt-quatre* and *quatre-vingts).*

Exercice 25/1   **Les chiffres, à l'oral et à l'écrit**   Travail à deux

Lisez à haute voix, à un(e) partenaire, un des numéros de téléphone ci–dessous; votre partenaire doit écrire chaque numéro en chiffres arabes: 02 76, etc.; vous pouvez répéter le numéro si votre partenaire vous le demande.

1   01 36 16 83 60

2   01 44 24 70 90

3   02 30 80 18 99

4   03 45 24 80 10

5   04 57 13 91 50

6   05 27 76 00 39

Numbers from 100–999

These are relatively straightforward, but note:

101	*cent un*	(English: 'a hundred and one')
200	*deux cents* (*-s* at end of exact hundreds, including when followed by a noun:	
	deux cents personnes: 'two hundred people')	
210	*deux cent dix* (no *-s* at end of *cent* if followed by other figures)	

Numbers above 1000

1000	*mille*	(English: a thousand')
20 000	*vingt mille*	(*mille* is invariable in all numbers)
300 000	*trois cent mille*	

French
Grammar
Explained

Dates

When saying dates up to 1999, it is important to include the word *cent*:

	in 1789	*en dix-sept **cent** quatre-vingt neuf*
	in about 1890	*vers dix-neuf **cent** quatre-vingt dix*
	the sixties, the 60s	*les années 1960 (les années dix-neuf **cent** soixante)*
or		*les années 60 (les années soixante)*
	(the year) 2000	*l'an deux mille*
	in 2003	*en deux mille trois*

Numbers above 1 000 000

1 000 000	*un million* (as in English)
10 000 000	*dix millions*
	(*-s* at end of *millions*, for all numbers of 2 000 000 and over)
20 000 000$	*20 millions de dollars*
	(*de*, always, between *million(s)* and a noun)
1 000 000 000	*un milliard*
3 000 000 000F	*trois milliards de francs*

Un milliard is similar in pronunciation to ***un millier*** ('about a thousand': **see 25.2**); make sure you can distinguish between the two: there's a lot at stake!

25.2 Approximate numbers

The following approximate numbers are in use in French; they are constructed with *de* before a following noun:

Singular		**Plural**	
une dizaine	about ten	*des dizaines*	dozens

(*dizaine(s)* corresponds to the use of 'dozen' as an approximate number in English: *il y en avait des dizaines*: 'there were dozens of them')

une douzaine	a dozen	*trois douzaines*	three dozen

(*douzaine(s)* is used as an approximate number, and as an exact number, in French)

une quinzaine	about a fortnight	–

(also *huit jours*: 'a week'; *quinze jours*: 'a fortnight')

une vingtaine	about twenty	–

(*un homme d'une vingtaine d'années*: 'a man of about twenty')

une trentaine	about thirty	–
une quarantaine	about forty	–
une cinquantaine	about fifty	–
une soixantaine	about sixty	–

(all four of these can also be used, with the definite article *la*, to refer to someone's age: *il approche de la cinquantaine*: 'he's nearly fifty')

une centaine	about a hundred	*des centaines*	hundreds

(*des centaines de personnes*: 'hundreds of people')

un millier	about a thousand	*des milliers*	thousands
		des millions	millions
		des milliards	billions

One can also use *quelques* ('a few') or *plusieurs* ('several') instead of *des* with the plural forms listed above:

quelques centaines (de)	a few hundred(s of)
plusieurs milliers (de)	several thousand(s of)

Approximate numbers can also be indicated by the use of *près de* ('nearly') or *autour de* ('around') before the number, or *à peu près* ('about', 'roughly') either before or after the number:

il y avait **près de** 50 000 spectateurs: le stade était plein à craquer

there were getting on for/just about 50 000 spectators: the ground was packed

on a fait 500 kilomètres **à peu près**

we've done about 500 kilometres

Exercice 25/2   **Chiffres approximatifs**   Travail individuel

Complétez les phrases ci-dessous en ajoutant un chiffre approximatif, au singulier ou au pluriel, selon le cas.

Exemple: C'était un jeune homme d' _ d'années.
Réponse possible: C'était un jeune homme d'**une vingtaine** d'années.

Exemple: C'est une entreprise gigantesque, avec un chiffre d'affaires de _ de dollars.
Réponse possible: C'est une entreprise gigantesque, avec un chiffre d'affaires de **plusieurs milliards** de dollars.

1   J'ai déjà essayé son numéro _ de fois.
2   Elle a hérité d'une grosse somme: _ de francs, je crois.
3   Elle adore les huîtres: hier soir, elle en a mangé trois _ !
4   La classe était trop nombreuse: près d' _ d'élèves.
5   Quelle ambiance! deux équipes au meilleur de leur forme, et _ de _ de spectateurs au stade.
6   Ils ont reçu _ d'appels, mais pas plus d' _ en tout.

25.3 Percentages, fractions, proportions

Percentages

'Per cent' is a Latin expression meaning 'for (each) hundred'; the French equivalent is two French words, **pour cent**. 'A percentage' is *un pourcentage* (one word). The same symbol, %, is used in both English and French.

A percentage followed by a singular noun is normally used with a singular verb, and one followed by a plural noun with a plural verb:

> *10% de la population active **est** au chômage*
> 10% of the working population is unemployed
> *60% des femmes entre 16 et 60 ans **travaillent***
> 60% of women aged between 16 and 60 have a job

or *60% de la population féminine entre 16 et 60 ans exerce une activité professionnelle* (N4)

Fractions

The following words are used for fractions. They are normally used with the definite article, unless otherwise shown:

la moitié	half, a half, one half
le tiers, un tiers	a third, one third
les deux tiers	two thirds
le quart, un quart	a quarter
les trois quarts	three quarters
le cinquième, un cinquième (etc.)	a fifth
les deux cinquièmes (etc.)	two fifths

Fractions are also used in adjective phrases beginning with *à*:

à moitié fini	half finished
à moitié prix	(for, at) half price
***aux** trois quarts vide*	three quarters empty

For numerical intensification of comparisons, **see 31.4**.

Proportions

The French equivalent of 'out of' (or 'in') is **sur** (see 27.2):

*un Français **sur** deux*	one out of two French people
*neuf fois **sur** dix*	nine times out of ten

Exercice 25/3   **Fractions**   Travail individuel

Dans les phrases ci-dessous, récrivez les fractions en toutes lettres:

1   Courage! on a déjà fait ($\frac{1}{2}$) du chemin.
2   Ils dépensent ($\frac{2}{3}$) de leur revenu pour s'alimenter.
3   Ces histoires laissent ($\frac{9}{10}$) des électeurs indifférents.
4   La banque a déjà épuisé ($\frac{3}{4}$) de ses réserves.
5   Dans certaines villes, ($\frac{1}{3}$) de la population vit au-dessous du seuil de pauvreté.
6   Profitez de nos soldes: ($\frac{1}{2}$) des articles ($\frac{1}{2}$) prix!

25.4 Rank, order

Premier, *dernier* and *seul* are placed **before** the noun, in everyday speech and writing:

le premier café de la journée   the first (cup of) coffee of the day
le dernier métro   the last underground train (at night)
le seul ennui, c'est que . . .   the only problem is that . . .

Numbers are normally placed before *premier* or *dernier*:

*les **deux** dernières années*   the last two years
*les **cinq** premières places*   the first five seats

Dernier is placed after days, weeks, months and years:

samedi dernier   last Saturday
l'année dernière   last year

Exercice 25/4   *Premier, dernier, seul*   Travail individuel

Ajoutez *premier*, *dernier*, *seul* aux phrases ci-dessous, selon le sens et à la place qui convient, et en faisant l'accord s'il le faut.

Exemple: ces deux années
Réponse: ces deux **dernières** années

1   Ils ont couru pour attraper le bus.
2   Les survivants étaient une femme et son enfant.
3   J'ai vu son nouveau film la semaine.
4   Les sprinters américains ont pris les trois places.
5   Interdire la publicité pour le tabac, c'est la politique raisonnable.
6   A la fin de la cérémonie, on a baissé le drapeau britannique pour la fois.

Second and ***deuxième***: *second* is associated with the idea 'and not first', and *deuxième* with a series of three or more items, but in practice they are interchangeable:

le second étage **or** *le deuxième étage*	the second floor
il est arrivé second **or** *deuxième*	he came in second

Troisième and ***tiers***: *troisième* is used, except in certain specific cases:

le Tiers État	the Third Estate
le Tiers Monde	the Third World

In French secondary schools, classes are numbered from *la sixième* (11–12 year olds) up to *la première* and *la terminale* (the last two years before *le bac*). Expressions used include:

*redoubler **la** sixième*	to repeat (stay down in) the first year
*passer/entrer **en** seconde*	to move up to the fifth year
*des élèves **de** terminale*	final year lycée students

In dates, the word *premier* (written *1ᵉʳ*) is used for the first day of the month, but numerals are used for the rest:

le 1ᵉʳ mars	the first of March
le 31 décembre	the thirty-first of December

With a superlative **(see 31.2)**, rank order is indicated as follows:

la 3ᵉ plus grande ville de France	the third largest city in France

26 Adjectives: position of the epithet adjective

26.1 *Grand, petit, beau, joli, jeune, vieux*
26.2 **Adjectives with different meanings**
26.3 **Use of adjectives for emphasis; two or more adjectives**

IN ENGLISH, an epithet adjective is placed before the noun. IN FRENCH, the usual position for an epithet adjective is after the noun:

la **Mer noire**	the Black Sea
la **forêt amazonienne**	the Amazonian forest
il écrit des **romans noirs**	he writes macabre novels

As a general rule, you should place an epithet adjective after the noun in French, unless you have reason to do otherwise.

In this position, an adjective can be separated by a pause, or the punctuation, from the rest of a statement:

il écrit **des romans. Noirs** (journalistic style)
he writes novels. Macabre ones
ses romans, noirs, sont lus dans le monde entier
his novels – which are macabre – are read all over the world

WHEN TO PLACE AN ADJECTIVE BEFORE THE NOUN

The main reasons for placing an adjective before the noun in French are:

● if the adjectives *grand, petit, beau, joli, jeune* or *vieux* are used without any particular emphasis, or if the adjective is obviously or traditionally associated with the noun (**see 26.1**);
● if the adjective is one which has different meanings, depending on whether it is placed before or after the noun (**see 26.2**);
● if the adjective is being used with particular emphasis, or if the presence of two or more epithet adjectives, or adjective phrases, makes it preferable to place one of them before the noun (**see 26.3**).

Sometimes two or more of these reasons can combine to determine the position of the adjective; in other cases, two reasons may conflict, and you (and French speakers) have to make a choice!

26.1 *Grand, petit, beau, joli, jeune* and *vieux*

Before the noun	After the noun
*salut, **jeune homme**!* (N2)	*soudain, il a vu une femme **jeune et jolie***
hello, young man!	*qui sortait du restaurant*
*c'est une **jolie robe**, ça!*	suddenly, he saw a young and pretty woman
that's a pretty dress!	leave the restaurant
*c'était un **bel homme**,*	*on ne peut pas dire de lui que c'est un homme*
tout de même!	***beau ou distingué***
he was a handsome man,	you can't say of him that he's a handsome or
though!	distinguished man
*lui, c'était un **grand homme**!*	*c'était une femme **grande et mince***
<u>he</u> was a great man!	she was a tall, slim woman

For word order with two or more adjectives, **see 26.3**.

Placed before the noun, the adjective forms part of a conventional phrase, made up of adjective + noun; placed after the noun, the adjective adds new information. In the case of *grand*, even the meaning is different.

Other adjectives can be placed before the noun if the association with the noun is traditional, conventional or obvious:

    *une **longue tradition***   a long tradition

(*longue* reinforces the idea contained in *tradition*; compare: *une tradition **récente**:* a recent tradition)

but: *les cheveux **longs***   long hair
        *les cheveux **courts***   short hair

Exercice 26/1   *Grand, petit* etc.   Travail à deux > Mise en commun

a   Avec un(e) partenaire, décidez quelle est la bonne position (avant ou après le nom souligné) de l'adjectif indiqué après chacune des phrases ci-dessous.

b   Ensuite, discutez vos choix avec le reste du groupe.

1	Attends une <u>seconde</u>!	(petit)
2	Là, on est dans le <u>Tours</u>.	(vieux)
3	C'était un <u>homme</u>, d'une trentaine d'années.	(jeune)
4	Pour accompagner ce plat, il faut un <u>vin</u>.	(vieux)
5	On lui a offert un <u>cadeau</u>.	(beau)
6	Elle avait grandi bien vite: c'était une <u>femme</u> déjà.	(jeune)
7	C'était un <u>homme</u>, mais gros.	(petit)
8	Tous leurs <u>mannequins</u> sont des <u>femmes</u>.	(jeune, beau)
9	C'était un <u>soulagement</u> pour lui d'avoir fini son livre.	(grand)

26.2 Adjectives with different meanings

Several adjectives, including *ancien*, *certain*, *cher*, *dernier*, *même*, *nouveau*, *pauvre*, *seul*, *simple* and *vrai* have different meanings, depending on whether they are placed before or after the noun.

In general, the meaning of these adjectives is conventional or intensive when placed before the noun, and literal or factual when placed after the noun:

Before the noun	After the noun
*le collège est installé dans un **ancien couvent*** the school occupies a former convent	*ils ont découvert des pièces de monnaie* ***anciennes*** they've discovered some old coins
*vous vous trompez, (mon) **cher ami**!* you're mistaken, dear friend!	*au théâtre, ils prenaient toujours les places **les plus chères*** at the theatre, they always booked the most expensive seats
*tu as lu son **dernier livre**?* have you read his latest book?	*j'ai vu ce film l'année **dernière*** I saw this/that/the film last year
*comment s'appelle leur **nouveau chien**?* what's their new dog called?	*ce qu'il nous faut maintenant, c'est des idées **nouvelles*** what we need now is fresh ideas
*il était le **seul survivant** du désastre* he was the sole survivor of the disaster	*il cherchait à escroquer les femmes **seules*** he tried to swindle women (living) on their own
*c'est une **simple formalité*** it's just a formality	*les fractures **simples** sont plus faciles à soigner que les fractures multiples* simple fractures are easier to treat than multiple fractures
*c'était un **vrai mystère*** it really was a mystery	*c'est une histoire **vraie*** it's a true story

---

Exercice 26/2   **Adjectifs: sens et position**   Travail à deux > Mise en commun

a   Avec un(e) partenaire, décidez quelle est la bonne position (avant ou après le nom souligné) de l'adjectif indiqué après chacune des phrases suivantes.

b   Ensuite, discutez vos choix avec le reste du groupe.

1   Il lui faut un <u>temps</u> pour comprendre.   (certain)
2   Tu sais, il y a des riches dans les <u>pays</u>.   (pauvres)
3   Mais tu te trompes, mon <u>ami</u>!   (pauvre)
4   Ce n'est pas un quartier idéal pour les <u>personnes</u>.   (seules)
5   Sans notre intervention, il se trouvait devant une <u>mort</u>. (certaine)
6   Elle dit toujours la <u>chose</u>.   (même)
7   C'est la <u>personne</u> à qui j'ai parlé aujourd'hui.   (seule)
8   C'était la <u>raison</u> de son départ.   (même)

26.3 Use of adjectives for emphasis; two or more adjectives

An adjective can be placed before the noun in order to emphasise or exaggerate its meaning; this can form a cliché:

l'immense Sibérie   the vast expanse of Siberia

(an obvious cliché; compare: *on a découvert un lac immense*: we discovered a vast lake – one did not expect the lake to be so large)

un charmant Italien   a charming Italian

(another cliché; compare: *un Allemand charmant*: a charming German)

un interminable cauchemar   an endless nightmare

(newspaper headline: a striking phrase, exaggeration; almost a cliché; compare:
30 ans d'un cauchemar interminable: 30 years' endless nightmare – headline for an interview on the same subject: the mention of a precise number restores the adjective to its 'informative' role)

ces shakespeariennes retrouvailles   this Shakespearean reunion

(in a magazine item on Saddam Hussein's eldest son welcoming Saddam's two sons-in-law at the frontier with Jordan: exaggeration used for ironic effect)

If there are two or more epithet adjectives, or if there is an adjective phrase (preposition + noun) qualifying the noun, it may be convenient to place an adjective before the noun, especially if it is qualitative, conventional or intensive:

une importante opération policière   a major police operation
un ingénieux système de refroidissement   an ingenious cooling system
l'heureux vainqueur des élections   the happy election winner

If two adjectives are both being used in a factual, descriptive way, they are placed after the noun:

> *c'était un homme **tranquille et discret***   he was a quiet, tactful man

Word order in compound nouns taken from English

In some compound nouns taken directly from English, the order adjective + noun is retained in French:

> *une standing ovation*   a standing ovation
> *un libre service* (originally un self-service)   a self-service (store)
> (but: *entrée libre*: come in and look round the shop)

In other cases, the English order is reversed:

> *un disque compact*   a compact disc
> (but the abbreviation used in French, *un CD*, reflects the English word order)

Nouns used as adjectives

A noun used as an adjective **(see 17.3c)** is placed after the noun it qualifies:

> *un homme grenouille*   a frogman
> *un coin pique-nique*   a picnic spot

Adjective phrases consisting of preposition + noun **(see 41.2)** are also placed after the noun:

> *un homme d'acier*   a man of steel
> *un port de pêche*   a fishing port

For adjective phrases consisting of preposition + infinitive, **see 41.1**.

Part
SIX

Building phrases

A **phrase** is a group of words which can be used on its own to make a meaningful statement, without the need for a tensed verb.

A phrase can contain:

- a preposition + a noun;   **(see 27–30)**
- a comparative or superlative adjective or adverb.   **(see 31)**

A phrase can also form part of a sentence **(see 32)**, or it can be added to a sentence **(see 43–44)**.

Prepositions and **adverbs** figure prominently in the next four sections **(27–30)**: before studying these, go back to **17** and study the grammatical function of prepositions and adverbs.

Prepositions are used with nouns to form adverb phrases **(see 30)** which are grammatically complete, and can be used to make a wide range of meaningful statements, especially in the course of a conversation:

> *Où vas-tu cette semaine? A Bruxelles*
> Where are you going this week? To Brussels
> *A quelle heure est-ce que le train part? A six heures*
> What time does the train leave? At six
> *Comment a-t-il marqué le but? Avec sa tête*
> How did he score the goal? With his head

These phrases are not sentences; a sentence normally contains a tensed verb **(see 32.1)**. However, a phrase containing a preposition + noun is one of the building blocks from which sentences are constructed. When a preposition is used between two nouns **(see 41.2)**, between a verb and a noun **(see 38.1)**, or with an infinitive **(see 38–40 and 41.1)**, it functions as a link between two parts of a sentence.

Words used as both prepositions and adverbs

Several prepositions, in English and French, can function either as a preposition (followed by a noun) or as an adverb (used on its own), in the same way that several verbs, in English and French, can be used transitively (with an object: noun or pronoun) or intransitively (without an object).

Compare the intransitive and transitive uses of the preposition 'up' and the verb 'climb', in English:

	Intransitive use	Transitive use
Preposition	up	up the stairs
Verb	to climb	to climb the stairs

Or, in French, the preposition *après* and the verb *suivre*:

	Intransitive use	Transitive use
Preposition	*après*	*après le guide*
	afterwards	after the guide
Verb	*suivre*	*suivre le guide*
	to follow (on)	to follow the guide

For words such as *avant* ('before') and *après* ('after'), which can function either as prepositions or as adverbs, see the table in **27.1**.

Some compound prepositions **(see 28)** consist of an adverb and a preposition, usually *de*:

Adverb	*près*	close by	**Preposition**	*près de*	near to
	à côté	next door		*à côté de*	next to

In Part Six, the following are examined:
27 **Single word prepositions**
28 **Compound prepositions**
29 **The prepositions *à, de, en***
30 **Adverbs and adverb phrases**
31 **Making comparisons**

27 Single word prepositions

27.1 Table of single word prepositions
27.2 Notes on single word prepositions

A **preposition** is a word or group of words used with a noun, pronoun or infinitive to situate it in time or space, or in any other relation with another noun, phrase, verb or sentence. A preposition plays a vital role in the communication of meaning in French, as it does in English. French is sometimes portrayed as a language in which verbs play the vital role in animating the sentence, as opposed to English, where this function is performed above all by prepositions (used as adverbs). There is some truth in this contrast:

French: verb	English: preposition
Vive les rouges!	*Up the reds!*
Qu'on l'**exécute**!/Qu'on lui **tranche** la tête!	*Off with his head!*

IN ENGLISH, a key role is played, not only by prepositions, but also by postpositions: little words which are used with verbs to provide (for the learner of English) a bewildering array of combinations. With the verb 'get', for example:

get on/out/in/away/into/up/down/over/under
get up to/away with/out of/over with/along with

IN FRENCH, a small number of prepositions play many and varied roles: as well as *à*, *de* and *en*, which are so widely used as to be almost invisible, *dans*, *pour* and *sur* are used in a wide variety of contexts. In this section, some of the main meanings and uses of a number of prepositions are illustrated.

For uses of prepositions, see also:

- **Adverb phrases** (*à*, *de*, *en* + noun): (30.2)
- **Verb** + preposition + noun or infinitive: (38)
- **Adjective** + preposition + noun or infinitive: (40)
- **Noun** + preposition + noun or infinitive: (41)
- **Adverb** + preposition + infinitive: (43.3)
- Adverb phrases used as **detached complements**; *en* + present participle (gerund) (44.2)

■ **Table of adverbs, single word prepositions, and conjunctions**
   (for *à*, *de* and *en*, see 29)

Adverb	Preposition	Preposition	Conjunction
used on its own	used with a noun	used with an infinitive **(see 43.3)**	used with *que* + indicative (I) or subjunctive (S) **(see 46–49)**
après afterwards	*après* after	*après* (+ *avoir/être*) after -ing	*après que* + I/S after he + verb
avant beforehand	*avant* before	*avant de* before -ing	*avant que* + S before he + verb
avec (N1) with it	*avec* with	–	–
–	*chez* at/to the house of	–	–
–	*contre* (up) against	–	–
dedans inside	*dans* in, into	–	–
depuis since then	*depuis* since	–	*depuis que* + I since he + verb
derrière behind it	*derrière* behind	–	–
–	*dès* right from	–	*dès que* + I as soon as he+verb
devant in front of it	*devant* in front of	–	–
–	*durant* (after noun) for (time)	–	–
–	*entre* between	–	–
–	*envers* towards (attitude, behaviour)	–	–
–	*jusqu'à* until, as far as	*jusqu'à* (N3) to the point of -ing	*jusqu'à ce que* + S until he + verb
–	*malgré* despite, in spite of	–	–

	par by, through	*(commencer/finir) par* by	*parce que* + I because he + verb
–	*parmi* among	–	–
cependant yet, however	*pendant* during	–	*pendant que* + I while he + verb
pour (N2) for it, in favour	*pour* for	*pour* to, in order to	*pour que* + S so that he + verb
puis then, next	–	–	*puisque* + I since he + verb
sans (N1) without it	*sans* without	*sans* without -ing	*sans que* + S without him -ing
–	*sauf* except for, save	*sauf à* (N3) unless he + verb	*sauf que* + I except that he + verb
dessous underneath (it)	*sous* below, beneath	–	–
dessus on top (of it)	*sur* on, about, in the region of, out of (etc.)	–	–
–	*vers* towards (movement)	–	–

Exercice 27/1   **Prépositions simples**   Travail individuel > Mise en commun

a   Complétez les phrases ci-dessous en ajoutant une préposition.

b   Après avoir vérifié vos réponses, écrivez l'équivalent en anglais de ces phrases, et discutez-en avec le reste du groupe.

Exemple: Son attitude _ lui est ambigüe.
Réponse: Son attitude **envers** lui est ambigüe.

1   Tiens! il y a une voiture arrêtée _ leur maison.
2   C'est abominable! Il faut l'arrêter _ tous les moyens.
3   Il n'y a plus de pain: ce soir, en rentrant, on passera _ le boulanger.
4   Dépêche-toi! Le train part _ deux minutes.
5   Il doit y avoir quelqu'un _ nous qui sait où elle se trouve.
6   Pour faire plus de place, on a repoussé le canapé _ le mur.
7   _ nos cris, l'enfant a continué de courir _ la rivière.
8   _ la circulation des départs en vacances, je ne serai pas rentré _ huit heures ce soir.

27.2 Notes on single word prepositions (for *à*, *de* and *en*, see 29)

Après 'after'

> *après avoir/être* + past participle: **see 44.3**
> *après que* + indicative or subjunctive: **see 46** and **48**

Avant 'before'

> *avant de* + infinitive: **see 43.3**
> *avant que* + subjunctive: **see 48**

Used as a preposition, *avant* refers to position in time, not in space (compare *devant*):

> *je suis sûr que vous arriverez **avant nous***
> I'm sure you'll get there before we do

Used as a noun, or as a prefix **(see 13)**, *avant* can refer to position in space; in these cases, it is opposed to *arrière*:

> *tout **l'avant**/tout **l'arrière** de la voiture était enfoncé*
> the whole of the front/the whole of the back of the car was crushed
> *il joue **avant** centre/**arrière** droit*
> he plays (in the) centre-forward/right back (position)

Avant is frequently used as an adverb:

> *j'ai un rendez-vous à deux heures, mais je peux te voir **avant***
> I've got an appointment at two, but I can see you before then
> ***avant**, il était toujours gai, mais maintenant il ne sourit jamais*
> before (then), he was always cheerful, but now he never smiles

Avec 'with'

Avec is used in many cases which correspond to English 'with', including descriptions of physical appearance:

> *le voilà **avec** son sourire éternel*
> there he is, with his permanent smile
> *il faut toujours accueillir les clients **avec** le sourire*
> you/one must always welcome/greet guests with a smile

But when English 'with' introduces a detached complement such as 'with a smile on his lips, he . . .', a preposition is not used in French **(see 43.2)**.

Avec can be used, in very informal situations (N1), as an adverb, generally to avoid using *avec lui*, *avec elle* to refer to an inanimate object:

> *il a pris le sac et il est parti **avec***   (N1)
> he took the bag and made off with it

Note: the equivalent in French of 'with no' is *sans*, not *avec* (see below).

Chez 'at/in/to the house of'

Chez is mainly used with this specific meaning:

> *ça fait longtemps qu'on n'est pas allés chez eux* (N2)
> it's been a long time since we went to their house
> *on est passés chez des amis*
> we dropped in on some friends
> *on est descendus chez des amis*
> we stayed with some friends

But *dans*, not *chez* is used in sentences such as:

> *elle a passé trois semaines dans une famille lyonnaise*
> she spent three weeks with a family in Lyon

Chez can also refer to a place of work:

aller chez le coiffeur	to go to the hairdresser's
passer chez le boucher	to go to the butcher's
travailler chez Renault	to work at the Renault factory/for Renault

Dans 'in', 'into'

Dans is mainly used when referring to place:

> *les voleurs ont pris tout ce qu'il y avait dans le coffre*
> the thieves took everything that was in the safe
> *on se demande comment ils avaient réussi à pénétrer dans la maison*
> one wonders how they managed to get into the house

Dans is used with the meaning 'in the centre of' (a city):

> *je n'aimerais pas vivre dans Paris même*
> I wouldn't like to live right in the centre of Paris (see also *sur*, below)

However, with a verb such as *prendre*, *dans* (or *sur*, etc., according to the position of the thing taken) is used, whereas in English the verb construction is 'take from', 'take out of', etc.:

> *prends un vase dans le placard/sur la table*
> take a vase out of/from the cupboard/from (off) the table

Dans is not used as an adverb: *dedans* is used instead:

> *le bébé a renversé la boîte mais il n'y avait rien dedans*
> the baby knocked the tin over, but there was nothing in it

With expressions of time, *dans* is used with the meaning of 'at the end of', 'in (three minutes') time':

> *dépêche-toi! notre car part dans trois minutes!*
> get a move on! our coach leaves in three minutes!

This contrasts with the use of *en*, which, used with expressions of time, means 'within the space of':

> *c'est le genre de réparation qu'on peut faire **en** trois minutes*
> it's the kind of repair you can do (with)in three minutes

Depuis   'since', 'ever since'

> *depuis que* + indicative: **see 46**
>
> *depuis* + present or imperfect tense (continuing process): **see 54.2**

Depuis is used to emphasise the whole period from the start of a process until the present (or a point in the past): compare this with *dès* below:

> *je n'ai rien fait **depuis** le début des vacances*
> I've done nothing since the beginning of the holidays
> ***depuis** son accident, il n'est plus le même*
> (ever) since his accident, he's not been the same

Depuis is most often used to refer to a situation in time, but its meaning can be extended to refer to place in a series or sequence, generally in conjunction with *jusqu'à*:

> ***depuis** le patron **jusqu'au** concierge, tous sont concernés par cette nouvelle*
> everyone, from the boss (right) down to the caretaker, is concerned by this news

Depuis can also be used as an adverb:

> *elle a publié un roman il y a cinq ans, mais rien **depuis***
> she published a novel five years ago, but nothing since then

Dès   'from', 'right from', 'at the start of'

> *dès que* + indicative: **see 46**

Dès is used to emphasise the start of a period of time, rather than a whole period up to the present (or a point in the past): compare this with *depuis* above:

> ***dès** son arrivée sur scène, le public l'a acclamé*
> from the moment he stepped onto the stage, the audience cheered/applauded him
> ***dès** le début du XXᵉ siècle, les femmes en Angleterre réclamaient le droit de voter*
> right from the beginning of the 20th century, women in England demanded the right to vote
> *ce matin-là, elle était levée **dès** six heures*
> that morning, she was up by six

Exercice 27/2   *Depuis* **or** *dès*?   Travail individuel

Complétez les phrases ci-dessous en ajoutant depuis ou dès, selon le sens.

Exemple: Cette voiture est garée là _ ce matin.
Réponse: Cette voiture est garée là **depuis** ce matin.

Exemple: Ce matin, j'étais levé _ six heures.
Réponse: Ce matin, j'étais levé **dès** six heures.

1   Chacun s'est senti concerné, _ le patron jusqu'au concierge.
2   _ le début de la saison, ils n'ont perdu qu'un seul match.
3   Leur meilleur buteur a été blessé _ le début du match.
4   _ sa première réplique, elle s'est imposée dans ce rôle.
5   J'ai faim: je n'ai rien mangé _ ce matin.
6   _ son arrivée, elle a transformé petit à petit toute l'organisation.

Devant   'in front of', 'outside'

Used as a preposition or as an adverb (see below), *devant* refers to position in space:

> *soudain, j'ai vu un camion **devant** moi*
> suddenly I saw a lorry in front of me

This spatial meaning is sometimes conveyed in English by the preposition 'before':

> *le match a été joué **devant** 50 000 spectateurs*
> the match was played before a crowd of 50 000

Devant can be used as an adverb:

> *elle était pressée, donc je l'ai laissée passer **devant***
> she was in a hurry, so I let her go first
> ***devant**, leur jardin n'est pas très grand*
> in the front, their garden's not very large

Entre   'between'

Entre is normally used, as is English 'between', when only two persons or things are mentioned (compare *parmi*):

> *leur maison est située **entre** deux vieilles granges*
> their house is between two old barns
> *cette information doit rester strictement **entre** nous*
> this piece of information must be kept strictly between ourselves

D'entre is used when one person or item is singled out from a group, in constructions such as:

> *il y avait un **d'entre** eux qui ne disait pas la vérité: mais lequel?*
> one of them wasn't telling the truth: but which one?

Jusqu'à   'until'

jusqu'à ce que + subjunctive: see 48

Jusqu'à can be used to refer to time or place:

> *ils ont dormi **jusqu'à** l'aube*
> they slept until dawn
> *elle a avancé **jusqu'à** la porte*
> she went up to/as far as the door

Pas avant is used, not *pas jusqu'à*, when the meaning is 'not until':

> *ils ne se sont **pas** endormis **avant** l'aube*
> they didn't get to sleep until dawn

Jusqu'à is a preposition, not a conjunction: the only direct equivalent of English 'until', used as a conjunction, is *jusqu'à ce que*, followed by a clause with the verb in the subjunctive:

> *continue à marcher **jusqu'à ce que** je te **dise** de t'arrêter*
> carry on walking until I tell you to stop

Jusqu'au moment où can also be used:

> *ils ont joué **jusqu'au moment où** il a commencé à pleuvoir*
> they played until it started to rain

Malgré   'despite', 'in spite of'

The preposition *malgré* offers a useful way of formulating sentences which would otherwise require **bien que** + a subordinate clause with the verb in the subjunctive (**see 48**):

> *malgré le mauvais temps, ils ont passé de bonnes vacances*
> they had a good holiday despite the poor weather/although the weather was bad, they had a good holiday
> *malgré tous leurs efforts, ils n'ont pas pu empêcher la rivière de déborder*
> although they worked hard, they couldn't stop the river overflowing

Par   by', 'by means of'

commencer/finir par + infinitive: see 38.2
Par is used to indicate the means or direction of an action:

> *prendre le taureau **par** les cornes*
> to take the bull by the horns
> *puisque je passais **par** là, je suis allé leur dire bonjour*
> since I was going that way, I dropped in to say hello

Par is used in a number of adverb phrases (**see 30.2**) describing the means, the medium, etc.:

> *ça va beaucoup plus vite **par** télécopie*
> it's much quicker by fax

Par is used in passive constructions (**see 35**) to indicate the agent of the action:

> *le message avait été transmis **par** un employé*
> the message had been passed on by an employee

Parmi 'among'

Parmi is used when a group of three or more (people or things) is described together (compare *entre*, above):

> *cette nouvelle a jeté la consternation **parmi** nous*
> this (piece of) news threw us into confusion
> *c'était une jolie rivière qui serpentait **parmi** les champs*
> it was a pretty river which wound its way among the fields

Pendant 'during', 'for'

> *pendant/pour:* **see 53.3**
> *depuis/pendant:* **see 54.2**
> *pendant que* + indicative: **see 46**

Pour 'for'

> *pendant/pour:* **see 53.3**
> *pour que* + subjunctive: **see 48**

Sans 'without', 'with no'

> *sans* + infinitive: **see 43.3**
> *sans que* + subjunctive: **see 48**

Sans is used in many adverb phrases (**see 30.2**):

> *elle est partie **sans** la moindre intention/**sans** aucune intention de revenir*
> she left without the least intention/with no intention of returning
> (*sans* + negative word: **see 34.5**)

Also: *ils sont **sans doute** arrivés*   they've probably arrived

   *ils sont arrivés, **sans aucun doute***   they've certainly arrived

   (**see also 50.1**)

Also in adjective phrases where the meaning corresponds to English 'with no':

> *sur le parking, il y avait une voiture abandonnée, **sans** roues*
> in the car park, there was an abandoned car, with no wheels

In French, a construction with *avec* and a negative word is not possible here.

Exercice 27/3   *Avec ou sans?*   Travail individuel

Complétez les phrases ci-dessous en ajoutant avec ou sans, selon le sens.

Exemple: La police a commencé l'enquête _ l'espoir de trouver bientôt le coupable.
Réponse: La police a commencé l'enquête **avec** l'espoir de trouver bientôt le coupable.

Exemple: L'avocat, _ beaucoup d'espoir, a posé plusieurs questions à ce témoin difficile.
Réponse: L'avocat, **sans** beaucoup d'espoir, a posé plusieurs questions à ce témoin difficile.

1   Il nous a servis _ le moindre sourire.
2   Ce sera lui le nouveau champion, _ aucun doute.
3   Il nous embête _ toutes ses histoires!
4   _ son intervention auprès des autorités, on attendrait encore la réponse.
5   _ son dynamisme, elle ira loin.
6   L'ouverture de leur nouveau restaurant a été accueillie _ enthousiasme.

Sauf 'except'

> *sauf* and *à part*: see 28.2
> *sauf que* + indicative: see 46

Sous

Sous is used in similar ways to its English equivalents: to indicate spatial and metaphorical position.

Sous is not used as an adverb: *dessous* is used instead:

> *il n'y a rien sur le lit: est-ce que tu as cherché **dessous**?*
> there's nothing on th bed: have you looked underneath?

Sur

Sur is used in a variety of contexts, with a wide range of meaning:

'on'   *Sur* is used when the meaning is 'on top of', 'resting on':

> *le livre est **sur** la table*
> the book is on the table
> *le prisonnier avait les mains **sur** la tête*
> the prisoner had his hands on his head

(For **'above'**, **'over'**   *au-dessus de* is used if no movement is implied, and *par-dessus* if movement is implied.)

'in', 'out of'   *Sur* is used when expressing proportions or fractions (**see 25.3**):

> *une personne **sur** cinq ne gagne pas assez pour vivre*
>
> one in five people do not earn a living wage
>
> *en France, tout est noté **sur** vingt*
>
> in France, everything is marked out of twenty

'about'

> *il avait lu plusieurs livres **sur** la guerre*
>
> he'd read several books about war
>
> *on pouvait écrire **sur** n'importe quel sujet*
>
> we could write about any topic

Sur is used here in preference to *au sujet de*: note, however, the following adverb phrases:

> *c'était **à quel sujet**?*
>
> what was it about?
>
> *il y aurait beaucoup à dire **à ce sujet***
>
> there would be many things to say on this/that matter

And also the use of *à propos de*:

> *je téléphone **à propos de** votre annonce*
>
> I'm phoning about/in connection with your advertisement
>
> (*sur* is not used in such cases)

'for (a distance of)'

> *la route est en mauvais état **sur** plusieurs kilomètres*
>
> the road is in poor condition for several kilometres

'in the area/region of'

> *dans son nouveau poste, elle travaille **sur** Paris*
>
> in her new job, she works in and around Paris
>
> ***sur** Lyon, le prix des maisons n'a pas beaucoup augmenté*
>
> the price of houses in the Lyon region hasn't gone up very much

One could also say *dans la région parisienne* and *dans l'agglomération lyonnaise*: for geographical adjectives, **see 14.6**.

'from'   *Sur* is used with the verb *prendre*, with the meaning 'to take from': see ***dans***, above.

Sur is not used as an adverb: ***dessus*** is used instead (just as *dessous* is used as an adverb, and not *sous*):

> *mets cela dans ta poche et ton mouchoir **dessus**!*
>
> put that in your pipe and smoke it!

Exercice 27/4   *Sur*   Travail à deux > Mise en commun

a   Avec un(e) partenaire, reformulez les phrases ci-dessous, de façon à employer la préposition **sur**.

b   Ensuite, lisez vos phrases au reste du groupe et discutez-en.

Exemple: Elle travaille dans la région parisienne.
Réponse: Elle travaille **sur** Paris.

1   On sait beaucoup de choses à son sujet.
2   Encore un livre où il est question des OVNI.
3   A cause de l'accident, plusieurs kilomètres de l'autoroute sont fermés.
4   Vous avez l'air d'être bien renseigné à ce sujet.
5   Cela les oblige à chercher un logement dans la région parisienne.
6   Pour dix appels à Police-Secours, neuf sont des canulars.

Vers   'towards'; 'about'

Vers is used in expressions of space to refer to 'movement towards':

> *j'ai compris que l'homme venait **vers** moi*
> I realised that the man was coming towards me
> *pour la cathédrale, il faut vous diriger **vers** le centre-ville*
> for the cathedral, you should aim for the city centre

In expressions of time, *vers* means 'about':

> *je ne sais pas à quelle heure on est rentrés: **vers** minuit, peut-être*
> I don't know what time we got home: perhaps about/around midnight

In expressions of space, *environ* is used to mean 'about':

> *le cimetière est à un kilomètre **environ** de l'église*
> the cemetery is about a kilometre (away) from the church

Envers, not *vers*, is used when 'towards' expresses behaviour or attitude, as opposed to physical movement:

> *sa conduite **envers** elle a toujours été irréprochable*
> his behaviour towards her has always been beyond reproach

28 Compound prepositions

28.1 Table of compound prepositions and adverbs
28.2 Notes on compound prepositions

Many adverbs and prepositions consist of more than one word (**see Table below**). The English equivalent of many of these is a single word.

IN FRENCH, using a compound preposition is one way of making up for the wide range of meanings and uses of a small number of one-word prepositions (**see 27.1**). Compound prepositions, which usually have a noun or an adverb at their centre, also enable a more precise meaning to be conveyed, if this is needed.

The table below shows some of the main compound prepositions in French.

■ **Table of compound prepositions and adverbs**

Compound preposition	Adverb phrase (see 30)	
	used alone	**including** *ce/son/quel/tout* **etc.**
à . . . de		
à côté de next to, beside	*à côté* next door *de côté* to one side	*à ses côtés* at his/her side *de ce côté* *de son côté* this way, for his/her part in this direction *de tous côtés* on all sides
à propos de about, concerning *à proximité de* near to, convenient for	*à propos* at the right moment *à proximité* near by	*à ce propos* *à quel propos?* on this subject what about?
au . . . de		
au bord de on the edge/verge of	*à bord* on board	

au cours de during			
au-dessous de below	*au-dessous* below (it)		
au-dessus de above	*au-dessus* above (it)		
à l'extérieur de outside	*à l'extérieur* (on the) outside		
à l'intérieur de inside	*à l'intérieur* inside, within		
au lieu de instead of			
au milieu de in the middle of	*au milieu* in the middle		
au niveau de at . . . level	*(passage) à niveau* level (crossing)	*à ce niveau* at this level	*à tous niveaux* at all levels
au sujet de about, concerning		*à ce sujet* about this/it	*à son sujet* about him/her

en . . . de

en bas de at the bottom of	*en bas* down (stairs)	
en cas de in case of		*en tout cas* in any case
en dehors de apart from, outside	*dehors* outside, outdoors	
en face de opposite	*en face* opposite (it)	
en haut de at the top of	*en haut* at the top, upstairs	

. . . de

auprès de close to	*auprès* nearby	
autour de around, about	*autour* (a)round (it)	
faute de for lack of		
hors de outside		
loin de far from	*au loin* in the distance	

près de near to	*(tout) près* close by *à peu près* approximately	
vis-à-vis de opposite, (feelings) about		
... *à*		
face à faced with, in front of *grâce à* thanks to		
***à* ...**		
à part apart from *à travers* across	*de travers* the wrong way	

Exercice 28/1   **Prépositions composées**   Travail individuel > Mise en commun

a   Complétez les phrases ci-dessous en ajoutant une préposition composée et, s'il le faut, un article.

b   Après avoir vérifié vos réponses, écrivez l'équivalent en anglais de ces phrases, et discutez-en avec le reste du groupe.

Exemple: Il a choisi une place _ président.

Réponses possibles: Il a choisi une place **près du** président.

Il a choisi une place **à côté du** président.

1   N'oubliez pas d'admirer la belle statue _ escalier!

2   La maison est très bien située, _ école primaire.

3   Tiens! je voulais justement te parler _ cette affaire.

4   _ problèmes de notre époque, il est facile de baisser les bras.

5   Les incertitudes financières ont mené son entreprise _ faillite.

6   L'enquête a révélé de sérieuses défaillances _ administration.

7   Personne, _ président de la République, n'a accès à ce dossier.

8   Malgré l'opération policière, le suspect a réussi à passer _ les mailles du filet.

9   _ hiver plutôt doux, les travaux ont été finis avec un mois d'avance.

10   Le projet a dû être abandonné, _ argent.

28.2 Notes on compound prepositions

Au-dessous de **'below'**
Au-dessus de **'above'**
  (Note the *de* in each case.)

These describe a position in space, a hierarchy, etc.:
  *il n'y avait personne **au-dessus de** lui*   there was no one above him

Par-dessous **'under'**
Par-dessus **'over'**
  (Note that there is no *de*.)

These describe movement in space (literally or figuratively):
  *tout cela lui est passé **par-dessus** la tête*   all that went over his/her head

---

Exercice 28/2   *Au-dessous de/au-dessus de; par-dessous/par-dessus; sur/sous*

Travail individuel > Mise en commun

a Complétez les phrases ci-dessous en ajoutant **une** de ces six prépositions, selon le sens.
b Après avoir vérifié vos réponses, discutez-en avec le reste du groupe.

Exemple: – Quel froid! – Oui, au moins dix degrés _ zéro.
Réponse: – Quel froid! – Oui, au moins dix degrés **au-dessous de** zéro.

1 Nous volons à plus d'un mille _ niveau de la mer.
2 Pour sortir du champ, les agneaux ont dû passer _ barrière.
3 Zut! j'ai laissé une casserole _ feu!
4 - Quelle sécheresse! – Oui, depuis cinq ans, la pluviosité est _ moyenne.
5 On va fixer la pendule au mur, _ cette table.
6 Je te conseille de passer _ ton chef et de t'adresser directement au patron.
7 La brigade des stupéfiants était _ ordres du ministère de l'Intérieur.

À part **'apart from', 'except for'**

This compound preposition is not followed by *de*:
  *j'ai tout compris, **à part** le dernier chapitre*
  I understood everything, apart from the last chapter
Sauf and *excepté* can be used with a similar meaning to *à part*.

En dehors de has the meaning 'away from', 'beyond':
  *je suis resté **en dehors de** leurs discussions*   I stayed out of their discussions
  *c'est **en dehors de** ses capacités*   it's beyond his/her capabilities

De la part de 'from', 'on behalf of'

> *dites-leur merci **de ma part***
>
> thank them for me
>
> *– Je voudrais parler à M. Dupont. – C'est **de la part de** qui?*
>
> – I'd like to speak to M. Dupont. – Who shall I say it is?

Près de

Près de describes physical proximity ('close to'); ***auprès de***, on the other hand, refers to emotional or organisational proximity:

> *il faut faire une demande **auprès de** la municipalité*
>
> you have to apply to the council

But one can say:

> *elle resta longtemps **auprès du** feu*
>
> she sat for a long time by the fire   (N3)

A travers 'through', 'across'

(this compound preposition is not followed by *de*)

Vis-à-vis de 'opposite'

(this compound preposition is followed by *de*)

USE OF PAST PARTICIPLES IN COMPOUND PREPOSITIONS

Certain past participles can form a compound preposition + *à* or *de*:

French	English equivalent (literal meaning)	(preposition)
situé à	situated at/in	at/in
doté de	endowed with	with
muni de	fitted with	with
pourvu de	provided with	with
dépourvu de	deprived of	without, with no
privé de	deprived of	without, with no

Examples:

> *une maison **située à** un kilomètre de la mer*
>
> a house half a mile from the sea
>
> *une moto **munie de** tous les derniers gadgets*
>
> a motorbike with all the latest gadgetry
>
> *cet homme est totalement **dépourvu de** scrupules*
>
> that man is completely unscrupulous

29 The prepositions *à, de, en*

29.1 **The preposition *à***
29.2 **The preposition *de***
29.3 **The preposition *en***
29.4 **Names of countries, regions, *départements***

Other sections where these three prepositions are discussed:

- *à* and *de* + noun which is an indirect object (**18.3**)
- *à*, *de* and *en* + noun in adverb phrases (**30.2**)
- verb constructions with nouns (**38.1**) and with infinitives (**38.2**)
- adjective constructions with nouns (**40.1**) and with infinitives (**40.2**)
- adjective phrases with *à* and *de* + infinitive (**41.1**) and + noun (**41.2**)
- *en* + present participle (gerund) (**44.2**)

IN ENGLISH, several prepositions such as 'by', 'for', 'from', 'in', 'of' and 'to' are used with a wide variety of meanings. Nevertheless, speakers of English would probably consider that each of these prepositions conveys a fairly straightforward mental picture to them.

IN FRENCH, the situation is different: three prepositions, *à*, *de* and *en* are used far more than any others, and in a wide variety of contexts. It would be hard to associate two of them (*à* and *de*) with any particular meaning at all (the notion 'in' is quite closely linked to the word *en*).

These three prepositions are the workhorses of the French phrase, just as the verbs *avoir*, *être* and *faire* are the workhorses of the French sentence.

The use of *à*, *de* or *en* in a particular context is more a matter of convention than of meaning. This is particularly the case with adverb phrases (**see 30.2**), where the preposition used with a particular noun may be quite different from its English counterpart in the equivalent English phrase. In some cases the meaning of the phrase depends on the use of the appropriate preposition.

You will find some of the principal uses of *à*, *de* and *en* in Section **29**, and their use in adverb phrases in Section **30.2**: you are advised to study, practise and learn most of these as set constructions and lexical phrases.

29.1 The preposition *à*

You may find it helpful to associate the preposition *à* (whether used after a verb, or before a noun or infinitive) with:

(à)   quality, intention, possibility, design, purpose

and contrast this mental image with that of *de*:

(de)   quantity, observation, factuality, result, composition

(**See** also **41.2**, especially *une tasse à thé* ('a teacup') as opposed to *une tasse de thé* ('a cup of tea'.)

In itself, *à* often does not mean very much at all; it takes its meaning from other words with which it is used. For example, there is movement in:

> *Marie est allée à la porte*   Marie went to the door

but no movement in:

> *Marie est restée à sa place*   Marie remained in her place/where she was

The sentence *Marie est allée à la porte* contains movement because of the verb, not because of the preposition; the preposition *à* indicates the direction, but that is all: did she go right up to the door, or just towards it? If the preceding sentence is *on a sonné* ('someone rang the bell/the bell rang'), we can assume that Marie went right up to the door. If there is no additional information of this kind, it may be preferable to replace *à* by a more informative preposition:

> *Marie est allée **vers** la porte*   Marie went towards the door

especially if the movement is interrupted:

> *Marie allait **vers** la porte, mais elle s'est arrêtée*
>
> Marie was going towards the door, but she stopped

Or one might wish to say:

> *Marie est allée **jusqu'à** la porte*   Marie went right up to the door

How *à* combines with an article

In the same way as *de* combines with the two definite articles *le* and *les* to give *du* and *des* (**see 29.2**), *à* combines with *le* and *les* to give **au** and **aux**:

à + le   *il retourne **au** pays de son enfance*

> he's going back to the land he grew up in

à + les   *elle rêve de participer **aux** Jeux Olympiques*

> she dreams of competing in the Olympics

When used with any other article, *à* does not combine with it:

> *cela ressemble **à du** fromage*
>
> it looks like cheese
>
> *sa musique fait plaisir **à des** millions de personnes*
>
> his/her music gives pleasure to millions

Like *de*, **à** does not combine with the direct object pronouns *le* and *les*:

> *son petit frère? elle prend plaisir à le taquiner*
>
> her little brother? she delights in teasing him
>
> *faites entrer les délégués: je suis prêt à les recevoir*
>
> show the representatives in: I'm ready to see them

■ Summary table: à + article

Definite article	*à* + *le* = **au**
	à + *l'* = *à l'*
	à + *la* = *à la*
	à + *les* = **aux**
Indefinite article	*à* + *un* = *à un*
	à + *une* = *à une*
	à + *des* = *à des*
Partitive article	*à* + *du* = *à du*
	à + *de l'* = *à de l'*
	à + *de la* = *à de la*

Exercice 29/1   *A* + article défini, partitif ou indéfini   Travail individuel

Récrivez les phrases ci-dessous en ajoutant à, et en changeant la forme de l'article s'il le faut.

Exemple: Il retourne (le) pays de son enfance.
Réponse: Il retourne **au** pays de son enfance.

1 Elle va participer (le) concours.
2 Il va en parler (un) professeur.
3 Cela ressemble (un) éléphant.
4 Ils ont émigré (les) États-Unis.
5 Ils ont communiqué leur message (des) millions de téléspectateurs.
6 Je vais me plaindre (le) patron.
7 Il faut toujours résister (les) tyrans.
8 L'appartement appartient (des) amis.

29.2 The preposition *de*

De is the least meaningful of all prepositions in French: although associated with quantity, facts etc. (see beginning of **29.1**), it often seems to serve no other purpose than to indicate a link between two nouns (as in *une salle de bains*: see **41.2**) or two phrases (such as *c'est très important de finir ce travail*: see **40.2**), or even simply to mark the boundary between them.

For example, in *le train de Paris* ('the Paris train') there is no indication as to whether the train in question is travelling to or from Paris. In many contexts, both speaker and listener know which direction is meant, perhaps because they've taken or met this train on previous occasions: the meaninglessness of *de* doesn't matter. In other cases, it may be necessary to replace *de* by a preposition with a more precise meaning:

*le train **en direction de** Paris*   the train going to Paris

This gives more information about the train, but does not say whether anyone is taking it all the way to Paris. This could be shown by using a verb:

*il a pris le train **pour aller** à Paris*   he took the train to (go to) Paris

To convey unambiguously the idea of 'from', a different preposition, or a verb, must be used:

*le train **en provenance de** Paris*   the train from Paris
*il **est arrivé de** Paris par le train*   he took the train from Paris, he arrived
                                                                    from Paris by train

De is used with a number of verbs to express the idea of 'away from', 'down from', etc.:

*revenir **de***   to return, come back from
*descendre **de***   to get down from, get out of (bus, train
                                         etc.)

(The opposite of *descendre de* is *monter dans*: 'to get into/onto'.)

De is used between two nouns when the first noun is part of, originates from, or belongs to the second noun:

*la porte **du** garage*   the garage door
*les saucisses **de** Francfort*   Frankfurter sausages
*'La Gloire **de** mon père'* (book by Pagnol)   'My father's fame'

When a noun is used in an adjective phrase to qualify another noun, the link word is often *de* (see **41.2**):

*une salle **de** bains*   a bathroom   *un terrain **de** golf*   a golf course

For *de ... en* ('from ... to'): see **31.4**.

How *de* combines with an article

Before working on this section, go back to **22.1**, and make sure you understand the meaning and use of definite, indefinite and partitive articles in French, and also to **24.1** (*beaucoup* etc. *de* + noun).

In some cases the combination of *de* with a definite article (*le, les*) produces a single word (*du, des*) which is identical in form, but not at all in meaning and grammatical construction, to the partitive article *du* or the indefinite article *des*. In other cases, the combination of *de* with a partitive or indefinite article (*du, de l', de la, des*) produces a single word (*de*) which is identical in form to the preposition *de*: see table below.

Like *à*, *de* does not combine with the direct object pronouns *le* and *les*:

*impossible **de le** voir*	no chance of seeing him
*j'étais content **de les** voir*	I was pleased to see them

In the examples in the table below, the choice of *du, d'un* or *de* in the right hand column depends on whether the noun is being used with the definite, indefinite or partitive article (see the left hand column). It is tempting, when faced with the problem noun + ? + noun, to put in *de* and hope for the best; instead, you should, at least when writing French, follow this golden rule:

> Work out <u>first</u> whether the article is definite, indefinite or partitive, and <u>then</u> how it combines with *de*.

■ How *de* combines with an article

Definite, partitive and indefinite articles	How these articles appear when used after *de*
Definite article (*le, l', la, les*)	***le, l', la, les + de = du, de l', de la, des***
le vin qu'on a bu hier	*une bouteille du vin qu'on a bu hier*
the wine we drank yesterday	a bottle of the wine we drank yesterday
la tarte qu'elle vient de faire	*la pâte de la tarte qu'elle vient de faire*
the flan she's just made	the crust of the flan she's just made
les cerises qu'il a cueillies	*le goût des cerises qu'il a cueillies*
the cherries he picked	the taste of the cherries he picked
Indefinite article (*un, une, des*)	***un, une, des + de = d'un, d'une, de***
on a acheté un gâteau au chocolat	*il reste la moitié d'un gâteau au chocolat*
we bought a chocolate cake	there's still half (of) a chocolate cake left
c'était une période difficile	*c'était le début d'une période difficile*
it was a difficult period	it was the start of a difficult period
ils ont distribué des prospectus	*la distribution de prospectus a été interdite*
they handed out (some) leaflets	the handing out of leaflets has been forbidden

Partitive article (*du, de l', de la*)	*du, de l', de la* + *de* = *de, de, de*
*on va lui acheter **du** vin*	*on va lui acheter **une bouteille de** vin*
we'll buy him/her some wine	we'll buy him/her a bottle of wine
*il faut ajouter **de l'**ail*	*il faut ajouter **un peu d'**ail*
you have to add (some) garlic	you have to add a bit of garlic
*au menu aujourd'hui il y a **de la** tarte*	*je prendrai **une petite part de** tarte*
on today's menu there's (some) flan	I'll have a small portion of flan

■ Summary table: *de* + article

Definite article	*de* + *le* = **du**
	de + *l'* = *de l'*
	de + *la* = *de la*
	de + *les* = **des**
Indefinite article	*de* + *un* = *d'un*
	de + *une* = *d'une*
	de + *des* = **de**
Partitive article	*de* + *du* = **de**
	de + *de l'* = **de**
	de + *de la* = **de**

Exercice 29/2   ***De* + article défini, indéfini, partitif**   Travail individuel

Récrivez les phrases ci-dessous en ajoutant les mots entre parenthèses + de, et en changeant la forme de l'article s'il le faut.

Exemple: Ajoutez de l'ail. (un peu)
Réponse: Ajoutez **un peu d'**ail.

1	On va acheter du vin.	(une bouteille)
2	Nous proposons des glaces.	(une sélection)
3	J'aime les framboises.	(le goût)
4	On a entendu les élèves.	(les réponses)
5	Il a mangé un gâteau.	(la moitié)
6	Elle a reçu des réponses.	(des centaines)
7	Ils ont écouté le concert.	(le début)
8	C'était une époque mouvementée.	(la fin)
9	Voilà le mystère.	(la clef)
10	Les observateurs avaient remarqué des voitures militaires.	(des mouvements)

29.3 The preposition *en*

The case of *en* is different from that of *à* or *de*: it is usually associated with the idea of 'in', but its use is restricted largely to set phrases and constructions, including:

- 'in'/'to' with names of countries etc. **(see 29.4)**;
- adverb phrases **(see 30.2)**;
- use with the present participle **(see 44.2)**.

In most other cases, the equivalent of English 'in' or 'into' is ***dans*** **(see 27.2**, including the different meanings of *en* and *dans* in expressions of time).

En is almost always used without an article, whereas *dans* is almost always used with an article **(see 29.4)**:

	en France	in France, to France
but	***dans la*** *France d'aujourd'hui*	in present-day France
	dans la *France contemporaine*	in contemporary France

The preposition *en* should not be confused with the pronoun *en*, which is used as an indirect object of a verb in place of *de* + noun **(see 18.4)**.

29.4 Names of countries, regions and *départements*

A definite article (*le, l', la, les*) is used with the names of all countries, regions and *départements* when these appear alone, or as subject or direct object of a verb:

Countries, continents	*le Canada*	*l'Europe*	*la Belgique*	*les Etats-Unis*
Regions, provinces	*le Limousin*	*l'Anjou*	*la Bretagne*	*les Pyrénées*
***Départements*, counties**	*le Lancashire*	*l'Ardèche*	*la Haute-Savoie*	*les Yvelines*

EXCEPTIONS: countries that are islands: *Chypre, Cuba, Malte*. Also: *Israël*

USE WITH PREPOSITIONS

IN ENGLISH, the prepositions most often used with geographical names are 'in', 'to' and 'from', and also 'of'. Definite articles are not used, except with plural names.

IN FRENCH, the system of prepositions used with geographical names does not correspond to the system used in English:

- a definite article is used in many cases;
- the choice of preposition depends on whether the geographical name is masculine or feminine, singular or plural, and even whether it begins with a consonant or vowel.

You should attempt to master the main elements of the system, in the following order:

● how to say 'in' and 'to', 'from' and 'of' with geographical names;
● the prepositions used with feminine singular names (the largest category);
● the prepositions used with masculine singular names beginning with a consonant, and with all plural names;
● the prepositions used with masculine singular names beginning with a vowel.

'In', 'to' + geographical names

The preposition used with a geographical name is the same, whether it corresponds to 'in' or 'to' in English. The idea of situation ('in') or movement ('to') is present in the preposition in English, but in the verb in French:

*elle **habite** en France*   she lives **in** France
*il **va** souvent en France*   he often goes **to** France

For feminine names, and masculine names of countries and regions beginning with a vowel, the preposition is *en*:

*habiter/aller **en** Allemagne/**en** Tunisie/**en** Normandie*
to live **in**/to go **to** Germany/Tunisia/Normandy

But if the name of the country or region is qualified by an adjective or adjective phrase, ***dans l'*** and ***dans la*** are used instead of *en*:

*se trouver/s'installer **dans la** France **profonde***
to be in/to go and live in a remote part of France/the depths of France
*voyager **dans l'**Irlande **des légendes***
to travel in the Ireland of folk tales

For masculine singular names of countries beginning with a consonant, and plural names, the preposition is *au* or *aux*:

*habiter/aller **au** Mexique/**aux** Etats-Unis*
to live in/to go to Mexico/the United States

For counties and ***départements***, and with *le nord, le sud* etc. + *de* + name of country, *dans* is used with the definite article:

*habiter/aller **dans le** Cumbria/**dans l'**Aveyron/**dans les** Alpes-Maritimes*
*habiter/aller **dans le** nord de l'Italie/**dans le** sud de la France*

Develop the habit of saying or writing *le* or *dans le* with counties and districts in the British Isles, except for *la Cornouailles* (Cornwall), which the French think of as a province: ***habiter/aller** en Cornouailles.*

'From' + geographical names

In all cases the word for 'from' is *de*; for geographical names used with *en* (see above), it is used without an article:

    *habiter/aller **en** Espagne/**en** Catalogne*   to live in/go to Spain/Catalonia
    *revenir **d'**Espagne/**de** Catalogne*   to return from Spain/from Catalonia

For names used with *au, aux* or *dans le* (see above), *de* combines with or is used with a definite article:

    *habiter/aller **au** Danemark/**aux** Pays-Bas/**dans le** Kent/**dans la** Somme*
    to live in/to go to Denmark/the Netherlands/Kent/the Somme
    *revenir **du** Danemark/**des** Pays-Bas/**du** Kent/**de la** Somme*
    to return from Denmark/the Netherlands/Kent/the Somme

'Of' + geographical names

The above pattern is followed when *de* + name corresponds to an adjective phrase:

    *les pommes **de** Normandie*   apples from Normandy/Normandy apples
    *les vins **d'**Anjou*   wines from Anjou/Anjou wines

except with masculine singular + consonant, and plural names of countries, regions etc.:

    *les routes **du** Portugal*   roads in Portugal/Portuguese roads
    *les habitants **des** Alpes*   inhabitants of the Alps

If a country is being mentioned as a political or economic entity (as opposed to a place of origin etc.), the definite article is always present:

    *la politique économique **de la** France*   France's economic policy
    *les problèmes industriels **de l'**Italie*   Italy's industrial problems

Names of towns

With the names of cities, towns and villages, *à* and *de* are used, but not *en*:

    *habiter/aller **à** Paris/**à** Londres*   to live in/to go to Paris/to London
    *revenir **de** Madrid/**de** Rome*   to return from Madrid/from Rome

For *dans* and *sur* with names of cities, towns, etc., **see 27.2**.

The names of a few towns in English, and of rather more in French, are used with a definite article, which is maintained after *à* and *de*:

    Le Caire   Cairo   ***au** Caire*   ***du** Caire*
    Le Havre   Le Havre   ***au** Havre*   ***du** Havre*

Exercice 29/3   Prépositions et articles: *à, en, de* + noms de pays etc.   Travail individuel

Complétez les phrases ci-dessous en ajoutant à, en, de, dans + article, selon le sens et le nom qui suit.

Exemple: vivre _ Inde
Réponse: vivre **en** Inde

Exemple: apporter une aide économique _ Inde
Réponse: apporter une aide économique **à l'**Inde

  1   Elle a toujours rêvé de faire un voyage _ nord _ Écosse.
  2   _ Allemagne, beaucoup de travailleurs immigrés viennent _ Turquie.
  3   Vite! Montez! c'est le train _ Londres!
  4   Depuis l'ouverture du Tunnel, plusieurs entreprises se sont installées _ Kent.
  5   La criminalité est assez répandue _ Var et _ Alpes-Maritimes.
  6   Ils reviennent _ Somme, où ils ont visité les champs de bataille de la Grande Guerre.
  7   Au cours des siècles, plusieurs peuples sont venus s'installer _ îles Britanniques.
  8   Les problèmes économiques _ Europe _ Ouest ne sont rien à côté de ceux _ Russie.
  9   Nous espérons faire un voyage _ sud _ Italie.
  10   Heureusement, les Britanniques deviennent moins méfiants à l'égard du reste _ Europe.

30 Adverbs and adverb phrases

30.1	**Formation of adverbs**
30.2	**Adverb phrases**
30.3	***A, de, en* in adverb phrases**

An **adverb** is a word that gives information about the circumstances (time, place, manner, etc.) of an action. An **adverb phrase** is a group of words, generally including a preposition and a noun, which functions as an adverb.

Examples of adverbs and adverb phrases:

Time	*hier*	yesterday	*à midi*	at noon
Place	*là-bas*	over there	*en haut*	at the top
Manner	*vite*	quickly	*à la hâte*	hastily

As these examples show, it is not an adequate description of the function of an adverb to say that it 'describes the verb': this is true – more or less – only of adverbs of manner (**see 30.1**).

An adverb (or adverb phrase), therefore, gives additional information about a verb, a phrase or a sentence. Unlike an adjective, which agrees with the noun it qualifies even if it is not placed next to it (**see 12**), an adverb is invariable. Its position in the phrase or sentence, although subject to some constraints (**see 32.3**), is relatively free; it can even stand apart from the sentence, forming an explanation of the action (**see 43.1**) or a commentary on it (**see 50.2**).

30.1 Formation of adverbs

Many adverbs of time or place have no particular distinguishing feature, such as a suffix:

Time	*hier*	*aujourd'hui*	*demain*	*maintenant*
Place	*ici*	*là-bas*	*près*	*loin*

Most adverbs of manner, however, are formed by adding ***-ment*** to the feminine form of an adjective; the English equivalent of these adverbs of manner is often a word ending in '**-ly**':

Masculine	**Feminine**		**Adverb**	
direct	*directe*	direct	*directement*	directly
doux	*douce*	gentle	*doucement*	gently
calme	*calme*	calm	*calmement*	calmly

In the case of some adverbs, this *e* becomes *é*, adding a syllable:

précis	*précise*	exact	*précisément*	precisely
aveugle	*aveugle*	blind	*aveuglément*	blindly
profond	*profonde*	deep	*profondément*	deeply

This *é* is added in order to break up a 'cluster' of consonants, making it easier to pronounce, but it is best to learn each one of these adverbs as a separate case. For example, the adverb *aveuglément* ('blindly') can be distinguished from the noun *l'aveuglement* ('blindness').

Adverbs formed from adjectives with a masculine ending in *-i* or *-u* do not add *e*:

joli	*jolie*	pretty	*joliment*	prettily
prétendu	*prétendue*	so-called	*prétendument*	supposedly

Vite: 'quickly'

The word *vite* is only ever used as an adverb, never as an adjective.

The closest corresponding adjective is *rapide*, from which is formed the adverb *rapidement*:

Adjective	Adverb
un train rapide	*ce train ne va pas bien vite*
a fast train	this train's not going very fast
prendre un déjeuner rapide	*ne mange pas si vite!*
to have a quick lunch	don't eat so fast/so quickly!

Adverbs used as modalisers (see 50.2)

Certain adverbs in *-ment* can be used, not to inform about the circumstances of an action or a sentence, but to provide a commentary on the action. An adverb like *sérieusement* can be used in both ways:

Adverb	*eux, ils travaillent **sérieusement***
	<u>they</u> work seriously
Modaliser	***sérieusement**, tu ne vas pas travailler par cette chaleur?*
	you aren't seriously going to work in this heat?

Heureusement or *évidemment*, on the other hand, are most likely to be used as modalisers:

***heureusement**, le train était presque vide*	fortunately, the train was almost empty
***évidemment**, elle n'avait rien préparé*	needless to say, she'd got nothing ready

IN ENGLISH many adverbs in '-ly' are used as modalisers, including 'fortunately', 'obviously', not to mention 'hopefully'.

Seulement and *seul*: 'only'

The adverb *seulement* is generally used between a verb and an adverb phrase or infinitive phrase:

*elle arrive **seulement** ce soir*	she won't be here until this evening
*ils venaient **seulement** de sortir*	they'd only just gone out

It can also be used with the object of a verb, as an alternative to the negative construction *ne . . . que*:

> *il y avait **seulement** une dizaine de personnes au restaurant*

or   *il **n'**y avait **qu'**une dizaine de personnes au restaurant*

> there were only about ten people in the restaurant

If a noun or pronoun is the subject of a verb, then the adjective *seul* is used, not the adverb *seulement*:

> ***seule**, la Grande-Bretagne s'est opposée au projet*
> only Britain opposed the plan
> *lui **seul** connaît la réponse*

or   *il **n'**y a **que** lui qui connaît la réponse*

> he's the only one who knows the answer

Exercice 30/1   *Seul* ou *seulement*?   Travail individuel

Complétez les phrases ci-dessous en ajoutant seul(e)(s) ou seulement, selon la construction grammaticale.

Exemple: Elle _ sait où le trouver.
Réponse: Elle **seule** sait où le trouver.

Exemple: Si _ elle savait où le trouver.
Réponse: Si **seulement** elle savait où le trouver.

1   La capacité de l'ascenseur est limitée: quatre personnes, _.
2   _ une infirmière avait entendu son cri.
3   Je le ferais moi-même, _ je n'ai pas le temps.
4   Depuis le début de la saison, l'équipe a marqué quatre buts _.
5   Lui _ connaît les risques.
6   _, les Anglais sont restés sceptiques.

For adjectives used as adverbs, **see 17.3e.**

30.2 Adverb phrases

You may find it helpful to study this small selection of examples for any or all of the following purposes:

●   to extend your vocabulary of French, which needs to consist of phrases (and longer units), as well as individual words;

● to become more aware of the wide range of communicative purposes served by adverb phrases in French;

● to note the differences in structure, including choice of preposition, between these phrases and their English equivalents.

Adverb phrases are listed here according to the preposition at the beginning of the phrase.

No preposition

Many time phrases consist of article + noun; the use of the definite article (**see 22**) suggests usual, habitual, regular, repeated action:

	vendredi	on Friday	*vendredi **dernier/prochain*** last/next Friday
	***un** vendredi*	one Friday	***ce** vendredi* this Friday
but	*le vendredi*	on Fridays	
	***tous les** vendredis soir*	every Friday night/evening	
	*la nuit **dernière***	last night	***cette** nuit* tonight
but	*les chats préfèrent sortir **la** nuit*	cats prefer to go out at night	

Longer phrases with no preposition at the beginning are used as detached complements (**see 43.2**):

> ***les mains dans les poches**, il regardait la vitrine*
> with his hands in his pockets, he was looking at the shop window

Avec, sans: 'with', 'without'

Adverb phrases consisting of *avec* or *sans* + noun (without article) are often equivalent in meaning to adverbs ending in *-ment*:

Avec	*travailler **avec sérieux**/sérieusement*	to work seriously
	*couper **avec soin**/soigneusement*	to cut carefully
	*parler **avec effort/avec difficulté***	to speak with difficulty
	*chanter **avec enthousiasme***	to sing enthusiastically
Sans	*nager **sans effort***	to swim effortlessly
	*chercher **sans espoir***	to seek without hope

In certain fixed phrases there is an article:

> *accueillir **avec le sourire***   to greet with a smile
> *être **sans le sou***   to be penniless

If the noun is qualified by an adjective or a longer phrase, an article is added:

> *avec **un** effort surhumain*   with a superhuman effort
> *sans **l'**espoir de les trouver vivants, nous aurions abandonné nos recherches*
> had it not been for the hope of finding them alive, we'd have called off the search
> (see also **Exercice 27/3**, p228)

249

Sans + infinitive (**see 43.3**); *sans que* + subjunctive (**see 48**).

Par: 'by'; 'as a'

Phrases without an article:

	par hasard	by chance		
but	*au hasard*	at random	*à tout hasard*	on the offchance
	par conséquent	as a result		
but	*en conséquence*	therefore, accordingly		

Phrases with article + noun + adjective:

*par **un** hasard extraordinaire*	by an extraordinary coincidence

Phrases with article + noun

	par le train	by train
but	*en voiture!*	please board the train!
	par le passé	in the past
but	*à l'avenir*	in the future

Commencer par, finir par + infinitive (**see list 38.3**).

Pour: 'for'

Phrases with an article:

	pour le plaisir	for pleasure
but	*au plaisir!*	(I hope to) see you soon!

Pour is also used in phrases with an infinitive:

pour rire	*pour s'amuser*	*pour voir*
for a laugh	for fun	(just) to see

Dans: 'in'

Dans is used in few adverb phrases: its place is largely occupied by *en*. It is, however, used in phrases with *mesure*:

dans quelle mesure	*dans la mesure où*	*dans une certaine mesure*
to what extent	to the extent that	to some extent

The use of *dans* with *mesure* can be contrasted with the use of *de* with *façon* and *manière* (**see 30.3,** *de*).

30.3 *A, de, en* in adverb phrases

A: *A* tends to be used in adverb phrases which indicate time or place.

A + noun (no article)

Means of travel

à cheval/à dos d'âne	on horseback/on a donkey
à bicyclette/à vélo	by bicycle/on a bicycle

One can also say *en vélo*, and one says *en moto* ('by/on a motor-bike'): see below, *en*.

Many adjective phrases **(see 41.2)** consist of *à* + noun:

un chapeau à plumes	a hat with feathers (on it)
un fer à cheval	a horseshoe

Time

	travailler à mi-temps/à temps partiel	to work part-time
also	*parler à mi-voix*	to speak softly
	arriver à mi-côte	to get half-way up

A *tout* + noun

	à tout hasard	on the offchance
but	*en tout cas*	in any case
	tout à l'heure + verb in past	just now
	tout à l'heure + verb in future	in a while
	tout à coup	all at once
but	*tout de suite*	straight away

A + article + noun

Time

	à l'avenir	in the future
but	*par le passé*	in the past
	à l'âge de treize ans	at (the age of) thirteen
	à l'époque des dinosaures	in the age of (the) dinosaurs
	au siècle dernier	in the previous century
	au mois d'août	in August
	à ce moment(-là)	at that (precise) moment
but	*en ce moment*	at the moment, now
	à la fois	at the same time
	*ce jeu est **à la fois** passionnant et exaspérant*	this game is both exciting and exasperating
but	*en même temps*	at the same time
	*ne répondez pas tous **en même temps***	don't all answer at once

Place

	à la radio, à la télé(vision)	on radio, on TV/television
but	*sur France 2, sur France Inter*	on Channel 2, on France Inter
	au téléphone	on the phone, by phone
	à l'université	at university
but	*en fac, en faculté*	at university, at college
	à l'étage	upstairs (on the first floor)
but	*en haut*	at the top

A ... de

The double structure *à* + time/distance + *de* + noun needs careful study: the *à* is easily forgotten:

> *la maison était à deux kilomètres de la mer*
> the house was two miles from the sea
> *nous sommes à une heure de route de l'aéroport*
> we're one hour's drive from the airport

De

De tends to be used in adverb phrases which indicate manner.

Phrases without an article include:

> *tuer de sang froid*   to kill in cold blood

Phrases with *tout* include:

	de toute façon	in any case
	tout de suite	straight away
but	*tout à l'heure*	just now, in a while

Phrases with *de* + article include:

de cette façon, de cette manière	in this/that way
de quelle façon, de quelle manière	in what way

Note that *de* is used before *façon/manière*, not *dans*.

Also

> *d'un côté . . . de l'autre*   on (the) one hand . . . on the other

De ... en

The double structure *de* + noun + *en* + noun corresponds to 'from ... to' **(see 31.4)**:

aller de maison en maison	to go from house to house
tomber de haut en bas	to fall from top to bottom

En

En tends to be used in adverb phrases which indicate time or place. Many of these phrases can be contrasted with similar phrases, with different meaning, constructed with *à* (see above):

Time	*en ce moment*	but	*à ce moment-là*
	en même temps	but	*à la fois*
Place	*en haut*	but	*à l'étage*
	en faculté	but	*à l'université*
Manner	*en tout cas*	but	*à tout hasard*

Also: *en plein air*   in the open air   *en plein visage*   right in the face

En tends to be used after particular verbs:

tomber en panne	*entrer en gare*	*fondre en larmes*
to break down	to come into the station	to burst into tears

Many connectors and modalisers **(see 50)** are formed by *en* + noun:

en principe	in theory	*en général*	in general

En + present participle (gerund): 'on -ing', 'by -ing':

*elle est partie **en courant*** she ran off **(see 44.2)**

Exercice 30/2 *A, de ou en?* Travail individuel

Complétez les phrases ci-dessous en ajoutant une de ces trois prépositions (avec un article s'il le faut).

Exemple: Qu'est-ce qu'elle compte faire _ avenir?
Réponse: Qu'est-ce qu'elle compte faire à l' avenir?

1 Elle avait appris à monter _ cheval.
2 Je n'en sais rien; _ toute façon, cela ne me concerne pas.
3 Ici, nous sommes _ trois minutes _ autoroute.
4 Je n'ai pas beaucoup de travail _ ce moment.
5 C'est _ ce moment-là qu'il a compris son erreur.
6 Il a préféré travailler _ mi-temps.
7 C'étaient des musiciens qui allaient _ ville _ ville.
8 J'espère que la voiture ne va pas tomber _ panne maintenant.
9 Est-ce qu'on était vraiment plus heureux _ siècle dernier?
10 Ils parlaient tous _ même temps.
11 Aller _ université avait toujours été son ambition.
12 Voilà: je te téléphone _ tout hasard.

31 Making comparisons

31.1 Comparative constructions
31.2 Superlative constructions
31.3 *Bon, meilleur, le meilleur; bien, mieux, le mieux*
31.4 Intensifiers

Comparative constructions and superlative constructions

A **comparative** construction is used when two items (or groups of item) are being compared; the point of comparison is usually an adjective or an adverb:

> *Pierre est **plus** intelligent **que** son cousin*
> Pierre's cleverer/more intelligent than his cousin
> *le train de 10 heures va **plus** vite **que** tous les autres*
> the 10 o'clock train goes faster than all the others

A comparative construction expresses a relative judgment: one item is judged alongside one or more other items in a similar category. There is no particular emphasis on the quality itself: Pierre might not be all that clever, and the 10 o'clock train might go pretty slowly.

A **superlative** construction also expresses a relative judgment, but it is used when one item (or group of items) is being singled out from a group or series of two or more items, in respect of a particular quality which forms the basis of comparison (often an adjective or adverb):

> *Madeleine est **la plus** intelligente **de** toute la famille*
> Madeleine is the cleverest/the most intelligent in the whole family
> *ce train va **le plus** vite **de** tous les TGV*
> this train goes the fastest of all the high-speed trains

IN ENGLISH, 'the more', 'the less' (or the -er form of the adjective or adverb) are used when there are only two items; IN FRENCH, the usual superlative constructions are used:

> *Madeleine est la plus/la moins intelligente des deux filles*
> Madeleine is the cleverer/the less clever of the two girls

For absolute superlatives, **see 31.4**.

254

French
Grammar
Explained

31.1 Comparative constructions

■ Comparative constructions in English and French

English	+ adjective or adverb	+ verb	+ noun	Link word
more . . . than	*plus*	*plus* *davantage* (N3)	*plus de* *davantage de* (N3)	. . . *que*
less . . . than	*moins*	*moins*	*moins de*	. . . *que*
as much/as many . . . as	*aussi*	*autant*	*autant de*	. . . *que*
not as much/as many . . . as	*pas si*	*pas autant*	*pas autant de*	. . . *que*

For *le même . . . que, différent de, supérieur à*, **see 40.1**.

Davantage, instead of *plus*, is useful to distinguish the comparative 'more' (*plus*) from the negative 'no longer' (*ne . . . plus*).

The linking word between the two parts of a comparative construction is ***que*** in French, corresponding to 'than' or 'as' in English.

Examples:
Plus . . . que ('more . . . than')
+ adjective
> *son jardin est **plus joli que** jamais*
> his/her garden is prettier than ever

+ adverb
> *cette année, je me sens **plus en sécurité que** l'année dernière*
> this year, I feel safer than last year

+ verb
> *elle **travaille plus que** son frère*
> she works more/longer than her brother

+ *de* + noun
> *son film a eu **plus de succès** en France qu'au Québec*
> his/her film was more successful/had more success in France than in Quebec

Moins . . . que ('less . . . than')
+ adjective or adverb
> *prendre l'avion est **moins dangereux qu'**autrefois*
> air travel is less dangerous than it used to be

+ verb
> *pendant l'Occupation, les paysans **ont moins souffert que** les ouvriers*
> during the Occupation, farmers were less badly hit than workers

+ *de* + **noun**

> *la Norvège a eu moins de points que l'Islande*
> Norway got fewer points than Iceland

Exercice 31/1   Quantité ou comparaison?: *plus/moins de* ou *plus/moins que*?

Travail individuel

Complétez les phrases ci-dessous en ajoutant de ou que, selon qu'il s'agit d'une **quantité** (plus de, moins de) ou d'une **comparaison** (plus que, moins que).

Exemple: Il y a eu plus _ problèmes _ prévu.
Réponse: Il y a eu plus **de** problèmes **que** prévu.

1   On a eu moins _ pluie _ l'hiver dernier.
2   Il a mangé plus _ deux hommes.
3   J'ai mangé plus _ cinq variétés de poire.
4   Ils ont déjà vendu plus _ parapluies _ l'année dernière.
5   Il a une fortune de plus _ trente milliards.
6   Il est plus riche _ ses concurrents.
7   Elle a eu moins _ ennuis _ son frère.
8   Il a plus _ bonne volonté _ _ véritable talent.

Aussi/Pas si ('as/not as . . . as')

+ adjective or adverb

> *je suis aussi curieux que toi de savoir le résultat*
> I'm as curious as you (are) to know the result
> *il n'est pas si bête qu'on pourrait penser*
> he's not as stupid as you might think

Autant ('as much/as many . . . as')

+ verb

> *bientôt, elle gagnera autant que son frère*
> sonn she'll be earning as much as her brother

+ *de* + noun

> *je n'ai pas autant d'expérience que toi*
> I haven't got as much experience as you

Aussi + **adjective** + *que* can be replaced by **adjective** + *comme*:

> *il est riche comme Crésus*

or   *il est aussi riche que Crésus*   he's as rich as Cresus

> *cette histoire est vieille comme la Terre*

or   *cette histoire est aussi vieille que la Terre*   that story's as old as the hills

The second term of a comparative construction does not have to be stated; it is often left understood or implied:

Wizzo lave plus blanc	*(. . . que les autres lessives)*
Wizzo washes whiter	(. . . than other washing powders)
maintenant, j'en suis moins sûr	*(. . . qu'hier, que l'année dernière)*
now I'm less sure	(. . . than yesterday, than last year)

Comparative clauses

The second term of a comparative construction can take the form of a comparative clause, with subject, verb (and object or other complement):

*le spectacle était **aussi** émouvant **qu'on avait espéré***

the show was as moving as we had hoped

*il s'est battu avec **autant** de courage **qu'il avait montré l'année précédente***

he fought with as much courage as he had shown the previous year

Other comparative conjunctions include:

ainsi que	just as, in the way that
dans la mesure où	to the extent that
comme	as
tel que	(just) as

*le spectacle était exactement **comme** on avait imaginé/**tel qu'**on avait imaginé*

the show was exactly as we'd thought it would be

After *plus . . . que, ne* is added in the second part of the sentence in formal French (N3), though not in conversational French (N2):

*il est plus tard **que tu ne penses***	(N3)
it's later than you think	
*elle est plus grande **que je n'avais imaginé***	(N3)
she's taller than I'd imagined	

This *ne* has no negative force in the sentence, but it does correspond to an underlying negative idea: 'you don't think it's (very) late'; 'I didn't imagine she was (very) tall'.

31.2 Superlative constructions

In French, as in English, there are two kinds of superlative:

● a relative superlative, in which one item or group of items is singled out from a wider group. This superlative construction is dealt with in this section;
● an absolute superlative, in which the meaning of an adjective or adverb is strengthened by the addition of 'very', 'most', 'highly', 'extremely', etc. These are forms of intensifiers, and are dealt with in **31.4**.

■ Superlative constructions in English and French

English	+ adjective	+ adverb	+ verb	+ noun	Link word
the most	*le/la/les plus*	*le plus*	*le plus*	*le plus de*	. . . *de*
the least	*le/la/les moins*	*le moins*	*le moins*	*le moins de*	. . . *de*

With adjectives that come after the noun, *le/la/les* is repeated; it is this *le/la/les* before the adjective or adverb which indicates a superlative, as opposed to a comparative, construction:

    *le jour **le plus** long*   the longest day

    *les régions **les moins** accessibles*   the least accessible regions

    Examples:

+ adjective

    *Paris est **la** ville **la plus** complète **du** monde*

    Paris is the city with the most to offer in the world

    *il faut opérer sur **un** nombre **le plus** élevé possible*

    we must work with the highest number possible

    *les plus grands crimes sont souvent **les moins spectaculaires***

    the greatest crimes are often the least sensational (ones)

+ adverb

    ***le plus souvent**, il y va en vélo*

    most times, he goes (there) by bike

    ***de** toutes ses collègues, c'est elle qui travaille **le plus** dur/**le moins** dur*

    (out) of all her colleagues, she's the one who works the hardest/the least hard

+ verb

    de** tous les manifestants, c'est lui qui criait **le plus/le moins

    (out) of all the demonstrators, he's the one who shouted the most/the least

+ noun

    ***de** tous ses camarades, c'est lui qui a eu **le plus de** problèmes/**le moins de** problèmes*

    (out) of all his workmates, he's the one who had the most/the fewest problems

When one states the category or group within which one item is singled out, the linking word in French is *de*, whereas in English it can be one of a number of prepositions: 'out of', 'of', 'among', 'in'. In other words:

Que is used in comparisons, but not in superlative constructions.

Examples:

Comparative	*plus vite **que** son frère*	faster than his/her brother
Superlative	*le plus vite possible*	the fastest possible/as fast as possible
Comparative	*une plus grande quantité **qu'**hier*	a larger amount than yesterday
Superlative	*la plus grande quantité possible*	the largest possible amount

One can also indicate the overall category or group by a relative construction (introduced for example by *qui* or *que*):

*le tremblement de terre est **le plus** violent **qui ait** jamais frappé la ville*

the earthquake is the most violent that has ever hit the town

*c'est le spectacle **le plus** merveilleux **que j'aie** jamais vu*

it's the most wonderful sight I've ever seen

The use of the subjunctive in the relative clause **(see 48.5)** draws attention to the surprising or dramatic nature of what is being described. If the relative clause contains a simple statement of fact, with no particular stress on the speaker's reaction to it, the indicative is used:

*c'est l'athlète **le plus** en forme **qui a** gagné la course*

it was the fittest athlete who won the race

Exercice 31/2   **Le superlatif**   Travail individuel

Complétez les phrases ci-dessous en ajoutant le, la ou les, et plus (1–5) ou moins (6–8). Attention! certains blancs correspondent à **deux mots**.

1   C'était _ jour _ long de ma vie.
2   C'est toujours elle qui crie _ fort.
3   C'est là que se trouvent _ prisonniers _ violents.
4   Il faut rénover _ quartiers _ défavorisés.
5   Ils sont parmi ceux qui ont résisté _ longtemps.
6   Ils ont réussi à trouver _ chemin _ difficile.
7   Ce soir-là c'était elle qui avait chanté _ bien.
8   Le chômage ne frappe pas toujours _ individus _ fortunés.

Exercice 31/3   **Emploi du comparatif et du superlatif**   Travail à deux > Mise en commun

Avec un(e) partenaire, choisissez **un** des sujets ci-dessous, et composez ensemble une dizaine de phrases: cinq sur votre 'candidat', cinq sur celui de votre partenaire. Vous pouvez, si vous voulez, donner aux phrases la forme d'un dialogue contradictoire. Chaque phrase doit inclure au moins **une** construction comparative ou superlative.

Sujets possibles:
1   Mon pays préféré
2   Ma région préférée
3   Mon chanteur préféré
4   Mon équipe de foot (etc.) préférée
5   Mon programme de télévision préféré

31.3 *Bon, meilleur, le meilleur; bien, mieux, le mieux*

Comparative and superlative of *bon* and *bien*

IN ENGLISH, the comparative and superlative forms of both 'good' (adjective) and 'well' (adverb) are 'better' and '(the) best'.

IN FRENCH, care must be taken when forming the comparative and superlative of *bon* (adjective) and *bien* (adverb: but see below for *bien* used as an adjective).

■	*Bon, bien* etc.	Comparative	Superlative
Adjective	*bon/bonne/* *bons/bonnes* good	*meilleur/meilleure/* *meilleurs/meilleures* better	*le/la/les meilleur(e)(s)* (the) best
Adverb	*bien* well	*mieux* better	*le mieux* (the) best
Intensifier **(see 31.4)**	*bien* well	*mieux* better	*le/la/les mieux* (the) best

Pronunciation

Meilleur is pronounced as two syllables: [me jœr]
Mieux is pronounced as one syllable: [mjø]

Examples:

Bon, meilleur, le meilleur (adjectives)
>   *les chocolats X sont **bons**, les chocolats Y sont **meilleurs** (**que** les chocolats X), et les chocolats Z*
>   *sont **les meilleurs** (**de** tous)*
>   X chocolates are good, Y chocolates are better (than X chocolates), and Z chocolates
>   are the best (of all)

Note that *meilleur* and *le meilleur* agree in all cases where *bon* would agree.

Bien, mieux, le mieux (adverbs)
>   *la soprano A chante **bien**, la soprano B chante **mieux** (**que** la soprano A), et la soprano C chante*
>   ***le mieux** (**de** toutes)*

French
Grammar
Explained

soprano A sings well, soprano B sings better (than soprano A), and soprano C sings (the) best (of all of them)

Note that *le mieux* is invariable when it qualifies a verb.

Bien, mieux, le/la/les mieux (intensifiers)

> *la maison L est **bien** isolée, la maison M est **mieux** isolée (**que** la maison L), et la maison N est **la mieux** isolée (**de** toutes)*
>
> house L is well insulated, house M is better insulated (than house L), and house N is the best insulated (of all)

Note that the definite article in *le/la/les mieux* agrees with the adjective which it intensifies.

Exercice 31/4   ***Bon, bien, meilleur, mieux** etc.*   Travail à deux > Mise en commun

a   Complétez les phrases ci-dessous en ajoutant bon, meilleur, le meilleur, bien, mieux, le mieux (etc.), selon le sens. Attention! certains blancs correspondent à **deux** mots.

b   Après avoir vérifié vos réponses, écrivez l'équivalent en anglais de chaque phrase.

Exemple: Elle chante _.
Réponse: Elle chante **bien**.

Exemple: C'est _ chanteuse de l'année.
Réponse: C'est **la meilleure** chanteuse de l'année.

1   Si tu as une _ solution, dis-le!
2   Il a été souffrant, mais maintenant il va beaucoup _.
3   C'est vrai qu'il a beaucoup de _ volonté.
4   Leurs journalistes sont toujours _ informés.
5   Avec cette voiture, on est _ protégé en cas d'accident.
6   Leurs résultats sont _ que ceux de leurs concurrents.
7   Elle a été _ contente de retrouver son appartement.
8   _ vins ne sont pas toujours les plus chers.
9   C'est toujours lui qui trouve _ réponse.
10   Ils ont la piscine _ équipée du pays.

Instead of *meilleur(e)(s) que* and *plus mauvais(e)(s) que*, one can say *supérieur(e)(s) à* and *inférieur(e)(s) à* (**see list, 40.1**).

Comparative and superlative of *mauvais* and *mal*

IN ENGLISH, the comparative and superlative forms of both 'bad' (adjective) and 'badly' (adverb) are 'worse' and '(the) worst'.

IN FRENCH, the comparative and superlative of *mauvais* (adjective) and *mal* (adverb) are usually formed by the addition of *plus* and *le/la/les plus*.

■	*Mauvais, mal* etc.	Comparative	Superlative
Adjective	*mauvais(e)(s)* bad	*plus mauvais(e)(s)* worse	*le/la/les plus mauvais(e)(s)* (the) worst
Adverb	*mal* badly	*plus mal* worse, less well	*le plus mal* (the) worst, (the) least well

Examples:

Adjective

*cette solution est encore **plus mauvaise que** la précédente*

this/that solution is even worse than the previous one

*cette solution est **la plus mauvaise de** toutes*

this/that solution is the worst of all

Adverb

*les choses vont encore **plus mal que** l'année dernière*

things are going even more badly/things are even worse than last year

*où avez-vous **le plus mal**?*

where does it hurt most?

Exercice 31/5   *Mauvais, plus mauvais, mal, plus mal*, etc.   Travail à deux > Mise en commun

a   Complétez les phrases ci-dessous en ajoutant (le) (plus) mauvais, (le) (plus) mal, selon le sens. Attention! certains blancs correspondent à **deux** ou même **trois** mots.

b   Après avoir vérifié vos réponses, écrivez l'équivalent en anglais de chaque phrase.

Exemple: Tout va _ pour lui en ce moment, le pauvre!
Réponse: Tout va **mal** pour lui en ce moment, le pauvre!

Exemple: Cette chanson n'est pas _ que l'autre.
Réponse: Cette chanson n'est pas **plus mauvaise** que l'autre.

1   Le temps est _ que prévu.
2   Cette ville ne mérite pas sa _ réputation.
3   A l'écouter, les choses vont toujours _ ici que là-bas.
4   De tous les candidats, c'était lui _ préparé.
5   Il trouvait qu'on l'avait _ conseillé.
6   C'est bien _ idée que j'ai jamais entendue!

Mauvais, *pire*, *le/la/les pire(s)* (adjectives); *mal*, *pis*, *le pis* (adverbs)

These comparative (*pire*, *pis*) and superlative (*le/la/les pire(s)*, *le pis*) forms of *mauvais* and *mal* respectively are mainly used in certain fixed phrases:

> *il va s'attirer **les pires ennuis***
>
> he's going to get into terrible trouble
>
> *tout va **de mal en pis***
>
> everything's going from bad to worse

Bien and *mal* as adjectives

The adverbs *bien*, *mieux*, *le mieux* and *mal*, and also *pas bien*, *pas mieux* and *pas mal*, are often used in French as adjectives. This can be confusing if you are still struggling to sort out:

> *bon*, *meilleur*, *le meilleur*, *mauvais*, *plus mauvais* and *le plus mauvais*

from   *bien*, *mieux*, *le mieux*, *mal*, *plus mal* and *le plus mal*

Bien (etc.) is used as an adjective when making value judgments (**see also 17.3f**):

> *il ne faut pas faire cela: ce n'est pas **bien***
>
> you/one shouldn't do that: it's not right   (morality)
>
> *il était très **bien**, ton article sur la manif* (N2)
>
> your article on the demo was great   (piece of work)
>
> *il est pas **mal**, ton copain/elle est pas **mal**, ta copine*
>
> your friend's not bad/quite nice   (appearance, manner)

With capital letters, *le Bien* and *le Mal* mean 'Good' and 'Evil' (N3). Note also:

> *j'ai fait ça pour **ton bien***
>
> I did that for your good
>
> *il lui a dit tout **le mal** qu'il pensait d'elle*
>
> he told her all the bad things he thought about her

Comparative and superlative adverb forms used as adjectives include *mieux*, *pas mieux* and *le mieux*:

> *une Jaguar, c'est bien, mais une Rolls c'est encore **mieux***   (N2)
>
> a Jag is great, but a Roller is even better

31.4 Intensifiers

An intensifier is an absolute superlative: by adding an adverb after a verb (*crier haut et fort; parler haut* etc.: **see 17.3e**) or before an adjective or adverb (see below), one can emphasise it, give it a stronger meaning, draw attention to one's own attitude or reaction, and so on.

Intensification of adjectives and adverbs

IN ENGLISH typical intensifiers used with adjectives are: 'very', 'highly', 'most', 'extremely', 'pretty' (N2), 'completely' or 'such a'.

IN FRENCH, typical intensifiers include:

très	*bien*	*énormément*	*extrêmement*	*fort* (N4)
very	very	very much	extremely	most
si	*tellement*	*tout*	*assez*	*trop*
so	so	completely	quite	too

In informal situations (N2), one can use prefixes (**see 13**) such as: *super- hyper- giga- méga-*

Examples:

French	English
très utile	very useful
bien lourd	very heavy
tout neuf	brand new
extrêmement difficile	extremely hard

Intensification of *plus, moins* and of *aussi, autant*

Plus, moins can be given added emphasis by the use of an intensifier such as *beaucoup, bien, encore, toujours*:

beaucoup *plus cher*	much/far more expensive
bien *moins amusant*	far less fun
encore *moins difficile*	even/still less difficult
toujours *plus loin*	still further, ever onwards

Aussi, autant can be emphasised by the addition of *tout*:

tout aussi dangereux	just as dangerous
tout autant	just as much, just as many

Superlative constructions can be emphasised with *bien/de loin*:

bien/de loin	*le plus/le moins/le meilleur (etc.)*
much/by far	the most/the least/the best

Exercice 31/6   **Intensification**   Travail individuel

Complétez les phrases ci-dessous en ajoutant un intensif (assez, beaucoup, bien, de loin, encore, toujours, tout, très, trop).

Exemple: Quand je lui ai dit ça, il a été _ surpris.
Réponses possibles: Quand je lui ai dit ça, il a été **bien** surpris.
Quand je lui ai dit ça, il a été **tout** surpris.

1   Son point de vue est _ aussi valable que le tien.
2   C'est _ plus cher que je n'avais imaginé.
3   Cette idée a été _ bien exploitée récemment, hélas!

4   C'est _ évident maintenant qu'il n'avait aucune intention de suivre nos conseils.

5   Sans tous ces livres, la valise serait _ moins lourde!

6   L'année dernière a été _ la plus difficile pour eux depuis dix ans.

7   Sa réponse a été reçu _ trop tard pour qu'on en tienne compte.

8   Je regrette _ autant que vous d'être obligé de dire non à la proposition.

9   Elle est _ ambitieuse; ' _ plus loin': voilà sa devise!

Numerical comparisons

IN ENGLISH, numerical comparisons are expressed through two constructions: 'as . . . as' ('nine times as heavy as . . .'), and 'more . . . than' ('nine times heavier than . . .')

IN FRENCH, numerical comparisons are expressed by the use of *plus/moins* + adjective (or *de*) + noun + *que*:

> une somme **trois fois plus** importante **que** *prévu*
> an amount three times greater than forecast/three times as great as expected
> *cette année, il est tombé* **moitié moins** *de pluie* **que** *d'habitude*
> this year there was half as much rain as usual

Intensification of a statement (*d'autant (plus) que, d'autant moins que*): see **46.2.**

Progressive process

The construction *de . . . en* ('from . . . to') is used with two nouns or two adverbs:

> *de temps en temps*   from time to time
> *de loin en loin*   at intervals (in time or space)

This construction is also used with *plus* and *moins*:

> *de plus en plus*   more and more
> *de moins en moins*   less and less

It can also be used on its own, as an adverb phrase:

> *j'y vais de moins en moins*   I go less and less (often)

or with an adjective:

> *dernièrement, elle se sent de plus en plus fatiguée*
> lately, she's been feeling more and more tired

or with a noun:

> *il y a de plus en plus de voitures en circulation*
> there are more and more cars on the roads

Part seven

Building sentences

So far, we have looked at how words are formed (**9–16**), and how they combine in groups (**17–26**) and phrases (**27–31**): the basic building blocks for communication in French. Most language, however, especially written language, consists of larger blocks: sentences.

Sentences can take various forms; these are examined in **32–37**:

32 **Basic sentence structure**
33 **Asking questions**
34 **Saying No: negative forms and uses**
35 **Passive constructions**
36 **Pronominal verbs and constructions**
37 **Impersonal verbs and constructions**

The traditional definition of a sentence is that it is complete in itself as regards both grammar and meaning, and contains a tensed verb. As we shall see (**32.5**), some parts of the sentence can be omitted, in speech and sometimes in writing, without loss of meaning, because they can be inferred from what has gone before.

32 Word order and meaning

32.1 The basic sentence
32.2 More complex sentences
32.3 Position of adverbs
32.4 *Aussi, ainsi, peut-être*
32.5 Verbless sentences

Word order is essential, in English and in French, to the communication of meaning: we only understand the difference in meaning between pairs of of sentences such as:

Pierre aime Marie   *Marie aime Pierre*
Peter likes Mary   Mary likes Peter

because all users of English or of French assume that the word before the verb is the subject of that verb, and the word after the verb is the object of that verb.

In other languages, such as Latin or, to a lesser extent, German, particular endings or articles often indicate whether a noun is subject or object of the verb. In these languages, word order is less important than it is in English or French for the communication of meaning.

IN ENGLISH and IN FRENCH, nouns carry no indication of whether they are being used as subject or object of the verb (though many pronouns do). Word order has a grammatical function: to indicate the subject (and the object, if there is one) of the verb. This does not mean, however, that word order is always fixed in French and in English: see, for example, **33** and **51**.

32.1 The basic sentence

The basic sentence in English and French is made up of two or three elements:
SV (subject + verb), or SVO (subject + verb + object, in that order):

SV   *elle a compris*   she (has) understood
SVO   *elle a compris la question*   she (has) understood the question

To this basic structure (SV or SVO), one or more complements (C), such as adjectives, adverbs or adverb phrases, can be added:

SVC	*la lune est* **ronde**	the moon is round
	Marie a réagi **rapidement**	Marie reacted swiftly
	Pierre part **à cinq heures**	Pierre's leaving at five
CSVCO	**aujourd'hui** *Marie a compris* **autrement** *la situation*	
CSVOC	today Marie saw the situation differently	

These complements give further information about the noun (adjectives: **see 12** and **26**), about the verb (adverbs: **see 30**), or about the circumstances (detached complements: **see 43–44**).

Sentences where the subject comes before the verb (SV, SVO, SVC etc.) constitute two-thirds of all sentences in non-literary written texts in French. Because of dislocation (**see 51.1**), this proportion is not so high in informal French, where the basic core of the sentence is expressed as pronouns (shown by the small letters s and o in the examples below). The nouns and phrases to which these pronouns correspond can occur at various points in the sentence:

S	V	C	O
mon père	*ne joue pas*	*souvent*	*à la Loterie*

can be expressed as:

	il n'y joue pas souvent, à la Loterie, mon père	(soVCOS)
or	*mon père il n'y joue pas souvent, à la Loterie*	(SsoVCO)
or	*la Loterie, il n'y joue pas souvent, mon père*	(OsoVCS)

With object pronouns, the SVO order is not followed in French: *je le vois*; *elle lui parle* (**see 18**).

32.2 More complex sentences

Within the basic structure, each element (S, V, O or C) can consist of several words:

S . . .	V . . .	O . . .
le Premier ministre, indisposé,	*n'a pas pu prononcer*	*le discours d'ouverture de la conférence internationale*
the Prime Minister, because of illness,	was unable to give	the opening address at the international conference

In more complex sentences, the basic sequence occurs more than once, for example when there is a relative clause (**see 42**):

S . . .	V . . .	C . . .	C . . .
l'homme **que la police recherchait depuis plusieurs jours**	*a été arrêté*	*hier soir*	*dans une banlieue de Paris*
the man the police had been looking for for several days	was arrested	last night	in a Paris suburb

The first part of the above sentence contains a further SVC sequence, where the object of the verb is represented by the pronoun *que*:

o	S	V	C
que	*la police*	*recherchait*	*depuis plusieurs jours*

Not all sentences consist of 'simple, neutral statements':

● instead of being a statement, a sentence can be a question **(see 33)**, or a negation **(see 34)**;

● instead of being simple, a sentence can have a phrase **(see 43–44)** or a coordinate clause **(see 45)** added to it, or a subordinate clause linked to it **(see 46–49)**;

● instead of being neutral, a sentence can be emphatic, or exclamative **(see 32.5)**;

● the basic word order can be changed by using a passive construction **(see 35)**, or dislocation or extraction **(see 51)**.

32.3 Position of adverbs

We have seen **(30)** that adverbs, whether single words such as *vite* or *lentement*, or phrases such as *à toute vitesse* or *à pas lents*, are not always as closely attached to the verb as their name ('ad-verb') suggests. Many adverbs refer, not directly to an action, but to the circumstances in which the action takes place:

hier	*à trois heures*	*ici*	*à trois kilomètres*
yesterday	at three o'clock	here	two miles away

We have also seen **(32.1)** that adverbs do not form part of the basic structure of a sentence, which is SV or SVO. In terms of this structure, adverbs are complements (C), and as such their position in the sentence is not wholly fixed.

The remarks that follow are intended to give some guidelines as to the usual place of adverbs in the French sentence.

After the verb

The usual position for an adverb in French is immediately after the verb:

*elle est arrivée **en retard*** — she arrived late
*il téléphone **souvent*** — he often rings

Two or more adverbs can occupy this position:

*elle n'arrive pas **souvent en retard pour son travail***
she doesn't often arrive late for work

But an adverb can be detached from this position, and placed at the beginning of the sentence:

***souvent**, il téléphone très tôt le matin* — he often rings very early in the morning

This has the advantage of keeping distinct the references to two different time scales: *souvent*, and *très tôt le matin*.

As a general rule, place adverbs after the verb, but be prepared to move one to the beginning of the sentence:

- if it might be confusing to have a string of adverbs together after the verb;
- if you want to give prominence to one adverb at the beginning of the sentence.

There is one position that the adverb does not occupy in French: between subject and verb. This contrasts with English, where some adverbs of time and manner can occupy this position:

he often rings   she quickly understood

IN FRENCH, adverbs of time and manner occupy this position only if the flow of the sentence is interrupted; this is indicated in speech by a pause and/or emphasis, and in writing by commas:

les hommes, ***souvent***, *sont cruels*   human beings are often cruel

This order of words represents a deliberate departure from the usual place of the adverb, which is after the verb.

With direct or indirect objects

If the verb has a direct object and one or more indirect objects, then any adverbs in the sentence are in competition with these for the position immediately after the verb:

Marie monte rapidement l'escalier   Marie hurries upstairs
(SVCO: simple description: no emphasis on the speed)
Marie monte l'escalier rapidement   Marie goes upstairs in a hurry
(SVOC: some emphasis on the speed)

In such cases, the difference in word order is not of great significance.

The adverb can be placed earlier, if the object consists of a particularly long phrase:

on parlera demain *de tous les détails de cette affaire*

or ***demain***, ***on parlera*** *de tous les détails de cette affaire*

or *tous les détails de cette affaire*, ***on en parlera demain*** (dislocation: **see 51.1**)

we'll talk about all the details tomorrow

With negative sentences

Several adverbs can form a unit with the negative word *pas*:

souvent	***pas souvent***	*vite*	***pas vite***
often	not often	quickly, fast	not quickly, not fast

In a complete sentence, this gives the following word order:

	*il ne voit **pas souvent** sa famille*	he doesn't often see his family
but	*il ne voit **pas** sa famille **très** souvent*	he doesn't see his family very often

An adverb used as an intensifier (**see 31.4**) is placed before *pas*:

*tu ne marches **vraiment pas** vite!*	you really don't walk fast!
*je n'ai **sûrement pas** l'intention d'y aller*	I certainly don't intend to go

This word order is more characteristic of informal than of formal usage, especially in the case of *même* ('even'):

*ils ne m'ont **même pas** répondu!*	they didn't even send a reply	(N2)
*ils ne m'ont **pas même** répondu!*	they didn't even send a reply	(N3)

Exercice 32/1   Position de l'adverbe 1: avec les temps simples

Travail à deux > Mise en commun

a   Complétez les phrases ci-dessous en ajoutant l'adverbe ou les adverbes (entre parenthèses) à la place qui vous semble la plus appropriée.

b   Avez-vous trouvé d'autres positions pour l'adverbe? Lesquelles? Pourquoi les trouvez-vous moins appropriées?

c   Présentez vos choix au reste du groupe, et discutez-en.

Exemple: On parlera de tout ça.   (ce soir)
Réponse possible: On parlera de tout ça ce soir.

1	Je lui dis bonjour.	(toujours)
2	Ne conduis pas!	(vite)
3	On ne le voit pas.	(à la bibliothèque; souvent)
4	Il y a des accidents.	(souvent; à ce carrefour)
5	J'ai fait trois heures de marche.	(hier; dans les collines)
6	Le brouillard se lèvera.	(rapidement; dans la matinée)
7	Je me lève.	(quelquefois; très tôt; le matin)
8	Je suis arrivé.	(ce matin; pour la première fois; depuis l'été; en retard)

With compound tenses

When there is no doubt as to which part of the sentence it refers to, an adverb can be placed before or after the past participle, as well as at the beginning or the end of the sentence:

*il est parti **vite***	he left quickly
*il est **vite** parti*	he soon left
*la voiture est partie **à toute vitesse** vers la ville*	the car sped off towards town
*la voiture est partie vers la ville **à toute vitesse***	the car went off towards town at great speed

*j'ai **tout de suite** compris ce qui se passait*   I realised at once what was going on

*j'ai compris **tout de suite** ce qui se passait*

***tout de suite**, j'ai compris ce qui se passait*

*j'ai compris ce qui se passait, **tout de suite***

In cases where it could apply to more than one part of the sentence, an adverb is placed as close as possible to the word or phrase it qualifies:

*j'ai compris **hier** ce qui se passait*   I realised yesterday what was going on

*j'ai compris ce qui s'était passé **hier***   I realised what had happened yesterday

If you are not sure where to place an adverb when writing French, try it out in more than one position, before you commit yourself.

With an infinitive

An adverb should be placed as close as possible to the verb to which it refers:

*elle apprend **lentement/peu à peu** à refaire sa vie*

she's slowly/gradually learning to put her life together again

*tu vas prendre **immédiatement** le train pour Paris*

you must take the train for Paris straight away

But   *tu vas prendre le train **immédiatement***   you must take the train at once

---

Exercice 32/2   **Position de l'adverbe 2: avec les temps composés ou l'infinitif**

Travail à deux > Mise en commun

a   Complétez les phrases ci-dessous en ajoutant l'adverbe (entre parenthèses) à la place qui vous semble la plus appropriée.

b   Avez-vous trouvé d'autres positions pour l'adverbe? Lesquelles? Pourquoi les trouvez-vous moins appropriées?

c   Présentez vos choix au reste du groupe, et discutez-en.

Exemple: Tu vas rentrer à la maison.   (immédiatement)

Réponse possible: Tu vas rentrer à la maison **immédiatement**.

1	On va découvrir qui est responsable.	(bientôt)
2	Je ne pourrai pas venir avec vous.	(demain)
3	J'ai entendu une voiture.	(distinctement)
4	Elle avait trouvé la réponse.	(tout de suite)
5	Je leur dis de faire attention.	(toujours)
6	Il a répondu à leurs questions.	(calmement)
7	Je me suis posé la même question.	(quelquefois)
8	Tu vas savoir ce qui se passe.	(demain)

32.4 *Aussi, ainsi, peut-être*

Aussi

The meaning and use of *aussi* can cause problems for learners of French, since it can mean either 'also' or 'therefore', depending on how it is used.

Meaning 1: 'also'

In everyday usage, *aussi* means 'also', 'as well', 'too', when used in the following ways:

et aussi	*j'en ai parlé à Pierre, **et aussi** à Paul/et à Paul **aussi***
	I mentioned it to Pierre, and (to) Paul as well
lui (etc.) *aussi*	*Qui veut de la tarte? Moi! **Moi aussi!***
	Who wants some flan? Me! Me too!
	*ensuite, je suis passé chez Boris. **Lui aussi** avait appris la nouvelle*
	then I went round to Boris's. He had heard the news as well

(Similarly: *toi aussi, vous aussi*: 'you too'; *eux aussi*: 'they too': **see 19.3**.)

In everyday speech and writing, *aussi* meaning 'also' is not used at the beginning of a statement or sentence.

IN ENGLISH, one says:	'Also', 'And also', 'And besides', 'And anyway'	
IN FRENCH, one says:	*D'ailleurs, . . .* or *Et puis, . . .*	(N2)
IN ENGLISH, one writes:	'And moreover', 'In addition'	
IN FRENCH, one writes:	*En outre, . . .* or *En plus, . . .*	(N3)

Meaning 2: 'therefore'

In formal usage, *aussi*, at the beginning of a sentence, means 'thus', 'therefore':

*les manifestations continuaient. **Aussi** le gouvernement **décida** de négocier*	(N3)
the demonstrations were still going on, and so the government decided to negotiate	

Ainsi ('thus', 'in this way') can be used in the same way as *aussi* at the start of a sentence:

*elle verrouilla toutes les portes. **Ainsi** elle se sentit en sécurité*	(N3)
she bolted all the doors; in this way, she felt safe	

Peut-être ('perhaps', 'maybe')

Three constructions, each with the same meaning but with a different word order, are possible with the adverb *peut-être* ('perhaps', 'maybe'):

a Inversion of verb and subject

peut-être sont-ils déjà arrivés	perhaps they have arrived already	(N3)

If the subject is a noun, not a pronoun, a dislocated construction (**see 51.1b**) is used:

***peut-être les autres sont-ils** déjà arrivés*	perhaps the others have arrived already	(N3)

This construction (with VS inversion) is characteristic of formal usage: you will generally find it more convenient to use **b** or **c** instead.

b   Use with *que* (no inversion)
   peut-être qu'ils *sont déjà arrivés*
   peut-être que les autres *sont déjà arrivés*

c   Postponement of *peut-être*
   ils/les autres sont ***peut-être*** *déjà arrivés*
   ils/les autres sont déjà arrivés, ***peut-être***

When you study the three ways of formulating a question in French (**see 33**), you will find that each of them corresponds to one of these three ways of using *peut-être*.

Exercice 32/3   *Aussi* et *peut-être*   Travail à deux > Mise en commun

a   Dans les phrases ci-dessous, ajoutez aussi (1–4) ou peut-être (5–8) à la place qui vous semble la plus appropriée (et en modifiant, s'il le faut, l'ordre des mots).

b   Après avoir vérifié vos réponses, donnez l'équivalent en anglais de chaque phrase.

(aussi)

Exemple: Le musée était fermé. Nous avons décidé de rentrer.
Réponse: Le musée était fermé, **aussi nous avons** décidé de rentrer.

1   Elle avait reçu une carte de ses parents et une de sa grand-mère.
2   Je ne voulais pas qu'elle s'inquiète: je ne lui ai rien dit.
3   Je viens d'apprendre la nouvelle: vous comprendrez si je n'ai pas grand-chose à vous dire.
4   J'ai téléphoné à Olga. Elle avait entendu l'explosion.

(peut-être)

Exemple: Vous avez entendu parler de ce philosophe.
Réponses possibles: Peut-être **avez-vous** entendu parler de ce philosophe.
   Peut-être **que** vous avez entendu parler de ce philosophe.
   Vous avez entendu parler de ce philosophe, **peut-être**.

5   Ils n'ont pas reçu notre lettre.
6   Vous allez trouver ma question naïve.
7   J'ai mal compris votre question.
8   Il avait trop mangé la veille.

32.5 Verbless sentences

Many spoken or written sentences do not fit the conventional definition of a sentence:

● a statement may not make sense on its own, but be perfectly meaningful to both speaker and listener, because the missing elements, although not actually spoken, are being pointed to, or referred to, or have already been said;
● many complete statements do not contain a tensed verb.

Incomplete sentences, that is to say sentences which do not contain a tensed verb, are used in a wide variety of contexts. They can consist of:

● truncated sentences, where the remaining part of the sentence keeps its grammatical markers;
● telegraphic sentences, where most grammatical links between words are omitted;
● one-word sentences.

Truncated sentences

Truncated sentences are used in recipes, stories, diaries, abbreviated constructions and exclamations:

Recipes The infinitive is sometimes used in recipes, in place of an imperative:

verser dans une casserole   pour into a saucepan

Stories A noun (word or phrase) is used on its own in the main clause to make an account more dramatic:

Un pas de plus, *et il était mort*   one step further and he'd be dead
(instead of: *s'il faisait un pas de plus*, . . .)

Sentences of this kind are called *phrases nominales* in French.

Diaries Any account of everyday life, etc., written in diary form, or in order to resemble such a style, can consist of verbless sentences such as:

Midi. Toujours pas de nouvelles. Tristesse.   Midday. Still no news. Feel sad.

Abbreviated constructions

Certain constructions can be abbreviated by the omission of *c'est* or *il est* at the beginning of a sentence:

- **adjective + à + infinitive** is used when the clause that is the object of the infinitive occurs before the adjective + *à* + infinitive construction:

quand est-ce qu'ils seront de retour? **Difficile à dire**
when will they be back? (It's) hard to say

- **adjective + *de* + infinitive** is used when the clause that is the object of the infinitive occurs after the adjective + *de* + infinitive construction:

> *les alpinistes sont partis avant l'aube.* ***Difficile de savoir*** *quand ils seront de retour*
> the mountaineers set out before dawn. It's hard to know when they will be back

Exclamations Exclamations (see below) can consist of incomplete sentences:

> *excellent, ce fromage!* (this is) fine cheese!
> (instead of: *il est excellent, ce fromage*)
> *mon rôti!* the joint!
> (instead of: *mon rôti est en train de brûler*)

Telegraphic sentences

Telegraphic sentences are used in headlines, notices, and instructions:

Headlines Headlines in French newspapers often consist of complete sentences, but a telegraphic style is also used:

> *Accident mortel à Evian* Fatal accident in Evian

Notices A telegraphic style can be used in notices:

> *Éviter jeter déchets. Merci* Please avoid dumping rubbish. Thank you
> (instead of: *Éviter **de** jeter **des** déchets*)

Instructions The infinitive, plus a telegraphic style, can be used in instructions:

> *agiter avant emploi* shake before using

One-word sentences

One-word sentences are used in exclamations, and in journalese and fiction:

Exclamations Exclamations can consist of interjections, imperatives or adverbs (and also of incomplete sentences: see above):

Interjections:	*hé!*	hey!	*hé ben!*	well!
Imperatives:	*dis donc!*	I say!	*eh ben dis donc!*	I don't believe it!
Adverbs:	*voyons!*	come on (now)!	*ben voyons!*	you don't say!

Journalese A single-word sentence is used in newspaper and magazine reports (and also in fiction, etc.) to dramatise an event:

> *ils pensaient être à l'abri des avalanches.* ***Erreur!*** *Dès le lendemain, . . .*
> they thought they were safe from avalanches. But they were wrong. The very next day, . . .
> *elle ouvrit le placard.* ***Stupeur!*** *Il était entièrement vide*
> she opened the cupboard. To her amazement, it was completely empty

Phrases nominales (etc.) Travail à deux > Mise en commun

a   Avec un(e) partenaire, composez à partir des phrases ci-dessous des phrases nominales, tronquées, télégraphiques, etc.

b   Pour chaque phrase, donnez aussi la situation dans laquelle elle pourrait être utilisée.

Exemple: Il y a eu une collision sur un passage à niveau.

Réponse possible: Collision sur le passage à niveau.   (titre dans un journal)

1   Cette glace à la vanille est délicieuse!

2   Il faut agiter la bouteille avant de s'en servir.

3   Ton idée est géniale!

4   Nous n'avons plus de pain.

5   Si j'entends encore un bang sonique, je vais téléphoner au ministère.

6   Pour avoir des renseignements, adressez-vous à la première porte à gauche, au premier étage.

7   C'était dimanche, et les enfants pleuraient parce qu'on n'avait rien à manger.

8   Il est défendu de déposer des ordures.

9   Elle a vérifié les numéros sur le billet, et elle a été surprise de découvrir qu'elle avait gagné.

Inferences

IN ENGLISH, phrases such as 'I am', 'I will', 'I can', 'he does', 'do they?', 'must you?' are a very concise and flexible way of referring to a verb that has just been used, without actually repeating it.

IN FRENCH, the equivalent phrases are often a little longer, and contain more grammatical information:

Vous êtes Mme Dupont? Oui, c'est moi.
Are you Mme Dupont? I am.

C'est vrai qu'ils ont des glaces à la rhubarbe? Oui, c'est vrai.
Do they really sell rhubarb ice cream? Yes, they do.

Tu lui téléphoneras, c'est sûr? Je n'y manquerai pas.
Will you definitely phone him/her? I will.

Exercice 32/5   **Réponses brèves**   Travail à deux > Mise en commun

Avec un(e) partenaire, posez tour à tour une des questions ci-dessous. La réponse (qui peut commencer par Oui ou Non) doit être suivi d'une phrase très courte, mais sans répéter le verbe et les détails contenus dans la question.

Exemple: Vous êtes sûr de les avoir vus?
Réponse possible: Oui, j'en suis sûr.

1   Tu as mis les valises dans le coffre?
2   On pourrait se voir samedi?
3   Vous avez bien réfléchi à ce que vous allez dire?
4   Est-ce qu'ils ont déjà annoncé notre vol?
5   C'est toi qui as décoré la chambre?
6   Tu promets de ne répéter cette histoire à personne?

33 Asking questions

33.1 Word order in Yes/No questions
33.2 WH- question words
33.3 WH- questions: word order
33.4 Indirect questions

Asking a question is different from making a statement: a question invites the listener or reader to make some form of response. This means that a question has to be formulated in such a way that it will be recognised as a question, and not as a statement.

There are several means of formulating a question, in speech and writing; often, two or more of these features occur together.

Means of indicating a question include:

- in speech or writing: using a different word order,
                                using a question word;
- in speech: using different intonation,
                                giving particular emphasis;
- in writing: adding a question mark at the end.

All of these means are used in both English and French, so that you will usually have no difficulty in spotting that a question is being asked in French. But there are differences between English and French in the use of question words (**see 33.2**) and of word order (**see 33.3**): you will need to know these in order to ask comprehensible questions in French.

Types of question

It is useful to distinguish two types of question:

Yes/No questions:	Q: Has he arrived yet?	A: **No**.
	Q: Did you see her?	A: **Yes**.
WH- questions:	Q: **What**'s the matter?	A: . . .
	Q: **Why** did he do that?	A: . . .

Intonation and emphasis   (see also 7.2)

In Yes/No questions in French, there is usually a rising intonation towards the end, with emphasis on one or more syllables of words which are part of the subject of the question:

alors, tu l'as fini, ton travail?

well, have you finished your work?

pourriez-vous m'indiquer le chemin de la gare, s'il vous plaît?

could you show me the way to the station, please?

In WH- questions, the question word is emphasised (wherever it comes), and there is a falling intonation towards the end:

pourquoi tu lui as parlé comme ça? (N2)

why did you speak to him/her like that?

bonjour, monsieur: comment allez-vous? (N3)

good morning/good afternoon: how are you?

33.1 Word order in Yes/No questions

Yes/No questions follow three different patterns in French:

a *Est-ce que* + usual word order   (SV, SVO)

b Usual word order   (SV, SVO)   (N2)

c Inversion of verb and subject pronoun   (Vs, VsO)   (N3)

a *Est-ce que* + usual word order

This form of Yes/No question can be used in all situations, formal or informal: the question phrase *Est-ce que* is useful as a means of alerting the listener that a question is being asked: at the start of a transaction, exchange or conversation, for example.

> When in doubt as to how to formulate a question, use the *Est-ce que* form.

Examples:

est-ce que le facteur a passé?	has the postman been?
est-ce que Marie habite toujours à Londres?	is Marie still living in London?

The question phrase *est-ce que/est-ce qu'* is invariable, and the word *est* has no function as a verb in the question as a whole:

*est-ce que ta mère **est** là?*	is your mother there/in?
*est-ce que ta mère **a** téléphoné?*	has your mother phoned?

The English form of the question is no guide to how it is formulated in French: in these examples, *est* or *a* cannot be omitted in French.

A noun which is the subject or object of the verb can be detached and replaced by a subject or object pronoun (**see 51.1b**):

*est-ce qu'**elle** est là, **ta sœur**?*	is your sister there?
*est-ce que vous **l'**avez vu, **mon chien**?*	have you seen my dog?

b   Usual word order

This form of Yes/No question (SV, SVO, with rising intonation at the end) is used when expressing a question in the course of an informal conversation:

> *tu sais ce qu'elle m'a dit?*
>
> d'you know what she told me/said (to me)?   (N2)
>
> *alors, c'est bientôt les vacances?*
>
> so, are you (off) on holiday soon?   (N2)

The subject or object of the verb can be detached (**see 51.1b**) and replaced by a subject or object pronoun:

> *et ton frère, il est toujours aussi actif?*   (N2)
>
> (and) is your brother as busy as ever?
>
> *tu l'as vue, sa nouvelle série à la télé?*   (N2)
>
> have you seen his/her new TV series?

c   Inversion of verb and subject pronoun

This form of Yes/No question is used in formal situations: when speaking to a stranger, or in writing. When the subject of the verb is a pronoun, the construction is straightforward (Vs, VsO):

> *pardon, monsieur: avez-vous vu un petit chat noir?*   (N3)
>
> excuse me: have you seen a little black cat?
>
> *auriez-vous une chambre pour ce soir?*   (N3)
>
> do you (happen to) have a room for tonight?

If the subject of the verb is a noun, it must be detached and replaced by a pronoun:

> *les étudiants ont-ils décidé de négocier?*   (N3)
>
> have the students decided to negotiate?
>
> *les personnes seules doivent-elles payer un supplément?*
>
> do people on their own have to pay extra?

In these examples, the sentences cannot begin with *ont* or *doivent*.

Exercice 33/1   **Comment formuler une question (interrogation totale: Oui/Non)**

Travail à deux > Mise en commun

a   Avec un(e) partenaire, formulez des questions à partir des phrases ci-dessous. Dans chaque cas, essayez de décider quelle est la meilleure formulation (a Est-ce que; b SVO ou c VSO), et pourquoi.

b   Ensuite, discutez vos conclusions avec le reste du groupe.

Exemple: Non, ils n'ont rien vu.

> *Questions possibles:*   a Est-ce qu'ils ont vu quelque chose?
>
> b Ils ont vu quelque chose?
>
> c Ont-ils vu quelque chose?

(Les trois formulations sont possibles; **b** est moins dramatique que **c**, qui est un peu plus formelle.)

1   Oui, je peux vous indiquer le chemin de la gare.
2   Oui, mes parents trouvent que c'était une bonne idée.
3   Non, je ne sais pas ce qu'elle t'a dit.
4   Non, Marie ne sait pas ce qui s'est passé.
5   Oui, je veux bien essayer votre gâteau.
6   Non, nous n'avons pas terminé les préparatifs pour Noël.

33.2 WH- question words

■ WH- words in English and French

	English	French
Persons *Qui*: who		
subject of verb	who	*qui, qui est-ce qui*
direct object of verb	who (N2), whom (N4)	*qui, qui est-ce que*
indirect object + *à*	who . . . to (N2), whose, to whom (N4)	*à qui*
indirect object + *de*	who . . . of (N2), whose, of whom (N4)	*de qui*
indirect object + *pour/avec*	who . . . for/with (N2), for/with whom (N4)	*pour qui/avec qui*
indirect object + compound preposition	who . . . about (N2), about whom (N4)	*à propos de qui*
Things, ideas *Que, quoi*: what		
subject of verb	what	*qu'est-ce qui*
direct object of verb	what	*que, qu'est-ce que* . . . *quoi* (N2) (at end)
indirect object + *à*	what . . . to (N2), to what (N3)	*à quoi* (not a place)
indirect object + *de*	what . . . of, whose (N2)	*de quoi*
indirect object + *avec*	what . . . with	*avec quoi*
Other WH- words	where (. . . to), what . . . to/ in/on, to/in/on what (N3)	*où* (place)
	when	*quand*
	how, in what way	*comment*
	how, to what extent	*combien*
	how much, how many	*combien*
	why, what . . . for	*pourquoi*

Persons, things *Quel*: which + noun		
subject/direct object	which + noun	*quel* + noun
indirect object + *à*	which + noun . . . to, to which + noun	*à quel* + noun
indirect object + *de*	which + noun . . . of	*de quel* + noun
indirect object + *avec* (etc.)	which + noun . . . with (etc.)	*avec* (etc.) *quel* + noun
Persons, things *Lequel*: which one		
subject/direct object	which one(s) (of)	*lequel (de)*
indirect object + *à*	to which one(s) (of), which one(s) (of) . . . to	*auquel (de)*
indirect object + *de*	of which one(s) (of), which one(s) (of) . . . of	*duquel (de)*
indirect object + *avec* (etc.)	with (etc.) which one(s) (of), which one(s) (of) ... with (etc.)	*avec* (etc.) *lequel (de)*

33.3 Word order in WH- questions

WH- questions in French follow the same three patterns as Yes/No questions (**see 33.1**), with the addition of a WH- word or phrase:

a WH- word + *est-ce que* + usual word order   (SV, SVO)

b WH- word + usual word order   (SV, SVO)   (N2)

c WH- word + inversion of verb and subject pronoun   (Vs, VsO and SVs, SVsO)   (N3)

a   WH- word + *est-ce que* + usual word order

This form of WH- question produces a fairly long formula at the start of the question, and is less frequently used than patterns **b** and **c**. It is a way of avoiding the informality of **b** and the formality of **c**:

> *à quelle heure est-ce que ta soeur est arrivée, finalement?*
> what time did your sister arrive, in the end?
> *pourquoi est-ce qu'il faut remplir tous ces formulaires?*
> why do we have to fill in all these forms?

The subject or object of the verb can be detached (**see 51.1b**) and replaced by a subject or object pronoun:

> *à quelle heure est-ce qu'elle est arrivée, ta sœur?*
> what time did your sister arrive?
> *où est-ce qu'on l'a vu, ce chanteur?*
> where was it that we saw that singer?
> *quand est-ce que tu y vas, à Paris?*
> when are you off to Paris?

b WH- word + usual word order

This form of WH- question is characteristic of everyday speech, and is not used in formal situations:

pourquoi tu pleures?	what're you crying for?	(N2)
à quoi tu penses?	what're you thinking about?	(N2)

If the subject or object of the verb is a noun, it can be detached and replaced by a subject or object pronoun:

*combien elle **en** a vendu, **de montres**?*	how many watches did she sell?	(N2)

The WH- word can come after the sequence SV/SVO, though this would sound impolite in formal situations:

*ton train arrive **à quelle heure**?*	when does your train get in?	(N2)

c WH- word + inversion of verb and subject pronoun

This form of WH- question is used in several everyday expressions. When the subject of the verb is a pronoun, the construction is straightforward:

quelle heure est-il? où allez-vous?	what's the time? where are you going?
à quoi pensez-vous?	what are you thinking about?
que pensez-vous de cette voiture?	what do you think of that car?

When the subject of the verb is a noun, the noun can be placed after the verb only if there is no direct object:

Où habite Paul?	Where does Paul live?
A qui sont ces chaussures?	Whose shoes are these?

But with ***pourquoi***, a dislocated construction is always used in formal situations:

Pourquoi les hommes sont-ils méchants?	(N3)
Why is mankind cruel/wicked?	

If there is a direct object, the subject noun is detached and replaced by a pronoun:

*Comment **les alpinistes** ont-ils retrouvé **la piste**?*	(N3)
How did the mountaineers find the track?	

Exercice 33/2 **Comment formuler une question (interrogation partielle: *qui*, etc.)**

Travail à deux > Mise en commun

a Avec un(e) partenaire, formulez des questions à partir des phrases ci-dessous. Dans chaque cas, essayez de décider quelle est la meilleure formulation (mot interrogatif + a est-ce que; b SVO et c VSO), et pourquoi.

b Ensuite, discutez vos conclusions avec le reste du groupe.

> **Exemple:** Elle a fait cette erreur parce qu'elle était fatiguée.
>
> *Questions possibles:* a Pourquoi est-ce qu'elle a fait cette erreur?
>
> (formulation b (Pourquoi elle a fait cette erreur?) est possible, mais un peu abrupte; c (Pourquoi a-t-elle fait cette erreur?) est possible dans une situation formelle: enquête, procès, etc.)
>
> 1 Ce sac est à moi.
> 2 C'est lui qui a préparé ce plat.
> 3 Il n'a rien dit concernant le chômage.
> 4 Le Président n'a rien dit concernant le chômage.
> 5 Je vais très bien, merci.
> 6 Les autorités s'inquiètent parce que la pollution s'aggrave.
> 7 Elle ne pensait à rien de précis.
> 8 Marie ne pensait à rien de précis.
> 9 J'ai rangé tes chaussettes dans le tiroir.
> 10 J'ai vu l'accusé devant le magasin vers minuit.

Exclamations   (see 32.5)

Some exclamations take the form of questions (to which an answer is not usually expected!):

qu'est-ce qu'il fait chaud! (N2)	(my,) it's hot!
où allons-nous!	where will it all end!

Answering WH- questions

When answering a WH- question, one can use various types of phrase or clause, without a main clause, when the main clause is implied in the question:

Où est-elle allée?	*A Paris/Chez sa mère*	(adverb phrase: **see 30**)
Where's she gone?	To Paris/To her mother's	
Comment fait-on cela?	*En la remuant doucement*	(gerund: **see 44.2**)
How does one do that?	By stirring it gently	
Pourquoi . . .?	*Parce que . . .*	(subordinate clause: **see 46–48**)
Quand . . .?/A quel moment . . .?	*Quand . . .*	
Qu'est-ce que tu dis?	*Qu'il faut partir*	(completive: **see 49**)
What are you saying?	That we must go	

Exercice 33/3   **Questions et réponses**   Travail à deux

a   Dites à haute voix une des phrases ci-dessous; votre partenaire doit poser une question, la plus brève possible, sur ce que vous venez de dire. (Vous pouvez vous servir de la **Table (33.2)** pour vous rappeler les mots interrogatifs en français.)

b   Essayez de répondre, le plus vite possible, à la question que votre partenaire vient de vous poser.

Exemple: Je suis allé à Paris.
Question possible: Avec qui?
Réponse possible: Avec ma sœur.

Exemple: J'ai posé mon sac quelque part.
Question possible: Où?
Réponse possible: Sur un fauteuil, peut-être.

1   J'ai trouvé la solution: c'était facile!
2   Cette statue lui a coûté une fortune!
3   On pourrait inviter quelques amis.
4   J'ai réussi à contacter un des clients qu'on cherchait.
5   Lionel a quitté son travail.
6   Sarah a eu le poste qu'elle voulait.

33.4 Indirect questions

A **direct** question is one which, when written down, ends with a question mark:
   Il a dit: 'A quelle heure arriverons-nous?'
   He said: 'What time will we arrive?'

An **indirect** question, when written down, does not end with a question mark; it is a factual report of a question that has been asked:
   Il m'a demandé à quelle heure nous arriverions
   He asked me what time we would arrive

Indirect questions can be either Yes/No questions or WH- questions.

Yes/No indirect questions are constructed in the same way as completives (**see 49**):

English		French	
I don't know	if/whether	*je ne sais pas*	*si*
I wonder	if/whether	*je me demande*	*si*
she asked me	if/whether	*elle m'a demandé*	*si*
I doubt	if/whether	*je doute*	*que*

287

I'm not sure	if/whether	*je ne suis pas sûr*	*que*
I know	that	*je sais*	*que*
I'm sure	that	*je suis certain*	*que*

WH- indirect questions use the same WH- words as the corresponding direct questions (**see table, 33.2**), with one exception: *ce qui*, *ce que* (see below):

Person	**English**	**French**
subject/direct object	who	*qui*
indirect object	who . . . to/of/with	*à/de/avec qui*
	in whose name	*au nom de qui*

Thing, Idea		
subject	what	***ce qui***
direct object	what	***ce que***
indirect object	what . . . to/of/with	*à/de/avec quoi*
	about which	*à propos de quoi*
	where (to)	*où*
	where . . . from	*d'où*

Person, Thing + Noun		
subject/direct object	which + noun	*quel* (etc.) + noun
indirect object	to/of/for/about	*à/de/pour/à propos de*
	which + noun	*quel* + noun

Other WH- words		
	how	*comment*
	how much, how many	*combien (de)*
	why	*pourquoi*
	when	*quand*

Word order in indirect questions

An indirect question is presented, not as a question, but as a piece of information, and so the order of words in all indirect questions is as for statements: SV/SVO.

Examples:

*elle m'a demandé **pourquoi j'avais fait** cela*
she asked me why I'd done that

*je ne savais pas **combien** de temps **il faudrait***
I didn't know how long it would take

With *(se) demander où*, the order of words can be either SV(O) or VS(O):

je te demande où Paul habite/où habite Paul
I'm asking you where Paul lives

But: *je sais où elle va*
I know where she's going

Ce qui, ce que in indirect questions

Ce qui and *ce que* are the only WH- words with a different form in indirect questions from their form in direct questions (*Qu'est-ce qui* and *Qu'est-ce que*):

Direct

    Elle a dit: 'Qu'est-ce qui se passe?'   She said: 'What's going on?'

Indirect

    *Elle a demandé **ce qui** se passait*   She asked what was happening

Direct

    *Il a dit: '**Qu'est-ce qu'**on va faire?'*   He said: 'What shall we do?'

Indirect

    *Il a demandé **ce qu'**on allait faire*   He asked what we were going to do

Je sais que . . . and *Je sais ce que . . .*

*Je sais **que*** ('I know that . . .') and *Je sais **ce que*** ('I know what . . .') are both indirect questions, and are similar in form, but one is followed by a completive clause, and the other by a relative construction:

Completive (see 49): *que*	**Relative (see 43.2):** *ce que*
('that' – or no link word – in English)	('what', in English)
*je sais **qu'**il est là*	*je sais **ce qu'**il fait*
I know (that) he's there	I know what he's doing
*on m'a dit **qu'**elle avait 20 ans*	*on m'a dit **ce qu'**elle avait*
I was told (that) she was 20	I was told what was the matter with her

---

Exercice 33/4   **Questions indirectes**   Travail individuel

Reformulez les phrases ci-dessous pour faire des questions indirectes. N'oubliez pas de faire tous les changements nécessaires.

Exemple: 'Qu'est-ce que tu as fait?', m'a-t-il demandé.

Réponse: Il m'a demandé **ce que** j'avais fait.

1   Qui a dit ça? Rappelez-moi.
2   'Combien de temps faudra-t-il?', nous a-t-elle demandé.
3   Qu'est-ce qu'elle a dit? J'ai essayé de me rappeler.
4   Quel train a-t-il pris? On ne pouvait pas savoir.
5   'Comment faites-vous pour écrire si vite?', m'a demandé l'employé.
6   Qu'est-ce qui le rend si dynamique? Je ne comprends pas.
7   Combien de coups de feu ai-je entendus? Je ne sais pas.
8   'Où allez-vous?', nous a demandé Laurent.
9   'Qu'est-ce qui se passe?, a demandé Laurence.
10 Qu'est-ce que tu veux? Voilà ce que j'aimerais savoir.

Comme, comment, combien in direct and indirect questions

	Comme	*Comment*	*Combien*
USE	not in direct Q in indirect Q not + adj or adv in exclamations	in direct Q in indirect Q not + adj or adv	in direct Q in indirect Q + adj or adv (N4)
MEANING	**time** ('as time passes') comparison ('as well as') cause ('since') degree ('how')	indicates **manner**	indicates **degree**

Alternatives

à quel point	*de quelle façon*	*dans quelle mesure*
to what extent	in what way	to what extent

Examples:

Comme

*tu vois **comme** il fait chaud*	you can see how hot it is
*voyez **comme** il est sage!*	look how well-behaved he is!

Comment

*je sais **comment** il a réussi à faire ça*	I know how he managed to do that
*j'aime **comment** elle travaille*	I like the way she works

Combien

*je sais **combien** elle travaille*	I know how much she works
*je sais **combien** tu souffres*	I know how hard it is for you
*remarquez **combien** ils sont différents*	notice how different they are (N3)

34 Saying No: negative forms and uses

34.1 When to use *ne . . . pas*, and when to use *pas*
34.2 Negative words and phrases
34.3 Order of words in negative expressions
34.4 Combinations of negative words
34.5 Using negative words without a verb

34.1 When to use *ne . . . pas*, and when to use *pas*

IN ENGLISH, the key negative word is '**not**'; the negative is expressed by adding 'not' after the verb, or 'do not' before the verb; in everyday speech (N2), 'not' is usually shortened:

Positive	he is here	she will be there	I know	
Negative	he is **not** here	she will **not** be there	I **do not** know	(N3)
	he is**n't** here	she **won't** be there	I **don't** know	(N2)

IN FRENCH, the key negative word is ***pas***; the negative is expressed, in formal situations (N3), by adding ***ne*** before the verb and ***pas*** after the verb; in everyday speech (N2), ***pas*** is, more often than not, used without *ne*:

Positive	*je sais*	*c'est possible*	*elle va arriver*	
Negative	*je **ne** sais **pas***	*ce **n'**est **pas** possible*	*elle **ne** va **pas** arriver*	(N3)
	*je sais **pas***	*c'est **pas** possible*	*elle va **pas** arriver*	(N2)

Try to develop two sets of reflexes for using negative expressions in French:

● with *ne*, for all formal situations (N3): this is what will be expected of you in academic work, interviews and job applications;

● without *ne*, for everyday conversation (N2): this is what French speakers do. They are more likely to include *ne* in subordinate clauses (**see 46–48**), which are themselves a sign of careful use of language, and also whenever they feel that correct French is called for – when speaking to a foreign visitor, for example!

Constructing negative expressions correctly in French means being able to apply more than one rule at once. The following explanations, examples and exercises take you step-by-step through each separate rule, and then give you practice in applying them together.

34.2 Negative words and phrases

As well as *pas* ('not'), other words and phrases are used, in English ('no more', 'no longer', 'nothing', 'no one' etc.) and in French, to give negative or restrictive meaning.

The following examples show how the main negative words are used in French. One can distinguish three categories of use:

a to negate a verb used intransitively;
b to negate a verb used transitively;
c to negate the object of a verb.

Ne . . . pas ('not')

a	*je ne crois pas*	I don't think so
b	*je ne comprends pas ce qu'il dit*	I can't understand what he says
c	*je ne le crois pas un seul instant*	I don't believe it for one moment

Ne . . . plus ('no longer', 'not now')

a	*il ne pleut plus*	it's stopped raining/it's not raining now
b	*je ne sais plus ce que j'ai dit*	I can't remember now what I said
c	*il n'y aura plus un seul arbre*	there won't be a single tree left

---

Ne . . . plus ('no longer') and *pas encore* ('not yet')

These two constructions do not mean the same thing: in fact, they have opposite meanings: *ne . . . plus* looks back in time, *pas encore* looks forward in time:

*elle n'est **plus** là*	she's not there any more/she's gone
*elle n'est **pas encore** arrivée*	she's not arrived yet
*ce n'est **plus** possible*	you can't do that now/any more
*ce n'est **pas encore** possible*	you can't do that yet

Exercice 34/1   *Ne . . . pas* et *ne . . . plus*   Travail individuel

Récrivez les phrases ci-dessous au négatif, en employant ne . . . pas ou ne . . . plus, selon le sens.

Exemple: Je sais où Marie habite en ce moment.
  Réponse: Je ne sais pas où Marie habite en ce moment.

Exemple: Je sais où j'ai mis mon stylo.
  Réponse: Je ne sais plus où j'ai mis mon stylo.

1 Mes lunettes sont où je les ai laissées.
2 Je suis allé en Allemagne cette année.
3 Je comprends ce qu'elle dit.
4 Les gens croient aux sorcières.
5 Il pleut depuis deux jours.
6 Dans les pays riches, on meurt de faim.
7 C'était une bonne idée.
8 A mon âge, ça m'intéresse.

Ne . . . jamais ('never')

a *cette machine ne se trompe jamais*   this machine never makes a mistake
b *il ne boit jamais d'alcool*   he never drinks (spirits)
c *ils ne mangent jamais avant huit heures*   they never eat before eight

Ne . . . rien ('nothing')

b *je n'entends rien*   I can't hear anything
       elle n'a peur de rien   she's afraid of nothing
c *il ne dira rien de nouveau*   he won't say anything new
       (*rien de, quelque chose de* + invariable adjective: **see 12.2**)

Pas rien can be used, with the meaning 'not nothing', 'quite something':
       c'est pas rien, ça!   (N2)   that's quite something!

Ne . . . personne ('no one')

b *je ne vois personne*   I can't see anyone
       je ne le dirai à personne   I won't tell anyone
c *on n'y rencontre personne d'intéressant*   you don't meet anyone interesting
                                                          there
       (*personne de, quelqu'un de* + invariable adjective: **see 12.2**)

Ne . . . aucun(e) ('not one', 'not any')

b *il n'y a aucun doute là-dessus*   there's no doubt about it
c *je n'aime aucun de ces tableaux*   I don't like any of these/those
                                                  paintings

Ne . . . nul(le) can be used, in formal situations (N3), instead of *aucun(e)*:
       *je n'avais **nulle** envie de les voir*   (N3)   I had no wish to see them

Ne . . . ni . . . ni ('neither . . . nor', 'not either . . . or')

a *elle ne fume ni ne boit*   (N3)   she neither smokes nor drinks
c *je n'écouterai ni lui ni elle*   I won't listen either to him or to her
       tu ne le diras ni à lui ni à elle   you're to tell neither him nor her

In spontaneous speech or writing, the first part of a 'neither . . . nor' sentence can be completed with *pas,* and the second part (with *ni*) added on:

*je ne l'ai **pas** vu, ni son frère*   (N2)   I didn't see him or his brother

Note: the use of *pas* with ***personne*** or ***aucun(e)*** is regarded as incorrect French.

Ne . . . que ('only')

a   *il ne fait que travailler*   all he does is work (***faire*** + infinitive: **see 39.3**)

c   *elle n'écoute que sa grand-mère*   the only one she listens to is her grandmother

IN ENGLISH, the word 'only' is often placed early in the sentence:

> she only arrived from Paris an hour ago
>
> I only understood the meaning of his question after the end of the discussion

IN FRENCH, the *que* of *ne . . . que* is placed later in the sentence, just before the noun it qualifies:

> *elle n'est arrivée de Paris **qu'**il y a une heure*
>
> *je n'ai compris le sens de sa question **qu'**après la fin de la discussion*

Compare the meaning and construction of ***ne . . . que*** ('only'), above, with ***ne . . . pas que*** ('not only'), **in 34.4**.

Exercice 34/2   **Expressions négatives**   Travail individuel

a   Récrivez les phrases ci-dessous au négatif, en employant une expression négative qui convient au sens de la phrase.

b   Écrivez l'équivalent en anglais de chaque phrase au négatif.

Exemple: J'aime tous ses disques.

Réponse: Je n'aime **aucun de** ses disques.

1   Comment lui répondre? J'ai une idée.
2   Elle tolérait ses silences et ses remarques acides.
3   Je suis sûr qu'elle racontera l'histoire à quelqu'un.
4   J'ai un doute quant à la vérité de ce qu'il dit.
5   En relisant le dossier, vous trouverez quelque chose de nouveau.
6   Quant à moi, j'approuve et je condamne sa conduite.
7   Oui, je sais que tu as envie de les rencontrer.
8   On a sonné; elle savait que ce serait quelqu'un d'intéressant.

Exercice 34/3   *Ne ... que*   Travail individuel

Reformulez, en employant ne ... que, les phrases ci-dessous.

Exemple: Ils sont arrivés il y a cinq minutes seulement.
Réponse: Ils ne sont arrivés qu'il y a cinq minutes.

Exemple: Lui seul parle bien.
Réponse: Il n'y a que lui qui parle bien.

1   Ce remède est le seul qui chasse la grippe.
2   J'ai appris la nouvelle il y a une heure seulement.
3   Je vous le dirai seulement quand ils seront partis.
4   Ma grand-mère est la seule personne qui écoute mon grand-père.
5   La seule chose qu'il respecte, c'est la force.
6   Il avait trouvé trois bonnes réponses sur six, seulement.

34.3 Order of words in negative expressions

All negative expressions (except *ne ... que* and *ne ... pas que*) can be used at the start of a sentence (as, or with, a negative subject of the verb), as well as after the verb (as or with a negative object of the verb, or to negate the verb).

Examples (the appropriate usage, with *ne*, for formal situations (N3) is shown)

Pas	***pas un seul** n'est venu*	(*pas un seul* is the subject of the verb)
	not one (of them) came	
Plus	***plus un arbre** n'est resté debout*	(*plus un arbre* is the subject of the verb)
	not a (single) tree remained standing	
Jamais	***jamais** il n'aurait dû faire cela*	(*jamais* is placed first for emphasis)
	he should never have done that	
Rien	***rien** ne peut l'arrêter*	(*rien* is the subject of the verb)
	nothing can stop him	
Personne	***personne** n'est venu*	(*personne* is the subject of the verb)
	nobody came	

Nul can be used, in formal situations (N3), in place of *personne*.
   ***nul** ne sait*   (N3)   no one knows

Aucun(e) **aucun doute** *n'est possible*   (*aucun doute* is the subject of the verb)
no doubt is possible

Ni . . . ni **ni lui ni son frère** *n'est venu/ne sont venus*
neither he nor his brother turned up
(*lui* and *son frère* are the subject of the verb, which can be singular or plural)

Exercice 34/4   **Mots négatifs au début de la phrase**   Travail individuel

Complétez les phrases ci-dessous en ajoutant, au début de la phrase, le mot négatif qui convient.

Exemple: _ n'est venu.

Réponse: **Personne n'est venu (ou: Aucun . . .)**

1   _ un seul taxi n'était libre.
2   _ ne trouve cela amusant.
3   _ je ne l'aurais cru capable d'une telle chose!
4   _ loi n'empêche de faire ce qu'il fait.
5   _ une feuille n'est restée sur les arbres.
6   _ ne m'a jamais demandé mon opinion.
7   _ de doute possible: on savait maintenant qui allait gagner.
8   _ la France, _ la Grande-Bretagne ne comptent plus parmi les grandes puissances.

Order of negative words with past participle and infinitive

Some negative words (*pas*, *plus*, *jamais*, *rien*) are placed before a past participle or infinitive; others are placed after:

Before a past participle

Pas

*elle n'avait **pas écouté** le message*
she hadn't listened to the message
*je ne l'ai **pas vu***
I haven't seen him

Plus

*depuis, elle n'a **plus participé** au projet*
since then, she has no longer taken part in the project

Jamais

*elle n'avait **jamais vu** un tel spectacle*
she'd never seen such a sight

Before an infinitive

*on ne peut **pas tourner** à gauche ici*
you can't turn left here
*je n'irai **pas** le **voir***
I won't go and see him

*tu ne dois **plus penser** à tout cela*
you must stop thinking about all that

*elle ne va **jamais voir** sa soeur*
she never visits her sister

Rien

> il n'a **rien appris**, **rien oublié**
> he's learnt nothing and forgotten nothing
> (But see below for *à/de/pour rien*.)

> je ne veux **rien écouter**
> I won't listen to anything (you say)

After a past participle	**After an infinitive**

Preposition + *rien*

> je ne l'aurais manqué pour rien
> I wouldn't have missed it for anything

> tu ne dois penser à rien
> you mustn't think about anything

Personne

> je n'ai vu personne
> I saw no one

> on ne peut rendre personne responsable de l'accident
> no one can be held responsible for the accident

Aucun(e)

> je n'y ai trouvé aucune erreur
> I could find no mistake (in it)

> cela ne peut faire aucun doute
> there can be no mistake about that

Ni . . . ni

> je n'ai vu ni le directeur ni son adjoint
> I saw neither the manager nor his assistant

> on ne va acheter ni l'un ni l'autre
> we'll buy neither of them

But in the construction *ni . . . ni* with two verbs, *ni* is placed before each past participle or infinitive:

> je ne les ai ni vus ni entendus
> I neither saw nor heard them

> je ne voudrais ni les voir ni leur écrire
> I'd rather not see or write to them

Ne . . . que

> je n'ai vu que l'adjoint
> I only saw the assistant

> il ne savait écrire que son nom
> all he could write was his name

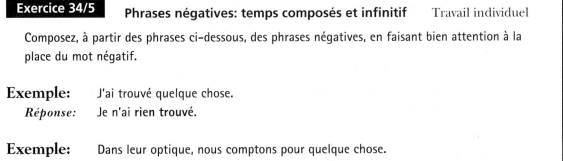

Exercice 34/5   **Phrases négatives: temps composés et infinitif**   Travail individuel

Composez, à partir des phrases ci-dessous, des phrases négatives, en faisant bien attention à la place du mot négatif.

Exemple: J'ai trouvé quelque chose.
Réponse: Je n'ai **rien trouvé.**

Exemple: Dans leur optique, nous comptons pour quelque chose.
Réponse: Dans leur optique, nous ne comptons **pour rien.**

1 Elle avait remarqué quelqu'un au coin de la rue.
2 Ce qu'il y a avec lui, c'est qu'il veut apprendre quelque chose.
3 Désormais, je vais penser à ce qu'il m'a dit.
4 Son adresse? Je l'ai notée!
5 Je sais que je pourrai oublier cette histoire.
6 Ses cousins? Après son déménagement, il leur avait écrit.
7 Les Dupont? On est allés les voir récemment.
8 C'était quelque chose qu'elle pourrait lui pardonner.

34.4 Combinations of negative words

IN ENGLISH, when two negative words are used together, only one of them remains in its negative form:

he hasn't ever told me	('not' + 'never' > 'not ever')
they never saw anyone	('never' + 'no one' > 'never anyone')
he doesn't live there any longer	('not' + 'no longer' > 'not any more', 'not now')

IN FRENCH, two negative words can also be used together, but neither of them changes.

ORDER OF WORDS

The order of negative words (when both are used after the verb) is:

plus		*rien*		*aucun(e)*	
jamais		*personne*		*ni*	*que*

Among the most usual combinations are:

plus jamais (or *jamais plus*)	never again, never any more
plus rien; plus personne	nothing left; no one . . . any more
plus aucun(e); jamais aucun(e)	no longer any/no . . . left; never any
jamais rien; jamais personne	never anything; never anyone

Ne . . . pas que, ne . . . plus que etc.

Combinations of another negative word with *ne . . . que* should be noted particularly. *Que* is used in so many different constructions (completive *que*, *que* in compound conjunctions, relative *que*, interrogative *que*, etc.), that its use as part of a negative construction is not always easy to spot:

Ne . . . que and *ne . . . pas que*

only	*il ne fait **que** travailler*	all he does is work
not only	*il ne fait **pas que** travailler*	he doesn't just work
only	*il n'y a **que** l'argent dans la vie*	money is all there is in life
not only	*il n'y a **pas que** l'argent dans la vie*	money isn't all there is in life

French
Grammar
Explained

Ne . . . plus que ('only . . . left', 'now only')

The meaning of *ne . . . plus que* is very close to the meaning of *ne . . . que* ('only'), whereas *ne . . . pas que* has the meaning 'not only'.

on ne voyait plus que les arbres	all you could see by now was the trees
il ne lui restait plus que trois litres d'eau	he/she (now) had only three litres of water left

Be careful to distinguish this construction from the use of *plus* in comparative constructions (**see 31.1**).

Ne . . . jamais que ('only ever')

après tout, ce n'est jamais qu'un jeu!	after all, it's only (ever) a game!

Ne . . . rien que ('merely', 'just')

ce n'est rien qu'une petite égratignure	it's only/it's just a little scratch

---

Exercice 34/6   **Deux mots négatifs: ordre des mots**   Travail individuel

a   Complétez les phrases ci-dessous en ajoutant, à la place qui convient, le mot négatif indiqué entre parenthèses.

b   Ensuite, écrivez l'équivalent en anglais des phrases que vous avez complétées.

Exemple: C'était trop tard: il n'y avait rien à faire.

Réponse: C'était trop tard: il n'y avait **plus** rien à faire.   (plus)

(It was too late: there was nothing more to be done.)

1	Il ne fait aucun effort pour élargir ses horizons.	(jamais)
2	Maintenant, il ne reste qu'une solution.	(plus)
3	Inutile de nous presser: il ne se passe rien avant minuit.	(jamais)
4	On sera tranquilles: il n'y a personne à cette heure-ci.	(plus)
5	Je n'ai eu aucun problème avec cet enfant.	(jamais)
6	Le jour baissait: on ne voyait que la silhouette des arbres.	(plus)

34.5 Using negative words without a verb

Pas, and other negative words, can be used, without a verb, to give negative meaning to a following word or phrase:

Pas	*pas du tout*	not at all
	pas un instant	not (for) a moment
Plus	*plus maintenant*	not any more
	plus d'histoires!	no more fuss!

Jamais	*jamais de la vie!*	never in your life!
Rien	*rien à faire!*	nothing doing! (N2)
Aucun(e)	*aucune solution*	no solution
Ni . . . ni	*ni fleurs, ni couronnes*	no flowers or wreaths
Que	*que par temps sec, svp*	only when the weather is dry, please
	(notice on letter box)	

Jamais, *rien* and *personne* can be used entirely on their own, for example in exclamations or questions:

*Qu'est-ce que tu as dit? Moi? **Rien!***	What did you say? Me? Nothing!
*moi, céder? **jamais!***	me, give in? never!
*qui sait la réponse? **personne?***	who knows the answer? no one?

Sans + negative word

IN ENGLISH, one can say 'without a', without ever', 'without any', etc., or one can say 'with no', 'with no one', etc.

IN FRENCH, *sans* (and not *avec*) is used with negative words:

+ noun (see 27.2 and 30.2)

| *sans rien* | with nothing, without anything |
| *sans aucun effort* | with no effort, without any effort |

+ infinitive (see 43.3)

sans plus parler	without saying anything more
sans jamais se fatiguer	without ever getting tired
sans rien dire à personne	without saying anything to anyone

For *sans que* + subjunctive: **see 48.**

Ne without *pas*

This usage is found only in very formal situations (N4):

- with four verbs: *cesser, oser, pouvoir, savoir*;
- in rhetorical questions after *Qui . . .?*;
- in certain circumstances after *si*;
- in a negative clause subordinate to a negative main clause.
- after *plus . . . que* in comparisons (see **31.1**).

Pas le or *pas de*? For articles in negative expressions, **see 22.4.**

35 Passive constructions

35.1 **Formation and use of the passive**
35.2 **Expressing the agent in a passive construction**
35.3 **Alternatives to the passive in French**

35.1 Formation and use of the passive

Passive constructions are a device for making the object of an active verb into the subject of a passive verb, putting this new subject in first place in the sentence. They are very common in English:

Active construction	Passive construction
something hit him	he was hit/he got hit
a ball hit him	he was hit by a ball
they/we don't allow that	that's not allowed
the law forbids that	that's forbidden by law

FORMATION OF THE PASSIVE IN ENGLISH

The passive in English is formed by using the appropriate person and tense of the verb 'to be', with the past participle of the verb which describes the action. The verb 'to get' can also be used as a passive auxiliary (see the first example above).

FORMATION OF THE PASSIVE IN FRENCH

The passive in French is formed in the same way as in English: subject + correct person and tense of *être* + past participle of the verb which describes the action.

Example: *blesser* **(Person 3)**

Présent	*il est blessé*	**Present**	he's injured
Passé composé	*il a été blessé*	**Present perfect**	he's been injured
Plus-que-parfait	*il avait été blessé*	**Past perfect**	he'd been injured
Passé simple	*il fut blessé* (N3)	**Simple past**	he was injured
Futur	*il sera blessé*	**Future**	he'll be injured
Conditionnel	*il serait blessé*	**Conditional**	he'd be injured
Futur + *aller*	*il va être blessé*	**Future + 'go'**	he's going to be injured
Passé + *venir de*	*il vient d'être blessé*	**Past + 'have just'**	he's just been injured

301

Past tenses in passive constructions

IN ENGLISH, in a passive construction describing an action in the past, 'was' and 'were' are used; IN FRENCH you must choose the appropriate tense of *être*:

- *était, étaient* etc. for the imperfect,
- *a été, ont été* etc. for the passé composé, and
- *fut, furent* etc. for the passé simple (**see 54.1**).

FORMATION OF THE PASSÉ COMPOSÉ AND THE IMPERFECT

Here is a list of the six persons of the passé composé, and of the imperfect, of a passive verb in French:

Person	Passé composé	Imperfect
1	*j'ai été blessé(e)*	*j'étais blessé(e)*
2	*tu as été blessé(e)*	*tu étais blessé(e)*
3	*il/elle/on a été blessé(e)*	*il/elle/on était blessé(e)*
4	*nous avons été blessé(e)s*	*nous étions blessé(e)s*
5	*vous avez été blessé(e)(s)*	*vous étiez blessé(e)(s)*
6	*ils/elles ont été blessé(e)s*	*ils/elles étaient blessé(e)s*

Exercice 35/1　　**Constructions passives**　　　　Travail individuel

Récrivez au passif les phrases ci-dessous, en faisant bien attention au temps du verbe, et à l'accord du participe passé.

Exemple:　　On a blessé Marie à la jambe.
Réponse:　　Marie **a été** blessée à la jambe.

1　On a refait le toit l'année dernière.
2　On tous les cinq ans.
3　On punira toute infraction.
4　On avait confirmé le résultat des élections.
5　On distribue les prix à la fin de la cérémonie.
6　On a sifflé l'arbitre pendant tout le match.
7　On annoncera la décision la semaine prochaine.
8　Ils espéraient qu'on arrêterait les provocateurs.
9　On vient d'annoncer les numéros gagnants.
10　On va mettre les troupes des Nations Unies en état d'alerte.

USE

When is a passive construction used in French?

A passive construction is used in French to give statements an air of precision and formality, which is not the impression given by the use of *on* with an active construction **(see 35.3a)**.

a   In official reports or documents (N3/N4):

*la proposition **a été approuvée***	(passé composé)
the proposal was passed	
*toute infraction **sera sanctionnée** par une amende*	(future)
any infringement will be subject to a fine	
*ce jour-là, le courrier **avait été distribué** normalement*	(pluperfect)
that day, the post had been/was delivered as usual	

b   In everyday speech or writing (N2/N3), when the agent, as well as the object, of the action are stated. In a passive construction, the agent of the action appears at the end of the sentence:

Active construction:

***un chien** m'a attaqué(e)*	a dog attacked me

Passive construction:

*j'ai été attaqué(e) **par un chien***	I have been/I was attacked by a dog

35.2 Expressing the agent in a passive construction: *par, de*

In a passive construction, the agent of the action is generally preceded by *par*, corresponding to 'by' in English:

la maison a été détruite par l'explosion	the house was destroyed by the explosion
elle vient d'être renversée par une voiture	she's just been knocked down by a car

The agent can be introduced by *de* when what is being described is habitual, ceremonial, etc.:

*comme d'habitude, le Président fut suivi **de** ses ministres*
as usual, the President was followed by his ministers
*les risques du tabac sont connus **de** tous*
the dangers of smoking are known to/by everyone
*elle est toujours accompagnée **de/par** son chien*
she always has her dog with her

Action (passive construction + *par*) or state (adjective + *de*)?

The first sentence below is an example of a passive construction, showing an action (*a été entouré*) and its agent (*par des policiers*). The second sentence, however, describes a state: there is neither action nor agent, and *entouré* functions as an adjective:

Action: passive construction + ***par***.

> *soudain, le petit groupe a été **entouré par** des policiers*
> suddenly, the little group was surrounded by policemen

State: *être* + adjective + ***de***:

> *le château était **entouré d'**un lac*
> the mansion was surrounded by a lake

Past participles commonly used as an adjective followed by *de* include:

entouré de	*rempli de*	*bourré de*	*couvert de*
surrounded by	filled with/full of	crammed with	covered with

Examples:

> *le tiroir était **bourré de** vieux papiers*
> the drawer was crammed with old papers
> *la salle était maintenant **remplie de** fumée*
> by now, the room was filled with smoke

One can also contrast the construction past participle (used as an adjective) + ***de*** + an unqualified noun (with no article) with the construction past participle + ***par le/la*** + a noun qualified by a further phrase:

> *les murs étaient noircis **de fumée***
> the walls were black with smoke
> *les murs étaient noircis **par la fumée** créée par l'incendie*
> the walls were blackened by the smoke from the fire
> *elle était accablée **de douleur***
> she was overwhelmed by pain

Exercice 35/2   **Constructions passives + *par* ou *de***   Travail individuel

Récrivez les phrases ci-dessous en employant une construction passive avec par ou de, selon le sens, en faisant attention au temps du verbe, et à l'accord du participe passé.

Exemple: L'explosion a détruit la maison.
Réponse: La maison a été détruite par l'explosion.

Exemple: Il y avait des arbres autour de la maison.
Réponse: La maison était entourée d'arbres.

1 Le résultat les a surpris.
2 Dix millions de téléspectateurs ont écouté l'allocution présidentielle.
3 Ses admirateurs l'entourent constamment.
4 Les sauveteurs n'ont pas abandonné tout espoir.
5 Un homme l'avait harcelée.
6 Il avait bourré des manuels scolaires dans son cartable.
7 La poussière noircit les mains et les visages.
8 Cette loi protégera-t-elle les citoyens?
9 Chaque participant a rempli un questionnaire.
10 Des fautes d'orthographe se trouvaient partout dans sa lettre.

35.3 Alternatives to the passive in French

IN ENGLISH, passive constructions such as 'he got hit' or 'that's not allowed' are used frequently; they are often more straightforward than the equivalent active constructions ('something hit him', 'we/they don't allow that' etc.), where the subject of the active verb has to be included, even though it may not add anything useful.

IN FRENCH, passive constructions are used about eight times less often than in English. Constructions used instead of the passive are shown below:

a use of *on* as an alternative to a passive construction
b use of *on* when a passive construction is not possible in French
c use of a pronominal verb in preference to a passive construction
d use of *se faire* as an alternative to a passive construction
e use of an active construction with a different verb

a Use of *on* as an alternative to a passive construction

A construction with *on* is often used in cases where a passive construction is also possible; note that *on* is more likely to be used in informal situations (N2):

Construction + *on*	Passive construction	
on va réparer le pont	*le pont va être réparé*	the bridge will be repaired
on a réparé le pont	*le pont a été réparé*	the bridge has been/was repaired
on annoncera la nouvelle	*la nouvelle sera annoncée*	the news will be announced

The construction with *on*, as an alternative to the passive, is useful in everyday conversation (N2), but it should not be over-used in formal situations (N3).

b Use of *on* when a passive construction is not possible in French

IN ENGLISH, some verbs are constructed with two direct objects ('she gave me the book', 'he asked them the way', etc.), or with a direct object + infinitive or subordinate clause ('they allowed her to leave', 'you told them (that) I'd left', etc.). In English all of these statements can be expressed in the passive, especially if the agent of the action is not stated:

> I was given the book (by her) they were asked the way (by him)
> she was allowed to leave (by them) they were told (by you) that I'd left

IN FRENCH, none of these statements can be expressed in the passive, for either or both of the following reasons:

- a verb can have only one direct object (**see 18.3**);
- the indirect object in an active construction cannot become the subject of a passive construction.

Examples (*dire, donner, permettre*):

Dire

English:	to tell someone something	(two objects, no preposition)
French:	*dire quelque chose **à** quelqu'un*	
	(the presence of a preposition shows that *quelqu'un* is an indirect object)	

	Active construction	**Passive construction**
English:	they told me that she was back	I was told that she was back
French:	*on **m'a dit** qu'elle était rentrée*	(not possible in French)

Donner

English:	to give someone something	(two objects, no preposition)
French:	*donner quelque chose **à** quelqu'un*	(one direct object, one indirect object)

	Active construction	**Passive construction**
English:	she gave me the book	the book was given to me by her
French:	*elle **m'a donné** le livre*	*le livre m'a été donné par elle*
English:		I was given the book by her
French:		(not possible in French)

Permettre

English:	to allow someone to do something	('someone' is the direct object of 'allow')
French:	*permettre **à** quelqu'un de faire quelque chose*	(*quelqu'un* is the indirect object of *permettre*)

	Active construction	**Passive construction**
English:	they allowed me to leave	I was allowed to leave
French:	*on **m'a permis** de partir*	(not possible in French)

Verbs constructed with one direct object and one indirect object in French include:

demander	*dire*	*donner*	*envoyer*
to ask	to say	to give	to send
offrir	*presenter*	*promettre*	*raconter*
to give (a present)	to introduce	to promise	to tell (a story)

Exercice 35/3   *Dire, donner, permettre, etc.*   Travail à deux > Mise en commun

Pour chacune des phrases ci–dessous:

a   Donnez l'équivalent en anglais, en employant une construction passive.

b   Récrivez au passif la phrase en français.

c   Donnez l'équivalent en anglais de cette nouvelle version de la phrase.

d   Laquelle des deux formulations de la phrase en français, et laquelle des deux formulations en anglais, est préférable? Discutez-en.

Exemple: On m'a donné ce livre.

Réponses: a I was given this book.

b Ce livre m'a été donné.

c This book was given to me.

1   On lui a offert trois cadeaux.

2   On ne leur a pas dit la vérité.

3   On leur avait promis une augmentation de salaire.

4   On ne m'a pas raconté cette histoire.

5   On va vous envoyer un chèque.

6   On nous a demandé une faveur.

---

c Use of a pronominal verb in preference to a passive construction

A pronominal verb (**see 36**) is preferred to a passive construction in cases such as the following:

> *ce plat **se mange** avec des baguettes*
> you use chopsticks to eat this/that dish
> *le tableau **s'est vendu** (pour) un million de livres*
> the painting sold/was sold for a million pounds

d Use of *se faire* as an alternative to a passive construction

Se faire + infinitive or *se voir* + past participle (N3) can be used instead of *être*:

Construction + *être*	**Construction + *se faire/se voir***
il a été arrêté par la police judiciaire	*il s'est fait arrêter par la police judiciaire*
he was arrested by the CID	
il a été obligé de vendre sa collection	*il s'est vu obligé de vendre sa collection* (N3)
he was forced to sell his collection	

e Use of an active construction with a different verb

When a passive construction is not possible, or a construction with *on* is not appropriate, an active construction, with a different verb altogether, is used:

French:	English:
Active construction	Active construction, or passive + different verb
*sa campagne **a reçu** un soutien inattendu*	his/her campaign received an unexpected boost
	his/her campaign was given an unexpected boost
*il **a été le sujet** de plusieurs articles*	he was written about in several articles
	several articles were written about him

36 Pronominal verbs and constructions

36.1 Formation of pronominal verbs

Pronominal verbs are used with a reflexive pronoun (*me, te, se, nous, vous*), which is placed immediately before the verb.

Example: *se réveiller*, note the place of the reflexive pronoun in the passé composé and with the future + *aller*.

Person	Present	Passé composé	Future + *aller*
1	*je me réveille*	*je me suis réveillé(e)*	*je vais me réveiller*
2	*tu te réveilles*	*tu t'es réveillé(e)*	*tu vas te réveiller*
3	*il/elle se réveille*	*il/elle s'est réveillé(e)*	*il/elle va se réveiller*
4	*nous nous réveillons*	*nous nous sommes réveillé(e)s*	*nous allons nous réveiller*
5	*vous vous réveillez*	*vous vous êtes réveillé(e)(s)*	*vous allez vous réveiller*
6	*ils/elles se réveillent*	*ils/elles se sont réveillé(e)s*	*ils/elles vont se réveiller*

In negative forms, the place of *ne* and *pas* (etc.) should be studied carefully, especially in the passé composé and the future + *aller*.

Person	Present	Passé composé	Future + *aller*
1	*je ne me réveille pas*	*je ne me suis pas réveillé(e)*	*je ne vais pas me réveiller*
2	*tu ne te réveilles pas*	*tu ne t'es pas réveillé(e)*	*tu ne vas pas te réveiller*
3	*il/elle ne se réveille pas*	*il/elle ne s'est pas réveillé(e)*	*il/elle ne va pas se réveiller*
4	*nous ne nous réveillons pas*	*nous ne nous sommes pas réveillé(e)s*	*nous n'allons pas nous réveiller*
5	*vous ne vous réveillez pas*	*vous ne vous êtes pas réveillé(e)(s)*	*vous n'allez pas vous réveiller*
6	*ils/elles ne se réveillent pas*	*ils/elles ne se sont pas réveillé(e)s*	*ils/elles ne vont pas se réveiller*

In all tenses, the reflexive pronoun is *se* only in Persons 3 and 6; for Persons 1, 2, 4 and 5, *me, te, nous* or *vous* must be used, even with the infinitive form:

*je vais **me** réveiller*   *tu dois **te** réveiller*

*nous n'aimons pas **nous** réveiller*   *vous n'essayez jamais de **vous** réveiller*

Agreement of the past participle   (see 44.4)

In compound tenses, the past participle agrees with the reflexive pronoun, if it is the direct object of the verb:

elle s'est réveillée   she woke up/she's woken up

ils se sont mariés   they (got) married

Exercice 36/1   **Verbes pronominaux: présent et passé composé**   Travail à deux

a   Avec un(e) partenaire, lisez tour à tour, à haute voix, une des phrases de la colonne de gauche (verbe au **présent**) ou de droite (verbe au **passé composé**), ci-dessous. Votre partenaire doit aussitôt, sans regarder la liste, dire à haute voix la phrase à l'**autre** temps du verbe.

b   Ensuite, récrivez au **négatif** toutes les phrases dans les deux colonnes.

c   Après avoir vérifié vos réponses (b), lisez-les tour à tour à haute voix.

1	les gens s'adaptent	les gens se sont adaptés
2	le temps s'améliore	le temps s'est amélioré
3	on s'amuse	on s'est amusés
4	ils se battent	ils se sont battus
5	ils se défendent	ils se sont défendus
6	la ville se développe	la ville s'est développée
7	il s'enfuit	il s'est enfui
8	ils s'enrichissent	ils se sont enrichis
9	je m'intéresse à la politique	je me suis intéressé à la politique
10	ils se marient	ils se sont mariés
11	je me sens triste	je me suis senti triste
12	vous vous spécialisez	vous vous êtes spécialisé(s)
13	tu te trompes	tu t'es trompé(e)
14	vous vous trouvez à Londres	vous vous êtes trouvé(s) à Londres

d   **Contrôle**   Travail individuel

Quelque temps après avoir fait cet exercice, couvrez la colonne de droite, et récrivez au passé composé (i) à l'affirmatif, (ii) au négatif, les phrases dans la colonne de gauche.

Exercice 36/2   **Forme du pronom réfléchi avec l'infinitif**   Travail individuel

Récrivez les phrases ci-dessous en employant comme auxiliaire le verbe entre parenthèses, et en mettant le verbe réfléchi à l'infinitif.

Exemple: Je ne me lève pas.   (aller)
Réponse: Je ne **vais** pas **me lever.**

1	Vous vous adaptez.	(devoir)	6	Je ne me force pas.	(aller)
2	Nous nous concentrons.	(aller)	7	Ils se marient.	(aller)
3	Je me défends.	(savoir)	8	Tu te rappelles.	(devoir)
4	Vous ne vous dérangez pas.	(vouloir)	9	Je ne me souviens pas.	(pouvoir)
5	Tu ne te fatigues pas.	(devoir)	10	Il ne se trompe pas.	(aimer)

36.2 Meaning and use of pronominal verbs

USE

Pronominal verbs are used more frequently in French than in English, where other constructions (including the passive: **see 35**) can be used instead.

MEANING

Pronominal verbs are used in several ways:
a   with reflexive meaning;
b   with reciprocal meaning;
c   instead of a possessive adjective;
d   to mean 'for myself', etc.;
e   in constructions with passive meaning, and in impersonal constructions.

a   Reflexive action

The subject of the verb is both the agent and the object of the action described by the verb:

je me réveille	I wake up	*nous nous asseyons*	we sit down
tu te lèves	you get up	*vous vous précipitez*	you rush
il se couche	he goes to bed	*ils s'amusent*	they're having fun
elle se marie	she's getting married	*elles s'installent*	they're settling in

Note, from these examples of reflexive verbs in French, how often the English equivalent is not a pronominal construction.

Most reflexive verbs can also be used as ordinary verbs, usually with an object (direct or indirect) which is distinct from the subject of the verb:

Verb + direct object		**Reflexive verb**	
réveiller	*elle a réveillé sa sœur* she woke her sister	*se réveiller*	*elle s'est réveillée* she woke up
coucher	*ils ont couché leur bébé dans son lit* they put the baby to bed	*se coucher*	*ils se sont couchés* they went to bed

améliorer	**s'améliorer**
*les techniciens ont amélioré **le système***	*leur productivité **s'**est beaucoup améliorée*
the technicians (have) improved the system	their productivity (has) greatly improved

adapter	**s'adapter**
*on a adapté **l'ancien moteur***	*les enfants **se** sont adaptés au nouveau système*
they adapted the previous engine	the children adapted to the new system

Certain intransitive verbs are used only pronominally:

s'évanouir	to faint	*s'enfuir*	to run away

Other intransitive verbs, however, are not used pronominally:

augmenter	to increase, go up	*diminuer*	to diminish, go down

Verb + indirect object	**Reflexive verb**
dire	*se dire*
je lui ai dit qu'il n'y avait rien à craindre	*elle s'est dit qu'il n'y avait rien à craindre*
I told her there was nothing to fear	she told herself there was nothing to fear

poser	*se poser*
je lui ai posé une question	*je me suis déjà posé cette question*
I asked him/her a question	I've already asked myself that question

demander	*se demander*
elle m'a demandé pourquoi il avait fait cela	*elle s'est demandé pourquoi il avait fait cela*
she asked me why he'd done that	she wondered why he'd done that

The English equivalents of many of these verbs have no pronominal form, but in French the pronominal form is used whenever there is no direct object:

(se) sentir, (se) trouver

Sentir is used when followed by a noun or completive clause:

je sens une douleur à la main gauche	I feel a pain in my right hand
(= j'éprouve une douleur . . .)	
on sent qu'il va réussir	you feel he's going to succeed
(= on a l'impression qu'il va réussir)	

Se sentir is used when followed by an adjective, adverb or infinitive:

je me sens capable de gagner	I feel I can win
elle s'est couchée: elle ne se sentait pas bien	she went to bed: she wasn't feeling well

Trouver can be used impersonally with *on*:

rassure-toi: on va trouver le chemin bientôt	don't worry: we'll soon find the way now
on trouve tout à la Samaritaine	you can find anything/you'll find everything at *'Samaritaine'* (a department store)

Se trouver is used with the meaning 'is':

le chemin se trouve un peu plus loin	the path is just a bit further on
la Samaritaine se trouve sur la rive droite	the *'Samaritaine'* is on the Right Bank

On se trouve is used only with the meaning 'one (etc.) is', 'one feels':

on se trouve au cœur de la vieille ville	we're in the heart of the old town
on se trouve tout bête (= on se sent . . .)	you feel/one feels quite stupid

---

Exercice 36/3   **Verbes employés avec ou sans pronom réfléchi**   Travail individuel

Complétez les phrases ci-dessous en ajoutant, s'il le faut, un pronom réfléchi.

Exemple: Ne ( ) réveillez pas le bébé!
Réponse: Ne réveillez pas le bébé!

Exemple: Ne ( ) réveille pas trop tard!
Réponse: Ne te réveille pas trop tard!

1   Qu'est-ce qui ( ) passe?
2   Je n'aimerais voir la ville ( ) développer trop.
3   Le mauvais temps va ( ) aggraver la situation.
4   Son intervention va ( ) produire un changement spectaculaire.
5   Le système va ( ) améliorer, j'espère.
6   Je ne ( ) sens pas très bien.
7   Les rumeurs ( ) répandent très vite.
8   Ne ( ) précipitons pas les choses!
9   On ( ) trouve toutes sortes de curiosités dans ce genre de magasin.
10   Je ( ) sens que quelque chose va arriver.
11   Elle va ( ) demander ce qui s'est passé.
12   Il n'aime pas ( ) poser trop de questions.

b   Reciprocal action

Some pronominal verbs are used in the plural to describe a reciprocal interaction between two people, groups or things:

> *ils se sont regardés avec étonnement*
>
> they looked at each other with amazement
>
> *ils ne se parlaient plus beaucoup*
>
> they no longer spoke very much to one another

If the reflexive pronoun is the indirect object of the verb, then in compound tenses the past participle does not agree **(see 44.4)**:

> *ils se sont parlé pour la première fois depuis deux jours*
>
> they spoke (to each other) for the first time in two days

c   Instead of a possessive adjective

A pronominal construction is used in French to describe an action done to a part of the body, whereas in English a simple verb + possessive adjective is used:

> *elle **se** lave **les** cheveux*   she washes her hair
>
> *il **s'**est cassé **la** jambe*   he has broken/he broke his leg

In these constructions, the reflexive pronoun (*se* etc.) is the indirect object of the verb, since the direct object slot is occupied by *les cheveux* or *la jambe*.

This means that in compound tenses, the past participle does not agree with the reflexive pronoun **(see 44.4)**:

> *elle s'est lavé les cheveux*   she (has) washed her hair
>
> *ils se sont brossé les dents*   they (have) brushed their teeth

d   'For myself'/'for himself', etc.

A pronominal construction, similar to **c**, is used in French with certain verbs where the meaning of the reflexive pronoun is 'for myself' (etc.):

> *elle s'est acheté un disque*   she (has) bought herself a record
>
> *ils se sont offert une croisière*   they (have) treated themselves to a cruise

In this construction, the reflexive pronoun is an indirect object, and so there is no agreement of the past participle.

If the meaning is not reflexive, then an indirect object pronoun (*lui*, *leur* etc.) is used:

> *je **leur** ai acheté un disque*   I bought them a record
>
> *son mari **lui** a offert une croisière*   her husband treated her to a cruise

---

Exercice 36/4   *Se ou lui/leur?*   Travail à deux > Mise en commun

a   Complétez les phrases ci-dessous en ajoutant se ou lui/leur.

b   Donnez l'équivalent en anglais de chaque phrase.

Exemple: Elle _ est acheté un disque pour son anniversaire.
Réponse: Elle **s'est** acheté un disque pour son anniversaire.
               (she bought herself a disc for her birthday)

Exemple: Elle _ a acheté un disque pour son anniversaire.
Réponse: Elle **lui** a acheté un disque pour son anniversaire.
               (she bought him/her a disc for his/her birthday)

1   On va _ acheter quelque chose pour les remercier.
2   Ils _ sont acheté un petit bateau.
3   J'espère qu'il ne _ est pas cassé la jambe.
4   On _ a proposé un très bon prix pour leur voiture.
5   Je _ ai offert un bijou pour Noël.
6   Elle a trouvé le temps de _ laver les cheveux.

---

e   Other categories

Other categories of pronominal verbs and constructions include:

- constructions with passive meaning (**see 35.3c**):   *cela ne se fait pas*
- impersonal constructions (**see 37**):   *il s'agit de* + noun (**37.2**);
    il se passe quelque chose (**37.3**)

36.3 Action or state?

The past participle of a pronominal verb can be used either as part of a compound tense, such as the passé composé or the pluperfect, to describe an action, or as an adjective, to describe a state.

Examples:

Action	State
Passé composé of *s'asseoir*:	**Present of *être* + past participle (*assis*):**
elle s'est assise she sat down	*elle est assise* she's sitting down
Pluperfect of *s'asseoir*:	**Imperfect of *être* + past participle (*assis*):**
elle s'était assise she had sat down	*elle était assise* she was sitting down

Action	State
Passé composé of *se lever*:	**Present of** *être* + **past participle** (*levé*):
elle s'est levée pour répondre au téléphone	*je suis levé(e) tous les jours avant sept heures*
she got up to answer the phone	I'm up every day by seven
Pluperfect of *se lever*:	**Imperfect of** *être* + **past participle** (*levé*):
ils s'étaient levés comme d'habitude à	*elle était levée depuis longtemps déjà*
l'entrée du président	she'd already been up for some time
they had stood up, as usual, when the	
chairman came in	

The form of these two constructions is so similar that they can easily be confused: it is worth practising some of them (for further examples, **see 54.3**).

Exercice 36/5   **Action ou état?**   Travail individuel

Complétez les phrases ci-dessous en choisissant une des alternatives (entre parenthèses), selon le sens de la phrase (action ou état).

1   Ils (se sont rendus/sont rendus) chez leurs amis, mais ceux-ci n'étaient pas à la maison.
2   Quand je l'ai vue, elle (s'était assise/était assise) près de la fenêtre.
3   A six heures déjà, elle (s'était levée/était levée), et bientôt elle (s'était penchée/était penchée) sur son travail.
4   Il (s'est réveillé/est réveillé) en sursaut: il a compris qu'il (s'était endormi/était endormi) devant la télé.
5   Le chien, attiré par la chaleur du feu, (s'est allongé/est allongé) sur le tapis.
6   On ne se repose que quand les enfants (se sont couchés/sont couchés).

---

37 Impersonal verbs and constructions

37.1 Impersonal verbs

37.2 Impersonal verb constructions

37.3 Verbs that can be constructed personally or impersonally

37.4 Making impersonal constructions refer to a specific topic

37.5 *Paraître* and *sembler*

37.6 Some differences between impersonal constructions in informal (N2) and formal (N3) situations

An **impersonal** verb or construction is one in which the subject position is occupied by the pronouns *il, ça* or *cela*:

il pleut	it's raining
il fait beau	it's fine
il est minuit	it's midnight
il y a eu un accident	there's been an accident
il s'agit de toi	it's about you
il faut partir	you/we must leave

Impersonal constructions can be used as a means of placing the subject of the verb at the end of the sentence; for example: *(il) se passe*:

*des choses terribles **se sont passées***

(normal word order: subject + verb)

***il s'est passé** des choses terribles*

(impersonal construction: the subject of the verb is at the end)

IN ENGLISH, impersonal constructions are introduced by 'it' (or 'there', as in 'there is', 'there are'). Certain impersonal constructions in French have no equivalent in English.

IN FRENCH, impersonal verbs and constructions are of three types: impersonal verbs (e.g. *il pleut*), impersonal verb constructions (e.g. *il faut*) and verbs that can be constructed personally or impersonally (e.g. *(il) se passe*).

37.1 Impersonal verbs

The only verbs in this category are:

- the 'meteorological' verbs *pleuvoir* (*il pleut*), *neiger* (*il neige*), *geler* (*il gèle*) etc., and *il fait beau* (etc.);
- expressions of time;
- the construction *il y a.*

Meteorological verbs

These can be followed by various noun or adverb phrases:

il pleuvait des torrents	it was raining buckets
il pleuvait fort	it was raining heavily

They can also be used (constructed personally or impersonally) with metaphorical, not meteorological, meaning:

il pleuvait des coups	blows rained down
les coups pleuvaient sur son dos	(the) blows rained down on his back

***Il fait* + noun or adjective**:

il ne fait pas très beau/chaud/froid aujourd'hui
it's not very fine/warm/cold today
il a fait du soleil/du brouillard hier
it was sunny/foggy yesterday

Also: *il fait jour*   it's daylight   *il fait nuit*   it's night

***Il fait un temps* + adjective; *le temps est* + adjective**:

il fait un *temps magnifique/un temps de chien*
it's lovely weather/dreadful weather
le temps est *doux pour la saison/**le temps est** meilleur en automne*
the weather is mild for the season/the weather is better in autumn

Expressions of time

quelle heure est-il?	what's the time?
il est cinq heures/il est midi	it's five o'clock/it's midday

Also: *il se fait tard*   it's getting late

Il y a

The three little words *il y a* are used as a unit in so many ways in French that one can overlook the fact that, as an impersonal construction of the verb *avoir*, they can be used in all tenses:

Positive forms		**Negative forms**	
Present indicative:			
il y a	there is/there are	*il n'y a pas*	there isn't/there aren't
Passé composé:			
il y a eu	there was/there were	*il n'y a pas eu*	there wasn't/there were no
Present subjunctive:			
(qu')il y ait	for there to be	*(qu')il n'y ait pas*	for there not to be
Past subjunctive:			
(qu')il y ait eu	for there to have been	*(qu')il n'y ait pas eu*	for there not to have been
Future:			
il y aura	there will be	*il n'y aura pas*	there won't be
Future + ***aller***:			
il va y avoir	there's going to be	*il ne va pas y avoir*	there's not going to be
Conditional:			
il y aurait	there would be	*il n'y aurait pas*	there wouldn't be
Past conditional:			
il y aurait eu	there would have been	*il n'y aurait pas eu*	there wouldn't have been
Past + ***venir de***:			
il vient d'y avoir	there's just been	*il ne vient pas d'y avoir*	there's not just been
Imperfect:			
il y avait	there was/there were	*il n'y avait pas*	there wasn't/there were no
Pluperfect:			
il y avait eu	there had been	*il n'y avait pas eu*	there hadn't been

The French equivalent of 'there was' is either *il y a eu* or *il y avait*, depending on whether something is viewed as an event, or as an ongoing state of affairs (**see 54.1**):

> *à quatre heures de l'après-midi, **il y a eu** une explosion*
> at 4pm, there was an explosion
> *deux jours après l'explosion, **il y avait** encore un nuage de poussière*
> two days after the explosion, there was still a cloud of dust

When ***il y a*** is used with auxiliary verbs, note the position of *y* (see also **39.2**):

+ *devoir*

*il **doit y avoir** une solution*	there must be a solution
il devrait y avoir une solution	there ought to/should be a solution
il devait y avoir/il a dû y avoir/il avait dû y avoir	there must have been

Note: for the appropriate choice of these three tenses, **see 39.2** and **54.1**.

+ pouvoir

il **peut y avoir**	there can be
il ne peut pas y avoir	there can't be
il ne pouvait pas y avoir/il ne pourrait pas y avoir	there couldn't be

Note: for the appropriate choice of these two tenses, **see 39.2** and **54.1**.

+ aller

il **va y avoir**	there's going to be
il vient d'y avoir	there's just been
il ne va pas y avoir de neige sur la route	there won't be any snow on the road

The construction *il y a* is always singular, since the subject of the verb *avoir* is the singular impersonal pronoun *il*:

il n'y a pas eu de problèmes	there were no problems

Exercice 37/1   *Il y a*   Travail à deux

a   Avec un(e) partenaire, lisez tour à tour, à haute voix, une des phrases ci-dessous, suivie du verbe auxiliaire (entre parenthèses). Votre partenaire doit reformuler la phrase en employant l'auxiliaire suivi de y avoir.

b   Ensuite, dites vous-même à votre partenaire la forme négative de la phrase que vous venez d'entendre.

Exemple: Il y avait une solution.   (devoir)

Réponse: **a** Il **devait y avoir** une solution.

  b Il **ne devait pas y avoir** de solution.

1	Il y aura des problèmes.	(pouvoir)
2	Il y a eu un accident.	(devoir)
3	Il y aurait des avantages	(pouvoir)
4	Il y a une discussion.	(aller)
5	Il y avait eu une erreur.	(devoir)
6	Il y aurait eu des bagarres.	(pouvoir)

37.2 Impersonal verb constructions

The main verb constructions in this category include: *il faut; il s'agit (de); il est question (de); (il n'est) pas question (de)*

Each of these can be used in three ways:

a   With a noun

b   With an infinitive
c   With a *que* clause + subjunctive

As you will see, the corresponding English constructions are often quite different, sometimes using different verbs.

Examples:
a   ***Il faut* + noun**
*il faut **trois heures** pour arriver au sommet*
it takes three hours to get to the top
(literally: 'three hours are needed'; prendre is not used here, though one can say *ça (nous) a pris trois heures:* 'it took (us) three hours')

***Il s'agit de* + noun**
*dans son livre il s'agit **d'un groupe** de jeunes scientifiques*
his/her book is about a group of young scientists

> The construction *il s'agit de* is always used impersonally.

To begin the sentence with *son livre*, one would have to use a different verb:
        *son livre **présente** . . .*   or   *son livre **raconte** l'histoire de . . .*

***Il est question de* + noun**
*de **quoi** est-il question?*   what's it about/what's the matter?
(one can also say *de quoi s'agit-il?*)

b   ***Il faut* + infinitive**
*il faut **comprendre** que c'est un travail épuisant*
you have to realise it's exhausting work
(the subject of *comprendre* is not stated; it will probably be clear from the context who has to 'realise . . .')

***Il s'agit de* + infinitive**
*maintenant, il s'agit **de trouver** le coupable*
now we/they have to find the criminal
(one can also say *il faut trouver . . .*; try to avoid always using *devoir* as the equivalent of 'must', 'have to')

***Il est question de* + infinitive**
*(il n'est) pas question **de sortir** par un temps pareil!*
no way are we/you going out in this weather!

c   ***Il faut que* + subjunctive**
*il faut **que tu comprennes** tout de suite*
you have to understand right away

321

Il s'agit que + **subjunctive**

> *il ne s'agit pas **que tu fasses** des bêtises!*

we can't have you fooling around

Il est question que + **subjunctive**

> *(il n'est) pas question **que tu ressortes** aujourd'hui*

(there's) no question of you going out again today   (For the subjunctive, **see 48**.)

Exercice 37/2   *Il faut, il s'agit (de), il est question (de)*   Travail individuel

Complétez les phrases ci-dessous en ajoutant, au temps qui convient, il faut, il s'agit (de), il est question (de), au **positif** (1–5) ou au **négatif** (6–9).

Exemple: Dans ce feuilleton, il _ deux jeunes couples.

Réponse: Dans ce feuilleton, il **s'agit de** deux jeunes couples.

1   On m'avait dit qu'il _ fermer ce cinéma.
2   Il _ que je te dise une chose: son idée ne marchera pas!
3   Maintenant, il _ décider ce qu'on va faire.
4   Je te laisse: il _ que je passe chez Claude.
5   Je n'ai pas très bien compris ce qu'il disait, mais je sais qu'il _ beaucoup d'argent.
6   Il _ traîner: on n'a plus beaucoup de temps!
7   Elle avait trop investi dans le projet: il _ l'abandonner.
8   Quand tu le verras, il _ oublier de lui parler de cette affaire.
9   Une fois qu'elle a compris qu'il _ elle, elle a été rassurée.

37.3 Verbs that can be constructed personally or impersonally

Among verbs which can be constructed either personally or impersonally are:

(il) vient	*(il) arrive*	*(il) se passe*	*(il) plaît*
(il) manque	*(il) suffit*	*(il) reste*	*(il) vaut mieux*

These verbs can be used in a personal or an impersonal construction; whichever is used, the meaning is similar: the impersonal construction is a device for shifting the subject of the verb to the end of the sentence (for other examples of dislocation and extraction, **see 51**).

Examples: + noun

(il) vient:

> *il **vient** peu de touristes en hiver*   few tourists come here in winter
> *peu de touristes **viennent** en hiver*

il n'est venu personne   nobody came
personne n'est venu

(il) arrive:
il arrive peu d'événements importants ici   not many important events happen
peu d'événements importants arrivent ici   here

(il) se passe:
il s'est passé quelque chose d'extraordinaire   something amazing (has) happened
quelque chose d'extraordinaire s'est passé

(il) reste:
il reste deux questions à résoudre   two questions remain to be resolved
deux questions restent à résoudre

(il) manque:
il manque un bouton à ta chemise   there's a button missing from your
un bouton manque à ta chemise   shirt

(il) suffit:
il suffit de deux mots   two words are enough
deux mots suffisent

(il) vaut mieux:
mieux vaut la pluie que la grêle   rain is better than hail
la pluie vaut mieux que la grêle

Examples: + infinitive
(il) suffit (de):
il suffit d'y croire   believing (in) it is enough
y croire suffit

(il) reste (de):
il restait à trouver les coupables   the criminals remained to be found
les coupables restaient à trouver

Exercice 37/3   **Construction personnelle ou impersonnelle?**   Travail à deux > Mise en
commun

a   Complétez les phrases ci-dessous en ajoutant, à la personne et au temps qui convient, un des
verbes suivants: arriver, manquer, se passer, rester, suffire, venir.

b   Pour chaque phrase, quelle construction (personnelle ou impersonnelle) trouvez-vous
préférable? Dans quelles circonstances?

c   Ensuite, discutez vos conclusions avec le reste du groupe.

Exemples: Hier, il ne s' _ rien _.   Rien ne _ hier.

Réponses: Hier, il ne s'est rien **passé**.   **Rien** ne s'est passé hier.

(Les deux formulations sont également possibles; la première suggère qu'il n'y a rien d'autre à dire, tandis que la deuxième semble annoncer qu'on va dire quelque chose de plus.)

1	Je suis sûr qu'il _ quelque chose entre eux.	Je suis sûr que quelque chose _ entre eux.
2	Hier, il me _ encore de l'espoir.	Hier, encore de l'espoir me _.
3	Il _ un élément essentiel à sa stratégie.	Un élément essentiel _ à sa stratégie.
4	On lui disait tout le temps qu'il allait lui _ un accident.	On lui disait tout le temps qu'un accident allait lui _.
5	Tu vas voir: il _ un temps où il regrettera son action.	Tu vas voir: un temps _ où il regrettera son action.
6	Il _ de l'écouter pour le croire.	L'écouter _ pour le croire.

37.4 Making impersonal constructions refer to a specific topic (person or thing)

All impersonal verbs and constructions refer to something or someone: even *il pleut, il fait beau* etc. are understood as referring to 'the weather'.

The topic of an impersonal construction can be very general:

    il faut trois heures pour arriver au sommet   it takes three hours to get to the top

The topic is assumed to be 'anyone', or at least to 'any normally healthy walker'.

The topic of an impersonal construction followed by *que* is assumed to be the subject of the verb in the *que* clause:

    *il faut que **tu** comprennes tout de suite*   you have to understand straight away

***Il (me) faut** etc.*

The topic (person or thing) of an impersonal construction followed by a noun or infinitive can be indicated by including it as the indirect object of the impersonal verb, using the indirect object pronouns *me/te/lui/nous/vous/leur*, or (but this can make the sentence cumbersome) *à* + noun:

    *il **me** faut une réponse immédiate*

    I need a quick answer

    *il **leur** a fallu trois heures pour arriver au sommet*

    they took three hours to get to the top

    *il a fallu **aux sauveteurs** trois heures pour repérer l'épave*

    it took the rescuers three hours to find the wreck

Impersonal constructions which can be personalised in this way include:

il faut	*il plaît*	*il manque*	*il suffit*
il arrive	*il reste*	*il vient*	
il semble	**(see 37.5)**	Also:	*il paraît*

Examples:

+ noun

*c'est Renault qu'il **vous** faut*	you need Renault (advertising slogan)
*il ne **me** restait plus que trois francs*	I had only three francs left
*il **m'**est venu un doute*	a doubt occurred to me
*il **lui** est arrivé un accident*	he's/she's had an accident
*il était arrivé un accident **à un des groupes***	one of the parties had had an accident

+ infinitive

*il ne **me** plaît pas d'y aller*	(N3)	I don't feel like going there
*ça **me** plaît pas d'y aller*	(N2)	

Exercice 37/4   *Il faut ou il me/lui faut (etc.)?*   Travail à deux

Avec un(e) partenaire, lisez à haute voix les phrases ci-dessous. Pour chacune, décidez s'il serait préférable d'ajouter un pronom personnel objet indirect (me, te, lui, nous, vous ou leur) à la construction impersonnelle. Quel pronom? Pourquoi?

Exemple: Il suffit de le voir pour être charmé.
Réponses possibles: Il suffit de le voir pour être charmé.
(il s'agit d'une déclaration d'ordre général: tout le monde, laisse-t-on supposer, est susceptible à son charme)

      Il **me** suffit de le voir pour être charmé.
(on parle de sa propre réaction)

      Il **te** suffit de le voir pour être charmé.
(possible, mais peu probable; mais il **te** suffirait . . ., avec le conditionnel, a un sens évident)

1   Pour ce poste, il faut un homme ou une femme très capable.
2   Il ne restait plus que cent francs.
3   Si ça continue, il va arriver un malheur.
4   Attendez! Il m'est venu une idée!
5   Ça plaît de faire la fête de temps en temps.
6   C'est un homme autoritaire: il ne faut jamais le contredire.

37.5 *Il paraît, il semble*

Paraître ('to appear') and *sembler* ('to seem') can be used in impersonal constructions. Like their English equivalents, both are used to put a distance between the speaker and what is being talked about:

● *il paraît* suggests that the speaker has made no effort to find out or check the information (compare, in English, 'apparently' and 'it would appear that');

● *il semble* suggests that the speaker believes something to be true, but may be mistaken (compare, in English, 'it looks as if', 'I think that').

Both can be used impersonally without a stated complement:

*Ils ont gagné? Oui, **il paraît*** (N2)
Have they won? They have, apparently
*vous oubliez une chose, **il me semble*** (N3)
I think you're forgetting one thing

(For *me semble-t-il* etc., see **49.5.**)

Examples:

+ adjective

Both are used in impersonal constructions with an adjective, which may be followed by *de* + infinitive or *que* + clause (**see also 52.3**):

y aller maintenant, ça me paraît difficile	I'd say it would be difficult to go now
ça me paraît difficile d'y aller maintenant	
il faut y aller, cela me semble évident	it seems obvious to me that we must go
cela me semble évident qu'il faut y aller	

+ infinitive

Il me/lui (etc.) *semble que* is used with an infinitive, as an alternative to a *que* clause:

*il me semblait te **l'avoir** déjà **dit***	(N3)	I thought I'd told you already
or *il me semblait **que je** te **l'avais** déjà **dit***		

+ *que* + subordinate clause

Both *il paraît* and *il semble* are used with *que* (**see 46** and **48**):

il paraît que, il me/lui (etc.) *semble que*	+ indicative
il semble que	+ indicative or subjunctive
il ne me/lui (etc.) *semble pas que, il semblerait que*	+ subjunctive
il paraît qu'elle vient de sortir	apparently she's just gone out
il ne me semble pas que tu aies compris	you don't seem to have understood

Both *paraître* and *sembler* can be used with a personal subject:

+ adjective

le résultat paraissait certain	the result seemed certain
elle semblait anxieuse	she seemed anxious

+ **infinitive**

    elle a paru hésiter   she appeared to hesitate

    elle semblait dire que c'était un hasard   she seemed to be saying it was by
                                        chance

Exercice 37/5   *Il paraît, il semble*   Travail individuel

Complétez les phrases ci-dessous en ajoutant paraître ou sembler au temps approprié, selon le cas.

Exemple: Ils vont gagner: ça me _ évident!
Réponse: Ils vont gagner: ça me **paraît** évident!

Exemple: Plus il y pensait, plus cela lui _ ridicule.
Réponse: Plus il y pensait, plus cela lui **semblait** ridicule.

1   Il _ évident que son témoignage était faux.
2   Il _ vrai que les étudiants de langues vivantes font toujours les mêmes fautes.
3   Allons vite au Gigamarché: il _ qu'ils liquident leur stock!
4   D'après les premières indications, il _ qu'il n'y ait pas eu de morts.
5   Désormais, le résultat lui _ certain, mais il ne pouvait pas en être sûr.
6   Garder tous ces vieux livres, ça ne me _ pas nécessaire.

37.6 Some differences between impersonal constructions in formal and informal situations

Certain impersonal constructions are appropriate for formal situations (N3) and others for informal situations (N2):

Informal situations (N2)	Formal situations (N3)

+ **infinitive**

    ***c'est mieux** d'y aller par le train*   ***il vaut mieux** y aller par le train*
    it's better to go (there) by train

    ***ça m'arrange** de le faire comme ça*   ***il/cela me plaît** de le faire ainsi*
    it suits me to do it that way

+ *que* + **subordinate clause**

    ***il n'y a qu'à** lui téléphoner*   ***il suffit de** lui téléphoner*
    all you have to do is phone him/her

    ***ça fait** longtemps **qu'**on ne l'avait pas vue*   ***il y a** longtemps **que** nous ne l'avions pas vue*
    we hadn't seen her for ages   (For other examples, **see 51.2.**)

Part eight

Linking groups of words

By combining words in groups (**see Part Five**) and phrases (**see Part Six**), and putting them in a particular order, one can construct a large number of meaningful sentences (**see Part Seven**).

But many sentences consist of more than a series of separate units: in order to convey a particular meaning, one often needs to make grammatical links between two units within the sentence. This is done by using **constructions**: a verb, adjective or noun which is linked by a particular preposition (*à, de, en, pour* or, in some cases, no preposition) to a following noun or infinitive.

In Part Eight, some of these verb, adjective and noun constructions are presented:

38   Verb constructions + noun/pronoun and + infinitive
39   Auxiliary verbs: tense and aspect auxiliaries; modal auxiliaries; *faire, laisser* etc. + infinitive
40   Adjective constructions + noun and + infinitive
41   Noun constructions: adjective phrases + infinitive and + noun
42   Relative constructions

38 Verb constructions

38.1 Verb constructions with nouns and pronouns

The basic sentence **(see 32.1)** consists of a subject (noun or pronoun, stated or implied) plus a tensed verb (present, passé composé, imperfect, etc.):

elle travaille   she works/she's working

This unit can be accompanied by other material, for example an adverb phrase **(see 30.2)** consisting of preposition + noun (*à Paris*: 'in Paris'):

elle travaille à Paris   she works/she's working in Paris

There is no grammatical link between the two parts of this sentence. Each is grammatically complete in its own right: the verb *travailler* is used intransitively, in other words without a direct or indirect object **(see 18.3)**; and the preposition *à* is not linked to the verb *travailler*: it forms part of the adverb phrase *à Paris*.

Very often, however, a verb is used transitively: it has a direct or indirect object **(see 18.3)**; there is a grammatical link between the verb and its object, and one can say that the verb is constructed with either a direct or an indirect object.

If a verb is constructed with a direct object, there is no preposition between the verb and its object:

*elle **commence son travail** à huit heures*   she starts work at eight

If a verb is constructed with an indirect object, there is a preposition (in most cases *à*, *de* or *en*) between the verb and its object:

*elle **s'intéresse à** son travail*   she takes an interest in her work

Unlike *à* in *à Paris*, the preposition *à* does not form part of a phrase *à son travail*: it forms part of the verb construction *s'intéresser à* + noun, just as, in the previous example, the verb construction is *commencer* + noun.

Two objects (double complementation)

Many verbs can be constructed with two (sometimes three) objects, either one direct object and one (sometimes two) indirect objects, or two indirect objects. Very often the verb construction is different in French and in English:

Direct object + indirect object

> *on a souhaité **bonne chance à toute l'équipe***
> we wished the whole team good luck
> *ils ont remercié **le maire de sa visite***
> they thanked the mayor for coming

Two indirect objects

> *il ne faut parler **de cela à personne***
> you mustn't tell anyone about it/that

Verb constructions with adjectives (attributive construction)

Certain verbs can be constructed with a noun as direct object, together with an adjective which qualifies the noun. Verbs used in this attributive construction include:

croire	*estimer*	*juger*	*supposer*	*trouver*
to believe	to consider	to consider/judge	to assume	to think/find

Examples:

> *on a jugé les deux hommes **capables** de gagner*
> the two men were considered capable of winning
> *j'ai trouvé ses explications assez **confuses***
> I found his/her explanations quite confused

Often the direct object appears as a pronoun:

> *tu **les** crois **capables** de gagner?*
> do you think they can win?
> *c'est une idée excellente, mais je **l'**estime **prématurée***
> it's an excellent idea, but I consider it to be premature

Rendre + noun + adjective; *faire de* + noun 1 + noun 2: 'to make . . .'

These two verb constructions are easily confused. Both are used with the meaning 'to make something into something (else)', but:

- *rendre* is used with a noun and an attribute adjective:

> *le bruit **a rendu** tout travail **impossible***
> the noise made all/any work impossible
> *la circulation **rend** l'air **irrespirable***
> the traffic makes the air unfit to breathe

- *faire de* is used with two different nouns:

> *l'abus de la drogue **a fait de** cet homme **une loque***
> drug abuse has made that man (into) a wreck

*il ne faut pas **faire de la Lune la poubelle de la Terre***
the Moon mustn't become Earth's dustbin

Coûter cher etc.: for constructions where the attributive adjective functions as an adverb, and is invariable, **see 17.3e.**

Exercice 38/1   **Constructions attributives (verbe + nom ou pronom + adjectif)**

Travail individuel

Complétez les phrases ci-dessous en ajoutant un des verbes suivants, selon le sens, et en employant le temps approprié du verbe: croire, estimer, juger, rendre, trouver.

Exemple: Je _ les deux projets valables.
Réponse: Je **trouve** les deux projets valables.
(j'**estime** ... et je **juge** ... sont possibles aussi)

1   Ah! vous voilà! Je vous _ partis.
2   Après plus de douze heures de discussion, les jurés _ l'accusé coupable.
3   Elle _ le prix trop élevé, mais d'un autre côté le tableau lui plaisait beaucoup.
4   Toute cette pluie va _ le terrain encore plus difficile.
5   Il est vraiment difficile de le _ innocent.
6   Son intervention hier _ l'enquête encore plus difficile.
7   La plupart des ministres _ les nouvelles mesures nécessaires, mais certains y étaient opposés.
8   Vous allez sans doute nous _ naïfs, mais nous _ sa conduite inacceptable.

38.2 Verb constructions with infinitives

The object of a verb can also be an infinitive; some verbs are constructed with a following infinitive without a preposition, others with a preposition (usually *à* or *de*):

No preposition

*j'**espère** aller en France l'année prochaine*	I'm hoping to go to France next year
*je **préfère** rester à la maison*	I'd rather stay at home
*elle **semble** connaître tout le monde*	she seems to know everyone
*nos ennuis **ne font que commencer***	our troubles are only just beginning

With *à* or *de*

*il **commence à** les comprendre*	he's beginning to understand them
*j'**ai essayé de** le prévenir*	I tried to warn him

In the last two examples, the preposition *à* or *de* forms part of the verb constructions *commencer à* + infinitive and *essayer de* + infinitive: it is not part of the infinitive phrase: *à* and *de* do not combine with object pronouns (for combination of *à* and *de* with the definite articles *le* and *les*, **see 29.1** and **29.2**).

A verb is not necessarily constructed in the same way with a noun, as with an infinitive: *commencer* + noun, but *commencer à* + infinitive, for example.

38.3 Verb constructions with nouns and with infinitives

Just as one needs to learn the pronunciation, spelling and gender (**see 11.1**) of nouns in French, so one needs to learn the pronunciation, the spelling, the conjugation (**see 9** and **10**) and the construction of verbs.

The following table lists over 100 verbs in French, together with their construction with nouns and with infinitives.

Note: the verbs marked with an **asterisk*** can also be constructed with a subordinate or completive clause introduced by *que* (**see 46–49**). The construction with *que* + subordinate clause, instead of an infinitive construction, is often essential when each of the two verbs has a different subject:

Same subject: infinitive construction
   le président a enfin accepté de démissionner
   the chairman finally agreed to step down
   (*le président* is the subject of both verbs: *accepter* and *démissionner*)

Different subject: *que* + subordinate clause
   le conseil a accepté que le président démissionne
   the board agreed to the chairman stepping down
   (each verb has a different subject: *le conseil* and *le président*)

Same subject: infinitive construction
   Boris a appris à conduire en très peu de temps
   Boris learnt to drive in a very short space of time
   (*Boris* is the subject of both verbs)

Different subject: *que* + subordinate clause
   Boris a appris que sa soeur était malade
   Boris heard/discovered his sister was ill
   (each verb has a different subject)

■ Table of verb constructions with nouns and infinitives

accepter	Noun	accept
	de Inf	accept to
accorder	Noun 1 *à* Noun 2	grant . . . to
	à Noun *de* Inf	allow . . . to
accuser	Noun 1 *de* Noun 2	accuse . . . of
	Noun *de* Inf	accuse . . . of -ing
s'adresser	*à* Noun	apply to
*il s'agit	*de* Noun	it's about
	de Inf	it's a matter of -ing
aider	Noun	help
	Noun *à* Inf	help . . . to
*aimer	Noun	love
	Inf	like to, like -ing
*apprendre	Noun	learn
	à Inf	learn (how) to
	Noun 1 *à* Noun 2	teach . . . to
	à Noun *à* Inf	teach . . . (how) to
*approuver	Noun	approve of
arrêter	Noun	stop
	de Inf	stop -ing
arriver	*à* Inf	manage to
en arriver	*à* Noun	to come to, reach (last in series)
	à Inf	to reach the point of -ing
assister	Noun	help
	à Noun	be present at
*attendre	Noun	wait for
*s'attendre	*à* Noun	expect
autoriser	Noun	allow
	Noun *à* Inf	allow . . . to
avoir l'air	Adjective	look
	de Noun	look like
	de Inf	appear to

cacher	Noun 1 *à* Noun 2	hide . . . from
cesser	Noun	stop
	de Inf	stop -ing
changer	Noun 1 *en* Noun 2	change . . . into
	de Noun	replace
chercher	Noun	look for
	à Inf	try to
choisir	Noun	choose
	de Inf	choose to
commencer	Noun	begin, start
	à (sometimes *de*) Inf	begin to, start -ing
	par Noun	begin with
	par Inf	begin by -ing
conseiller	Noun (thing)	advise, suggest
	Noun (person)	give advice to
	à Noun *de* Inf	advise . . . to
consentir	*à* Noun	agree to
	à Inf	agree to
consister	*en* Noun	consist of
	à Inf	consist in -ing
continuer	Noun	continue
	à (or *de*) Inf	continue -ing
*craindre	Noun	fear, be afraid of
	de Inf	fear to
*décider	*de* Inf	decide to
	Noun *à* Inf	make (someone) do, bring (someone) to
se décider	*à* Inf	make up one's mind to
*défendre	Noun 1 *à* Noun 2	rule out . . . for
	à Noun *de* Inf	forbid . . . to
*demander	Noun	ask for
	Noun 1 *à* Noun 2	ask . . . of
	à Inf	ask permission to
	à Noun *de* Inf	ask (someone) to
se dépêcher	*de* Inf	make haste to

dépendre	*de* Noun	depend on
*détester	Noun	dislike
	Inf	not like, hate -ing
devoir	Noun	owe
	Inf	have to, must
*dire	Noun 1 *à* Noun 2	tell . . . to, tell Noun 2 about Noun 1
	à Noun *de* Inf	tell . . . to
donner	Noun 1 *à* Noun 2	give . . . to, give Noun 2 Noun 1
*douter	*de* Noun	doubt
	de Inf	doubt if/whether
*se douter	*de* Noun	suspect, think as much
échapper	*à* Noun	avoid, get away from
s'échapper	*à* Noun	escape from
*empêcher	Noun	prevent
	Noun *de* Inf	prevent . . . from -ing, stop . . . -ing
emprunter	Noun 1 *à* Noun 2	borrow from
encourager	Noun *à* Inf	encourage . . . to
enlever	Noun 1 *à* Noun 2	remove, take away . . . from
*espérer	Noun	hope for, expect
	Inf	hope to
essayer	Noun	try (on)
	de Inf	try to
en être	*à* Noun	to have reached, be at (in a series)
	à Inf	to be at the point of -ing
		(stage in a process)
*éviter	Noun	avoid
	de Inf	avoid -ing
s'excuser	*de* Inf	be sorry to, apologise for -ing
faillir	Inf	almost do something, nearly do something (used in Past tenses only)
faire	*de* Noun 1 Noun 2	make Noun 2 of Noun 1, make Noun 1 into Noun 2 (see also *rendre*)

ne faire que	Inf	be just -ing, be only -ing
finir	Noun	finish (off), complete
	de Inf	stop -ing
	par Inf	end up (by) -ing
forcer	Noun *à* Inf	force . . . to
fournir	Noun 1 *à* Noun 2	provide Noun 2 with Noun 1
s'inquiéter	*de* Noun	worry about, be worried about
	de Inf	worry about -ing, be worried about -ing
insister	*sur* Noun	stress, emphasise
	pour Inf	insist on -ing
*interdire	Noun 1 *à* Noun 2	rule out . . . for
	à Noun *de* Inf	forbid . . . to
s'intéresser	*à* Noun	take an interest in
inviter	Noun 1 *à* Noun 2	invite . . . to
	Noun *à* Inf	invite . . . to
jouer	*à* Noun	play (a sport)
	de Noun	play (an instrument)
manquer	Noun	miss (train, opportunity)
	à Noun	be missed by
	de Noun	lack, be short of
il manque	Noun 1 *à* Noun 2	Noun 1 is missing from Noun 2
*mériter	Noun	deserve
	de Inf	deserve to
nuire	*à* Noun	harm
obéir	*à* Noun	obey
obliger	Noun *à* Inf	make, force
être obligé	*de* Inf	have to
s'occuper	*de* Noun	look after, deal with
	de Inf	see about -ing
oser	Inf	dare to
*oublier	Noun	forget
	de Inf	forget to

*paraître	Adjective	appear
	Noun	appear
	Inf	appear to
pardonner	Noun 1 à Noun 2	forgive Noun 2 for Noun 1
	à Noun de Inf	forgive . . . for -ing
parler	Noun	speak (language)
	à Noun 1 de Noun 2	tell . . . about
	de Inf	talk about -ing
payer	Noun 1 à Noun 2	pay . . . to
	Noun 1 Noun 2	pay (amount) for
*penser	à Noun	think about (have in mind)
	à Inf	be thinking of -ing
	de Noun	think of (have an opinion of)
*permettre	Noun 1 à Noun 2	allow Noun 2 Noun 1
	à Noun de Inf	allow . . . to
*persuader	Noun de Inf	parsuade . . . to, get . . . to
pouvoir	Pronoun	be capable of (something)
	Inf	be capable of -ing
*préférer	Noun 1 à Noun 2	like . . . better than . . .
	Inf	prefer to, prefer -ing
	Inf 1 que de Inf 2	prefer -ing to -ing, would rather . . . than
présenter	Noun 1 à Noun 2	introduce . . . to
*promettre	Noun 1 à Noun 2	promise . . . to, promise Noun 2 noun 1
	à Noun de Inf	promise . . . to
*proposer	Noun 1 à Noun 2	suggest . . . to
	à Noun de Inf	suggest to . . . to
*rappeler	Noun 1 à Noun 2	remind Noun 2 of Noun 1, recall Noun 1 to Noun 2
	à Noun de Inf	remind . . . to
*se rappeler	Noun (formal)	remember
	de Noun (informal)	
	de Inf	remember to
*refuser	Noun 1 à Noun 2	deny . . . to
	de Inf	refuse to
	à Noun de Inf	not allow . . . to

remercier	Noun 1 *de* Noun 2	thank . . . for
	Noun *de* Inf	thank . . . for -ing
rendre	Noun Adjective	make Noun Adjective,
		cause Noun to be Adjective
	Noun 1 *à* Noun 2	return, give back . . . to
		(see also *faire*)
renoncer	*à* Noun	give up
	à Inf	give up -ing
reprocher	Noun 1 *à* Noun 2	blame, criticise Noun 2 for Noun 1
	à Noun *de* Inf	blame, criticise . . . for -ing
résister	*à* Noun	resist
réussir	Noun	make a success of (dish, exploit)
	à Noun	pass (exam)
	à Inf	succeed in -ing
risquer	Noun	risk, run the risk of
	de Inf	be likely to
*savoir	Noun	know (a fact, etc.)
	Inf	know how to
*sembler	Adjective	seem
	Noun	seem
	Inf	seem to
*sentir	Noun	feel (a pain etc.)
se sentir	Adjective	feel (tired etc.)
servir	Noun	serve (a meal); work in someone's favour
	à Noun	be of use for
	à Inf	be of use for -ing
se servir	*de* Noun	use, make use of
*souhaiter	Noun 1 *à* Noun 2	wish Noun 2 Noun 1
	à Noun *de* Inf	want (someone else) to
*se souvenir	*de* Noun	remember
	de Inf	remember to
suffire	*à* Noun	be enough for
	à Inf	be enough to

il suffit	*de* Noun	Noun is enough
	à Noun *de* Inf	all Noun has to do is
tenir	*à* Noun	be fond of, keen on
	à Inf	be keen on -ing, insist on -ing
en venir	*à* Noun	to come to (last in a series)
	à Inf	to come to the point of -ing
*vouloir	Noun	want
	Inf	want to

Note: as well as studying and practising these verbs, their meaning and their constructions, it would be advisable to learn them by heart, systematically.

Exercice 38/2   **Constructions verbales 1: + nom**   Travail individuel

Complétez les phrases ci-dessous en ajoutant à ou de (parfois en ou sur), s'il le faut.

1   Nous pensons qu'il s'agit ( ) un accident.
2   Je n'approuve pas du tout ( ) son action.
3   Elle a décidé de cacher ( ) sa déception ( ) son mari.
4   J'ai conseillé ( ) mon frère de ne rien dire.
5   Leur défense consistait ( ) trois points essentiels.
6   On avait défendu ( ) cet homme de revenir en France.
7   Les enfants ont demandé ( ) leur mère.
8   Les enfants ont demandé ( ) leur mère s'ils pouvaient sortir.
9   La réponse dépend ( ) la façon dont on pose la question.
10   Je ne doute pas ( ) sa sincérité.
11   Permettez-moi d'insister ( ) cette question.
12   Pour se détendre, il joue ( ) la guitare.
13   Je veux être sûr qu'ils ne manquent ( ) rien.
14   Tout excès finit par nuire ( ) la santé.
15   Il aimait la vie militaire, mais il détestait obéir ( ) ses supérieurs.
16   Qu'est-ce que tu penses ( ) mes nouvelles chaussures?
17   Il avait l'esprit libre, et ne pensait ( ) rien.
18   Ce que je reproche ( ) tes camarades, c'est qu'ils sont trop bruyants!
19   Jette ce vieux sac: il ne sert ( ) rien!
20   Tu ne te sers plus ( ) ce sac: on peut le jeter?

Exercice 38/3   **Constructions verbales 2: + infinitif**   Travail individuel

Complétez les phrases ci-dessous en ajoutant à ou de (parfois pour), s'il le faut.

1   Maintenant, il s'agit ( ) savoir qui aura le plus de patience!
2   Elle aidait sa vieille mère ( ) faire la vaisselle.
3   Ce n'est pas ainsi qu'on apprendra aux enfants ( ) être de bons citoyens.
4   Arrête ( ) pleurer, veux-tu!
5   Le travail consiste ( ) vérifier les comptes.
6   C'est un comique qui ne craint pas ( ) offenser chaque secteur de son public.
7   C'est vendredi: tout le monde se dépêche ( ) rentrer.
8   Vous êtes libre: rien ne vous empêche ( ) partir.
9   J'espère ( ) pouvoir finir avant minuit.
10   Elle a essayé ( ) les contacter, mais en vain.
11   J'étais si furieux que j'ai failli ( ) lui dire ( ) ne jamais revenir.
12   J'ai insisté ( ) voir le malade.
13   On l'a obligé ( ) rendre l'argent.
14   Il a été obligé ( ) rendre l'argent.
15   Comment osez-vous ( ) dire cela?
16   Il a paru ( ) hésiter, puis il a continué.
17   Moi, je serais bien venu, mais lui il préfère ( ) rester à la maison.
18   Ils ont promis ( ) ne plus recommencer.
19   C'est quand les choses semblent ( ) aller le plus mal qu'il faut rester calme.
20   Tiens! Je ne me souviens pas ( ) avoir laissé la porte ouverte.

Exercice 38/4   **Constructions verbales + nom et + infinitif**   Travail en groupe

Tour à tour, chaque étudiant lit à haute voix un des débuts de phrase ci-dessous. L'étudiant à sa droite doit compléter la phrase avec une construction + **nom**, et l'étudiant à sa gauche doit la compléter avec une construction + **infinitif**.

Exemple: Il faut arrêter . . .
Réponses possibles:(+ nom)   . . . ce jeu tout de suite.
                  (+ infinitif)   . . . **de faire** des bêtises.

1 Silence! On commence ...	11 La plupart des gens acceptent ...
2 Ce jeu consiste ...	12 Personnellement, je préfère ...
3 Je vais essayer ...	13 L'année prochaine, j'espère ...
4 Personne ne doute ...	14 Il ne faut jamais permettre ...
5 Je pense ...	15 Ce matin j'ai réussi ...
6 Les hommes aiment ...	16 Je vais vous apprendre ...
7 Les femmes cherchent ...	17 Je me souviens ...
8 Est-ce qu'on peut choisir ...?	18 Le conducteur a réussi à éviter ...
9 Ce que je crains, c'est ...	19 Celui qui a inventé ce jeu mérite ...
10 Demain, je vais demander ...	20 Ça y est! Je refuse ...

39 Auxiliary verbs

39.1 Tense and aspect auxiliaries
39.2 Modal auxiliaries
39.3 *Faire, laisser; voir, entendre* + infinitive

Certain verbs, in English and in French, can function as auxiliary verbs: used with another verb (present participle, past participle or infinitive), they determine the status of this verb. The subject of the auxiliary verb is the agent of the action described by the second verb.

One can distinguish three main kinds of auxiliary verb: tense auxiliaries, aspect auxiliaries, and modal auxiliaries.

The system of auxiliary verbs is different in certain key respects, between English and French: in order to understand and use French auxiliary verbs with confidence, it is helpful to understand how the system works in English, and the ways in which the French system is different.

39.1 Tense and aspect auxiliaries

Tense auxiliaries

English	French
has, had + past participle	*avoir*, *être* + past participle
will, would + infinitive	(no auxiliary in French)
do, did + infinitive	(no auxiliary in French)

Tense	English	French
Passé composé:	he has worked	*il **a** travaillé*
	he has left	*il **est** parti*
Pluperfect:	he had worked	*il **avait** travaillé*
	he had left	*il **était** parti*
Future:	he will work	*il travaillera*

343

Conditional:	he would work	*il travaillerait*
Present:	he does work	*il travaille*
	he doesn't work	*il ne travaille pas*
	does he work?	*est-ce qu'il travaille?*
Past:	he did work	*il **a** travaillé*
	he didn't work	*il n'**a** pas travaillé*
	did he work?	*est-ce qu'il **a** travaillé?*

Aspect auxiliaries

English	French
is, was + present participle	(no equivalent in French)
is/was going to + infinitive	present/imperfect of **aller** + infinitive
has/had just been + pres participle	present/imperfect of **venir de** + infinitive

Aspect	English	French
Present continuous:	he is working	*il travaille*
		*il **est en train de** travailler*
Past continuous:	he was working	*il travaillait*
		*il **était en train de** travailler*
Immediate future:	he's going to work	*il **va** travailler*
	he was going to work	*il **allait** travailler*
	he's about to work	*il **est sur le point de** travailler*
	he was about to work	*il **était sur le point de** travailler*
Immediate past:	he's just been working	*il **vient de** travailler*
	he'd just been working	*il **venait de** travailler*

39.2 Modal auxiliaries

Devoir

IN ENGLISH, the auxiliary 'must' has two meanings: an obligation ('has to'), and a probability ('is due to').

IN FRENCH, the auxiliary *il doit* has both these meanings, and is also used to express a supposition ('he probably works').

Tense	English	French
Present:	he has to/has got to work	*il **doit** travailler*
	he probably works/he must work	*il **doit** travailler*
	he's due to work	*il **doit** travailler*
Past:	he had to work	*il **devait**/**a dû** travailler*
		(depending on **aspect: see 54**)
	he probably worked/	*il **a dû**/**avait dû** travailler*
	he must have worked	(depending on **tense:** see **53**)
	he was due to work	*il **devait** travailler*
Pluperfect:	he'd had to work	*il **avait dû** travailler*
Future:	he'll have to work	*il **devra** travailler*
Conditional:	he should work/he ought to work	*il **devrait** travailler*
	he should have worked/	*il **aurait dû** travailler*
	he ought to have worked	

To express the meaning of an obligation, the impersonal construction ***il faut*** is often used (**see 37.2**). To express a weaker form of obligation, ***avoir à*** is used:

> *j'ai ce travail à faire*   or   *j'ai à faire ce travail*
> I have this work to do   I have to do this work

For the difference between *il a dû* (passé composé) and *il devait* (imperfect), **see 54.1**.

Exercice 39/1   *Devoir*   Travail individuel

Récrivez les phrases ci-dessous en ajoutant, au temps qui convient, l'auxiliaire devoir, et en récrivant à l'infinitif le verbe souligné.

Exemple: Il ne <u>travaille</u> pas.
Réponse: Il ne **doit** pas **travailler**.

1   Le train <u>est parti</u>.
2   Les générations futures <u>se souviendront</u>.
3   Tu les <u>aurais prévenus</u>.
4   Elle ne <u>serait</u> pas <u>venue</u>.
5   Cela ne <u>compterait</u> pas pour lui.
6   Il <u>avait subi</u> une interrogation.
7   Ils ne <u>réfléchissaient</u> pas trop.
8   Ils <u>ont eu</u> de la chance.

Exercice 39/2   *Devoir, avoir à, il (me/lui) faut*   Travail à deux > Mise en commun

a   Reformulez les phrases ci-dessous en employant avoir à + infinitif et/ou il (me/lui) faut + infinitif. Pour chaque phrase, mettez-vous d'accord avec votre partenaire sur la ou les formulations (y compris celle avec devoir) que vous jugez préférables ou acceptables.

b   Présentez vos conclusions au reste du groupe.

Exemple: Je dois partir.
Réponse: Il me faut partir.
(Il faut partir: avec cette construction impersonnelle, on ne sait pas de qui il est question;
J'ai à partir: difficile d'imaginer dans quelles circonstances cette formulation serait employée.)

1   Je dois finir ma dissertation.
2   Elle devait faire énormément de choses.
3   Tu devrais bientôt penser à ton avenir.
4   Il devait faire une tournée d'inspection toutes les deux heures.
5   Tu ne devais pas oublier de lui écrire.
6   On doit apporter trop de choses avec soi.

Pouvoir

IN ENGLISH, the auxiliary 'could' has two meanings: imperfect, or conditional.

IN FRENCH, care must be taken, before using either *pouvait* or *pourrait*, to be sure which of these two tenses is appropriate.

The auxiliary *il peut/il pouvait/il pourrait* is used to describe:

● a capability ('is/was/would be able to');
● an authorisation ('is/was/would be allowed to');
● a possibility ('may/might').

Tense	English	French
Present:	he can work/he's able to work	*il **peut** travailler*
	he may work/he's allowed to work	*il **peut** travailler*
Past:	he managed to work	*il **a pu** travailler*
	he could work/he was able to work	*il **pouvait**/**a pu** travailler* (depending on aspect: **see 54.1**)
	he was allowed to work	*il **pouvait**/**a pu** travailler*

Pluperfect:	he'd been able to work	*il **avait pu** travailler*
Future:	he'll be able to work	*il **pourra** travailler*
Conditional:	he could work/he might work	*il **pourrait** travailler*
	he'd be able to work	*il **pourrait** travailler*
	he could have worked/ he might have worked	*il **aurait pu** travailler*

Note the difference in meaning between *pouvoir* and *savoir*:

    *le drapeau est vert: on **peut** se baigner*

    the flag's green: we can (we're allowed to) go in the water

    *il n'aime pas se baigner: il ne **sait** pas nager*

    he doesn't like going in the water: he can't (doesn't know how to) swim

---

Exercice 39/3   ***Pouvoir***   Travail individuel

Récrivez les phrases ci-dessous en ajoutant, au temps qui convient, l'auxiliaire pouvoir, et en récrivant à l'infinitif le verbe souligné.

Exemple: Il ne <u>travaille</u> pas.

Réponse: Il ne **peut** pas **travailler**.

1   Là, on <u>faisait</u> ce qu'on voulait.
2   Il m'a dit qu'il n'<u>avait</u> pas fini le travail à temps.
3   Si tu le lui demandais, il te <u>donnerait</u> l'adresse.
4   Je <u>comprenais</u> son point de vue.
5   On lui a dit qu'elle <u>commencerait</u> au début de la semaine suivante.
6   Après six mois de travail, il <u>a</u> enfin <u>pris</u> quinze jours de vacances.

Vouloir

Tense	English	French
Present:	he wants to work/he's willing to work	*il **veut** travailler*
Past:	he wanted to work/he was willing to work	*il **voulait** travailler*
	he tried to work	*il **a voulu** travailler*
Pluperfect:	he'd wanted to work/he'd been willing to work/he'd tried to work	*il **avait voulu** travailler*
Future:	he'll be willing to work	*il **voudra** travailler*
Conditional:	he'd like to work/he'd want to work	*il **voudrait** travailler*

IN ENGLISH, the auxiliary 'want' can be used with a direct object (noun or pronoun) which becomes the agent of the verb in the infinitive:

he wants me to work   I want these people to work

IN FRENCH, the subject of *vouloir* is the agent of the verb in the infinitive: *il veut travailler*. 'he wants to work'. An infinitive construction is not possible when there is a change of subject; instead, a construction with *que* + subjunctive must be used (**see 48**):

qu'est-ce que tu veux que je fasse?   what do you expect me to do?

Other verbs, such as ***espérer***, ***souhaiter*** and ***préférer***, can be constructed in the same two ways:

Same subject
j'espère arriver avant minuit   I hope I get back by midnight
Different subject
j'espère qu'ils vont arriver avant minuit   I hope they get back by midnight
Same subject
il souhaitait finir à trois heures   he hoped he could finish by three
Different subject
il souhaitait qu'ils puissent finir à trois heures   he hoped they could finish by three
Same subject
je préfère ne pas y penser   I'd rather not think about it
Different subject
je préfère qu'il n'en parle pas   I'd rather he didn't mention it

---

Exercice 39/4   *Vouloir*   Travail individuel

a   Complétez les débuts de phrase ci-dessous (i) avec un infinitif, (ii) avec que + proposition subordonnée (le verbe doit être au subjonctif!). Employez le même verbe pour (ii) que pour (i).
b   Écrivez l'équivalent en anglais de chaque phrase (i) et (ii) que vous avez complétée.

Exemple: Il ne veut pas ...   (i) travailler   (ii) je
Réponses: (i) Il ne veut pas travailler.   (He doesn't want to work.)
          (ii) Il ne veut pas **que** je **travaille**. (He doesn't want me to work.)

1   J'ai voulu ...   (i) répondre   (ii) ils
2   Je ne voudrais pas ...   (i) y penser   (ii) elle
3   Ils voulaient ...   (i) signer   (ii) je
4   Elle aurait voulu ...   (i) gagner   (ii) il
5   Il n'avait pas voulu ...   (i) en parler   (ii) on
6   Nous ne voulons pas ...   (i) y retourner   (ii) ils

There are verb constructions with the infinitive in French which do involve a change of subject, such as *aider quelqu'un à, dire à quelqu'un de, obliger quelqu'un à* and *remercier quelqu'un de* (**see 38.2** and **38.3**).

39.3 *Faire, laisser; voir, entendre* + infinitive

Faire, laisser + infinitive: making someone do something/making something happen
Voir, entendre + infinitive: seeing/hearing someone do something/something happen

In these constructions, the subject of the auxiliary verb (*faire, voir,* etc.) is not the agent of the second verb; the object of the first verb is also the subject of the second verb:

   *le patron **a fait venir** la police*
   the landlord called the police in
   *les douaniers **ont laissé passer** les trois camions*
   the customs officers let the three lorries through
   *on **voyait arriver** les premiers nuages*
   we could see the first clouds coming
   *on **entendait crier** une chouette*
   we could hear an owl calling

The construction used in English is similar, but not always identical, to the one used in French. Note the order of words in the second part of each sentence: the infinitive comes immediately after the auxiliary, and the agent (subject) of the infinitive comes at the end.

Faire + infinitive

In this construction, the two verbs (*faire* + infinitive) function as one unit: only one direct object (**see 18.3**) is possible in the sentence. This presents no problem when the second verb is intransitive (is not followed by an object at all) or is constructed with an indirect object:

   *c'est un prof qui **fait parler** ses élèves*
   he's a teacher who gets his students to speak
   (*parler* is used intransitively – with no object at all)
   *cette image **fait penser** les enfants à la guerre*
   this picture makes children think of war
   (*penser à* is followed by an indirect object)

But when the second verb is followed by a direct object, the subject of the second verb becomes an indirect object, preceded by *à* or *par*.

+ *par*   *elle avait fait peindre son portrait **par un ami***
       she'd had her portrait painted by a friend

This is similar to a passive construction **(see 35)**, where the agent (*un ami*) of the verb *peindre* is preceded by *par*:

> *son portrait avait été peint **par un ami***
>
> her portrait had been painted by a friend

+ *à*   *j'ai enfin fait comprendre **au directeur** la raison de mon absence*

   I finally got the manager to understand the reason for my absence

In this sentence, the direct object (the noun phrase *la raison de mon absence*) could also be an indirect question **(see 33.4)** or a completive clause **(see 49)**:

> *j'ai enfin fait comprendre au directeur **pourquoi j'avais été absent***
>
> *j'ai enfin fait comprendre au directeur **que mon absence avait été nécessaire***

Exercice 39/5   *Faire* + **infinitif** + **nom**   Travail individuel

Composez des phrases à partir des éléments donnés ci-dessous, en employant faire (au temps indiqué) + infinitif.

Exemple: (tu) les autorités comprendront pourquoi c'est urgent   (futur)
Réponse: **Tu feras comprendre aux** autorités pourquoi c'est urgent.

1 (ils)	le projet avance lentement	(présent)
2 (ils)	des spécialistes ont refait leur toit	(passé composé)
3 (elle)	un artisan faisait ces objets	(imparfait)
4 (je)	le jeune homme a répété le message	(passé composé)
5 (tu)	le prix a baissé	(passé composé)
6 (je)	ces gens réfléchiront aux conséquences de leur action	(futur)

Object pronouns in *faire* + infinitive constructions

When an object pronoun **(see 18)** is used in a *faire* + infinitive construction, it is placed before *faire*, not before the infinitive.

If the second verb is intransitive, or constructed with an indirect object, a direct object pronoun can be used:

> *il **les** fait parler*   he gets them to speak
>
> *cette image **les** fait penser à la guerre*   this picture makes them think of the
>   war

If the second verb is constructed with a direct object (or an indirect question or a completive clause), then an indirect object pronoun is used:

> *elle **lui** avait fait peindre son portrait*
>
> she had got him to paint her portrait

*je **lui** ai fait comprendre pourquoi j'avais été absent*
I got him to understand why I'd been absent

Two object pronouns (one direct, one indirect: **see 18.3**) can be used in the *faire* + infinitive construction:

*elle **le lui** avait fait peindre*   she'd got him to paint it

*je **le lui** ai fait comprendre*   I got him to understand this/why

The neuter direct object pronoun *le* stands for the phrase *pourquoi j'avais été absent* (**see 18.4 and 52.5**).

Exercice 39/6   ***Faire* + pronom + infinitif**   Travail individuel

Reformulez les phrases ci-dessous en employant faire + infinitif.

Exemple: Après avoir vu ce film, j'ai pleuré.
Réponse: Ce film m'a fait pleurer.

1   Après avoir écouté le premier ministre, il a changé d'avis.
2   Grâce aux encouragements de leurs supporters, ils ont gagné le match.
3   Malgré sa mélancolie, il n'a pas renoncé à travailler.
4   Malgré la crise financière, nous ne perdrons pas beaucoup d'argent.
5   A cause de ce projet, je néglige certaines autres choses.
6   A cause de leurs remarques, tu perdais souvent ton sang-froid.

Se faire + infinitive

This pronominal construction is used as an alternative to a passive construction (**see 35.3d**):

il s'est fait arrêter par la police   he got/was arrested by the police

It is also used when the meaning of the reflexive pronoun (*me, te, se* etc.) is 'for oneself':

*je **me** suis enfin fait couper les cheveux*   I finally had my hair cut

Alternatives to a *faire* + infinitive construction

Treating two verbs as one for grammatical purposes can lead to sentences where the meaning is unclear, or the grammatical structure unsatisfactory. In such cases, alternative constructions are used in French.

If you find that a *faire* + infinitive construction of the kinds illustrated above does not seem to work, or the meaning does not seem clear, try using constructions such as:

obliger quelqu'un à + infinitive   *faire que* + subjunctive
to oblige someone to   to make something happen

pousser quelqu'un à + infinitive   *demander à quelqu'un de* + infinitive
to encourage someone to   to ask someone to

Examples:

je lui ai demandé de le réparer   I asked him/her to mend it

qu'est-ce qui fait qu'elle l'aime?   what makes her love him?

Laisser + infinitive

This construction is similar to *faire* + infinitive:

+ noun	*cela **fait passer** le temps*	it passes the time
	*laissons **passer** le temps!*	we must let time pass!
+ pronoun	*ne me **fais** pas **rire**!*	don't make me laugh!
	*je te **laisse faire***	I'll let you do it/I'll leave it to you

But it is possible to construct *laisser* + infinitive as two separate verbs, grammatically speaking:

*je **lui** ai fait finir le travail*   I made him/her finish the work

*je **lui** ai laissé finir le travail*   I let him/her finish the work

*je **l'**ai laissé finir le travail*   I left him/her to finish the work

Se laisser + infinitive

This construction is similar to *se faire* + infinitive:

ils **se sont laissé** enfermer par la routine

they let themselves be caught up by routine

je **me suis laissé** tenter par le gâteau au chocolat

I allowed myself to be tempted by the chocolate cake

Voir, entendre, regarder, écouter + infinitive:

to see/hear/watch/listen to s.o. doing sth./sth. happening

When these verbs are used in a construction with the infinitive, the structure can be the same as for *faire* and *laisser*, or the two parts can be treated as separate:

+ noun	*il n'avait pas **vu arriver** l'autre voiture*	
	he hadn't seen the other car coming	
	*il n'avait pas **vu** l'autre voiture **arriver** sur lui*	
	he hadn't seen the other car coming towards him	
	*j'ai **entendu chanter** les oiseaux*	
	I heard the birds singing	
	*j'ai **entendu** les oiseaux **chanter** dans le bois*	
	I heard the birds singing in the wood	
+ pronoun	*il ne **l'**avait pas **vu arriver***	he hadn't seen it coming
	*je les **ai entendus chanter***	I heard them singing

Entendre dire que + **clause;** *entendre parler de* + **noun**

- *entendre dire que* is used with a completive clause (**see 49**):

j'ai entendu dire qu'elle n'est plus à l'hôpital   I've heard she's out of hospital

(one can also say *j'ai appris qu'elle n'est plus à l'hôpital*)

- *entendre parler de* is used with a noun or pronoun:

cela, je n'en ai jamais entendu parler!   I've never heard of it/that!

Se voir etc.: this pronominal construction is used as an alternative to the passive (**see 35.3**):

il s'est vu réclamer 10 000F par le fisc

he was asked to pay 10 000F by the Inland Revenue

It is also used with a reflexive meaning:

il s'écoute parler   he listens to himself speak

je ne me vois pas faire cela   I can't see myself doing that

Alternatives to a *voir* (etc.) + infinitive construction

The infinitive construction is only one way in which these verbs (*voir, entendre, regarder, écouter*) can be used. Depending on the meaning, a number of different grammatical constructions are possible:

Basic sentence (SVO)   **(see 32.1)**

*j'ai vu **ses tableaux***   I've seen his paintings

Indirect question with WH- word plus clause   **(see 33.4)**

*j'ai vu **comment il travaille***   I've seen how he works

Infinitive construction   **(see 39)**

*je l'ai vu **travailler***   I've seen him working/at work

Relative construction   **(see 42)**

*je l'ai vu **qui travaillait dans son atelier***   I saw him working in his studio

Subordinate clause   **(see 46–48)**

*je l'ai vu **alors qu'il travaillait dans son atelier***   I saw him while he was working in his studio

Completive clause   **(see 49)**

*j'ai vu **qu'il travaillait dans son atelier***   I saw/noticed that he was working in his studio

40 Adjective constructions with nouns and with infinitives

40.1 Adjective constructions with nouns and with infinitives
40.2 Adjective constructions followed by either *à* or *de* + infinitive

40.1 Adjective constructions with nouns and with infinitives

One usually thinks of an adjective as a word (or phrase) that describes a noun (**see 12.1**), but many adjectives can introduce phrases made up of:

adjective + preposition (usually *à* or *de*) + noun/pronoun

and/or adjective + preposition (*à* or *de*) + infinitive

Examples:

Habitué à	*elle est **habituée à** la pluie*	she's used to rain
	*elle est **habituée à** gagner*	she's used to winning
Sûr de	*il est **sûr de** lui*	he's sure of himself
	*il est **sûr de** gagner*	he's certain of winning/sure to win

The group adjective + preposition forms an adjective construction, in a similar way to verb constructions (**see 38**).

In adjective constructions used with an infinitive, the agent of the verb in the infinitive is assumed to be the person or thing the adjective refers to. If the sentence as a whole refers to two different people or things, then a subordinate clause (**see 46–48**), not an infinitive, must be used after these adjectives, enabling the second subject to appear as the subject of the verb in the subordinate clause:

Same subject	*je suis content **d'être** là*
	I'm pleased to be here, I'm pleased I'm here
Different subject	*je suis content **que vous soyez** là*
	I'm pleased you're here, I'm pleased for you to be here

The following Table lists some adjectives which can be constructed with nouns and/or infinitives, together with the preposition (usually *à* or *de*) which is used with each adjective.

Note: the adjectives marked with an **asterisk*** can also be constructed with a subordinate or completive clause introduced by *que* (**see 46–49**).

■ Table of adjective constructions with nouns and infinitives

apte	*à* Noun	fit for
	à Inf	fit to
***autre**	*que* Noun	other than
avide	*de* Noun	eager for
	de Inf	eager to
bon	*à* Noun	fit for
	à Inf	fit to
capable	*de* Noun	capable of
	de Inf	capable of -ing
***certain**	*de* Noun	sure of
	de Inf	certain of -ing, sure to
***conscient**	*de* Noun	aware of
	de Inf	aware of -ing
***content**	*de* Noun	pleased with
	de Inf	pleased to, content with -ing
coupable	*de* Noun	guilty of
	de Inf	guilty of -ing
cruel	*envers* Noun	cruel towards
décidé	*à* Inf	determined to
le dernier	*de* Noun	the last of, the last in
	à Inf	the last to
***désolé**	*de* Inf	(very) sorry to
différent	*de* Noun	different from
doué	*pour* Noun	good at, with a gift for
égal	*à* Noun	equal to, up to
***enchanté**	*de* Noun	delighted at
	de Inf	delighted to
***étonné**	*de* Noun	surprised at
	de Inf	surprised to
expert	*en* Noun	(an) expert at

*****fâché**	*contre* Noun	annoyed with (person)
	de Noun	annoyed at (thing)
fatigué	*de* Noun	tired with, tired of
	de Inf	tired of -ing
*****fier**	*de* Noun	proud of
	de Inf	proud to
forcé	*de* Inf	forced to
fort	*en* Noun	good at
fou	*de* Noun	wild with, mad with
*****furieux**	*contre* Noun	furious with
habitué	*à* Noun	used to
	à Inf	used to -ing
*****heureux**	*de* Noun	happy with
	de Inf	glad to
impatient	*de* Inf	impatient to, in a hurry to
impuissant	*à* Inf	powerless to, unable to
incapable	*de* Noun	incapable of
	de Inf	incapable of -ing
inférieur	*à* Noun	inferior to, not as good as
*****inquiet**	*de* Noun	worried about
	de Inf	worried at -ing
lent	*à* Inf	slow to
long	*à* Inf	taking a long time to
le même	*que* Noun	the same as
obligé	*de* Inf	obliged to
occupé	*à* Inf	busy with -ing
plein	*de* Noun	full of
le premier	*de* Noun	the first of
	à Inf	the first to
proche	*de* Noun	close to, near to

propre	*à* Inf	likely to
responsable	*de* Noun	responsible for, in charge of
***satisfait**	*de* Noun	pleased with
semblable	*à* Noun	similar to
le seul	*de* Noun *à* Inf	the only one of, the only one in the only one to
supérieur	*à* Noun	superior to, better than
***sûr**	*de* Noun *de* Inf	sure of certain to
***surpris**	*de* Inf	surprised to
susceptible	*de* Inf	likely to, capable of -ing
utile	*à* Noun	useful for

Exercice 40/1   **Constructions adjectivales 1: + nom**   Travail individuel

Complétez les phrases ci-dessous en ajoutant à ou de (parfois pour ou contre).

1 Elle est toujours avide _ nouvelles sur la famille.
2 Je pense qu'il n'était pas conscient _ son erreur.
3 Était-il coupable _ tous les crimes dont on l'accusait?
4 Son nouveau disque est différent _ ce que j'avais imaginé.
5 On a découvert qu'il était doué _ les maths.
6 Au début, elle a été fâchée _ son fils.
7 Je ne suis pas très fort _ mécanique.
8 C'est vrai de dire qu'au début elle était folle _ lui.
9 Quand j'ai lu l'article, j'ai été furieux _ la mairie.
10 Dans ce quartier, les revenus familiaux sont bien inférieurs _ la moyenne.
11 Elle était inquiète _ ce qu'il allait penser.
12 L'incident n'était que le premier _ toute une série.
13 C'est à de tels moments qu'on se sent proche _ sa famille.
14 Il a toujours insisté qu'il n'était pas responsable _ l'incendie.
15 Pour une fois, elle s'est déclarée satisfaite _ son travail.

Exercice 40/2   **Constructions adjectivales 2: + infinitif**   Travail individuel

Complétez les phrases ci-dessous en ajoutant à ou de.

1   Toutes les vérités ne sont pas bonnes _ dire.
2   Méfiez-vous de lui: il est capable _ dire n'importe quoi.
3   Je suis content _ vous voir guéri.
4   Elle était décidée _ découvrir la vérité sur cette affaire.
5   Pour ces choses-là, je suis toujours le dernier _ savoir.
6   Je suis désolé _ ne pas pouvoir vous en dire plus.
7   J'ai été étonné _ apprendre qu'il était mort.
8   Il était fatigué _ entendre toujours les mêmes arguments.
9   Elle était maintenant habituée _ entendre ce genre de remarques.
10 Quand je l'ai questionné, il a été incapable _ me donner une réponse cohérente.
11 Cette machine est toujours lente _ démarrer.
12 Ça, c'est bien lui: toujours occupé _ dire du mal de quelqu'un.
13 Sa grand-mère était la seule _ apprécier son talent.
14 Je suis bien surpris _ vous entendre dire cela.
15 Je vous préviens: cette voiture est susceptible _ tomber en panne à tout moment.

40.2 Adjectives followed by either *à* or *de* + infinitive

In the above Table (see 40.1), the two words (adjective + preposition) should be learnt as one unit, in the same way as verb constructions (see 38.3), but there are some adjectives which can be followed by *à* + infinitive, or by *de* + infinitive. One cannot say, of these adjectives, either that 'they are constructed with *à*' or that 'they are constructed with *de*': the choice of *à* or *de* depends on the way the whole sentence is constructed.

Adjectives that can be used in this way include:

agréable	*amusant*	*difficile*	*ennuyeux*
pleasant	funny	difficult	boring
facile	*impossible*	*intéressant*	*triste*
easy	impossible	interesting	sad

All these adjectives express a subjective judgment: they refer both to what is observed, and to the observer's impression (if something is 'difficult' or 'boring', that may be because of what it is, or because of what the observer is).

Noun + *être* + adjective + *à* + infinitive

The construction with *à* is made up of noun + *être* + adjective + *à* + infinitive: the preposition *à* forms a unit with the infinitive (*à visiter, à trouver, à lire*), not with the adjective (*agréable, difficile, intéressants*):

*le parc est **agréable à visiter***	the grounds are pleasant to walk round
*la réponse est **difficile à trouver***	the answer is hard to find
*ses livres sont **intéressants à lire***	his/her books are interesting to read

The agent of the infinitive is anyone who might walk round the grounds, find the answer, or read the books, not *le parc, la réponse* or *les livres: le parc* is the object of *visiter, la réponse* is the object of *trouver, ses livres* is the object of *lire*.

In the above examples, the adjective (+ *à* + infinitive) refers to a specific noun. A similar construction, beginning with *c'est*, is used when referring back to an idea or a sentence:

est-ce une bonne ou une mauvaise chose? C'est difficile à dire

is it a good or a bad thing? It's hard to say

The construction can be abbreviated to adjective + *à* + infinitive (**see 32.5a**):

*est-ce une bonne ou une mauvaise chose? **Difficile à dire***

is it a good or bad thing? Hard to say

C'est/il est + adjective + *de* + infinitive

The construction with *de* is made up of ***c'est/il est*** + adjective + ***de*** + infinitive: the sentence *Pierre est facile à contenter* ('Pierre is easy to please') is a statement about *Pierre*, saying that he's easy to please.

The same facts can be expressed as a statement about what is easy, expressed as *contenter Pierre* ('pleasing Pierre'):

c'est facile de *contenter Pierre*	(N2)	it's easy to please Pierre

In formal situations, this sentence is formulated with *il est*, not *c'est*:

il est facile de *contenter Pierre*	(N3)	it is easy to please Pierre

The construction can be abbreviated to adjective + *de* + infinitive (see **32.5a**):

difficile de savoir *ce qui plaît à Pierre*		(it's) hard to know what Pierre likes

Infinitive + noun + *est* + adjective

Another way of expressing the same idea is:

contenter Pierre est facile	(N3)	pleasing Pierre is easy
or *contenter Pierre, c'est facile*	(N2)	

Now the infinitive phrase (*contenter Pierre*) has become the subject of the sentence, and there is no preposition, either *à* or *de*.

For more examples of these constructions, **see 52.3**, but first, practise each of the constructions described here, by converting from one formulation to another. This will help you:

- to make an association in your mind between each of the three types of construction and the use of *à*, *de* or no preposition before the infinitive, and
- to develop a sense for when one formulation is more appropriate than the other.

Exercice 40/3   **Constructions avec *à*, avec *de*, et sans préposition**   Travail à deux > Mise en commun

a   Composez des phrases à partir des éléments donnés ci-dessous. Essayez chaque fois de composer trois phrases différentes.

b   Donnez l'équivalent en anglais de chacune de ces trois formulations.

c   Décidez si certaines formulations sont préférables à d'autres, et pourquoi.

d   Présentez vos phrases et vos conclusions au reste du groupe.

Exemple: Pierre et Marie   facile(s)   contenter
Réponses: avec à   Pierre et Marie sont faciles à contenter.
                     avec de   C'est/Il est facile de contenter Pierre et Marie.
                     sans préposition   Contenter Pierre et Marie est facile.

1	cette question	impossible	résoudre
2	les coupables	difficile(s)	trouver
3	les mots croisés	ennuyeux	faire
4	son histoire	triste	écouter
5	un vin fin	agréable	boire
6	les bandes dessinées	amusant(es)	lire

41 Noun constructions: adjective phrases

41.1   Adjective phrases with *à/de/pour* + infinitive
41.2   Adjective phrases with *à/de/en* + noun

41.1 Adjective phrases with *à/de/pour* + infinitive

In both French and English, a noun is often constructed with a following infinitive:

'*appartement **à** louer*'	'flat to let'
*le droit **de** vivre*	the right to live
*un effort **pour** respirer*	an effort to breathe

IN ENGLISH, the linking preposition between noun and infinitive is always 'to'.

IN FRENCH, the linking preposition can be *à*, *de* or *pour*, and it is not easy to formulate simple guidelines as to which preposition to use in each case. The link between a particular noun and a particular preposition (*à*, *de* or *pour*) is weaker than for verb constructions **(see 38.1)**, or for adjective constructions **(see 40.1)**.

Noun + *à* + infinitive
This group includes constructions such as *maison à vendre* ('house for sale'), where the phrase *à vendre* functions as an adjective. The adjective phrase formed by *à* + infinitive describes some feature of the noun which involves action by someone else; you could think of the full meaning of the phrase as: *une maison que quelqu'un veut vendre* ('a house that someone wants to sell'):

*une machine **à écrire***	a typewriter
	(a machine that someone writes with)
*la salle **à manger***	the dining room
	(the room where people eat their meals)
*c'est une occasion **à saisir***	it's a bargain not to be missed
	(that anyone should take)
*c'est un homme **à abattre***	he's a man with a price on his head
	(that anyone should shoot)

Avoir/il y a + noun + *à* + infinitive
The verb *avoir* forms part of several compound verbs, such as *donner lieu, faire mal* **(see 15.2)**, which can be used with *à* + infinitive.

Avoir (or *il y a*) is also used to introduce noun + *à* + infinitive constructions where *avoir* does not form a compound verb with the noun; the noun (or pronoun) is the object of both verbs: *avoir* and the infinitive.

*j'ai beaucoup de choses **à faire***	I've lots of things to do
*on a quelque chose d'urgent **à discuter***	we've got something urgent to discuss
*ils n'ont pas d'idées **à nous proposer***	they have no ideas to suggest
*il n'y a rien d'intéressant **à voir***	there is nothing interesting to see
*qu'est-ce qu'il y a **à voir** à la télé?*	what's there to see on TV?

A noun used with an indefinite or partitive article **(see 22)** or a qualifier/quantifier **(see 23–24)** used with or without a noun, is usually constructed with *à* + infinitive: *avoir/il y a + un/une/des* + noun/*beaucoup de* (etc.) + noun/*quelque chose/rien* (etc.)

and:	*mettre du temps/une heure à*	to take time/an hour to
	passer du temps/une heure à	to spend time/an hour -ing
also:	*rester assis(e)/debout à*	to remain sitting/standing -ing, to sit/stand -ing

Noun + *de* + infinitive

As a general rule, a noun used with a definite article **(see 22)**, or with a possessive or demonstrative adjective **(see 20–21)** is constructed with *de* + infinitive:

avoir or *il y a*	+	*le/son/ce* (etc.)	+	noun	+ *de* +	infinitive

*elle a **la** volonté **de** réussir*	she has the will to succeed
*j'admire **cette** passion **de** vivre*	I admire such a passion to live/for life
***sa** tentative **de** former un gouvernement a échoué*	his/her attempt to form a government (has) failed
*il a toujours eu **le** désir **de** voyager*	he has always wanted to travel

Nouns constructed with *à* or *de* + infinitive

Because of their meaning, and/or the overall meaning of the phrases in which they are often used, certain nouns tend to be followed by *à*, and others by *de*, + infinitive.

Nouns likely to be followed by *à* + infinitive include:

aptitude	*inclination*	*rapidité*	*lenteur*
aptitude	inclination	speed	slowness
habileté	*impuissance*	*tendance*	*timidité*
skill	powerlessness	tendency	shyness

Nouns likely to be followed by *de* + infinitive include:

crainte	*souci*	*désir*
fear	concern	desire
tentation	*obligation*	*nécessité*
temptation	obligation	need, necessity

(im)possibilité	*occasion*	*chance*
(im)possibility	opportunity	luck
pouvoir	*devoir*	*droit*
power	duty	right
moyen	*façon*	*manière*
means	way	manner

Nouns followed by *à* or *de* + infinitive include:

(in)capacité	*intelligence*	*volonté*
(in)capacity	intelligence	will
(im)patience	*appétit*	*hâte*
(im)patience	appetite	haste

Making use of constructions consisting of noun + *à/de* + infinitive is an economical and adaptable way of extending your powers of expression in French.

Noun + *pour* + infinitive

Pour + infinitive is used when the infinitive phrase expresses a sense of purpose; there is no particular link between the noun and *pour* + infinitive: the noun simply happens to come at the end of the preceding phrase:

> *c'est une bonne méthode **pour se débarrasser** des mouches*
> it's a good way of getting rid of flies
> *il a fallu deux grues **pour sortir** le camion de l'eau*
> it took two cranes to get the lorry out of the water
> *ils n'ont fait aucun effort **pour trouver** le coupable*
> they made no effort to find the criminal

Exercice 41/1   **Nom + *à/de/pour* + infinitif**   Travail individuel

Complétez les phrases ci-dessous en ajoutant à, de ou pour.

1   Est-ce qu'on a le droit _ faire tout ce qu'on veut?
2   Parlez-lui si vous voulez, mais vous aurez du mal _ le convaincre.
3   Tu peux me rappeler? J'ai quelque chose d'important _ te dire.
4   J'ai une idée _ résoudre le problème.
5   Voilà ma dernière offre: c'est _ prendre ou _ laisser.
6   Je désapprouve totalement leur façon _ vivre.
7   On a eu la malchance _ arriver juste avant la fermeture.
8   Il nous a fallu deux heures _ aller à l'aéroport.
9   Les partis politiques n'ont rien de nouveau _ proposer.
10 Il faut résister à la tentation _ les condamner.

41.2 Noun constructions with *à/de/en* + another noun

In phrases consisting of noun 1 + *à/de* + noun 2, the group *à/de/en* + noun 2 functions as an adjective, qualifying noun 1.

IN ENGLISH, the noun (or other word) being used as a adjective is placed before the noun being qualified, and there is no need for the linking preposition 'of':

un trèfle à quatre feuilles	a four-leaf clover
un donneur de sang	a blood donor
l'abus d'alcool	alcohol abuse
un policier en uniforme	a uniformed policeman

IN FRENCH, the noun being qualified comes first, followed by an adjective phrase beginning with *à*, *de* or *en*.

How to know when to use one or other of these prepositions between two nouns?

A or *de*?

In general, the difference between these two prepositions when used with a noun corresponds to the difference when they are used with an infinitive:

- *à* has an idea of purpose, function, capacity, potential (**see 29.1**);
- *de* is associated with description, observation, appearance, fact (**see 29.2**).

One illustration of this difference can be seen in the two phrases:

	une tasse à thé	a teacup
and	*une tasse de thé*	a cup of tea

The first phrase, with *à*, refers to the function of the cup: there may well be no tea in it at all; the second phrase, with *de*, describes a cup containing tea.

De or *en*?

As before, *de* is associated with description, appearance; *en*, on the other hand, emphasises substance, design, etc.:

la porte d'entrée	the front door
la langue de bois	empty slogans (media, business, politics)
une porte en bois	a wooden door

A or *en*?

A refers to fittings, equipment, etc., whereas *en* refers to substance, design, etc.:

une montre à quartz	a quartz watch
une montre en or	a (solid) gold watch
un cahier à spirale	a spiral bound exercise book
un escalier en spirale	a spiral staircase

Exercice 41/2   **Nom 1 + à/de/en + nom 2**   Travail individuel

Complétez les phrases ci-dessous en ajoutant à, de ou en.

1   On a découvert que la sortie _ secours avait été fermée à clef.
2   En deux ans, ils ont constitué une banque _ données impressionnante.
3   Leur appartement est très petit: on dirait un placard _ balais.
4   La meilleure pièce est une armoire _ chêne massif.
5   Tiens! C'est le général: _ civil, on ne le reconnaît pas.
6   Cette chaise _ dossier haut est sûrement un Louis treize.
7   Maintenant la lionne est _ bout _ souffle: elle ne peut plus poursuivre sa proie.
8   Le circuit cycliste est _ forme _ huit.

Preposition + noun: with or without article?

In all the above examples, the second noun forms part of an adjective phrase: the second noun does not exist in its own right, and there is no article. The more the second noun (after *à* or *de*) exists in its own right in a sentence, separately from the first noun, the more likely it is to be accompanied by a definite article: *au, à la, aux* in the case of *à*, and *du, de la, des* in the case of *de*:

l'homme à la canne   the man with the/a walking-stick
(man and stick are separate entities, equally present in the description)
la cantine du personnel   the staff canteen
(canteen and staff are seen as separate entities: the idea is: 'the canteen for the staff')
l'industrie du disque   the record industry
(which makes and sells records)
la capitale de l'Europe   Europe's capital
(*l'Europe* as opposed to *l'Asie*, etc.)
la baisse des ventes   the drop in sales
(*les ventes ont baissé*)
une photo des jardins   a photo of the gardens

In some cases both *de* and *du/de la/des* are used:
Val de Loire. Pays des châteaux   (motorway sign in Touraine)
(the phrase *pays de châteaux* might suggest that *châteaux* were the only thing of note in the region)
l'office de tourisme   the tourist office
or *l'office du tourisme*

365

In the last example above, the meaning can be either 'tourist office' or 'office for tourism'. This distinction can be applied to a number of expressions, such as:

le service de réanimation	the intensive care unit
le service des urgences	the casualty department ('for emergencies')
le service de presse	the press office
le service du personnel	the personnel department ('for personnel matters')

If the second noun is itself qualified by an adjective phrase, and is presented as a separate entity, a definite article is used:

*l'homme **à la** barbe **blanche*** the man with a white beard

Whereas in phrases such as

*une chemise **à** manches courtes* a short-sleeved shirt

the second noun, although qualified by an adjective, is still part of an adjective phrase.

Other prepositions can be used in noun 1 + preposition + noun 2 constructions:

*un film **avec Depardieu***	a film with/featuring Depardieu	
*un jour **sans pluie***	a rainless day	**(see 27.2)**

An adjective phrase composed of preposition + noun is not the only way of giving an extended description of a noun; one way of giving further information about a noun is to use a **relative construction**: see **42**.

■ Summary

Noun + adjective	**(see 26)**
*un jour **sombre***	a dull day
*un bureau **vide***	an empty office
Noun 1 + preposition + noun 2	**(see 41.2)**
*un jour **de pluie***	a rainy day
Noun + preposition + infinitive	**(see 41.1)**
*un bureau **à louer***	an office to rent
Noun + relative construction	**(see 42)**
*un jour **où il pleut beaucoup***	a day when it rains a lot
*un bureau **que personne ne veut occuper***	an office (that) nobody wants to take

Exercice 41/3   **Comment compléter une phrase**   Travail à deux ou en groupe

a   Complétez chacun des débuts de phrase ci-dessous de **quatre** façons différentes: (i) avec un adjectif, (ii) avec une préposition + nom, (iii) avec une préposition + infinitif, (iv) avec qui ou que + proposition relative.

b   Ensuite, comparez et discutez les phrases que vous avez inventées.

Exemple: Le mien, c'est un bureau ...

Réponses possibles:(i)   sombre

(ii)   sans caractère

(iii)   à fuir

(iv)   que personne ne m'envie

1   Le onze novembre est un jour ...
2   Le football est un sport ...
3   Mon rêve, ce serait une maison ...
4   Je ne voudrais jamais avoir une voiture ...
5   Le printemps est une saison ...
6   Allumer une cigarette dans un endroit public est une action ...
7   La petite enfance est un âge ...
8   Chercher un emploi est une activité ...

42 Relative constructions

42.1 Simple relative constructions
42.2 More complex relative constructions
42.3 Other relative constructions

A **relative construction** is one way of providing further information about a noun or pronoun; one can think of a relative construction as an extended adjective:

+ adjective	*un chien endormi*	a sleeping dog
+ relative	*un chien **qui** dort*	a dog that sleeps
+ adjective	*un tyran détesté*	a hated tyrant
+ relative	*un tyran **qu'**on déteste*	a tyrant who is hated

42.1 Simple relative constructions

IN ENGLISH, the main words used to introduce simple relative constructions are 'who', 'whom' (N4), 'that' and 'which':

	Subject	Direct object
Persons	who	who (N2), whom (N4)
	that	that (or no link word)
Things, ideas	which	which
	that	that (or no link word)

IN ENGLISH, it is possible to use a different word for a person ('who') and for a thing or idea ('which'), but the link word 'that' can be used for both persons and things or ideas. These link words are used whether they are the subject or the direct object of the verb that follows, except for the use of 'whom' instead of 'who' in very formal situations. In many cases where 'who(m)', 'that' or 'which' is the direct object of the verb that follows, it can be omitted altogether:

   'the man I saw' 'the book she bought'
This construction, with no link word, is not possible in French.

IN FRENCH, only two words are used to introduce simple relative constructions: *qui* and *que*. No distinction is made between persons and things or ideas.

> *Qui* is used if it is the subject of the verb that follows, and *que/qu'* if it is the direct object of the verb that follows.

Qui and *que/qu'* have a double function in relative constructions:

● they refer back to a particular noun or pronoun (called the **antecedent** of the relative construction), and;

● they refer forward to the verb in what follows (called the **relative clause**).

Qui is spelt in full, even before a vowel:

une idée **qui** *m'intéresse*	an idea that interests me
une ville **qui** *a beaucoup changé*	a town that has changed a lot

Que is shortened to *qu'* before a vowel:

une chose **que** *j'adore*	a thing (that) I love
la maison **qu'***on peut voir*	the house (that) one can see

In standard French (spoken or written), *qui* or *que* is never omitted:

l'homme **que** *j'ai vu*	the man I saw
le livre **qu'***elle a acheté*	the book she bought

Exercice 42/1   *Qui* **et** *que*   Travail individuel

Complétez les phrases ci-dessous en ajoutant qui ou que/qu'.

1   C'est un livre _ on lit avec plaisir.
2   Les gens _ disent cela ne sont pas sincères.
3   C'est une invention _ a permis de sauver beaucoup de vies.
4   C'est quelqu'un _ j'admire beaucoup.
5   L'air _ on respire est souvent pollué.
6   Voilà l'équipe _ va gagner la coupe.

Exercice 42/2   **Composer des propositions relatives avec** *qui* **et** *que*

Travail en groupe

Quand c'est son tour, chaque étudiant doit compléter, à haute voix, et le plus promptement possible, un des débuts de phrase ci-dessous, en employant qui ou que/qu' + construction relative. Si le professeur a dit qui, tous les étudiants doivent employer qui, jusqu'à ce que le professeur dise que, et alors tous les étudiants doivent employer que.

1	J'aime les hommes . . .
2	Je ne comprends pas les gens . . .
3	Je n'achète pas les vêtements . . .
4	J'achète souvent des choses . . .
5	Je n'aime pas la musique . . .
6	Je déteste les politiciens . . .

42.2 More complex relative constructions

The simple relative constructions (those where the link word is the subject (*qui*) or the direct object (*que/qu'*) of the verb that follows) are by far the most commonly used in French. More complex constructions, where the relative pronoun is the indirect object of the verb that follows, are used mainly in formal, written situations (N3/N4), and can cause problems for native speakers of both English and French.

IN ENGLISH, relative pronouns used to introduce more complex relative constructions include:

Relative pronoun used . . .

when the antecedent is a:	when the verb that follows is constructed with:		
	'to'	'of'	other prepositions
Person	to whom (N3)	of whom (N3)	for whom (N3)
	(who) . . . to (N2)	whose	(who) . . . for (N2)
Thing, idea	to which (N3)	of which (N3)	with which (N3)
	(that) . . . to (N2)	whose (N2)	(that) . . . with (N2)

The forms labelled (N3) are not used in spontaneous, informal situations; people prefer to use the forms with the preposition at the end of the relative clause:

the man I gave the book to (N2)   the knife he cut the bread with (N2)

IN FRENCH, relative pronouns used to introduce more complex relative constructions (those where the relative pronoun is the indirect object of the verb that follows) include:

Relative pronoun used . . .

when the ante-cedent is a:	when the verb that follows is constructed with:			
	à	*de*	*pour/avec* etc.	*au nom de* etc.
Person	*à qui*	*dont*	*pour qui*	*au nom de qui*
			avec qui	*à propos de qui*
Thing	*auquel,*	**dont*	*avec lequel,*	*à propos duquel,*
	à laquelle,		*avec laquelle,*	*à propos de laquelle,*
	auxquels,		*avec lesquels,*	*à propos desquels,*
	auxquelles		*avec lesquelles*	*à propos desquelles*

| Place, time | *où | d'où | par où | jusqu'où |

*You should associate *où* with the preposition *à* (+ place or time), and *dont* with the preposition *de*:

à + noun

| *à ce moment-là* | at that moment | *à cette époque* | at that time |

où

| *le jour où* | the day when | *au moment où* | at the time when |
| *l'époque où* | the period when | *la fois où* | (on) the occasion when |

de + noun

| *de cette façon* | in this/that way | *de cette manière* | in this/that way |

dont

| *la façon dont* | the way in which | *la manière dont* | the way in which |

Relative constructions where the verb is constructed with *à*, *de* or other preposition (see 38)

With verbs constructed with *à*

Person	*non, ce n'est pas la personne à qui je pensais*	(*penser à*)
	no, that's not the person I was thinking of	
Thing	*c'est la chose à laquelle il tient le plus*	(*tenir à*)
	it's the thing he is most attached to	
Place	*on m'a indiqué le bureau où il fallait s'adresser*	(*s'adresser à*)
	I was shown the office you had to apply to/where you had to ask	

With verbs constructed with *de*

Person, thing	*voilà la personne dont je t'ai parlé*	(*parler de*)
	there's the person I told you about	
Place	*elle est retournée à la ville d'où elle était*	(*partir de*)
	partie à l'âge de 20 ans	
	she went back to the town she'd left when she was 20	

'Whose'

Dont is also used to link the antecedent with a noun in the relative clause:

*c'est un homme **dont le courage** est remarquable*
he's a man whose courage is remarkable
*c'est un homme **dont** on peut admirer **le courage***
he's a man whose courage one can admire

IN ENGLISH, the words 'whose courage' stick together, whether 'courage' is the subject or the direct object of the verb that follows; IN FRENCH, the usual word order (SVO) is maintained in the relative clause, so that in the second example *le courage* is placed at the end.

Exercice 42/3   *Où* et *dont*   Travail individuel

a   Complétez les phrases ci-dessous en ajoutant où ou dont.

b   Donnez l'équivalent en anglais de chaque phrase.

1   Je peux recommander un petit hôtel _ on est descendus l'année dernière.
2   C'est une affaire _ le président s'occupe personnellement.
3   A l'époque _ je parle, j'étais encore jeune.
4   A l'époque _ ma grand-mère est née, une femme mariée n'avait pas le droit d'être fonctionnaire.
5   Le jour _ la guerre a été déclarée, mon grand-père venait d'entrer au lycée.
6   C'était une journée _ on s'est souvenu longtemps après.
7   Elle détestait les réunions _ tout le monde parlait en même temps.
8   Le bureau _ il faut s'adresser n'est pas ici.
9   Je n'aime pas la manière _ les négociations ont été conduites.
10   Venise? C'est une ville _ je rêve depuis des années.

With verbs constructed with *avec*, *pour* etc.

Person	*je ne connais pas l'homme **avec qui** tu parlais*	*(parler **avec**)*
	I don't know the man you were talking with	
Thing	*c'est un produit **pour lequel** on a fait tant de publicité*	(N3)
	it's a product for which there's been so much advertising	
Place	*c'était un tiroir **où** (**dans lequel**: N3) elle mettait tous ses bijoux*	
	it was a drawer where she kept all her jewellery	
	*voici une photo de la maison **près de laquelle** on avait vu la victime*	(N3)
	here's a photo of the house near which the victim had been seen	

Exercice 42/4   Composer des propositions relatives sans employer *qui/que*

Travail en groupe

Quand c'est son tour, chaque étudiant doit compléter, à haute voix, et le plus promptement possible, un des débuts de phrase ci-dessous, en employant une construction relative (où, dont, à qui, pour lesquels, etc.) qui ne commence ni par qui ni par que.

1   J'aime les femmes . . .
2   Je déteste les films . . .
3   J'aimerais voyager dans les pays . . .
4   Je trouve ennuyeux les livres . . .
5   J'en ai assez des programmes . . .
6   Je préfère les profs . . .

Use of the infinitive in a relative construction

A relative construction can consist of a relative pronoun + an infinitive, if the meaning is clear:

*il me faut une pièce **où travailler***	I need a room to work in
il me faut une pièce où je pourrais travailler	I need a room I can work in
*il n'y a personne **à qui** s'adresser*	there's no one to ask
il n'y a personne à qui on pourrait s'adresser	there's no one one could ask

42.3 Other relative constructions

a Relative constructions where the antecedent is not a noun

In relative constructions, the antecedent is not always a noun: it can be a demonstrative pronoun (*celui/celle, (tous) ceux/(toutes) celles*) or a notion/sentence/idea (*(tout) ce*).

■	Simple constructions		Complex constructions		
	Relative pronoun used when it is the:				
	Subject	**Direct object**	**Indirect object**		
			+ *à*	**+ *de***	**+ *avec, pour* etc.**
Antecedent: **Person** *celui, celle* the one *(tous)* ***ceux*** *(toutes)* ***celles*** (all) those	*qui*	*que*	*à qui*	*dont*	*pour qui*
Thing *celui, celle* the one *(tous)* ***ceux*** *(toutes)* ***celles*** (all) those	*qui*	*que*	*auquel, à laquelle, auxquels, auxquelles,*	*dont*	*avec lequel, avec laquelle, avec lesquels, avec lesquelles,*
Notion 'what' (sentence, idea)	*ce qui*	*ce que*	*ce à quoi* (N4)		*ce dont* (N4) *ce avec quoi* (N4)
	tout ce qui 'all that', 'everything that'	*tout ce que*			

Simple constructions

It is important that you should be able to formulate these easily, in speech and in writing, especially when it comes to making the correct choice between

ceux qui/que	those who	*(tous)* **ceux** qui/que	everyone who
and *ce* qui/que	what	*(tout)* **ce** qui/que	everything that

Examples:

Celui, (tous) ceux + relative construction

> **celui qui** *a fait cela est un criminel*
> whoever did that is a criminal
> *la police a interrogé* **toutes celles que** *l'homme avait approchées*
> the police (have) questioned all the women whom the man had approached
> **tous ceux à qui** *on a fait cette injection sont tombés malades*
> everyone who had this injection was taken ill

Ce, tout ce + relative construction

> *je vais te dire* **ce qui** *s'est passé*   (*ce qui*: subject of *se passer*)
> I'll tell you what's happened
> *elle avait envie de faire* **tout ce qui** *lui plaisait*   (*tout ce qui*: subject of *plaire*)
> she felt like doing anything she pleased
> *je n'oublierai pas* **ce que** *tu m'as dit*   (*ce que*: direct object of *dire*)
> I won't forget what you told me
> **tout ce qu'**on y achète est trop cher*   (*tout ce que*: direct object of *acheter*)
> everything you buy there is too expensive

Complex constructions

You are unlikely to need to formulate these very often, but it is useful to be able to recognise them.

Exercice 42/5   *Qui, que* ou *ce qui, ce que*?   Travail individuel

a   Complétez les phrases ci-dessous en ajoutant qui, que ou ce qui, ce que, selon le sens.
b   Donnez l'équivalent en anglais de chaque phrase.

1   _ il a fait est complètement inacceptable.
2   On voit bien _ lui fait dire ça.
3   C'est impossible d'exagérer le bien _ ce voyage m'a fait.
4   _ est fait, est fait: n'en parlons plus!
5   Les clefs? Mais c'est toi _ les avais tout à l'heure!
6   Il n'est plus l'homme _ il était.
7   Je vais te dire _ je pense de cette affaire.
8   Il avait décidé d'ignorer les histoires _ commençaient à circuler.

Exercice 42/6   *Tout ce qui* etc., ou *tous ceux qui*, etc.?   Travail individuel

Complétez les phrases ci-dessous en ajoutant tout ce qui, tout ce que, ou tous ceux qui, tous ceux que, selon le sens.

Exemple: _ il dit m'intéresse.
Réponse: **Tout ce qu'il dit m'intéresse.**

Exemple: _ l'ont vu ont remarqué sa pâleur.
Réponse: **Tous ceux qui l'ont vu ont remarqué sa pâleur.**

1   _ l'intéresse, c'est l'argent.
2   Le musée est ouvert pour _ veulent le visiter.
3   N'oublions pas _ n'ont pas de travail.
4   Quant à moi, je suis d'accord avec _ il a fait.
5   _ on peut savoir, c'est qu'il y a eu une explosion.
6   _ j'ai pu interroger m'ont raconté à peu près la même chose.
7   Il se passionne pour _ concerne la musique du 18ᵉ siècle.
8   Le service d'ordre a expulsé _ n'avaient pas leur carte de membre.

---

b   Relative construction without an antecedent

A relative construction can be used without an antecedent:

	English	**French**
Person	who	*qui*
	I wonder who'll be there	*je me demande **qui** sera là*
	they asked him who he'd seen	*on lui a demandé **qui** il avait vu*
Thing	what	*ce qui* (subject)
	what	*ce que* (direct object)
	she told him what was the matter	*elle lui a dit **ce qui** n'allait pas*
	I know what you mean	*je sais **ce que** tu veux dire*

This construction is an indirect WH- question (**see 33.4**).

c Relative construction with postponed antecedent

A relative construction can be used before the antecedent to which it refers:

	English	French
Person	the one(s) who, the one(s) that	*celui* (etc.) *qui* (subject)
		celui (etc.) *que* (direct object)
	the one who gets on my nerves is X	*celui qui m'agace, c'est X*
	the one (that) I can't stand is Y	*celui que je déteste, c'est Y*
Thing, Idea	what, the thing that	*ce qui* (subject)
		ce que (direct object)
	the thing that relaxes me is music	*ce qui me détend, c'est la musique*
	what I find moving is his/her voice	*ce que je trouve émouvant, c'est sa voix*

This construction is called a pseudo-cleft construction **(see 51.3)**.

Part nine

Extending and linking clauses

A **phrase** is a group of words which does not contain a tensed verb; a phrase centred on an adjective, adverb or noun, or a present or past participle can be used, alongside a main clause, as a detached complement (**see 43–44**).

A **clause** is a group of words which contains a tensed verb (e.g. present, passé composé, future).

A **main clause** is a clause which does not depend grammatically on any other clause. It may be linked to another main clause by a coordinating conjunction (for example, *et/mais/ou*: **see 45**), or by a connecting adverb such as *alors/puis* (**see 50.1**); in these cases the two clauses become coordinate clauses: they stand equal. Or two main clauses can be placed side by side in correlative constructions (**see 45.2**), or in juxtaposition (**see 45.3**).

A **subordinate clause** is one which is linked to a main clause by a subordinating conjunction, such as *parce que*, *quand* or simply *que*: the presence of this conjunction makes the clause grammatically subordinate to (and indicates that it is dependent for its meaning on) another clause, which is either stated or implied/understood (**see 46–48**).

A **completive clause** is a grammatically subordinate clause following statements such as *je sais que*, *je crois que*, which serve to introduce the main statement (**see 49**).

You will find examples of these ways of linking a phrase or a clause to a main clause in the next seven sections (**43–49**):

43   **How to extend a clause 1: detached words and phrases**
44   **How to extend a clause 2: present and past participles**

43 How to extend a clause 1: detached words and phrases

43.1   Detached complements
43.2   Detached phrases: noun + adjective
43.3   Detached phrases: preposition + infinitive

Spoken and written communication

When speaking, especially in informal situations (N2), one tends:

- to omit certain sounds **(see 5–7)** and certain words (e.g. impersonal *il*, negative *ne*), and to shorten words **(see 16.2)**, but;
- to lengthen phrases and clauses **(see 45 and 51)**, and to add words and phrases **(see 50)**, and one adds pauses, hesitations (*euh* . . . etc.) and false starts.

The effect of all this on spoken communication is that individual words and phrases are shorter, but that there is more time for the speaker to think them up, and for the listener to take them in.

When writing, especially in formal situations (N3), on the other hand, the above processes are reversed; one tends:

- to use longer, perhaps more technical or learned words **(see 4.2)**, in more complex grammatical structures **(see 46–48)**, but;
- to reduce the overall number of words, by using infinitive constructions **(see 38–41)** wherever possible; also by avoiding repetition and eliminating superfluous information.

In these ways, written communication involves economy: giving as little information as possible, but as much information (lexical and grammatical) as is necessary for the text to be understood.

43.1 Detached complements

Detached complements help to achieve the goal of economy by reducing the number of words and the grammatical complexity of your text, while still making clear what you are talking or writing about, and what you have to say about it.

The detached word or phrase can take a variety of forms:

Detached adjective   (see 12.1)

*les Américains, **inquiets**, ont alerté leurs alliés*
the Americans were worried, and alerted their allies
***inquiets de la situation**, les Américains ont alerté leurs alliés*
worried by the situation, the Americans alerted their allies

Detached adverb   (see 30.1)

***posément**, je lui ai demandé ce qu'il voulait*
calmly, I asked him/her what he/she wanted
*elle m'a répondu, **le plus tranquillement du monde**, que c'était impossible*
she replied, cool as a cucumber, that it was impossible

Detached phrase: preposition + noun   (see 30.2)

***depuis son mariage**, Paul ne voit plus ses copains*
since he got married, Paul no longer sees his mates
***d'après ce rapport**, il faudra s'attendre à une période difficile*
according to this report, we must expect difficult times ahead

Detached phrase: noun + adjective   (see 43.2)

*il est allé la voir, **un bouquet de fleurs à la main***
he went to see her, with a bunch of flowers in his hand

Detached phrase: preposition + infinitive   (see 43.3)

*il faut que je passe à la banque **avant de partir***
I must pop into the bank before I leave

Present participle + complement   (see 44.1)

sortant de chez le coiffeur, . . .   (on) leaving the hairdresser's, . . .

Gerund + complement   (see 44.2)

(tout) en travaillant, . . .   at the same time as working,/while
                                                working, . . .

Past participle + complement   (see 44.3)

arrivés au sommet, . . .   on reaching the top, . . .

Subordinate clause   (see 46–48)

pendant que j'étais là, . . .   while I was there, . . .

Using a detached complement is an economical way of presenting the circumstances
(time, manner, etc.) in which an action takes place, without having to construct a
subordinate clause using a conjunction and a tensed verb **(see 46–48)**.

Although they are detached from the main clause by a comma (hence their name), these
words and phrases are attached to the main clause, in that they are dependent on it,
sometimes grammatically and always for their meaning.

43.2 Detached phrases: noun + adjective

IN ENGLISH, the preposition 'with' is often added to detached complements consisting of noun + adjective.

IN FRENCH, the corresponding detached complements begin with the definite article (*le, l', la, les*), and there is no preposition:

le regard assuré, elle a répondu à sa question

with a firm look, she answered his/her question

M. Dupont, la tête penchée sur les documents, cherchait la confirmation de son idée

M. Dupont, bent over the documents, was looking for confirmation of his hunch

---

Exercice 43/1   **Nom + adjectif**   Travail individuel ou à deux

a   Récrivez les déclarations suivantes, en employant un complément détaché (nom + adjectif).
b   Dans chaque cas, quelle est la meilleure place (avant, après ou au cours de la proposition principale) pour le complément détaché?

Exemple: Elle avait le regard assuré. Elle a répondu à sa question.
a Réponse: Le regard assuré, elle a répondu à sa question.
b Réponse possible: La meilleure place est avant la proposition principale, parce que le complément détaché contient la partie la plus importante du message.

1   Je pourrais faire cet exercice même si j'avais les yeux fermés.
2   Pierre se promène partout. Il a toujours un pull sur les épaules.
3   Marie a traversé la foule; elle avait la tête haute.
4   On a aperçu M. Dupont qui venait vers nous; il avait les mains dans les poches.
5   La réceptionniste, qui avait le sourire aux lèvres, a accueilli les nouveaux clients.
6   Les enfants grandissent et ils ont la tête pleine d'idées nouvelles.

43.3 Detached phrases: preposition + infinitive

The Tables of adverbs and prepositions (**see 27.1** and **28.1**) show several prepositions which are followed by *de* both before a noun and before an infinitive (notable exceptions are *pour* and *sans*; *avant*, however, is followed by *de* only before an infinitive).

Examples:

après avoir vu le médecin, elle s'est sentie rassurée

after seeing the doctor, she felt reassured

les vacances se sont très bien passées, à en juger par votre mine

you've had a very good holiday, by the look of you

le temps de passer un coup de fil, et je vous rejoins (N2)

I've just got to make a phone call, then I'll be with you

Avant de, avant **and** *avant que*

There are three possible ways of constructing the French equivalent to an English sentence such as 'come and see me before you leave', using:

a   *avant de* + **infinitive**

b   *avant* + **noun**

c   *avant que* + **subjunctive**

a   *Avant de* + **infinitive**

   venez me voir avant de partir

   come and see me before you leave/before leaving

In English the gerund ('-ing'), not the infinitive, is often used in such constructions.

In this infinitive construction, the subject/agent of the infinitive (*partir*) is assumed to be the subject of the main verb (*venez*): both speaker and listener have probably just been speaking about the listener's future departure.

b   *Avant* + **noun**

Alternatively, an adverb phrase **(see 30.2)** can be used:

   venez me voir avant votre départ

   come and see me before your departure/before you leave

This has the advantage of making clear, through the possessive adjective *votre*, whose departure is being referred to; compare:

   venez me voir avant mon départ

   come and see me before I leave

c   *Avant que* + **subjunctive**

A subordinate clause introduced by the conjunction *avant que* (*avant que vous partiez*) is grammatically possible, but is unlikely to be used in practice, since it is not needed in order to make the meaning clear **(see also 48.2)**.

A subordinate clause is used instead of an infinitive construction if it is necessary to specify the subject of the verb in the second part of the sentence. Consider, for example, the following sentence:

   ils m'ont téléphoné au moment de partir

   they phoned me just as (I was?/they were?) leaving

In French, one assumes that the same person is the subject of both verbs (*ont téléphoné* and *partir*), and so the infinitive construction is sufficient if the meaning is '. . . just as they were leaving'. But if the meaning is '. . . just as I was leaving', a different construction must be used:

either   *ils m'ont téléphoné **au moment de mon départ***

          (but this makes the departure sound almost ceremonial)

or   *ils m'ont téléphoné **au moment où je partais***

Exercice 43/2   Préposition + nom ou préposition + infinitif

Travail individuel ou à deux

Récrivez les déclarations ci-dessous en employant, à la bonne place dans la phrase, un complément détaché (préposition + nom ou préposition + infinitif).

Exemple: Paul ne voit plus ses copains depuis qu'il s'est marié.

Réponse possible: **Depuis son mariage**, Paul ne voit plus ses copains.

Exemple: Je vais partir, mais il faut d'abord que je passe à la banque.

Réponse possible: Il faut que je passe à la banque **avant de partir**.

1   La secrétaire était de bonne humeur ce jour-là, donc elle est allée le chercher à la gare.
2   Il voulait avoir la paix, donc il a accédé à leur demande.
3   Les dernières informations indiquent que l'accident avait été causé par la négligence.
4   Je vais vous dire la vérité: cette affaire ne m'intéresse pas.
5   Il joue de la guitare parce que cela lui fait plaisir.
6   Quand vous aurez vu l'exposition, vous pourrez juger pour vous-même.
7   Ils sont passés près de nous mais ils ne nous ont pas salués.
8   C'est vraiment un spectacle qu'il ne faut pas manquer.

---

44 How to extend a clause 2: present and past participles

44.1 Present participles (*-ant*)
44.2 Gerunds (*en -ant*)
44.3 Past participles
44.4 Agreement of the past participle

44.1 Present participles

FORM

The present participle in French is the **-ant** form of the verb. Just as the present participle of English verbs ends in '-ing', the present participle of French verbs ends in *-ant*.

MEANING

On their own, 'going' or *allant* do not provide enough information to act as a verb in their own right: * 'she going' or * *elle allant* would probably be understood by a native speaker as meaning 'she's going' or *elle va*, but these would not be acceptable as standard English or French.

FUNCTION

English '-ing' and French *-ant* have a similar meaning, but their function is different:

IN ENGLISH, '-ing' is used with 'is'/'are' as a tense auxiliary to form the continuing present or continuing past: 'she is trying to help', 'she was trying to help'.

IN FRENCH, *-ant* is not used in this way; instead, one uses:
- the simple present: *elle essaie d'aider*   she's trying to help
- or *en train de*:   *elle est en train d'aider*   she's helping
- or, in past contexts, the imperfect:

elle essayait d'aider	she was trying to help
elle était en train d'aider	she was helping
	(see 54.4)

IN ENGLISH, '-ing' is also used when a verb is used as a noun: 'running keeps you fit'. The verb can even become a noun in its own right: 'she's in the running for the top job'. This use of '-ing' in English has been adopted in French to create nouns such as *le shopping*, *le parking*, some of which do not exist as nouns in English: *le shampooing*.

IN FRENCH, when a verb is used as a noun, the infinitive form (*-er*, *-ir*, *-re*), not the present participle form, is used (**see 52.3**):

> *voir c'est croire*   seeing is believing

When is the *-ant* form of a verb used in French?

a   As an adjective

The use of the present participle as an adjective is more widespread in French than in English:

> *avec l'eau **courante***
>
> with running water
>
> *elle était là, heureuse, **souriante**, détendue*
>
> there she was, happy, smiling, relaxed

Used as an adjective, the present participle always agrees with the noun or pronoun it qualifies:

> *on a retrouvé les trois alpinistes, **encore vivants**, dans un ravin*
>
> the three mountaineers were found/have been found, still alive, in a ravine

b   To introduce a detached complement (see 43)

This gives additional information about something described in a main clause:

> *des explorateurs ont découvert une tribu **vivant** (encore) à l'Age de pierre*
>
> explorers (have) discovered a tribe (still) living in the Stone Age

Used in this way, to describe an action actually taking place, the present participle functions as a verb, not as an adjective, and is invariable in French: *vivant* does not agree with *tribu*. Since the present participle carries no indication of the subject of the verb, it can only be used when the listener/reader can infer from the context who or what is the subject of the verb. In cases such as *une tribu **vivant** à l'Age de pierre*, the meaning of the utterance as a whole, and the proximity of *tribu* and *vivant*, are enough to indicate that the subject of *vivant* is *tribu*.

In both English and French, the sentence could be reformulated to include a relative clause:

> *une tribu **qui vivait** (encore) à l'Age de pierre*
>
> a tribe which was (still) living in the Stone Age

c   For the first of two actions which are in a sequence

The sequence can be either one of:

- time (Action 1, then Action 2) or of
- cause and effect (Action 1, therefore Action 2; Action 2 because of Action 1).

385

IN ENGLISH, a present participle can be used in these cases, though sometimes a time clause or a causal clause, or even two clauses linked by 'and', is preferred.

Examples:

Time sequence (in English: 'on doing something'); the first action takes place just before the action described in the main clause:

ramassant ses affaires, **elle a quitté** la pièce

she picked up her things and left the room

baissant la tête, il entra dans la vieille maison

lowering his head, he entered the old house

The meaning is similar to ***il baissa la tête** et entra* ... which could be used instead.

Cause and effect; the first action can be seen as what explains or causes the action in the main clause:

étant donné qu'il avait déjà passé un an en prison, **on l'a libéré** aussitôt

seeing that he'd already spent a year in prison, he was freed immediately

(= *puisqu'il* avait ...: 'in view of the fact that ...', 'since ...')

pensant (sans doute) **qu'il n'y avait pas de voiture**, il commença à traverser

(probably) believing/thinking (that) there was no car coming, he began to cross

(= *puisqu'il pensait* qu'il n'y avait pas ...: 'since he thought there was no ...')

(The constructions shown in brackets are grammatically correct, but would not normally be necessary.)

A present participle can be used, even though each of the two verbs has a different subject, by adding the subject before the present participle:

l'opposition ayant critiqué le gouvernement, la situation s'aggrave

now that the opposition has criticised the government, the situation is deteriorating

---

Exercice 44/1   Emploi du participe présent: séquence temporelle, ou cause-effet

Travail individuel ou à deux > Mise en commun

Récrivez les phrases suivantes en remplaçant une des propositions par un complément détaché commençant par un participe présent.

Exemple: Ils sont sortis du magasin et puis ils ont traversé la rue.

Réponse: **Sortant du magasin**, ils ont traversé la rue.

Exemple: Elle a vu qu'il n'y avait personne dans la salle, donc elle n'est pas restée.

Réponse: **Voyant qu'il n'y avait personne dans la salle**, elle n'est pas restée.

1   Il nous a dit au revoir puis il est monté dans le train.

2   Je suis descendu au bar parce que j'espérais y trouver mes camarades.

3 Il a fermé les yeux et puis il a sauté dans l'eau.

4 Elle pleurait la mort de son père, donc elle était inconsolable.

5 Elle a levé la main et puis elle a commencé à poser sa question.

6 Ils n'ont pas attendu, parce qu'ils croyaient qu'on était déjà partis.

44.2 The gerund

The gerund (*en* + present participle: *en travaillant*) is used in two ways:

    a to describe one of two simultaneous actions, and;

    b to describe one action which is the cause of another action.

a Simultaneous action

The gerund is used to introduce a detached complement which describes an action going on at the same time as the action described in the main clause (in English: 'while doing something').

The difference in meaning between the gerund (*en* + present participle) and the present participle used without *en* can be seen in the first two examples below:

    me regardant dans les yeux, elle s'est détournée

    she looked me full in the face and (then) turned away

    en me regardant dans les yeux, elle m'a dit ce qu'elle avait sur le coeur

    looking me straight in the eye, she told me what was bothering her

*elle a descendu l'escalier **en courant***	she ran downstairs/down the stairs
*elle est tombée **en descendant** l'escalier*	she fell while coming/going downstairs
***en arrivant**, j'ai donné mon nom au surveillant*	on arriving, I gave my name to the security clerk

(the 'arrival' includes giving one's name, so the two actions can be seen as simultaneous)

Tout

Tout is added to emphasise the simultaneous nature of the two actions (for example, because their happening together is surprising or contradictory):

    *tout en travaillant, **il a réfléchi** aux événements de la veille*

    while/at the same time as he was working, he pondered on/went on thinking about the previous day's events

    *tout en comprenant votre point de vue, **je ne peux pas** l'approuver*

    while/although I understand your point of view, I can't approve of it

Passer du temps (etc.) *à* + infinitive

The gerund (*en . . . -ant*) is not used after certain verbs and verb constructions. Instead, a construction with *à* + infinitive is used:

mettre du temps	mettre une heure (etc.)	+ à + infinitive
to take/spend time	to take spend an hour (etc.)	+ -ing
être/rester assis	être/rester debout (etc.)	+ à + infinitive
to sit	to stand (etc.)	+ -ing

Examples:

*j'ai **mis** plus d'une heure **à traverser** la ville*
it took me more than an hour to come through town
*pendant longtemps, elle est **restée** assise **à regarder** par la fenêtre*
for a long time, she sat looking out of the window

b Means

The gerund is used for one action which is the means whereby another action takes place
(in English: '**by** doing something'):

en travaillant, on apprend à mieux travailler
by working, one learns how to work better
en disant ça, tu bloques toute discussion   (N2)
by saying that, you're stopping any (further) discussion

If using the present participle or the gerund could lead to ambiguity as to the subject of
the verb, you should use other constructions:

*(?) la police a arrêté l'assassin **en essayant** de passer la frontière*
the police arrested the murderer trying to cross the border

This is not a satisfactory sentence: one would normally link the gerund (*en essayant*) to the
subject of the main verb (*la police*), but since it is unlikely that it was the police who tried
to cross the border, it is better to use a different construction altogether:

*la police a arrêté l'assassin **qui essayait** de passer la frontière*
the police arrested the murderer, who was trying to cross the border
*la police a arrêté l'assassin **alors qu'il essayait** de passer la frontière*
the police arrested the murderer while he was trying to cross the border

---

Exercice 44/2   **Emploi du gérondif**   Travail individuel ou à deux > Mise en commun

a   Reformulez le phrases suivantes, en employant un gérondif (en + -ant/tout en +
-ant), à la place d'un des verbes finis;
b   Avec un(e) partenaire, décidez laquelle des deux formulations est préférable, et pourquoi, ou si
les deux ont chacun un sens (légèrement) différent.

Exemple: Je comprends ton point de vue, mais je ne peux pas l'approuver.
Réponse: Tout en comprenant ton point de vue, je ne peux pas l'approuver.

1	Quand tu dis ça, tu ne sais pas ce que tu dis.
2	Pendant qu'elle travaillait, elle a sifflé doucement.
3	Je sais que je prendrais un risque si je faisais cela.
4	Quand on conduit plus lentement, on économise le carburant.
5	Il savait que c'était urgent, mais il n'avait pas le temps de s'en occuper.
6	Les forces lui sont revenues pendant qu'elle dormait.
7	L'appétit vient quand on mange.

44.3 Past participles

FORMATION

For the formation of the past participle, **see 10.2**.

USE

The past participle (*étonne, sorti, vu* etc.) can be used as a detached complement:

    a in a time sequence;
    b to describe cause and effect.

a   Time sequence

This use of the past participle is similar to the use of the present participle in time sequences, but here the action is viewed as completed:

    *après être **sortie** de la réunion, **Marie s'est demandé** ce qu'elle allait faire ensuite*   (N3)
    having left the meeting, Marie wondered what to do next

Une fois can be added, especially in informal situations:

    ***une fois sortie** de la réunion, Marie s'est demandé ce qu'elle allait faire ensuite*   (N2)
    once she'd left the meeting, Marie wondered what to do next

If the subject of the past participle is not the same as the subject of the verb in the main clause, it can be stated:

    ***une fois Marie sortie**, nous avons décidé . . .*
    once Marie had left, we decided . . .

or a separate clause can be used instead:

    ***une fois que** Marie était sortie, **nous** avons décidé . . .*
    once Marie had left, we decided . . .

    ***après que** Marie était sortie, nous . . .*
    after Marie had left, we . . .

b   Cause and effect

In sequences of cause and effect, the past participle is used in the same way as the present participle:

> *étonnée de n'y trouver personne, **elle s'est demandé** ce qu'elle allait faire*
> she was surprised to find no one there, and wondered what to do
> *attristée par la mort de son chien, **elle a perdu** deux kilos en trois semaines*
> she was saddened by the death of her dog, and lost five pounds in three weeks

If the subject of the two verbs is different, a subordinate clause is used instead:

> *puisqu'elle était attristée par la mort de son chien, **ses voisins ont** . . .*
> since she was saddened by the death of her dog, her neighbours . . .

Exercice 44/3   **Emploi du participe passé**   Travail individuel ou à deux > Mise en commun

a   Reformulez les phrases suivantes, en remplaçant un des verbes finis par un participe passé.
b   Vérifiez vos réponses en regardant le corrigé (57).
c   Avec un(e) partenaire, décidez si chacune des deux formulations a le même sens; si oui, laquelle est préférable, et pourquoi.

Exemple: Elle est arrivée de bonne heure à la gare, et elle a acheté un journal.
Réponse: **Arrivée de bonne heure à la gare**, elle a acheté un journal.

Exemple: Puisque nous avons été surpris par l'orage, nous avons trouvé refuge dans un cabanon.
Réponse: **Surpris par l'orage**, nous avons trouvé refuge dans un cabanon.

1   Nous sommes partis avant l'aube, et nous sommes arrivés au sommet à midi.
2   L'actrice a refusé d'ouvrir sa porte parce qu'elle était harcelée par les journalistes.
3   Le film avait été tourné il y a trois ans, mais il ne sortira que l'année prochaine.
4   Nous avons assisté à son enterrement parce que nous avions été bouleversés par sa mort.
5   L'équipe a été encouragée par les supporters, et elle a commencé à mieux jouer.
6   Puisqu'elle avait été écrite à la main, la lettre était illisible.

44.4 Past participle: agreement

In detached complements

When used as a detached complement as in **44.3**, the past participle agrees with the subject of the main clause.

The past participle, like the present participle, can be used as an adjective, in which case it agrees with the noun it qualifies:

*ce sont des cadeaux très **appréciés***
these are very popular presents

*maintenant, elle se sent bien **enracinée** dans le pays*
now, she feels well rooted in the country

*elle était **fatiguée***	she was tired
*ils étaient **bouleversés***	they were very upset

Sentences such as the last two above have the same structure as passive constructions (**see 35**), where the past participle also agrees with the subject:

*elle **a été fatiguée** par une journée difficile*
she was exhausted after a difficult day

*les habitants **ont été bouleversés** par cet événement*
the inhabitants were shocked by the event

In compound tenses

When it is used as part of a compound tense (**see 10.3**) – for example, the **passé composé** (*il a travaillé*) or the **pluperfect** (*il avait travaillé*) – the past participle agrees only if certain conditions are met. These conditions are different for each of the three ways in which compound tenses are constructed:

a   **verbs conjugated with *être***
b   **verbs conjugated with *avoir***
c   **pronominal verbs**

a   Verbs conjugated with *être*

The most clear-cut case where the past participle agrees is in compound tenses of verbs conjugated with *être*:

il est sorti	*elle est sortie*	*ils sont rentrés*	*elles sont rentrées*
he went out	she went out	they came back	they came back

The past participle agrees with the subject of the verb, as if it were an adjective. You should make this agreement, whether you are speaking or writing French.

For the two possible meanings of sentences such as those above (*il est sorti* can be a passé composé: 'he went out/he has gone out', or a present + adjective/adverb: 'he's out'), **see 54.3**.

b   Verbs conjugated with *avoir*

In the case of compound tenses of verbs conjugated with *avoir*, the past participle never agrees with the subject; it agrees with an object of the verb, if the answer to both the following questions is YES:

Does the verb have a direct object?

A direct object is one where there is no preposition between the verb and a noun object; if there is a preposition, such as *à*, *de* or *avec*, the object is indirect.

Does this direct object come earlier than the verb, in the sentence?

In most cases, in French, a noun which is the object of a verb comes later than the verb (see 32.1):

ils achètent une nouvelle voiture	*ils ont acheté une nouvelle voiture*
they're buying a new car	they've bought a new car

Here are the main cases where the direct object of a verb comes earlier than the verb:
- when the object appears as a pronoun, not a noun:

*ils ont acheté **une nouvelle voiture***	*ils **l'ont achetée** hier*
they've bought a new car	they bought it yesterday
*on a déjà fait **les courses***	*on **les a faites** ce matin*
we've already done the shopping	we did it this morning

- when the object appears as the relative pronoun *que:*

*ils ont acheté **une voiture***	*voilà **la voiture qu'ils ont achetée***
they've bought a car	there's the car they bought

- when the object appears as part of a question:

*ils ont acheté **une voiture***	*quelle voiture est-ce qu'ils **ont achetée**?*
they've bought a car	what car did they buy?

This agreement is made when writing or speaking French in formal situations (N3); but not when speaking spontaneously (N2). Note that, in all the above examples except *fait/faites*, the past participle is pronounced the same, with or without agreement.

Exercice 44/4   **Verbes + *avoir*: accord du participe passé**   Travail individuel

Dans chacune des phrases ci-dessous, remplacez le groupe nominal (entre parenthèses) par un pronom (le, l', la, les, lui, leur, you, en), et faites l'accord du participe passé si c'est nécessaire.

Exemple: Tu as vu (cette femme)?
Réponse: Tu l'as vue?

Exemple: Tu as parlé (à cette femme)?
Réponse: Tu lui as parlé?

1	J'ai approuvé (sa décision).	6	Elle n'a pas trouvé (la solution).
2	On a choisi (nos délégués).	7	On a étudié (le problème).
3	Tu n'as pas écrit (à grand-mère).	8	Ils ont traversé (la frontière).
4	J'ai parlé (de la ville).	9	On n'a rien reproché (aux parents).
5	J'ai pensé (à ce qu'il avait dit).	10	Vous n'avez pas compris (sa question).

Exercice 44/5   **Verbes + *avoir*: accord du participe passé**   Travail à deux > Mise en
commun

Reformulez chacune des phrases suivantes de trois façons différentes, a, b et c, en faisant chaque
fois, s'il le faut, l'accord du participe passé. Si vous voulez, vous pouvez ajouter d'autres
compléments (d'information) pour compléter le sens.

a   en remplaçant un nom par un **pronom** (voir 18);

b   en employant une construction **relative** (voir 42);

c   en formulant une **question** (voir 33).

Exemple (avec accord):   Ils ont fait cette erreur
   Réponses possibles: **a** Ils l'ont faite sans réfléchir
                                  b L'erreur qu'ils ont faite n'est pas grave
                                  c Quelle erreur ont-ils faite?

Exemple (sans accord):   Elle a parlé à mes professeurs
   Réponses possibles: **a** Elle leur a parlé hier soir
                                  b Les professeurs à qui elle a parlé étaient contents.
                                  c A quels professeurs a-t-elle parlé?

1   On a consulté les experts.
2   Ils ont détruit les paysages.
3   J'ai réfléchi à cette question.
4   Elle en a parlé à mes parents.
5   J'ai tout expliqué au directeur.
6   Tu as trouvé la réponse.

---

c   Pronominal verbs

These are conjugated with *être* in compound tenses: *elle se réveille, elle s'est réveillée.* However,
the agreement here of the past participle is not with the subject, but with the preceding
direct object, which is *se.*

In **Exercice 44/6** (see over), the reflexive pronoun (*se* etc.) is the direct object of the verb:

Exercice 44/6   Verbes pronominaux: accord du participe passé   Travail individuel

a   Récrivez les phrases suivantes au passé composé (si la phrase est au présent) ou au plus-que-parfait (si la phrase est à l'imparfait), en faisant l'accord du participe passé chaque fois que c'est nécessaire.

b   Ensuite, écrivez l'équivalent en anglais des phrases que vous venez d'écrire.

Exemple: (présent)   Elle se couche
Réponse: (passé composé)   Elle s'est couchée   (She went to bed)

Exemple: (imparfait)   Il se lavait
Réponse: (plus-que-parfait)   Il s'était lavé   (He had got washed)

1   Elle s'adapte au nouveau système.
2   Le temps s'améliorait.
3   La ville se développe.
4   Elle s'intéresse à son cas.
5   Les vacances se passaient sans problèmes.
6   Elle s'amusait au bal.
7   Ils se spécialisent.
8   Nous nous sentions à l'aise.
9   Ils se trouvaient sans travail.
10   Je me dépêche de finir l'exercice.

With some pronominal verbs and constructions, however, the reflexive pronoun is an indirect, not a direct object of the verb.

Consider the following sentences:

elle se lave; elle s'est lavée

Here *se* is the direct object of *laver*, and precedes the past participle, and so the past participle agrees.

But in:

elle se lave les mains

the direct object is *les mains*; since a verb in French can have only one direct object **(see 18)**, *se* in the above sentence is an indirect object, so the past participle does not agree with *se*:

elle s'est lavé les mains.

Verbs which take an indirect object, and which are commonly used in pronominal form, include:

*se dire (dire quelque chose **à** quelqu'un)*	to say to oneself/to each other
*se parler (parler **à/avec** quelqu'un)*	to speak to each other
*se faire mal (faire mal **à** quelqu'un)*	to hurt oneself

So that one writes:

elle s'est dit qu'elle n'aurait pas le temps	*ils se sont parlé longtemps*
she thought she wouldn't have time	they talked (together) for a long time

And sentences such as the following are perfectly correct:

les choses qu'il s'est dites	*le malheur qu'ils se sont fait*
the things he told himself	the unhappiness they caused each other

Can you explain why?

In **Exercice 44/7**, the past participle agrees only if the reflexive pronoun is the direct object of the verb:

Exercice 44/7 **Verbes pronominaux: accord du participe passé?** Travail individuel

a Construisez des phrases en remplaçant les groupes de mots soulignés par des pronoms, et en employant la forme **pronominale** du verbe. N'oubliez pas de faire l'accord du participe passé chaque fois qu'il le faut.

b Ensuite, récrivez toutes les phrases au négatif.

Exemple: Mme Dupont et Mme Durand (regarder)
Réponse a: Mme Dupont et Mme Durand se sont regardées
Réponse b: Mme Dupont et Mme Durand ne se sont pas regardées

Exemple: Mme Dupont et Mme Durand (parler)
Réponse a: Mme Dupont et Mme Durand se sont parlé
Réponse b: Mme Dupont et Mme Durand ne se sont pas parlé

1	Ils se font mal.	4	Ils se rendent compte.
2	Nous nous voyons.	5	Elle se casse la jambe.
3	Elle se trompe.	6	Elle se défend.

---

45 Coordination and juxtaposition

45.1 Coordination
45.2 Parallel process: correlative constructions
45.3 Juxtaposition

In sections **43–44**, we saw how a phrase (a group of words without a tensed verb) can be added or attached to a main clause (a group of words with a tensed verb).

In section **45**, we look at ways of linking two clauses of equal value, grammatically speaking (for subordinate clauses, see **46–49**):

45.1 Coordination: the second clause is added to the first, using a coordinating conjunction

45.2 Parallel process: correlative constructions: each of the two clauses is headed by the same word or phrase

45.3 Juxtaposition: the two clauses are spoken or written one after the other, without any linking or heading words

45.1 Coordination

With **coordination**, two statements are treated as being in some way equivalent. Four main words are used in French as coordinating conjunctions: *et* ('and'), *ou* ('or'), *ni* ('nor'), and *mais* ('but').

These four words are widely used, especially in spontaneous conversation, for two main reasons:

● because the second clause is added to the first, there is no need to think out the whole statement in advance – it can be made up as one goes along;

● *et*, and to a lesser extent *ou* and *ni* can be used repeatedly, to add a new idea, to continue a narrative, and so on.

Et

Two (or more) statements added together, or in sequence, can be joined by *et*:

*il a sauté en bas du mur, **et** (puis) il a commencé à courir*
he jumped down from the wall, and (then) began to run

> *c'était une surprise, **et** c'était (en même temps) agréable*
> it was a surprise, and (at the same time) it was pleasant

Et is often used together with a connector (**see 50.1**), which helps to situate the second clause (in time, etc.) relative to the first: *et puis, et en même temps, et alors, et donc,* for example.

Et que (and ***ou que***) can be used to link two subordinate clauses introduced by *parce que, puisque* etc., instead of repeating the full conjunction:

> *la vie est agréable **quand** on est en vacances **et qu'**on peut prendre son temps*
> life is pleasant when one is on holiday and one can take one's time
> ***puisque** vous êtes tous là **et qu'**il est quatre heures, on peut commencer*
> since you're all here and it's four o'clock, we can begin

or two relative constructions:

> *M Dupont est un homme **qui** est intelligent **et qui** le sait*
> M Dupont is a man who's clever and who knows it

Et non, et non pas, et pas + noun or infinitive

Et non (N3), *et non pas, et pas* (N2) are used, in the same way and with the same meaning as English 'and not', to include one noun, adjective or adverb, and exclude another:

> *c'est en France, **et (non) pas** à l'école qu'il a appris à parler français*
> he learnt to speak French in France, and not at school

Et à/de, mais à/de etc.

The prepositions *à* and *de* are usually repeated after *et* and *mais*:

> *je le dirai **à** ta mère **et à** ton père*
> I'll tell your mother and your father
> *elle a besoin **de** cette valise-ci **mais pas de** celle-là*
> she needs this case but not that one

Other prepositions (*avec, pour* etc.) are not usually repeated.

Ou

If two (or more) statements are presented as alternatives, they can be linked by *ou,* or *ou bien*:

> *allons, décide-toi: tu restes **ou** tu pars?*
> come on, make up your mind: are you staying or leaving?
> *elle a dû rentrer, **ou bien** est elle dans un autre bureau*
> she must have gone home, or else she's in another office

Ou, like *et,* can be used with an additional connector: *ou alors, ou peut-être,* for example.

Ni

Ni is used to link two (or more) negative statements (**see 34**):

> *il ne fume **ni ne** boit*　　　　　　(N3)　　　　　　he neither smokes nor drinks

including after *sans* ('without'):

> **sans** *tambour* **ni** *musique* (N3) without drums or music

In less formal situations, a different construction is used:

> *il ne fume pas, et il ne boit pas* **non plus**
> he doesn't smoke, and he doesn't drink either

Mais

If two statements are presented as in some way in contradiction with each other, they can be linked by **mais**, or *(et) cependant*:

> *j'aurais préféré y aller à pied,* **mais** *il pleuvait et j'étais fatigué(e)*
> I'd have preferred to walk there, but it was raining and I was tired

Mais, like *et* and *ou*, can be used with an additional connector: *mais néanmoins* (N3), for example.

45.2 Parallel process: correlative constructions

Another way of linking two clauses or two phrases, while keeping them on an equal footing, is to begin each clause or phrase with the same word or phrase, or with two different words.

Three of the four coordinating conjunctions can be used in this way:

Et ... et

Et ... et ... ('both ... and') is used to link two phrases, or sometimes two clauses, and is used in formal situations (N3):

> **et** *les maisons* **et** *l'église ont disparu sous la coulée de lava* (N3)
> the houses and the church all disappeared under the flow of lava

Other constructions are often preferred:

non seulement ... mais (aussi) ...		not only ... but (also) ...
tant ... que ...	(N3)	both ... and ...
aussi bien ... que ...	(N3)	... as well as ...
à la fois ... et ...		... and at the same time ...

Ou ... ou; ou bien ... ou bien

Ou ... ou ... ('either ... or ...') and *ou bien ... ou bien ...* ('either ... or else ...') are used with clauses as well as phrases:

> *l'après-midi, c'est toujours pareil:* **ou** *il regarde la télé,* **ou** *il s'endort*
> in the afternoon, it's always the same: he either watches TV or falls asleep
> *l'oiseau était* **ou bien** *une grive* **ou bien** *un merle*
> the bird was either a thrush or else a blackbird

Soit . . . soit

Soit . . . soit . . . ('either . . . or . . .') can also be used to mark a choice between two alternatives:

> *vous avez le choix: **soit** l'un, **soit** l'autre*
> you have the choice: one or the other
> ***soit** on faisait ce qu'il nous disait, **soit** on était punis*
> either we did what he said, or we were punished

Que . . . + subjunctive; *ou que* . . . + subjunctive

Que . . . + subjunctive, or *ou que . . .* + subjunctive, is used when the choice makes no difference:

> *que tu y ailles à pied **ou** (**que** tu y ailles) en vélo, cela revient au même*
> whether you walk or go by bike it comes to the same thing

Ni . . . ni . . . 'neither . . . nor . . .' **(see 34)**

Plus . . . plus: 'the more . . . the more'
Moins . . . moins: 'the less . . . the less'
Autant X . . . autant Y: 'X . . . as much as Y', 'X . . ., but Y'

There are differences between English and French in the way the above constructions are formed:

IN ENGLISH
- each part begins with 'the':
> the more I see him, the less I like him
- the complement (noun, adjective, adverb) is placed early in the structure:
> the more she listened, the more anxious she became

IN FRENCH
- there is no *le*, and no *que*; the two parts can be linked by *et*:
> ***plus** je le vois (et) **moins** il me plaît*
- the order of words in each part is *plus/moins* + SV or SVO **(see 32.1)**:
> ***plus** elle écoutait, **plus elle devenait** anxieuse*

Examples:
> ***plus** je lis de romans, **moins** j'ai envie de regarder la télé*
> the more novels I read/the more I read novels, the less I feel like watching TV
> (the two parts are seen as exactly parallel)
> ***moins** tu parleras (et) **plus** tu comprendras*
> the less you talk, the more you'll understand
> (in French, the same tense is used in both parts, whereas in English, the meaning is similar to 'if you talk less, you'll understand more')
> ***autant** j'apprécie ses chansons, **autant** je déteste sa manière de vivre*
> I appreciate his songs, but I don't like his lifestyle

When appropriate, *mieux* (as in *c'est mieux, cela vaut mieux*) can be used in this kind of construction:

> ***plus tôt** il répondra (et) **mieux** ce sera/mieux cela vaudra*
>
> the sooner he answers the better

This comparative construction is easily confused with the superlative construction used in cases such as the following:

> *il doit répondre: **le plus tôt** sera **le mieux***
>
> he's got to answer, and the sooner the better

Exercice 45/1   **Processus parallèles**   Travail individuel

Complétez les phrases ci-dessous en ajoutant plus, moins ou mieux, selon le sens.

Exemple: _ tu écouteras et _ tu comprendras.
Réponse: Plus tu écouteras et **mieux** tu comprendras.

1 _ je pense à cette affaire, _ je la trouve bizarre.
2 _ tôt cette question sera résolue, et _ cela vaudra pour nous.
3 L'affaire est délicate: _ on en parlera, _ cela vaudra.
4 _ on va vers le nord, _ le ciel devient gris.
5 C'est exaspérant: _ je lis et _ je comprends!
6 _ j'étudie le français, _ j'ai envie de continuer.

45.3 Juxtaposition

Juxtaposition is when two statements are placed one after the other, without any grammatical indication of how they are linked. This device can be used when the link between two statements is obvious to both the speaker or writer and the listener or reader. It provides a means of conveying a message quickly and clearly.

Juxtaposition instead of coordination

Two statements can be juxtaposed, instead of being linked by *et, ou* or *mais* (**see 45.1**). This can be done by punctuation (use of a comma, or of a semi-colon) or, in speech, by a pause:

(instead of *et*)   *le ciel s'assombrit; bientôt il commença à neiger*   (N3)
              the sky grew dark, and soon it began to snow
              (the two events are presented as happening one after the other)

(instead of *ou*)   *partir, rester: il n'arriva pas à se décider*   (N3)
              he couldn't make up his mind whether to leave or to stay
              (the two events are presented as equal alternatives)

(instead of ***mais***)   *je ne cherche pas, je trouve (Picasso)*

I don't look, I find

(the two actions are presented as two choices; one is preferred to the other)

Juxtaposition instead of subordination

Two statements can be juxtaposed, instead of being linked by a subordinating conjunction. Juxtaposition is more usual in spontaneous speech, in informal situations (N2); subordination is characteristic of written French, in formal situations (N3) **(see 46–48)**:

Temporal   (see 46.1)

*j'étais à peine rentré **que** le téléphone a sonné*

or ***aussitôt que** j'étais rentré, le téléphone a sonné*

no sooner had I got home than the phone rang

*je n'étais pas sorti depuis trois minutes **qu'**il a commencé à pleuvoir*

or ***quand** il a commencé à pleuvoir, je n'étais pas sorti depuis trois minutes*

I hadn't been out three minutes (when) it began to rain

Note this use of ***que*** as a link between two juxtaposed clauses describing an event which follows quickly after another.

Causal   (see 46.2)

je ne viendrai pas: il y aura sûrement un accident

or *je ne viendrai pas, **car/parce qu'**il y aura sûrement un accident*

I'm not coming: (because) there's bound to be an accident

Consecutive   (see 46.3)

il a neigé toute la nuit; le toit du garage s'est effondré

or *il a neigé toute la nuit, **si bien que** le toit du garage s'est effondré*

it snowed all night (with the result that) the garage roof fell in

Conditional   (see 47)

on serait à Nice, on aurait plus chaud   (N2)

or ***si on était** à Nice, on aurait plus chaud*

if we were in Nice, we'd be warmer

Concessive   (see 48)

***on a beau** lui dire, il n'écoute jamais*

or ***bien qu'**on le lui dise, il n'écoute jamais*

there's no point in telling him, he never listens

> *j'ai beau* essayer, je ne m'en souviens plus
>
> or *bien que* j'essaie, je ne m'en souviens pas
>
> or *malgré mes efforts*, je ne m'en souviens pas   (N3)
>
> I've tried, but I can't remember

Note this use of ***avoir beau*** to indicate the opposition between the two juxtaposed clauses.

Completive   **(see 49)**

> *je sais bien: vous n'êtes pas d'accord*
>
> or *je sais bien* **que** *vous n'êtes pas d'accord*
>
> I know: you don't agree

> *vous le voyez bien: il n'y a rien*
>
> or *vous voyez bien* **qu'**il n'y a rien*
>
> you can see for yourself: there's nothing there

Exercice 45/2   **Juxtaposition ou subordination?**   Travail à deux > Mise en commun

a   Reformulez chacune des phrases ci-dessous en remplaçant la construction **subordonnée** par une construction **juxtaposée**.

b   Après avoir vérifié vos réponses, décidez **dans chaque cas** si l'une ou l'autre formulation est préférable, pourquoi, et dans quelle situation.

Exemple: Je t'ai bien dit qu'ils ne sont pas là.
Réponse: Je te l'ai bien dit: ils ne sont pas là.

Exemple: Si on se levait plus tôt, on serait moins pressé.
Réponse: On se lèverait plus tôt, on serait moins pressé.

1   Je vois bien que tu ne veux pas partir.
2   Elle a travaillé jusqu'à trois heures du matin, si bien que le lendemain elle dormait debout.
3   Je me doutais qu'ils seraient là avant nous.
4   Bien que j'aie téléphoné vingt fois, personne n'a répondu.
5   Aussitôt que nous nous étions levés pour danser, la musique a changé.
6   S'il boit un verre de trop, il devient agressif.

46 Subordination 1: the indicative

46.1 Temporal clauses
46.2 Causal clauses
46.3 Consecutive clauses

Circumstantial clauses indicate a link in reality (time, cause, effect) between two actions (etc.). The nature of this link is expressed in the subordinating conjunction (*dès que*, *puisque*, *à tel point que*, in the examples below).

Although one clause is grammatically subordinate to the other, both clauses are equally based in reality, and this is shown by the use of the indicative for the verb in each clause.

46.1 Temporal clauses

A typical temporal clause, with its conjunction, indicates the situation in time (before, after, simultaneous, etc.) of the action (etc.), in relation to the action (etc.) described in the main clause:

> *appelez-moi **dès que** vous serez arrivés*
> phone me as soon as you get there

46.2 Causal clauses

A typical causal clause, with its conjunction, indicates a cause, a reason, a justification for the situation (etc.) described in the main clause:

> ***puisque** tu insistes, je viendrai avec toi*
> since you insist, I'll come with you

46.3 Consecutive clauses

A typical consecutive clause, with its conjunction, indicates a result, a consequence of the action (etc.) described in the main clause:

> *Marie a insisté, **à tel point que** sa mère s'est fâchée*
> Marie kept on about it, with the result that her mother became angry

Conjunctions followed by the conditional or the subjunctive

Certain subordinating conjunctions introducing circumstantial clauses present the speaker's or the writer's perspective on reality, making the action in the subordinate clause conditional on the action in the main clause, or negating altogether the reality of what is stated in the subordinate clause. In these cases, the verb in the subordinate clause is in the conditional (**see 47**) or in the subjunctive (**see 48**).

The lists and examples in **46.1–46.3** show some of the constructions used to introduce circumstantial clauses, and how they can be used.

46.1 Temporal clauses

+ **indicative** (describes situation in reality)

quand, lorsque (N3)	when	*(jusqu')au moment où*	(until) the moment
en même temps que	at the same time as	*dès que, aussitôt que*	when as soon as
une fois que	once	*depuis que*	(ever) since
pendant que	while	*comme*	as, while
tandis que	whereas	*alors que*	whereas

+ **indicative or subjunctive** (perhaps influenced by *avant que* + subjunctive)

après que   after

Examples:

quand je suis arrivé, ils étaient déjà partis
when I arrived, they'd already left
nous sommes arrivés à la gare au moment où le train partait
we arrived at the station just as the train was leaving

The tense in the subordinate clause can be quite different from the tense used in English, in French it matches the tense in the main clause:

une fois que j'aurai fini ce travail, je pourrai vous aider
once I've finished this work, I'll be able to help you
on lui parlera quand il rentrera/sera rentré
we'll speak to him when he gets back/is back
j'allais lui parler quand il rentrerait/serait rentré
I was going to speak to him when he got back

Exercice 46/1   **Les temps du verbe avec *quand***   Travail individuel

Complétez les phrases ci-dessous en mettant les verbs indiqués entre parenthèses au temps qui convient.

1   On préfère faire nos courses quand il y _ moins de monde.   (avoir)
2   Quand on _ les autorités, elles ont réagi très vite.   (contacter)
3   On en parlera quand tu _ te temps.   (avoir)
4   Je lui avais dit qu'on en parlerait quand elle _ le temps.   (avoir)
5   Promets-moi que tu ne diras rien quand il _.   (téléphoner)
6   Elle m'avait promis qu'elle ne dirait rien quand il _.   (téléphoner)

46.2 Causal clauses

+ **indicative** (describes situation in reality)

parce que	because	*puisque*	since
vu que/étant donné que	seeing that	*car*	for
comme	as, since	*d'autant (plus) que*	all the more so since

Examples:

*je ne pourrai pas te voir après tout, **car** j'ai encore du travail à faire*
I won't be able to see you after all, as I've still got work to do

***puisque** tu insistes, je viendrai avec toi*
since you insist, I'll come with you

Car always comes after the consequence has been stated; it introduces the cause or reason for the first time; *puisque*, on the other hand, refers to a consequence which is already apparent.

***comme** j'ai trop de travail, je ne pourrai pas te voir*
since I've got too much work, I won't be able to see you

*on ne pouvait pas expulser les squatters, **étant donné que** c'était l'hiver*
the squatters couldn't be thrown out, seeing that it was winter

Intensification of a statement (or of an adjective or adverb)

IN ENGLISH, a number of phrases can be used to bring in additional material in support of a statement already made:

especially since	particularly + adjective/adverb + because
above all because	all the more + adjective/adverb + because

IN FRENCH, similar phrases can be used, such as *surtout que* (N2), but one construction, for which there is no direct equivalent in English, is particularly useful:

d'autant plus (adjective/adverb) *que*
d'autant moins (adjective/adverb) *que*
d'autant que

This construction has a double function: to intensify an adjective or adverb (**see 31.4**), and to give the reason for this intensification:

*elle était **d'autant plus** fatiguée **qu'**elle avait mal dormi la veille*
she was all the more tired for having slept badly the previous night

D'autant que (without *plus*) can be used when referring to a fact rather than a single adjective or adverb:

*je suis sûr qu'il va y avoir des problèmes, **d'autant que** les prix n'ont pas été fixés*
I'm sure there will be problems, especially since the prices haven't been fixed

In everyday speech, *d'autant que* can be used, without *plus*, to intensify an adjective or adverb:

> *je suis fâché qu'il soit pas là, **d'autant** que je lui avais bien dit l'heure* (N2)
>
> I'm annoyed he's not here, seeing that I made a point of telling him what time to come

46.3 Consecutive clauses

When the description of the action (etc.) in a subordinate clause after a consecutive conjunction comes later in time than the description of the action (etc.) in the main clause, it can be viewed in two ways:

- in its situation in reality, as a consequence of the action in the main clause. In this case, the verb in the subordinate clause is in the indicative;
- from the perspective of the agent of the action in the main clause, as an aim, a purpose. In this case, the verb in the subordinate clause is in the subjunctive (**see 48**).

+ indicative <u>or</u> subjunctive (depending on the way the action in the main clause is being viewed)

de façon que/de sorte que	so that
de (telle) manière que	in such a way that
à tel point que	to such an extent that
si + adjective + *que*	so + adjective + that
si bien que	with the result that

Examples:

Consequence: indicative used

> *le soleil s'était couché, **de sorte qu'**on ne **voyait** plus le lac*
>
> the sun had set, so (that) one could no longer see the lake

Purpose: subjunctive used

> *on avait disposé les chaises **de sorte que** tout le monde **puisse** voir le conférencier*
>
> the chairs had been arranged so that everyone could see the speaker

Study, with their meaning, the conjunctions listed in **46.1**, **46.2** and **46.3**, before attempting Exercice 46/2.

Exercice 46/2　　**Propositions circonstancielles**　　　　　　Travail individuel

Complétez les phrases ci-dessous en ajoutant une conjonction.

Exemple:　　　_ tu insistes, je viendrai avec toi.

Réponse:　　Puisque tu insistes, je viendrai avec toi.

---

1 Elle n'aime pas qu'on la dérange _ elle travaille.
2 La journée avait été très bien organisée, _ tout le monde était content.
3 _ on aura fait les courses, il sera déjà midi.
4 J'aimerais qu'on se voie bientôt, _ j'ai beaucoup de choses à te raconter.
5 _ elle m'a dit ça, j'ai été très surpris.
6 Il a plu plus de vingt-quatre heures de suite, _ le terrain était entièrement inondé.
7 Je te téléphonerai _ je pourrai.
8 Elle était très fatiguée après l'excursion, _ elle avait la migraine ce jour-là.
9 On n'avait pas voulu l'envoyer en prison, _ elle était enceinte.
10 Ils n'ont envoyé que deux caisses, _ on en avait commandé cinq.

Alternative constructions

Using a subordinate clause amounts to introducing the equivalent of a whole new sentence into what one is saying or writing. This may be necessary in order to make the meaning clear (for example by indicating that the subject of the two verbs is not the same), but often there are shorter ways of conveying the same information, without changing or losing the meaning of the statement as a whole.

The following table shows some cases where an adverb phrase (preposition + noun), or a construction with an infinitive or a past participle, is grammatically possible, instead of a subordinate clause with the indicative:

■ Table of conjunctions and prepositions + noun or infinitive

Conjunction + subordinate clause	Preposition + noun	Preposition + infinitive or past participle
(Temporal: 46.1)		
quand il est parti	*au moment de son départ*	*au moment de partir*
when he left	at the time he left	at the time of leaving
lorsqu'il est parti (N3)	*lors de son départ* (N3)	
when he left	at the time of his departure	
après qu'il est parti	*après son départ*	*après être parti, il . . .*
after he left	after he left	after leaving, he . . .
		lui parti, je . . . (N3)
		when he'd left, I . . .
aussitôt qu'il est parti		
as soon as he left		
dès qu'il est parti	*dès son départ*	
as soon as he left	as soon as he left	

une fois qu'il est parti once he'd left		*une fois parti, il . . .* having left, he . . .
depuis qu'il est parti since he left	*depuis son départ* since he left	
pendant qu'il partait while he was leaving	*pendant son départ* while he was leaving	
il était à peine parti que . . . he'd just left when . . .		*à peine parti, il . . .* having just left, he . . .
(Causal: 46.2) *parce qu'il est parti* because he left	*à cause de son départ* because he left	
étant donné qu'il est parti seeing that/since he's left	*étant donné son départ* seeing that/since he's left	

Some subordinating conjunctions also appear in the tables in **27.1** and **28.1**: study these, as well as those in the above table, before attempting Exercice 46/3.

Exercice 46/3   Construction + *que*, ou + infinitif, ou + nom

Travail à deux > Mise en commun

Voici dix phrases avec une proposition subordonnée (entre parenthèses).

a   En discutant avec votre partenaire, décidez si une **construction + infinitif**, et/ou une **construction + nom** peut remplacer la construction + que + indicatif, sans changer le sens de la phrase.

b   Après avoir formulé les constructions qui vous semblent possibles, vérifiez-les, puis essayez de décider, avec le reste du groupe, pourquoi telle ou telle construction n'est pas possible dans certains cas.

1   Je suis allé la voir (quand elle était malade).
2   (Depuis qu'elle est revenue du Québec), elle n'arrive pas à se réhabituer à l'Europe.
3   (Après que j'ai téléphoné à l'hôpital), je me suis senti rassuré.
4   Nous nous sommes inquiétés (parce qu'il était parti précipitamment).
5   (Pendant qu'elle était en vacances en Écosse), elle a visité plusieurs monuments historiques.
6   (Une fois que sa mère est rentrée), l'enfant s'est calmé.
7   Je te raconterai tout cela (dès que je serai de retour).
8   (Une fois qu'il était arrivé en France), il s'est senti beaucoup mieux.
9   (Étant donné qu'elle était malade), elle n'a pas pu assister au concert.
10   (Après que mon frère m'a écrit), j'ai commencé à me poser quelques questions.

47 Subordination 2: the conditional

> **47.1 The three types of construction with *si***
> **47.2 Other meanings and uses of *si***
> **47.3 Other conditional constructions in French**

A **conditional** clause sets out the circumstances which the speaker or writer regards as necessary for the events in the main clause to take place.

The words most commonly used to introduce conditional clauses are the conjunction *si* ('if') and the intensified form *même si* ('even if'). *Si* reduces to *s'* before *il, ils*: *s'il, s'ils*, but not otherwise: one says and writes *si on, si elle, si elles, si un, si une*, etc.

Some conjunctions used to introduce conditional clauses, including *quand, quand même* ('even if', 'even though'), *au cas où* ('in case'), are followed by the conditional tense in French (**see 10.1**).

Other conjunctions, including *à condition que* ('on condition that'), *pourvu que* ('provided that') and *à moins que* ('unless'), are followed by the subjunctive in French (**see 48**).

47.1 The three types of construction with *si*

The key to using *si* ('if') successfully lies in using the correct tenses, both in the main clause and in the subordinate clause introduced by *si* (for verb forms and tense markers, **see 9–10**).

There are three basic types of 'if' construction, in each of which two different tenses are used; these six tenses are the same in both English and French:

	Subordinate clause: the condition	Main clause: the consequence
Type 1	*si* + present tense	, future tense
Type 2	*si* + imperfect tense	, conditional tense
Type 3	*si* + pluperfect tense	, past conditional tense

Depending on the meaning and the effect sought by the speaker or writer, the order of the two parts of a conditional statement can be reversed, so that the main clause comes before the 'if' clause:

	Main clause: the consequence	Subordinate clause: the condition
Type 1	future tense	, *si* + present tense
Type 2	conditional tense	, *si* + imperfect tense
Type 3	past conditional tense	, *si* + pluperfect tense

Examples:

Type 1	*s'il **pleut**, on se **fera** mouiller*	if it rains, we'll get wet
Type 2	*s'il **pleuvait**, on se **ferait** mouiller*	if it rained, we'd get wet
Type 3	*s'il **avait plu**, on se **serait fait** mouiller*	if it had rained, we'd have got wet

The difference in meaning between each of these three statements depends entirely on the tenses used: if you are unsure of one of the tenses needed to formulate Types 2 and 3 correctly, and fall back on the present tense (and perhaps the future tense), you will not be able to get your meaning across. In short, know your verb forms and tenses (**see 9–10**) before reading on!

Type 1 (*si* + present tense, future tense in main clause)

This type of statement represents an open condition, with immediate effect. It is used to refer to acual, present situations. Its use suggests immediate action on the part of the listener, or a commitment to action on the part of the speaker:

> *si **tu manges** trop de glaces, tu te **rendras** malade*
> if you eat too many ice creams, you'll make yourself sick

> *je le **ferai** demain **si j'ai** le temps*
> I'll do it tomorow if I have the time

Variants

The future tense in the main clause can be replaced by an imperative:

> *apportez-moi le livre demain, si vous préférez*
> bring the book tomorrow, if you'd rather do that

or by a present tense:

> *vous me l'apportez demain, si vous préférez*
> you can bring it tomorrow, if you prefer

especially to describe habitual actions:

> *s'il risque de pleuvoir, je prends toujours mon parapluie*
> if it looks like rain, I always take my umbrella

The present tense in the 'if' clause can be replaced by a passé composé, to emphasise that one action is to be completed before the next one begins:

> *si vous avez déjà fini l'exercice, vous pouvez faire l'exercice suivant*
> if you've already finished the exercise, you can do the next one

Type 2 (*si* + imperfect tense, conditional tense in main clause)

This type of statement also represents an open condition, but one that does not have immediate effect. It is used to refer to possible events or situations. Its use does not imply any immediate action on the part of either the listener or the speaker:

> *si quelqu'un me **parlait** comme ça, je **serais** fâché(e)*
>
> if anyone spoke to me/were to speak to me like that, I'd be cross
>
> *j'**irais** la voir **si j'avais** moins de travail, je t'assure*
>
> I'd go and see her if I hadn't got so much work, honestly

Variants

The conditional tense in the main clause can be replaced by an imperative; this variant is widely used in the marketing of consumer products:

> *si ce produit ne vous donnait pas satisfaction, renvoyez-le-nous*
>
> if this product were to prove/should this product prove unsatisfactory, send it back to us

The *si* + imperfect tense part of the construction can be used on its own, to express an invitation, a wish, a dream, etc.:

> *et si on allait au cinéma ce soir?*
>
> what about going to the cinema this evening?
>
> *si seulement j'étais jeune encore!*
>
> if only I were still young!

The conditional tense in the main clause can be replaced by an imperfect tense to describe habitual action:

> *s'il se sentait fatigué, il allait se coucher*
>
> if he felt tired, he went to bed

Type 3 (*si* + pluperfect tense, past conditional tense in main clause)

This type of statement represents a closed condition. It is used when referring to past events or situations, in order to suggest what might have been. No action, by listener or speaker, is possible:

> *si elle **avait été** plus prudente, l'accident ne **serait pas arrivé***
>
> if she'd been more careful, the accident wouldn't have happened
>
> *on **aurait réagi** plus vite **si** les autorités nous **avaient prévenus***
>
> we'd have reacted sooner if the authorities had given us a warning

Variant

The *si* + pluperfect tense part of the construction can be used in the same way as *si* + imperfect tense, on its own, to express a wish, a regret, etc.:

> *si (seulement) j'avais su!*   if (only) I'd known!

Même si

The construction with *même si* ('even if') is exactly the same as with *si*: all three types of sentence combinations, and the usual variants of these can be used:

*j'**irai** voir son nouveau film*, **même si** *les critiques en* **disent** *du mal*

I'll go and see his/her new film, even if the critics pan it

même si *on me* **payait**, *je n'**irais** pas le voir*

even if they paid me, I wouldn't go and see it

The construction *même que* is not a synonym of *même si*: *même que* is used in very informal situations (N1) with the meaning 'and anyway' (followed by the indicative) or 'although' (followed by the subjunctive).

Exercice 47/1   **Le temps du verbe dans les phrases avec *si***   Travail individuel

Dans chacune des phrases ci-dessous, mettez le verbe entre parenthèses au temps qui convient, selon que la phrase est de Type 1, 2 ou 3.

Exemple (Type 3):   Si tu m' (dire) ça plus tôt, j'aurais préparé quelque chose.
Réponse: Si tu m'**avais dit** ça plus tôt, j'aurais préparé quelque chose.

1   Je (venir) avec toi, si tu veux.
2   Si quelqu'un m'avait parlé comme ça, j' (être) très fâché.
3   S'il ne se remet pas de sa blessure, il ne (pouvoir) pas jouer samedi.
4   Il a dit qu'il y (aller) s'il avait le temps.
5   S'ils (jouer) avec plus de détermination, ils auraient gagné.
6   Il (pouvoir) le faire s'il avait voulu.
7   On n' (entendre) rien si tu cries tout le temps.
8   Si elle avait le choix, elle (vivre) en Italie.

Exercice 47/2   **Le temps du verbe avec *si***   Travail à deux

Dans chacune des phrases ci-dessous, les deux verbes (entre parenthèses) sont à l'infinitif. Avec un(e) partenaire,

a   Décidez si la phrase est de Type 1, 2 ou 3 (ou s'il y a plus d'une possibilité).
b   Mettez-vous d'accord sur la forme de chaque verbe, au temps que vous avez choisi.
c   Vérifiez vos réponses, puis donnez l'équivalent en anglais de chaque phrase.

Exemple: Si on (partir) maintenant, on y (être) à temps pour le film.
Réponses: Si on **part** maintenant, on **sera** à temps pour le film.   (Type 1)
           Si on **partait** maintenant, on serait à temps pour le film.   (Type 2)
           (Type 3 n'est pas possible, à cause du mot maintenant.)

1   S'il nous (dire) ça la semaine dernière, on (pouvoir) faire des préparatifs.
2   Si tu (manger) trop de biscuits, tu n' (avoir) plus d'appétit!
3   Si les études (être) gratuites, tout le monde (aller) à l'université.
4   Ce (être) dommage si tout le monde (avoir) les mêmes idées.
5   J' (aller) moi-même si personne d'autre ne (vouloir) y aller.
6   Si Dieu (vouloir) que les êtres humains volent, Il nous (donner) des ailes.
7   Si on (arriver) plus tôt, on (trouver) de meilleures places.
8   Le monde (se détruire) si on ne (protéger) pas la nature.

Exercice 47/3   **Avec des si . . .**   Travail en groupe

Tour à tour, chaque étudiant doit formuler une proposition commençant par Si . . .: c'est aux autres étudiants de formuler une proposition principale appropriée.
(**Note:** il vaut mieux choisir des phrases de Type 2.)

Exemple: Si on vivait au 18ᵉ siècle, . . .
Réponses possibles: . . . on s'éclairerait à la bougie.
. . . on aurait froid l'hiver.
. . . on ne ferait pas d'études supérieures.

47.2 Other meanings and uses of *si*

With an **explanation**:
*si je vous dis ça, **c'est que** je m'y connais un peu*   (N2)
(je vous dis cela parce que je m'y connais un peu)
if I tell you that, it's because I know a thing or two about it   **(see also 51.2)**

With a **concessive** meaning, close to English 'although':
*(même) **si** son idée est intéressante, elle n'est pas pratique*
even though/although his/her idea is interesting, it's not practical
***si** les résultats définitifs ne sont pas encore connus, on prévoit déjà une défaite pour le*
gouvernement   (N3)
although the official results aren't out yet, a government defeat is forecast

Used in this way, *si* or *même si* can be followed by any tense, including the future or the conditional, appropriate to the overall meaning of the statement.

Comme si

Comme si ('as if') introduces a comparative clause:
*il parle **comme s'**il avait déjà quarante ans*
he talks as if he were already forty

But with an infinitive ('as if to'), ***comme*** is used without *si*:

> *elle ouvrit la bouche **comme pour** parler* (N3)
>
> she opened her mouth as if (she were about) to speak

47.3 Other conditional constructions in French

Quand, *quand même* and juxtaposition (with or without *que*)

These constructions are widely used in French, but show certain differences from the corresponding constructions in English. Here, for example, are some alternative ways of expressing the following statement:

> ***même si** on le lui **disait** dix fois, il ne **comprendrait** pas* (N3)
>
> even if you told him ten times, he wouldn't understand

a *Quand même* + conditional, + conditional
> ***quand même** on le lui **dirait** dix fois, il ne **comprendrait** pas* (N3)

b *Quand* + conditional, + conditional
> ***quand** on le lui **dirait** dix fois, il ne **comprendrait** pas* (N3)

c Conditional + *que* + conditional
> *on lui **dirait** dix fois **qu'il comprendrait** pas* (N2)

d Conditional, + conditional
> *on lui **dirait** dix fois, il **comprendrait** pas* (N2)

e Conditional (+ inversion of verb and subject) + *que* + conditional
> *le lui **dirait-on** dix fois qu'il ne **comprendrait** pas* (N4)

All of these statements are similar in meaning, and the conditional is used in both parts of each statement;

- ● in **a** and **b**, the use of the conditional for the first verb announces to the listener or reader that the first part has a conditional meaning;
- ● in **c–e**, the conditional used for the first verb, together with the *que* (or pause) between each part, signals the conditional relationship between the two parts.

Au cas où

Au cas où ('in case') is used with the conditional in statements such as:

> elle avait fait de la soupe **au cas où** on **aurait** faim
>
> *she'd made some soup in case we were hungry*

48 Subordination 3: the subjunctive

48.1 **Subjunctive forms**

48.2 **When to use the subjunctive instead of the indicative**

48.3 **Principal constructions which are followed by the subjunctive in French**

48.4 **Examples of the subjunctive in use in French**

48.5 **Relative constructions: indicative, conditional, subjunctive?**

'The subjunctive' looms large in the minds of many learners of French, like an Everest that can be conquered only by a select few, with the help of expert guides and favourable conditions. Yet every French-speaking five-year-old produces statements containing the subjunctive, before learning about 'the subjunctive' at school. The subjunctive is used in everyday communication in French: this means that you need to be able to recognise and understand it, and to extend your own powers of expression in French by using it when it is called for.

You are unlikely to use the subjunctive if you are unsure of how it is formed: in **48.1**, you can see how the present subjunctive of regular and some irregular verbs is formed (see also the Verb tables, **56**), together with the use of the subjunctive of *avoir* and *être* to form the past (passé composé) subjunctive.

48.1 Subjunctive forms

The **present subjunctive** is identical to the present indicative in Persons 1, 2, 3 and 6 of all verbs where these endings are *-e*, *-es*, *-e*, *-ent*. This means that you may not have always noticed, when reading or listening to French, that a particular construction is followed by the subjunctive.

Where the form of the present subjunctive is different from that of the present indicative, the difference often involves adding the sound [s]:

pouvoir	*elle peut*	[pø]	*qu'elle puisse*	[pɥis]
faire	*je fais*	[fɛ]	*que je fasse*	[fas]
être	*tu es*	[ɛ]	*que tu sois*	[swa]
-ir **verbs**	*on choisit*	[ʃwa zi]	*qu'on choisisse*	[ʃwa zis]

The singular forms (Persons 1, 2 and 3) of the present subjunctive often sound like the plural form (Person 6):

	Present indicative	Present subjunctive	Present indicative/subjunctive
-ir verbs	*je finis*	*que je finisse*	*(ils finissent)*
-re verbs	*j'attends*	*que j'attende*	*(ils attendent)*
prendre	*il prend*	*qu'il prenne*	*(ils prennent)*

Exercice 48/1   **Formation du subjonctif**   Travail individuel

a   Complétez les phrases ci-dessous au présent du subjonctif, en employant le verbe entre parenthèses.

b   Donnez l'équivalent en anglais de chaque phrase.

1   Je suis content qu'il _ enfin son permis de conduire.   (avoir)
2   Je ne veux pas que tu _ triste.   (être)
3   C'est impossible qu'elle _ déjà les résultats.   (savoir)
4   Comment veux-tu qu'on _ travailler avec tout ce bruit?   (pouvoir)
5   Quoi qu'ils _, nous saurons y faire face.   (faire)
6   Où que tu _, tu entendras le même refrain.   (aller)
7   Le nouveau système est conçu pour qu'on n' _ pas trop longtemps.   (attendre)
8   Voilà ma réponse: que voulez-vous que je _ de plus?   (dire)

Present subjunctive and past subjunctive

Only two tenses of the subjunctive are in everyday use in French:

● the present subjunctive (*que je **sois**, qu'il **fasse***, etc.), and;
● the past subjunctive (*que j'**aie été**, qu'il **ait fait***, etc.).

The **present subjunctive** is so called because its forms are based on (and in some cases are identical to) the forms of the present indicative. It has no particular temporal meaning, and can be used whatever the tense of the verb in the main clause:

*j'aimerais **que vous finissiez** le plus tôt possible*
I'd like you to finish as soon as possible

The **past subjunctive** is formed from the passé composé, using the present subjunctive forms of the auxiliaries *avoir* and *être*, in place of the present indicative forms. It is used for an event (etc.) that is seen or imagined as taking place at a point in time earlier than the one the speaker is referring to:

*j'aimerais **que vous ayez fini** avant ce soir*
I'd like you to have finished before this evening

Exercice 48/2   **Le subjonctif: présent ou passé composé?**   Travail individuel

a   Complétez les phrases ci-dessous en employant le présent du subjonctif ou le passé composé
du subjonctif du verbe entre parenthèses, selon le sens.

b   Donnez l'équivalent en anglais de chaque phrase.

1   Je doute qu'on _ lui faire parvenir le message avant demain.   (pouvoir)
2   Il est indispensable que les gens _ bien informés sur ces questions.   (être)
3   Je suis content que vous _ à l'heure ce matin.   (arriver)
4   Je n'aimerais pas qu'on _ cela.   (faire)
5   Je regrette qu'ils _ cela sans m'informer d'abord.   (faire)
6   Ils donnent ces explications pour qu'on _ mieux de quoi il s'agit.   (comprendre)
7   C'est dommage qu'elle _ avant la naissance de son petit-fils.   (mourir)
8   C'est trop tard: je ne peux pas attendre que tout le monde _.   (finir)

48.2 When to use the subjunctive instead of the indicative

In main clauses, you do not need to think about using the subjunctive at all: it is used only
in certain set phrases.

In subordinate clauses (introduced in French by . . . *que*: **see 48.3** and **48.4**) and relative
constructions (introduced by *qui, que, où*, etc.: **see 48.5**), the use of the subjunctive instead
of the indicative is triggered by something particular in the meaning of the statement as a
whole (main clause + subordinate clause).

The subjunctive is used when the status of the subordinate clause is modified in one of
the following ways by the main clause:

a   Intention concerning potential situation
The main clause expresses an intention concerning a potential or hypothetical situation
or outcome.

b   Attitude towards actual situation
The main clause expresses an attitude to an actual (past, present or future) situation.

c   Contradiction, doubt or supposition
The main clause contradicts, denies or doubts the information in the subordinate
clause; or the information in the subordinate clause is a matter of question or
supposition.

Informal and formal situations

The subjunctive is used less often in informal situations (N2) than in formal situations (N3). There are two main reasons for this:

1 Apart from simple completive constructions (*je crois que, je sais que*, etc.: **see 49**) and presentatives (*ça fait longtemps que, c'est que*, etc.: **see 51.2**), and the subordinating conjunctions *parce que, quand* and *si*, all of which are followed by the indicative, including the conditional (**see 46** and **47**), there are fewer subordinate clauses in spontaneous speech (N2), compared to more formal speech and writing (N3). This means that there are fewer opportunities to use the subjunctive.

2 After certain constructions (such as *il (me) semble que, je ne crois pas que, il n'y a personne qui, je ne dis pas que*), the subjunctive is more likely to be used in formal situations (N3), and the indicative in informal situations (N2).

There is nothing quaint or old-fashioned, for French speakers, about the subjunctive: in certain constructions and expressions, its use is automatic; in other contexts, it has an expressive function. In other cases, use of the subjunctive is both automatic and fulfils an expressive function, particularly after constructions such as *pour que, je veux que, comment veux-tu que...?, il faut que*.

This contrasts with the subjunctive in English, which is used only in a few fossilised expressions, such as 'if I were you' (subjunctive of 'was'), 'were he to come' (= 'if he came'), 'if this be true' (subjunctive of 'is'), and 'be that as it may'.

Exercice 48/3   **Indicatif ou subjonctif?**   Travail à deux > Mise en commun

a   Complétez les phrases ci-dessous en mettant le verbe indiqué entre parenthèses à l'indicatif ou au subjonctif, selon que vous jugez que les faits donnés dans la proposition subordonnée sont situés plutôt dans la réalité (employez l'indicatif) ou dans l'attitude du locuteur (employez le subjonctif).

b   Ensuite, discutez et défendez vos jugements devant le reste du groupe.

1	Je crois qu'il _ pleuvoir.	(aller)
2	Je trouve ridicule qu'on ne _ pas consulter ces documents.	(pouvoir)
3	Je ne pense pas que ce _ une bonne idée.	(être)
4	Je pense que tu _ raison.	(avoir)
5	Je dis qu'on ne _ pas sortir par un temps pareil.	(pouvoir)
6	Je veux que vous me _ la vérité.	(dire)
7	Je souhaite qu'il _ les choses un peu plus au sérieux.	(prendre)
8	J'espère que tout le monde _ content.	(être)

When to use *que* + subjunctive, and when to use an infinitive construction

Do not use a construction with *que* + subjunctive if the meaning can be made clear with an infinitive construction. Many infinitive constructions refer to the subject of the main clause; a construction with *que* + subjunctive is necessary only if there is a change of subject (**see also 43.3**):

Infinitive construction: same subject	*que* + subjunctive: change of subject
*viens me voir **avant de partir***	*viens nous voir **avant que je parte***
come and see me before you leave	come and see me before I leave
*j'ai téléphoné **pour avoir** des nouvelles*	*je te téléphone **pour que tu saches***
I phoned in order to find out the latest news	I'm phoning you so that you know
*je veux **savoir***	*je veux **que tu saches***
I want to know	I want you to know

Exception: *dire* + **infinitive and** *dire* + **que:**

je lui ai dit de partir	*je lui ai dit que je partais*
I told him/her to leave	I told him/her I was leaving

Exercice 48/4 **Construction + subjonctif ou construction + infinitif?**

Travail à deux > Mise en commun

a Dans chaque question ci-dessous, combinez les deux propositions en une seule phrase en employant une construction + que + subjonctif, ou une construction + infinitif.

b Dans certains cas, une construction + infinitif n'est pas possible sans changer le sens de la phrase: lesquels? Discutez-en avec le reste du groupe.
(Constructions à employer: avant de/avant que, il faut/il faut que, j'ai peur de/j'ai peur que, pour/pour que, sans/sans que.)

1	Il a fait ça.	Il s'amuse.
2	Il a fait ça.	On s'amuse.
3	Venez me voir.	Je pars.
4	Venez me voir.	Vous partez.
5	Répondez.	Ne regardez pas la liste.
6	Répondez.	Je ne vous dis pas les mots.
7	Dépêche-toi!	On part dans cinq minutes.
8	Dépêche-toi!	Tu t'habilles vite.
9	Je ne me présente pas à l'examen.	Je vais échouer.
10	Je ne me présente pas à l'examen.	Les questions seront trop difficiles.

48.3 Principal contexts in which the subjunctive is used

The three groupings:

a Intention concerning potential situation;

b Attitude towards actual situation;

c Contradiction, doubt or supposition

correspond to those described at the beginning of **48.2**.

The examples in **bold type** indicate constructions frequently used in French.

a Intention concerning a potential situation

Wish	*je veux que X*	*j'aimerais que X*	*je permets que X*
	I want X to	I'd like X to	I allow X to
	Qu'il fasse	*il faut que X*	
	Let him do	X must	
Purpose	*pour que*	*de façon/manière que*	
	so that	so that	

b Attitude towards an actual situation

Feeling	*j'aime que X*	*je suis content/fier etc. que*
	I like X to	I'm pleased/proud etc. that
Opinion	*c'est dommage que*	*c'est/je trouve ridicule/rare etc. que X*
	it's a pity that	it's/I find it ridiculous that/unusual for X to
	il vaut mieux que	*c'est/il est **important**/urgent etc. que X*
	it's better if	it's important/urgent that X/for X to
	***bien que**, quoique*	*trop/assez* (+ adj/ad) *pour que*
	although	too (+ adj/adv) to/(adj/adv) enough to
	que ce soit X ou Y	***qu'il/elle soit** (adj) **ou** (adj)*
	whether it's X or Y	whether he/she/it is (adj) or (adj)
	quoi qu'il fasse	*où qu'il aille*
	whatever he does	wherever he goes
	je comprends que	*je conçois que*
	I realise that	I can see how

c Contradiction, doubt or supposition

Negation	*sans que X*
	without X -ing

Future time	*avant que X*	*jusqu'à ce que*	
	before X	until	
	j'attendrai que	*j'attends que X*	
	I'll wait until	I'm waiting for X to	
Condition	*à moins que*	*à condition que*	
	unless	on condition that	
Doubt	*je doute que*		
	I doubt if/whether		
Denial	*je ne crois/pense/dis pas que*	*c'est/il est impossible que X*	
	I don't believe/think/say that	it's impossible for X to	
Question	*croyez-/pensez- etc. vous que?*		
	do you believe/think that?		
Possibility	*il se peut que*	*c'est/il est possible que*	
	it could be that	it's possible that	
Fear	*j'ai peur que*	*je crains que*	
	I'm afraid that	I fear that	

For the subjunctive in relative constructions, **see 48.5**; for other examples of **completives** followed by the subjunctive, **see 49.3 and 49.4**.

48.4 Examples of the subjunctive in use in French

You may find it helpful to study these examples in two different ways:

● look at each example with its English equivalent, noting how often an infinitive construction is used in English, but is not possible in French;
● say each French example aloud (on your own or with a partner), as a way of beginning to make an automatic association between certain constructions and the subjunctive.

a Intention

Wish	*il voulait que je parte tout de suite*
	he wanted me to set off straight away
	je n'aimerais pas que cela devienne une obligation
	I wouldn't like it to become an obligation
	il faudra que j'en parle avec ma femme
	I'll have to discuss it with my wife
	il n'est pas content? eh bien, qu'il fasse ce qu'il veut!
	so he's not pleased? well, let him/he can do what he likes!
Purpose	*ils ont vraiment tout fait pour qu'on soit heureux*
	they really did all they could to make us happy

b   Attitude

Feeling	*je suis content que tu sois là*
	I'm glad you're here
Opinion	*c'est important que tu répondes tout de suite*
	it's important for you to answer straight away
	c'est rare qu'il pleuve si fort
	it's unusual for it to rain so heavily
	la voiture était trop endommagée pour qu'on puisse la faire réparer
	the car was too badly damaged for us to have it repaired
	ils lui ont parlé en allemand, bien qu'elle ne comprenne pas un mot de cette langue
	they spoke to her in German, even though she didn't/doesn't understand a word of the language
	elle regardait tous les films, qu'ils soient bons ou mauvais
	she watched all the films, whether they were good or bad
	quoi qu'il fasse désormais, je ne m'en occuperai pas
	whatever he does from now on, I'll keep out of it

c   Contradiction, doubt or supposition

Negation	*elle a compris sans qu'il soit nécessaire de le lui dire une deuxième fois*
	she understood without having to be told a second time
Future time	*surtout, ne faites rien avant que les pompiers soient là*
	above all, don't do anything until the fire brigade gets here/there
Condition	*prenez celles-là, à moins que vous cherchiez quelque chose de plus léger*
	take these, unless you wanted/want something lighter
Doubt	*je doute qu'on puisse arriver à l'heure, maintenant*
	I doubt if we can get there on time, now
Fear	*j'ai bien peur qu'ils n'aient rien compris*
	I really fear that they haven't understood a thing

Je ne pense pas que, croyez-vous que?, c'est/il est possible/impossible que: for examples, **see 49.3.**

48.5 Relative constructions: indicative, conditional or subjunctive?

In certain circumstances, the verb in a relative construction is likely to be in the subjunctive, or the conditional, and not the indicative. Why?

Any relative construction is an extended description of the noun or pronoun which is its antecedent (**see 42**):

	Antecedent	**Relative construction**
j'ai vu	*l'homme*	*que la police recherchait*
I saw	the man	the police were looking for
je connais	*quelqu'un*	*qui pourra vous aider*
I know	someone	who'll be able to help you

In the above examples, *l'homme* and *quelqu'un* are presented as existing in reality: the speaker says *j'ai vu l'homme*, and *je connais quelqu'un*. This basis in reality is shown by the use of the indicative in the relative construction: *recherchait* (imperfect tense) and *pourra* (future tense).

The **conditional** is used in relative constructions as a half-way house between the indicative (basis in reality) and the subjunctive (no basis in reality):

> *je connais quelqu'un qui **pourrait** vous aider*
> I know someone who might be able to help you
> (the person exists, but it is not certain that they will be able to help)

Also after a question:

> *est-ce que tu connais quelqu'un qui **serait** capable de faire ce travail?*
> do you know someone/anyone who'd be capable of doing this work?
> (the competence would be there – if such a person exists)

The subjunctive is used in relative constructions when the speaker's feelings are involved, and he/she is expressing a personal stake in the matter:

> *il me faudrait quelqu'un qui **soit** capable de faire ce travail*
> I'd need someone who'd be capable of doing this work

Also after an imperative:

> *cherchez-moi quelqu'un qui **soit** capable de faire ce travail*
> find me someone who'd be capable of doing this work

The subjunctive can be used after a negative statement – one where the existence of the matter in question is denied:

> *je ne connais personne qui **puisse** faire/**soit** capable de faire ce travail*   (N3)
> I don't know anyone who's capable of/who'd be capable of doing this work

In this example, the speaker's personal investment in the matter is less than in the previous two examples, and use of the subjunctive here is more likely in formal situations. In everyday conversation, one might say:

> *je ne connais personne qui **serait** capable de faire ce travail* or even:
> *je ne connais personne qui **est** capable de faire ce travail*   (N2)

The use of a superlative construction (*le plus, le moins, le seul, le premier*, etc.: **see 31.2**) often indicates the expression of a personal view, a personal feeling etc., and for this reason the subjunctive is often used in a following relative construction:

> *des cinq romans qu'elle a écrits, c'est **le seul qui ait été** publié*
> of the five novels she wrote, this is the only one that has been published
> *c'est **le moins qu'on puisse** dire!*   that's the least one could say!

But in everyday speech, referring to actual events, the indicative can be used after a superlative:

> *c'est bien la première fois qu'on me dit ça!*   (N2)
> that's certainly the first time I've been told that!

And the indicative is always used after a superlative when one is making a simple statement of fact:

> *c'est le plus fort des trois qui a gagné*   the strongest of the three was the winner

This sentence is an expansion of *le plus fort a gagné* into a cleft construction: (**see 51.2**).

Exercice 48/5   **Constructions relatives: indicatif, conditionnel ou subjonctif?**

Travail à deux > Mise en commun

a Complétez les phrases ci-dessous en mettant le verbe (entre parenthèses) à l'indicatif, au conditionnel, ou au subjonctif, selon le sens. Mettez-vous d'accord avec votre partenaire sur vos raisons pour préférer l'indicatif, le conditionnel ou le subjonctif (ou pourquoi deux ou même trois solutions semblent également possibles).

b Ensuite, défendez vos jugements devant le reste du groupe.

1 Voici justement quelqu'un qui _ nous renseigner, j'en suis sûr.   (pouvoir)
2 Il n'y a personne qui _ jouer ce rôle mieux que lui.   (pouvoir)
3 C'est le seul véhicule qui _ adapté à ce genre de terrain.   (être)
4 C'est l'équipe française qui _ sûre de gagner.   (être)
5 Où vas-tu trouver une machine qui _ ce genre de travail?   (faire)
6 C'est bien la première fois qu'on me _ ça!   (dire)

Exercice 48/6   Emploi du subjonctif: 'Mon/ma partenaire idéal(e)'

Travail à deux > Mise en commun

Avec un(e) autre membre du groupe, composez le portrait de votre partenaire idéal(e). Vous pouvez, si vous voulez, composer un seul portrait ou, si vos goûts sont trop différents, composer deux portraits différents.

Pour composer votre portrait, employez le plus possible de constructions qui sont suivies d'un **subjonctif**. Voici quelques suggestions:

J'aimerais qu'il/qu'elle ...	Je n'aimerais pas qu'il/qu'elle ...
Je voudrais qu'il/qu'elle ...	Je ne voudrais pas qu'il/qu'elle ...
Il faudrait qu'il/qu'elle ...	Il ne faudrait pas qu'il/qu'elle ...
Ce serait important qu'il/qu'elle ...	Ce serait indispensable qu'il/qu'elle ...
Je ne permettrais pas qu'il/qu'elle ...	Je préférerais qu'il/qu'elle ...

Vous pourrez également consulter la liste des constructions suivies du subjonctif (voir **48.3**).

Variante   Si les membres du groupe le préfèrent, on peut choisir un sujet différent: 'Ma maison idéale', par exemple ...

49 Completive clauses, interpolations and parentheses

49.1 Completive clauses
49.2 Completives followed by the indicative
49.3 Completives followed by the subjunctive
49.4 Completives followed by either the indicative or the subjunctive
49.5 Interpolations and parentheses

49.1 Completive clauses

FORM

Whenever we make a statement (making an observation, expressing an opinion, etc.), we are in effect saying to our listener 'I see that . . .', 'I think that . . .', as well as making the statement itself. It is not necessary actually to say 'I think that . . .' before each and every statement: we accept (as speakers and listeners) that statements do represent what the speaker thinks. Observations such as *il fait beau* ('it's fine') or *tu es fatigué* ('you're tired') can therefore be made without any introductory clause; but we can also say:

je vois qu'il fait beau and *j'ai l'impression que tu es fatigué*
I see (that) it's fine   I think you're tired/you look tired to me

Note that in English the equivalent to the link word *que* ('that') is very often omitted.

In conversation, one also uses phrases such as *je crois que*: 'I think (that)' and *je trouve que*: 'in my view'. These are completive constructions.

When someone is asked to repeat a statement, this implied introductory clause reappears, in full (*je dis que*) or reduced to the link word (*que*):

Il va pleuvoir. Qu'est-ce que tu dis?   *Je dis qu'il va pleuvoir*
or: *Qu'il va pleuvoir*

> In a completive construction, the second clause, beginning with *que*, is grammatically subordinate to the first clause, but communicatively necessary to complete the meaning of the first clause.

426

The status of each of the two clauses in a completive construction can be summed up as follows:

	je crois	*qu'il va pleuvoir*
Grammatical status:	main clause	completive clause
Communicative status:	secondary importance	central importance
	(prepares for the main message)	(this is the main message)

FUNCTION

The function of a completive construction is to give one's listener some clue as to the statement we are about to make: for example, indicating the extent to which one takes responsibility for it, or suggesting what one feels about it. Another way of doing this is by the use of modalisers: **see 50.2**.

The first clause in a completive construction can, for example:
- confirm or doubt what is in the completive clause:

je sais que	*je suis certain que*	*c'est vrai que*	*je doute que*
I know that	I'm sure that	it's true that	I doubt whether

- express an intention about what is in the completive clause:

je veux que	*il faut que*
I want . . .	. . . must

- express an attitude to what is in the completive clause:

heureusement que	*j'espère que*	*je souhaite que*	*c'est étonnant que*
fortunately	I hope that	I wish that	it's surprising that

If the meaning of the main clause is such as to cast doubt on, or to set aside, the statement in the completive clause, this can be reflected in the use of the subjunctive (**see 48** and **49.3**), or sometimes the conditional (**see 47**), instead of the indicative in the completive clause.

49.2 Completives followed by the indicative

If the effect of the first clause is to confirm or support the statement in the completive clause, then the verb in the completive clause is in the indicative.

Here are some phrases used to introduce completive clauses in the indicative:

c'est/il est évident/certain que	*il est probable que*
it's obvious/certain that	it's probable that
peut-être que	*sans doute que*
perhaps/maybe (that)	no doubt
je suis certain/sûr que	*je crois que/je pense que*
I'm certain/sure that	I believe/think that

le fait est que	*il (me/lui) semble que*
the fact is that	I/he/she think(s) that
je sais que/je vois que	*voici que/voilà que*
I know/I can see that	and now . . ./and then . . .

Examples:

c'est/il est probable qu'elle rentrera demain	it's likely she'll be back tomorrow
je crois que/je pense qu'il va pleuvoir	I think it's going to rain

Introductory phrases which support the statement that follows, can also appear after the statement, as parentheses (**see 49.5**):

*il va pleuvoir, **je crois/je pense***	it's going to rain, I think

49.3 Completives followed by the subjunctive

Other completive constructions, far from supporting the statement that follows, change its value, for example:

- by emphasising its importance;
- by denying or casting doubt on its value or existence;
- by expressing a wish that an idea becomes (or does not become) a reality.

In all these cases, the completive construction is followed by the subjunctive (**see 48.3** and **48.4**):

je préférerais que	*c'est/il est important que*
I'd rather that	it's important that
c'est extraordinaire que	*ça/cela m'étonnerait que*
it's extraordinary that	I'd be surprised if
c'est ennuyeux que	*je trouve normal que*
it's a nuisance that	it seems right to me that

Examples:

je crains qu'il soit trop tard maintenant
I fear it might be too late now
je doute qu'ils aient déjà reçu ma lettre
I doubt if/whether they've got my letter yet
moi je trouve normal qu'on fasse un effort pour l'environnement (N2)
I think it's natural to do something for the environment

49.4 Completives followed by either the indicative or the subjunctive

The indicative is used when the speaker is using the opening phrase to confirm the reality of what follows, and the subjunctive is used when the speaker is using it to doubt or deny the reality of what follows.

From the above lists and examples, it can be seen that the borderline between the use of the indicative or the subjunctive in the completive clause lies somewhere between

         *c'est/il est **probable** qu'il **viendra***   it's likely he'll come   (indicative)

and   *c'est/il est **possible** qu'il **vienne***   it's possible he'll come (subjunctive)

But what about ***peu** probable* ('unlikely'), or ***bien** possible* ('very possible')? With phrases where the meaning falls between *probable* and *possible*, a French speaker may use either the indicative or the subjunctive, possibly on the spur of the moment, and perhaps according to his/her perception of the communication situation as more, or less, formal.

This is the case with phrases such as *crois-tu que?*, *penses-tu que?*, *j'imagine que*, *je suppose que* and *en supposant que*, all of which can be followed by the indicative or the subjunctive, depending on the speaker's intention:

    *tu crois qu'ils **sont** arrivés maintenant?*   (N2)

    do you think they've arrived yet?

    (a casual, matter-of-fact enquiry, in an informal situation)

    *pensez-vous vraiment qu'ils **soient** arrivés?*   (N3)

    do you really think they've arrived?

    (the speaker emphasises the doubtful nature of the matter, there is perhaps tension, the situation is more formal)

Le fait que: 'the fact that'

If this construction is used to introduce new information, it is followed by the indicative; if it is used to introduce a comment on information already known, it is followed by the subjunctive.

  Constructions complétives: + indicatif ou + subjonctif?

                               Travail à deux > Mise en commun

a   Complétez les phrases ci-dessous en ajoutant le verbe (entre parenthèses) à l'indicatif ou au subjonctif, selon le sens.

b   Y a-t-il des phrases pour lesquelles vous avez hésité entre l'indicatif et le subjonctif? Lesquelles? Pourquoi?

c   Présentez vos conclusions – et vos problèmes – au reste du groupe.

1	C'est vrai que cette valise _ lourde.	(être)
2	Je constate que souvent on _ courir deux fois plus vite pour arriver au même résultat.	(devoir)
3	C'est étonnant qu'on n'y _ pas pensé avant.	(avoir)
4	Je trouve normal qu'on _ payer les vandales.	(faire)
5	Il est certain qu'on _ traverser une période difficile.	(aller)
6	Je pense qu'il _ réfléchir un peu plus sur cette question.	(falloir)
7	C'est ennuyeux que tu ne _ pas venir avec nous.	(pouvoir)
8	C'est curieux qu'il n'y _ aucune trace d'effraction.	(avoir)
9	Je suis sûr que les diplômes _ utiles.	(être)
10	Est-ce que vous pensez qu'ils _ vraiment compris?	(avoir)

49.5 Interpolations and parentheses

Interpolations

An **interpolation** is used with direct quotation of speech or thoughts, etc., to indicate who is speaking or thinking the thoughts.

If the interpolation comes first, normal word order (SV, SVO) is used:

> *le cinéaste cria: 'Coupez!'*   the director shouted: 'Cut!'
> *j'ai dit à ma femme: 'Où sont-ils?'*   I said to my wife: 'Where are they?'

If the interpolation comes in the course of, or at the end of the direct quotation, the verb is placed before its subject (VS, VSO):

> *'Hé!' me **cria-t-il**. 'Qu'est-ce que vous faites là?'*
> 'Hey!' he shouted. 'What're you doing there?
> *'Nous sommes arrivés', **dit/a dit** M. Dupont à sa femme.*
> 'We've arrived', said M. Dupont to his wife.
> *'Heureusement', **pensa-t-elle/a-t-elle pensé**.*
> 'Fortunately', she thought.

When an interpolation is made, in very casual speech (N1), in the course of or at the end of a direct quotation, it takes the form *que* + normal word order (SV, SVO):

> *'Hé!' qu'il me crie/qu'il m'a crié. 'Qu'est-ce que vous faites là?'*   (N1)

Parentheses

A **parenthesis** is a phrase, generally consisting of subject pronoun + verb, added in the course of or at the end of a statement. It forms a comment on the statement, or a way of involving the listener in it, and is an alternative to a completive construction (**see 49.1**):

Parenthesis   *Paul viendra aussi, **j'espère***
                 Paul will be coming as well, I hope

Completive	*j'espère que Paul viendra aussi*
	I hope Paul will be coming as well
Parenthesis	*il n'est pas venu*, **vous pensez bien**
	he didn't turn up, as you can guess
Completive	**vous pensez bien** *qu'il n'est pas venu*
	as you can guess, he didn't turn up

The addition of the neuter object pronoun *le* to link the parenthesis grammatically to the topic of the statement, is characteristic of more formal or deliberate speech or writing (**see 52.5**).

Common parentheses include:

..., *vous savez*, ...	you know
..., *comme vous le savez*, ...	as you are aware
..., *je sais bien*, ...	I know, I'm well aware
..., *c'est bien connu*, ...	as is well known
..., *j'en conviens*, ...	I agree, I admit
..., *il est vrai*, ... (N3)	it is true

Others have VS word order, or are introduced by *(à ce) que*:

..., *me semble-t-il*, ... (N3)	it seems to me
..., *qu'il me semble*, ... (N2)	it seems to me
..., *à ce qu'il paraît*, ...	it would appear, apparently

Exercice 49/2 **Parenthèse ou construction complétive?** Travail à deux

a Reformulez les phrases ci-dessous en employant une parenthèse au lieu d'une construction complétive.

b Lisez tour à tour à haute voix les deux formulations l'une après l'autre: laquelle jugez-vous la meilleure? Est-ce que les deux vous semblent également possibles?

c Discutez-en avec le reste du groupe.

Exemple: J'espère que tu n'as pas oublié le vin.
Réponse: Tu n'as pas oublié le vin, j'espère.

1 Tu as remarqué qu'il n'a rien dit?
2 Il est vrai qu'elle n'a pas l'air d'être en bonne santé.
3 Je sais bien que ça nous fait faire des dizaines de kilomètres en plus.
4 Il paraît qu'il n'y aura pas de feu d'artifice cette année.
5 Tu crois qu'il va neiger?
6 C'est bien connu qu'aujourd'hui on est tous la victime de quelque chose ou de quelqu'un.

Part
ten

Constructing texts

Coherence refers to the way in which the ideas in a spoken or written text are organised so as to make sense to the listener or reader.

Cohesion refers to the use of linguistic items which show explicitly how different parts of a text are linked, for example by using a conjunction or other connector to indicate how a particular phrase or sentence relates to another sentence, or to the rest of the text.

If a text is incoherent, no amount of linguistic cohesion can make it comprehensible – indeed, over-use of complex constructions and frequent linguistic markers can only make a bad text worse. Conversely, if the speaker or writer, and the listener or reader, share a set of assumptions about the meaning of certain words, letters and figures, a coherent message or conversation can be produced without the usual linguistic markers of cohesion, for example in a conversation between a small child and a parent **(see 3.1)**, or in a small ad for a flat **(see 32.5)**.

When speaking or writing French, you need to strike the right balance between over-use and under-use of markers of cohesion. Generally speaking, formal, written communication requires the use of grammatical structures such as subordinating conjunctions, to make explicit the links between different parts of a text; informal, spoken communication, on the other hand, makes less use of grammatical structures, and relies more on adverbs **(see 30.1)**, adverb phrases **(see 30.2)**, interpolated phrases and sentences **(see 49.5)**, and connectors, modalisers and fillers **(see 51)**.

In the preceding sections of this book, we progressed from the most basic to more complex structures of French: forms and combinations of words, phrases and sentences. In the next five sections **(50–54)**, we look at ways in which the various forms, structures and combinations of the French language can be used to construct texts: spoken or written productions which make sense not only at the level of individual words, groups, phrases or sentences, but on a wider scale: between sentences and throughout a paragraph or conversational exchange.

Sections **50–54** show some of the choices you can make, when applying the rules of French grammar:

50   **How to link arguments and present ideas**
51   **How to highlight a word or phrase**
52   **How to refer back or forward**
53   **Tense use: situation in time**
54   **Tense use: aspect**

50 How to link arguments and present ideas

50.1 Connectors
50.2 Modalisers and fillers
50.3 Imperative forms

50.1 Connectors

The words and phrases used to organise a text fall into several grammatical categories; many of these are dealt with in other sections of this book, including: Adverbs **(see 30)**, Conjunctions **(see 45–48)**, Parentheses **(see 49.5)** and Forms of reference **(see 52)**.

The following table lists a number of connectors. Many of these can be used with more than one type of text; for example *d'un côté . . . de l'autre côté* and *d'une part . . . d'autre part* can be used:

- in a description (see list **a** below: **Reality**), with spatial meaning ('in one direction', 'on one side' . . . 'in the other', 'on the other'), or
- in an argument (see list **b** below: **Ideas**), indicating opposition ('on (the) one hand . . . 'on the other').

■ **Table of adverbs and adverb phrases used as connectors**

a **Reality: organising a narrative text**

	Words		Phrases	
Time	*ensuite* next *enfin* finally	*après* afterwards *soudain* suddenly	*tout à coup* suddenly	*d'abord* at first
Space	*ici/là* here/there		*en haut* at the top *au-dessus* above	*en bas* at the bottom *plus loin* farther (away)

b   Ideas: organising an argument or a description

	Words		Phrases	
Opposition	*cependant* however *néanmoins* nevertheless	*pourtant* and yet	*en revanche* on the other hand	*au contraire* quite the opposite
Explanation, **justification**	*justement* as it happens		*en effet* indeed	*au fond* basically
Complementation			*d'ailleurs* besides	*de plus* moreover
Conclusion	*donc* therefore *Aussi* and so *enfin* finally	*Ainsi* thus *finalement* eventually	*par conséquent* consequently *en tout cas* in any case	*malgré tout* nevertheless *de toute façon* anyway
Enumeration	*ensuite* next, then *aussi* also	*enfin* last (of all) *également* as well	*d'abord* first (of all) *en plus* as well	*de même* similarly *en outre* besides
Reformulation	*bref* in a word		*en somme* in short *en fin de compte* in the end	*autrement dit* in other words *en conclusion* in conclusion

Exercice 50/1   **Récit oral > récit écrit**   Travail à deux > Mise en commun

Le texte ci-dessous est un sketch du comique Raymond Devos. Il s'agit donc d'un texte originellement destiné à être écouté et non à être lu.

a   En respectant l'ordre du récit, récrivez avec votre partenaire ce texte de manière à en faire un texte destiné à être lu. Vous pouvez, si vous le jugez nécessaire, modifier le vocabulaire du texte, mais les changements à_faire sont essentiellement de deux types:

(i) emploi de conjonctions **subordonnantes** (voir 46–49), et

(ii) emploi de **connecteurs** (voir 50.1).

b   Avec le reste du groupe, composez une seule version du texte, à partir des suggestions formulées au moment du travail à deux.

LES NEUF VEAUX

Savez-vous ce qui s'est passé

lors de la dernière conférence

des Neuf sur l'Europe agricole?

Pendant que les neuf ministres de l'agriculture

débattaient du prix du porc,

il y a un paysan mécontent

qui a fait entrer neuf veaux dans la salle.

Une confusion!

On ne savait plus qui était qui!

A la fin de la conférence,

le paysan, au lieu de remporter ses neuf veaux,

dans la bousculade qui a suivi

n'en a remporté que huit!

Il a emmené un ministre avec.

On ne dit pas lequel!

Ce n'est qu'en arrivant sur le marché

qu'il s'en est aperçu.

Au moment de vendre les veaux, il y en avait un qui était invendable.

C'était le . . . eh oui!

Parce qu'un ministre, ça ne se vend pas!

Ça s'achète parfois! Mais ça ne se vend pas!

Une fois (je l'avoue à ma grande honte),

je me suis vendu pour pas cher,

et quand j'ai voulu me racheter,

je me suis payé un prix fou!

(les Neuf: à l'époque de ce sketch, la Communauté européenne comptait neuf pays membres)

50.2 Modalisers and fillers

Modalisers

Many words and phrases prepare our listener or reader for what we are about to say, for example by expressing our attitude to something that has just been mentioned. To achieve this, various types of connectors (**see 50.1**) and other words and phrases are used as modalisers.

Modalisers present a commentary on the topic; they are used early in the sentence if it is important to guide the listener or reader, or later in the sentence if the commentary is more of an afterthought.

Modalisers fall into several grammatical categories:

Adverbs   (see 30)

évidemment	*manifestement*	*heureusement*
of course	obviously	fortunately
peut-être	*sans doute*	*sans aucun doute*
perhaps	maybe, doubtless	certainly

Interjections   (see 32.5)

bravo!	*mais oui!*	*mais non!*
well done!	oh yes (he did)! etc.	not at all!
justement!	*parfaitement!*	*(eh ben) dis donc!*
precisely!	(most) certainly!	(well) I say!

Modal verbs   (see 39.2)

je pourrais	*tu devrais*	*je voudrais*
I could	you should	I'd like to

Detached complements   (see 43–44)

à mon avis	*à vrai dire*
in my opinion	in (actual) fact

Completive constructions   (see 49.1)

je crois que	*il est vrai que*	*il est certain que*
I think that	it's true that	it's certain that

Parentheses   (see 49.5)

Imperative forms of a verb   (see 50.3)

French
Grammar
Explained

Fillers

The main reason for using fillers in spoken communication is to give yourself a breathing-space within which to gather your thoughts and the words with which to express them. Another use for fillers is to include the listener in the construction of the conversation; in this respect, fillers also function as modalisers.

There are considerable differences between speaking and writing, in respect of the relative importance and usefulness of modalisers and fillers.

Writing

As readers, we expect to be guided into and through any text we read, not only typographically by the layout and division of material, numbering, headings and sub-headings, etc., but linguistically by the ways in which sentences are introduced, constructed and combined, and the presence of signposts: words and phrases which indicate what is being written about, how it is being viewed, and so on. Many of the devices presented in **43–49** are used in written texts for this purpose, for example to show how one piece of information is related to another.

Speaking

Both modalisers and fillers can be useful when speaking.

Modalisers: if you do not use modalisers, your listener may become confused by not being able to work out what your attitude is, and by not having sufficient information to piece together about your message. Any shortcomings in your vocabulary, grammar or pronunciation of French will stand out.

Fillers: if you do not use fillers, you will find yourself obliged to find several new ideas (and the necessary vocabulary) per minute, and you will either express them too rapidly for your listener to take them in, or lapse into hesitant speech with long pauses while you search for a particular word.

Examples of fillers (see also table of connectors, **50.1**)

mais	*non mais*	*alors*	*donc*
but, oh ...	hey, now look here	so, then	(and) so
après tout	*finalement*	*à vrai dire*	
after all	in the end	to tell the truth	
tu vois	*n'est-ce pas?*	*si vous voulez*	
you see	isn't it? (etc.)	if you like, so to speak	

A word of warning

It is possible to overdo the use of fillers (especially *alors*), to the point where it becomes difficult for a listener to discern any message at all in what you are saying. It is best to use fillers only when you need to gain time, since in themselves they add nothing to the coherence or the cohesion of your message.

Le texte ci-dessous est un des Exercices de style de R Queneau (1947). L'auteur a choisi
délibérément d'employer le plus de fois possible le connecteur alors, avec le résultat que vous
constaterez.

a   En respectant l'ordre du récit, récrivez ce texte sans employer le mot alors, mais en marquant,
     par l'emploi de conjonctions subordonnantes et d'autres connecteurs, les liens entre chaque
     partie du texte.

b   Lisez à haute voix votre texte au reste du groupe, et discutez-en.

ALORS

Alors l'autobus est arrivé. Alors j'ai monté dedans. Alors j'ai vu un citoyen qui m'a saisi l'œil. Alors
j'ai vu son long cou et j'ai vu la tresse qu'il y avait autour de son chapeau. Alors il s'est mis à pester
contre son voisin qui lui marchait alors sur les pieds. Alors, il est allé s'asseoir.

   Alors, plus tard, je l'ai revu Cour de Rome. Alors il était avec un copain. Alors, il lui disait, le
copain: tu devrais faire mettre un autre bouton à ton pardessus. Alors.

(Il m'a saisi l'œil: je l'ai remarqué; la tresse: 'braid', 'trimming'; Cour de Rome: devant la gare Saint-
Lazare, à Paris)

Many of the devices used in spoken French to get started, to keep talking, or to announce
the topic, consist of various forms of dislocation and extraction (**see 51**).

50.3 Imperative forms

The imperative form of a verb functions as a modaliser: it gives the listener (or reader)
some advance notice as to what to expect. Imperative forms are used to give orders,
instructions, etc. They are formed from the present indicative of a verb, with a few
exceptions, including:

être	*sois*	*soyons*	*soyez*
avoir	*aie*	*ayons*	*ayez*
savoir	*sache*	*sachons*	*sachez* (see also Verb tables, **56**)

Persons 2 and 5 are used to give orders (etc.) to someone else:

   va voir si le facteur est passé   go and see if the postman's been
   allez la France!   come on France!

Person 4 is used to make a suggestion in which one includes oneself:

   ***Allons**, enfants de la Patrie!*   (opening of *la Marseillaise*)

In Person 2, the *-s* is dropped from *-er* verbs (and *aller*: see example below), unless the imperative is followed by *-y* or *-en*:

tu restes?   are you staying?   *reste!*   stay!   *restes-y!*   stay there!

With imperative forms of pronominal verbs **(see 36)**, the reflexive pronoun is placed after the verb:

*reposons-**nous**!*   let's have a rest!   *lève-**toi**!*   get up!   *asseyez-**vous**!*   sit down!

This use of the reflexive pronoun after the verb in the imperative should not be confused with the subject pronoun of other verbs, in questions with inversion of verb and subject **(see 33)**:

Question	*écoutez-vous ce qu'il dit?*	are you listening to what he is saying?	(N3)
Imperative	*écoutez ce que je vais dire!*	listen to what I'm about to say!	
Question	*où allons-nous?*	where are we going?	(N3)
Imperative	*allons nous reposer!*	let's go and rest!	
	(*nous* is part of the pronominal verb *se reposer*)		

Other ways of expressing the imperative

Not all commands (in English or in French) are expressed directly by using the imperative. Alternatives include:

- the **future tense**, or ***aller*** + infinitive. This has the effect of making the imperative less abrupt, but more insistent:

*tu **feras** ce que je te dis!*   you'll do as I say!
*vous **allez** me trouver cette lettre!*   I'm telling you to find the letter!

- a **question form**:

veux-tu te taire!   will you be quiet!

- an **infinitive**. This is used to make a polite or public request:

*ne pas **déranger** svp*   please do not disturb
***Ralentir**. Travaux*   Slow down. Roadworks   **(see 32.5)**

- an **adverb phrase**:

hors d'ici!   get out of here!

- a **noun**:

silence! (instead of taisez-vous!)   silence! (instead of 'be quiet!')
***prière** de ne pas déranger*   please do not disturb (polite request)
***défense** de déposer des ordures*   no rubbish to be tipped here (public notice)

The subjunctive **(see 48)** can be used to express an imperative involving another person or other people:

qu'il vienne ici!   let him come here!
qu'ils essayent!   (just) let them try!

51 How to highlight a word or phrase

51.1 Dislocation
51.2 Extraction: cleft constructions
51.3 Extraction: pseudo-cleft constructions

In both English and French, the usual order of material in a sentence is subject – verb – object or complement: SV, SVO or SVC **(see 32.1)**.

This basic order can be changed when asking questions **(see 33)**, and the use of passive, pronominal and impersonal constructions **(see 35, 36** and **37)** can involve changes to the order in which material is presented. Within each of these constructions, the order of material follows a conventional pattern: changing this word order would lead, in many cases, to a change of meaning, or even the loss of meaning altogether.

But there are other devices which involve changes in the order of material and/or the addition of new words (pronouns repeating a particular noun, for example). These devices are useful for highlighting one element in the sentence, for example.

In speech, an element in the sentence can be highlighted by putting stress on particular words or syllables (by saying them more loudly), together with a change of tone, a slowing-down of the speech rate, or a pause before or after the words or syllables to be emphasised:

*il a fait **quoi**?*	he did what?	(N2)
*je m'occupe de **mes** affaires*	I mind my own business	

In writing, emphasis is denoted by the use of **bold** type, *italics*, or <u>underlining</u>.

The use of emphasis on its own as a device for highlighting material within a sentence is more suited to English, which has word-stress (the same syllable(s) in a word are always stressed wherever the word appears in the sentence) than to French, which has group stress **(see 7.2)**.

In French, greater use than in English is made of dislocation **(51.1)** and extraction **(51.2** and **51.3)**.

51.1 Dislocation

> **Dislocation** refers to the moving of one or more elements in a sentence from their usual place. The element (noun, pronoun, adverb, etc.) which is moved is said to be detached.

In some cases, dislocation can take place without making any additions or other changes to the material:

- an adverb is easily moved in French from its usual position after the verb to the start of the sentence:

    *j'ai vu Paul **à Paris***   >   ***à Paris**, j'ai vu Paul*   **(see 32.3)**

- a noun which is a direct object can be moved to the start of the sentence in order to focus on it:

    *j'adore **le chocolat***   >   ***le chocolat**, j'adore*   (N2)

But dislocation involves other changes to the material; for example, the noun can be repeated in the form of the corresponding object pronoun:

    j'adore le chocolat   >   *le chocolat, je **l'**adore*

In other cases, a noun or tonic pronoun can be repeated as a subject pronoun, without any rearrangement of material:

    j'adore le chocolat   >   ***moi** j'adore le chocolat*   (N2)

Dislocation in French takes a number of different forms, depending on whether the detached element:

- is a noun or tonic pronoun;
- is the subject, direct object or indirect object of the verb;
- is moved to the start (left dislocation) or to the end (right dislocation) of the sentence.

In some cases, dislocation is characteristic of usage in formal situations (for example in certain forms of question: see below, and **33**); in other cases, it is characteristic of usage in informal situations.

Cases of dislocation are considered below in three groups:

a   Dislocation of tonic pronouns (as subject or direct object);
b   Dislocation of nouns (as subject or direct object);
c   Dislocation of tonic pronouns or nouns as indirect object.

a   Dislocation of tonic pronouns

As subject of the verb   (see also 19.3)

Left dislocation of a detached tonic pronoun does not involve any change to basic
SV/SVO word order. It is a common feature of spontaneous spoken French:

moi je *te dis qu'il est parti*	I tell you he's gone	(N2)
nous on *va au cinéma ce soir*	we're going to the cinema this evening	(N2)

The detached tonic pronoun (*moi, nous*) serves mainly to reinforce the subject pronoun
(*je, on*); it does not carry much emphasis.

Right dislocation of the detached tonic pronoun in the same sentences as those given
above carries greater emphasis:

je *te dis qu'il est parti,* *moi!*	<u>I</u> tell you he's left!	(N2)
on *va au cinéma ce soir,* *nous!*	<u>we're</u> going to the cinema this evening	(N2)

As direct object of the verb

A tonic pronoun used as the direct object of a verb can be dislocated to left or to right:

Left	*toi, je te connais*	**Right**	*je te connais,* *toi*	I know <u>you</u>
Left	*elle, je l'admire*	**Right**	*je l'admire,* *elle*	I admire <u>her</u>

Exercice 51/1   Dislocation: détachement du pronom   Travail à deux > Mise en commun

a   Reformulez les phrases ci-dessous en ajoutant un pronom tonique (détaché (i) à gauche, (ii) à
     droite) correspondant au pronom souligné. Avec votre partenaire, lisez à haute voix les deux
     versions de chaque phrase, et essayez de décider laquelle est préférable et pourquoi.

b   Ensuite, discutez-en avec le reste du groupe.

Exemple: <u>Je</u> te dis qu'elle n'est pas là!

Réponses possibles: (i)   **Moi** je te dis qu'elle n'est pas là!

                (ii)   Je te dis qu'elle n'est pas là, **moi!**

                (dans (ii), il y a plus d'insistance que dans (i))

1	<u>Il</u> n'avait rien fait.	5	<u>Tu</u> restes ici, hein!
2	Je <u>la</u> déteste.	6	<u>On</u> n'est pas si bêtes!
3	<u>On</u> a les pieds sur terre.	7	<u>Je</u> n'ai rien compris.
4	<u>Ils</u> ne sont jamais contents.	8	<u>Il</u> sait manipuler les gens.

b   Dislocation of nouns

As subject of the verb

In left dislocation of a detached noun which is the subject of a verb, the basic SV/SVO word order is retained. It is the most widely-used of all forms of dislocation involving a noun:

mon patron m'en a parlé	>	*mon patron **il** m'a parlé de ça*	(N2)
my boss mentioned it/that to me			

Left dislocation of a detached noun is common in questions (**see 33.1c** and **33.3c**):

Yes/No	*(et) **ton frère, il** est toujours aussi actif?*	what about your brother? is he as active as ever?	(N2)
WH-	*où **Pierre** a-t-**il** trouvé ce livre?*	where did Pierre find this/that/the book?	(N3)
	*pourquoi **les gens ils** sont si bêtes?*	why are people so stupid?	(N2)

Right dislocation of a detached noun which is the subject of the verb is also possible:

	il** est bien, tu sais, **le nouveau directeur	the new head is a good sort, you know	(N2)

Right dislocation also occurs in questions:

Yes/No	***elle** est là, **ta soeur**?*	is your sister there?	(N2)
WH-	*à quelle heure est-ce qu'**elle** est arrivée, **ta soeur**?*	what time did your sister arrive?	

As direct object of the verb

A detached noun which is used as the direct object of a verb can be dislocated to left or right:

Left	***ses histoires**, on **les** a trop entendues*	we've heard his stories too many times
Right	*je **l'**aimais bien, **cette table***	I used to like this/that table

A detached noun which is the direct object of a verb can be dislocated in questions:

Yes/No	*tu **l'**as vue, **sa nouvelle série** à la télé?*	have you seen his/her new TV series?	(N2)
WH-	*où est-ce qu'on **l'**a vu, **ce chanteur**?*	where was it we saw that singer?	

For dislocation after *Aussi, peut-être* etc. (N3/N4) **see 32.4**. For the use of ***c'est*** (or *ça/cela* + other verb) in dislocation, **see 52**.

Double dislocation, of subject and object, is a feature of spontaneous speech (N2):

moi les épinards je déteste ça	(N2)	*quant à moi, je déteste les épinards*	(N3)
(as for) me, I hate spinach			
moi ma femme ses robes elles me coûtent une fortune			(N2)
my wife costs me a fortune in dresses			

Exercice 51/2   **Dislocation: détachement du nom**   Travail à deux > Mise en commun

a   Reformulez les phrases ci-dessous en détachant (i) à gauche, (ii) à droite le nom souligné
et en ajoutant un pronom à la place du nom. Avec votre partenaire, lisez à haute voix les
deux versions de chaque phrase, et essayez de décider laquelle est préférable, et
pourquoi.

b   Ensuite, discutez-en avec le reste du groupe.

Exemple: <u>Les autres</u> sont déjà arrivés?

Réponses possibles:(i)   Les autres, ils sont déjà arrivés?

(ii)   Ils sont déjà arrivés, les autres?

1   <u>Le nouveau directeur</u> a rencontré le personnel?
2   Tu as vu <u>le documentaire sur la mafia</u>?
3   A quelle heure est-ce que <u>la bibliothèque</u> ferme?
4   <u>Celui-là</u> a toujours son mot à dire.
5   On voit <u>celle-là</u> partout.
6   Où est-ce que tu as acheté <u>cette montre</u>?
7   Tu écoutes souvent <u>les informations</u>?
8   Quand est-ce qu'ils annoncent <u>les résultats</u>?

---

c   Dislocation of an indirect object and other complements

Dislocation of the indirect object of the verb, or of an adverb phrase beginning with a
preposition (**see 30.2** and **30.3**), is usually to the left. The preposition is generally omitted
before the noun or pronoun, but an indirect object pronoun is used:

on ne m'a rien dit	>	***moi** on m'a rien dit* (N2)
no one told me anything		
on ne peut pas demander des miracles	>	***les enfants** on (ne) peut pas **leur** demander*
aux enfants		*des miracles* (N2)
you can't expect miracles from children		
j'avais peur de ce professeur	>	***ce prof**, j'**en** avais peur* (N2)
I was scared of that teacher		
je ne vais pas souvent à Paris	>	***Paris** j'**y** vais pas souvent* (N2)
I don't go to Paris very often		

In WH- questions (**see 33.3**), there is right dislocation, and the appropriate preposition is
used with the detached noun:

*quand est-ce que tu **y** vas, **à Paris**?*	when do you go to Paris?	(N2)
*combien elle **en** a vendu, **de montres**?*	how many watches has she sold?	(N2)

51.2 Extraction: cleft constructions

Extraction involves the use of *c'est* ... *qui/que* or *ce qui/que* ..., *c'est* to highlight one element (noun, tonic pronoun, adverb) in a sentence; this is done by the use of a cleft construction **(see 51.2)** to highlight a word at the beginning of a sentence, or a pseudo-cleft construction **(see 51.3)** to highlight a word at the end of a sentence.

A cleft construction highlights an element at the start of the sentence by the use of *c'est* ... *qui/que*:

je voulais te voir	> *c'est toi que je voulais voir*

IN ENGLISH, a cleft construction ('it's ... that') can be used for the same purpose:

I wanted to see you	> it's you that I wanted to see

but it is not the most usual way of highlighting 'you'. This is done simply by emphasising the noun, pronoun or adverb:

you're the one I wanted to see	(emphasis on 'you're')

IN FRENCH, a relative construction (*celui qui*, *celui que*, etc.), corresponding to 'you're the one ...' can be used:

tu es celui/celle que je voulais voir dans ce rôle
you're the one I wanted to see in that role

but the cleft construction with *c'est* ... *qui/que* is the usual way to isolate a word or phrase in French.

Examples:
C'est + **noun**/**pronoun** + *qui/que* (relative construction)
- to highlight a noun or pronoun which is the subject or the direct object of the main verb:

c'est lui qui gagnera	he's the one who'll win
c'est lui qu'on aime	he's the one people like

In this cleft construction, *c'est* can change to *ce sont* (N3), or to *c'était, ce sera* etc., but this is not essential in everyday speech:

c'est (N2)/*ce sont* (N3) *toujours les plus forts qui gagnent*
it's always the strongest who win/the strongest always win
c'est/ce sera la petite Parisienne qu'ils choisiront, tu verras
they'll choose the Parisian girl, you'll see

C'est à + noun/pronoun + *de* + infinitive (infinitive construction)
- to express the idea of 'it's up to ...' + noun/pronoun:

c'est à vous de jouer	it's your turn
c'est au directeur de décider	it's for the manager to decide

Exercice 51/3   **Construction clivée ou construction simple?**   Travail à deux > Mise en commun

a   Reformulez les phrases ci-dessous en employant une construction clivée; dans certains cas, plus d'une formulation est possible.

b   Décidez, dans chaque cas, si la construction clivée est préférable à la construction simple. Pourquoi? Dans quelles circonstances?

c   Discutez-en avec le reste du groupe.

1   Vous devez décider.
2   Les chiens aboient quand il fait de l'orage.
3   J'ai pensé à vous pour cette mission difficile.
4   Après la fermeture des bureaux, il n'y a plus personne dans le quartier.
5   Elle a tout organisé.
6   L'entraîneur doit choisir l'équipe.
7   Elle est déprimée quand les jours raccourcissent.
8   En arrivant à l'aéroport, il a découvert qu'il n'avait pas son passeport.
9   Il ne faut pas s'adresser ici.
10   Dans une telle dispute, tout le monde est perdant.

C'est + **adverb** (etc.) + *que*   (completive construction)
- to highlight a noun/pronoun as indirect object, an adverb, a gerund, or a subordinate clause:

c'est à vous que je parle	you're the one(s) I'm speaking to
c'est à ce moment-là qu'il a compris son erreur	that was when he realised his mistake
c'est en forgeant qu'on devient forgeron	practice makes perfect (proverb; *forgeron*: blacksmith)
c'est surtout quand elle sourit qu'elle est jolie	she's prettiest when she smiles

Other cleft constructions

Other cleft constructions are used in French, particularly in informal situations (N2):
- *il y a* + **noun** + *qui/que*

   et puis il y a mon frère que je n'ai pas vu depuis longtemps
   and then there's my brother – I haven't seen him for ages

- *j'ai* + **noun** + *qui/que*

   j'ai ma mère qui est malade   (you see,) my mother's ill

French
Grammar
Explained

The table below lists some cleft constructions, together with equivalent constructions which are more likely to be used in formal situations (N3):

Cleft constructions (N2)	Equivalent constructions (N3)
Il y a des ... qui/que *il y a des gens qui pensent qu'il a raison* *il y a des bruits qu'elle déteste*	*Certains* *certains pensent qu'il a raison* some people think he's right *elle déteste certains bruits* she dislikes some noises
Il n'y a que ... qui/que *il n'y a que lui qui travaille* *il n'y a que les imbéciles qui approuveront*	*Seul* *lui seul travaille* he's the only one working *seuls les imbéciles approuveront* only fools will agree
Ça fait (time) *que ...* *ça fait longtemps que je n'y pense plus* *ça fait des heures qu'on attend le courrier*	*Depuis* (time) *je n'y pense plus depuis longtemps* I stopped thinking about that long ago *on attend le courrier depuis des heures* we've been waiting hours for the post
Si ... c'est que *si j'ai dit ça, c'est que c'est la vérité*	*Parce que* *j'ai dit cela parce que c'est la vérité* I said that because it's the truth

Exercice 51/4   **Constructions clivées**   Travail individuel

Après avoir étudié la **table** (ci-dessus), composez une construction clivée (N2) à partir des phrases simples (N3) ci-dessous, en faisant d'autres changements si vous le jugez nécessaire.

1   On ne les a pas vus depuis longtemps.
2   Il a affirmé cela parce qu'il le croit.
3   Je n'aime que toi.
4   Seul le sport l'intéresse.
5   Je propose cela parce que je ne vois pas d'autre solution.
6   Certains approuvent encore le châtiment corporel.
7   Il essaie depuis des années de faire avancer son procès.
8   Ils parlent comme cela parce qu'ils ne savent pas faire autrement.

51.3 Extraction: pseudo-cleft constructions

A pseudo-cleft construction highlights one element at the end of the sentence by the use of:

> *celui qui/celui que* . . ., *c'est* + **noun** (person, thing):
>
> | *Pierre a gagné* | > | *celui qui a gagné, c'est Pierre* |
> |---|---|---|
> | Pierre's won | | the one who's won is Pierre |

or *ce qui/ce que* . . ., *c'est* + **noun** (idea):

> | *elle cherche le bonheur* | > | *ce qu'elle cherche, c'est le bonheur* |
> |---|---|---|
> | she's looking for happiness | | what she's looking for is happiness |

or *ce qui/ce que* . . ., *c'est que* + **completive clause**:

> | *je veux qu'elle travaille* | > | *ce que je veux, c'est qu'elle travaille* |
> |---|---|---|
> | I want her to work | | what I want is for her to work |

Pseudo-cleft constructions are used frequently in English ('the one (that)/what . . . is'), and in French; you should practise these until they are automatic:

celui qui/celui que etc.

le nouveau modèle automatique	>	*se vend bien **celui qui** se vend bien, c'est le nouveau modèle automatique*
the new automatic model sells well	>	the one that sells well is the new automatic model
je voulais te voir dans ce rôle	>	***celui/celle que** je voulais voir dans ce rôle, **c'est** toi*
I wanted to see you in that part	>	the person I wanted to see in that part was you

ce qui/ce que

son instabilité m'inquiète	>	*ce qui m'inquiète, **c'est** son instabilité*
his instability worries me	>	what worries me is his instability
il vous faut de l'imagination	>	*ce qu'il vous faut, **c'est** de l'imagination*
you need vision	>	what you need is vision

Exercice 51/5   **Constructions pseudo-clivées**   Travail à deux > Mise en commun

a Reformulez les phrases ci-dessous en employant une construction pseudo-clivée (ce qui (etc.) ..., c'est ou celui qui (etc.) ..., c'est).

b Vérifiez vos réponses.

c Dans certaines phrases, une autre formulation, par exemple une construction clivée (c'est ... qui/que) est également possible: essayez de trouver d'autres formulations pour chaque phrase.

d Présentez vos conclusions au reste du groupe.

Exemple: La situation économique m'inquiète.

Construction pseudo-clivée: Ce **qui** m'inquiète, **c'est** la situation économique.

Construction clivée: **C'est** la situation économique **qui** m'inquiète.

(également possible, si on veut souligner **la situation** par rapport à **d'autres** sujets d'inquiétude)

1 Elle déteste la musique moderne.
2 Buster Keaton me fait rire.
3 Il faut dire tout de suite que je n'ai pas encore vu ce film.
4 Il a l'air de croire qu'il joue bien: c'est amusant.
5 On oublie qu'il y a beaucoup de jeunes qui n'ont jamais travaillé.
6 Hitler a fait le plus de mal dans le monde.
7 Ils n'ont rien dit: c'est curieux.
8 Je préfère la guerre de 14–18.

Other pseudo-cleft constructions

As well as *celui qui/celui que* and *ce qui/ce que*, other groups of words can be extracted and followed by *c'est que*:

Où clause

> *où il s'est trompé, c'est dans la conception du moteur*
> where he went wrong was in the design of the engine

Noun

> *l'ennui, c'est qu'on n'a presque plus de carburant*
> the problem is, we've hardly any fuel left
> *moi **mon idée** c'est qu'il est parti seul*   (N2)
> what I think is that he set off on his own
> *lui **son problème** c'est qu'il veut tout contrôler*   (N2)
> the problem with him is that he wants to keep an eye on everything

52 How to refer back or forward

52.1 **Referring (back or forward) to nouns and pronouns**
52.2 **Noun or pronoun +** *c'est* **or** *il/elle est*
52.3 **Infinitive +** *c'est* **or** *ça/cela* **+ other verb**
52.4 **Completive clause +** *c'est* **or** *ça/cela* **+ other verb**
52.5 *Ça, cela* **and** *le, y, en*

52.1 Referring (back or forward) to nouns and pronouns

Constantly, in speech and writing, we make reference to something which is not named directly. Instead of repeating the same nouns, names, phrases, etc., we use a pronoun that refers our listener/reader to someone or something we and/or they have just seen, heard, said or thought about:

who said **that**?

he won't know

that's what I think, anyway

she soon recovered

Most often, as in the above examples, we are referring back to something, but the same or similar pronouns are also used to refer forward:

now listen to **this**!   just look at **him**!   I'll tell you **what**

IN ENGLISH, the system of pronouns used when referring (back or forward) to a specific noun (person or thing) is 'he/she/it/they' (subject) or 'him/her/it/they' (object); these pronouns can be stressed for emphasis: 'not <u>him</u>!' etc.

When referring back to a notion rather than to a specific noun, 'it' or 'that' are used, and 'that' can be stressed for emphasis: 'not <u>that</u>!' etc. When referring forward to a notion, 'this' is used: 'this is what I have to tell you'.

IN FRENCH, subject pronouns (see **9.1**) or object pronouns (see **18.2**) are used when referring (back or forward) to a specific noun (person or thing), without particular emphasis. For emphasis, tonic pronouns (see **19.1**) are used to refer to specific persons; demonstrative pronouns (see **21.4**) are used to refer to specific persons or things.

Demonstrative adjectives (see **21.1**) can be used the second time a noun is mentioned:

*on avait abattu un arbre . . . **cet** arbre . . .*

a tree had been felled . . . this tree . . .

or with a more general noun, standing for a specific noun:

> *un jeune homme à l'aspect menaçant . . .* ***cet*** *individu . . .*
>
> a threatening-looking young man . . . this individual . . .

For reference back to an idea, a fact, a statement, an event, etc., *ce* is used with *être* (as in *c'est*), and *ça* (N2) or *cela* (N3) with other verbs. For reference forward, *c'est* and *ceci* are used.

> The *ce* used in *c'est, c'était, ce sera*, etc. is an invariable neuter subject pronoun, unlike the demonstrative adjective *ce*, which is one of the series *ce/cet/cette/ces*.

For the difference between ***il/elle*** *est médecin* and ***c'est un*** *médecin célèbre*, **see 22.5**.

52.2–52.4 *C'est* and *ça/cela*

Ce (as in *c'est*) and, with other verbs, *ça* (N2) or *cela* (N3) are used to refer to a **topic** (noun, infinitive or completive clause), before making a **comment** (adjective, noun, infinitive, verb) on it. When speaking, there is a pause before *c'est*, and in writing this is usually marked by a comma:

	Topic		Comment	
52.2	**Noun**	*les voyages,*	*c'est facile*	(*c'est* + adjective)
	'travel'		*c'est un plaisir*	(*c'est* + noun)
			ça/cela forme la jeunesse	(*ça/cela* + verb)
	Pronoun	*ça*	*c'est facile*	(*c'est* + adjective)
	'that'		*c'est un plaisir*	(*c'est* + noun)
52.3	**Infinitive**	*voyager,*	*c'est passionnant*	(*c'est* + adjective)
	'going on		*c'est une aventure*	(*c'est* + noun)
	a journey'		*c'est découvrir le monde*	(*c'est* + infinitive)
			ça/cela ouvre des perspectives	(*ça/cela* + verb)
52.4	**Completive**	*que les jeunes*	*c'est indispensable*	(*c'est* + adjective)
	clause	*voyagent,*	*c'est une nécessité*	(*c'est* + noun)
	'that/if young		*ça/cela fait plaisir à tout le monde*	(*ça/cela* + verb)
	people travel'			

If the topic (*les voyages, voyager, que les jeunes voyagent*) has already been mentioned or is implied or understood, it need not be stated: the comment (*c'est* + adjective/noun/infinitive) is used on its own.

IN ENGLISH, 'that' (+ 'is' or other verb) is used in similar ways, but less often than *c'est* in French. In the examples below, the English equivalents show that other devices, including word stress, are often preferred. Compare these examples of dislocation using *c'est* or *ça/cela* with the examples in **51.1**, where subject pronouns or object pronouns are used.

52.2 Noun or pronoun + *c'est* or *il/elle est*

Noun + *c'est* + adjective

Followed by an adjective, *c'est* refers to the topic as a whole, not to the specific noun:

Topic + comment		Comment + topic
noun + *c'est* + adjective		***c'est* + adjective, + noun**
les cours de grammaire, c'est passionnant	or	*c'est passionnant, les cours de grammaire!*
grammar classes are great!		
des hommes sur la planète Mars,	or	*c'est inimaginable! des hommes sur la*
c'est inimaginable		*planète Mars!*
it's hard to imagine men on Mars		

When the focus is on the noun itself, rather than on the topic as a whole, ***il/elle est*** is used, not *c'est*:

Topic + comment		Comment + topic
*j'ai rencontré **son frère**: il est très gentil*	or	***il est** très gentil, **son frère**: je l'ai rencontré*
I've met his/her brother: he's very nice		his/her brother's very nice: I've met him
*tu as vu **sa nouvelle voiture**? elle est sensationnelle!*	or	***elle est** formidable, **sa nouvelle voiture**: tu l'as vue?*
have you seen his/her new car? it's terrific!		his/her new car is great: have you seen it?

C'est or *il/elle est* + adjective?

The following examples show when to use *c'est* + adjective, and when to use *il/elle est* + adjective:

General	*tu as essayé la Grande Roue? **c'est** sensationnel!*
	have you had a go on the Big Wheel? it's great!
	(c'est: the reference is to the experience, not to the specific noun)
Specific	*on devrait fermer la Grande Roue: **elle est** dangereuse*
	they should close the Big Wheel: it's dangerous
	(il/elle est: the reference is to the specific noun)
Specific	***elle est** belle, ma ville*
	my city is beautiful
	(il/elle est: the reference is to the specific noun)

General	*c'est beau, une ville bien fleurie/une ville bien fleurie, c'est beau*
	a city with lots of flowers is beautiful
	(c'est: the reference is to the experience of seeing a city full of flowers)

Noun 1 + *c'est* + noun 2

Followed by a noun, *c'est*, not *il/elle est*, is used to refer (back or forward) to another specific noun or pronoun:

Person	*c'est un très bon ami: **il** nous a beaucoup aidés*
	he's a very good friend: he's helped us a lot
	*j'ai rencontré **son frère**: c'est un homme charmant*
	I've met his/her brother: he's a charming man
Thing	*c'est une vieille maison: **elle** a été construite au 18ᵉ siècle*
	it's an old house: it was built in the 18th century
	*tu as vu **sa nouvelle voiture**? c'est une Rolls!*
	have you seen his/her new car? it's a Rolls!

In 'noun 1 is noun 2' constructions such as the following, there is no need for *c'est* (or *ce sont*):

les affaires sont les affaires	business is business
les hommes sont des imbéciles	men are idiots

C'est is also used with a noun or tonic pronoun to draw attention to a person, in the same way as 'it is', 'it's' in English:

*regarde! **c'est** le Premier Ministre!*	look! it's the Prime Minister!
*mais je te dis que **c'est** lui/**c'est** elle!*	I tell you it's him/it's her!

Ça, c'est + noun or adjective

This construction is used in speech to refer to a topic which speaker and listener are aware of or have just mentioned, and then to make a comment on it:

ça, c'est le comble!	that's the last straw!	(N2)

The order of items can be reversed, so that the comment comes first:

c'est une bonne idée, ça!	that's a good idea!	(N2)

Noun + ça/cela + verb other than être

If the comment contains a verb other than *être*, then *ça* (N2) or *cela* (N3) is used, not *ce*:

*le sport, **ça** rapproche les nations*	sport brings countries closer together
***ça** marchera pas, son truc* (N2)	his/her idea won't work

But if the comment refers to a specific noun, a personal pronoun (*il/elle*), not *ça*, is used **(see 51.1b)**:

*cette invention, **elle** va révolutionner l'industrie*	or	***elle** va révolutionner l'industrie, cette invention*
		this invention will revolutionise industry

Exercice 52/1 · Thème + propos ('topic' + 'comment'): ordre des éléments

Travail à deux > Mise en commun

a Composez des phrases en combinant les éléments séparés ci-dessous. Employez c'est ou ça/cela + autre verbe.

b Pour chaque phrase que vous venez de composer, essayez (i) d'abord l'ordre Thème + propos, puis (ii) l'ordre Propos + thème: lequel vous semble préférable? Pourquoi? Discutez-en, puis présentez vos conclusions au reste du groupe.

Exemple: (thème) les examens (propos) stressant
  Réponses: (i) Les examens, c'est stressant.
        (ii) C'est stressant, les examens.
        (les deux formulations sont également possibles)

1 les vacances   toujours trop court
2 la famille   parfois encombrant
3 son idée   ridicule
4 la publicité à la télé   souvent enfantin

Exemple: (thème) sa voiture préférée (propos) une BMW
  Réponses: (i) Sa voiture préférée, c'est une BMW.
        (ii) C'est une BMW, sa voiture préférée.
        (la formulation (ii) est possible, mais avec un sens différent: 'it's/there's a BMW, his/her favourite car')

5 ce tableau   un chef d'oeuvre
6 ma chambre   un bazar
7 tous ces sans-abri   un scandale
8 la destruction de l'environnement   un crime

Exemple: (thème) les matchs internationaux (propos) ne rapprochent pas toujours les nations
  Réponses: (i) Les matchs internationaux, ça ne **rapproche** pas toujours les nations.
        (ii) Ça ne **rapproche** pas toujours les nations, les matchs internationaux.
        (possible, surtout si les mots les matchs internationaux viennent d'être dits par quelqu'un d'autre)

9 les études   servent toujours à quelque chose
10 le sport   fournit des sujets de conversation
11 les vols transatlantiques   consomment énormément de carburant
12 les partis politiques   devront s'adapter au monde d'aujourd'hui

French
Grammar
Explained

Exercice 52/2   *C'est* ou *il/elle est* + adjectif?   Travail individuel

Composez des phrases à partir des éléments ci-dessous, en ajoutant ce/c' ou il/elle + le verbe être au temps qui convient.

Exemple: il faut voir la tour Eiffel   extraordinaire
Réponse: Il faut voir la tour Eiffel: **elle est** extraordinaire.

Exemple: il faut aller jusqu'au troisième étage de la tour Eiffel   extraordinaire
Réponse: Il faut aller jusqu'au troisième étage de la tour Eiffel: **c'est** extraordinaire.

1	elle ne se rappelle absolument rien	curieux
2	va voir Madeleine	très inquiète
3	tu as vu Charlot dans ses premiers films?	très amusant
4	je ne sais pas pourquoi cette machine ne fonctionne pas	presque neuf
5	le conseil municipal n'a toujours pas pris de décision	ridicule
6	il m'a tout raconté sur l'affaire	incroyable

52.3 Infinitive + *c'est* + adjective or noun   (see 40.2)

In this construction, the infinitive functions as a noun. The order of items is reversible:

Topic	Comment		Comment	Topic
Infinitive +	*c'est* + adj/noun	or	*C'est* + adj/noun	+ *de* + infinitive

*faire ce travail
  pour demain*
	c'est impossible	or	*c'est
			  impossible*
				*de faire ce travail
				  pour demain* (N2)

it's impossible to do this job by tomorrow

*ne pas finir
  ce travail*
	ce serait dommage	or	*ce serait
			  dommage*
				*de ne pas finir
				  ce travail*

it'd be a pity not to finish this job

When the comment (*c'est* + adjective/noun) comes before the topic (infinitive), *de* is added between the two parts (compare, in English, the use of 'to' with an infinitive: 'it's going to rain', etc.). In French, this *de* adds no meaning: it corresponds to the pause or comma used when the topic is a noun:

    c'est fatigant, le travail   *c'est fatigant de travailler tout le temps*   (N2)

In all the above examples, the part beginning *c'est* is complete and self-contained: the words form a meaningful statement on their own. This use of a series of grammatically and semantically complete words, phrases or sentences is characteristic of communication in informal situations (N2).

In formal situations (N3), on the other hand, grammatical means are more often used to link words, phrases and sentences. In the case of the structures illustrated above, this linkage is achieved by the use of the impersonal pronoun *il*, not *ce*, at the start of the sentence.

This means that there are three ways of formulating the same sequence in French:

faire ce travail pour demain, c'est impossible
c'est impossible de faire ce travail pour demain (N2)
il est impossible de faire ce travail pour demain (N3)

In the formulation with *il*, the first three words (*il est* + adjective) are incomplete on their own: the listener or reader expects the speaker or writer to continue the sentence, either with *de* + infinitive, or with *que* + completive clause **(see 52.4)**.

Depending on the situation (formal or informal) – and on the order in which the ideas and words come to your mind – you will need to use each of these three formulations, so it is worth practising them all.

Exercice 52/3   Thème + propos: infinitif + *c'est* + adjectif/nom

Travail à deux > Mise en commun

a   Composez des phrases en combinant les éléments séparés ci-dessous. Employez c'est, et, dans la série (ii), de avec l'infinitif.

b   Pour chaque phrase que vous venez de composer, essayez (i) d'abord l'ordre thème + propos, puis (ii) l'ordre propos + thème: lequel vous semble préférable? Pourquoi? Discutez-en, puis présentez vos conclusions au reste du groupe.

Exemple: (thème) les voir dans cet état   (propos) pénible
Réponses: (i)   Les voir dans cet état, **c'est** pénible.
              (ii) **C'est** pénible de les voir dans cet état.
              (les deux réponses sont également possibles)

1	travailler huit heures sans temps de repos	inhumain
2	arriver et partir comme ça, sans rien dire	bizarre
3	avoir trouvé deux bonne places	une chance
4	faire les courses avec deux enfants en bas âge	tout un exploit
5	acheter un chien ou un chat et puis l'abandonner	cruel
6	pénaliser les gens les plus défavorisés	un scandale

Infinitive + *c'est* + infinitive

Two infinitives can be linked by *c'est*; the second infinitive provides a definition or an extension of the meaning of the first infinitive:

voir c'est croire	seeing is believing/to see is to believe
partir c'est mourir un peu	going away is like dying a little

The corresponding construction in English is usually a gerund (ending in '-ing'), though an infinitive with 'to' can also be used.

Infinitive + *ça/cela* + verb other than *être*

If the comment contains a verb other than *être*, then *ça* (N2) or *cela* (N3) is used, not *ce*.

lui demander de l'argent, ***ça me gêne***	(N2)
asking him/her for money embarrasses me	
se rendre à l'aéroport, ***cela prend*** *de plus en plus de temps*	(N3)
getting to the airport takes longer and longer	

As with the constructions studied earlier, when the comment (*ça/cela* + verb) comes before the topic (infinitive), ***de*** is added before the infinitive:

ça me gêne ***de*** *lui demander de l'argent*	(N2)
cela prend de plus en plus de temps ***de*** *se rendre à l'aéroport*	(N3)

Note that *cela*, not *il* (N3) and *ça*, not *ce* (N2), are used with verbs other than *être*.

52.4 Completive clause + *c'est* or *ça/cela* + other verb

Completive clauses (**see 49**) usually come after the construction which introduces them:

c'est évident qu'il est toujours là	it's obvious he's still there

Alternatively, the topic (completive clause) can come before the comment (*c'est* + adjective). In informal situations (N2), topic and comment are simply juxtaposed, without *que*:

il est toujours là, c'est évident	he's still there, that's obvious	(N2)

But in formal situations (N3), grammatical means are used to link topic and comment:

- *que* is retained;
- the subjunctive is used, instead of the indicative, in the completive clause, to show that the information is dependent on what is still to come:

qu'il soit *toujours là,* ***c'est*** *évident*	that he's still there is obvious	(N2)
que Pierre soit *tombé,* ***cela amuse*** *Paul*	Paul finds it amusing that Pierre fell over	(N3)

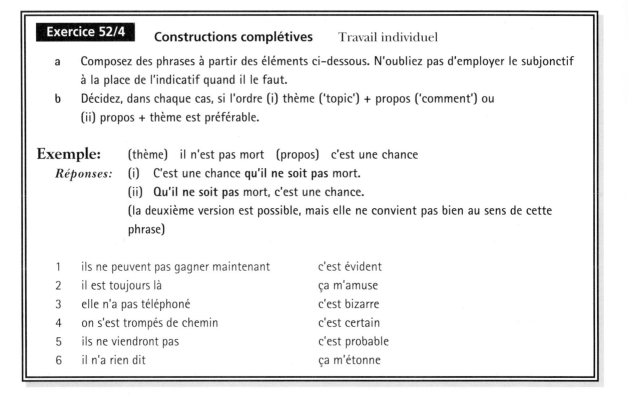

Exercice 52/4   **Constructions complétives**   Travail individuel

a   Composez des phrases à partir des éléments ci-dessous. N'oubliez pas d'employer le subjonctif à la place de l'indicatif quand il le faut.

b   Décidez, dans chaque cas, si l'ordre (i) thème ('topic') + propos ('comment') ou (ii) propos + thème est préférable.

Exemple: (thème) il n'est pas mort   (propos)   c'est une chance
Réponses: (i)   C'est une chance **qu'il ne soit pas mort.**
              (ii) **Qu'il ne soit pas mort,** c'est une chance.
              (la deuxième version est possible, mais elle ne convient pas bien au sens de cette phrase)

1   ils ne peuvent pas gagner maintenant   c'est évident
2   il est toujours là   ça m'amuse
3   elle n'a pas téléphoné   c'est bizarre
4   on s'est trompés de chemin   c'est certain
5   ils ne viendront pas   c'est probable
6   il n'a rien dit   ça m'étonne

52.5 *Ça* (N2), *cela* (N3) and *le* (N3), *y*, *en*, neuter pronouns

Just as *y* and *en* are used as neuter indirect object pronouns after verbs constructed with *à* and *de*, respectively (**see 18.5**), *le* can be used as a neuter direct object pronoun.

This use of *le* occurs when one is referring back, not to a particular noun (which would be represented by one of the pronouns *le*, *la* or *les*, as appropriate), but to a fact, an idea, a sentence:

*tout le monde dit que c'est vrai, mais moi je ne **le** crois pas*
everyone says it's true, but I don't believe it
(*le* refers back to *ce* in *c'est*, which refers to a fact, a phenomenon, etc., not to a specific noun)
*qu'il soit parti/intelligent/un escroc, on **le** savait*
we knew he'd left/he's clever/he's a crook
*Il va renoncer à jouer? On **le** dit*
Is he going to give up playing? So people say

The use of ça as a neuter pronoun is characteristic of informal usage (N2). In more formal situations (N3), *cela* is used instead of *ça*; *le*, *y* or *en* can be used when there is no particular emphasis (when the English equivalent is 'it' rather than 'that').

Informal (N2)	Formal (N3)	Formal (N3)
ça	*cela*	*le/y/en*
Subject		
ça change tout	*cela change tout*	–
that changes everything		
ça prend du temps	*cela prend du temps*	–
that takes time		
Direct object		
on dit ça	*on dit cela*	*on le dit*
that's what they say		
je trouve ça formidable	*je trouve cela formidable*	*je le trouve formidable*
I find that/it great		
Indirect object		
je pense à ça	*je pense à cela*	*j'y pense*
I'm thinking about that/it		
qu'est-ce que tu penses de ça?	*qu'est-ce que tu penses de cela?*	*qu'est-ce que tu en penses?*
what do you think of that/it?		

Exercice 52/5   Emploi de *le, y, en*   Travail individuel

Récrivez en style soutenu (N3) les phrases ci-dessous, qui sont rédigées en style familier (N2).

Exemple: On dit ça.
Réponse: On le dit.

1   Je ne vais pas dire ça.
2   Tu vas me dire ce que tu penses de ça.
3   Je ne doute pas de ça.
4   On imagine ça facilement.
5   Il n'avait pas pensé à ça.
6   On ne croit plus à ça.
7   Il est allé raconter ça à tout le monde.
8   Je me souviens de ça.

53 Tense use: situation in time

53.1 Two standpoints: in present or past reality
53.2 Direct speech and reported speech
53.3 Situation in time: use of adverbs and adverb phrases
53.4 *Venir de* + infinitive and *aller* + infinitive

Before working on this section, revise the names of various tenses used in French, and how these tenses are formed with regular and irregular verbs (**see 10**, noting from the English equivalents of the example sentences the meanings of these tenses, and see also the Verb tables, **56**). Now you are ready to look more closely at some of the ways in which tenses are used in French.

A list of the various tenses in French (present, future, passé composé, etc.) suggests that each tense occupies a fixed place, and has a meaning that can be defined independently of the others. In fact, the tenses together form a system, and their meaning comes from the place they occupy in that system, relative to one or more other tenses. How does this system relate to reality?

53.1 Two standpoints: in present or past reality

When we communicate in any language, we adopt one of two standpoints in relation to reality:

   1   **A standpoint in present reality**, the here and now, the situation we find ourselves in at the moment of speaking (or, sometimes, of writing);
   2   **A standpoint in past reality**, giving an account of an event or series of events viewed as over and done with, separate from the moment of writing (or, sometimes, of speaking).

1   Standpoint in present reality

From the standpoint of here and now, we can look back to an hour ago, to yesterday (etc.), or forward to this evening, or to next week (etc.). To let our listener know whether we are talking about the present moment, or are looking back or forward from the present, we use two kinds of markers (one or the other, or both):

- **adverbs**, including adverb phrases **(see 30.2)** and detached complements **(see 43–44)**;
- **verbs**, including different tenses **(see 10)** and certain auxiliary verbs **(see 39.1)**.

Present standpoint in English

Here are some examples of adverbs and verb tenses used in English to talk about the present, and to look back or forward from the present:

	Looking back from the present	Talking about the present	Looking forward from the present
	←———————————		———————————→
Adverbs	yesterday just now	now at the moment	tomorrow in a moment
Verbs	I saw him he was running	I know you're telling me!	I'll think about it

Depending on what has been said or is understood already, and on the amount of information one wants to convey, one uses:

- an **adverb** on its own: (When will you see her again?) **Tomorrow**.
- a **verb** on its own: (What did you do yesterday?) **I went** to the cinema.
- adverb + verb: **I'm feeling** quite tired **at the moment**.

Present standpoint in French

Here are some examples of adverbs and verb tenses used in French to talk about the present, and to look back or forward from the present:

	Looking back from the present	Talking about the present	Looking forward from the present
	←———————————		———————————→
Adverbs	*hier* *l'autre jour*	*maintenant* *en ce moment*	*demain* *l'année prochaine*
Verbs	*il pleuvait* *je l'ai vu*	*je sais*	*on verra* *je vais réfléchir*

Depending on what has been said or is already understood, and on the amount of information one wants to convey, one uses:

- an **adverb** on its own: *(Tu vas la voir bientôt?) Oui,* **demain**
- a **verb** on its own: *(Qu'est-ce que vous avez fait hier?) On* **est sortis**
- adverb + verb: *ça ne m'**intéresse** plus* **maintenant**

2   Standpoint in past reality

From a standpoint somewhere in the past, the narrator can look back to an even earlier period, or forward to something that happened at a later date. To indicate to the reader how each event is situated in time relative to the basic past standpoint, adverbs (etc.) and verb tenses (etc.) are used as markers, but a different set from those used for present reality. Here are some examples :

	Looking back from a point in the past	**Writing about a point in the past**	**Looking forward to a point in the past**
	←		———————→
Adverbs	*avant*	*alors*	*après*
	before(hand)	at that time	after(wards)
	la veille	*ce jour-là*	*le lendemain*
	the previous day	that day	the following day
Verbs	*ils avaient gagné*	*il était encore jeune*	*elle partirait*
	they had won	he was still young	she would leave
	ils venaient de gagner	*il devint roi*	*elle allait partir*
	they had just won	he became king	she was going to leave

Summary table showing the tenses which, in French, are used to indicate the six main relative positions in time:

1 **Standpoint: present reality**	(The different tenses relate to the present)	
Looking back from the present	**Talking about the present**	**Looking forward from the present**
←		———————→
PASSÉ COMP. or IMPERF.	PRESENT	FUTURE
j'ai travaillé I worked	*je travaille*	*je travaillerai*
il pleuvait it was raining	I work/I'm working	I will work
2 **Standpoint: past reality**	(The different tenses relate to a point in the past)	
Looking back from a point in the past	**Writing about a point in the past**	**Looking forward to a point in the past**
←		———————→
PLUPERFECT	PAST HIST. or IMPERF.	CONDITIONAL
elle avait travaillé	*elle travailla* she worked	*elle travaillerait*
she had worked	*il pleuvait* it was raining	she would work

The difference between the use of the passé composé and the imperfect in 1, and the past historic and the imperfect in 2, is one of aspect: **see 54**.

These two sets of three tenses can be mapped on to each other: each of the three tenses in 2 corresponds to a tense in 1, but moved from a present to a past standpoint. That is why the conditional tense is sometimes called the 'future in the past', and why the pluperfect tense is also called the 'past perfect'.

Standpoint 1 (present reality) is the normal standpoint one adopts when speaking: even when one is not talking about oneself, or about the present moment, one is openly involved in what one is talking about. Standpoint 1 is adopted in everyday conversation and in more formal situations such as interviews or presentations to an audience. It is also the natural standpoint for personal correspondence (paper or electronic), eyewitness accounts, 'feature' articles in the press, practical books, etc. Notice that the past historic does not appear in the set of tenses used for Standpoint 1.

Standpoint 2 (past reality) is the normal standpoint adopted for certain styles of writing: historical accounts, (auto)biographies, novels, etc., including accounts using the first person (*je*). Standpoint 2 is above all adopted in story-telling, including reading aloud or telling stories to children of all ages.

Exercice 53/1   **Point de vue: la réalité passée > Point de vue: la réalité présente**

Travail à deux > Mise en commun

Récrivez, en adoptant le point de vue de la réalité **présente**, et en faisant bien attention au temps de chaque verbe, le passage ci-dessous.

Début suggéré: Le Bressan **se dit** qu'en décembre, il **sera** appelé ...
                  Un jeune paysan envisage son avenir

Le Bressan s'est dit qu'en décembre, il serait appelé au service militaire. A sa libération, il se marierait avec la fille d'un voisin, qui lui apporterait trois hectares en dot; cela avait déjà été réglé. Il trouverait trois ou quatre autres hectares à louer et il paierait en journées de travail la paire de boeufs que son beau-père lui prêterait pour les labours et les charrois. Il devrait économiser pour acheter des bestiaux et du matériel et prendre un jour une ferme à son compte. Plus tard, économiser pour payer le fermage, et, plus tard encore, quand il aurait des enfants, pour prendre une ferme plus grande. La femme tiendrait la bourse.

Changing standpoint

The same standpoint (1 or 2) is not necessarily maintained throughout a conversation, a presentation, a book or an article:

- in the course of a conversation or a presentation centred on Standpoint 1 (present reality), a speaker might adopt Standpoint 2 (past reality) for a certain length of time, while giving an account of family or social history, for example;
- whenever conversations or trains of thought are quoted (within speech marks) in a novel, a biography, etc. centred on Standpoint 2 (past reality), these are likely to be centred on Standpoint 1 (present reality).

Passé composé and past historic

Although the passé composé is used in standpoint 1, and the past historic in standpoint 2, it is in fact possible to use them both in the course of the same text:

In spoken French, the past historic of the verb *être* is sometimes used, in Person 3 (*il/elle fut, ce fut*), to mark, perhaps humorously, a single event:

> *on n'avait pas pensé aux orages; ce **fut** la catastrophe!*
> we'd forgotten about the storms; it was a disaster!

In written French, the passé composé and the past historic can be used in the same text, and even in the same sentence: the past historic can be used to give a number of details about what happened, while the passé composé is used to describe the result, the outcome, the point that still affects things at the time of writing:

> *les auditions au Sénat ne **durèrent** qu'une journée. La bataille **fut** féroce; la Maison Blanche l'**a emporté***
> the Senate hearings lasted just one day. After a fierce battle, the White House was the winner

53.2 Direct speech and reported speech

Direct speech consists of words quoted, in a novel, for example, within quotation marks. In French, these can consist of «...», "...", '...'or –.... The words within these quotation marks are presented as if they had actually been said aloud (or thought). In common with all conversation, direct speech is normally centred on Standpoint 1 (present reality).

Reported speech consists of material presented (in a novel etc.), as having originated as actual speech (or thoughts). This is reworded in the form of a report, and integrated without quotation marks into the text as a whole. The text is likely to be centred on Standpoint 2 (past reality). To convert direct speech into reported speech, one transposes each of the three tenses, each time it occurs, from 1 to 2:

Standpoint 1		Standpoint 2
the present tense	→	a past tense (imperfect, passé composé, past historic)
a past tense (passé composé, imperfect)	→	the pluperfect
the future	→	the conditional

Looking back from the moment of speaking	Talking about the moment of speaking	Looking forward from the moment of speaking
← ———————————		——————————— →
1 Direct speech: *Elle dit/Elle a dit:*		
'J'ai travaillé'	*'Je travaille'*	*'Je travaillerai'*
'Il pleuvait'		
2 Reported speech: *Elle dit/Elle a dit*		
qu'elle avait travaillé	*qu'elle travaillait*	*qu'elle travaillerait*
qu'il avait plu	*qu'elle a travaillé*	
	qu'elle travailla	

The difference between the passé composé/past historic and the imperfect, is one of Aspect (**see 54**).

Pluperfect and conditional

These tenses are often used in subordinate clauses (**see 46**) and relative constructions (**see 42**) to provide details or explanations which originated in someone's thoughts, even though they are not presented as reported speech:

Direct	*Paul s'arrêta. 'Zut! se dit-il, j'ai oublié mon parapluie!'*
	Paul stopped. 'Drat!' he said, 'I've forgotten my umbrella!'
Reported	*Paul s'arrêta parce qu'il avait oublié son parapluie*
	Paul stopped because he'd forgotten his umbrella
Direct	*Marie s'est dit: 'Je vais économiser l'argent qu'il me faudra pour le voyage'.*
	Marie said: 'I'll save up the money I'll need for the trip'.
Reported	*Marie a enfin économisé l'argent qu'il lui faudrait pour le voyage*
	Marie managed to save up the money she needed/would need for the trip

Other changes are involved in transposing direct speech into reported speech:

● with direct speech, the originator of the words is indicated by an interpolation (**see 49.5**):

'J'arriverai demain', dit-il/a-t-il dit.

● with reported speech, *il dit* is used to introduce a completive clause (**see 49.1**):
*Il dit/il a dit **qu'il arriverait** le lendemain.*

● with reported speech, direct questions are transposed to indirect questions (**see 33.4**):

Direct speech; direct question: *'**Qu'est-ce qui** se passe?' demanda-t-elle.*
Reported speech; indirect question: *Elle demanda **ce qui** se passait.*

The above examples illustrate direct and reported speech in written texts; in spoken production, particularly spontaneous conversation, there are of course no speech marks, and the distinction between direct and reported speech tends to be ignored:

je lui ai demandé ce qu'il avait   (N3)

je lui ai demandé qu'est-ce qu'il avait   (N2)

I asked him what was the matter

Exercice 53/2   **Point de vue: la réalité présente > Point de vue: la réalité passée**
Travail à deux > Mise en commun

Récrivez, en adoptant le point de vue de la réalité passée, et en employant le discours indirect à la place du discours direct, le passage ci-dessous. Faites bien attention au temps de chaque verbe.

Début suggéré: J'ai dit à l'aumônier qu'**il avait** l'air si certain …
                             Un condamné à mort découvre la valeur de la vie

J'ai dit à l'aumônier: 'Vous avez l'air si certain, n'est-ce pas? Pourtant, aucune de vos certitudes ne vaut un cheveu de femme. Vous n'êtes même pas sûr d'être en vie puisque vous vivez comme un mort. Moi, j'ai l'air d'avoir les mains vides. Mais je suis sûr de moi, sûr de tout, plus sûr que vous, sûr de ma vie et de cette mort qui va venir. Oui, je n'ai que cela. Mais du moins, je tiens cette vérité autant qu'elle me tient. J'ai eu raison, j'ai encore raison, j'ai toujours raison. J'ai vécu de telle façon et j'aurais pu vivre de telle autre. J'ai fait ceci et je n'ai pas fait cela. Je n'ai pas fait telle chose, alors que j'ai fait telle autre. Et après? C'est comme si j'avais attendu pendant tout le temps cette minute et cette petite aube où je serai justifié. Rien, rien n'a d'importance et je sais bien pourquoi. Vous aussi savez pourquoi.'

L'Étranger, A Camus, © Éditions Gallimard (adapté)

53.3 Situation in time

The tense of the verb is used to situate an action or an event, not in 'absolute' time, but in time relative to the standpoint of the speaker or writer:

le train est parti   the train has left
le train partira   the train will leave

To situate the action or event more precisely, one uses adverbs (**see 53.1**):

le train est parti	*déjà*	already
	à l'instant (même)	a moment ago
	il y a dix minutes	ten minutes ago
	à midi vingt	at 12.20 p.m.
le train partira	*bientôt*	soon
	à l'instant	right away
	dans dix minutes	in ten minutes
	à minuit	at midnight

Some adverb phrases can refer back or forward, depending on the sense and tense of the verb:

tout à l'heure	just now	or	later
à l'instant	a moment ago	or	straight away

Pendant or *pour?*

Pendant is used when referring to past events, *pour* when referring to possibilities or intentions about the future:

> *la maison est restée vide **pendant** trois ans/**pendant** longtemps*
> the house remained empty for three years/for a long time
> *nous partons **pour** trois jours/**pour** plusieurs mois*
> we're going to be away for three days/for several months

53.4 *Venir de* + infinitive and *aller* + infinitive

Two verb constructions are used to situate an event in the immediate past or future:

a *venir de* + infinitive for the immediate past, and
b *aller* + infinitive for the immediate future.

Strictly speaking, these are aspect auxiliaries (**see 54**), but it is convenient to deal with them here.

Standpoint 1 When the standpoint is present reality, the present tense of *venir de* is used to look back from the present, and the present tense of *aller* is used to look forward from the present:

Looking back from the present	Talking about the present	Looking forward from the present
←		→
le train vient de partir	*le train part*	*le train va partir*
the train has just left	the train is leaving	the train is going to leave

Standpoint 2   When the standpoint is past reality, the imperfect tense of *venir de* is used to look back from the point in the past, and the imperfect tense of *aller* is used to look forward from the point in the past:

Looking back from a point in the past	Writing about a point in the past	Looking forward to a point in the past
←		→
le train venait de partir	*le train partait*	*le train allait partir*
the train had just left	the train was leaving	the train was going to leave

a   Referring back in time: *venir de* + infinitive

Only two tenses of the verb *venir* are used in this construction: present and imperfect.

The present tense is used when the reference is to present reality:

    'Vous arrivez trop tard: le train vient de partir'
    'You're too late: the train's just left'

The imperfect tense is used when the reference is to past reality:

    quand je suis arrivé à la gare, le train venait de partir
    when I arrived at the station, the train had just left

The equivalent construction in English, 'has just', 'had just', presents the fact as an event in the past, whereas *il vient de, il venait de* views the event as still present in the mind of the speaker or narrator.

Exercice 53/3   *Venir de*   Travail individuel

Récrivez les phrases ci-dessous en employant, au temps qui convient, la construction venir de + infinitif.

Exemple: Le train est parti.
Réponse: Le train **vient de partir.**

Exemple: Le train était parti.
Réponse: Le train **venait de partir.**

1   Ils ont vendu leur maison.
2   J'ai compris ce qui se passe.
3   Il avait trouvé la solution.
4   L'avion avait atterri.
5   Ils avaient nommé un nouveau directeur.
6   On a appris la nouvelle.
7   Ta mère a téléphoné.
8   Une idée affreuse lui était venue à l'esprit.
9   Elle avait terminé son premier roman.
10   Les enfants sont rentrés.

The *venir de* construction is used to draw attention to the fact that an event has just happened, but its meaning is weaker than 'has/had just'. It can be made more dramatic by the addition of *juste* or *à l'instant*:

c'était trop tard: le bus venait juste de partir

it was too late: the bus had just that minute left

vous vouliez voir Mme X? ah, c'est dommage, elle vient de sortir à l'instant

so you wanted to speak to Ms X? what a pity: she went out just this minute

USE OF PRESENT TENSE TO REFER TO PAST REALITY

IN ENGLISH, the use of the present tense to recount past events is characteristic of very informal situations (N1): 'so this fellow comes up to me and he says ...'

IN FRENCH, considerable use is made of the present tense for dramatic effect:

● in conversation, the passé composé is used at the start of a story, to situate it in the past; then the present is used to tell the rest of the story:

je vais vous dire ce qui s'est passé vendredi matin: me voilà dans mon bureau, et quelqu'un frappe à la porte. Je dis 'Entrez!' et la porte s'ouvre ...

I'll tell you what happened Friday morning: there I was in my office, when there was a knock at the door. I called 'Come in!' and the door opened ...

● in newspaper and radio/TV reports, when it is clear that an account is being given of events in the past: for example, in a summary of the events leading up to the release of a political prisoner:

peu de temps après, sa condamnation est transformée en détention à perpétuité; fin décembre, les autorités le grâcient ...

shortly afterwards, his sentence was commuted to life imprisonment; at the end of December, the authorities granted him a reprieve ...

What happens in such cases is that the speaker or writer, although adopting Standpoint 2 (centred on past reality), uses the tense system associated with Standpoint 1: present tense for the flow of events, plus past and future tenses to refer back or forward in time.

In an obituary, for example, the writer might describe a sequence of events in the present tense, but then look forward from this sequence to a point later in time:

en 1913 il écrit 'Le Vent' qui ne sera publié qu'après sa mort en 1938

in 1913 he wrote 'The Wind' which was not published until after his death in 1938

This example underlines the importance, for understanding and using the system of tenses in French, of seeing the system as a set of relativities, not of absolutes.

b   Referring forward in time: *aller* + infinitive

Only two tenses of the verb *aller* are used in this construction: present and imperfect.

The present is used when the reference is to present reality:

> '***Courez*** *vite au quai numéro 3: votre train* ***va*** *partir!*'
> 'Hurry to platform 3: your train is about to leave!'

The imperfect is used when the reference is to past reality:

> *on a couru au quai numéro 3 parce qu'on nous* ***a dit*** *que notre train* ***allait*** *partir*
> we ran to platform 3 because they told us our train was about to leave

In this construction, the same tenses are used in both the English and the French versions: present, or imperfect: the event is viewed from the standpoint of the speaker or narrator, rather than as an event in the future.

Exercice 53/4   *Aller*   Travail individuel

Récrivez les phrases ci-dessous en employant, au temps qui convient, la construction aller + infinitif.

Exemple: Je lui téléphonerai.
Réponse: Je vais lui téléphoner.

Exemple: Je lui téléphonerais.
Réponse: J'allais lui téléphoner.

1   Elle repassera le bac.
2   Ils ne seront pas contents.
3   Elle m'a dit qu'elle ne partirait pas.
4   Je ne rentrerai pas à la maison.
5   Vous m'avez dit que vous rangeriez votre chambre.
6   J'ai appris qu'il ne donnerait plus de concerts.
7   On aura une contravention.
8   Vous comprendrez tout à l'heure.
9   Je lui ai répété que je réparerais les dégâts.
10   Il m'a informé qu'il préviendrait la police.

The *aller* construction is used instead of the future tense to stress, not necessarily that something will happen immediately, but that the speaker intends it to happen, or feels certain that it will happen:

> je **vais rentrer** *à la maison; ça* **ira** *mieux là-bas*
> I'm going home; I'll feel better there
> je **vais téléphoner** *au médecin; il me* **donnera** *quelque chose*
> I'll phone the doctor; he'll prescribe something

Compare, for example, *tu vas voir* and *tu verras*:
- *tu vas voir* leads the listener to expect an immediate demonstration;
- *tu verras* stresses that something will happen, however long it takes.

The *aller* construction is one way of expressing the imperative in French:

> *Messieurs, vous allez me dire ce qui s'est passé*
> now tell me what happened

Other ways of expressing the imperative include: *dites-moi* **(see 50.3)** and *je veux que vous me disiez* **(see 48)**.

USE OF PRESENT TENSE TO REFER TO FUTURE REALITY

In French, even more than in English, the immediate future can be expressed by using the present tense:

> *qu'est-ce qu'on fait demain/ce soir/maintenant?*
> what shall we do tomorrow/tonight/now?
> *le directeur vient d'arriver; je vous le passe*
> the manager's just got in; I'll put you through (to him)
> *et voici mon fils aîné; il passe son bac cette année*
> and this is my oldest boy; he's taking his A levels this year

This use of the present tense (and of the passé composé) presents the event or action as certain to happen: the speaker invites the listener to see a promised action or event as being already completed:

> *j'arrive!*   I'll be right with you!
> *j'ai bientôt fini*   I'll soon be finished

54 Tense use: aspect

- **54.1 Imperfect or passé composé/past historic? what difference does it make?**
- **54.2 *Pendant* or *depuis*? which tense?**
- **54.3 Verbs used with *être*: *elle est sortie*; *il (s')est couché*: two meanings**
- **54.4 Aspect auxiliaries: *être en train de, être sur le point de***

Tense

In **53.1**, we saw how two sub-sets of tenses (past – present – future, and pluperfect – past – conditional) are used in French to situate actions, events (etc.) in time relative to either:

- present reality: the moment when the speaker is speaking or the writer is writing, or
- past reality: a point in past time from which past events are viewed by the speaker or writer.

Aspect

In **54**, we look at some of the ways in which certain tenses in French (in particular the passé composé and the past historic on one hand, and the imperfect on the other) are used not only to situate events in time relative to Standpoint 1 or Standpoint 2, but also relative to each other.

Various either/or definitions can be made of the ways in which aspect functions in French: perfective/imperfective, non-secant/secant, and so on. At the risk of simplification, one main distinction, as regards aspect, will be made here: presentation of a process as completed (*aspect accompli*) or continuing (*aspect non accompli*).

The aim of this section is to help you to choose the appropriate tense, generally when you are hesitating between the passé composé (or the past historic) on one hand, and the imperfect tense on the other.

54.1 Imperfect or passé composé/past historic?

There are important differences between English and French in the way that the distinction between completed and continuing aspect is expressed.

Present tenses in English and French

IN ENGLISH, there are two forms of the verb: the simple present, 'she runs', which can be used in almost all cases (completed, habitual and even continuing action), and the present continuous, 'she is running', which can be used to express continuing aspect.

IN FRENCH, there is only one form of the verb: the simple present, *elle court*, which is usable in all cases. To emphasise continuing aspect, one can use an aspect auxiliary **(see 54.4)**: *elle est en train de* courir.

Past tenses in English and French

IN ENGLISH, there are three forms of the verb:

- the past continuous, ('she was running'), which can be used to express continuing aspect;
- the present perfect, ('she has run'), which can be used to express completed aspect;
- the simple past, ('she ran'), which is neutral as regards aspect, and can be used to express either continuing or completed aspect.

An additional aspectual function can be provided by the use of the auxiliary 'used to': 'she used to run' (habitual aspect). The auxiliary 'did' can be used for emphasis ('she did run'), and in questions ('did she run?').

IN FRENCH, there are also three forms of the verb, but their distribution as regards aspect is different:

- the imperfect (*elle courait*) is used to express continuing aspect, but also habitual action (English 'used to run');
- the passé composé (*elle a couru*) and the past historic (*elle courut*) are used to express completed aspect.

This means that the simple past in English ('she ran') has three equivalents in French: *elle courait, elle a couru, elle courut*. To choose correctly between these three, you have to know:

- the forms of French tenses (stems and endings) **(see 9–10)**;
- the difference in meaning and use between the passé composé and the past historic **(see 53.1)**;
- the difference as regards aspect between the imperfect and the other two past tenses.

> **Passé composé and past historic**
> Both are used when describing a series of events in time, in the order in which they happened: the listener or reader follows a moving film where each successive sequence answers the question 'What happened next?'.

One will hear (or say) a succession of verbs in the passé composé in an everyday conversation where an account is given of a series of actions:

j'ai entendu un bruit, alors j'ai regardé par la fenêtre, mais je n'ai rien vu d'extraordinaire
I heard a noise, so I looked out of the window, but I didn't see anything unusual

One will read (or write) a succession of verbs in the past historic in a historical account:

*Napoléon **gagna** plusieurs batailles, **devint** premier Consul en 1799, et **se fit couronner** Empereur cinq ans plus tard* (N3)
Napoleon won several battles, became First Consul in 1799, and was crowned Emperor five years later

The passé composé and the past historic are used to describe any process, however long, which is presented as completed, or where the starting or finishing point is explicitly situated in time:

*le train **est parti** à 10h30*
the train left at 10.30

*après son accession au trône en 1837, Victoria **régna** jusqu'à sa mort en 1901* (N3)
after her accession to the throne in 1837, Victoria reigned until her death in 1901

Imperfect tense

The imperfect tense is used to take a snapshot or make a freeze frame of a moving film: the process described in the imperfect is taken out of time, and answers the question: 'What was going on at that point in time?'

Many processes can be described either in the passé composé/past historic or in the imperfect, depending on whether they are being presented as completed (passé composé/past historic) or continuing (imperfect).

Completed: *il **a plu/il a fait beau** toute la journée*
it rained/it was fine all day
(passé composé: the rain/the fine weather is presented as a whole process which is completed; this is indicated by the phrase *toute la journée*)

Continuing: *quand on s'est réveillés, **il pleuvait/il faisait beau***
when we woke up, it was raining/it was fine
(imperfect: the rain/fine weather, which in reality had a beginning and an end, is presented as a process which is not in any sequence of events; there is no indication of start or finish, it happened to be going on at a particular point in time)

The same event, therefore, can be described using either the passé composé/past historic or the imperfect, depending on how it relates to another event.

For example, suppose that M. Dupont is telling a friend what happened when he and his wife discovered that their house had been broken into:

j'ai téléphoné à la police, et puis ma femme est allée chez les voisins
I phoned the police, and then my wife went round to the neighbours'
(the passé composé presents the two actions as events that took place one after the other)

Or M. Dupont might have said:

pendant que je téléphonais à la police, ma femme est allée chez les voisins
while I was phoning the police, my wife went round to the neighbours'
(the first action has probably already been described; now the imperfect presents this action not as an event, but as the context in which the other action, presented in the passé composé, took place)

Or M. Dupont might have said, possibly in answer to a question from his friend:

j'ai téléphoné à la police pendant que ma femme était chez les voisins
I phoned the police while my wife was at the neighbours'
(M. Dupont has probably already said that his wife had gone to the neighbours'; now, the imperfect presents this action as the context in which the other action, presented in the passé composé, takes place)

The use of the appropriate past tense (passé composé or imperfect) in each case forms part of the organisation and presentation of the account M. Dupont gives of the break-in.

Exercice 54/1   **Imparfait ou passé composé?**   Travail individuel

Complétez chacune des phrases ci-dessous en ajoutant le verbe (entre parenthèses) à l'imparfait ou au passé composé, selon le sens de la phrase.

Exemple: Elle _ l'anglais pendant six ans.   (étudier)
Réponse: Elle **a étudié** l'anglais pendant six ans.

Exemple: Je lui ai demandé pourquoi il _ le japonais.   (étudier)
Réponse: Je lui ai demandé pourquoi il **étudiait** le japonais.

1	Il _ de fumer il y a deux ans.	(arrêter)
2	Elle était très énervée: elle n' _ pas de regarder autour d'elle.	(arrêter)
3	Quand je suis arrivé, il _ de faire la vaisselle.	(finir)
4	Alphonse! Est-ce que tu _ tes devoirs?	(finir)
5	Dans son rêve, elle _ un oiseau qui _ à_un aigle.	(voir, ressembler)
6	Quand ils _ de se marier, ils se _ depuis cinq ans.	(décider, connaître)
7	Quand ils _ chez nous, on _ se promener au bord de la mer.	(venir, aller)
8	On _ au restaurant parce qu'il ne _ plus rien à la maison.	(aller, rester)
9	Quand elle _ la porte, elle _ qu'il _ à torrents.	(ouvrir, découvrir, pleuvoir)

Part ten: Constructing texts

Key to the exercise 54/2
verbi di not matur :9, 26

Exercice 54/2   Imparfait ou passe compose?   Travail individuel

Complétez cet extrait du roman de A Camus, L'Étranger (1942) en ajoutant, à l'imparfait ou au passé composé selon le sens, les vingt-sept verbes dans la liste ci-dessous.

1	vouloir	8	avancer	15	retarder	22	nager
2	descendre	9	ajouter	16	avoir	23	laisser
3	se jeter	10	dire	17	finir	24	être
4	attendre	11	avoir	18	plonger	25	être
5	parler	12	être	19	entrer	26	s'éloigner
6	remarquer	13	faire	20	se jeter	27	se sentir
7	avoir	14	commencer	21	perdre		

A la plage

Masson voulait se baigner, mais sa femme et Raymond ne (1) pas venir. Nous (2) tous les trois et Marie (3) immédiatement dans l'eau. Masson et moi, nous (4) un peu. Lui (5) lentement et j' (6) qu'il (7) l'habitude de compléter tout ce qu'il (8) par un "et je dirai plus", même quand, au fond, il n' (9) rien au sens de sa phrase. A propos de Marie, il m' (10): "Elle est épatante, et je dirai plus, charmante." Puis je n' (11) plus attention à ce tic parce que j' (12) occupé à_éprouver que le soleil me (13) du bien. Le sable (14) à chauffer sous les pieds. J' (15) encore l'envie que j' (16) de l'eau, mais j' (17) par dire à Masson: "On y va?" J' (18). Lui (19) dans l'eau doucement et (20) quand il (21) pied. Il (22) à la brasse et assez mal, de sorte que je l' (23) pour rejoindre Marie. L'eau (24) froide et j' (25) content de nager. Avec Marie, nous (26) et nous (27) d'accord dans nos gestes et dans notre contentement.   © Éditions Gallimard

---

Exercice 54/3   **Imparfait ou passé simple?**   Travail individuel

Complétez cet extrait du roman de M Duras, Le Marin de Gibraltar (1952) en ajoutant, à l'imparfait ou au passé simple selon le sens, les vingt verbes dans la liste ci-dessous.

1	devoir	6	avoir	11	descendre	16	demander
2	monter	7	allumer	12	voir	17	être
3	être	8	grogner	13	être	18	dire
4	être	9	se réveiller	14	remonter	19	savoir
5	dormir	10	être	15	réveiller	20	être

A bord d'un yacht

(Après une discussion sur la possibilité d'un voyage en Afrique, le narrateur s'endort.)

Je dormis longtemps. Je (1) me réveiller un peu avant le dîner. Je (2) aussitôt au bar. Elle n'y (3) pas. Seul Épaminondas y (4), allongé sur deux fauteuils. Il (5) profondément. Il n'y (6) personne d'autre à bord. J' (7). Épaminondas (8), mais ne (9) pas. Les chauffe-plats (10) éteints, on n'avait pas fait le dîner. Je (11) en courant à la cale et je (12) que les deux autos (13) là. Je (14) lentement au bar, je (15) Épaminondas, et je lui (16) où elle (17). Il me (18) ce que je (19), qu'elle (20) dans sa cabine.   © Éditions Gallimard

Six verbs to note: *être, avoir, devoir, pouvoir, savoir, vouloir*

The past tense you will meet and use most often of these verbs is the imperfect: *était, avait, devait, pouvait, savait, voulait.* But you will also need to recognise and to use the passé composé forms of these verbs: *a été, a eu, a dû, a pu, a su, a voulu,* and to recognise the past historic forms: *fut, eut, dut, put, sut, voulut.* With these verbs, the difference of aspect (between the imperfect and the passé composé/past historic) is particularly important for the meaning of the sentence as a whole:

Être

> *j'**étais** surpris(e) par son attitude*   I was surprised by his/her attitude
>
> (imperfect: part of a general description of the speaker's impressions)
>
> *j'**ai été** surpris(e) par son attitude*   I was surprised by his/her attitude
>
> (passé composé: a reference to a particular occasion which caused surprise)

Avoir

> *il y **avait** une foule rassemblée devant*   there was a crowd outside the Town Hall
> *l'Hôtel de ville*
>
> (imperfect: the speaker is describing the scene as (s)he found it)
>
> *il y **a eu** un long silence*   there was a long silence
>
> (passé composé: the silence is presented as the next thing that happened)

Devoir

> *Pierre **devait** parler de cette affaire au directeur*
>
> Pierre had to/he was due to mention the matter to the manager
>
> (imperfect: the action is presented as something in Pierre's mind, not as something that has (yet) taken place in reality)
>
> *Pierre **a dû** parler de cette affaire au directeur*
>
> Pierre had to/was obliged to mention/must have mentioned the matter to the manager
>
> (passé composé: the action is presented as having actually taken place, or the speaker assumes that it has)

Pouvoir

> *que faire? on **pouvait** forcer la serrure, mais on a préféré téléphoner à la police*
>
> what should we do? we could break the lock, but we decided to phone the police instead
>
> (imperfect: the speaker presents breaking the lock as a possibility which was in their minds, but which did not take place in reality)
>
> *heureusement, on **a pu** forcer la serrure sans trop de mal*
>
> fortunately, we managed to break the lock without too much difficulty
>
> (passé composé: the speaker describes an event which actually took place, probably as one of a sequence of events all described using the passé composé)

Savoir

> *je ne **savais** jamais ce qu'il fallait faire dans ces occasions*
>
> I never knew what to do on these occasions
>
> (imperfect: the speaker describes a habitual state of affairs, without situating it in time, or giving a starting or finishing point)
>
> *je n'**ai** jamais **su** ce qui s'était passé*　　　　I never found out what had happened
>
> (passé composé: the speaker has tried to find out, but has given up: the process is presented as completed, over and done with; compare *je ne sais toujours pas . . .*, where the speaker suggests that (s)he'd still like to know)

Vouloir

> *Paul n'a rien dit: il **voulait** que tout s'arrange sans violence*
>
> Paul said nothing: he wanted everything to be sorted out peacefully
>
> (imperfect: the speaker describes Paul's intention, a state of mind which lasted for an unspecified period)
>
> *M. Dupont **a voulu** parler, mais sa femme est intervenue*
>
> M. Dupont tried to/was about to speak, but his wife intervened
>
> (passé composé: the speaker describes an actual attempt by M. Dupont to speak)

Exercice 54/4　　*Etre, avoir, devoir, pouvoir, savoir, vouloir*: imparfait ou passé composé?　　　　　　　　　　　　　　　　　Travail individuel

Complétez les phrases ci-dessous en ajoutant être, avoir, devoir, pouvoir, savoir, vouloir, à l'imparfait ou au passé composé, selon le sens de la phrase.

Exemple:　Quand elle m'a téléphoné, j' _ trop fatigué pour lui parler sérieusement.　(être)
Réponse:　Quand elle m'a téléphoné, j'**étais** trop fatigué pour lui parler sérieusement.

Exemple:　Quand elle m'a téléphoné, j' _ très surpris par le ton de sa voix.　　　　(être)
Réponse:　Quand elle m'a téléphoné, j'**ai été** très surpris par le ton de sa voix.

1　Il y _ tellement de circulation qu'elle _ attendre cinq minutes avant de pouvoir traverser la rue.
　　　　　　　　　　　　　　　　　　　　　　　　　　　　　　　(avoir, devoir)
2　Il _ ouvrir la porte, mais elle _ coincée.　　　　　　　　　　(vouloir, être)
3　Soudain, elle _ l'intuition qu'il _ à quoi elle pensait.　　　　(avoir, savoir)
4　Heureusement, le directeur _ de bonne humeur ce jour-là, et on _ lui expliquer notre problème.
　　　　　　　　　　　　　　　　　　　　　　　　　　　　　　　(être, pouvoir)
5　Après plusieurs efforts, on _ ce qu'ils _.　　　　　(savoir, vouloir)
6　Il _ pris de panique quand il a compris qu'il _ terminer le rapport pour le
　　lendemain.　　　　　　　　　　　　　　　　　　　　　　　(être, devoir)

54.2 *Pendant* or *depuis*? Which tense?

Pendant

Pendant is used to express the duration in time or space of a process, when the process is completed, over and done with; if the reference is to past reality, the verb to which the adverb phrase is attached is in the passé composé/past historic:

> *j'y **ai travaillé pendant** six mois, puis j'ai trouvé autre chose*
> I worked there for six months, then I found something else
> *il **est resté** prisonnier des guérilleros **pendant** plusieurs années*
> he was held prisoner by the guerillas for several years

Pendant can be omitted, if the meaning remains clear:

> *j'y ai travaillé six mois, puis . . .*
> *il est resté plusieurs années prisonnier . . .*

Pendant can be replaced by **durant** (at the end of the phrase) to emphasise the duration or the length of the process:

> *j'y ai travaillé six mois durant*

Used at the start of the phrase, *durant* corresponds to English 'during':

> *quelqu'un a essayé de forcer la porte durant la nuit*
> someone tried to break in during the night

In general, the use of ***pendant*** with the passé composé/past historic or the pluperfect leads the listener/reader to expect, not only that a particular stage or process is over, but that some information will be given about what else happened next. The use of ***depuis***, on the other hand, takes the listener/reader right up to the present (or past) point in time.

Depuis

Depuis, like *pendant*, is used in adverb phrases expressing the duration of a process, but with the idea that the process is continuing up to the present time or to a particular point in the past.

This continuity, and the incomplete nature of the process, are usually reflected in the tense of the verb: present (for Standpoint 1: present reality) or imperfect (for Standpoint 2: past reality):

> *on **habite** ici **depuis** dix ans déjà*   we've been living here for ten years now
> *quand il a perdu son emploi, ils **habitaient** à Londres **depuis** dix ans*
> when he lost his job, they'd been living in London for ten years

IN ENGLISH, past and pluperfect continuous tenses are used ('have been -ing' and 'had been -ing').

The passé composé (or the pluperfect) is used with *depuis* if the verb is in the negative:

depuis cinq ans, il n'a plus travaillé au projet

for the past five years, he hasn't worked on the project

depuis cinq ans, il n'avait plus travaillé au projet

for the previous five years, he hadn't worked on the project

In everyday conversation (N2), a cleft construction **(see 51.2)**, *ça fait (longtemps/ quelques jours/des années* etc.) *que* is used in preference to *depuis*:

ça fait dix ans déjà qu'on habite ici   (N2)

ça fait des années que je travaille sur ce projet   (N2)

Exercice 54/5   *Depuis* + présent ou imparfait, ou *pendant* + passé composé?

Travail à deux > Mise en commun

a   Complétez les phrases ci-dessous en ajoutant (i) depuis ou pendant, (ii) le verbe (indiqué entre parenthèses) au présent, à l'imparfait ou au passé composé, selon le sens de la phrase.

b   Si vous jugez que plus d'une réponse est possible, notez les deux réponses, et discutez-en avec le reste du groupe.

Exemple: C'est vrai qu'elle _ sur ce projet _ plusieurs années. (travailler)

*Réponses possibles:*C'est vrai qu'elle **travaille** sur ce projet **depuis** plusieurs années.

(sens: le projet n'est pas terminé; elle y travaille encore)

C'est vrai qu'elle a **travaillé** sur ce projet **pendant** plusieurs années.

(sens: le projet est terminé)

1   Je _ là-bas _ six mois seulement, puis je suis revenu.   (rester)

2   Quand je les ai connus, ils _ mariés _ quinze ans.   (être)

3   On _ cette maison _ dix ans.   (habiter)

4   Ah! vous voilà! On _ de vous contacter _ ce matin.   (essayer)

5   _ deux jours, la police _ sans rien trouver, et puis elle est tombée sur un indice significatif.

(chercher)

6   L'année dernière à Noël, le mistral _ _ huit jours.   (souffler)

54.3 Verbs used with *être: elle est sortie, il (s')est couché*: two meanings

The compound tenses case of verbs which are conjugated with *être* **(see 10.3b)** have two meanings, depending on whether one is presenting an event as:

a   an action in the past, or

b   the present state resulting from that action.

a Action (passé composé of the verb): the past participle is part of the verb form:

il *est resté à la maison*	he stayed at home
il *est passé chez le boulanger*	he stopped at/called in at the baker's

b State (present tense of *être* + past participle of the verb): the past participle functions as an adjective:

il est *resté à la maison*	he's still at home
l'orage est *passé maintenant*	the storm is over now

Other examples:

French: action or state	English: action	state
elle est sortie	she went out	she's (gone) out
il est parti	he went away/he left	he's (gone) away
il est mort	he died	he's dead
elle est rentrée	she returned/she came home	she's back/she's home
ils sont arrivés	they arrived	they're here

If the standpoint **(see 53.1)** is not present reality, as in the above examples, but past reality, the difference of aspect (**a** an action in the past, or **b** the present result of the action) is marked in the same way:

a Action (pluperfect) The past participle is part of the verb form:

il *était resté à la maison*	he'd stayed at home
il *était passé chez le boulanger*	he'd stopped at/he'd called in at the baker's

b State (imperfect) The past participle functions as an adjective:

il était *resté à la maison*	he was still at home
l'orage était *passé*	the storm was over

Other examples:

French: action or state	English: action	state
elle était sortie	she'd gone out	she was out
il était parti	he'd gone away/he'd left	he was away
il était mort	he'd died	he was dead
elle était rentrée	she'd returned/she'd come home	she was back/she was home

Pronominal verbs: *elle (s')est assise* etc.: double aspect

The same difference of aspect is found with pronominal verbs **(see 36.3)**, but there is a difference in the way they are used:

a Action (passé composé of *s'asseoir*)

The past participle is part of the verb form, which includes the reflexive pronoun:

se trouvant soudain mal, elle s'est assise sur une chaise

she suddenly felt faint, so she sat (down) on a chair

b State (present of *être* + past participle *assise*)

The past participle functions as an adjective; there is no reflexive pronoun:

> *chaque fois que je vais la voir, elle est **assise** sur une chaise devant la télé*
>
> each time I visit her, she's sitting on a chair in front of the TV

Examples:

(Standpoint 1: present reality)

Action	*(se coucher)*	*il s'est couché*	he went to bed/he lay down
State	*(être couché)*	*il est couché*	he's in bed/he's lying down
Action	*(se décider)*	*elle s'est décidée*	she's made up her mind
State	*(être décidé)*	*elle est décidée*	her mind's made up

(Standpoint 2: past reality)

Action	*(se coucher)*	*il s'était couché*	he'd gone to bed/he'd lain down
State	*(être couché)*	*il était couché*	he was in bed/he was lying down
Action	*(se décider)*	*elle s'était décidée*	she'd made up her mind
State	*(être décidé)*	*elle était décidée*	her mind was made up

(see Exercice 36/5, page 316)

54.4 Aspect auxiliaries (for *venir de* and *aller*, see 53.4)

Certain verbs or phrases are used as auxiliaries, followed by the verb in the infinitive, to indicate aspect:

Etre en train de: continuing process

This construction is used, in the absence of a present continuous in French (which would correspond to English 'is -ing'), to emphasise that a process is still continuing at the time of speaking; it can also be used in the imperfect:

> *il **est** toujours **en train de** maltraiter son chien*
>
> he's always ill-treating his dog
>
> *non, tu ne me déranges pas du tout: j'**étais** (juste) **en train de** ranger de vieux papiers*
>
> no, you're not disturbing me at all: I was (just) sorting out some old papers

Etre sur le point de: process about to begin

This construction is used to describe something that is or was about to happen:

> *ah, te voilà! j'**étais sur le point de** m'inquiéter*
>
> ah, there you are! I was nearly beginning to get worried

This construction has a similar meaning to *aller* + infinitive **(see 53.4)**.

Avoir l'habitude de: **habitual process**

This construction corresponds to English 'usually', and to the French imperfect tense with the meaning of 'used to':

> *je n'ai pas l'habitude de mentir!*
>
> I don't usually lie!
>
> *elle avait l'habitude de sortir faire un tour tous les après-midi*
>
> she used to go out/she was in the habit of going out for a walk every afternoon

Commencer à, cesser de **etc.: marking the start or end of a process**

These verbs, constructed with an infinitive are used to mark the start of a process (*commencer à, se mettre à*) or the end of a process (*cesser de, finir de, achever de*).

Part
eleven

Using appropriate language

55 Using appropriate language

55.1 **Language in use**
55.2 **Degrees of formality**
55.3 **Hybrid language**
55.4 **Examples of spontaneous, informal French**

55.1 Language in use

In any language, most of what you hear, read and use remains the same in all situations. However, certain ways of speaking, certain words or phrases, certain ways of constructing sentences, are appropriate in some situations, but less so in others depending on whether the situation is public or private, formal or informal, involving family, friends, strangers, foreigners, teachers, and so on: think of the choice of *vous* or *tu* as a form of address, or whether the negative is expressed by *ne* + verb + *pas* or just verb + *pas* (**see 34.1**).

As a learner of French, you need above all to practise and understand standard French (N3) (usually, but not always, written) and conversational French (N2) (usually, but not always, spoken). In *French Grammar Explained*, examples of usage appropriate to very formal (N4) and very informal (N1) situations have been kept to a minimum.

The following table shows the types of situation for which the examples labelled N1, N2, N3, N4 would be appropriate.

■ Table of types of language, with examples of situations

Label used in *French Grammar Explained*:			
N4	**N3**	**N2**	**N1**
Type of language — French used for special purposes, e.g. professional	Standard French	Conversational French	French used for special effects, e.g. slang
Situation: Very formal	Relatively formal	Relatively informal	Very informal
Examples: **(1) speech** — Public speech, including special occasions e.g. wedding/funeral	Radio/TV news bulletin	Conversation with older people or in mixed age group	Conversation in groups of young people
	Formal interview e.g. for job	Radio/TV interview Sports commentary	Conversation among workmates etc.,
Official announcement	Oral exposé/ presentation	Class discussion/ debate/follow-up to exposé	e.g. doctors, police, drivers, labourers
		Large committee meeting (+ some N3) Small working group meeting (+ some N1)	
(2) writing — Scientific/ medical/legal article/document (using specialist terms)	Formal letter e.g. job application Report/serious article in magazine/newspaper Student report, essay etc.	Personal letter (+ some N1)	
N4 + N3 + N2 + N1: Creative/imaginative writing, literature: N4 + N3 + N2 + N1			

55.2 Degrees of formality

No label Most examples (words, phrases, sentences) in *French Grammar Explained* are unlabelled. This means that they can be used in all situations, formal and informal: they are part of both standard French (N3) and everyday French (N2).

N3 **Standard French.** Used in these situations, N3 words/phrases do not draw attention to themselves; if used in everyday conversation they stand out as relatively formal.

N2 **Everyday French.** Used in these situations, N2 words/phrases do not draw attention to themselves; if used in reports, essays, business letters, etc., they stand out as relatively informal.

N4 **French for special purposes.** Used in any situation other than very formal, N4 words/phrases draw attention to themselves. In dictionaries, N4 words and expressions are labelled 'formal'/*soutenu*, 'archaic'/*archaïque*, 'dated'/*vieilli*, or 'management'/*entreprise*, 'literary'/*littéraire*, etc.

N1 **French for special effects.** Used in any situation, N1 words/phrases draw attention to themselves. Sometimes they are used deliberately, in order to shock; at other times they are used inadvertently, constituting a *faux pas*. In dictionaries, N1 words and expressions are labelled 'informal'/*familier*, 'very informal'/*populaire*, 'very colloquial'/*très familier*, 'slang'/*argot*, or 'vulgar', 'taboo', 'racist'/*vulgaire, tabou, raciste*, etc.

No label, N3 and N2 mean 'safe to use', but N4 and N1 mean 'handle with care!'

No label, **N3 and N2** denote words and phrases which are valid for all. They constitute your entry ticket to the French language game: N3 corresponds to what most French speakers regard as correct French, and N2 corresponds to what most French speakers actually say in spontaneous conversation. Most French speakers will expect you, as a non-native speaker, to avoid extremes of formality and informality. Practise two kinds of French: one for informal, one for formal communication; link the two in your mind (use or non-use of *ne*, for example), but keep them distinct.

N4 and N1, on the other hand are like a membership card to a particular French language club: use them in the wrong places, and you have to take the consequences. N4 or N1 words/phrases draw attention to themselves – and to their user.

In all academic work, avoid slang, and do not use impressive-sounding phrases as a substitute for ideas and clear expression.

55.3 Hybrid language

We tend to equate spoken language with informality, and written language with formality, and indeed this is often the case in reality. However, much of the language we encounter is in fact a hybrid of spoken and written language.

Interviews and many **quotations** in newspapers and magazines started life as recordings of spontaneous speech, which has been rewritten or re-drafted so as to make it easier to read. A literal transcription of spontaneous speech, with all its natural pauses, hesitations, repetitions, false starts, slips of the tongue and so on, is difficult, even irritating, to read.

Personal correspondence consists largely of spontaneous thoughts. Since the original message is expressed through the written code of the language, a certain amount of sorting and tidying-up takes place, compared with, say, a telephone conversation.

News bulletins, on radio and television, begin life as written reports; the result, for the listener/viewer, is speech that is more formal than anything we would say ourselves in conversation. We accept this kind of language as appropriate for the purpose.

Other forms of **public speaking**, such as presentations or exposés which you make in front of a group or class, or talks or lectures which you listen to, are generally based on written notes prepared beforehand. As with news bulletins, the result is more formal than spontaneous spoken communication, but the speaker can make it acceptable and understandable by delivering it in a semi-spontaneous manner: varying the tone and pace of delivery, making sufficient pauses, being audible without shouting, and not reading verbatim from a fully written-out text.

55.4 Examples of spontaneous, informal French

Here are some of the main features of spontaneous, informal French (N2) which you may wish to imitate, when speaking or writing informally.

In the right-hand column, the equivalent version in careful, formal French (N3) is given; you should use this version whenever you are speaking or writing in a formal situation.

N2 (informal)	**N3 (formal)**
Use of *tu, te, ton* etc. instead of *vous, votre* etc. (9.1)	
salut, Jean! Qu'est-ce que tu racontes?	*bonjour, monsieur! Comment allez-vous?*
ciao, Jeanne! Je te passerai un coup de fil	*au revoir, madame! Je ne manquerai pas de vous téléphoner*
Use of *on* instead of *nous* (9.1)	
on a fait un bon gueuleton	*nous avons fait un repas excellent*
nous on y est pas allés	*nous nous sommes abstenus*

Silent *l* in *il, ils*

il [i] *travaille; ils* [iz] *arrivent* | *il* [il] *travaille; ils* [ilz] *arrivent*

No inversion in questions (33.1, 33.3)

ils sont arrivés, tes copains? | *vos amis sont-ils arrivés?*

pourquoi tu as fait ça? | *pourquoi avez-vous fait cela?*

Absence of *ne* in most negative constructions (34.1)

c'est pas vrai; je crois pas | *ce n'est pas vrai; je ne crois pas*

Use of *c'est* instead of *il est* (40.2)

c'est pas facile de savoir ce qui se passe | *il n'est pas facile de savoir ce qui se passe*

Non-agreement of past participle with preceding direct object (44.4)

c'est une chose que j'ai jamais compris | *c'est une chose que je n'ai jamais comprise*

alors, tu l'as écrit, cette lettre? | *cette lettre, l'avez-vous écrite?*

Use of fillers (50.2)

ben, c'est-à-dire qu'il était pas content | *(je peux vous assurer qu')il n'était pas content*

moi tu sais j'aime pas les animaux | *(quant à moi,) je n'aime pas les animaux*

False starts, unfinished sentences

je crois que c'est . . . enfin, elle m'a dit | *elle m'a dit qu'elle n'approuvait pas*

qu'elle trouvait ça pas normal

Dislocation of subject or object (51.1)

Pierre il a rien dit | *Pierre n'a rien dit*

tu les a vus, tes copains? | *avez-vous vu vos amis?*

Use of *ça* instead of *cela* (52.5)

ça m'a fait un choc | *cela m'a bouleversé*

Part
twelve

Reference section

56 Verb forms and tenses; Verb tables

56.1 **Verb forms and tenses**
56.2 **Verb tables**

56.1 Verb forms and tenses

Present participle
The present participle is shown for each verb in the **Verb tables (56.2)**; for use of the present participle, **see 44.1**.

Past participle
The past participle is shown for each verb in the **Verb tables (56.2)**; for use of the past participle, **see 44.3**.

Present indicative
The forms of all 6 persons are shown for each verb in the **Verb tables (56.2)**.

Present subjunctive
The forms of all 6 persons are shown for each verb in the **Verb tables (56.2)**. For *-er* verbs (except *aller*), the forms of the present subjunctive are identical to the present indicative in persons 1, 2, 3 and 6.

Future tense ('they will finish', etc.)
For all regular and some irregular verbs, the **stem** is formed from the infinitive (*parler, finir, vendre*), without the ending (*-r, -r, -re*): *parle-, fini-, vend-*. **Exceptions** include many common irregular verbs: see **Verb tables (56.2)**.

The **endings** are:

Person	Ending	Example
1	*-rai*	*parlerai*
2	*-ras*	*parleras*
3	*-ra*	*parlera*
4	*-rons*	*parlerons*
5	*-rez*	*parlerez*
6	*-ront*	*parleront*

Conditional ('they **would** finish', etc.)

The **stem** is the same as for the future tense.

The **endings** are:

Person	Ending	Example
1	-rais	parlerais
2	-rais	parlerais
3	-rait	parlerait
4	-rions	parlerions
5	-riez	parleriez
6	-raient	parleraient

Imperfect indicative

The **stem** is formed from persons 4 and 5 of the present tense (*parlons, parlez*), without the ending (*-ons, -ez*): *parl-*. **Exception**: *être*, where the stem is *ét-*.

The **endings** are:

Person	Ending	Example	
1	-ais	parlais	étais
2	-ais	parlais	étais
3	-ait	parlait	était
4	-ions	parlions	étions
5	-iez	parliez	étiez
6	-aient	parlaient	étaient

Past historic tense

For most verbs, the **stem** is the same as the stem of the past participle: *parler, parlé, parl-; finir, fini, fin-, vendre, vendu, vend-*, but there are several exceptions, including verbs where the 'stem' is a single consonant: *faire, fait, f-; ouvrir, ouvert, ouvr-; voir, vu, v-*: see **Verb tables (56.2)**.

The **endings** are:

		Verb type	
Person	-er	-ir, -re (regular and some irregular)	-oir, -re (some irregular)
1	-ai	-is	-us
2	-as	-is	-us
3	-a	-it	-ut
4	-âmes	-îmes	-ûmes
5	-âtes	-îtes	-ûtes
6	-èrent	-irent	-urent

Imperfect subjunctive

The **stem** is as for the past historic tense.

The **endings** are:

Person	-er	-ir, -re (regular and some irregular)	-oir, -re (some irregular)
		Verb type	
1	-asse	-isse	-usse
2	-asses	-isses	-usses
3	-ât	-ît	-ût
4	-assions	-issions	-ussions
5	-assiez	-issiez	-ussiez
6	-assent	-issent	-ussent

The imperfect subjunctive is used mainly in **very formal** situations (N4); in most other cases, the present subjunctive is used instead. Nevertheless, it is useful to be able to recognise the imperfect subjunctive.

Passé composé (indicative)

For all verbs, the passé composé is formed from the present indicative of the auxiliary verb + past participle (for agreement of the past participle, **see 44.4**).

For most verbs, the auxiliary is *avoir*; for certain verbs (see list, **10.3b**), and for all pronominal verbs **(see 36)**, the auxiliary is *être*.

Passé composé (subjunctive)

For all verbs, the subjunctive of the passé composé is formed from the present subjunctive of the auxiliary verb + past participle.

Examples: *qu'on ait parlé; qu'elle soit partie; qu'ils se soient réveillés.*

Pluperfect indicative ('they **had** finished', etc.)

For all verbs, the pluperfect indicative is formed from the imperfect indicative of the auxiliary verb + past participle.

Examples: *on avait parlé; elle était partie; ils s'étaient réveillés.*

Pluperfect subjunctive

For all verbs, the pluperfect subjunctive is formed from the imperfect subjunctive of the auxiliary verb + past participle.

Examples: *qu'on eût parlé; qu'elle fût partie; qu'ils se fussent réveillés.*

The pluperfect subjunctive is used almost exclusively in **very formal** situations (N4); in most other cases, the subjunctive form of the passé composé is used instead. Nevertheless, it is useful to be able to recognise the pluperfect subjunctive.

Future perfect ('they **will have** finished', etc.)

For all verbs, the future perfect is formed from the future tense of the auxiliary verb + past participle.

Examples: *on aura parlé; elle sera partie; ils se seront réveillés.*

Past conditional ('they **would have** finished', etc.)

For all verbs, the past conditional is formed from the conditional of the auxiliary verb + past participle.

Examples: *on aurait parlé; elle serait partie; ils se seraient réveillés.*

Past anterior ('(when) they **had** finished', etc.)

For all verbs, the past anterior is formed from the past historic of the auxiliary verb + past participle.

The **meaning** of the past anterior is similar to that of the pluperfect ('had finished', etc.).

The past anterior is used only in texts where the **past historic** is used as the main narrative tense. It occurs in time clauses (introduced by *quand, dès que, aussitôt que*, etc.), describing an action which is **anterior** to the action in the main clause:

> *quand il eut fini, il sortit*
> when he had finished, he went out
> *dès qu'elle fut partie, les problèmes commencèrent*
> as soon as she had left, the problems began

It also occurs with *à peine* and *bientôt*:
> *elle eut à peine commencé à parler qu'il y eut une interruption*
> she had hardly begun to speak when there was an interruption
> *il eut bientôt trouvé la solution*
> he had soon found the solution

56.2 Verb tables

Infinitive	Present participle Past participle	Present indicative Present subjunctive (stem + endings for persons 1–6)	Future (person 3) Past historic (person 3)
a Regular verbs			
parler	*parlant* *parlé*	*parl- e es e ons ez ent* *parl- e es e ions iez ent*	*parlera* *parla*
finir	*finissant* *fini*	*fini- s s t ssons ssez ssent* *fini- sse sses sse ssions ssiez ssent*	*finira* *finit*
attendre	*attendant* *attendu*	*attend- s s − ons ez ent* *attend- e es e ions iez ent*	*attendra* *attendit*
b Irregular verbs			
(s')accroître	see *croître*		
accueillir	see *cueillir*		
acquérir	*acquérant* *acquis*	*acqu- iers iers iert érons érez ièrent* *acqu- ière ières ière érions ériez ièrent*	*acquerra* *acquit*
aller	*allant* *allé*	*vais vas va allons allez vont* *aille ailles aille allions alliez aillent*	*ira* *alla*
apercevoir	see *recevoir*		
(s')appeler	*appelant* *appelé*	*appel- le les le ons ez lent* *appel- le les le ions iez lent*	*appellera* *appela*
apprendre	see *prendre*		
arranger	see *manger*		
assaillir	*assaillant* *assailli*	*assaill- e es e ons ez ent* *assaill- e es e ions iez ent*	*assaillira* *assaillit*
s'asseoir	*s'asseyant* *assis*	*ass- ieds ieds ied eyons eyez eyent* also: *ass- ois ois oit oyons oyez oient* *ass- eye eyes eye eyions eyiez eyent* also: *ass- oie oies oie oyions oyiez oient*	*assiéra* *assoira* *assit*

Infinitive	Present participle Past participle	Present indicative Present subjunctive (stem + endings for persons 1–6)	Future (person 3) Past historic (person 3)
atteindre	see *craindre*		
avancer	*avançant* *avancé*	avan- *ce ces ce çons cez cent* avan- *ce ces ce cions ciez cent*	*avancera* *avança*
avoir	*ayant* *eu*	*ai as a avons avez ont* *aie aies ait ayons ayez aient* **Imperative:** *aie ayons ayez*	*aura* *eut*
(se) battre	*(se) battant* *battu*	bat- *s s – tons tez tent* bat- *te tes te tions tiez tent*	*battra* *battit*
boire	*buvant* *bu*	b- *ois ois oit uvons uvez oivent* b- *oive oives oive uvions uviez oivent*	*boira* *but*
combattre	see *battre*		
commencer	see *avancer*		
commettre	see *mettre*		
comprendre	see *prendre*		
concevoir	see *recevoir*		
conclure	*concluant* *conclu*	conclu- *s s t ons ez ent* conclu- *e es e ions iez ent*	*conclura* *conclut*
conduire	*conduisant* *conduit*	condui- *s s t sons sez sent* condui- *se ses se sions siez sent*	*conduira* *conduisit*
connaître	*connaissant* *connu*	conn- *ais ais aît aissons aissez aissent* conn- *aisse aisses aisse aissions aissiez aissent*	*connaîtra* *connut*
construire	see *conduire*		
contredire	see *dire*, except that person 5 of the present indicative is *contredisez*		
convaincre	see *vaincre*		
corrompre	see *rompre*		

Infinitive	Present participle Past participle	Present indicative Present subjunctive (stem + endings for persons 1–6)	Future (person 3) Past historic (person 3)
courir	*courant* *couru*	*cour- s s t ons ez ent* *cour- e es e ions iez ent*	*courra* *courut*
couvrir	see *ouvrir*		
craindre	see *joindre*		
croire	*croyant* *cru*	*cr- ois ois oit oyons oyez oient* *cr- oie oies oie oyions oyiez oient*	*croira* *crut*
croître	*croissant* *crû, crue*	*cr- oîs oîs oît oissons oissez oissent* *cr- oisse oisses oisse oissions oissiez* *oissent*	*croîtra* *crût*
cueillir	*cueillant* *cueilli*	*cueill- e es e ons ez ent* *cueill- e es e ions iez ent*	*cueillera* *cueillit*
décrire	see *écrire*		
détruire	see *conduire*		
devenir	see *tenir*		
devoir	*devant* *dû, due*	*d- ois ois oit evons evez oivent* *d- oive oives oive evions eviez oivent*	*devra* *dut*
dire	*disant* *dit*	*di- s s t sons tes sent* *di- se ses se sions siez sent*	*dira* *dit*
dormir	see *partir*		
écrire	*écrivant* *écrit*	*écri- s s t vons vez vent* *écri- ve ves ve vions viez vent*	*écrira* *écrivit*
(s')émouvoir	*(s')émouvant* *ému*	*ém- eus eus eut ouvons ouvez euvent* *ém- euve euves euve ouvions ouviez* *euvent*	*émouvrai* *émut*
s'enfuir	*s'enfuyant* *enfui*	*enfu- is is it yons yez ient* *enfu- ie ies ie yions yiez ient*	*enfuira* *enfuit*
envoyer	*envoyant* *envoyé*	*env- oie oies oie oyons oyez oient* *env- oie oies oie oyions oyiez oient*	*enverra* *envoya*

Infinitive	Present participle Past participle	Present indicative Present subjunctive (stem + endings for persons 1–6)	Future (person 3) Past historic (person 3)
essayer	*essayant* *essayé*	*essa-* ie ies ie yons yez ient also: *essa-* ye yes ye yons yez yent *essa-* ie ies ie yions yiez ient also: *essa-* ye yes ye yions yiez yent	*essaiera* *essayera* *essaya*
être	*étant* *été*	*suis es est sommes êtes sont* *sois sois soit soyons soyez soient* **Imperative:** *sois soyons soyez* **Imperfect:** *était*	*sera* *fut*
extraire	*extrayant* *extrait*	*extra-* is is it yons yez ient *extra-* ie ies ie yions yiez ient	*extraira* (not used)
faillir	(present participle and present tense not often used) *failli*		*faillira* *faillit*
faire	*faisant* *fait*	*f-* ais ais ait aisons aites ont *f-* asse asses asse assions assiez assent	*fera* *fit*
falloir	(not used) *fallu*	*(il) faut* *(qu'il) faille*	*faudra* *fallut*
fuir	*fuyant* *fui*	*fu-* is is it yons yez ient *fu-* ie ies ie yions yiez ient	*fuira* *fuit*
haïr	*haïssant* *haï*	*ha-* is is it issons issez issent *ha-* isse isses isse issions issiez issent	*haïra* *haït*
inclure	see *conclure*, except that the past participle is *inclus, incluse*		
interdire	see *dire*, except that person 5 of the present indicative is *interdisez*		
jeter	*jetant* *jeté*	*jet-* te tes te ons ez tent *jet-* te tes te ions iez tent	*jettera* *jeta*
joindre	*joignant* *joint*	*joi-* ns ns nt gnons gnez gnent *joi-* gne gnes gne gnions gniez gnent	*joindra* *joignit*
(se) lever	*(se) levant* *levé*	*l-* ève èves ève evons evez èvent *l-* ève èves ève evions eviez èvent	*lèvera* *leva*

Infinitive	Present participle Past participle	Present indicative Present subjunctive (stem + endings for persons 1–6)	Future (person 3) Past historic (person 3)
lire	*lisant* *lu*	*l- is is it isons isez isent* *l- ise ises ise isions isiez isent*	*lira* *lut*
manger	*mangeant* *mangé*	*mang- e es e eons ez ent* *mang- e es e ions iez ent*	*mangera* *mangea*
mentir	see *partir*		
mettre	*mettant* *mis*	*m- ets ets et ettons ettez ettent* *m- ette ettes ette ettions ettiez ettent*	*mettra* *mit*
mourir	*mourant* *mort*	*m- eurs eurs eurt ourons ourez eurent* *m- eure eures eure ourions ouriez eurent*	*mourra* *mourut*
naître	*naissant* *né*	*n- ais ais aît aissons aissez aissent* *n- aisse aisses aisse aissions aissiez aissent*	*naîtra* *naquit*
nuire	*nuisant* *nui*	*nui- s s t sons sez sent* *nui- se ses se sions siez sent*	*nuira* *nuisit*
offrir	see *ouvrir*		
ouvrir	*ouvrant* *ouvert*	*ouv- re res re rons rez rent* *ouv- re res re rions riez rent*	*ouvrira* *ouvrit*
paraître	see *connaître*		
partir	*partant* *parti*	*par- s s t tons tez tent* *par- te tes te tions tiez tent*	*partira* *partit*
payer	see *essayer*		
peindre	see *joindre*		
plaire	*plaisant* *plu*	*pl ais ais aît aisons aisez aisent* *pl- aise aises aise aisions aisiez aisent*	*plaira* *plut*
pleuvoir	*pleuvant* *plu*	*(il) pleut* *(qu'il) pleuve* **Imperfect:** *pleuvait*	*pleuvra* *plut*

French
Grammar
Explained

Infinitive	Present participle Past participle	Present indicative Present subjunctive (stem + endings for persons 1–6)	Future (person 3) Past historic (person 3)
pouvoir	*pouvant* *pu*	*p-* eux eux eut ouvons ouvez euvent *p-* uisse uisses uisse uissions uissiez 　　uissent	*pourra* *put*
préférer	*préférant* *préféré*	*préf-* ère ères ère érons érez èrent *préf-* ère ères ère érions ériez èrent	*préférera* (old) *préfèrera* (new) *préféra*
prendre	*prenant* *pris*	*pr-* ends ends end enons enez ennent *pr-* enne ennes enne enions eniez 　　ennent	*prendra* *prit*
prévoir	*prévoyant* *prévu*	*prév-* ois ois oit oyons oyez oient *prév-* oie oies oie oyions oyiez oient	*prévoira* *prévit*
produire	see *conduire*		
recevoir	*recevant* *reçu*	*re-* çois çois çoit cevons cevez çoivent *re-* çoive çoives çoive cevions ceviez 　　çoivent	*recevra* *reçut*
réduire	see *conduire*		
rejoindre	see *joindre*		
reproduire	see *conduire*		
résoudre	*résolvant* *résolu*	*réso-* us us ut lvons lvez lvent *réso-* lve lves lve lvions lviez lvent	*résoudra* *résolut*
revêtir	*revêtant* *revêtu*	*revêt-* s s - ons ez ent *revêt-* e es e ions iez ent	*revêtira* *revêtit*
rire	*riant* *ri*	*ri-* s s t ons ez ent *ri-* e es e ions iez ent	*rira* *rit*
rompre	*rompant* *rompu*	*romp-* s s t ons ez ent *romp-* e es e ions iez ent	*rompra* *rompit*
savoir	*sachant* *su*	*s-* ais ais ait avons avez avent *s-* ache aches ache achions achiez 　　achent	*saura* *su*

French Grammar Explained

Infinitive	Present participle Past participle	Present indicative Present subjunctive (stem + endings for persons 1–6)	Future (person 3) Past historic (person 3)
sentir	see *partir*		
servir	see *partir*		
sortir	see *partir*		
souffrir	see *ouvrir*		
sourire	see *rire*		
suffire	*suffisant* *suffi*	*suffi- s s t sons sez sent* *suffi- se ses se sions siez sent*	*suffira* *suffit*
suivre	*suivant* *suivi*	*sui- s s t vons vez vent* *sui- ve ves ve vions viez vent*	*suivra* *suivit*
(se) taire	*(se) taisant* *tu*	*t- ais ais ait aisons aisez aisent* *t- aise aises aise aisions aisiez aisent*	*taira* *tut*
tenir	*tenant* *tenu*	*t- iens iens ient enons enez iennent* *t- ienne iennes ienne enions eniez iennent*	*tiendra* *tint*
vaincre	*vainquant* *vaincu*	*vain- cs cs c quons quez quent* *vain- que ques que quions quiez quent*	*vaincra* *vainquit*
valoir	*valant* *valu*	*va- ux ux ut lons lez lent* *va- ille illes ille lions liez illent*	*vaudra* *valut*
venir	see *tenir*		
vivre	*vivant* *vécu*	*v- is is it vons vez vent* *v- ive ives ive vions viez vent*	*vivra* *vécut*
voir	*voyant* *vu*	*v- ois ois oit oyons oyez oient* *v- oie oies oie oyions oyiez oient*	*verra* *vit*
vouloir	*voulant* *voulu*	*v- eux eux eut oulons oulez eulent* *v- euille euilles euille oulions ouliez euillent* **Imperative:** *veuille veuillons veuillez*	*voudra* *voulut*

57 Key to exercises

6/1 Words pronounced with [s]: *islam, conséquence, renverser, législation*. Words pronounced with [z]: *peser, comparaison, névrose, épuisé, épouser, économiser*.

6/2 1 *entreprise; réussie* 2 *s'intéresse; possessions* 3 *choisissez; succès* 4 *saisissent; occasion* 5 *assistance; connaissance*

6/3 Left column: silent final consonant; right column: sounded final consonant.

7/1 1 *pre-mier* 2 *sé-vé-ri-té* 3 *l'o-pé-ra* 4 *s'o-ccu-per* 5 *té-lé-vi-sé* 6 *struc-ture* 7 *é-tran-ger* 8 *sur-tout* 9 *res-pon-sable* 10 *re-pré-sen-ter*

8/1 *Le matin du 16 avril, le docteur Bernard Rieux sortit de son cabinet et buta sur un rat mort, au milieu du palier. Sur le moment, il **écarta** la **bête** sans y prendre garde et descendit l'escalier. Mais, **arrivé** dans la rue, la **pensée** lui vint que ce rat n'**était** pas à sa place et il retourna sur ses pas pour avertir le concierge. Devant la **réaction** du vieux M. Michel, il sentit mieux ce que sa **découverte** avait d'insolite. La **présence** de ce rat mort lui avait paru seulement bizarre tandis que, pour le concierge, elle constituait un scandale. La position de ce dernier **était** d'ailleurs **catégorique**: il n'y avait pas de rats dans la maison. Le docteur eut beau l'assurer qu'il y en avait un sur le palier du premier **étage**, et probablement mort, la conviction de M. Michel restait **entière**. Il n'y avait pas de rats dans la maison, il fallait donc qu'on eût **apporté** celui-ci du dehors. Bref, il s'agissait d'une farce.* (from *La Peste*, A Camus, © Éditions Gallimard)

8/2 1 *les Bretons; breton* 2 *la mer; du Nord* 3 *un Anglais; française* 4 *le président; la République* 5 *l'italien; les Français*

10/2 1b *elle est restée* 1e *elle était restée* 2b *ils sont devenus* 2e *ils étaient devenus* 3b *nous sommes sortis* 3e *nous étions sortis* 4b *ils sont morts* 4e *ils étaient morts* 5b *vous êtes parti(s)* 5e *vous étiez parti(s)*

11/1 1 *une banlieue* – suburb 2 *un chiffre* – (numerical) figure 3 *un cimetière* – cemetery 4 *un comité* – committee 5 *un commerce* – (retail) business 6 *une enquête* – investigation 7 *une façon* – way, manner 8 *une fierté* – pride 9 *une fin* – end, purpose 10 *une honte* – shame 11 *un luxe* – luxury 12 *un modèle* – model 13 *un régime* – regime, diet 14 *un risque* – risk 15 *une saison* – season 16 *un siècle* – century 17 *un trimestre* – term

12/1 **a** 1 *quelqu'un d'actif* 2 *quelque chose de différent* 3 *quelqu'un d'exceptionnel* 4 *quelque chose de passionnant* 5 *quelque chose de nouveau* 6 *quelqu'un d'intéressant*

b 1 *elle n'a trouvé personne d'actif* 2 *il ne cherche rien de différent* 3 *ce n'est personne d'exceptionnel* 4 *son livre ne contient rien de passionnant* 5 *ce changement n'offre rien de nouveau* 6 *il n'a rencontré personne d'intéressant*

12/2 1 *amicale* 2 *familiale* 3 *individuelle* 4 *industrielle* 5 *locale* 6 *naturelle* 7 *normale* 8 *principale* 9 *traditionnelle* 10 *universelle*

12/3 1 *commerciaux* 2 *égaux* 3 *locaux* 4 *mondiaux* 5 *naturels* 6 *principaux* 7 *professionnels* 8 *sociaux* 9 *spéciaux* 10 *traditionnels*

13/1 (Use a French–English dictionary to check your answers to this exercise.)

14/1 1 *la bonté* 2 *la communauté* 3 *la comptabilité* 4 *l'évidence* 5 *une exagération* 6 *la faiblesse* 7 *la féminité* 8 *le gouvernement* 9 *l'habitation* 10 *l'ignorance* 11 *l'inévitabilité* 12 *l'inquiétude* 13 *un logement* 14 *la masculinité* 15 *l'organisation* 16 *la rentrée* 17 *le sauvetage* 18 *le sentiment* 19 *une suggestion* 20 *la violence*

14/2 1 *commercial; commerçant* 2 *communautaire* 3 *coûteux* 4 *égalitaire* 5 *familial* 6 *féminin* 7 *financier* 8 *gouvernemental* 9 *historique* 10 *honteux* 11 *individuel* 12 *luxueux* 13 *mondial* 14 *normal* 15 *systématique*

14/3 1 *allemand, allemande; un Allemand, une Allemande*
2 *alsacien, alsacienne; un Alsacien, une Alsacienne*
3 *bavarois, bavaroise; un Bavarois, une Bavaroise*
4 *californien, californienne; un Californien, une
Californienne* 5 *canadien, canadienne; un Canadien, une
Canadienne* 6 *catalan, catalane; un Catalan, une Catalane*
7 *florentin, florentine; un Florentin, une Florentine* 8 *gallois,
galloise; un Gallois, une Galloise* 9 *britannique, britannique;
un Britannique, une Britannique* 10 *hambourgeois,
hambourgeoise; un Hambourgeois, une Hambourgeoise*
11 *japonais, japonaise; un Japonais, une Japonaise*
12 *lorrain, lorraine; un Lorrain, une Lorraine* 13 *lyonnais,
lyonnaise; un Lyonnais, une Lyonnaise* 14 *marseillais,
marseillaise; un Marseillais, une Marseillaise* 15 *napolitain,
napolitaine; un Napolitain, une Napolitaine* 16 *norvégien,
norvégienne; un Norvégien, une Norvégienne* 17 *hollandais,
hollandaise; un Hollandais, une Hollandaise* 18 *portugais,
portugaise; un Portugais, une Portugaise* 19 *strasbourgeois,
strasbourgeoise; un Strasbourgeois, une Strasbourgeoise*
20 *suédois, suédoise; un Suédois, une Suédoise*

15/1 1 *avait* – He ran because he was afraid of arriving
late. 2 *prendre* – If he won't do anything, it's up to you
to take the initiative. 3 *mise* – They sold their house six
months after putting it on the market. 4 *prendre* –
Gradually, his big plan began to take shape. 5 *a* – He
says he built it himself, but it's hard to believe it/him.
6 *mettre* – Right! that's enough talk. Let's get to work. 7
fait – Don't shout like that; you frightened me!
8 *mettre* – Ten o'clock already! It's time to get going.
9 *mis* – When he died it was discovered that he had
saved a lot of money. 10 *prennes* – Close the window! I
wouldn't want you to catch cold. 11 *a* – With a fair
wind, we might be able to reach port before nightfall.
12 *faire* – His plan is liable to fall through for lack of
money.

17/1 *is* – verb   *figure* – noun   *modern* – adjective
anywhere – adverb   *because* – conjunction
the – determiner   *appeared* – verb
manifestly – adverb   *for* – preposition   *it* – pronoun

17/2 *parcmètres* – noun   *une* – determiner
que – conjunction   *rapporte* – verb   *pouvoirs* – noun
le – pronoun   *parce que* – conjunction
petit – adjective   *retirer* – verb   *bien* – adverb

17/3 1 verb; noun 2 verb; noun 3 verb; noun 4 verb;
noun 5 verb; noun 6 verb; noun 7 adjective; noun
8 preposition; noun 9 preposition; noun 10 noun;
adjective 11 noun; adverb

17/4 1 *(travailler) dur* 2 *(coûter) cher* 3 *(gagner) gros*
4 *(parler) bas* 5 *(couper) court* 6 *(casser) net* 7 *(sonner) faux*
8 *(crier) fort* 9 *(dire) haut et fort*

18/1 1 *je le connais* 2 *vous ne la savez pas* 3 *il ne leur
racontera pas* 4 *elle lui téléphonait souvent* 5 *vous le
cherchiez* 6 *nous ne les mangerons pas* 7 *je l'apporterai* 8 *je
lui transmettrai* 9 *elle ne la conduisait pas* 10 *il les
accueillait* 11 *ils ne le détruiront pas* 12 *nous les repeindrons*
13 *vous ne leur écrivez pas* 14 *je la choisirai* 15 *je lui
parlerai*

18/2 1 *le train s'en approchait* 2 *on s'y adressera*
3 *j'y pense souvent* 4 *elle y résistera* 5 *il n'y renonce pas* 6 *je
ne m'en occuperai pas* 7 *ils en dépendaient* 8 *je m'en doutais*
9 *il y participait* 10 *que j'en entends parler*

18/3 1 *Oui, elle les a aidés. Non, elle ne les a pas aidés.*
2 *Oui, je lui en avais parlé/nous lui en avions parlé. Non, je
ne lui en avais pas parlé/nous ne lui en avions pas parlé.*
3 *Oui, il lui a rendu visite. Non, il ne lui a pas rendu visite.*
4 *Oui, ils les avaient prévenus. Non, ils ne les avaient pas
prévenus.* 5 *Oui, je leur ai demandé la réponse. Non, je ne
leur avais pas demandé la réponse.* 6 *Oui, je l'ai fini/nous
l'avons fini. Non, je ne l'ai pas fini/nous ne l'avons pas fini.*

18/4 1 *je ne veux pas l'écouter* 2 *on doit les surveiller* 3 *je
vais vous dire un secret* 4 *ils ne pouvaient pas nous écrire
souvent* 5 *personne ne doit lui parler* 6 *on ne pouvait pas les
voir tous les jours* 7 *j'allais leur dire au revoir* 8 *il a dû
m'oublier* 9 *ils avaient voulu nous donner un cadeau* 10 *je
n'ai pas pu leur en parler*

19/1 1 *toi* 2 *eux* 3 *moi* 4 *lui* 5 *nous* 6 *toi* 7 *lui/elle;
lui/elle* 8 *moi-* 9 *eux/elles* 10 *soi*

19/2 1 *ne le regarde pas!* 2 *ne te réveille pas!* 3 *ne me surprenez pas!* 4 *ne leur demande pas!* 5 *ne l'aidons pas!* 6 *ne nous écoutez pas!* 7 *abandonnons-le/-la!* 8 *imagine-toi!* 9 *parle-lui!* 10 *asseyez-vous!* 11 *raconte-moi cette histoire!* 12 *écoutez-les!*

20/1 1 *il a augmenté son offre* 2 *je cherche mon inspiration* 3 *elle connaît son public* 4 *tu t'intéresses à ton travail* 5 *il s'ennuie à son école* 6 *ils augmentent leurs revenus* 7 *nous suivons nos propres idées* 8 *elles réforment leurs organisations* 9 *vous cultivez vos légumes* 10 *ils soignent leurs malades*

20/2 1 *ma/ta/sa photo* 2 *mon/ton/son choix* 3 *mon/ton/son exercice* 4 *mon/ton/son enquête* 5 *ma/ta/sa surprise* 6 *mon/ton/son histoire* 7 *ma/ta/sa couleur* 8 *mon/ton/son invention* 9 *mon/ton/son système* 10 *mon/ton/son image*

20/3 1 *son école* 2 *leur enthousiasme* 3 *son impatience* 4 *ses parents* 5 *leur valeur* 6 *leurs amis* 7 *ses avantages et ses inconvénients*

20/4 1 *(lever) la main* 2 *son visage* 3 *ses mains* 4 *(me casser) la jambe* 5 *(lui serrer) la main* 6 *(lever) les bras* 7 *(croiser) les bras* 8 *de sa main* 9 *son visage; son chapeau* 10 *(garder) les mains sur la tête*

21/1 1 *ce vin* 2 *ce mois-ci* 3 *ce jour-là* 4 *cette question* 5 *ces fleurs-là* 6 *cet homme là-bas* 7 *cette maison* (this house) or *cette maison-là* (that house) 8 *cette idée*

21/2 1 *celles-là* 2 *ceux qui* 3 *ceux du* 4 *celle qui* 5 *celui qui* 6 *celui qui*

21/3 1 *celui qui* 2 *celles-ci; celles-là* (or vice-versa) 3 *celui de* 4 *celui d'* 5 *celles qu'* 6 *celle-ci* (this one) or *celle-là* (that one)

21/4 1 *cela/ça* 2 *celles-là* 3 *ça* 4 *celle-là* 5 *cela* 6 *ça* (that) or *celle-là* (her, that one)

22/1 1 *des questions* – If the Mayor were here, I'd have some questions to ask him. 2 *les magazines; les mêmes* – Women's magazines are all the same. 3 *les services* – There were so many accidents that the emergency services couldn't cope. 4 *des négociations; des discussions* – The demonstrators demanded negotiations but they were offered only discussions. 5 *les véhicules; les voitures* – The police were stopping all vehicles except for foreign cars. 6 *les questions* – For their exam, the questions are set by one man. 7 *des raisons* – He claimed it was true, but she had reasons to believe otherwise.

22/2 1 *le sucre* – Sugar is good for health, but bad for the/your teeth. 2 *la peine* – I know it's true because I took the trouble to check. 3 *du lait; de la crème* – Would you like milk or cream in your coffee? 4 *le thé; le café* – Tea and coffee are products whose price varies enormously. 5 *le succès* – I'm delighted to see the success of your business. 6 *du sucre* – For this recipe, you need (some) sugar, but not too much. 7 *de la peine* – This story about deserted children distressed me. 8 *du mal* – He speaks so quietly that it's hard to understand him.

22/3 1 *je n'aime pas les pêches* – I don't like peaches (or: *je n'aime plus les pêches* – I don't like peaches any more). 2 *il n'a pas mangé de fruits* – He didn't eat any fruit. 3 *ils ne travaillent pas le dimanche* – They don't work on Sundays (or: *ils ne travaillent plus le dimanche* – They don't work on Sundays any more). 4 *il ne cherche pas le succès* – He's not looking for success. (or: *il ne cherche plus le succès* – He's not looking for success any more). 5 *elle n'avait pas d'objections* – She had no objections (or: *elle n'avait plus d'objections* – She no longer had any objections). 6 *elle n'a pas fait de progrès* – She's made no progress. 7 *ce n'est pas la fin du monde* – It's not the end of the world. 8 *vous n'avez pas de fromage* – You have no cheese (or: *vous n'avez plus de fromage* – You have no cheese left). 9 *sa nouvelle pièce n'a pas eu de succès* – His/Her new play wasn't a success. 10 *il ne faut plus tolérer la faim dans le monde* – Hunger in the world should no longer be tolerated.

22/4 1 *Défense de fumer* 2 *Vends Fiat 500 (pour) 10 000 F* 3 *Soldes d'été. Dernier jour* 4 *Hôpital. Silence* 5 *(Vendons) lait frais* 6 *Sens interdit* 7 *Chute de pierres. Route barrée* (or vice-versa) 8 *Produits non toxiques* 9 *Missiles en Irak: rebondissement* 10 *Renseignements, inscriptions: s'adresser ici*

23/1 1 *chaque fois* – Every time we went to see her, she made us tea. 2 *toute infraction* – Offenders will be prosecuted. 3 *tout le temps* – If you keep shouting, no one will be able to hear anything. 4 *chaque lettre* – All letters will be answered. 5 *toutes les cinq minutes* – I can't be looking after him every five minutes. 6 *chaque spectateur* – Each/every spectator had a good view of the pitch. 7 *chaque matin* – Every morning he called in (on him/her) to say hello. 8 *toute idée* – The walls were so thick that all/any idea of escape was out of the question.

23/2 1 *tout* – He knew he could tell him/her anything/everything. 2 *tous* – I wish you all goodnight. 3 *tous* – They're all pleased she's here/there. 4 *tout* – There you are: that makes 80 francs altogether. 5 *tout* – Above all, I wanted to know that you were all right. 6 *tous* – The programme is called 'Music for everyone'. 7 *tous* – I've seen everyone I wanted to see. 8 *tout* – That's all I've been able to do.

23/3 1 *plusieurs choses* – Could we meet soon? I've several things to tell you. 2 *certains jours* – Some days, he lost heart. 3 *quelques dizaines* – I've just got a few dozen (more) envelopes to address. 4 *plusieurs* – I've listened to several of his speeches: he's a good (public) speaker. 5 *quelques jours* – He didn't have to wait long: the reply came a few days later. 6 *quelques-uns* (or: *certains*) – All his/her paintings are very good, and some are masterpieces. 7 *plusieurs* (or: *certaines*) – You can see he's clever: several/certain of his answers are interesting. 8 *plusieurs millions* – This series/serial/soap is watched regularly by several million viewers.

23/4 1 *d'autres questions* 2 *les autres* 3 *d'autres chaussures* 4 *d'autres idées* 5 *tous les autres* 6 *du mal des autres*

23/5 1 *l'une et l'autre* 2 *l'un sans l'autre* 3 *les uns les autres* 4 *les uns les autres/les uns avec les autres* 5 *l'un de*

l'autre 6 *les uns avec les autres/les uns aux autres* 7 *les uns et les autres* 8 *l'un l'autre*

24/2 1 *pas autant* 2 *tant travaillé* 3 *tant rêvé* 4 *autant que toi* 5 *pas autant* 6 *tant ri* 7 *tant de micro-ordinateurs* 8 *pour autant*

24/3 1 *la plupart de ses réponses* 2 *la plus grande partie de l'inscription* 3 *la plus grande partie de sa collection* 4 *la plupart de ses livres* 5 *la plupart sont restés* 6 *la plus grande partie de l'année*

25/2 Possible answers include: 1 *des dizaines de fois* 2 *plusieurs millions de francs* 3 *trois douzaines* 4 *une quarantaine d'élèves* 5 *des dizaines de milliers de spectateurs* 6 *des centaines d'appels; un millier*

25/3 1 *la moitié* 2 *les deux tiers* 3 *les neuf dixièmes* 4 *les trois quarts* 5 *le tiers* 6 *la moitié; à moitié*

25/4 1 *le dernier bus* 2 *les seuls survivants* 3 *la semaine dernière* 4 *les trois premières places* 5 *la seule politique raisonnable* 6 *pour la dernière fois*

26/1 1 *une petite seconde* 2 *le vieux Tours* 3 *un homme jeune* 4 *un vin vieux* 5 *un beau cadeau* 6 *une jeune femme* 7 *un homme petit* 8 *leurs jeunes mannequins; des belles femmes* 9 *un grand soulagement*

26/2 1 *un certain temps* 2 *les pays pauvres* 3 *mon pauvre ami* 4 *les personnes seules* 5 *une mort certaine* 6 *la même chose* 7 *la seule personne* 8 *la raison même*

27/1 1 *devant* – Look! there's a car parked outside their house. 2 *par* – That's appalling! We must do everything we can to stop it. 3 *chez* – We're out of bread: we'll call in at the baker's on our way home tonight. 4 *dans* – Get a move on! The train leaves in two minutes. 5 *parmi* – There must be someone here who knows where she is. 6 *contre* – To make more room, we/they pushed the sofa up against the wall. 7 *malgré; vers* – Although we called out, the child went on running towards the river. 8 *avec; avant* – What with the holiday traffic, I won't be back until/before eight tonight.

27/2 1 *depuis* 2 *depuis* 3 *dès* 4 *dès* 5 *depuis* 6 *dès*

27/3 1 *sans* 2 *sans* 3 *avec* 4 *sans* 5 *avec* 6 *avec* (or: *sans*)

27/4 1 *sur lui/sur elle* 2 *un livre sur les OVNI* 3 *l'autoroute est fermée sur plusieurs kilomètres* 4 *de savoir beaucoup (de choses) sur ce sujet* 5 *un logement sur Paris* 6 *neuf appels sur dix*

28/1 Possible answers include: 1 *en haut de l'escalier* – Don't miss the lovely statue at the top of the staircase. 2 *près d'une école primaire* – The house is very well located, near a primary school. 3 *à propos de cette affaire* – Ah! you're the very person I wanted to talk to about all this. 4 *face aux problèmes* – Faced with the problems of our times, it's easy to give up. 5 *au bord de la faillite* – Financial uncertainties brought his business close to bankruptcy. 6 *au sein de l'administration* – The inquiry showed up serious shortcomings within the administration. 7 *à part le président* – No one, apart from the President, is allowed to see this file. 8 *à travers les mailles* – Despite the police operation, the suspect managed to slip through the net. 9 *grâce à un hiver* – Thanks to a fairly mild winter, the work was completed a month ahead of schedule. 10 *faute d'argent* – The plan had to be abandoned, for lack of money.

28/2 1 *au-dessus du niveau de la mer* 2 *par-dessous une/la barrière* 3 *sur le feu* 4 *au-dessous de la moyenne* 5 *au-dessus de cette table* 6 *par-dessus ton chef* 6 *sous les ordres*

29/1 1 *au concours* 2 *à un professeur* 3 *à un éléphant* 4 *aux États-Unis* 5 *à des millions de téléspectateurs* 6 *au patron* 7 *aux tyrans* 8 *à des amis*

29/2 1 *une bouteille de vin* 2 *une sélection de glaces* 3 *le goût des framboises* 4 *les réponses des élèves* 5 *la moitié d'un gâteau* 6 *des centaines de réponses* 7 *le début du concert* 8 *la fin d'une époque* 9 *la clef du mystère* 10 *des mouvements de voitures*

29/3 1 *dans le nord de l'Écosse* 2 *en Allemagne; de Turquie* 3 *le train de Londres* 4 *dans le Kent* 5 *dans le Var et dans les Alpes-Maritimes* 6 *de la Somme* 7 *dans les îles Britanniques* 8 *de l'Europe de l'Ouest; de la Russie* 9 *dans le sud de l'Italie* 10 *de l'Europe*

30/1 1 *seulement* 2 *seule* 3 *seulement* 4 *seulement* 5 *seul* 6 *seuls*

30/2 1 *monter à cheval* 2 *de toute façon* 3 *à trois minutes de l'autoroute* 4 *en ce moment* 5 *à ce moment-là* 6 *à mi-temps* 7 *de ville en ville* 8 *tomber en panne* 9 *au siècle dernier* 10 *en même temps* 11 *aller à l'université* 12 *à tout hasard*

31/1 1 *moins de pluie que* 2 *plus que* 3 *plus de* 4 *plus de parapluies que* 5 *plus de* 6 *plus riche que* 7 *moins d'ennuis que* 8 *plus de bonne volonté que de*

31/2 1 *le jour le plus long* 2 *le plus fort* 3 *les prisonniers les plus violents* 4 *les quartiers les plus défavorisés* 5 *le plus longtemps* 6 *le chemin le moins difficile* 7 *le moins bien* 8 *les individus les moins fortunés*

31/4 1 *meilleure* – If you have a better solution, let's hear it! 2 *mieux* – He's been unwell, but he's much better now. 3 *bonne* – It's true he has plenty of goodwill. 4 *bien* – Journalistes are always well informed. 5 *mieux* – With this car, one is better protected if there's an accident. 6 *meilleurs* – Their results are better than their competitors'. 7 *bien* – She was very glad to be back in her flat. 8 *les meilleurs* – The best wines aren't always the most expensive ones. 9 *la bonne* (or: *la meilleure*) – He's always the one who finds the right (or: the best) answer. 10 *la mieux* – Theirs is the best equipped pool in the country/area.

31/5 1 *plus mauvais* – The weather is worse than (was) forecast. 2 *mauvaise* – The town doesn't deserve its bad reputation. 3 *plus mal* – To hear him/her talk, things are always worse here than over there. 4 *le plus mal* – Of all the candidates, he was the least/the worst prepared. 5 *mal* – He thought he'd been badly advised. 6 *la plus mauvaise* – That's certainly the worst idea I've ever heard!

31/6 Possible answers include: 1 *tout aussi valable* 2 *encore plus cher* 3 *trop bien* 4 *bien évident* 5 *beaucoup*

moins lourde 6 *de loin la plus difficile* 7 *beaucoup trop tard*
8 *tout autant que vous* 9 *très; toujours*

32/1 Possible answers include: 1 *je lui dis toujours
bonjour* 2 *ne conduis pas vite!* 3 *on ne le voit pas souvent à
la bibliothèque* 4 *il y a souvent des accidents à ce carrefour*
5 *hier, j'ai fait trois heures de marche dans les collines* 6 *dans
la matinée, le brouillard se lèvera rapidement* 7 *quelquefois je
me lève très tôt le matin* 8 *ce matin, je suis arrivé en retard
pour la première fois depuis l'été*

32/2 Possible answers include: 1 *on va bientôt découvrir
qui est responsable* 2 *je ne pourrai pas venir avec vous demain*
3 *j'ai entendu distinctement une voiture* 4 *elle avait trouvé la
réponse tout de suite* 5 *je leur dis toujours de faire attention*
(or: *je leur dis de faire toujours attention*) 6 *calmement, il a
répondu à leurs questions* 7 *je me suis quelquefois posé la
même question* 8 *demain, tu vas savoir ce qui se passe* (or: *tu
vas savoir ce qui se passe demain*)

32/3 Possible answers include: 1 *et aussi une de sa
grand-mère* – She'd had a card from her parents and also
one from her grandmother. 2 *aussi ne lui ai-je rien dit* – I
did not want her to worry, (and) so I said nothing to
her. 3 *aussi comprendrez-vous* – I've just heard the news,
so you will understand if I have not very much to say.
4 *elle aussi avait entendu* – I phoned Olga. She'd heard
the explosion as well. 5 *peut-être qu'ils n'ont pas reçu* –
Perhaps they've not received our letter. 6 *vous allez peut-
être trouver* – Perhaps you will find my question naïve.
7 *peut-être ai-je mal compris* – Perhaps I (have) misheard
your question. 8 *peut-être qu'il avait trop mangé* – Perhaps
he'd eaten too much the day before.

32/4 Possible answers include: 1 *Délicieuse, cette glace à
la vanille!* 2 *Agiter avant emploi/avant usage.* 3 *Géniale,
ton idée!* 4 *Plus de pain.* 5 *Encore un bang sonique, et je
téléphone au ministère.* 6 *Renseignements: premier étage,
première porte à gauche.* 7 *Dimanche. Rien à manger. Les
enfants pleurent.* 8 *Défense de déposer des ordures.* 9 *Elle
vérifie les numéros. Surprise! elle a gagné.*

32/5 Possible answers include: 1 *Oui, c'est fait. / Non,
pas encore.* 2 *Oui, d'accord. / Non, c'est impossible.* 3 *Oui,*

t'inquiète pas. / Non, mais ça ira. 4 *Oui, il faut y aller. /
Non, pas encore.* 5 *Oui, tout(e) seul(e). / Non, j'avais pas le
temps.* 6 *Oui, tu peux compter sur moi.*

33/1 Possible answers include: 1c *Pourriez-vous
m'indiquer le chemin de la gare?* 2a *Est-ce que tes parents ont
trouvé que c'était une bonne idée?* 3b *Tu sais ce qu'elle m'a
dit?* 4a *Est-ce que Marie sait ce qui s'est passé?* 5c *Voulez-
vous essayer mon gâteau?* 6b *Vous avez terminé les préparatifs
pour Noël?*

33/2 Possible answers include: 1c *A qui est ce sac?*
2b *Qui a préparé ce plat?* 3a *Qu'est-ce qu'il a dit concernant
le chômage?* 4c *Qu'a dit le Président concernant le chômage?*
5c *Comment allez-vous?* 6a *Pourquoi est-ce que les autorités
s'inquiètent?* 7c *A quoi pensait-elle?* 8a *A quoi est-ce que
Marie pensait?* 9c *Où as-tu rangé mes chaussettes?*
10c *Quand avez-vous vu l'accusé devant le magasin?*

33/3 Possible questions and answers include:
1 – *Comment?* – *L'idée m'est venue tout d'un coup.*
2 – *Combien?* – *Plusieurs millions, je crois.*
3 – *Lesquels?* – *Les Duquesne, peut-être.*
4 – *Comment?* – *En laissant un message chez lui.*
5 – *Quand?* – *La semaine dernière.*
6 – *Lequel?* – *Celui de Marseille.*

33/4 1 *rappelez-moi qui a dit/avait dit ça.* 2 *elle nous a
demandé combien de temps il faudrait* 3 *j'ai essayé de me
rappeler ce qu'elle avait dit* 4 *on ne pouvait pas savoir quel
train il avait pris* 5 *l'employé m'a demandé comment je faisais
pour écrire si vite* 6 *je ne comprends pas ce qui le rend si
dynamique* 7 *je ne sais pas combien de coups de feu
j'ai/j'avais entendu* 8 *Laurent nous a demandé où nous
allions/on allait* 9 *Laurence a demandé ce qui se passait*
10 *j'aimerais savoir ce que tu veux*

34/1 1 *mes lunettes ne sont plus* 2 *je ne suis pas allé* 3 *je
ne comprends pas* 4 *les gens ne croient plus* 5 *il ne pleut plus*
6 *on ne meurt plus* (or: *pas*) 7 *ce n'était pas* 8 *ça ne
m'intéresse pas* (or: *plus*)

34/2 1 *je n'ai aucune idée* – How to answer him/her?
I've no idea. 2 *elle ne tolérait ni ses silences ni ses remarques
acides* – She couldn't put up with his silences or his

cutting remarks (or: *elle ne tolérait plus ses silences et ses remarques acides* – She could no longer put up with his silences or his cutting remarks.) 3 *je suis sûr qu'elle ne racontera l'histoire à personne* – I'm sure she won't tell the story to anyone (else). 4 *je n'ai aucun doute* – I have no doubt as to the truth of what he says. 5 *vous ne trouverez rien de nouveau* – If you reread the file, you'll find nothing new. 6 *je n'approuve ni ne condamne sa conduite* – For my part, I neither approve nor condemn his behaviour. 7 *je sais que tu n'as aucune envie de les rencontrer* – Yes, I know you've no desire to meet them. 8 *elle savait que ce ne serait personne d'intéressant* – The doorbell rang; she knew it would be nobody interesting.

34/3 1 *il n'y a que ce remède qui chasse/pour chasser la grippe* 2 *je n'ai appris la nouvelle qu'il y a une heure* 3 *je ne vous le dirai que quand ils seront partis* 4 *il n'y a que ma grand-mère qui écoute mon grand-père* 5 *il ne respecte que la force* 6 *il n'avait trouvé que trois bonnes réponses sur six*

34/4 1 *pas un seul taxi* 2 *personne ne trouve* 3 *jamais je ne l'aurais cru* 4 *aucune loi n'empêche* 5 *plus une feuille n'est restée* 6 *personne ne m'a jamais demandé* 7 *plus de doute* 8 *ni la France, ni la Grande-Bretagne*

34/5 1 *elle n'avait remarqué personne* 2 *c'est qu'il ne veut rien apprendre* 3 *je ne vais plus penser* 4 *je ne l'ai pas notée* 5 *je ne pourrai jamais oublier* 6 *il ne leur avait jamais écrit* (or: *il ne leur avait plus écrit*) 7 *on n'est pas allés les voir* 8 *qu'elle ne pourrait jamais lui pardonner*

34/6 1 *il ne fait jamais aucun effort* – He never makes any effort to broaden his horizons. 2 *il ne reste plus qu'une solution* – Now, there's only one solution left. 3 *il ne se passe jamais rien* – No need to hurry: nothing ever happens before midnight. 4 *il n'y a plus personne* – We'll have the place to ourselves: there's nobody (still) around at this time (of day). 5 *je n'ai jamais eu aucun problème* – I've never had any problem with the child. 6 *on ne voyait plus que la silhouette* – It was getting dark: by now, all you could see was the outline of the trees.

35/1 1 *le toit a été refait* 2 *les murs étaient repeints* 3 *tout infraction sera punie* 4 *le résultat avait été confirmé* 5 *les prix

sont distribués* 6 *l'arbitre a été sifflé* 7 *la décision sera annoncée* 8 *ils espéraient que les provocateurs seraient arrêtés* 9 *les numéros gagnants viennent d'être annoncés* 10 *les troupes vont être mises en état d'alerte*

35/2 1 *ils ont été surpris par le résultat* 2 *l'allocution a été écoutée par dix millions de téléspectateurs* 3 *il/elle est constamment entouré(e) de ses admirateurs* 4 *tout espoir n'a pas été abandonné par les sauveteurs* 5 *elle avait été harcelée par un homme* 6 *son cartable était bourré de manuels scolaires* 7 *les mains et les visages étaient noircis de poussière* 8 *les citoyens seront-ils protégés par cette loi?* 9 *un questionnaire a été rempli par chaque participant* 10 *sa lettre était remplie/bourrée de fautes d'orthographe*

35/3 1a he was given three presents 1b *trois cadeaux lui ont été offerts* 1c three presents were given to him 2a they were not told the truth 2b *la vérité ne leur a pas été dite* 2c the truth was not told to them 3a they had been promised a wage increase 3b *une augmentation de salaire leur avait été promise* 3c a wage increase had been promised to them 4a I was not told this story 4b *cette histoire ne m'a pas été racontée* 4c this story was not told/has not been told to me 5a you'll be sent a cheque 5b *un chèque va vous être envoyé* 5c a cheque will be sent to you 6a we were asked a favour 6b *une faveur nous a été demandée* 6c a favour was asked of us

36/1 **b** 1 *les gens ne s'adaptent pas; les gens ne se sont pas adaptés* 2 *le temps ne s'améliore pas; le temps ne s'est pas amélioré* 3 *on ne s'amuse pas; on ne s'est pas amusés* 4 *ils ne se battent pas; ils ne se sont pas battus* 5 *ils ne se défendent pas; ils ne se sont pas défendus* 6 *la ville ne se développe pas; la ville ne s'est pas développée* 7 *il ne s'enfuit pas; il ne s'est pas enfui* 8 *ils ne s'enrichissent pas; ils ne se sont pas enrichis* 9 *je ne m'intéresse pas à la politique; je ne me suis pas intéressé à la politique* 10 *ils ne se marient pas; ils ne se sont pas mariés* 11 *je ne me sens pas triste; je ne me suis pas senti triste* 12 *vous ne vous spécialisez pas; vous ne vous êtes pas spécialisés* 13 *tu ne te trompes pas; tu ne t'es pas trompé(e)* 14 *vous ne vous trouvez pas à Londres; vous ne vous êtes pas trouvé(s) à Londres*

36/2 1 *vous devez vous adapter* 2 *nous allons nous concentrer* 3 *je sais me défendre* 4 *vous ne voulez pas vous déranger* 5 *tu ne dois pas te fatiguer* 6 *je ne vais pas me forcer* 7 *ils vont se marier* 8 *tu dois te rappeler* 9 *je ne peux pas me souvenir* 10 *il n'aime pas se tromper*

36/3 1 *qu'est-ce qui se passe?* 2 *voir la ville se développer trop* 3 *le mauvais temps va aggraver la situation* 4 *son intervention va produire un changement* 5 *le système va s'améliorer* 6 *je ne me sens pas très bien* 7 *les rumeurs se répandent* 8 *ne précipitons pas les choses* 9 *on trouve toutes sortes* 10 *je sens que quelque chose va arriver* 11 *elle va se demander* (she'll be wondering) or: *elle va demander* (she's going to ask) 12 *il n'aime pas se poser trop de questions* (he doesn't like asking himself) or: *il n'aime pas poser* (he doesn't like asking)

36/4 1 *on va leur acheter* – Let's buy them something to say thank you. 2 *ils se sont acheté* – They've bought themselves a little boat. 3 *j'espère qu'il ne s'est pas cassé la jambe* – I hope he's not broken his leg. 4 *on leur a proposé* – We offered them a very good price for their car. 5 *je lui ai offert* – I gave him/her a jewel for Christmas. 6 *le temps de se laver les cheveux* – She found time to wash her hair.

36/5 1 *ils se sont rendus* 2 *elle était assise* 3 *elle était levée; elle était penchée* 4 *il s'est réveillé; il s'était endormi* 5 *le chien s'est allongé* (stretched out) or: *est allongé* (is stretched out) 6 *quand les enfants sont couchés*

37/1 1 *il pourra y avoir des problèmes; il ne pourra pas y avoir de problèmes* 2 *il a dû y avoir un accident; il n'a pas dû y avoir d'accident* 3 *il pourrait y avoir des avantages; il ne pourrait pas y avoir d'avantages* 4 *il va y avoir une discussion; il ne va pas y avoir de discussion* 5 *il avait dû y avoir une erreur; il n'avait pas dû y avoir d'erreur* 6 *il aurait pu y avoir des bagarres; il n'aurait pas pu y avoir de bagarres*

37/2 1 *il était question de fermer* 2 *il faut que je te dise* 3 *il s'agit de décider* (or: *il faut décider*) 4 *il faut que je passe* 5 *il était question de beaucoup d'argent* (or: *il s'agissait de*) 6 *il ne faut pas traîner* (or: *il ne s'agit pas de traîner*, or: *il n'est*

pas question de traîner) 7 *il n'était pas question de l'abandonner* 8 *il ne faudra pas oublier* 9 *il ne s'agissait pas d'elle*

37/3 1 *il s'est passé quelque chose; quelque chose s'est passé* (or: *il est arrivé quelque chose; quelque chose est arrivé*) 2 *il me restait encore de l'espoir; encore de l'espoir me restait* 3 *il manque un élément essentiel; un élément essentiel manque* 4 *il allait lui arriver un accident; un accident allait lui arriver* 5 *il viendra un temps; un temps viendra* 6 *il suffit de l'écouter; l'écouter suffit*

37/4 Depending on the meaning, possible answers include: 1 *il faut; il me faut; il nous faut* 2 *il ne restait plus; il ne me restait plus; il ne lui restait plus* 3 *il va arriver un malheur; il va t'arriver un malheur; il va nous arriver un malheur* 4 *il m'est venu une idée* 5 *ça me plaît; ça lui plaît; ça leur plaît* 6 *il ne faut jamais le contredire*

37/5 1 *il paraissait évident* (or: *il semblait évident*) 2 *il semble vrai* 3 *il paraît qu'ils liquident* 4 *il semblerait qu'il n'y ait pas eu* 5 *le résultat lui paraissait certain* 6 *ça ne me paraît pas nécessaire* (or: *ça ne me semble pas*)

38/1 1 *je vous croyais partis* 2 *les jurés ont trouvé l'accusé coupable* 3 *elle estimait le prix trop élevé* (or: *elle trouvait*, or: *elle jugeait*) 4 *toute cette pluie va rendre le terrain encore plus difficile* 5 *de le croire innocent* 6 *son intervention hier a rendu l'enquête encore plus difficile* 7 *la plupart des ministres jugeaient les mesures nécessaires* (or: *estimaient*; or: *trouvaient*) 8 *vous allez nous croire* (or: *nous trouver*) *naïfs; nous trouvons sa conduite inacceptable*

38/2 1 *il s'agit d'* 2 *je n'approuve pas du tout son action* 3 *cacher sa déception à son mari* 4 *j'ai conseillé à* 5 *consistait en* 6 *défendu à* 7 *ont demandé leur mère* 8 *ont demandé à* 9 *dépend de* 10 *je ne doute pas de* 11 *insister sur* 12 *il joue de la guitare* 13 *ils ne manquent de rien* 14 *nuire à* 15 *obéir à* 16 *tu penses de mes chaussures* 17 *ne pensait à rien* 18 *je reproche à* 19 *il ne sert à rien* 20 *tu ne te sers plus de*

38/3 1 *il s'agit de* 2 *elle aidait sa mère à* 3 *on apprendra aux enfants à* 4 *arrête de* 5 *consiste à* 6 *ne craint pas d'* 7 *se dépêche de* 8 *ne vous empêche de* 9 *j'espère pouvoir* 10 *elle a* essayé de 11 *j'ai failli lui dire de* 12 *insisté pour* 13 *on l'a obligé à* 14 *il a été obligé de* 15 *osez-vous dire* 16 *il a paru hésiter* 17 *il préfère rester* 18 *ils ont promis de* 19 *semblent aller* 20 *je ne me souviens pas d'*

39/1 1 *le train a dû partir* 2 *devront se souvenir* 3 *tu aurais dû les prévenir* 4 *elle n'aurait pas dû venir* 5 *cela ne devrait pas compter* 6 *il avait dû subir* 7 *ils ne devaient pas trop réfléchir* 8 *ils ont dû avoir*

39/3 1 *on pouvait faire* 2 *il n'avait pas pu finir* 3 *il pourrait te donner* 4 *je pourrais comprendre* 5 *elle pourrait commencer* 6 *il a enfin pu prendre*

39/4 1 *j'ai voulu répondre; j'ai voulu qu'ils répondent* – I wanted to answer; I wanted them to answer. 2 *je ne voudrais pas y penser; je ne voudrais pas qu'elle y pense* – I wouldn't like to think about it; I wouldn't want her to think about it. 3 *ils voulaient signer; ils voulaient que je signe* – They wanted to sign; they wanted me to sign. 4 *elle aurait voulu gagner; elle aurait voulu qu'il gagne* – She'd have liked to win; she'd have liked him to win. 5 *il n'avait pas voulu en parler; il n'avait pas voulu qu'on en parle* – He hadn't wanted to talk about it; he hadn't wanted us to talk about it. 6 *nous ne voulons pas y retourner; nous ne voulons pas qu'ils y retournent* – We don't want to go back (there); we don't want them to go back (there).

39/5 1 *ils font avancer le projet lentement* 2 *ils ont fait refaire leur toit par des spécialistes* 3 *elle faisait faire ces objets par un artisan* 4 *j'ai fait répéter le message par le jeune homme* (or: *au jeune homme*) 5 *tu as fait baisser le prix* 6 *je ferai réfléchir ces gens aux conséquences de leur action*

39/6 1 (*écouter*) *le premier ministre l'a fait changer d'avis* 2 *les encouragements de leurs supporters leur ont fait gagner le match* 3 *sa mélancolie ne l'a pas fait renoncer à travailler* 4 *la crise financière ne nous fera pas perdre beaucoup d'argent* 5 *ce projet me fait négliger certaines autres choses* 6 *leurs remarques te faisaient souvent perdre ton sang-froid*

40/1 1 *avide de* 2 *conscient de* 3 *coupable de* 4 *différent de* 5 *doué pour* 6 *fâchée contre* 7 *fort en* 8 *folle de* 9 *furieux*

contre 10 *inférieurs à* 11 *inquiète de* 12 *le premier de* 13 *proche de* 14 *responsable de* 15 *satisfaite de*

40/2 1 *bonnes à* 2 *capable de* 3 *content de* 4 *décidée à* 5 *le dernier à* 6 *désolé de* 7 *étonné de* 8 *fatigué de* 9 *habituée à* 10 *incapable de* 11 *lente à* 12 *occupé à* 13 *la seule à* 14 *surpris de* 15 *susceptible de*

41/1 1 *le droit de* 2 *du mal à* 3 *quelque chose d'important à* 4 *une idée pour* 5 *c'est à prendre ou à laisser* 6 *leur façon de* 7 *la malchance d'* 8 *deux heures pour* 9 *rien de nouveau à* 10 *la tentation de*

41/2 1 *la sortie de secours* 2 *une banque de données* 3 *un placard à balais* 4 *une armoire en chêne massif* 5 *en civil* 6 *chaise à dossier haut* 7 *à bout de souffle* 8 *en forme de huit*

42/1 1 *qu'on lit* 2 *qui disent cela* 3 *qui a permis* 4 *que j'admire* 5 *qu'on respire* 6 *qui va gagner*

42/3 1 *où* – I can recommend a small hotel where we stayed last year. 2 *dont* – It's a matter which the chairman is dealing with personally. 3 *dont* – At the time I'm speaking about, I was still young. 4 *où* – At the time my grandmother was born, a married woman wasn't allowed to be a civil servant. 5 *où* – The day war was declared, my grandfather had just started at grammar school. 6 *dont* – It was a day we remembered for a long time. 7 *où* – She hated meetings where everyone spoke at once. 8 *où* – The office you have to apply to is not on this floor/in this building. 9 *dont* – I don't like the way the negotiations have been conducted. 10 *dont* – Venice? That's a city I've dreamt about for years.

42/5 1 *ce qu'il a fait* – What he did is completely unacceptable. 2 *ce qui lui fait dire ça* – It's obvious what makes him/her say that. 3 *le bien que ce voyage m'a fait* – It's impossible to exaggerate the good this trip has done me. 4 *ce qui est fait* – What's done is done: let's not talk about it any more. 5 *qui les avais* – The keys? Well, you're the one who had them just now. 6 *l'homme qu'il était* – He's no longer the man he used to be. 7 *ce que je pense* – I'll tell you what I think of this business. 8 *les* *histoires qui commençaient* – He'd decided to ignore the stories that were starting to go around.

42/6 1 *tout ce qui l'intéresse* 2 *tous ceux qui veulent* 3 *tous ceux qui n'ont pas* 4 *tout ce qu'il a fait* 5 *tout ce qu'on peut savoir* 6 *tous ceux que j'ai pu interroger* 7 *tout ce qui concerne* 8 *tous ceux qui n'avaient pas*

43/1 Possible answers include: 1 *je pourrais faire cet exercice les yeux fermés* 2 *Pierre se promène partout, un pull sur les épaules* 3 *la tête haute, Marie a traversé la foule* 4 *on a aperçu M. Dupont qui venait vers nous, les mains dans les poches* 5 *le sourire aux lèvres, la réceptionniste a accueilli les nouveaux clients* 6 *les enfants grandissent, la tête pleine d'idées nouvelles*

43/2 1 *la secrétaire, de bonne humeur, est allée le chercher* 2 *pour avoir la paix, il a accédé* 3 *selon les dernières informations, l'accident avait été causé* (or: *aurait été causé*) 4 *à vrai dire, cette affaire ne m'intéresse pas* 5 *il joue de la guitare pour le plaisir* 6 *après avoir vu l'exposition, vous pourrez juger* 7 *ils sont passés près de nous sans nous saluer* 8 *c'est vraiment un spectacle à ne pas manquer*

44/1 1 *nous disant au revoir, il est monté* 2 *espérant y trouver mes camarades, je suis descendu au bar* 3 *fermant les yeux, il a sauté* 4 *pleurant la mort de son père, elle était inconsolable* 5 *levant la main, elle a commencé* 6 *croyant qu'on était déjà partis, ils n'ont pas attendu*

44/2 Preferable answers include: 1 *en disant ça, tu* 2 *tout en travaillant, elle* 3 *je prendrais un risque en faisant cela* 4 *en conduisant plus lentement, on* 5 *tout en sachant que c'était urgent, il* 6 *les forces lui sont revenues en dormant* 7 *l'appétit vient en mangeant*

44/3 1 *partis avant l'aube, nous* 2 *harcelée par les journalistes, l'actrice* 3 *tourné il y a trois ans, le film* 4 *bouleversés par sa mort, nous* 5 *encouragée par les supporters, l'équipe* 6 *écrite à la main, la lettre*

44/4 1 *je l'ai approuvée* 2 *on les a choisis* 3 *tu ne lui a pas écrit* 4 *j'en ai parlé* 5 *j'y ai pensé* 6 *elle ne l'a pas trouvée* 7 *on l'a étudié* 8 *ils l'ont traversée* 9 *on ne leur a rien reproché* 10 *vous ne l'avez pas comprise*

44/5 Possible answers include: 1a *on les a consultés plusieurs fois* 1b *les experts qu'on a consultés ont approuvé le projet* 1c *quels experts a-t-on/avez-vous consultés?* 2a *ils les ont détruits pour le profit* 2b *les paysages qu'ils ont détruits sont irremplaçables* 2c *quels paysages ont-ils détruits?* 3a *j'y ai réfléchi longtemps* 3b *cette question, à laquelle j'ai réfléchi, est difficile à résoudre* 3c *à quelle question avez-vous/as-tu réfléchi?* 4a *elle leur en a parlé* 4b *mes parents, à qui elle en a parlé hier, sont d'accord* 4c *à qui en a-t-elle parlé?* 5a *je lui ai tout expliqué ce matin* 5b *le directeur, à qui j'ai tout expliqué, est d'accord* 5c *à qui avez-vous/as-tu tout expliqué?* 6a *tu l'as trouvée bien vite* 6b *la réponse que tu as trouvée est juste* 6c *quelle réponse ai-je/as-tu trouvée?*

44/6 1 *elle s'est adaptée* – She (has) adapted to the new system. 2 *le temps s'était amélioré* – The weather had improved. 3 *la ville s'est développée* – The town/city has grown/developed. 4 *elle s'est intéressée* – She took/has taken an interest in his/her case. 5 *les vacances s'étaient passées* – The holidays had gone well. 6 *elle s'était amusée* – She had had a good time at the dance. 7 *ils se sont spécialisés* – They (have) specialised. 8 *nous nous étions sentis* – We had felt at ease/comfortable. 9 *ils s'étaient trouvés* – They had found themselves out of a job. 10 *je me suis dépêché* – I hurried to finish the exercise.

44/7 1 *ils se sont fait mal; ils ne se sont pas fait mal* 2 *nous nous sommes vus; nous ne nous sommes pas vus* 3 *elle s'est trompée; elle ne s'est pas trompée* 4 *ils se sont rendu compte; ils ne se sont pas rendu compte* 5 *elle s'est cassé la jambe; elle ne s'est pas cassé la jambe* 6 *elle s'est défendue; elle ne s'est pas défendue*

45/1 1 *plus je pense . . . plus je la trouve* 2 *plus tôt . . . et mieux cela vaudra* 3 *moins on en parlera, mieux cela vaudra* 4 *plus on va . . . plus le ciel* 5 *plus je lis et moins je comprends* 6 *plus j'étudie . . . plus j'ai envie* (or: *moins . . .*)

45/2 Possible juxtaposed sentences include: 1 *je le vois bien: tu ne veux pas partir* 2 *elle a travaillé jusqu'à trois heures du matin; le lendemain elle dormait debout* 3 *je m'en doutais: ils seront là avant nous* 4 *j'ai eu beau téléphoner* *vingt fois, personne n'a répondu* 5 *nous nous étions à peine levés pour danser que la musique a changé* 6 *un verre de trop, et il devient agressif*

46/1 1 *quand il y a moins de monde* 2 *quand on a contacté les autorités* 3 *quand tu auras le temps* 4 *quand elle aurait le temps* 5 *quand il téléphonera* 6 *quand il téléphonerait*

46/2 1 *pendant qu'elle travaille* 2 *si bien que tout le monde était content* 3 *quand on aura fait les courses* 4 *parce que j'ai beaucoup de choses à te raconter* 5 *quand elle m'a dit ça* 6 *si bien que le terrain était entièrement inondée* 7 *dès que je pourrai* 8 *d'autant (plus) qu'elle avait la migraine ce jour-là* 9 *étant donné qu'elle était enceinte* 10 *alors qu'on en avait commandé cinq*

46/3 a Possible answers include: 1 *pendant sa maladie* 2 *depuis son retour du Québec* 3 *après avoir téléphoné* 4 *à cause de son départ précipité* 5 *pendant ses vacances en Écosse* 6 *après le retour de sa mère* 7 *dès mon retour* 8 *dès son arrivée en France* 9 *étant donné sa maladie* 10 *après avoir reçu la lettre de mon frère*

47/1 1 *je viendrai* 2 *j'aurais été* 3 *il ne pourra pas* 4 *il y irait* 5 *s'ils avaient joué* 6 *il aurait pu* 7 *on n'entendra rien* 8 *elle vivrait*

47/2 Possible answers include: 1 (Type 3) *s'il nous avait dit . . . on aurait pu* – If he'd told us that last week, we could have started preparing. 2 (Type 1) *si tu manges . . . tu n'auras plus* – If you eat too many biscuits, you won't have any appetite (left). 3 (Type 2) *si les études étaient . . . tout le monde irait* – If (higher) education was free, everyone would go to university. 4 (Type 2) *ce serait dommage . . . si tout le monde avait* – It'd be a pity if evryone had the same ideas. 5 (Type 1) *j'irai . . . si personne d'autre ne veut* – I'll go myself if no one else wants to. 6 (Type 3) *si Dieu avait voulu . . . Il nous aurait donné* – If God had wanted human beings to fly, He'd have given us wings. 7 (Type 3) *si on était arrivés . . . on aurait trouvé* – If we'd got there sooner, we'd have had better seats. 8 (Type 1) *le monde se détruira . . . si on ne protège pas* – The world will be destroyed if we don't protect nature.

48/1 1 *qu'il ait* – I'm pleased he's passed his driving test at last. 2 *que tu sois* – I don't want you to be sad. 3 *qu'elle sache* – It's impossible for her to know the results already. 4 *qu'on puisse* – How do you expect us to be able to work with all this/that noise? 5 *quoi qu'ils fassent* – Whatever they do, we'll be able to cope. 6 *où que tu ailles* – Wherever you go, you'll hear the same (old) story. 7 *pour qu'on n'attende pas* – The new system is designed so that you don't have too long to wait. 8 *que je dise* – That's my answer: what more do you want me to say?

48/2 1 *qu'on puisse* – I doubt if we'll be able to get the message to him/her before tomorrow. 2 *que les gens soient* – It's essential for people to be well informed on these issues. 3 *que vous soyez arrivé(e)s* – I'm pleased that you got here on time this morning. 4 *qu'on fasse* – I wouldn't like them/us to do that. 5 *qu'ils aient fait* – I'm sorry they did that before telling me first. 6 *pour qu'on comprenne* – They give these explanations so that people have a better idea of what it's about. 7 *qu'elle soit morte* – It's a shame she died before her grandson was born. 8 *que tout le monde ait fini* – (It's) too late: I can't wait until everyone has finished/for everyone to have finished.

48/3 1 *qu'il va* 2 *qu'on ne puisse pas* 3 *que ce soit* 4 *que tu as* 5 *qu'on ne peut pas* 6 *que vous me disiez* 7 *qu'il prenne* 8 *que tout le monde est/sera*

48/4 1 *il a fait ça pour s'amuser* 2 *il a fait ça pour qu'on s'amuse* 3 *venez me voir avant que je parte* 4 *venez me voir avant de partir* 5 *répondez sans regarder la liste* 6 *répondez sans que je vous dise les mots* 7 *dépêche-toi! Il faut qu'on parte dans cinq minutes* 8 *dépêche-toi! Il faut que tu t'habilles vite* (or: *dépêche-toi de t'habiller*) 9 *je ne me présente pas à l'examen, de peur d'échouer* 10 *je ne me présente pas à l'examen, de peur que les questions soient trop difficiles*

48/5 Possible answers include: 1 *qui pourra; qui pourrait* 2 *qui pourrait; qui puisse* 3 *qui soit* 4 *qui est* 5 *qui ferait; qui fasse* 6 *qu'on me dit*

49/1 Possible answers include: 1 *est* 2 *doit* 3 *ait*
4 *fasse* 5 *va* 6 *faut* 7 *puisses* 8 *ait* 9 *sont* 10 *aient* (or
possibly: *ont*)

49/2 a Possible answers include: 1 *il n'a rien dit: tu
l'as remarqué?* 2 *elle n'a pas l'air d'être en bonne santé, c'est
vrai* 3 *ça nous fait faire des dizaines de kilomètres en plus, je
sais bien* 4 *il n'y aura pas de feu d'artifice cette année, paraît-
il* (or: *à ce qu'il paraît*) 5 *est-ce qu'il va neiger, tu crois?*
6 *aujourd'hui on est tous les victimes . . . c'est bien connu*

50/1 Possible version: *Je vais vous dire ce qui s'est passé
lors de la dernière conférence des Neuf sur l'Europe agricole.
Pendant que les neuf ministres de l'agriculture débattaient du
prix du porc, un paysan mécontent a fait entrer neuf veaux
dans la salle, ce qui a créé beaucoup de confusion, car on ne
savait plus qui était qui. A la fin de la conférence, le paysan,
au lieu de remporter ses neuf veaux, dans la bousculade qui a
suivi n'en a remporté que huit, mais il a emmené aussi un
ministre. Cependant, on n'a pas annoncé* (or: *je ne vous dirai
pas*) *lequel. Or, ce n'est qu'en arrivant sur le marché qu'il s'est
aperçu de son erreur. Malheureusement, quand le moment est
venu de vendre les veaux, il y en avait un qui était
invendable, à savoir le . . . oui, vous l'avez deviné! Car un
ministre, voyez-vous, ne se vend pas, bien qu'il arrive parfois
qu'un ministre s'achète. Mais, je le répète, un ministre ne se
vend pas. D'ailleurs, je dois avouer à ma grande honte que
moi-même, une fois, après m'être vendu à bas prix, j'ai voulu
me racheter, mais cela m'a coûté une somme énorme.*

50/2 Possible version: *Quand l'autobus est arrivé, je suis
monté. Une fois à bord, j'ai remarqué quelqu'un dont
l'apparence m'a frappé à cause de son long cou et du ruban de
son chapeau. Soudain il s'est mis à pester contre son voisin qui
avait dû lui marcher sur les pieds; ensuite, il est allé s'asseoir.
Chose curieuse, je l'ai revu plus tard Cour de Rome. Cette fois-
ci, il était avec un copain qui lui disait qu'il devrait faire
mettre un autre bouton à son pardessus. Voilà.*

51/1 Possible answers include: 1 *lui, il n'avait rien fait*
2 *elle, je la déteste* 3 *nous, on a les pieds sur terre* (or: *on a les
pieds sur terre, nous*) 4 *eux, ils ne sont jamais contents* (or:

ils ne sont jamais contents, eux) 5 *toi, tu restes ici, hein!*
6 *on n'est pas si bêtes, nous!* 7 *moi je n'ai rien compris* 8 *lui,
il sait manipuler les gens*

51/2 Possible answers include: 1 *il a rencontré le
personnel, le nouveau directeur?* 2 *tu l'as vu, le documentaire
sur la mafia?* 3 *à quelle heure est-ce qu'elle ferme, la
bibliothèque?* 4 *il a toujours son mot à dire, celui-là* 5 *c'est
elle qui a tout organisé* 6 *c'est l'entraîneur qui doit choisir*
7 *c'est quand les jours raccourcissent qu'elle est déprimée*
8 *c'est en arrivant à l'aéroport qu'il a découvert* 9 *ce n'est pas
ici qu'il faut s'adresser* 10 (a cleft construction is unlikely
in this case)

51/4 1 *il y a longtemps qu'il (ne) les a pas vus* 2 *s'il a
affirmé ça, c'est qu'il le croit* 3 *il n'y a que toi que j'aime*
4 *il n'y a que le sport qui l'intéresse* 5 *si je propose ça, c'est que
je ne vois pas* 6 *il y en a encore qui approuvent* 7 *ça fait des
années qu'il essaie de* 8 *s'ils parlent comme ça, c'est qu'ils ne
savent pas*

51/5 Possible answers include: 1 *ce qu'elle déteste, c'est
la musique moderne* (also: *c'est la musique moderne qu'elle
déteste*) 2 *celui qui me fait rire, c'est Buster Keaton* (also: *c'est
BK qui me fait rire*) 3 *ce qu'il faut dire tout de suite, c'est que
je n'ai pas* 4 *ce qui est amusant, c'est qu'il a l'air* 5 *ce qu'on
oublie, c'est qu'il y a* 6 *celui qui a fait le plus de mal dans le
monde, c'est Hitler* (also: *c'est H qui a fait*) 7 *ce qui est
curieux, c'est qu'ils n'ont rien dit* 8 *celle que je préfère, c'est la
guerre de 14–18* (also: *c'est la guerre de 14–18 que je préfère*)

52/1 Possible answers include: 1 *les vacances, c'est
toujours trop court; c'est toujours trop court, les vacances* 2 *la
famille, c'est parfois encombrant; c'est encombrant parfois, la
famille* 3 *c'est ridicule, son idée* (also: *elle est ridicule, son
idée*); *son idée, c'est ridicule* (also: *son idée, elle est ridicule*)
4 *c'est souvent enfantin, la publicité à la télé; la publicité à la
télé, c'est souvent enfantin* 5 *ce tableau, c'est un chef d'œuvre*
6 *ma chambre, c'est un bazar* 7 *tous ces sans-abri, c'est un
scandale* (or possibly: *c'est un scandale, tous ces sans-abri*)
8 *la destruction de l'environnement, c'est un crime* 9 *les
études, ça sert; cela/ça sert toujours à quelque chose, les études*
10 *le sport, ça fournit* 11 *les vols transatlantiques, ça*

consomme; ça consomme énormément de carburant, les vols transatlantiques 12 *les partis politiques, ça devra s'adapter*

52/2 1 *c'est curieux* 2 *elle est très inquiète* 3 *il est très amusant* 4 *elle est presque neuve* 5 *c'est ridicule* 6 *c'est incroyable* (referring to what he told me), or: e*lle est incroyable* (referring to *l'affaire*)

52/3 Possible answers include: 1 *travailler . . . c'est inhumain; c'est inhumain de travailler* 2 *arriver . . . c'est bizarre; c'est bizarre d'arriver* 3 *c'est une chance d'avoir trouvé* 4 *faire les courses . . . c'est tout un exploit* 5 *c'est cruel d'acheter* 6 *pénaliser . . . c'est un scandale*

52/4 Possible answers include: 1 *c'est évident qu'ils ne peuvent pas* 2 *ça m'amuse qu'il soit toujours là* 3 *c'est bizarre qu'elle n'ait pas téléphoné* 4 *c'est certain qu'on s'est trompés* (or: *qu'on se soit trompés . . . c'est évident*) 5 *c'est probable qu'ils ne viendront pas* 6 *ça m'étonne qu'il n'ait rien dit* (or: *qu'il n'ait rien dit, ça m'étonne*)

52/5 1 *je ne vais pas le dire* 2 *ce que tu en penses* 3 *je n'en doute pas* 4 *on l'imagine* 5 *il n'y avait pas pensé* 6 *on n'y croit plus* 7 *il est allé le raconter* 8 *je m'en souviens*

53/1 *Le Bressan* **se dit** *qu'en décembre, il* **sera** *appelé au service militaire. A sa libération, il* **se mariera** *avec la fille d'un voisin, qui lui* **apportera** *trois hectares en dot; cela* **était** *déjà réglé. Il* **trouvera** *trois ou quatre autres hectares à louer et il* **paiera** *en journées de travail la paire de bœufs que son beau-père lui* **prêtera** *pour les labours et les charrois. Il* **devra** *économiser pour acheter des bestiaux et du matériel et prendre un jour une ferme à son compte. Plus tard, économiser pour payer le fermage, et, plus tard encore, quand il* **aura** *des enfants, pour prendre une ferme plus grande. La femme* **tiendra** *la bourse.* (from *325 000*, Roger Vailland, © Buchet Chastel)

53/2 *J'ai dit à l'aumônier qu'***il avait** *l'air si certain, n'est-ce pas? Pourtant, aucune de* **ses** *certitudes ne* **valait** *un cheveu de femme.* **Il n'était** *même pas sûr d'être en vie* **puisqu'il vivait** *comme un mort. Moi,* **j'avais** *l'air d'avoir les mains vides.*

Mais **j'étais** *sûr de moi, sûr de tout, plus sûr que* **lui***, sûr de ma vie et de cette mort qui* **allait** *venir. Oui,* **je n'avais** *que cela. Mais du moins, je* **tenais** *cette vérité autant qu'elle me* **tenait***.* **J'avais eu** *raison,* **j'avais** *encore raison,* **j'avais** *toujours raison.* **J'avais** *vécu de telle façon et j'aurais pu vivre de telle autre.* **J'avais fait** *ceci et je* **n'avais pas fait** *cela. Je* **n'avais pas fait** *telle chose, alors que* **j'avais fait** *telle autre. Et après?* **C'était** *comme si j'avais attendu pendant tout le temps cette minute et cette petite aube où je* **serais** *justifié. Rien, rien* **n'avait** *d'importance et je* **savais** *bien pourquoi.* **Lui** *aussi* **savait** *pourquoi.* (adapted from *L'Étranger*, Albert Camus, © Éditions Gallimard)

53/3 1 *ils viennent de vendre* 2 *je viens de comprendre* 3 *il venait de trouver* 4 *l'avion venait d'atterrir* 5 *ils venaient de nommer* 6 *on vient d'apprendre* 7 *ta mère vient de téléphoner* 8 *une idée affreuse venait de la frapper* 9 *elle venait de terminer* 10 *les enfants viennent de rentrer*

53/4 1 *elle va repasser* 2 *ils ne vont pas être* 3 *qu'elle n'allait pas partir* 4 *je ne vais pas rentrer* 5 *que vous alliez ranger* 6 *qu'il n'allait plus donner de concerts* 7 *on va avoir* 8 *vous allez comprendre* 9 *que j'allais réparer* 10 *qu'il allait prévenir*

54/1 1 *il a arrêté* 2 *elle n'arrêtait pas* 3 *il finissait* 4 *tu as fini* 5 *elle a vu . . . qui ressemblait* 6 *ils ont décidé . . . ils se connaissaient* 7 *ils venaient . . . on allait* 8 *hier, on est allé . . . il ne restait plus* 9 *quand elle a ouvert la porte, elle a découvert qu'il pleuvait*

54/2 1 *voulaient* 2 *sommes descendus* 3 *s'est . . . jetée* 4 *avons attendu* 5 *parlait* 6 *ai remarqué* 7 *avait* 8 *avançait* 9 *avait* 10 *a dit* 11 *ai . . . fait* 12 *étais* 13 *faisait* 14 *commençait* 15 *ai retardé* 16 *avais* 17 *ai fini* 18 *ai plongé* 19 *est entré* 20 *s'est jeté* 21 *a perdu* 22 *nageait* 23 *ai laissé* 24 *était* 25 *étais* 26 *nous sommes baignés* 27 *nous sentions*

54/3 1 *dus* 2 *montai* 3 *était* 4 *était* 5 *dormait* 6 *avait* 7 *allumai* 8 *grogna* 9 *se réveilla* 10 *étaient* 11 *descendis*

12 *vis* 13 *étaient* 14 *remontai* 15 *réveillai* 16 *demandai* 17 *était* 18 *dit* 19 *savais* 20 *était*

54/4 1 *avait . . . a dû* 2 *a voulu . . . était* 3 *a eu . . . savait* 4 *était . . . a pu* 5 *a su . . . voulaient* 6 *a été . . . devait*

54/5 1 *suis resté . . . pendant* 2 *étaient . . . depuis* 3 *habite . . . depuis* ('we've been living . . . for'), or: *a habité . . . pendant* ('we lived . . . for') 4 *essaye . . . depuis* 5 *pendant . . . a cherché* 6 *a soufflé . . . pendant*

French
Grammar
Explained

58 Glossary of grammatical terms used in *French Grammar Explained*

Acronym *un sigle*
The use of the initial letters of each word in a group of words, with the same meaning as the original group of words: *l'Organaisation des nations unies > l'ONU.*

Active construction See **Passive**.

Adjective *un adjectif*
One of the four major parts of speech. Adjectives describe nouns, providing details about appearance, character, value or other qualities.

Adverb *un adverbe*
One of the four major parts of speech. Adverbs describe the manner or circumstances in which a process or action takes place. They can refer either to a single verb or to a whole sentence or series of sentences. An adverb can consist of a single word: *demain; vite*, or a group of words: *tout à l'heure; à la hâte.*

Agreement See **Gender**.

Article *un article*
A **determiner** which is used to place a noun in a category ranging from general to specific.

    Definite article *un article défini*
One of *le, l', la, les*, used, as is 'the' in English, to refer to a specific item: *l'argent qu'elle a économisé.* Also used to refer to the whole class of such items: *l'argent ne fait pas le bonheur*; in English, no article is used in such cases.

    Indefinite article *un article indéfini*
One of *un, une, des*, used to refer to an unspecified item ('a/an', in English) or to an unspecified number ('some', or no article, in English) of items: *j'ai acheté **une** baguette et **des** croissants.* As in English, *un/une* + singular noun can also stand for a whole class of items: ***un** enfant a besoin d'encouragement.*

    Partitive article *un article partitif*
One of *du, de l', de la*, used, as is 'some' in English, to refer to a limited amount of a substance: *donnez-moi **de l'eau**, s'il vous plaît.* Also used when naming the substance itself: *c'est **de l'eau***; in English, no article is used in such cases.

Aspect   *l'aspect*

Tenses are used to situate an event, a process in time relative to the speaker or writer, or relative to another event. But tenses are also used to indicate the way an event or process is viewed by the speaker or writer: this is aspect. For example, the passé composé (or the past historic) can be used in French to indicate completed aspect: one particular event is set within stated time limits, or it is presented as one of a series of actions. The imperfect tense, on the other hand, can be used to indicate uncompleted aspect: the process is not set within time limits, it is part of the circumstances in which another event takes place. The imperfect tense is also used to indicate an event which is repeated an unspecified number of times. Aspect is also indicated by aspect auxiliaries + infinitive, such as *venir de, aller, être en train de, être sur le point de, avoir l'habitude de, commencer à, cesser de.*

Auxiliary verb   *un verbe auxiliaire*

A verb used with the present or past participle, or the infinitive, of another verb in order to indicate **tense**: *elle **est** arrivée*, **aspect**: *elle **vient d'**arriver* or **mood**: *elle **doit** arriver.*

Clause   *une proposition*

Independent clause   *une proposition indépendante*

A statement containing a **tensed verb** and making sense on its own: *notre chat a attrapé une souris.*

Main clause   *une proposition principale*

A statement containing a tensed verb and making sense when used with a **coordinate** or **subordinate clause**.

Coordinate clause   *une proposition coordonnée*

A statement containing a tensed verb and linked to a main clause by a coordinating conjunction (*et, ou* etc.).

Subordinate clause   *une proposition subordonnée*

A statement containing a tensed verb and linked to a main clause by a subordinating conjunction: *on est rentrés **parce qu'il pleuvait***, or ***quand je l'ai vue**, elle était souriante*, or a statement containing an infinitive or participle and linked to a main clause by a preposition (in some cases, there is no linking preposition): *venez me voir **avant de partir***, or *elle espère **finir demain***, or *l'appétit vient **en mangeant**.*

Completive clause   *une proposition complétive*

A subordinate clause introduced by a construction such as *je sais que, je suis certain que, c'est vrai que*. *je sais **qu'il est là**; c'est vrai **qu'elle est belle**.* In the sentence as a whole, the introductory construction, although grammatically the main clause, is the **comment**: it prepares for the main message, or **topic**, which is in the completive clause. See also **Phrase, Sentence; Correlative construction, Juxtaposition**.

Cleft construction   *une construction clivée*

The use of *c'est/il y a* + noun/pronoun/adverb + *qui/que* to highlight one element by detaching it and placing it at the beginning of the sentence: *je t'aime* > ***c'est toi que** j'aime*.

Pseudo-cleft construction   *une construction pseudo-clivée*

The use of *celui* (etc.) */ce qui/que* + noun + *c'est* (etc.) to highlight one element by detaching it and placing it at the end of the sentence: *la grammaire est difficile* > ***ce qui** est difficile, **c'est** la grammaire*.

Coherence   *la cohérence (textuelle)*

The ways in which the ideas in a text (etc.) are chosen, organised and presented so as to make sense to a reader or listener.

Cohesion   *la cohésion*

The ways in which language is used to make clear the links between different parts of a text, for example by the use of pronouns (instead of repeating nouns) or conjunctions (instead of separate sentences).

Comment   See **Topic**.

Comparative construction   *une construction comparative*

A way of expressing a relative judgment by comparing one item or set with another or others in a similar category: ***plus** grand **que** l'autre; **moins** difficiles **que** les autres*. See also **Superlative construction**.

Complement   *un complément*

A word or group of words which is linked grammatically to one of the four major parts of speech. **Verb** complements include direct and indirect **objects**, **infinitive** constructions and **completive** clauses; **noun** complements include preposition + noun or infinitive: *l'idée du départ; l'idée **de** partir*, and *que* + completive clause: *l'idée **qu'on va partir***, **adjective** complements include preposition + noun or infinitive: *content **qu'ils soient partis***; the complement of a **comparative** adjective or adverb is introduced by *que*, and of a superlative by *de*.

Detached complement   *un complément circonstantiel*

A word or phrase consisting of or centred on an adjective, an adverb, a noun, a present or past participle, or an infinitive, and not linked grammatically to another phrase or clause. A detached complement can appear at the beginning or end, or at a suitable point in the middle of a clause. It gives information on the circumstances in which the action takes place; the meaning is often equivalent to a subordinate clause introduced by conjunctions such as *pendant que, parce que, pour que*.

521

Completive construction   *une construction complétive*
See **Clause: Completive clause**.

Compound tense   *un temps composé*
A tense formed with a tense **auxiliary** (*avoir* or, in some cases, *être*) + past participle.

Compound word   See **Group of words, (a)**.

Conditional   *le conditionnel*
One of the tenses of the verb: *il finirait*, which, together with the past conditional: *il aurait fini*, belongs to the **indicative** mood of the verb. The conditional, including the past conditional, can also be used instead of the present or the passé composé, when the use of one of these two tenses is felt to be too direct, or to claim too much. Used in this way, the conditional functions as a **mood** of the verb, occupying an intermediate position between the indicative and the **subjunctive**.

Conjunction   *une conjonction*
One of the four minor parts of speech. A conjunction introduces a **clause** centred on a **tensed verb**: *quand le temps s'améliorera; avant que les autres soient partis.*

Connector   *un connecteur*
A word or group of words (adverb or conjunction) used to indicate the nature of the link between two clauses: *donc, parce que* (cause-effect); *mais, alors que* (opposition); *puis, après que* (time sequence), for example. A similar function is performed by **parentheses** and forms of **reference**: *c'est, voilà* etc. Connectors play a vital role in textual **cohesion**.

Consonant   *une consonne*
In written French, one of the letters of the alphabet other than the vowels *a e i o u* (and *y*). In spoken French, one of 18 consonant sounds, each produced with some degree of closure or constriction. Each spoken **syllable** consists of a single vowel, on its own, or with one or more consonants.

Construction   *une construction*
The way in which a group of words is linked to what follows. Certain verbs and adjectives are used with a particular preposition when followed by a noun, or an infinitive: *commencer à* + infinitive; *douter de* + noun; *apte à* + noun or infinitive. Certain verbs and phrases are constructed with *que* + **indicative**: *espérer que; il est certain que*, and others are constructed with *que* + **subjunctive**: *souhaiter que; il est impossible que.*

Correlative construction *une construction corrélative*

Two clauses or phrases, each beginning with the same word or group of words: *ou bien . . . ou bien*, or with two different words or groups: *aussi bien . . . que*, which are used to place two processes, two objects, etc., on an equal or parallel footing.

Demonstrative adjective *un adjectif démonstratif*

One of *ce, cet, cette, ces*. A demonstrative adjective is a **determiner**; it is always used with a noun, and agrees with that noun in number and gender.

Demonstrative pronoun *un pronom démonstratif*

One of *celui, celle, ceux, celles*. A demonstrative pronoun is used in place of a demonstrative adjective + noun, and agrees in number and gender with the noun it replaces. The **tonic pronoun** *ça, cela*, on the other hand, refers to a topic, an idea, etc., not to a specific noun.

Detachment See **Dislocation**.

Determiner *un déterminant*

One of the four minor parts of speech, specifying a function of a noun. The class of determiners includes **possessive** and **demonstrative** adjectives, definite, indefinite and partitive **articles**, and indefinite adjectives such as *plusieurs, certains*.

Diphthong *une diphtongue*

A spoken vowel consisting of two different sounds, produced as a single **syllable**, with or without consonants. There are eight diphthongs in spoken English, but none in spoken French; the closest equivalent to a diphthong in French is the unit **semivowel** + vowel, or vowel + semivowel.

Dislocation *la dislocation*

The moving of one or more elements (nouns or pronouns) from their usual place in a sentence: *Pierre, je le connais* (left dislocation); *je ne sais pas, moi!* (right dislocation). The element which is moved is said to be detached; in many cases it is repeated as a **subject** or **object** pronoun. Dislocation is one means of drawing attention to a particular element, whether it is the **topic** or the **comment**, in a statement.

Elision *l'élision*

The non-pronunciation of a vowel, usually *-e*, at the end of a word followed by a word beginning with a vowel. In certain cases, elision is marked in spelling by an apostrophe: *que + elle > qu'elle; si + il > s'il*. In other cases, the elided *-e* remains in the spelling: *on est presque arrivés*. When elision does not take place, there is *enchaînement* between two vowels.

523

Emphasis *l'accent d'insistance*

In speech, in order to draw attention to a word, an idea, etc., a syllable can be emphasised by making it longer and/or louder than the syllables around it. In English, any word can receive emphasis, wherever it appears in a group of words; words of more than one syllable are emphasised by placing additional **stress** on the syllable that is usually stressed. In French, emphasis is achieved by placing additional stress on the initial syllable of a word or group of words, or by pausing in the middle of a group, just before the syllable which is emphasised, and also by adding tonic pronouns, by repeating words, and through the use of **dislocation** or **extraction**.

Enchaînement

The production, without a break, of a series of syllables within a **rhythmic group**. If, within a rhythmic group, a word ending in a consonant is followed by one beginning with a vowel, the consonant is pronounced at the start of the next syllable, not at the end of the previous one. *Enchaînement* is a distinctive feature of spoken French, compared to spoken English or German, for example. See also **Liaison**.

Extraction See **Cleft construction**; **Pseudo-cleft construction**.

Gender *le genre*

In English, there are three genders: masculine, feminine and neuter, but these are differentiated only in certain personal pronouns ('he, she, it'; 'him, her, it'), possessive adjectives ('his, her, its') and possessive pronouns ('his, hers, its'). In French, there are two genders, masculine and feminine, which are differentiated in respect of nouns (including determiners and adjective agreement) and pronouns; but grammatical gender ('masculine', 'feminine') represents sex ('male', 'female') only in respect of people and certain creatures. Adjectives used with certain indefinite pronouns are invariable: *il m'a dit quelque chose **d'intéressant**; il n'y a personne **d'intéressant**.*

Grammar *la grammaire*

(a) The expression of meaning through the form of words and the structure and combination of **groups**, **phrases**, **clauses** and **sentences**.
(b) The system of forms, structures and combinations used in a particular language, such as English or French.
(c) The study of the grammatical resources and constraints of **language** in general (see **(a)** above).
(d) The study of the grammatical system and conventions of a particular **language** (see **(b)** above).

Grammatical class *une catégorie grammaticale*
or Part of speech *une partie du discours*

Each word in a language can be seen as belonging to a particular grammatical class or part of speech: verb, noun, adjective, adverb; determiner, pronoun, preposition, conjunction. These grammatical classes provide convenient labels for individual words, reminding one to 'make adjectives agree' in French, or to 'use the appropriate verb ending'. In order to understand how **language** in general, and particular **languages**, work, however, it is important to consider the grammatical functions which these labels represent. The same word can have different grammatical functions: the word 'table' can function as a verb or as a noun, and the word 'shock' can function as a verb, a noun or an adjective. A particular grammatical function can be performed by a group of words: *avoir peur* (verb); *une salle à manger* (noun); *avec soin* (adverb); *à côté de* (preposition). Understanding **grammar** therefore involves understanding a system of grammatical relationships: how adjectives and determiners relate to nouns, how nouns and pronouns relate to verbs, and so on.

Group of words

(a) *une locution*

Many verbs, nouns, etc are formed from a group of words instead of a single word: *faire partie de* (verb); *un sous-marin* (noun); *sous-équipé* (adjective); *tout à coup* (adverb); *à côté de* (preposition); *pendant que* (conjunction). These can also be called **compound** words (nouns, prepositions, etc.).

(b) *un groupe de mots*

Other groups consist of two or more words which are linked grammatically: *je **te parle*** (verb + object pronoun); ***cet homme**-là* (determiner + noun); *il **commence à pleuvoir*** (verb + preposition + infinitive); *c'est **facile à faire*** (adjective + preposition + infinitive). See also **Phrase, Clause, Sentence**.

(c) Rhythmic group *un groupe rythmique*

French is written as separate words, unless there is an apostrophe: *l'Inde*, or a hyphen: *la Grande-Bretagne*; but French is spoken as a series of syllables without any pause between words. Pauses occur after 2–5 (sometimes more) syllables, depending on the meaning and the need to take breath; each sequence of syllables is called a rhythmic group, or a 'breath group'. **Stress** normally ocurs at the end of a rhythmic group.

Idiom *une locution idiomatique, une expression idiomatique*

A **group, phrase** or **sentence** which has a meaning other than that of the individual words in it: *il y a* ('there is', 'there are'); *se casser la tête* ('to give oneself a headache' – by thinking or worrying about something).

Imperative *l'impératif*

The imperative is the **mood** of the verb which is used to give a direct order or instruction. The imperative is formed from persons 2, 4 and 5 of the verb, without the subject pronoun (but with the reflexive pronoun of a pronominal verb): *viens! assieds-toi! sortons! venez! asseyez-vous!* An imperative for persons 3 and 6 is formed by using *que* + subject + subjunctive: *que le meilleur gagne! qu'ils s'en aillent!*

Impersonal construction *une construction impersonnelle*

A construction in which the subject of the verb is *il* (*il fait froid; il faut partir*), *ça* or *cela* (*ça m'ennuie d'y aller*), or is not stated (*reste à savoir qui va gagner*).

Impersonal pronoun *un pronom impersonnel*

Subject, object and **tonic** pronouns are called 'personal' pronouns; they are used to refer to specific persons, creatures, things, or ideas. However, certain 'personal' pronouns are used impersonally, in that they do not refer to a specific person, thing or idea: *il* as the subject of impersonal verbs and constructions: *il pleut, il faut partir, il est difficile de décider*; *ce* as the subject of *être*: *c'est moi; c'était la fin; ce sera difficile*; *ça* or *cela* as the subject or object of other verbs: *cela l'a fait rire; tu comprends ça, toi?*; *on* when used as the impersonal subject of a verb: *on dit ça; on a fait venir le médecin*; *se* with pronominal verbs when used with impersonal meaning: *cela ne se fait plus; il s'agit de toi*; *le* as the impersonal direct object (replacing a noun or adjective) of a verb: *je le veux; es-tu certain? oui, je le suis*; *y* or *en* as the impersonal indirect object (replacing *à* + noun or *de* + noun) of a verb (often in set phrases and constructions): *y voir clair; s'en aller*.

Indefinite pronoun *un pronom indéfini*

A word or group such as *quelqu'un, quelque chose; tous, certains.*

Indicative *l'indicatif*

The indicative is the **mood** of the verb which is used unless there is a particular reason to use the **subjunctive** mood. The names of the various **tenses** (present, imperfect, future, etc.) are assumed to refer to the indicative unless the subjunctive is explicitly mentioned.

Infinitive *l'infinitif*

The verb form, ending in *-er, -ir* or *-re* (corresponding to English 'to' + verb), which is listed in dictionaries, etc.: *parler, finir, attendre.* In use, the infinitive corresponds to a noun; it can be the subject or object of a **tensed verb**: *chanter lui plaît; elle aime chanter*, and it can be used with prepositions: *pour rire; sans hésiter.*

Intensifier *un intensif*

a Certain prefixes (*sur-, super-, hyper-*, for example) can be used as intensifiers.
b For the use of certain adverbs as intensifiers, see **Superlative construction**: **Absolute superlative**.

Interlanguage   *l'interlangue*

A person's map of a particular **language**, made up of more or less explicit notions and more or less unformulated assumptions about the sounds, meanings, words, forms, structures and conventions of that language. The word interlanguage is usually applied to the notions and assumptions of a learner of a second language: about his/her native language, about the second language, and about **language** in general. See also **Grammar**.

Interpolation   *une proposition incise*

Used with direct quotation of speech or thoughts, to indicate their source: *Au secours! cria-t-il*. See also **Parenthesis**.

Interrogative pronoun   *un pronom interrogatif*

A pronoun used to introduce a WH- question, for example *Qui? Qu'est-ce que? Où?*

Juxtaposition   *la juxtaposition*

Two clauses can be juxtaposed, instead of being linked by a **coordinating** (*et* etc.) or **subordinating** (*parce que* etc.) conjunction; this can be done when the nature of the link between the two clauses is clear from the meaning of the statement as a whole: *je n'ai pas faim, je viens de manger*.

Language

(a) *le langage*

The human capacity to express and understand meaning through sounds and written signs, corresponding to words (vocabulary) and forms, structures and combinations (**grammar**).

(b) *une langue*

A particular system of sounds (and written signs), vocabulary and **grammar**, such as English or French.

Liaison   *une liaison*

The pronunciation, before a following vowel, of a final consonant which is normally silent: *les* [le] *garçons*, but *les* [le z] *enfants*. When liaison takes place, there is usually *enchaînement*: the liaison consonant is pronounced at the beginning of the following syllable.

Modaliser   *un modalisateur*

A word or phrase placed before a sentence (or later), and forming a commentary on the sentence: *malheureusement, il n'y a plus de pain; il n'y a plus de pain, malheureusement*. A modaliser can consist of an adverb or adverb phrase, an interjection or parenthesis, an imperative, a completive construction, or a modal verb (*devoir, pouvoir* etc.). A modaliser can be seen as a type of **connector**.

527

Mood *un mode*

There are three personal moods of the verb: **indicative, subjunctive, imperative**, and two impersonal moods: **infinitive, participle**. See also **Modaliser**.

Noun *un nom*

One of the four major parts of speech. Nouns are the name or label for people, creatures, things, ideas or concepts.

Object *un complément d'objet*

The object of a verb is indicated by a noun or pronoun; the object is the target of the action indicated by the verb: *je reçois **un cadeau**; on **leur** a parlé; elle doute de **sa sincérité***. See also **Subject**.

Direct object *un complément d'objet direct*

If no preposition is used between a verb and a noun which is the object of that verb, the object is said to be the direct object of that verb: *elle a aidé **sa mère***. If the direct object is a pronoun, the direct object form of the pronoun is used: *elle **l'**a aidée*.

Indirect object *un complément d'objet indirect*

If a preposition (*à, de, par, pour*, for example) is used between a verb and an object of that verb, the object is said to be the indirect object of that verb: *elle a parlé **à sa mère***. If the indirect object is a pronoun, the indirect object form of the pronoun (*lui, leur, y*, for example) is used instead of *à* + noun; other prepositions are used with the **tonic** pronoun (*moi, elle, eux* etc.): *elle a parlé **avec sa mère** > elle a parlé **avec elle***. Instead of *de* + noun (thing, idea), *en* is used: *elle a parlé **de cette affaire** > elle **en** a parlé*.

Object pronoun *un pronom personnel objet*

One of *me, te, le, la, se, nous, vous, les* (direct object pronouns) or *me, te, lui, se, y, en, nous, vous, leur* (indirect object pronouns). See also **Tonic pronoun**.

Parenthesis *une proposition incidente*

A phrase added in the course of or at the end of a statement, and forming a comment or a way of involving the listener: *il sera là, **j'espère***. A parenthesis is an alternative to a **completive construction**: *j'espère qu'il sera là*. See also **Interpolation**.

Part of speech See **Grammatical class**.

Participle *un participe*

An impersonal form (or **mood**) of the verb, unlike the forms of the various **tenses** (in the indicative or the subjunctive) which, together with the subject (noun or pronoun), indicate one of the six persons.

Present participle *le participe présent*

The verb form ending in *-ant*, corresponding to the English verb form in '-ing'; it can be used as an adjective, as a **detached complement**, or to describe the first of two actions in a sequence.

Gerund *le gérondif*

The unit *en* + present participle, corresponding to English 'on -ing' or 'by -ing'; it can be used as a detached complement to describe an action which is simultaneous with another, or is the means to another.

Past participle *le participe passé*

The verb form ending in *-é, -i, -u* (or *-is, -it, -ait, -ert, -aint* etc., in the case of certain irregular verbs); used with the **auxiliaries** *avoir* or *être* to form **compound tenses**, or as an adjective or a **detached complement**.

Passive *le passif*

Active and passive constructions *constructions actives et passives*

In an active construction, the **subject** of the verb is the agent of the action indicated by the verb: *elle sourit*. In a passive construction, formed by the use of *être* + the past participle of the verb which indicates the action, the subject of *être* is not the agent of the action indicated by the past participle: *le message avait été reçu*. The passive is one way in French of placing the **topic** (*le message*, in the above example) before the **comment** (*avait été reçu*).

Person *une personne*

A convenient way of referring to the **subject** of a verb (+ the verb ending). The six persons are often called 'first/second/third person singular/plural'; in *French Grammar Explained*, they are called 'person 1 ... person 6'. For person 1, the subject is *je*, person 2 *tu*, person 3 *il, elle, on* or any singular noun, person 4 *nous*, person 5 *vous*, person 6 *ils, elles* or any plural noun.

Phrase *un groupe, un syntagme*

A group of words which makes sense on its own, without a verb: *un homme compétent* (noun + adjective); *dans la rue* (preposition + noun); *plus fort que moi* (comparison). See also **Group, Clause, Sentence**.

Set phrase (or **lexical phrase**) *une expression figée*

A group of words which is habitually used with a particular meaning, which is different from the meaning of each word in the phrase, analysed separately. See also **Idiom, Construction**.

Possessive adjective *un adjectif possessif*

One of *mon, ma, mes, ton, ta, tes, son, sa, ses; notre, nos, votre, vos, leur, leurs*. A possessive adjective is a determiner; it is always used with a noun, and agrees with that noun in number and gender.

Possessive pronoun *un pronom possessif*

One of *le mien, la mienne, les miens, les miennes* etc. and *le nôtre, la nôtre, les nôtres* etc. A possessive pronoun is used in place of a possessive adjective + noun, and agrees in number and gender with the noun it replaces.

Prefix *un préfixe*

A letter of group of letters which, added at the beginning of a word, forms a new word with a different meaning; in some cases, the new word is in a different grammatical class from the original word. See also **Suffix**.

Preposition *une préposition*

One of the four minor parts of speech. A preposition introduces a **phrase** centred on a noun or pronoun: *devant la maison; devant moi*. A preposition can consist of a single word, or a group of words: *près de; à côté de*. Certain prepositions (*avant, devant,* for example) can be used without a noun or pronoun, in which case they function as **adverbs**.

Pronominal verb *un verbe pronominal*

A verb used with a reflexive pronoun (*me, te, se, nous, vous*). The meaning of a pronominal verb can be reflexive: *il se lave*, reciprocal: *ils se parlent*, or simply intransitive: *tout le monde doit s'adapter*.

Pronoun *un pronom*

One of the four minor parts of speech. A pronoun has the same grammatical function as a noun in relation to **prepositions**: *avec cet homme > avec lui, avec celui-ci*, and in relation to **verbs**: *Pierre arrive > il arrive, qui arrive?; j'ai vu Marie > je l'ai vue, j'ai vu quelqu'un; c'est mon chien > c'est le mien*. See also **Subject pronoun, Object pronoun, Tonic pronoun, Indefinite pronoun; Possessive pronoun, Demonstrative pronoun; Relative pronoun, Interrogative pronoun**.

Pseudo-cleft construction See **Cleft construction**.

Question

Direct question   *une question directe*

A question which, when written down, ends with a question mark: *Où allez-vous?*

Indirect question   *une question indirecte*

A factual report of a question that has been asked: *il m'a demandé **où j'allais**,* or a reference to a question that could be asked: *je me demande **s'il est arrivé**.* See also **completive construction**.

Yes/No question = *l'interrogation totale*

A question that can be answered by Yes or No: *c'est vrai? est-ce qu'il est là?* etc.

WH- question = *l'interrogation partielle*

A question that cannot be answered by Yes or No: ***comment** le savez-vous? **où** est-il?* etc.

Reduction   *la réduction*

The use of one word with the same meaning as a group of words: *une route nationale > une nationale; bleu marine > marine.* See also **Truncation**.

Reference   *la référence*

To avoid constant repetition of a name or group of words which have already been mentioned, we use **subject/object/tonic/demonstrative pronouns**, or **demonstrative adjectives**, for example. In particular, *il/elle/ils/elles*, and *il/ce* (in *c'est*)/*ça/cela* are used in French to refer to a particular noun, or to a particular fact or notion.

Register   *niveau de langue* See **Situation**.

Relative construction   *une construction relative*
or Relative clause   *une proposition relative*

A way of providing further information about a noun: *un chien **qui dort**,* or a pronoun: *celui **qu'ils recherchent**.* It can also replace a noun: *ce qu'il dit,* instead of *ses propos* or *son discours.* The noun (*un chien*) or the pronoun (*celui*) is called the 'antecedent' of the relative construction. The basic form of a relative construction is either: relative pronoun (subject) + verb: *qui dort,* or relative pronoun (object) + subject + verb: *qu'ils recherchent.*

Relative pronoun   *un pronom relatif*

One of *qui, que, ce qui, ce que, où, dont* or preposition + *qui, quoi, lequel* etc. (including *auquel* etc.), when used to introduce a relative construction.

Semivowel, Semiconsonant or Glide   *une semi-voyelle, une semi-consonne*

One of the three sounds [j], [ɥ], [w], corresponding to the three full vowel sounds [i], [y], [u], and usually written as *i, u, ou.* A semivowel is pronounced in the same **syllable** as another vowel. The combination semivowel + vowel (or vowel + semivowel) is the closest equivalent to a **diphthong** in spoken French.

Sentence   *une phrase*

A complete statement consisting of an **independent clause**, or a **main clause** together with one or more **coordinate** or **subordinate clauses**. The beginning of a sentence is indicated in writing by a capital letter, and the end by a full stop; if two sentences are part of the same point, this can be indicated by the use of a semicolon, as in the two sentences you have just read. See also **Verbless sentence**.

Situation

Communicative situation   *la situation de communication, le contexte situationnel*

The particular circumstances in which language is used by speakers and writers, and understood by listeners and readers: the occasion (formal or informal) and the purpose of the exchange, the ages and the socioeconomic and geographical status and origins of the participants, the relation between the participants (foreigners, strangers, colleagues, friends, family). All these factors can affect the type of language used by each of the participants. In *French Grammar Explained*, examples of language more likely to be used in one kind of situation than another are labelled N1, N2, N3, N4, corresponding to very informal, relatively informal, relatively formal and verb formal situations. N stands for *niveau de langue* (in English: 'register').

Stress   *l'accent tonique*

In speech, a **syllable** is said to be stressed when it is longer and/or louder than the syllables around it. Stress is a regular feature of all speech, and should be distinguished from **emphasis** (*l'accent d'insistance*), which occurs only when a speaker wishes to draw attention to a particular word, phrase or idea.

Word stress   *l'accent lexical*

In English, a word of more than one syllable always has the same stress pattern: wherever it appears in a group of words, the same syllable (or syllables) is always stressed: this is called word stress.

Group stress   *l'accent rythmique*

In French, stress is placed on the final syllable of each group of syllables; this pattern is called group stress, and is achieved by making the syllable longer than the others in the group. There is also some stress on the initial syllable of each group.

Subject   *un sujet*

The subject of a verb is usually indicated by a noun or pronoun. In an **active** construction, the subject is the agent of the action indicated by the verb: *la nuit tombe, je reçois un cadeau; elle rêve*. In a **passive** construction (*être* + past participle), however, the subject of the verb *être* is not the agent of the action indicated by the past participle: *l'alerte a été donnée*, 'the alarm was raised'. See also **Object**.

French
Grammar
Explained

Subject pronoun   *un pronom personnel sujet*

One of *je, tu, il, elle, on, nous, vous, ils, elles.* These pronouns are used only as the subject of a **tensed verb**: *on arrive,* **ils** *sont partis* etc. See also **Tonic pronoun**.

Subjunctive   *le subjonctif*

The subjunctive is used instead of the **indicative** in **subordinate clauses** when the meaning of the main clause challenges in some way the reality of the action in the subordinate clause, by denying or doubting it, or by setting it aside, etc. In everyday French, only two **tenses** are used in the subjunctive: the present and the passé composé; the imperfect subjunctive and the pluperfect subjunctive are used only in certain specialised and particularly formal situations.

Suffix   *un suffixe*

A group of letters which, added at the end of a word, forms a new word with a different meaning, and often in a different grammatical class, from the original word. See also **Prefix**.

Superlative construction   *une construction superlative*

Relative superlative   *un superlatif relatif*

A way of expressing a relative judgment by singling out one item or set from a group of two or more items, in respect of a particular quality: *le **plus** grand **de** tous* etc. See also **Comparative construction**.

Absolute superlative   *un superlatif absolu*

A way of expressing an absolute judgment by using an adverb as an **intensifier** after a verb: *parler **fort***, or before an adjective or adverb: ***extrêmement*** *difficile;* ***très*** *utile.*

Syllable   *une syllabe*

In speech, a syllable contains one, and only one, **vowel**, on its own or with one or more **consonants** or **semivowels**: *ah!* [a] (vowel); *c'est* [sɛ] (consonant + vowel); *bien* [bjɛ̃] (consonant + semivowel + vowel); *belle* [bɛl] (consonant + vowel + consonant); *tact* [takt] (consonant + vowel + consonant + consonant). In writing, two or even three vowels can correspond to a single vowel sound: *beau* [bo] The letter *e* can form part of a new syllable in writing, but not in speech: *bel - le* (two syllables) in writing and in song, but [bɛl] (one syllable) in speech. See also **Group: Rhythmic group**.

Open syllable   *une syllabe ouverte*

A syllable that, when spoken, ends in a vowel: *mois* [mwa].

Closed syllable   *une syllabe fermée*

A syllable that, when spoken, ends in one or more consonants: *masse* [mas]; *mars* [mars].

Tense   *le temps (du verbe)*

The name of particular verb forms and endings: the present tense, the imperfect tense, the pluperfect tense, and so on. The system of tenses in French is used for three purposes:

● to situate an event or state of affairs in time relative to the standpoint of the speaker or writer (past or present time);

● to situate an event (etc.) in time relative to another event (before, simultaneous with or after);

● to indicate whether an event (etc.) is/was completed or continuing at a particular point in time, or whether it was habitual, etc (**aspect**).

Any **tensed verb** in spoken or written French may be fulfilling one, two or three of these different purposes, though in practice the system is often simplified, for example by beginning a spoken anecdote/story with one or two verbs in past tenses, and then using the present tense for the events in the rest of the story.

Tensed verb   *une forme personnelle du verbe*

A verb used in a particular tense (present, passé composé, etc.), whether in the **indicative** or the **subjunctive** (or in the **imperative**), and in one of the six **persons**. The traditional definition of a **sentence** is that it should contain a tensed verb; in fact, it is possible in French to have **verbless sentences**.

Tense forms

Simple tense forms   *les formes simples des temps*

Tenses expressed in a single word: verb stem + ending to indicate tense (and person); these include the present indicative, the present subjunctive, the future, the conditional, the imperfect and the past historic.

Compound tense forms   *les formes composées des temps*

Tenses expressed by the use of *avoir* or *être* (as **auxiliary**) + **past participle**; these include the passé composé, the past subjunctive, the pluperfect, the past conditional and the future perfect.

Text   *un texte*

A series of sentences organised to make a statement which makes sense as a whole: a brief description, an anecdote, a commentary, a letter, a report, a poem, a play, a novel, etc.

Tonic pronoun   *un pronom tonique*
One of *moi, toi, lui, elle, soi, ça, cela, nous, vous, eux, elles*. A tonic pronoun is used, alone or with a **subject pronoun**:

- to reinforce or emphasise the **subject** or the **object** of a verb: *moi je sais la réponse; eux sont partis avant nous; on te connaît, toi!*;
- after a preposition (except when an **indirect object pronoun** is used instead of *à +* noun): *je l'ai fait pour toi; avec elle, on est tranquille*;
- alone or after *c'est* etc.: *qui est là? moi!; mais c'est lui!*

Topic and comment   *le thème et le propos*
In a statement, the topic is what is being spoken or written about, and the comment is what one has to say about the topic. This way of looking at the information in a statement is different from a grammatical analysis: the topic can be the **subject** or the **object** of a verb, or a **detached complement**, for example: *le chat* (topic) *dormait devant le feu* (comment); *l'argent, l'argent* (topic), *tu ne penses qu'à ça!* (comment); *tous les jours* (topic), *elle se posait la même question* (comment). The topic can appear after the comment: *ce fromage est excellent!* or *excellent, ce fromage!* See also **Dislocation** and **Extraction**.

Transitive; intransitive   *transitif; intransitif*
A **verb** used with an **object** (**direct** or **indirect**, noun or pronoun) is said to be transitive; a verb used without an object is said to be intransitive. Many verbs can be used either transitively or intransitively, depending on the meaning of the sentence: *j'ai fini le travail* or *j'ai fini*. Several verbs, when used intransitively, become **pronominal verbs**: *il cultive son jardin* but *il se cultive*. A **preposition** (which is always used with a noun or pronoun) can be seen as a transitive **adverb**, and an adverb (which is not used with a noun or pronoun) as an intransitive preposition: *venez me voir après le cours* (transitive: *après* is used as a preposition) or *venez me voir après* (intransitive: *après* is used as an adverb).

Truncation   *la troncation*
The use of a shortened form of a word with the same meaning as the original word: *la faculté > la fac; la télévision > la télé*. See also **Reduction**.

Verb   *un verbe*
One of the four major parts of speech. Verbs describe actions, processes and states.

Verbless sentence   *une phrase nominale/adjectivale/adverbiale*
A sentence which does not contain a **tensed verb**, but which makes sense on its own, or in a particular context: *Tempête sur la Manche*, or *Impossible de dormir*, or *Enfin du nouveau!* A verbless sentence can consist of a **topic**: *La porte!* or a **comment**: *Au secours!* or topic + comment or vice-versa: *Excellent, ce fromage!* It can take the form of an abbreviated or truncated sentence, or be centred on an **infinitive**: *Ne pas déranger svp.*

535

Vowel *une voyelle*

In written French, one of the letters *a e i o u* (and *y*). In spoken French, one of 16 vowel sounds (12 **open vowels**, 4 **nasal vowels**), each pronounced with the mouth open. Almost all words are spelt with at least one vowel, and all words are pronounced with at least one vowel sound. Each spoken **syllable** consists of one vowel, with or without one or more **consonants**. Another way of saying this is that a vowel constitutes the nucleus of each spoken syllable. See also **Semivowel, Diphthong**.

Open (or **oral**) vowel *une voyelle orale*

A vowel sound produced entirely through the mouth, which remains open.

Nasal vowel *une voyelle nasale*

A vowel sound produced partly through the mouth and partly through the nasal cavity; the mouth remains open.

French
Grammar
Explained

59 Indexes

How to use this section

These indexes offer three ways of finding the section(s) where a particular grammar point appears:

- if the word you have in mind is a **grammatical term** (passive or subjunctive, for example), use the Index in **59.1**;
- if the word you have in mind is an **English** word ('if' or 'most', for example), use the Index in **59.2**;
- if the word you have in mind is a **French** word (*on* or *meilleur*, for example), use the Index in **59.3**.

59.1 Index of grammatical terms

* An asterisk denotes a term which also appears in the **Glossary (58)**.

Accent 8.3
*Acronym 16.3
*Active construction 35
*Adjective 3.2, 8.2, 14.4, 14.5, 17.3, 31.4, 41
   agreement 12
   construction 40
   position 25.4, 26, 43.2
*Adverb 3.2, 17.3, 27.1, 28.1, 30, 31.4, 53.3
   position 32.3, 32.4, 43.2, 50.1
*Agreement
   of adjective 12
   of past participle 44.4
   of verb 9.2
*Article 22
   definite, indefinite, partitive 22.1, 22.2, 22.4, 29.1, 29.2, 29.4
   not used 22.1, 22.5, 29.3, 29.4, 41.2
*Aspect 54
Attributive construction 38.1
*Auxiliary verb 39

aspect auxiliary 39.1, 53.4, 54.4
modal auxiliary 18.5, 37.1, 39.2
passive auxiliary 35.1
tense auxiliary 10.3, 18.5, 37.1, 39.1, 44.4

Capital letter 8.3
*Clause
   completive 33.4, 49, 52.4
   coordinate 45.1, 45.3
   main 45–49
   subordinate 45.3, 46–48
*Cleft construction 51.2
   pseudo-cleft construction 42.3, 51.3
*Comment: *see* Topic
*Comparative construction 24, 31
*Complement
   detached 43
*Completive construction: *see* Clause, completive
*Compound tense: *see* Tense forms

59.2 Index of English keywords

59.3 Index of French keywords